2
EDITION

PARENTING

PARENTING

A Dynamic Perspective

GEORGE W. HOLDEN
Southern Methodist University

Los Angeles | London | New Delhi
Singapore | Washington DC

Los Angeles | London | New Delhi
Singapore | Washington DC

FOR INFORMATION:

SAGE Publications, Inc.
2455 Teller Road
Thousand Oaks, California 91320
E-mail: order@sagepub.com

SAGE Publications Ltd.
1 Oliver's Yard
55 City Road
London EC1Y 1SP
United Kingdom

SAGE Publications India Pvt. Ltd.
B 1/I 1 Mohan Cooperative Industrial Area
Mathura Road, New Delhi 110 044
India

SAGE Publications Asia-Pacific Pte. Ltd.
3 Church Street
#10-04 Samsung Hub
Singapore 049483

Acquisitions Editor: Reid Hester
Associate Editor: Nathan Davidson
Editorial Assistant: Lucy Berbeo
Production Editor: Jane Haenel
Copy Editor: Erin Livingston
Typesetter: C&M Digitals (P) Ltd.
Proofreader: Jeff Bryant
Indexer: Sylvia Coates
Cover Designer: Janet Kiesel
Marketing Manager: Shari Countryman

Printed in the United States of America

Library of Congress Cataloging-in-Publication Data

Holden, George W.

Parenting : a dynamic perspective / George W. Holden, Southern Methodist University — 2nd Edition.

pages cm
Includes bibliographical references and index.

ISBN 978-1-4833-4748-6 (pbk. : alk. paper)
1. Parenting. I. Title.

HQ755.8.H625 2014
649'.1—dc23 2014020354

This book is printed on acid-free paper.

14 15 16 17 18 10 9 8 7 6 5 4 3 2 1

Contents

Detailed Contents

PART III: CONTEMPORARY ISSUES

Preface

The word *parenting* is derived from the Latin verb *parere,* a word that can be defined as "That from which something springs or is derived; a source, cause, origin" (Oxford English Dictionary). That word defines much of our lives. During most of our first two decades of life, our parents (or parent) fed, clothed, and nurtured us. They also decided or influenced (at least for a while) where we lived, what we ate, whom we associated with, and how we spent our time. Then, after perhaps 10 or 15 years of independence, child rearing once again returned to the forefront of our lives, but this time, we encountered it from the other side of the equation—as parents. Parenthood changes the structure of our lives, and it also changes us as individuals. For most of us, it is the most important activity of our lives.

By the time most people are 30 or 35 years old, they have two sets of defining relationships—one with their parents and one with their children. Both sets of relationships converge to give focus and meaning to our lives. Although it is true that parenting is a major challenge and can be the cause of considerable "misery," children are also the source of great joy (Nelson, Kushlev, English, Dunn, & Lyubomirsky, 2013). The famous attorney Clarence Darrow (1857–1938) made this point in a different way. He once quipped that parents ruin the first half of our lives and that children ruin the second half.

The prominence of parenting is not limited to our personal lives. Scan through a daily newspaper. Virtually every day, you can find multiple articles that address issues related to parenting. Articles concern issues about pregnancy, how to intellectually stimulate infants, the epidemic of obesity in children, childrearing practices in different cultures, and shocking articles about middle-school-age children committing crimes or appalling new ways parents have invented to abuse their children. Childrearing controversies continue to be debated in newspapers: Should infants be breastfed? Does daycare negatively affect children? Is spanking harmful? And discussion of many social problems, including adolescent pregnancy, children's behavior problems, school dropouts, drug abuse, divorce rates, crime and violence, and the effects of poverty on children are incomplete unless they address the issue of child rearing.

Personal relationships, continuing controversies, and chronic social problems are just three examples indicating that parenting is central to all of our lives. Not surprisingly, researchers from a variety of disciplines are investigating questions related to child rearing. Psychologists are now joined in their research efforts by sociologists, anthropologists, biologists, geneticists, physicians, nurses, economists, and investigators from other disciplines. Consequently, links between child rearing and child outcomes are appearing in scientific journals with unprecedented frequency.

Indeed, research into parenting has exploded in the past 35 years; new information is published virtually every day. Today, there is an excellent journal dedicated to parenting research (*Parenting: Science and Practice*), and every month, dozens of other journals publish articles addressing childrearing issues. It is an exciting time for parenting research!

New empirical discoveries as well as conceptual insights frequently appear in the journals. Along with the rapidly accruing knowledge, our understanding of the topic is getting progressively more sophisticated and complex. It is increasingly clear that child rearing is multidimensional and can be highly differentiated. This book describes and summarizes that changing landscape of research.

At the heart of this domain is at least one relationship: You cannot parent without a child. Child rearing then must be recognized as a two-person, bidirectional process rather than how it used to be thought of—determined simply by parental characteristics. Of course, child rearing is strongly influenced by the child's characteristics, such as age, gender, and behavior. However, parenting is affected by many other considerations as well and reflects a dynamic and ongoing process. That process is characterized, in part, by change. Change comes in response to many variables, including the situation, environment, parental emotions, stressors, culture, and even the time of the year. The histories of interactions as well as future childrearing goals are yet two more influences on parental behavior. Such a view—one that captures the dynamics of parenting—will be fleshed out in the following pages.

My goals in writing this book were threefold. Foremost, I sought to provide an up-to-date and accurate summary of the parenting research that would be geared toward undergraduate students. A large number of ideas, information, and research has been summarized and condensed to create this book. In light of the importance of repetition for recall, the book is structured so that many of the key ideas build on information presented in earlier chapters and appear more than once. My hope is that students will finish reading the book with a solid understanding about what is known about parenting, an appreciation for childrearing research, and a renewed recognition of the centrality of parenting in their lives.

Although readers should come away better equipped to evaluate new childrearing information, studies, and news reports they will hear about parenting, this book is not a childrearing manual. However, in dozens of places throughout the book, it will be clear what the research tells us about the attributes of effective parenting.

The ever-increasing amount and complexity of research conflicts with my second goal: to present the material in an interesting and accessible way. I resolved this dialectic by selecting topics, examples, and studies that should have wide interest. To maintain interest and provide some visual variation for the reader, I have incorporated numerous tables, figures, and boxed materials. Similarly, I frequently cite recent statistics to highlight social changes related to the family and the magnitude of the contemporary problems.

My third goal was to prompt readers to become advocates for parents and children. Good parenting plays a fundamental role in a healthy society. Nelson Mandela, the late president of South Africa, said, "There can be no keener revelation of a society's soul than the way in which it treats its children." And if a society cherishes its children, it must also nurture their parents. After all, who does not want to help children have healthy and happy childhoods so they, in turn, will develop into good parents? No one wants the words of Clarence Darrow to ring true.

Acknowledgments

Although a new edition does not require as much effort as the first edition, it nevertheless represents a substantial commitment of time and energy. My wife, the Rev. Dr. Anne Cameron, deserves much credit for not only tolerating the consequences of a spouse working on a book but also for masterfully editing the chapters. She deserves, as always, my thanks, gratitude, and steadfast love. Thanks also go to my graduate student, Rose Ashraf, and four undergraduate research assistants—Hani Gazal, Natalie Raymondi, Shradha Singh, and Lesta Stay—who helped compile the research studies.

I am also indebted to the reviewers of the book's first edition, who provided many excellent and constructive comments. I tried to incorporate as many of their suggestions into this edition as space and time permitted. The reviewers included the following:

Elaine S. Barry, Penn State Fayette, the Eberly Campus

Dixie R. Crase, University of Memphis

Nerissa LeBlanc Gillum, Texas Woman's University

Desalyn De-Souza, PhD, Empire State College, State University of New York

Patricia E. Gross, University of Northern Iowa

David MacPhee, Colorado State University

Laura Nathans, University of North Texas

Lucinda O. Payne, Appalachian State University

Aya Shigeto, Nova Southeastern University

Tammy Lowery Zacchilli, Saint Leo University

Finally, I thank the staff at SAGE. In particular, Reid Hester, a senior acquisition editor, was both supportive and patient. Lucy Berbeo, an editorial assistant, was cheerful and instrumental in the final stages of the manuscript preparation. Also, this book greatly benefited from the diligent attention of Jane Haenel (production editor) and Erin Livingston (copy editor). I am most grateful to all these individuals.

About the Author

George W. Holden, PhD, is Professor of Psychology at Southern Methodist University in Dallas, Texas. After receiving his BA from Yale University and his PhD from the University of North Carolina at Chapel Hill, he was a member of the psychology faculty at the University of Texas at Austin for 23 years. Holden's research interests are in the area of social development, with a focus on parent-child relationships. His work into the determinants of parental behavior, parental social cognition, and the causes and consequences of family violence has been supported by grants from the National Institute of Child Health and Human Development, National Institutes of Justice, Department of Health and Human Services, the Guggenheim Foundation, the Hogg Foundation for Mental Health, the Timberlawn Research Foundation, and, most recently, the U.S. State Department. He is the author of numerous scientific articles and chapters as well as two books: *Parenting: A Dynamic Perspective* (2010) and *Parents and the Dynamics of Child Rearing* (1997). In addition, he coedited *Children Exposed to Marital Violence* (1998) and the *Handbook of Family Measurement Techniques* (2001). Holden is a Fellow of the American Psychological Society and a member of the Society for Research in Child Development, the International Society for the Prevention of Child Abuse & Neglect, and the Society for Research in Human Development, where he served as president. He has been or is on the editorial boards of *Child Development*, *Developmental Psychology*, *Journal of Emotional Abuse*, *Journal of Family Psychology*, and *Parenting: Science and Practice.* He was a member of the State of Texas Task Force to Address the Relationship between Domestic Violence and Child Abuse and Neglect. He is a founding member of the U.S. Alliance to End the Hitting of Children. Dr. Holden received the Outstanding Mentor Award in 2010 from the Society for Research in Human Development and the Lightner Sams Foundation Child Advocate Prism Award in 2011. He is the president-elect of the board of Family Compass, an organization devoted to preventing child maltreatment in the Dallas community. He is married and is the father of three wonderful adult children.

PART I

Understanding Parents and Child Rearing

CHAPTER 1

Introduction

From Beliefs to Evidence

Chapter Preview: True or False?

- The concept of childhood as a separate phase of life did not exist in the Middle Ages.
- In the past, pediatricians and psychologists warned parents not to kiss their children.
- Systematic research into parenting began in 1950.

PARENTING BELIEFS THROUGHOUT HISTORY

Take a moment to look around you. Depending on where you are reading this book right now, you may see various kinds of people. Young, old, **immigrant**, native. Affluent, poor, introverted, outgoing. Multiple skin tones and a myriad of accents. But there is one thing we all share in common. Each one of us has been a child. We are all born into the world helpless and unformed, needy and full of potential. And for most of us, the primary source of learning—about the world, how to think and feel, and how to behave—was our parents.

It's no wonder then, that for millennia, people have asked important questions about parenting. How *do* parents affect children's development? Are parents the single most important influence on children's development? Do mothers and fathers make unique contributions to their children's development, or are their roles interchangeable? How does parental behavior change as children grow? What role did parents play in rearing a child who became a pioneer of nonviolent civil disobedience (Mahatma Gandhi, 1869–1948) in contrast to that of another child (Adolf Hitler, 1889–1945), who became the architect of the genocide of six million Jews? More currently, consider the 35th President the United States, Barack Obama. Born in 1961, he was reared by a single mother and his grandparents. Or Sonia Sotomayor, the third woman to be a Supreme Court Justice. She was raised by her immigrant mother after her alcoholic father died when she was nine. How did their unique experiences shape them? To what extent does the way a parent treats his or her child—childrearing practices—actually affect the child's personality, social competence, intelligence, occupations, athleticism, eating habits, aggression, and a variety of other potential outcomes?

The role that parents play in child development is commonly referred to as **socialization**. The meaning of the word has evolved over the past one hundred years (Morawski & St. Martin, 2011) but an accepted definition now is "the processes whereby naïve individuals are taught the skills, behavior patterns, values, and motivations needed for competent functioning in the **culture** in which the child is growing up" (Maccoby, 2007, p. 13). As we will see, the answer to the question of *how* parents socialize their children is not a simple one. But our scientific understanding of the question has grown dramatically since the 1960s.

Researchers have been studying parents and socialization for a long time. However, early efforts to study parents, begun in the 1920s and 1930s, were both limited and one dimensional, as we will see. Researchers tended to focus on parental love or **discipline** and how that related to a child's behavior. But it is increasingly apparent that parents socialize their children in multiple domains, including gender development, **emotion regulation**, school success, and perhaps racial relations and religious **beliefs** (Holden, 2010). Furthermore, the role of parents is not limited to socialization. Rather, as Robert Bradley (2007) identified, parents have many other important childrearing functions besides providing love and discipline. These include ensuring safety, structuring the child's environment and day, stimulating and instructing the child, and providing social connections (see Table 1.1).

New research is also revealing that beliefs about and **perceptions** of children and how to raise them differ over time and across cultures. Ideas about what is good and bad for a child's development are being increasingly informed by scientific investigations. Through the scientific processes of observing behavior, testing hypotheses, and replicating findings, the knowledge base about child rearing has expanded exponentially over the past quarter century.

In his book, *Centuries of Childhood* (1962), French historian Philippe Ariès proposed the idea that beliefs about children change over time. He contended that childhood, as we think today of that developmental stage, did not exist during the Middle Ages (476–1453 CE) [Preview Question]. During that period, children beginning at about seven years of age

Table 1.1 Six Fundamental Tasks of Parenting

Ensuring Safety and Sustenance	Stimulating and Instructing
• Providing food, housing, clothing • Accessing health care • Protecting	• Making available toys and learning materials • Coaching • Encouraging achievement
Giving Socioemotional Support	**Monitoring and Surveillance**
• Loving • Disciplining • Modeling	• Watching • Collecting information • Communicating with the child
Structuring	**Providing Social Connectedness**
• Structuring the environment • Organizing the child's day • Providing routines	• Connecting with family and relatives • Forming peer relationships • Joining institutions/organizations (e.g., religious, sports)

Source: Adapted from Bradley, 2007.

were considered to be small adults—physically smaller but essentially no different from adults. Children did not enjoy a special status, adults did not consider childhood to be a unique developmental period, and children were not protected from abuse. Ariès believed that this **adult-centered** view of children only began to change in the late 16th century, when a new **child-centered** approach in the upper classes recognized childhood as a distinct time of life and a time when it was important to begin education.

Ariès based his thesis, to a large extent, on inferences derived from examining children's portraits and other paintings depicting children. Paintings of young children portrayed them as adultlike, as if they were simply miniaturized adults. Their expressions and portrayed activities did not suggest that adults treated that period of life as a special and unique time. For example, take a look at the childhood portrait of King Edward VI of England, painted around 1538 by Han Holbein the younger. He is portrayed as amazingly regal for an infant or young toddler. In contrast, the painting by Thomas Eakins almost 340 years later depicts a child of approximately the same age but engaged in behavior that looks much more characteristic of a toddler (see Photos 1.1a and 1.1b).

Historians have carefully scrutinized Ariès's thesis and have refuted some of his claims with counterexamples (e.g., French, 2002; Shanahan, 2007). Take, for example, the ancient Greeks (1100–146 BCE). They conceptualized childhood as divided into three stages: *infantia* (birth to age 7 years), *pueritia* (ages 7 to 12 for girls, 7 to 14 for boys), and *adolescentia* (ages 12 to 21 for girls, 14 to 21 for boys) (Heywood, 2001). Thus Ariès's thesis was not entirely accurate. Nevertheless, the central point—that the way we perceive children is a product of the times—is valid. Phrased differently, beliefs about children and parents are **social constructions**.

There have also been dramatic historical shifts in parents' views about children. In antiquity, children were considered the property of parents; parents had the right to do whatever they wanted with their offspring, even kill them. Typically, it meant putting the child to work as soon as possible in an effort to help the family survive, whether it was working in the garden or the fields, hunting food, or helping out in the home. Hendrick (2002) presents an interesting conceptualization of various "themes" of childhood throughout British history, beginning with the "natural child" in the late 17th century through the "delinquent child" in the mid-19th-century and on to the "psychological child" of the early 20th century (see Table 1.2) Gradually, parents began to perceive children as individuals with unique psychological needs. Not until the late 19th century (the Industrial Revolution) did the idea of a dedicated time period of childhood spread into the lower and lower-middle classes.

Photo 1.1a Portrait of King Edward VI as a young child, Han Holbein the younger, ca. 1538.

Source: Wikimedia Commons

AUTHORITIES' PARENTING BELIEFS THROUGHOUT HISTORY

In contrast to Ariès's approach of making inferences from art, a more direct way to examine how children and parents were thought about throughout history is by reading the published views about children. The writings of influential thinkers or authorities reveal changing views to such questions: How do parents influence their children? Is the nature of children basically good or evil? What role does society play? The best known types of individuals in

Photo 1.1b Baby at play, Thomas Eakins, 1876.

Source: Wikimedia Commons

Table 1.2 Changing Conceptualization of Children in Great Britain

18th Century Views	Natural Child (Rousseau's Emile)
	Romantic Child (in literature, poetry)
	Evangelical Child (religious views)
	Wage-Earner Child (child labor)
19th Century Views	Delinquent Child (unsocialized, misbehaving)
	Schooled Child (compulsory schooling)
	Child-Study Child (beginning of research)
	Children of the Nation (child reforms)
20th Century Views	Psychological Child (in the family)

Source: Adapted from Hendrick, 2002.

influencing Western conceptions about socialization have been religious leaders, philosophers, physicians (often pediatricians), and, most recently, psychologists. Below are some prominent examples from these four professions, with examples drawn primarily from Western culture.

Religious Leaders

In sacred writings, one can find many examples of views about children and parents. However, the descriptions are often limited to such topics as the significance of love and discipline, what is proper behavior, and the importance of children's learning of morality—a sense of right and wrong. All three of the world's great theistic religions (Christianity, Judaism, and Islam) share an emphasis on the family and encourage parents to devote considerable time and attention to their children. In Judaism (the Torah) and Christianity (the Old Testament), one of the Ten Commandments ("Honor thy father and thy mother," Exodus 20:12) as well as several proverbs and other scriptures give prescriptions as to how parents should treat their children, how children should behave, and the virtues that children should develop (e.g., being honest, having humility, caring for others, and respecting parents as well as elders).

Parents are also important in Islamic views of development. Topics related to the family concern about one-third of the injunctions in the Qur'an (Frosh, 2004). Like other religions, Islam promotes character development and such values such as patience, honesty, forgiveness, and respect for parents (Husain, 2006). But it differs by emphasizing the importance of family honor. Maintaining family *izzat* (pride, honor, self-respect) is an important value and a determinant of behavior in Islamic families (Stewart et al., 1999). The prominence of that value explains why Muslim men sometimes kill their female relatives if they are suspected of bringing dishonor on the family.

In China, Confucius (circa 551–479 BCE), the father of the Confucianism, also emphasized filial piety ("Parents are always right") as well as respect for elders, **interdependence**, group identification, harmony, self-discipline, and achievement (Lin & Fu, 1990). Although it is debated whether Confucius can be considered a religious leader, he talked about heaven and the afterlife and addressed ethics, morality, and values.

Given the fundamental role that religion plays in the lives of many people, it is not surprising that childrearing is often a topic of religious writers. Many Christian leaders wrote about parents' influence in their children's development. One of the first and most influential was the theologian known as St. Augustine of Hippo (354–430 CE). He developed the religious doctrine that children were tainted by **original sin**: "No man is clean of sin, not even the infant who has lived but a day upon earth" (Augustine, 397/1960, p. 49). This doctrine refers to how Adam and Eve disobeyed God in the Garden of Eden through an act of free will (eating the forbidden fruit). Consequently, their nature became corrupt. Because all people are direct descendants of Adam and Eve, St. Augustine reasoned, everyone has inherited their sinful and guilty state. Therefore, infants are born willful and even evil. A German preacher from the 1520s went so far as to warn parishioners that infants' hearts craved "adultery, fornication, impure desires, lewdness, idol worship, belief in magic, hostility, quarrelling, passion, anger, strife, dissension, factiousness, hatred, murder, drunkenness, gluttony" (Heywood, 2001, p. 33).

The Protestant Reformation of Martin Luther and others prompted changes in parenting. Luther (1483–1546 CE), adopting a **patriarchal** view of families, considered fathers to be the authority and moral guide. Consequently, it was the father's duty to teach religion and lead the family in prayer. He also believed that fathers should be involved in parenting. He wrote that "when a father washes diapers and performs some other menial task for his child, and someone ridicules him as an effeminate fool, . . . God with all his angels and creatures is smiling" (Gillis, 1996, p. 186).

John Calvin (1509–1564 CE; see Photo 1.2), the influential French Protestant religious reformer, promoted the idea that children are, by nature, sinful and parents had an important role in correcting this problem. Calvin is well known for his doctrine of *total depravity*, the concept that all humans are born into sin and that human nature (without God) is destined for depravity. In his most significant work, *The Institutes of the Christian Religion* (1536/1960), Calvin wrote:

> Even infants bear their condemnation with them from their mother's womb; for though they have not yet brought forth the fruits of their own iniquity [sinfulness], they have the seed enclosed within themselves. Indeed, their whole nature is a seed of sin thus it cannot but be hateful and abominable to God. (p. 1311)

Calvin, a stepfather of two children, advocated that parents must educate and discipline their children in order to help save them from their sinful ways. Parents should not be overly indulgent. In fact, he recognized that children need frequent *admonitions* (gentle or friendly corrections). However, those reprimands need to be administered in a kind way so that children will cheerfully obey.

Photo 1.2 John Calvin argued that infants are sinful.

Source: Wikimedia Commons

Calvin influenced the thinking of many Protestant ministers, including John Robinson (1575–1625), a Puritan and spiritual leader of the Plymouth pilgrims. Robinson voiced concern about saving the child's soul:

> And surely there is in all children, though not alike, a stubbornness, and stoutness of minds arising from natural pride, which must in the first place, be broken and beaten down. . . . This fruit of natural corruption and root of actual rebellion both against God and man must be destroyed and in no manner or way nourished. (Greven, 1973, p. 13)

Robinson's childrearing advice consisted mostly of harsh punishment. Fathers should be the disciplinarians. Because of their greater wisdom, authority, and strength, they were in a position to correct "the fruits of their mother's indulgence" (Cable, 1972, p. 4). Puritan ministers also advocated educating children in conjunction with restraining children's innate evil, because those practices would lead them to become faithful adults.

During the next century, John Wesley (1703–1791), an Englishman and founder of the Methodist Church, also promoted parental discipline as essential for children's development. He viewed disobedience to parents as synonymous with moral disorder and warned of the dangers of losing control of a child. He advocated frequent use of corporal (also called *physical*) punishment:

> A wise parent . . . should begin to break their [the child's] will the first moment it appears. In the whole of Christian education, there is nothing more important than this. The will of the parent is to a little child in the place of the will of God. Therefore, studiously teach them to submit to this while they are children, that they may be ready to submit to his will, when they are men. (Greven, 1973, pp. 59–60)

Wesley's views likely come directly from his mother, Susannah. She bore 19 children (though only nine survived past the age of two years) and developed a detailed childrearing philosophy. In a letter to her son, written in 1732, she described her childrearing philosophy in the form of rules. Those rules are centered on four principles: establishing habits, developing morals, disciplining, and encouraging religious beliefs. Many of her rules are listed in Box 1.1.

Historians of the colonial and postcolonial period now believe that the authoritarian childrearing practices advocated by the Reverends Robinson, Wesley, and others were limited to certain segments of the Puritan population and not representative of childrearing practices in colonial America (Greven, 1977). In fact, Puritan childrearing manuals discouraged spanking, a topic that we will return to in this book. Harsh punishments, whippings, and beatings were to be used only as a last resort—to combat the cardinal sins of stubbornness and disobedience. Instead, the use of **shaming** (such as public displays of the offending person) was considered a more effective technique for developing a strong sense of right and wrong.

Box 1.1 Outdated or Enduring? Susannah Wesley's Rules for Child Rearing (from 1732)

On Daily Routines:

- Establish routines right from birth.
- For older children, do not allow snacking between meals.
- Children are to be in bed by 8 P.M.
- Girls should be taught to read before they are taught to do housework.

On Morality:

- Teach children about individual property rights, even in smallest matters.
- Commend and reward obedient behavior.
- Acts intended to please the parent, even if poorly performed, should be accepted kindly.
- Do not beat children who confess to misbehavior.

On Punishment:

- Never allow a sinful act to go unpunished.
- Never punish a child twice for the same misbehavior.
- Teach children to fear the rod by 12 months of age and to cry softly.

On Religion and Sin:

- Teach children to pray as soon as they can speak.
- Conquer a child's will; self-will is the root of all sin and misery.

Source: Adapted from Clarke, E. (1886). *Susanna Wesley*. Boston, MA: Roberts Brothers. Reprinted in P. J. Greven Jr. (1973). *Child-rearing concepts, 1628–1861: Historical sources*. Itasca, IL: F.E. Peacock.

Over time, corporal punishment fell out of favor among many of the clergy. Some preachers even decried punishing children. Horace Bushnell (1802–1876), a Congregationalist minister in Connecticut, wrote a book called *Christian Nurture* (1908/2000). He proposed that infants were not born depraved but rather were "formless lumps." The parental role, he believed, should be one of providing good guidance in order to let children thrive. Today, vestiges of the harsh punishment orientation to socialization can be found among some conservative Christian writers (e.g., Rosemond, 2007) who continue to advocate hitting children to make them subservient. However, many other Christians do not subscribe to such views. For example, the United Methodist Church, in contrast to the beliefs of its founder, passed two resolutions in 2004 and reaffirmed them in 2012, calling for an end to corporal punishment of children both in the schools and in the home. The Presbyterian Church USA also passed, in 2012, a resolution against the use of corporal punishment. See Table 1.3 for more information.

Table 1.3 A Time Line of the Views of Clergy and Churches About Children and Punishment

354–430	St. Augustine	North Africa	Original Sin
1483–1546	Martin Luther	Germany	Patriarchy Emphasis
1509–1564	John Calvin	France	Total Depravity
1575–1625	John Robinson	England	Harsh Corporal Punishment
1703–1791	John Wesley	England	Frequent Corporal Punishment
1802–1876	Horace Bushnell	United States	Parental Guidance
2004	United Methodist Church Resolution to end corporal punishment		
2012	Presbyterian Church USA Resolution to end corporal punishment		

Philosophers

Philosophers have long pondered the nature of children, the influence of parents, and the impact of society on development. One recurring theme in philosophy has been the lifelong significance of the early years of life. This idea is captured in the Chinese proverb, "As the twig is bent, the tree inclines." The importance of childhood is also captured in a phrase from Virgil (40 BCE): "The child is the father of the man." The Greek philosopher Aristotle (384–322 BCE) advanced the idea that children were blank tablets, waiting to be written on by parents and life experiences. Thus he emphasized the importance of the environment in shaping children. He also recognized the unique role that fathers play in their sons' development (French, 2002). Aristotle espoused a patriarchal society, where a women's primary role was to produce male heirs and supervise households.

John Locke, the English physician and philosopher (1632–1704; see Photo 1.3), had a revolutionary and enduring impact on childrearing practices. The son of Puritan parents, Locke wrote a childrearing manual titled *Some Thoughts Concerning Education* (1693/1996). Its radical view of child rearing became the dominant guide to raising children in Western Europe and America during the first half of the 1700s. Besides advocating a **blank slate** position and thereby rejecting the notion of children as innately sinful, Locke proposed a novel view of a child's development. He appreciated the influence of the environment, recognized the need for early stimulation, and promoted parental encouragement of mature behavior: "The sooner you treat him as a man, the sooner he will begin to be one" (p. 72). Locke's view that children are rational beings meant that parents should reason with children rather than punish or reward them.

Photo 1.3 John Locke recognized the role of the environment in shaping how children turn out.

Source: Wikimedia Commons

> For I am very apt to think, that great severity of punishment does but very little good, nay, great harm in education [socialization]; and I believe it will be found that *ceteris paribus* [other things being equal] those children who have been most chastised seldom make the best men. (p. 32)

He stressed the importance of the first few years of life, and his work prompted parents in Europe and America to be more loving, nurturing, and egalitarian (Clarke-Stewart, 1998). In many ways, Locke's childrearing philosophy foreshadowed contemporary childrearing views. However, not all of his recommendations are currently regarded as sensible. Some of Locke's more unusual childrearing proposals can be found in Box 1.2.

Box 1.2 Childrearing Practices Advocated by John Locke Now Viewed as Abusive or Unusual

John Locke promoted a warmer, more sympathetic orientation toward children. However, he also proposed certain practices that are now regarded as unorthodox or even bizarre. Many pages of his manual are devoted to the virtues of "**hardening**" infants as a way of trying to defend against **infant**

(Continued)

(Continued)

mortality. His suggestions included immersing infants in cold baths, building endurance and toughness by dressing them in light clothing and thin shoes in cold weather, administering low levels of pain as a way of firming up their minds, and avoiding certain fruits (peaches, melons, grapes) because of their "unwholesome" juices. Although vegans would not find this suggestion unusual, Locke recommended a vegetarian diet for young children—at least, during the first three years of life.

Source: Adapted from Locke, 1693/1996.

Another influential philosopher was Swiss-born Frenchman Jean-Jacques Rousseau (1712–1778; see Photo 1.4). In his book, *Emile* (1762/1956), Rousseau described methods for raising a child free from the corrupting influences of society. Rousseau, like Locke, rejected the idea of original sin in children: "Let us lay it down an incontrovertible rule that the first impulses of nature are always right; there is no original sin in the human heart, the how and why of the entrance of every vice can be traced" (p. 56). Children are born innocent and amoral; it is society that corrupts them. Rousseau wrote, "All things are good as they come out of the hands of the creator, but everything degenerates in the hands of man." In contrast to Locke, Rousseau believed that children were not rational—at least, not until age 12. "If children understood reason, they would not need education [to be raised]. . . . Nature would have them [wants them to be] children before they are men" (1911, pp. 53–54). Consequently, punishment for misbehavior made little sense to him: "Before the age of reason we do good or ill without knowing it, and there is no morality in our actions" (p. 34).

Photo 1.4 Rousseau believed that society corrupts the innocent nature of children.

Source: Wikimedia Commons

The parental role, according to Rousseau, is not to discipline, educate, or train but rather to facilitate natural development. Rousseau believed that children have positive inclinations and needed little help from their parents to develop naturally. He encouraged mothers to breastfeed their babies themselves (rather then send infants off to wet nurses), to avoid all use of physical punishment, and to bring children up as vegetarians (something Locke also advocated). *Emile* ends with the description of the boy as a grown man: someone appropriately socialized who cares for people in need and has a capacity for loving others. As enlightened as Rousseau was by today's standards, he did not advocate bringing up girls the same way as boys. Girls required a specialized education in order to prepare them for motherhood.

Physicians

Physicians represent a third group of individuals who provided a strong dose of childrearing beliefs to society, beginning with the ancient Greek physician Hippocrates (460–370 BCE). Many of their directives regarding child health or child rearing were based on unsubstantiated personal ideas rather than medical knowledge. Given that a central goal of the early physicians was to combat the high rate of infant illnesses and deaths—the causes of which were largely mysterious at the time—much of their advice concerned infant feeding and nutrition (Ruhrah, 1925; Wickes, 1953). Box 1.3 contains some of the stranger advice from premodern physicians.

Box 1.3 Antiquated Pediatric Treatments

For good health: Give infants warm baths and diluted wine (Hippocrates, 460–370 BCE).

To treat excessive hair: Rub the body with powder of burned dry figs (Aetius, 527–565 CE).

To soothe teething: Smear the infant's gums with hare's brains (Oribasius, 325–403 CE).

For crying infants: Give them a drink of "quietness": boiled-down extract of black poppies or poppy seeds (otherwise known as opium; 1520 until 20th century).

To cure bedwetting: Scatter dried and powdered rooster's comb over child's bed without his knowledge (Rhazes, ca. 900 CE).

Sources: Adapted from Beekman, 1977; Colon, 1999.

In the United States, two American physicians stand out as particularly influential on childrearing practices. The first one was Dr. Luther Emmett Holt (1855–1924; see Photo 1.5), who first published *The Care and Feeding of Children* in 1894. It, along with its 15 revisions, became the leading book on child care in the United States for almost 50 years (and was translated into Spanish, Russian, and Chinese). The book contains information about daily care of infants, milestones of child development, feeding recommendations, and remedies for common ailments or behaviors (e.g., dealing with "the bad habits of [thumb-]sucking, nail-biting, dirt-eating, bed-wetting, and masturbation;" Holt, 1929, p. 230). Many of Holt's recommendations sound reasonable by today's standards. For example in the 14th edition (1929) of his book, he advocated breastfeeding with the rationale that there was "no perfect substitute" and justified it as resulting in lower rates of infant mortality, an observation repeatedly confirmed by scientific studies (Kozuki et al., 2013). Nevertheless, he recognized that some mothers would not or could not breastfeed their infants and therefore included detailed information about alternative feeding methods. He created highly detailed recommendations for when and how much formula should be fed to infants that gave the appearance of being scientific.

Photo 1.5 The first prominent American pediatrician, Dr. Luther Emmett Holt, was the author of a popular childcare book.

Source: Library of Congress

Dr. Holt also advocated some practices that we now consider medically and developmentally unsound or even outlandish. For example, he recommended that parents avoid kissing infants because "tuberculosis, diphtheria, syphilis, and many other grave diseases may be communicated in this way" (Holt, 1929, p. 205) [Preview Question]. Holt also warned against soothing crying babies or playing with infants, which could cause "nervousness" in children:

> Babies under six months should never be played with; and the less of it [play] at any age the better for the infant. . . . They are made more nervous and irritable, sleep badly, and suffer from indigestion and cease to gain in weight. (p. 201)

Dr. Holt also considered thumb-sucking to be another serious problem. His solution: tying an infant's arms to the sides of the crib at night. Other techniques tried in the early 1900s in an effort to control thumb-sucking included tying large mittens on infants' hands or putting foul-tasting ointments on their thumbs.

The influence of physicians' beliefs on popular parenting culture was captured by an early 20th-century postcard reproduced in Photo 1.6. This is a whimsical depiction of children, because they don't ride cows nor can they drink from udders with long straws. The absurdity is presumably intended to highlight the message that parents should not feed cow's milk to infants.

One child raised strictly according to Dr. Holt's precepts grew up to become an even more influential physician. After working for several years as a pediatrician, Dr. Benjamin Spock (Photo 1.7) recognized the need for a new and radically different guide to child care. In 1945, he wrote *The Common Sense Book of Baby and Child Care*. The book rapidly became a best seller, along with the shorter *The Pocket Book of Baby and Child Care* (1946). These books corrected some of Holt's peculiar recommendations and encouraged parents to enjoy parenting. Parents were instructed to trust themselves in deciding how to raise their baby. His message to mothers was that "you know more than you think you do" (1946, p. 3). Dr. Spock advocated less emphasis upon strict regularity of feeding and sleeping schedules for infants and toddlers, encouraging parents to treat their children as individuals. He changed his opinion about male circumcision, later suggesting it might best be avoided.

Although Spock received a reputation as encouraging permissive parenting, it was largely undeserved—although he did recommend that parents avoid physical punishment. His book has been the most widely read and influential child care manual ever published.

Photo 1.6 This postcard from the early 20th century was intended to warn the public of the dangers of cow's milk for babies.

Dr. Spock's books have been translated into 42 languages and have sold well over 50 million copies. Throughout its first 52 years, *Baby and Child Care* was the second-best-selling book, after the Bible, and indeed, it has often been called "the Bible of child rearing." In addition to *Baby and Child Care*, Spock authored multiple books on child rearing. In subsequent books, he addressed feeding issues, mothering, parental problems, caring for disabled children, adolescence, and dealing with difficult contemporary issues. Even after Dr. Spock's death in 1998, the book lives on in its ninth edition with the help of the latest coauthor (Spock & Needlman, 2012). See Table 1.4 for a closer look at the contributions of philosophers and physicians.

Psychologists

Besides pediatricians, many types of professionals have contributed to the understanding of parenting. For example, since the late 1800s, family life educators under various disciplines (e.g., home economics, parent education, family studies, human ecology, family science) have focused on understanding the welfare of parent and children and the importance of strengthening families. European-born psychologists Sigmund Freud (1856–1939), Alfred Adler (1870–1937), Jean Piaget (1896–1980), and Erik Erikson (1902–1994) each theorized about children's development and, to varying degrees, the vital role played by parents. Both Freud and Adler were trained as physicians (Freud in psychiatry, Adler in

Photo 1.7 Dr. Spock.

Source: © MDCarchives/Wikimedia Commons/ CC-BY-SA-3.0/GFDL

ophthalmology) but both were seminal thinkers in the just-emerging field of psychology. Two early American psychologists who played important roles in developing research in the area of parenting were G. Stanley Hall and John B. Watson. Hall (1844–1924) was a pioneer in American psychology and is considered one of its fathers. At Harvard in 1878, he received the first PhD in psychology conferred in the United States. He established the earliest working psychology laboratory in the country, founded several journals, and became president of Clark University in Massachusetts, where he brought Sigmund Freud for a famous visit in 1909 (see Photo 1.8). Hall established a program of research on children, parents, and adolescents and pioneered the use of questionnaires in research. Although he is not remembered for his intellectual contributions, he was an influential figure in initiating research into children's development. With regard to child rearing, Hall favored physical punishment: "We need less sentimentality and more spanking" (Cable, 1972, p. 172).

Another early American psychologist who played a more influential role than Hall on how we think about parenting was John B. Watson (1878–1958). Watson, known as the "father of behaviorism" for advocating the study of behavior, espoused an extreme environmentalism perspective in his writings about parents. He gained fame by his learning studies of "Little Albert," a nine-month-old infant (Watson &

Table 1.4 Time Line of Philosophers and Physicians and Their Key Contribution Regarding Children

460–370 BCE	Hippocrates	Specific prescriptions for child treatment
384–322 BCE	Aristotle	Children are blank tablets
40 BCE	Virgil	Child is father to the man
1632–1704	John Locke	Importance of environmental influences
1717–1778	Jean-Jacques Rousseau	Children are arational
1855–1924	Luther Emmett Holt	1894 *Care and Feeding of Children*
1903–1998	Benjamin Spock	1946 *Baby and Child Care*

Photo 1.8 One of the fathers of American psychology, G. Stanley Hall (*front row, center*), invited Sigmund Freud (*seated on Hall's right*) and Carl Jung (*seated on Hall's left*) to Clark University in 1909.

Source: Library of Congress/Science Faction/Getty Images

Rayner, 1920). By scaring Albert with the sound of a gong when a white rat was brought into view, Watson taught Albert to be afraid of the sight of a white rat. This was the first study to use classical conditioning on an infant. This form of learning, made famous by Soviet psychologist Ivan Pavlov (1849–1936), involves pairing a conditioned stimulus (in Albert's case, the rat) with an unconditioned stimulus (fear caused by the loud sound of the gong).

The famous study was flawed in various ways (both ethically and methodologically), and recent evidence indicates that Albert was neurologically impaired and had several serious medical conditions (Fridlund, Beck, Goldie, & Irons, 2012). Nevertheless, Watson developed a theory of child rearing. His book, *Psychological Care of Infant and Child* (1928), provided a psychological companion to Holt's manual. Watson believed that classical conditioning (operant conditioning had not yet been developed) could account for how children learned, and he ignored the role of genetic inheritance. See Table 1.5 for a look at how various psychologists contributed to how children were viewed.

Watson (1928) subscribed to some of Dr. Holt's views (e.g., not to kiss children) but developed his own views based on his theoretical orientation. For example, in contrast to Hall, Watson did not endorse the use of punishments at all. He wrote: "Punishment is a

Table 1.5 A Time Line of Psychologists and Their Key Contribution Regarding Children

1844–1924	G. Stanley Hall	American	First working research lab
1856–1937	Sigmund Freud	Austrian	Psychosexual development
1870–1937	Alfred Adler	German	Individual psychology
1878–1958	John B. Watson	American	Behaviorism
1896–1980	Jean Piaget	Swiss	Cognitive stage theory
1902–1994	Erik Erikson	German	Psychosocial stage theory

word which ought never to have crept into our language" (p. 111). He thought spanking was misguided for three reasons: It occurred well after the misbehavior, so it was not **contingent**; it served as an outlet for parental aggression; and it was unlikely to be used "scientifically" and thus appropriately. His parenting views will be discussed more fully in the next chapter.

Box 1.4 Personal Experience and the Experts

Where did the authorities get their information about how to parent? In some cases, they were informed by their interpretation of sacred texts. More commonly, individuals' personal experience in their own families and their unsystematic observations about children and parents informed their views. Many of the advice givers identified in this chapter were parents. Aristotle and Dr. Spock each had two children. Dr. Holt had five. Some of the early childrearing "experts," however, appear to have lacked extensive experience with children and therefore based their views on casual rather than systematic observations. Rousseau fathered five children, but he did not raise any of them. Because all his children were born out of wedlock (although to the same mother), they were sent to an orphanage. Rousseau thus based his beliefs on three sources: his work as a tutor, his observations of French peasant children, and what he had heard about children in primitive cultures (Damrosch, 2005). Locke, on the other hand, was a bachelor and did not have any offspring. Of the influential "authorities" cited, the only one who gained a rich background of experience with children and parents before writing his book was Dr. Spock. Spock wrote his book only after a decade of work as a pediatrician and fathering two children. Even so, he questioned the wisdom of his own advice and admitted that, "when a young man writes a book about how to raise children, in a sense, it's his reflection on the way his mother raised him" (Morgan & Spock, 1989, p. 136).

OTHER SOURCES OF PARENTING BELIEFS

Social and Political Forces

Writings by prominent religious leaders, philosophers, physicians, and psychologists provided influential sources of beliefs about children and parenting. However, those were not the only sources of beliefs. Society in general, politics, and the legal system also contribute to the way we think about children. Sandin (2014) provided a detailed history of how children have been treated in different societies, with a focus on social-political influences. How these forces shape views and treatment of children can be clearly seen in the areas of child labor, children's education, child welfare, and children's **rights**.

In all too many societies, children have been treated very poorly through history. According to the historian Lloyd deMause (1975),

> The history of childhood is a nightmare from which we have only recently begun to awaken. The further back in history one goes, the lower the level of child care, and the more likely children are to be killed, abandoned, beaten, terrorized, and sexually abused. (p. 1)

deMause documented widespread practices of **infanticide** (the killing of newborns and infants), child physical and **child sexual abuse**, selling or abandoning of children, sending infants to live with wet nurses, restraining infants with **swaddling** clothes during waking hours so they could not move, and practices such as Locke's "hardening" of infants (see Box 1.2).

It is not difficult to find additional examples of harsh and abusive childrearing practices in history. The earliest evidence, dating back to around 1750 BCE, of abusive practices appears on the clay tablets found in Mesopotamia (present-day Iraq). These tablets contain 282 codes or laws of conduct in ancient Babylon. Named the Code of Hammurabi, after the king who established them, the laws describe penalties for specific unacceptable behavior. The tablets reveal a patriarchal orientation toward offspring: Children were legally the property of their father and had none of their own rights. Codes dealt with a wide range of topics, including fathers' rights, property, slaves, payments and debts, inheritance and dowries, divorce, and adoption (Johns, 1903). Examples of some Babylonian directives include the following: *Code 14:* If someone steals a child, he shall be put to death; *Code 186:* If an adopted son injures his adoptive father or mother, the son shall be returned to his biological father's house; and *Code 195:* If a son strikes his father, they shall cut off his fingers. Indeed, children have also been disfigured, injured, and maimed throughout history to suit adult beliefs and desires. Child maltreatment will be discussed at length in Chapter 14. However, some of the abusive or controversial practices that have been or are being conducted in China, Italy, Arab countries, and the United States are described in Box 1.5.

Box 1.5 Mutilation of Children Across Time and Cultures

The Chinese practice of foot binding was performed on as many as 1 billion girls over a thousand years (10th to early 20th century). Girls, beginning as early as four years old, would have their feet tightly wrapped so the arch would not grow and their foot length would be no longer than four to six inches. Despite the pain and long-term crippling effects, mothers practiced this on their daughters so the children would be perceived as beautiful and marriageable. This practice was not officially banned until 1949 (Jackson, 1997).

Another example of mutilation—this time of boys—occurred in Italy from the mid-16th century until it was outlawed in 1870. Prepubescent boys were surgically castrated so their vocal chords would not develop and they could continue to sing in the soprano range. It is estimated that during the peak of this practice, as many as 4,000 boys were castrated annually in order to supply opera houses (Peschel & Peschel, 1987). A recording of a "castrato," Alessandro Moreschi—who died in 1922—can be found on the Internet.

A widely recognized example of a physical mutilation practice that continues today on some females is benignly called **female genital circumcision**. Another term that more accurately reflects the practice is *cutting*. To ensure against sexual activity and enjoyment, 80 to 100 million girls in Africa and the Middle East have had their clitoris removed and the labia partly cut away and then sewn together. The surgery is often unsanitary, with immediate and long-term medical problems. Surprisingly, many mothers condone the practice on their daughters so that men will want to marry them (otherwise the girls are considered promiscuous and unclean). The practice has been outlawed in many places but still continues, even occasionally in the United States (Sundby, Essén, & Johansen, 2013).

Thankfully, not all historical evidence points to abusive practices toward children. The childrearing orientation in ancient Egypt (ca. 3000–1000 BCE) was quite to the contrary. Based on what information can be gleaned from tomb paintings, hieroglyphics, medical literature, and archeological evidence, Egyptians—from pharaohs to peasants—parented in a child-centered way. Large families (with eight to 12 children) were common, and parents reared their offspring with love, care, and enjoyment (French, 2002). Mothers breastfed their children until age three. By the age of five or six, children began to prepare for their adult occupations, with the exception of the privileged children who attended school until age 14.

Greeks in the classical era (490–323 BCE) also enjoyed their children. They viewed their offspring as unformed and impressionable but also inheriting both physical and psychological characteristics from their parents and ancestors (Pomeroy, 1998). Ancient Greeks attended to their children and comforted them when they were frightened. Children were viewed as innocent, loving, happy, and playful. Aristotle (as had Plato before him) developed a **stage theory** about children and their proper care. He also recognized the individuality of each child and advised parents to tailor their child rearing to each particular child. In general, Greek child rearing had a nurturing orientation rather than a disciplinary one (French, 2002).

The Romans (510 BCE–476 CE) built upon Greek childrearing ideas. Roman parents believed in the importance of the early years of life and devoted considerable time and attention toward influencing their children's physical, moral, and intellectual development. They loved their children and worked to promote close relationships. At the same time, patriarchal power was primary. Fathers had absolute authority as embodied in the concept of ***patria potestas*** ("power of the father"). This doctrine gave fathers the right to kill anyone in the household, including grown children. Although this authority was tempered by various factors (e.g., the wishes of the mother, the legal obligation to rear sons to adulthood), historians have discovered many examples of fathers exercising their power, both with infants and older children (French, 2002). It took both religious (e.g., Prophet Mohammed) and political leaders to end the widespread practice of **filicide** (a parent deliberately killing his or her own child). Emperor Constantine, the first Christian emperor (280–337 CE), enacted two measures to discourage the practice, and it was subsequently banned.

Historical documents also reveal that childhood has always been an extremely hazardous period of life. Until only the recent past, a high percentage of children died at early ages. The Belgian social statistician Adolphe Quetelet (1796–1874) determined that 10% of infants died in the first month of life and 25% in the first year of life (Routh, 1879). Written records indicate that during the 16th century, the rate of **child mortality** (child death prior to age five) ranged from 20% to 42.6%. Of those children who died in childhood, about one-third died during childbirth and another 50% to 60% died during the first month of life (Shahar, 1990). In 17th-century New England, the infant mortality (death during the first 12 months of life) rate ranged from 10% to 33% (Mintz & Kellogg, 1988). Today, the highest infant mortality rate in the world is in Afghanistan, with an estimated rate for 2014 of 117 for every 1,000 births. In contrast, in 2004, the last year with complete data, the United States had a rate of 61 per 1,000 and was ranked 169th in the world (Central Intelligence Agency, 2014).

Children frequently died from accidents. During the central and late Middle Ages (12th through the 15th century), children faced many hazards. Common dangers included being smothered by sleeping adults, falling into wells or rivers, and getting burned by cooking fires or house fires (Shahar, 1990). A study of death records from this time period revealed the six most common causes of children's deaths: drowning, being crushed or pierced, falling, choking, being burned, and being killed by animals (Finucane, 1997).

Despite historically high rates of infant and child mortality, there is evidence that parents loved their babies, worried about their health, and grieved at their death. For example, the New England Puritan merchant Samuel Sewall, who lost seven of his 14 children before they reached age two, wrote in his diary of the "general sorrow and tears" when his two-year-old daughter died. In addition, he blamed himself for not being adequately careful about guarding her health (Mintz & Kellogg, 1988, p. 2).

Family economic needs were another determinant of childrearing practices. To survive, parents have often required that their young children work. This may have meant having children work alongside parents, assigning them to become apprentices, or sending them off to work on their own. It was not uncommon for children—sometimes as young as three years old—to work. The grim face of child labor occurring outside the family setting became common during the Industrial Revolution (roughly 1750–1850). At that time, as families migrated from countryside to towns, children toiled in factories, mines, manufacturing mills,

Photo 1.9 A young girl at work at a brick factory in Kabul, Afghanistan.

Source: © iStockphoto.com/EdStock

and on street corners. Exploitation was rampant: Children worked long hours, received very low pay, and were placed in dangerous, unregulated conditions. In England, many children worked 16-hour days before Parliamentary acts (e.g., the Factory Health and Morals Act of 1802) limited workdays in factories and cotton mills to a maximum of 12 hours. In the United States, children worked in a variety of jobs, including those in mines, canneries, textile and glass factories, and as newsboys and peddlers.

Over time, child labor was outlawed in the United States. Child labor laws were enacted as early as 1836 in Massachusetts, but it took another 82 years for all states (except Alaska) to pass compulsory education laws in which children were mandated to attend school. In 1938, a federal law (the Fair Labor Standards Act) was passed that established the minimum age of employment and number of hours worked. With the exception of the agricultural industry, child labor is no longer a social concern in the United States. However, it continues to be widely practiced, particularly in developing nations (see Photo 1.9). The International Labour Organization estimates that 306 million children between the ages of 5 and 17 work (Diallo, Hagemann, Etienne, Gurbuzer, & Mehran, 2010). Child labor is primarily in agriculture but also in illegal activities including child prostitution and house slaves.

Clearly, beliefs about children and how to rear them have undergone many "domestic revolutions" (Mintz & Kellogg, 1988). Ancient beliefs concerning the value of children, their roles in society, and the moral state of newborns ranged widely in the ancient world (as they do today). Other influences include economic shifts and hardships, politics, cultural changes, and (especially) statements and advice from those we view as authorities, such as pediatricians and psychologists. As new childrearing ideas are proposed and gain acceptance, practices shift, and subsequent generations are guided by evolving and evidence-based understandings about children's development and parenting.

Modern Media

In our modern world, we are bombarded by multiple sources of information about children and child rearing. The Internet is already strongly influencing our culture and certainly shaping the way we think about parenting. With a few clicks of the mouse, a parent today has Internet access to more than 42,000 parenting book titles. Type in "parenting" on a search engine and you will come up with somewhere around 87.7 *million* hits.

Consider Facebook, Twitter, blogs, posts, and texting on cell phones. We are no longer limited to advice from published experts, popular locals, or our grandmothers. Anyone with access to the Internet can offer an opinion online on everything from talking to your kids about drugs to ending bed-wetting to preparing nutritious snacks for a picky toddler. It is true that the Internet has made sound, scientific articles easily available. But it has also given a voice to many ideas with no reasonable basis. Even so-called "expert advice" discovered on the Internet might be based on a single, small sample or unpublished study. And with the many product endorsements, it can be hard to tell the advertisers from the advisors.

As for print media, more than three dozen parenting magazines can be found on the market, hundreds of books are readily available, and newspaper columnists regularly dispense parenting advice. Television broadcasts educational shows about how to rear children (both on public and cable television) as well as reality shows about the challenges of parenting (e.g., *Nanny 911*). If that's not enough, advertisements tell us what we *must* buy to make our children brighter, happier, and healthier.

Children's Rights

In some countries in the world, a relatively new perspective on children is beginning to affect how children are treated. That perspective involves recognizing children's rights as separate from parental rights. Children are the most vulnerable major subgroup of the human family, but in many parts of the world, they are still treated as the parent's property (Hart, 1991). The United Nations recognized this worldwide problem and created the **Convention on the Rights of the Child** in 1989 in an effort to bolster the recognition of their inherent dignity and as well as the inalienable rights of children (Melton, 2008). To date, all but three countries have ratified that convention—Somalia, South Sudan, and the United States (Scherrer, 2012).

USING RESEARCH TO UNDERSTAND PARENTING

Only through careful, systematic research can fact be culled from opinion. However, "facts" about children, parents, and social development in general are rarely fixed or immutable. The facts that do exist are not like laws of physics or chemical interactions, since each child is unique. The science of parenting consists more of the understanding of how children develop and the roles that parents play in influencing developmental processes—such as socialization and **individuation** (the process of becoming an autonomous person). The scientific efforts to study parenting have seen considerable development over the past century (see Photo 1.10).

Research Beginnings

Systematic research into child rearing, involving the collection of data and the testing of beliefs, began in earnest during the 1920s [Preview Question]. Studies were initiated to provide answers for parents. Beliefs about children and parents, once only the province of ministers, philosophers, physicians, and politicians, could now be tested with research. A few early research milestones warrant mentioning. The first parenting study involved a questionnaire about parents' views of child-discipline techniques (Sears,

Photo 1.10 The author's paternal ancestors photographed in 1899 in Cincinnati, Ohio.

Table 1.6 Early Landmark Studies Into Parenting

	Sample Size	Methods	Key Finding
Baldwin, Kalhorn, & Breese, 1945	150 children and their families	Interview	Parents who were democratic in childrearing styles had the most competent children.
Sears, Maccoby, & Levin, 1957	306 mothers	Interview	Maternal practices varied widely.
Baumrind, 1971	109 families	Interview, questionnaire, and observation	The typology of authoritative, authoritarian, and permissive parenting was established.

1899), conducted under the direction of G. Stanley Hall. However, it was only in the 1920s that studies began to appear in scientific journals with some regularity. The first child study center, established in Iowa in 1917, required many years of effort by an activist named Cora Bussey Hillis before it was funded. She recognized that the state was devoting considerable expense to studying how to breed better hogs. So, she argued, why not also focus on how to raise better children (Sears, 1975)? Child study centers were subsequently founded at Yale, Cornell, and the University of Minnesota. In 1930, *Child Development*, the leading journal in the field of developmental psychology, began publication. Even the concept of the *socialization* of the individual child is a relatively recent development in the social sciences, first being utilized and studied in the mid-20th century (Morawski & St. Martin, 2011).

Attention to understanding the role of parenting in development began in earnest in the mid-1940s. Table 1.6 lists three early landmark studies into parenting. These studies by psychologists made a variety of contributions, including methodological approaches to studying parents, testing new concepts, and identifying associations between parenting practices and child outcomes. They also served to establish child rearing as an important area of scientific inquiry.

Research and Expert Advice

How do contemporary childrearing expert advice and empirical research match up? One effort to address that question can be found in a book by Jane Rankin (2005). She analyzed the writings of five experts: two pediatricians (Drs. Spock and T. Berry Brazelton) and three psychologists (Dr. James Dobson, Dr. Penelope Leach, and John Rosemond) on six common childrearing issues. Rankin arrived at several conclusions. Foremost, the experts disagreed. For some issues, the disagreements were minor. But for others (including how to discipline children), their differences in opinion were dramatic. Given the conflicting advice, it was evident that experts do not necessarily base their advice on scientific

child-centered Thinking about children from the child's perspective or with the child's needs in mind.

child mortality The death of infants and children under the age of five.

child sexual abuse A type of child abuse that occurs when a child is used for the sexual gratification of an adult or adolescent. The abuse may take a variety of forms, ranging from exposing genitals to fondling or raping a child.

contingent Something, such as a behavior, that is dependent on or conditioned by something else.

Convention on the Rights of the Child A United Nations document designed to promote the rights of children around the world.

culture The way of life shared by members of a society.

discipline Training in order to produce a specific outcome or pattern of behavior. Often, this involves some type of punishment.

emotion regulation The ability to control one's own emotions.

female genital circumcision The practice of altering female genital organs for nonmedical reasons. Also called *female genital mutilation* or *female genital cutting*.

filicide A parent deliberately killing his or her own child.

hardening A variety of practices intended to toughen up infants in an effort to promote their survival.

immigrant An individual born in one country but living in another.

individuation The process of becoming an autonomous individual.

infanticide The killing of a child during the first year of life; the killing of newborns and infants.

infant mortality Child death during the first 12 months of life.

interdependence A belief system that, in contrast to independence, recognizes and values the interconnected nature of human relationships.

lay theories Folk beliefs that have not been empirically verified.

original sin The Christian theological concept that all children are born with sin.

patria potestas *The power of the father*—a doctrine in ancient Roman law giving authority to the father over his children, including decisions about life and death.

patriarchal The structuring of society where fathers in family units have the primary authority.

perceptions Recognition and interpretation of sensory stimuli.

rights Freedoms to which all humans are entitled.

shaming A disciplinary technique intended to make the child feel bad, guilty, or sad.

social constructions Beliefs about children and parents that are invented or constructed by participants in a culture or society. Also known as *cultural inventions*.

socialization The processes whereby children are taught to become competent individuals.

stage theory A type of theory based on the idea that there are discrete stages or steps and that children pass sequentially from the lower stages to the higher ones.

swaddling Wrapping an infant tightly in a blanket or some type of material.

CHAPTER 2

Theoretical Perspectives on Parenting

Chapter Preview: True or False?

- Freud proposed one of the earliest theories about development but gave little attention to the role that parents have.
- Evolutionary theory seeks to explain how parent-child behavior developed from hunter-gatherer societies.
- Twin studies of parental influence have found only a very small percentage of children's behavior to be impacted by their social environment or other nongenetic factors.

INTRODUCTION TO THEORY

Johnny Depp, in the movie *The Libertine,* portrays the fascinating John Wilmot, Second Earl of Rochester (1647–1680). Wilmot lived the life of a libertine, ignoring and even spurning religious norms, contemporary morals, and culturally acceptable behavior. Wilmot spent much of his time drinking excessive amounts of alcohol, chasing women, and partying. He also wrote poetry that today would be called pornographic. However, he is also remembered for a witty sentence attributed to him about theories of child development: "Before I got married, I had six theories about bringing up children; now I have six children and no theories." He was exaggerating: He only had four children when he died at age 33 from sexually transmitted diseases and alcoholism. But his quote underscores two key themes: First, *everyone* has ideas about child rearing. This idea was introduced in Chapter 1 with the description of *lay theories*. Wilmot's second point is that once you actually have children to rear, the task is considerably more complicated than anticipated. Your prior theories often do not hold up.

Lay Beliefs and Parental Behavior

Lay theories of parent-child relations are sometimes captured in aphorisms and clichés. In the English language, several expressions highlight the theme of parental influence: "Like father, like son; like mother, like daughter;" "Chip off the old block;" "The apple doesn't fall far from the tree;" "He's the spitting image of his father;" and "Following in his father's footsteps."

Theories about child rearing—whether lay or scientific—are important, because they help us understand parenting and prescribe the ways in which parents should behave. For example, some parents are under the mistaken notion that you can spoil infants by giving them too much attention. This lay misperception may have its roots in classical learning theory, but it is obviously an oversimplification of a complex interactional process. Learning theory is the implicit orientation here: If you give infants too much attention, they will learn to want it all the time. Recall from the last chapter the psychologist credited as being the father of behaviorism, John B. Watson. Based on his theoretical orientation, Watson (1928) warned about the dangers of love and affection. He wrote,

> Never hug and kiss them, never let them sit in [*sic*] your lap. If you must, kiss them once on the forehead when they say good night. Shake hands with them in the morning. Give them a pat on the head if they have done an extraordinarily good job of a difficult task. Try it out. In a week's time you will find how easy it is to be perfectly objective with your child and at the same time kindly. You will be utterly ashamed of the mawkish, sentimental way you have been handling it. (pp. 81–82)

Another example of how different childrearing beliefs result in different actions occurs with sleep problems. Bedtime can be a time of conflict in many households. Most parents have some problems trying to get a toddler or preschooler to sleep. Unless they are ill or exhausted, most children would rather stay up. In medieval times, parents resorted to drugging their children using the "quietness" concoction (see Box 1.3). We can certainly see how this practice has changed! Today, parents tend to deal with bedtime struggles using behavioral means. If a mother believes she is encouraging noncompliance and giving in to a child who resists bedtime and is allowed to stay up, she is operating under a learning-theory orientation. Her solution might be to ignore the child's cries or bids for a glass of water or another story. Ignoring may require shutting (or even locking) the child in his room and letting him plead or cry until he falls asleep (see Photo 2.1).

An alternative parental orientation might be based more on emotions and would result in a very different course of action. Here, a father might perceive his son as scared of the dark and in need of attention and reassurance. Consequently, he comforts the child and may read another story, lie down with him, or bring him into the parents' bed. Whether he knows it or not, this father's behavior and beliefs reflect the theory of attachment, which will be discussed later in this chapter.

Often, groups of parents can adhere to certain theories together. For instance, Puritans in colonial America had a clear theory of the source of problems in children and how to deal with them. Children were viewed as inherently evil or sinful and the parents' job was to drive this "evil instinct" away. This religiously driven theory about evil in children colored their perceptions and influenced parental practices. Today, most parents do not see their children in such a unidimensional way. Rather, parents' beliefs about children are varied and eclectic, and they often change over time with experience and changing circumstances.

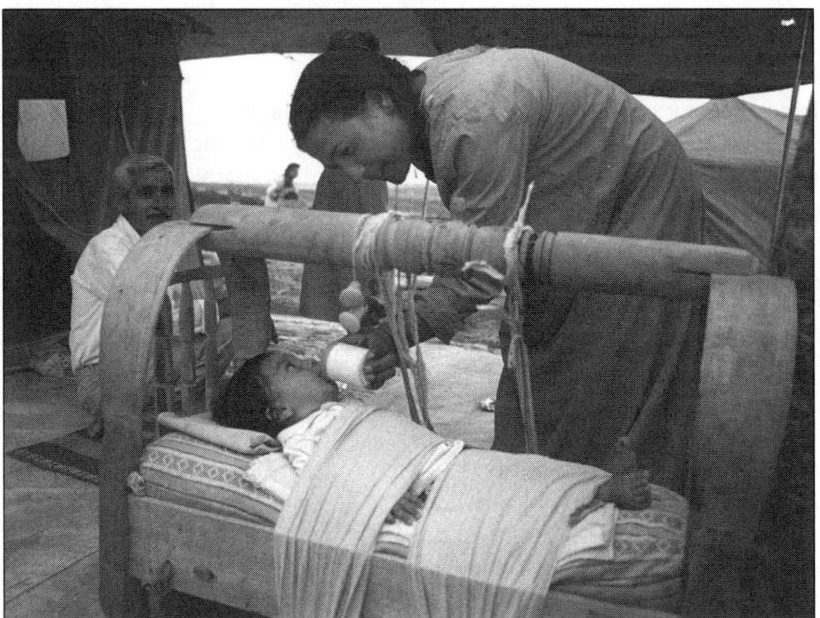

Photo 2.1 A Kurdish infant in northern Iraq lies in a crib with cloth bindings to keep the baby on the mattress in bed while the cradle is rocked from side to side.

Source: Photograph by J. P. Bell

One of the first theories about children's development was proposed by Sigmund Freud (1856–1939). Although Freud is famous for his rich theory of the conscious and unconscious mind, his psychosexual theory (1936) is less well known. Freud paid scant attention to the role that parents play in child development, with the exception of ensuring a smooth transition through each of the five psychosexual (and largely internalized) stages [Preview Question]. Freud hypothesized that children's development progressed in a fixed and orderly sequence through discrete stages that include oral, anal, phallic, and genital stages. Between the phallic and genital stage is a period (stage) of latency in which the sexual energy is repressed and not located in any body part. During each stage, the child's sexual energy is focused on a particular region or erogenous zone.

When the theory was put to the test, researchers found little support for it. Sewell and Mussen (1952) used Freud's theory to generate predictions concerning infant feeding practices and their development. They hypothesized that children who were breastfed versus bottle fed, those who were fed on demand rather than on a timetable, and those who were gradually weaned (versus abrupt weaning) would be more likely to successfully pass through the oral stage than other children and therefore be less likely to show personality or behavioral problems. However, they did not detect any significant effects as a consequence of different feeding histories. Due to studies such as that one, Freud's theory lost favor among researchers and was not the topic of much scientific work. Despite the shortcomings of his theory and the failure of other empirical research to support it, Freud's work opened the scientific door to the study of child rearing and parental influences on children.

Scientific Theories Addressing Parenting

There is no comprehensive theory of parenting, although various investigators have attempted to formulate one. As early as 1959, Benedict (1949) recognized parenthood as a developmental phase of life. Sameroff and Feil (1985) proposed four cognitive stages of parents' thinking about their children, with more advanced levels of thinking reflecting increasing differentiation of the parent and child. Ellen Galinsky (1981) developed a theory of parenting comprised of six orderly stages that are tied to the age of the child. The stages are (1) *image-making* (preparing for parenthood); (2) *nurturing* (birth–2 years); (3) *authority* (2–5 years); (4) *interpretive*, or helping the child understand the world (5–12 years); (5) *interdependent*, when parents need to develop anew their relationships (adolescence); and (6) *departure* (late adolescence). Although there are few empirical efforts to validate this theory, Galinsky's work has been critiqued on both methodological and theoretical grounds (e.g., Demick, 2002, 2006). It is no longer actively investigated.

Instead of specific theories about parenting, researchers frame their work based on more general theories about development or parent-child relationships. There are many such theories to choose from. For more than 100 years, formal theories about children's development—and how parents influence that progress—have been proposed. Theoretical approaches to the study of parent-child relationships differ widely on a variety of fundamental dimensions. They contrast in their scope, viewing parent-child relationships either from a **phylogenetic** (development of the species over time) or an **ontogenetic** (development of individuals over their life span) perspective. The approaches also differ markedly

Photo 2.3 Attachment theory is based on the importance for development of the love between a parent and a child. Here, a young father comforts his baby daughter with close contact and loving attention.

Source: Jupiterimages/Stockbyte/Thinkstock

by satisfying their needs and helping to regulate their emotions. In turn, infants learn to trust that the caregiver will take care of their needs. That trust develops into a secure attachment that promotes exploration of the environment, supports the development of social and cognitive competence, and establishes feelings of efficacy (Ainsworth & Bowlby, 1991; Easterbrooks, Bartlett, Beeghly, & Thompson, 2013).

Ainsworth, after observing how mothers and infants interacted in the Ganda tribe in Uganda (Ainsworth, 1967) and conducting a **longitudinal** study in Baltimore, designed a clever laboratory procedure to assess the quality of the attachment relationship (Ainsworth, Blehar, Waters, & Wall, 1978). In this 22-minute procedure, 12-month-old infants were put through increasingly stressful situations. The eight episodes listed in Table 2.1 involve a carefully orchestrated series of departures and reunions of the parent and an unfamiliar adult in order to gauge the infant's quality of attachment with his or her parent. The key episodes are numbers 5 and 8, when the parent returns to the room after the infant has been left with the unfamiliar adult or alone.

Ainsworth's early work was almost exclusively focused on maternal attachment, though now we consider these concepts to apply equally to fathers and other primary caregivers. How infants respond to the parent during these reunions is thought to reveal the essence of children's emotional ties to their parents—that is, children's learned behavior strategy of interacting with the mother. To determine the quality of the parent-child relationships, video recordings of infants in Ainsworth's Strange Situation procedure are painstakingly coded in order to classify a child into attachment types. The classification is based primarily on how infants behave when the mother leaves and returns. Other information that contributes to the coding includes how upset the infants become, how much they cry, and whether and when they show positive emotion.

One might expect all infants to be upset when their mothers leave them and, upon their return, to eagerly approach and hug them. These children are considered *secure* in their attachment to their mothers. However, depending on the sample, approximately 40% of infants respond quite differently. Some barely notice their mother's reentering the room or even ignore her return. These children are classified as **anxious-avoidant**. Another pattern of response is to be upset when the mother leaves and, upon reunion, approach her but resist being held. These children are classified as **anxious-resistant,** also called *ambivalent*.

Table 2.1 Ainsworth's Strange Situation Procedure

Episode	Actions	Comments
1	Introduction of Experimenter, Parent, and Child	Lasts only 30 seconds
2	Parent and Child alone	Parent watches Child
3	Stranger enters, talks with Parent, approaches Child. Parent leaves	Stranger silent first minute, then talks to Parent, then in 3rd minute to Child; first separation of Parent
4	Child alone with Stranger	Key question is whether Child gets comfort from Stranger
5	Parent returns, Stranger leaves	Reunion #1 of Parent and Child; Parent leaves at end of episode
6	Child is alone	Episode often lasts less than 3 minutes due to Child's distress
7	Stranger enters	Key question is whether Child gets comfort from Stranger
8	Parent returns, Stranger leaves	Reunion #2

Note: Each episode lasts 3 minutes except for Episode 1 and those episodes where the child becomes very distressed.

The final type of *insecure* attachment does not follow either pattern but instead shows a mixture of responses. These children do not have an organized behavioral strategy to deal with stresses and therefore are labeled **disorganized**.

Attachment theory holds that the way a child responds to the maternal absence is due to the history of parent-child interaction. Infants who received **sensitive parenting** over their first year of life developed secure attachments. **Sensitive parenting** means that, at a minimum, the parent responds promptly and appropriately as well as is available to help calm a distressed infant and help him or her to self-regulate (Easterbrooks et al., 2013). Furthermore, parents of secure children are also flexible, balanced, and integrated (Solomon & George, 2008). Imagine an infant who is in pain because she is hungry. She begins to cry. If her distress signal is responded to quickly and appropriately (she gets fed), she will begin to trust that caregiver to meet her needs. Over time, if the caregiver quickly and correctly addresses the infant's needs (such as hunger, boredom, and discomfort), the infant learns that the caregiver can be relied on. In this way, the infant feels secure in the presence of this adult.

Some mothers and fathers do not respond sensitively to their infants. It could be because the parent is depressed, angry, or stressed. Or the parent could be operating under the erroneous belief that infants do not need responsive care or that such care might even be damaging (for instance, they are afraid of spoiling the infant). In some cases, parents did not plan or want to have children, and they resent the demands of parenting. These parents may provide inconsistent care or even ignore or reject the infant's bids for attention. Parents who fail to respond sensitively are likely to have children who develop insecure attachment relations. If the parent does not attend regularly to the infant's needs, the child will develop an *anxious-avoidant* relationship pattern. Such children learn that the parent cannot be expected to provide for their needs, so they do not bother going to their parents later when stressed or in need.

Other parents may love their infants, but for various reasons, they have a poor sense of timing, misjudge their infants' needs, and are subsequently quite inconsistent in their care. For example, a mother may misread her infant son's fussiness and think he wants to play. Or a father may be preoccupied with his troubles and so responds inconsistently to his crying daughter. Consequently, the message the infant receives is that the parent is an unreliable caregiver. The infant learns that "my parent is unpredictable and cannot be counted upon to help me when I am in distress." As a result, that child will show an ambivalent—that is, *anxious-resistant*—pattern of behavior.

The third category of insecurely attached children—that is, *disorganized*—was created to describe children who could not otherwise be classified as *avoidant* or *resistant*. These infants did not show the typical strategies of avoiding their caregivers or responding to them with ambivalence. Instead, these infants did not display any consistent pattern of response. These disorganized children are believed to be survivors of abuse or some **trauma** and thus show peculiar and incoherent response patterns.

In the 1980s and 1990s, hundreds of studies were conducted using the Strange Situation procedure. A wealth of questions addressed such topics as the relation between maternal versus paternal attachment, the relation between child **temperament** and attachment, whether day care causes insecure attachments, the relations between maternal caregiving and attachment classification, cross-cultural differences in attachment patterns, and outcomes of secure attachment patterns in terms of social competence and school success. Some findings from these studies will be examined in subsequent chapters.

The newest frontier of attachment theory lies in understanding how early parent-child relationships influence a growing child's understanding of how reliable and trustworthy other people are. As their social world expands, children carry these views of others with them into their new relationships. These views are called **internal working models** (Bretherton & Munholland, 2008). As children develop, they build an understanding of the world that contains ideas and expectations about how other people will behave toward them.

According to attachment theorists (e.g., Bowlby, 1988; Cassidy, 2008), there is something else infants are learning from interacting with caregivers—their own worth or lack of worth. If a caregiver does not provide sensitive care, then infants get the message they are unworthy of care and perhaps unlovable. The theory has been extended to capture how individuals' internal representation of self and others influence their behavior in later childhood and adulthood (Ainsworth, 1989). Psychologists (e.g., Mikulincer & Shaver, 2008) also study the influence of early attachment relations as it relates to dating relationships and functioning in married couples.

Here is a rough example of how an internal working model may apply to a college student. Suppose a friend sets you up for a blind date. You show up at the appointed time and at the right place, but your date does not. What is your first thought? Do you suspect that your date was an unreliable person (i.e., suggesting a distrust of others)? Or do you think that perhaps the date arrived, checked you out from a distance, and decided you were not a good match (i.e., negative view of self)? Our immediate, uncensored reactions provide a glimpse of the working models of ourselves and of others that we carry around in our heads.

According to attachment theory, the implications of attachment classifications are profound because individuals base their interpersonal behavior on their internal working models, even into adulthood. Insecurely attached individuals are expected to behave differently from **securely attached** ones, whether interacting with their parents or others such as peers and teachers. In particular, investigations have linked adults' working models with how they form romantic relationships and how they parent their own children. However, these internal working models are just cognitions, and they can be changed. If an insecurely attached individual reevaluates her thinking, perhaps with the help of a therapist, she can establish new representations about herself and others. Such an individual can then shift into an "earned" secure status.

Attachment theory was developed to account for the development and significance of parent-child love. Another theory centered on the love (or lack thereof) between a parent and child is called **parental acceptance-rejection theory**. Developed by Ronald Rohner (1986), the theory is based around the idea that parental love results in positive outcomes, but rejection negatively affects a child's psychological adjustment and behavioral functioning. The four key questions this theory attempts to address are (1) What happens to children who perceive themselves to be loved or unloved by their parents? (2) Do the effects of childhood rejection extend into adulthood? (3) Why are some parents warm and accepting and others are cold, neglecting, and rejecting? and (4) What happens to a society when children in general are either accepted or rejected?

The tenets of Rohner's theory have been tested in more than 400 studies around the world. For example, a **meta-analysis** (a review that involves combining and comparing the results of multiple studies using a common and quantifiable measure of effect size) found largely universal effects of parental rejection on personality. A total of 43 studies (representing more than 7,500 children and adults from America, Africa, Asia, Europe, South America, and the Caribbean) were reviewed (Khaleque & Rohner, 2002). The theory correctly predicted most (about 80%) of the participants' personality scores. Rejected children are more likely to be fearful, insecure, attention seeking, jealous, hostile, and lonely. However, a small percentage of rejected children appeared to be resilient and were functioning well. Similarly, some children from accepting families showed symptoms of rejection. Rohner accounts for that finding with the explanation that these individuals may have experienced rejection by someone other than the parent, such as a peer or romantic partner.

Theories about parent-child love continue to hold interest for researchers and parents alike because they address one of the fundamental experiences of parenting. Next, we move on to a very different approach to the parent-child relationship coming from the behavioral tradition.

Behavioral Theory

John B. Watson (1878–1958) was a prominent and colorful early behavioral theorist. Though the centerpiece of his theory was observable behavior, Watson's work acknowledged the importance of social learning as well. Known as the "father of behaviorism"

candy. When the child stops fussing, the parent's action has been negatively reinforced because an unpleasant stimulus (the noxious child fussing) was withdrawn. The next time the parent takes the child shopping, the parent is more likely to buy candy quickly so as to avoid the fussing altogether. In this case, the parent is the one being trained! Interestingly, the candy has also positively reinforced the child's fussing, so the child is more likely to fuss again—and more vigorously—on the next shopping trip unless given the candy. This example highlights the potential **bidirectional** (or dynamic) aspect of something so basic as simple reinforcement of behavior.

To add complexity to the picture, reinforcement may be social as well as material. In fact, most parent-child interactions will involve social reinforcement or punishment rather than material consequences. We can see, then, how Skinner's theory of operant conditioning can be used to uncover the causes of some seemingly mysterious behavioral outcomes. It can be useful in explaining how children acquire bad habits from their parents and how parents inadvertently reinforce behaviors they do not like, such as whining, noncompliance, and temper tantrums.

According to behavior theorists, parents often make at least three basic operant conditioning mistakes. Perhaps most commonly, they give attention to undesired behaviors and thereby reinforce them. A child misbehaves and the parent reacts by reprimanding. The child then gets attention, which can be reinforcing, even if the attention is of an unpleasant form. This is a difficult concept for most parents to grasp—that negative attention can actually be reinforcing to the child. The child may not enjoy the parent yelling at her, but if the child's target behavior increases, it has been reinforced. A second problem is that parents fail to positively reinforce desired behaviors. When a child is playing nicely with a peer, parents generally do not notice and so miss the opportunity to reward the behavior with positive attention and compliments. The third type of error parents commonly make is to overly rely on punishments rather than reinforcements.

There are two types of fundamental problems with punishments. First, they generally are ineffective because parents do not punish correctly. Punishment is only effective if it is used consistently (any time the misbehavior occurs), contingently (right after the misbehavior), and—at least following the initial instance of the misbehavior—firmly and decisively (Gershoff, 2013; Holden, 2002). However, most parents are reluctant to punish firmly, are likely to postpone punishment (i.e., "Wait until we get home!"), and are inconsistent in dispensing punishment. A second type of problem with punishment is that it introduces fear and anxiety into what should be constructive and pleasant child-parent interactions.

As with any theory, there is the danger of oversimplifying or misapplying the practice of conditioning. Although candy, allowance, and gold star stickers can function as rewards (material reinforcers), the most powerful parental reinforcer is attention and approval (a social reinforcer). No amount of monetary or material reward can substitute for the attention that children crave. Unfortunately, these days, at least with older children, rewards for good grades often come in the form of money, iPods, or gift cards. One of the concerns with that practice is that when external rewards are given for educational goals, students will not be internally motivated and will not develop a love of learning. Later, when the reward is no longer offered, children may not continue to want to learn or to be self-motivated to do well in school or college.

Behavioral principles for understanding learning have stood the test of time and continue to be relevant as we seek to understand such topics as child discipline, learning, and behavior change, including therapeutic interventions for problem behaviors such as anxiety disorders and phobias. The principles of reinforcement, punishment, and classical conditioning, however, do not address more complex human systems, which we will now explore as we consider other kinds of influences on children's behavior that may inform parents' behavior as well.

BIOLOGICAL, GENETIC, AND ENVIRONMENTAL INFLUENCES

Evolutionary Developmental Psychology

Charles Darwin shocked the world and revolutionized the scientific community when, in 1859, he published his theory about the **evolution** of humans and animals. His core conceptualization was deceptively simple. According to the concept of **natural selection**, not all individuals have the same chances for survival in a particular environment. Those better suited for their environment will survive longer and more often, leaving behind more offspring than will those individuals who are less well adapted. Characteristics, then, that are a better match for the environment will be more likely to be genetically transmitted to the next generation. They are thus "selected." Through this process, particular traits and characteristics become more or less common in any given population. According to contemporary applications of Darwinian theory, natural selection operates on individuals (and therefore their genetic material) with the goal of having our **genes** survive in subsequent generations. Thus, as the biologist Richard Dawkins (1976) phrased it in his celebrated book, our genes are "selfish."

When the evolutionary approach is applied to parenting, researchers seek to understand how patterns of child rearing have been modified and selected—at least, during the past 35,000 years, when anatomically modern humans emerged and lived in **hunter-gatherer** communities [Preview Question]. Given that 99% of human generations (each generation lasts roughly 25 years) have lived in hunter-gatherer societies, the aim of the evolutionary approach is to explicate how contemporary parent behavior reflects and is affected by selection processes within these societies.

Individuals have evolved to be particularly attuned to certain environmental events or stimuli in order to promote their survival. The fear of heights or fear of snakes are good fears to have if one wants to live long. The same evolutionary theory has led researchers to look for characteristics and behaviors in organisms that promote the survival of the young. It is easy to recognize that the cry of an infant is a powerful and aversive behavior designed to elicit rapid caregiver attention. Thus it is an example of a human behavior that probably evolved to increase the survival prospects of the **altricial** (an organism requiring care and feeding to survive) human infant. Parents may not appreciate the positive aspects of the lusty cries of their newborn, but they certainly know they are effective in getting their attention! There are also more subtle stimuli that have been linked to caregiving behavior. The unique facial characteristics of human infants and other young animals that we perceive as

Photo 2.4 Evolutionary psychologists argue that the distinctive features of infants that make them appear cute have been selected in order to ensure parental care and investment.

Source: Photograph by J. P. Bell

cute (e.g., large forehead, round cheeks, small nose and chin) represent a special class of stimuli that are believed to literally "turn on" caregiving behavior—whether it be in animals or humans (Eibl-Eibesfeldt, 1970; see Photo 2.4). Who can deny the impulse to cuddle or care for such an adorable creature?

Evolutionary theorist Kevin MacDonald (1992) argued that the feeling of love for a child has been selected over hundreds of thousands of years. That emotion has served to ensure cohesive family relationships and paternal involvement in child rearing, thus increasing the likelihood of child survival. Although love is a complex concept, one can imagine that it can prompt better and more self-sacrificial parenting behaviors. Another concept of interest to evolutionary researchers is **parental investment** (Trivers, 1974). Parents (especially mothers in traditional societies) devote a great deal of time, energy, money, and thought to rearing their children. But why do some parents spend so much time with some children while other parents may be largely uninvolved? According to evolutionary theory, the answer lies in the amount of shared genetic material, the offspring's likelihood of survival, and the future likelihood that the child will have children (e.g., Geary, 2006). For example, evolutionary psychologists argue that it was adaptive for our ancestors with scarce resources not to care for premature or handicapped newborns who were unlikely to survive—thus providing a phylogenetic basis for the widespread practice of infanticide, discussed in the previous chapter. In addition, cultural, social, and environmental factors may also have contributed to the frequent use of this practice.

Differential parental investment has also been proposed as the explanation of why some parents physically abuse their children. Two researchers (Daly & Wilson, 1996) proposed that serious child abuse—when children are killed—can be explained by evolutionary theory. When they analyzed Canadian child fatality data, they discovered that the annual rate of child homicides was about 500 victims per million for fathers living with stepchildren. In contrast, the child homicide rate for fathers and their biological children was less than 20 victims per million. Stepfathers, then, were 25 times more likely to murder their stepchildren than were biological fathers. Although there are social interaction explanations for this effect, and other investigators have not replicated that finding (e.g., Malkin & Lamb, 1994), the results are provocative.

It is important to point out that an evolutionary view of development does not claim that any action is inevitable. Rather, current proponents of **evolutionary psychology** (e.g., Bjorklund & Jordan, 2013) view our heritage as providing a propensity or bias *toward* behaving or reacting in particular ways due to selection pressures. It is possible to counteract that bias, but a person needs to be conscious of that bias and then work to compensate for it.

Behavioral Genetics Theory

In contrast to big-picture focus of evolutionary theory, the field of human behavioral genetics is more concerned with evaluating the possibility of how human traits and even behaviors might be directly impacted by genetic inheritance. This field of inquiry has often focused on understanding the origins of aggression and other problem behaviors.

Willie Bosket was a bright and appealing child, but by the time he was 15 years old, he was also a double murderer. Social cognitive as well as ecological systems theories, which will be covered later, would explain Willie's violent behavior by analyzing how he was reared and other environmental influences: His mother was a poor, single parent who relied on harsh physical punishment in her efforts to socialize him; as a preteen, he spent considerable time with **delinquent** peers who encouraged him to be violent.

Behavioral genetics theory takes a different approach to explaining behavior. It focuses on genetic inheritance and environmental contributions to behavior or particular characteristics. The behavioral genetics theory explanation of Willie's behavior would be that he was genetically predisposed to violent behavior. After all, Willie's father, whom Willie had never met, had a long criminal history that had started before he was eight years old. The family history of violence and criminality did not end there. Willie's grandfather and great-grandfather also had violent histories (Butterfield, 1995). The fact that four generations of Bosket men had violent criminal records suggests another possible influence on behavior—that of genetic inheritance.

The goal of behavioral genetics theory is to understand both genetic and environmental influences on human behavior (McGuire, Segal, & Hershberger, 2012; Plomin, 1990). This orientation upon genetic determinants began with the English scientist Sir Francis Galton (1822–1911) and was pursued by the American physician Arnold Gesell (1880–1961). Trained as an educator, developmental psychologist, and physician, Gesell posed a **nativist** theory of development. He believed that children's genetic constitution determined the natural unfolding of their inherited predispositions. Gesell pioneered a variety of photographic methods to carefully document children's growth. Parents' central role was to support this unfolding by providing an environment appropriately matched to the child's state of maturational readiness (Thelen & Adolph, 1992).

Gesell's legacy can be readily seen in contemporary behavioral genetics theory; however, in contrast to Gesell, who was primarily interested in charting the normative course of development, modern behavioral geneticists typically study how variations in genetic similarity are associated with variations in personal traits. Most behavioral genetics studies involve either *twin studies* or *adoption* research. In twin studies, the similarities in children's characteristics within a family are compared in identical, fraternal, and non-twin siblings. Adoption studies are used to compare the similarities between adopted and biological offspring with their biological and adoptive parents. Clearly, behavioral geneticists are not only interested in a child's **genotype**, or genetic makeup, but they are also focused on the child's **phenotype**, how traits are expressed behaviorally. No child is a perfect copy of his or her parents. Though a child receives 50% of his or her genes from each parent, not even these are all exact copies. Behavioral geneticists also recognize that the environment plays an important role in the child's phenotype, beginning with the environment when the child was *in utero*.

Ecological Systems Theory

Ecological systems theory was created by Urie Bronfenbrenner to capture how the developing child is embedded in a series of environmental systems or contexts that interact with one another and with the person (e.g., Bronfenbrenner, 1979; Bronfenbrenner & Morris, 2006). A serious problem with previously proposed theories (such as attachment or social cognitive theories) was that they did not explicitly consider the roles that environment and context play in influencing behavior.

Bronfenbrenner's theory expands on Kurt Lewin's (1935) classic formula of behavior, $B = f(P,E)$, or a person's behavior is a function of (or caused by) a combination of the person and the environment. Ecologists believe that one cannot and should not separate out the person from the environment; the two are integrally connected. This constant interaction between the two is described as **transactional influence**. In the case of parent-child relationships, this means that the child's behavior or characteristics can influence both the parent and the context in which the interactions occur. In turn, the context influences the child's subsequent behavior and characteristics. For example, an athletic child may persuade her parents to allow her to join a soccer team. That involvement, in turn, may result in family trips to attend soccer tournaments, summers at soccer camp, and new friends for both the child and the parents. Those new experiences and relationships then influence the child and result in new experiences.

The central contribution of Bronfenbrenner's theory lies in explicating how children's biologically influenced characteristics interact with multiple levels of the natural environment. These levels of context are hierarchically organized and nested, each within the next. The innermost environmental context is called the **microsystem** and refers to the immediate settings that a person encounters and the interactions and activities within those settings. So interactions at home, in the classroom, or in the mall are examples of the microsystem context. The interactions a child has in this context are often bidirectional: The child influences the surroundings, and the surroundings influence the child. For example, a friendly and attentive child is more likely to evoke positive and patient childrearing behaviors in contrast to a high-activity child who may elicit more restrictions and reprimands. These bidirectional interactions recur over time and can have a lasting effect on development.

The second level of the model is the **mesosystem**, which refers to the connections or interrelations between microsystems. Children's development is promoted when there are supportive links between microsystems. An example is school success. Performance at school depends, in part, on whether the child is ready for school. **School readiness** depends on what goes on in the home or in child care centers to prepare the child for school. Thus the links between home, child care centers, and school contribute to school success and represent part of the mesosystem (see Figure 2.1).

The next level, called the **exosystem**, refers to contexts that do not ordinarily contain children but nevertheless affect their development. The parent's place of employment is one such setting. That setting influences children's development through employment policies (e.g., sick leave) as well as the work climate. A parent who has had a hard day at work will come home in a different mood than another parent who has had a positive day (Matjasko & Feldman, 2006). A parent's group of friends or **social support** network is another example of an exosystem.

Figure 2.1 The Ecological Framework

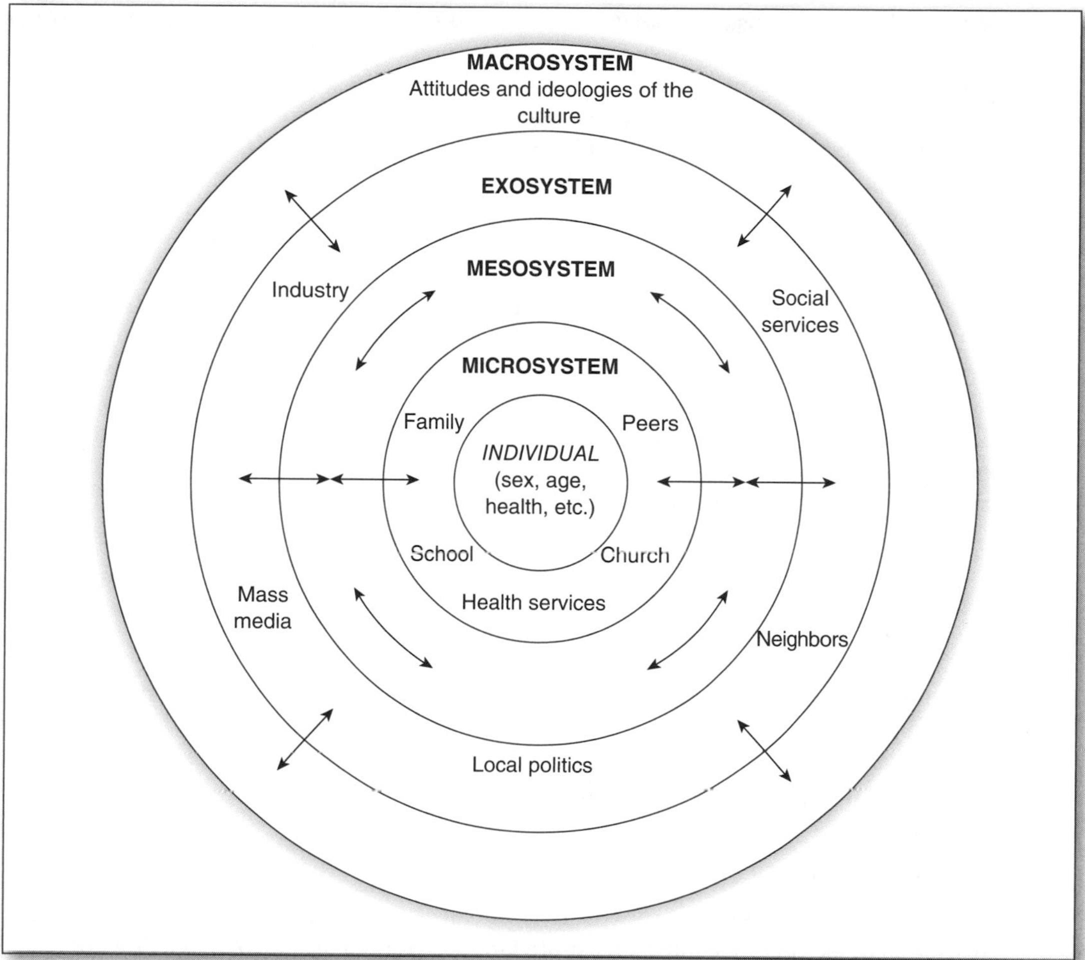

Source: ©Hchokr/Wikimedia Commons/CC-BY-SA-3.0/GFDL

The final and outermost level of Bronfenbrenner's model is the **macrosystem**. This level refers to the subcultural or cultural context in which microsystems, mesosystems, and exosystems are embedded. It includes the cultural values, laws, and customs of a particular society. What happens at this level affects each of the inner levels. Governmental policies about children and cultural institutions (such as the church) and general cultural beliefs about children and parenting are captured at this level of analysis. Simply put, these are the **social policies**, customs, and practices that have an impact on the society's children. Several examples of the legal/political macrosystem were discussed in Chapter 1, including the banning of infanticide and the instigation of child labor laws.

Bronfenbrenner recognized that past experiences influence present behavior, that environments change over time, and that children change, so he included the **chronosystem** in his model. This system refers to how nested systems of interactions influence future behavior as well as change as the child gets older. For example, maturational changes that occur in puberty are linked to increased parent-child conflict, as will be discussed in Chapter 10 (Paikoff & Brooks-Gunn, 1991).

The ecological systems theory has been particularly influential in at least two ways. First, it has helped to focus attention on the role that context plays in the lives of children and their parents. Second, it has afforded a theoretical structure within which to integrate diverse research results, such as the influence of different types of external environments (e.g., work, social networks, and neighborhoods) on the adaptive and maladaptive functioning of families. Bronfenbrenner's theory provides a useful framework for recognizing the different contextual influences on an individual and how those influences help to shape a child's development. It also recognizes the role that children can play in their own development, a topic we will address later in this chapter (self-determination theory).

Bronfenbrenner's multifaceted approach provides a good segue now for us to consider another broad area of theoretical inquiry into children's development: social learning theory. We will look at examples of **social learning theories** from Patterson and Bandura and also view some examples of theories that either put their accent on parental determinants or on children's behavior within the broader context of socialization and social learning.

SOCIAL LEARNING AND SOCIAL THEORIES

Children change as they grow, and at least some of this change relates to what they learn as they interact with others in their world. This concept is the basis for social learning theories and their derivative, **social cognitive theory**. These theories address how social behavior is modified through specific social experiences.

Social Cognitive Theory

Bandura (2001) was one of the theorists who developed social learning theory. His early work was based on modeling, as illustrated in the postcard of the girl modeling her mother's behavior (see Photo 2.5). Contemporary theories have evolved from a mixture of previous theories, including psychoanalytic theory, behavioral learning theory, and cognitive theories (Cairns, 1979; Grusec, 1992).

Gerald Patterson is a social learning theorist who recognized the power of operant conditioning in parent-child relationships. For many years, he carefully analyzed the behavioral interactions of antisocial boys and their families and made several important insights into the development of **conduct disorder** and delinquency. At the heart of his model are **coercive cycles**, problematic interactions in which parent and child compete to see who can gain the upper hand. The cycle may start with a mundane event, such as a mother nicely requesting that John, her six-year-old son, pick up the mess of toys and clothes strewn across his room. If he is like most children, he will ignore the first request. When the mother returns to inspect

Box 2.4 Scaffolding Two-Year-Olds in the Supermarket Study

Everyone has witnessed out-of-control young children in the supermarket. You have seen them running up and down the aisles, fussing for food, or throwing a tantrum. At the same time, other children of the same age are sitting nicely in shopping carts, perhaps assisting their mothers with the shopping task. What differentiates the two types of behavior? Lev Vygotsky, if he were alive today, would say it was the parental behavior that determined their children's behavior. Parents who scaffold (or support) positive behavior elicit much more mature behavior from their children than other parents.

To investigate how others did this, the author (Holden, 1983) followed mothers (with their permission) and their two-year-old children during two weekly trips to the market. After placing a tape recorder in a cereal box in the mother's cart (in order to collect verbalizations), the author followed the mother-child dyad from behind, pushing a shopping cart and taking notes about the mothers' and children's behavior. It was immediately evident that most of the mothers were actively engaged in promoting good behavior. Mothers had a variety of tricks they used to ensure good behavior: They brought toys from home, bought bananas for the child to eat, avoided problematic aisles, or gave the child a task to perform, such as being on the lookout for a certain item. But the technique used most commonly was to engage the child in the shopping task. By doing this, mothers were structuring and supporting more mature child behavior. Through **scaffolding**, mothers moved children into the zone of proximal development, an area of more mature behavior than the child would be able to achieve on his or her own. Experiences in the zone were what Vygotsky believed provided a major engine for development.

The fundamental way that parents are able to elicit more mature behavior is through the process of scaffolding. Parents erect a structure around a desired behavior to support children's more advanced behavior. As children grow more advanced in their linguistic, cognitive, or social interactional ability, parents no longer need to provide that structure. Eventually, children are able to navigate through a toy store on their own without parents closely monitoring and controlling their every move. Thus parents occupy a central role in their children's acquisition of mature behavior, according to **Vygotsky's theory**.

Although it may be easiest for adults to relate to their importance and influence in the parent-child relationship, the dynamic nature of human relationships insists that we also consider there may be times when children demonstrate a great deal of agency in their own development. Deci and Ryan's theory (2012), which we now turn to, presents an intriguing counterbalance to the adult-centric emphasis postulated by most theorists.

Box 2.5 Control Theory

A very different type of theory was developed by Richard Bell to account for parental regulation of child behavior. Rather than focusing on attachment and emotions, **control theory** concerns the ongoing *reciprocal* nature of interactions (Bell, 1979; Bell & Chapman, 1986). It reflects the view that parents and children regulate each other's behavior. According to Bell, parents have an upper and lower limit of tolerance for the intensity, frequency, and situational appropriateness of their children's behavior. These limits are based on expectations and previous interactions. Parents attempt to keep their children within the ideal boundary set by these upper and lower limits.

Young children often violate a parent's *upper limits*. This might mean the child is too loud, too active, or engaged in unacceptable behavior. The parent reacts by reducing or redirecting the child's excessive behavior so it falls back into the acceptable range. Alternatively, a "couch potato" child (perhaps "addicted" to television or video games) might violate a parent's *lower limits*. The parent would be motivated to try to make the child more active. Bell argued that the model holds equally well from the child's perspective. If a parent gives a child inadequate attention (violating the child's lower limit), the child might act in such a way as to stimulate the parent to action.

This theory of mutual regulation has received support from observational studies of parents and children, focusing on such child characteristics as activity level, independence, and responsiveness (Bell & Chapman, 1986). However, the model is best suited to account for parent-child relationships during times of disequilibrium. When the parent-child dyad is in a period of stability and the individuals are meeting each other's expectations, the model has little explanatory power (Maccoby & Martin, 1983).

Child Emphases: Self-Determination Theory

Self-determination theory is a theory about what motivates individuals to act (Deci & Ryan, 2012; Ryan & Deci, 2000). All individuals have three basic needs: autonomy, competence, and relatedness. Children want to be able to do things for themselves, master their environment, engage in activities they like, and persist in goal-directed behavior. This theory focuses upon the agency of the child, understanding that even from a very young age, children are motivated for mastery—they have a strong desire to have a say in the way in which they develop.

We can see an early example of this in Western culture, the so-called *terrible twos*. Children even as young as two years of age exhibit a strong will and a desire to do things their own way, in their own time, and as independently as possible. This is a common and vexing phenomenon to parents. Some parents regard that behavior as problematic, although this theory considers that behavior to be not only normative but also an indication the child is developing appropriately.

Parents, according to this theory, need to be involved, provide structure, and support the child's developing autonomy. Involvement means showing an interest in, being knowledgeable about, and staying active in their children's lives. Through this, children will feel connected and related to the parent. By structuring the environment to promote competence, the environment becomes predictable and understandable. Children know what is expected of them and how others will respond to them. Autonomy support means taking the child's perspective, encouraging their initiations, and providing them with developmentally appropriate choices. These three parenting qualities promote children's well-being (Farkas & Grolnick, 2010).

FAMILY SYSTEMS THEORY

Murray Bowen (1913–1990) was trained as a physician in psychiatry. At the time of his education, mainstream psychiatric thinking was exclusively informed by Freudian psychodynamic theory. Bowen's life experiences in World War II caused him to consider a different way of thinking about disease and mental illness. As a result of Bowen's early research at the Menninger Foundation, **family systems theory** was born. In contrast to the individual or even dyadic focus of most child development and parenting theories, systems theory views the *family* as the basic emotional unit. Any change in the emotional functioning of one member of the family is predictably and automatically compensated for by changes in the emotional functioning of other members of that family. Family systems theory attempts to explain social behavior and patterns of social interactions via an understanding of these interacting systems. Systems theory also posits that multigenerational patterns of family interaction, assigned roles within the family, social triangulation, and the tendency for all emotional systems to seek and maintain homeostasis function to affect behavior and emotional health.

To fully understand behavior in the family, one cannot simply focus on an individual child in isolation or only on the parent-child dyad. Rather, relationships among all members of the family must be recognized in order to understand how the behavior of individuals is supported by, encouraged, or reacted to other family members (e.g., Carter & McGoldrick, 2005; Minuchin, 1985; Nichols & Schwartz, 2007). For example, the parent-child relationship is often disrupted in families experiencing marital discord. In such a situation, in order to understand the parent-child relationship (and perhaps why a child was experiencing behavior problems), it is not only necessary to recognize the conflict between the husband and wife (e.g., Buehler et al., 1997) but to understand how the child's behavior may play a direct role in maintaining family equilibrium. Children do not want their parents to fight with each other. Systems theory might predict that, in such situations, children might develop serious psychological or behavioral problems. Subsequently, the emotional energy of the parents turns away from each other and toward the child, thus often reducing parental conflict (at the cost of a symptomatic child). A family systems theorist is careful to examine *all* family members and their interrelationships in order to appreciate the behavioral dynamics operating within a family (e.g., Cox & Paley, 2003).

Family systems theory has uncovered a number of useful concepts for understanding triadic family interactions that involve a mother, a father, and a child. For example, **second-order effects** refers to the observation that one parent may interact differently

Photo 2.6 Family systems theory considers the interrelationships between all of the family members. This cartoon illustrates the concept of triangulation.

Source: © The New Yorker Collection 2006 Danny Shanahan from cartoonbank.com.

toward a child when someone else—in this case, a spouse—is present. An example of this occurs in violent homes, where mothers or fathers might alter their childrearing behavior when in the presence of an abusive partner. For instance, in one study mothers were found to modify their disciplinary practices when in the presence of an abusive spouse. They did this in order to appease their partners and avoid inciting their anger. There was not one consistent way mothers attempted to pacify their violent husbands; some women used more strict discipline with their children, whereas others became more permissive (Holden & Ritchie, 1991).

The most frequently studied construct in parenting that derives from family systems theory is **co-parenting**. This concept refers to how mothers and fathers function together in their roles as parents and, in particular, whether the parents are mutually supportive and involved. For example, if one parent takes over the tasks of an ill parent, that would be an example of mutual support and cooperation. If one parent disparages the efforts of the other parent, that would be an example of negative co-parenting. Systems theorists also call this *triangulation*. Investigators have identified a number of separate components of co-parenting, including conflict, disparagement, cooperation, and triangulation (McHale & Lindahl, 2011). An example of triangulation can be seen in the cartoon (see Photo 2.6).

OTHER EMOTION-BASED THEORIES

The next theoretical orientation we will look at examines a specific application of family dynamics to the problem of interpersonal conflict in families. In particular, it addresses the question of how children are affected by parental conflict.

Emotional Security Theory

This theory focuses on the effects of children's reactions to interparental conflict. According to the theory proposed by Patrick Davies and Mark Cummings (1994), children who see their parents arguing become fearful that this conflict indicates impending separation and divorce. This fear results in emotional distress. Thus the **emotional security theory** focuses on children's perceptions of and exposure to parental conflict. If parents engage in frequent acrimonious exchanges, children will feel insecure and worry about whether their parents will get divorced—and what will happen to themselves. Alternatively, children who are exposed to little or no marital discord, or to conflict that gets resolved amicably, develop feelings of emotional well-being and develop an improved capacity for regulating their emotions.

This theory has been empirically tested in a number of experimental and naturalistic studies with similar results. Children exposed to adult arguments experience physiological arousal, emotional distress, and health problems (Troxel & Matthews, 2004) as well as behavioral problems (Cummings, Schermerhorn, Davies, Goeke-Morey, & Cummings, 2006). However, if a conflict is resolved in a respectful, constructive way (such as coming to an agreement or agreeing to disagree), the negative effects associated with the conflict are greatly diminished.

DEVELOPMENTAL STAGE THEORIES

We turn our attention now to two developmental stage theories that have informed an enormous body of research in the 20th century and that have proved important to understanding the ways in which parents view the changing child. Every parent knows that children change dramatically over a short period of time. The tasks, problems, and joys of each stage of children's development require a dynamic understanding in order to best meet children's needs and optimize their development. Both Piaget's and Erikson's theories recognized that children think and behave differently as well as have different motivations at different points in their childhood.

Piaget

Swiss-born Jean Piaget (1986–1980) began his academic career not in the field of psychology, but studying mollusks! He received a doctorate when he was only 21 years old but was unable to obtain a faculty appointment in his field. He moved to Paris and started teaching at a boy's school run by Alfred Binet, a pioneer in the development of intelligence tests. His observations of children's errors led him to develop groundbreaking ideas on the nature of children's cognitive skills as they grow and develop.

It may seem strange to us today, but at the time, Piaget's claim that cognitive development proceeds through a series of universal and invariant stages was both bold and controversial. Piaget's stage theory is found in Box 2.6. His monumental contributions lay in revealing that the ways children think and process information are fundamentally different from adults.

Box 2.6 Piaget's Stage Theory

Period	Ages	Core
Sensorimotor	birth to 2 years	reflexive responding
Preoperational	2 to 7 years	symbol use begins
Concrete operational	7 to 11 years	use of logical relations
Formal operations	onset at 11 to 15 yrs	abstract thought

The core of Piaget's cognitive theory was formed as a result of hundreds of interviews, experiments, and observations of how children think (and what they communicate about that) at various ages. The implication for parenting is that at different stages of cognitive development, children process information and think as well as reason very differently from adults.

Erikson

Erik Erikson (1902–1994) was a German-born child psychoanalyst who developed a unique personality stage theory. Similar to Piaget, Erikson's early interests had nothing to do with psychology or even children. He was an aspiring artist with little formal schooling when he was hired to teach art to children of Americans studying Freudian psychoanalysis in Vienna. This accidental introduction to psychiatry launched what would be Erikson's life's work.

Erikson's work was an extension of Freudian psychoanalytic thinking into the full life span. Much of his focus was on the development of identity, with the concept that each life stage presents humans with psychosocial challenges that must be met and resolved before successfully moving on to the next stage.

His eight life stages are (1) basic trust versus mistrust (infancy), (2) autonomy versus shame (one–three years), (3) purpose initiative versus guilt (four–five years), (4) competence industry versus inferiority (six years–puberty), (5) fidelity identity versus role confusion (adolescence), (6) intimacy versus isolation (early adulthood), (7) generativity versus stagnation (middle adulthood), and (8) ego integrity versus despair (late adulthood). Each stage consists of a developmental task the individual must struggle through.

Parents play a key role in helping their children successfully navigate through at least the first five stages. The first was forming a basic trust of others in infancy (i.e., developing a secure attachment). Here, Erikson mainly focused on the maternal role in attachment. The second was developing a healthy autonomy without feelings of shame or doubt, and the infant's expanding social circle was thought to include both parents and other adults functioning as parents. The third stage presents the growing child with the dilemma of identifying with his or her parents versus who he or she will be independent of the parental identity. The family plays a key role here. In the fourth stage, children move beyond the family to a larger social group involving school and peers, with competency and competition being primary foci. Finally, in stage five, the young adolescent is confronted head-on with the challenges of adult identity formation, moving beyond the confines of home and school into a more broadly based peer experience.

CHAPTER SUMMARY

This chapter has reviewed fourteen theories that help to reveal the nature of the parent-child relationship. Much of the contemporary research into parent-child relationships is framed around one of the major theoretical approaches presented in this chapter: attachment theory, behavioral theory, evolutionary developmental psychology, social cognitive theory, behavioral genetics theory, ecological systems theory, and family systems theory. The other newer or more narrowly focused theories, including social relational theory, parental role theory, Vygotsky's theory, self-determination theory, and emotional security theory, also help to shape parenting research. Each theory views the parent-child relationship from a slightly different perspective, asks different questions, and provides different answers. Developmental stage theories also continue to inform research in that the theories capture some of the many changes in children that help to influence the ways in which parents think about and interact with their children.

Although the many theories presented in this chapter are far from integrated (and in some cases, they are contradictory), four themes about parenting can be identified. First, parent and child behavior is influenced by a variety of variables, including genetic predispositions, learning experiences, role expectations, and perceptions of the child. Second, the role of context in behavior has to be recognized. Parents and children behave differently in different contexts, and multiple levels of context influence the behavior. A third theme is that children play a key role in eliciting parental behavior: Parenting is not unilaterally determined by the mother or father. Finally, parenting is increasingly recognized as being dynamic and changeable rather than static and rigid. Parental behavior changes in response to different child behavior, different children, different contexts, and across time.

THOUGHT QUESTIONS

- What are the strengths and weaknesses of each theoretical perspective for understanding parent and child behavior?
- Give an example of a how an older theory continues to inform our current thinking about child rearing.
- Of the theories presented in this chapter, which inform your own perspectives about children or parenting? How so? Which do you wish to explore further?
- Suppose a mother subscribed to an attachment theory of development but her husband believed in a learning theory approach. How might each approach the question of whether to hold back their young kindergarten child for another year in kindergarten? Where would they agree/disagree?

CHAPTER GLOSSARY

altricial An organism requiring care and feeding after birth to survive.

anxious-avoidant An insecure attachment classification based on an infant's pattern of behavior, characterized by avoiding or ignoring the parent when he or she returns from a separation.

anxious-resistant An insecure attachment classification based on an infant's pattern of behavior, characterized by little exploration of the environment, wariness of unfamiliar persons, and ambivalence about the parent upon his or her return follow a separation.

attachment theory A theory about development that focuses on the establishment, maintenance, and consequences of affectionate bonds between parents and children.

behavioral genetics theory A theory that seeks to understand genetic and environmental contributions to variations in human behavior and characteristics.

bidirectional Refers to the idea that dyadic behavior is influenced by both individuals.

child effects The effects a child can have on a parent as a consequence of a child characteristic or behavior.

chronosystem This system refers to how nested systems of interactions can change over time.

classical conditioning A form of associative learning that typically involves presentations of a neutral stimulus along with a stimulus of some significance.

coercive cycles Problematic interactions in which two individuals compete with increasing force to see who can gain control.

conduct disorder A group of behavioral and emotional problems in children involving difficulties in following rules or behaving in socially acceptable ways. Problematic behaviors include aggression, property destruction, lying, stealing, and truancy.

constructs Ideas about a psychological entity.

control theory A narrow theory of parent-child relationships focusing on how both parents and children perceive and respond to the intensity, frequency, and situational appropriateness of behavior shown by the other.

co-parenting From the family systems perspective, how well and in what ways mothers and fathers work together in their roles as parents. The term is also used to refer to the shared responsibility for a child of two parents who are separated or divorced.

delinquent A youth who persistently engages in misdeeds such as aggression.

disorganized According to attachment theory, when a child shows a confused and inconsistent pattern of response to stress, he or she has a disorganized attachment style.

ecological systems theory A theory that focuses on the interrelations of different levels of context and how they relate to child's behavior and development.

emotional security theory A theory focusing on children's feelings of insecurity as a consequence of marital conflict.

evolution A theory about the origins of plants and animals as well as processes of change.

evolutionary psychology A theory that seeks to understand human behavior and characteristics as a result of adaptive processes over tens of thousands of years.

exosystem The layer of context or settings in the ecological systems theory that affects children but does not directly include children (e.g., parents' workplace).

family structure The composition of the family, including the number and gender of parents and children.

family systems theory A theory that focuses on the system of interactions, interrelations, and interconnections between family members.

gene-environment interaction The idea that a particular phenotypic expression is due to the interaction between genes and the environment.

genes Blueprints of development, comprised of a segment of DNA and made up of amino acids.

genotype An individual's genetic makeup, comprised of some 20,000 to 25,000 genes.

group socialization theory A theory of development that highlights the role that peers and peer-group processes play, particularly during adolescence.

hunter-gatherer A society where food is procured primarily by hunting animals and gathering edible foods.

internal working model Ideas and expectations about oneself and others derived from previous attachment-related experiences.

longitudinal A study that follows an individual over time and includes repeated observations or data collection points.

macrosystem The outermost level of the ecological systems theory. This level refers to the major, overarching characteristics or structures of a culture or subculture that affect children.

mesosystem A layer of the ecological systems theory that refers to the system of processes or linkages taking place between two or more microsystems.

meta-analysis A type of review of research literature that involves combining and comparing the results of multiple empirical studies using a common measure, called an *effect size*.

microsystem A term in the ecological systems theory that refers to the contexts where children interact (e.g., the home, school, and playground).

nativist A view that espouses that children's genetic makeup or innate characteristics are the key determinants of development rather than the environment.

natural selection The process whereby heritable traits that are better suited for an environment will survive and other traits will become less common.

nonshared environment Aspects of the environment (e.g., activities, social interactions, and friendships) that are unique to each child in a family.

novelty seeking According to attachment theory, children will seek new activities and experiences when they feel safe in their environment. Through this behavioral system, children acquire new competences.

ontogenetic Development of individuals over their life span.

operant conditioning Also known as *Skinnerian conditioning*, this refers to a form of learning where the consequences of an act modify the likelihood of its recurrence.

parental acceptance-rejection theory A theory concerning children's development that is centered around the presence or absence of love between a parent and child.

parental investment A concept in human evolutionary theory referring to the time, energy, and resources parents devote to rearing their children.

parental self-efficacy Parents who believe they can control their children typically are more competent in their parenting abilities and have children who are better adjusted.

parent effects A term that refers to changes in a child caused by a parent.

phenotype The physical expression or manifestation of an individual's genotype.

phylogenetic The development of the species over time.

problem solving Thought processes involved in dealing with a solving a problem.

proximity seeking When children feel threatened or scared, they will retreat to being held by or being near the parent in an effort to regain feelings of being safe, according to attachment theory.

punishment effect From Skinner's theory of operant conditioning, a punishment is any action in response to a behavior that decreases the likelihood that the behavior will recur.

reinforcement effect According to operant conditioning principles, a reinforcement is any action that increases the likelihood that a prior behavior will recur.

role conflict Occurs when an individual experiences conflict between two or more roles of different status. For example, many parents experience problems balancing their roles of parent and employee.

role strain Strain in roles occurs when there is tension between roles that share the same status, such as caring for a child and caring for an elderly parent.

role theory A theory from sociology that examines behavior from the perspective of the multiple socially defined categories an individual has (e.g., mother, wife, sister, and employee).

scaffolding Social interactions that support a child's behavior in a way that allows the child to exhibit more advanced behavior.

school readiness Refers to when children have the skills, knowledge, and attitudes to enable them to succeed in kindergarten.

second-order effects How individuals adjust their behavior when in the presence of a third individual.

securely attached A pattern of behavior from which it is inferred that infants or young children trust their parents to protect and care for them in times of need.

self-efficacy An individual's beliefs about his or her ability to affect changes in the environment.

sensitive parenting A quality of parenting (also called *responsive parenting*) characterized by responding timely, appropriately, and reliably to the infant or child.

shared environment Aspects of the environment (activities, social interactions, and friendships) experienced by two or more siblings in the same family.

social cognitive theory A theory of behavior that focuses on the cognitive and information-processing capacities of individuals as central influences on their social behavior.

social learning theories A collection of theories that address how children learn from their social environment.

social policies Principles that guide decisions or efforts to achieve desired goals (and avoid undesired results) concerning human needs and welfare.

social support Material, emotional, or instrumental forms of assistance provided by other people.

socioeconomic status (SES) The term used to describe the relative social position of an individual or family. Typically, it is based on income, education, and occupation.

temperament Refers to the biologically based behavioral style of the child.

transactional influence The idea that there is a continuous mutual influence of the person and environment on development. In turn, individuals change and then influence the environment around them.

trauma A physical or emotional injury.

Vygotsky's theory A theory developed by Lev Vygotsky that focused on the role of particular types of social interactions as the central influence on children's cognitive and social development.

warmth The expression of parental affection and love.

zone of proximal development Refers to the distance between an individual's ability to do something independently and the ability of the individual to perform a task under adult (or more-advanced peer) guidance. Learning occurs when in this zone, according to Vygotsky.

CHAPTER 3

Approaches to Parenting Research

Chapter Preview: True or False?

- Researchers have given little attention to the child's effect on parental behavior.
- How parents think about child rearing has been studied for more than 75 years.
- Large-scale studies, sometimes with 10,000 participants or more, are able to analyze the complexities in family life.

Considering the multiple roots that feed into the study of child rearing (Chapter 1), coupled with dissimilar and often competing theoretical perspectives (Chapter 2), it should come as no surprise that investigators choose to study parents in a number of different ways. Whereas in Chapter 2, we discussed the various theories (and theorists) behind much of parenting research, this chapter describes the more practical concept of *approaches* to research—that is, what determines the priorities of the research, what questions it seeks to answer, and how the research is carried out.

If you were to sample 20 to 30 parent studies, you would likely notice distinct approaches. We will identify eight of them in this chapter. Each approach adopts different assumptions, focuses on different aspects of the parent-child relationship, and addresses different questions about parents and child rearing. The eight approaches we will survey are parenting traits, child effects and transactions, social learning, social address, ecological momentary assessment, parent cognition, behavioral genetics, and **large datasets approach**.

APPROACHES

Parenting Traits

Vanderbilt is our first choice. We'd like to get into Sigma Nu there, but if we don't, we'll look into another fraternity.

—One middle-age parent to another, speaking of her son's college admissions choices

You have probably heard of "**helicopter parents**." These parents are characterized by their "hovering" as they intrude and generally over-involve themselves in their children's lives. College admissions officers report that these types of parents are a serious problem for emerging adults. Helicopter parents write their high school student's college entrance essays, speak for their children during admissions interviews, and subsequently telephone their children's professors to protest low grades.

Over the past few years, researchers have begun to systematically study helicopter parents. These highly involved parents have strong concern for the well-being of their children. However, they become inappropriately intrusive and overly managing (Padilla-Walker & Nelson, 2012). Ironically, over-involved parenting is negatively associated with the psychological well-being of their offspring. The children tend to be narcissistic, have poor coping styles, and report high levels of anxiety, stress, and depression (LeMoyne & Buchanan, 2011; Segrin, Woszidlo, Givertz, & Montgomery, 2013).

Characterizing parents by a single major childrearing quality or characteristic is the oldest approach to conceptualizing and studying parents (see Photo 3.1). A pioneer of this approach was the psychiatrist David Levy, who wrote in 1943 about the dangers of "overprotective" mothers.

This approach can be recognized under different names, including parenting *style*, *typology*, *syndrome*, or *pattern*. The core idea of the **parental traits approach** is that parents can be classified into a one-word category that captures the essence of their parenting behavior. That essential childrearing quality is believed to affect a child's development. Depending on the researcher's focus, the traits of interest have concerned parental love, **sensitivity**, discipline practices, level of involvement (as illustrated by helicopter parents), or any of a wide range of other childrearing behaviors. A trait of interest among early parent researchers was whether parents had a "democratic" childrearing style (i.e., a high level of communication in the family, consulting the child on policy decisions, giving the child choices, and encouraging self-reliant behavior). Children in democratic families were found to be the most socially competent (Baldwin, Kalhorn, & Breese, 1945). Table 3.1 lists nine parenting traits that have been studied since the 1940s.

Photo 3.1 The parenting traits approach distills the quality of interactions between parents and children into one characteristic.

Source: Photograph by J. P. Bell

The best-known scheme of childrearing traits was developed by Diana Baumrind (1971, 2013a). Her tripartite conceptualization focuses on differentiating how much warmth and control parents exhibit. The three patterns of child rearing are labeled **authoritarian, authoritative,** and **permissive**. *Authoritarian* parents are those individuals who insist on

Table 3.1 Some of the Parenting Traits That Have Been Investigated

• Accepting vs. rejecting	• Involved vs. autonomous
• Child-centered vs. parent-centered	• Lax disciplinarians vs. strict disciplinarians
• Democratic vs. autocratic	• Overprotective, indifferent, and conflicted
• Dictators, cooperators, and appeasers	• Sensitive, less sensitive, and hypersensitive
• Facilitator vs. regulator	• Warm vs. hostile

Sources: Grolnick, 2003; Holden & Miller, 1999.

obedience, use punishment, and typically exhibit little warmth toward their children. Imagine the stereotypical Marine Corps drill sergeant, and that image captures an extreme authoritarian parent. In contrast, *authoritative* parents do not bark commands and expect immediate compliance but rather control their children with reasoning and warmth. They also encourage the development of autonomy in their children. They are able to balance responsiveness with demandingness. The final major category is *permissive* parents. These mothers and fathers are warm and loving but exert little control over their children. They rarely punish or restrict their children nor do they require mature behavior. Instead, indulgence is the theme, as these parents let their children make nearly all their own decisions. Bedtimes, behavioral rules, and punishment are unlikely in these types of homes.

To test her classification scheme, Baumrind (1971) conducted an extensive assessment of 133 parents of preschoolers in northern California. Based on observations, interviews, and questionnaire results, she was able to classify about 75% of the parents. Authoritarian parents formed about 20% of the sample; authoritative parents accounted for another 19%; and permissive parents made up 30% of the group. A fourth group—8% of the parents—consisted of *rejecting-neglecting* parents, who rejected their children and did not encourage independence. Baumrind found that the three primary typologies were associated with different levels of child competence. Children of authoritative parents were the most competent. In contrast, children of authoritarian and permissive parents had various problems, as will be discussed in the next chapter.

Many investigators followed suit and used Baumrind's typology, although they have not been as thorough in their efforts to assess the quality of parents. In fact, researchers have typically measured parenting traits with short questionnaires completed by parents or by children. For example, below are three statements from John Buri's (1991) Parental Authority Questionnaire, a questionnaire often given to college students so they could report on how their parents reared them. Each statement corresponds to one of Baumrind's three typologies—it is not difficult to figure it out which statement represents which type of parenting.

- As the children in my family were growing up, my mother/father consistently gave us direction and guidance in rational and objective ways.
- Most of the time as I was growing up, my mother/father did what the children in the family wanted when making family decisions.
- My mother/father felt that wise parents should teach their children early just who is boss in the family.

Various critiques have surfaced about limitations of Baumrind's parenting traits approach. Lewis (1981) argued that the so-called parenting traits are more reflections of the nature of the children than the parents. That is, difficult children elicit more control and less warmth than easy, compliant children. Lewis's argument was essentially one of child effects: Parental behavior is often determined by the child's behavior or characteristics [Preview Question].

Another critique focused on the two childrearing dimensions. To be more systematic in classifying parents, Eleanor Maccoby and John Martin (1983) argued that parenting styles could be divided into four cells, depending on whether the parent was demanding or not and responsive or not. Consequently, a demanding but responsive parent is classified as *authoritative;* a demanding, nonresponsive parent is labeled *authoritarian;* a nondemanding, responsive parent would be labeled *permissive;* and a nondemanding, nonresponsive parent is classified as *neglecting* or *uninvolved.*

Baumrind's work and the parenting traits approach in general represent a very useful beginning for examining how variations in parenting may be related to different child outcomes. (Some of those findings will be described in subsequent chapters.) Many other traits have been studied (and are listed in Table 3.1). However, the traits approach can be faulted for being too vague, too simple, too static, and failing to reveal the parenting processes that are actually at work. Another problem is the assumption that one trait is always the best form of child rearing, irrespective of age, child characteristics, racial group, or culture. Despite its limitations, the traits approach has served as an important opening act for understanding how parents influence their children's development.

Child Effects and Transactions

This child is making me crazy!

—A frazzled young father speaking to his own mother.

The **child effects and transactions approach** grew out of a reaction to the unidirectional view—embodied in the parental traits approach—that parental behavior determines a child's behavior. That view can be diagrammed as (P → C).

However, everyone knows that children often can have a major impact on their parents' behavior. They voice their preferences about what and where to eat. They let you know what they like and dislike. Many advertisements are geared toward children because marketers know the truth: Children 4 to 12 years old directly influence how their parents spend an estimated $330 billion per year (Schor, 2004). In the psychological domain, children's behavior—good or bad—can powerfully influence child rearing. Documenting the child's role in influencing key adults is the focus of the child effects approach.

This approach was spearheaded by a review paper by Richard Bell (1968) in which he argued for a reinterpretation of the **direction of effect**. Bell reasoned that the prevailing model of parents influencing children in a unidirectional way was not always accurate. Sometimes children can, through their specific actions, elicit particular parental responses (C →P). Since Bell's review paper, investigators have documented many types of child characteristics that have an important influence on parents. These features of children or their behavior can be organized into three major categories: general child features (e.g., age, gender), physical attributes (e.g., attractiveness), and behavior (e.g., hyperactivity). Examples of some of the characteristics that have been investigated over the last forty years are listed in Table 3.2.

One behavior characteristic that has received considerable attention is a child's activity level—potentially a powerful determinant of parental behavior or concern (recall Bell's control theory, described in Chapter 2). For example, children who are diagnosed with **attention-deficit/hyperactivity disorder (ADHD)** are a serious challenge in homes and in classrooms

Table 3.2 Child Effects: Examples of Child Characteristics That Influence Parenting

General Child Features	
Age	Gender
Biological, step, foster, or adoptive child	Twin status
Birth order	
Physical or Personal Attributes	
Attractiveness	Health
Appearance (height and weight)	Intelligence
Disability	Prematurity
Behavior	
Activity level	Quality of attachment to parents
Frequency and type of misbehavior	Relationships with others
Performance (in school, sports, and music)	Temperament

because they have difficulty controlling their own behavior (Hinshaw & Scheffler, 2014). As many as 11% of children (and more than twice as common in boys) received this diagnosis in the United States (Centers for Disease Control and Prevention, 2013). That translates to approximately 6.4 million children.

As the name indicates, these children typically have three types of behavior problems: inattention, hyperactivity, and impulsivity. These children are easily distracted, have trouble following instructions, are unable to pay attention to details, and are constantly in motion. They are restless, fidgety, and generally hard to keep quiet. Many children with ADHD are also impulsive, both verbally and behaviorally. They make inappropriate, unrestrained comments. They may be unable to wait their turn. As you might imagine, it is stressful to rear children with ADHD, as has been replicated in numerous studies (Theule, Wiener, Tannock, & Jenkins, 2013).

Investigations by clinical psychologists and other researchers into the problem of ADHD clearly illustrate the potent role that children play in influencing parental behavior. In one prototypic study in this area, hyperactive boys were randomly assigned to receive either ADHD medication or a placebo (Barkley & Cunningham, 1979). This study was blind, so neither the boys nor their mothers knew which pill they had been assigned. The boys who received the medication responded favorably to the medication by showing greater behavioral improvements than those boys who received the placebo. But the researchers did not just evaluate the boys; they observed the mothers, too. They found that the mothers of the boys with improved behavior also acted differently. This experimental study (framed to evaluate medication effects) also provided clear evidence about the influence of child behavior on parent behavior.

Box 3.1 The Overdiagnosis of Attention-Deficit/Hyperactivity Disorder

Almost 20% of high-school-age boys in the United States and 11% of school-age children overall have received a diagnosis of ADHD, according to the Centers for Disease Control and Prevention (http://www.cdc.gov/ncbddd/adhd/?s_cid=cdc_homepage_topmenu_001). These rates are a dramatic increase over the last decade. Consequently, many people suspect that the ADHD diagnosis and its medication are overused.

An estimated 6.4 million children, from 4 through 17 years of age, will receive an ADHD diagnosis. This is a 41% percent rise in the past decade. Roughly two-thirds of those diagnosed are given stimulants such as Ritalin or Adderall. Although these drugs can be highly effective, they can also lead to addiction, anxiety, and other problems.

Recent revisions in the *Diagnostic and Statistical Manual* (*DSM-V*, 5th edition), published by the American Psychiatric Association, have attempted to more accurately reflect the experience of ADHD across the life span, although the diagnostic criteria have not changed. Controversies continue to rage as to what degree this common behavioral problem is actually a medical problem, a social problem, or a pharmaceutical industry marketing ploy to greatly increase the use of extremely profitable drugs. The costs in the United States associated with ADHD are estimated to be as high as $100 billion per year (Hinshaw & Scheffler, 2014).

Source: Schwarz & Cohen, 2013.

In addition to eliciting parent reaction, children affect their parents in other, more subtle ways. First, through their personality and interests, children can contribute to the overall quality of the parent-child relationship. A parent may decide to become his son's basketball coach in response to the child's interest in playing the sport. In turn, this newfound joint activity may enhance the quality of their relationship. Second, children's perceptions of their parents' behavior may, in turn, influence the child rearing. Children perceive and react to the same parental behavior differently. An aggressive child may react to physical punishment with anger and perhaps seek retaliation. In contrast, a shy child might respond with sadness and withdrawal to the exact same type of physical punishment. Thus temperamental characteristics of a child can affect how that child responds to parental behavior.

A relatively new idea that falls under the umbrella of child effects is that of **differential susceptibility**. Jay Belsky (1997) proposed that parenting and the environment does not affect all children equally. Rather, using evolutionary reasoning, it can be expected that some children will be more vulnerable to negative experiences than others, just as some children may benefit more from positive experiences than others. In one empirical test of that hypothesis, van Zeijl and colleagues (2007) tested the role of children's temperament and maternal discipline in the development of behavior problems. They found that children with difficult temperaments were indeed more likely to develop behavior problems (i.e., aggression) if their mothers used negative disciplinary practices. However, other difficult children who had mothers who used positive disciplinary techniques showed fewer problems. In contrast, children with easy temperaments did not develop behavior problems. van Zeijl and colleagues concluded that temperament was a moderating variable between the maternal discipline and behavior problems. Since Belsky proposed his idea, many more studies have been published that support the idea (Belsky & Pluess, 2009).

The child effects approach was never intended to explain the whole story. Rather, it emerged as a counter to the one-sided parenting traits view. The whole story is better told from bidirectional and transactional perspectives, both of which recognize that parent and child influence each other. The bidirectional approach, put simply, highlights the mutual effects that each person has on the other (P ⟷ C) (Pettit & Arsiwalla, 2008). A bidirectional model is useful for depicting ongoing interaction, but it does not reflect the changes over time that can result from these interactions. Consider a parent interacting repeatedly with a child who has ADHD, or consider the infant who is trying to gain the attention of a depressed mother. In both cases, the parent and the child will be learning from their interactions, and subsequent interactions will reflect that learning. This idea, captured by transactional development, of how an individual is changed based on interactions with another person, is depicted below:

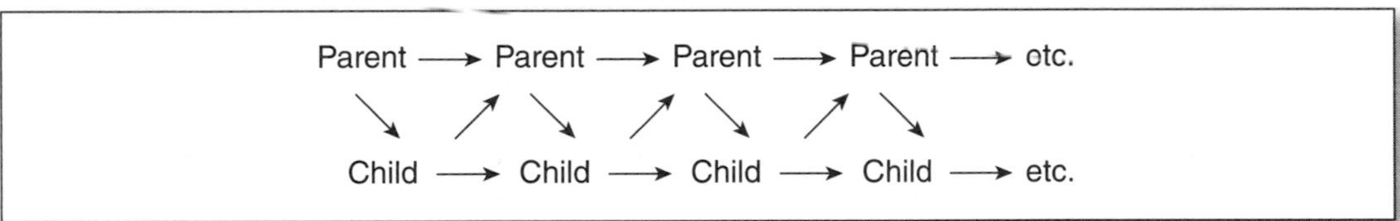

Many contemporary researchers examine not only child effects or parent effects but also relationship effects—the unique contribution attributed to the quality of the parent-child relationship. These investigations help to reveal the multiple ways in which participants in personal relationships can influence each other. Such research is indicative of the *transactional* model of development, which developed out of the child effects approach. The core idea of is that children are not just affected by others and the environment in which they live, but children also affect those others (Sameroff, 2009; Sameroff & Chandler, 1975).

The transactional model is helpful in trying to understand why some children are particularly affected in negative environments. According to Fruzzetti, Shenk, and Hoffman (2005), the model can explain why certain children develop borderline personality disorder, a particularly complex psychiatric disorder. They argued that some children are more genetically and biologically susceptible to the ill effects of trauma. Once a child has experienced the trauma (such as sexual abuse), those children who are more susceptible will show behavioral symptoms reflecting the abuse. In turn, parents and perhaps siblings in the child's social environment will respond to the child's behavior in a negative way, such as being critical, invalidating, and generally unsupportive or empathetic. Those reactions then help to shape the child's subsequent behavior. The reciprocal interactions between all the family members continue to influence the child and family members in a downward cycle, resulting in a potentially serious psychiatric problem.

Social Learning

You may have a cookie once you've eaten all your vegetables.

—Nearly every mom in the Western world

Social learning refers to how individuals learn from the social environment. Not surprisingly, this approach to understanding parents relies heavily upon traditional social learning theories (Domjan, 2015) to interpret and understand child rearing and its effects. Recall from the last chapter that John B. Watson focused exclusively on classical conditioning as a mechanism for understanding how the child learns from the environment. The work on social learning has changed considerably since then, in part influenced by the work of B. F. Skinner. Skinner (Chapter 2) played a major role in developing this approach by articulating the principle of *operant conditioning*. With its emphasis on learned behavior, reward, and punishment, operant conditioning is the basic theoretical launching pad of the social learning approach.

Parenting researchers who adopt a social learning approach do not attempt to identify character differences among parents but rather focus on the learning principles that parents exhibit—or fail to exhibit—in their child rearing. These learning principles are embodied by parents in two ways. Foremost, parental influence occurs through dispensing contingencies and through modeling. Second, parental behavior is determined through a parent's own prior social learning experiences. Different proponents of the social learning approach focus on different principles, such as positive and negative reinforcement, punishment, or learning associations through classical conditioning. Although they espouse different learning mechanisms, researchers adopting this approach share the common belief that the essence of parenting can be captured by social learning constructs.

These researchers interpret child behaviors—and misbehaviors—through the lens of social learning. They investigate how parents inadvertently reinforce undesired behaviors. Some have claimed that parents can reduce their infant's frequency of crying, stop bed-wetting, and even get more sleep by only reinforcing certain child behaviors (Pumroy & Pumroy, 1978). Studies of parenting continue to document how parents positively reinforced their young children for eating healthy foods, being active, and completing homework (e.g., Rollins, Loken, Savage, & Birch, 2014).

The investigations of Gerald Patterson also provide an excellent model of the social learning approach to understanding parenting, as discussed in the last chapter. When studying boys who were coercive and difficult to manage, Patterson looked for the ways in which the boys were *learning* this behavior. And as we have already discussed, he found his answer in the boys' "inept" mothers and their ineffective parenting habits. These frustrated mothers resorted to behaviors that were ineffective for controlling their children, such as "nattering" (fussing at) their sons. When the mothers finally gave up, the boys would then "win" the interaction, thus reinforcing their strategies (Granic & Patterson, 2006; Patterson, 1982).

According to the social learning approach, these mothers were inadvertently reinforcing their sons' aversive behavior in these commonly occurring interactions. By giving up fussing or other coercive efforts, the mothers were actually *negatively reinforcing* (removing a negative stimulus) their sons' behavior, thereby increasing the likelihood that the behavior will be repeated in the future. Mothers of these aggressive boys have also been observed to positively reinforce the noxious behavior by giving attention to, laughing at, or even verbally encouraging the misbehavior. Through these coercive cycles, the boys were learning that coercive behavior is effective. It is no surprise, then, that they would attempt to use this acquired style of interaction with peers and others.

Patterson's work nicely illustrates how one can apply social learning principles to understanding parenting and how it can go awry. See Box 3.2 for some other common errors that parents make, according to social learning researcher, Susan O'Leary. Searching for these types of mistakes would be a priority for someone studying parenting from a social learning perspective. Such approaches to understanding parenting have proven to be useful and powerful—as far as they go. However, there are many domains of child rearing, such as attachment or cultural influences, about which social learning theories have little to say. The issue of cultural influences is addressed by the next approach.

Box 3.2 Common Parenting Errors From a Social Learning Perspective

Clinical psychologist Susan O'Leary (e.g., O'Leary, 1995; O'Leary & Vidair, 2005) has carefully studied the interactions between parents and misbehaving children. From a social learning perspective, she identified several common types of errors parents make when interacting with their children. These are considered errors because the behaviors are not effective in managing or improving the child's behavior.

1. Parents inadvertently reinforce the wrong behaviors by giving attention to them. Parents laugh when a preschooler uses "adult" language, or they give in to their children to get them to stop bothering them. Children learn what behaviors get attention and get results.
2. Parents forget to reward the behavior they *want* to see in their children. For example, parents should make an effort to say things such as, "You are playing so nicely with your brother. I like how you are getting along."
3. Parents overreact. A common manifestation of this overreaction is to rely on punishment to try to eliminate undesired behavior. However, punishment is difficult to administer correctly (so that it is effective). Parents, then, should be oriented toward promoting desired behavior rather than eliminating undesired behavior.
4. Parents give long, verbal explanations about misbehavior. Young children are often unable to cognitively process long-winded explanations about problematic behavior and may experience even this kind of parental attention as reinforcing.

Social Address

You can take the child out of Kansas, but you can't take Kansas out of the child.

The **social address approach**, termed by Urie Bronfenbrenner (1979), typically involves comparing parents from different locations or "addresses" (see Photo 3.2). These addresses can be different cultures, geographic locals, religious backgrounds, racial or ethnic groups, or socioeconomic status groups. The underlying assumption is that membership in a larger cultural group is the variable that not only determines how parents rear their children but also accounts for how those parents affect their children's development. Variation within a cultural group is typically ignored. This approach is, in essence, a traditional sociological approach to studying parents.

Long before Bronfenbrenner articulated his theory, cultural anthropologists used a comparative sociological approach to investigate different cultures. One of the first such studies was conducted by Margaret Mead (1928), who studied the inhabitants of the island of Samoa. She wanted to observe how development was influenced by culture. She had heard that, in contrast to American adolescents, youth there did not rebel. Mead's method was to interview carefully chosen informants as representatives of the Samoan culture. Although some of the data she collected—particularly the wild accounts of sexual relations among the Samoan youth—were subsequently criticized as apparent fabrications by the informants (Freeman, 1983), her watershed study laid the groundwork for other investigations exploring cultural differences in childrearing practices and children's development.

Photo 3.2 The social address approach consists of the study of parents from different locations, such as this mother with her child in Tanzania, East Africa.

Source: Photograph by J. P. Bell

Although anthropologists were the first to use what would later be termed the *social address approach*, psychologists soon began to conduct their own such studies both across and within cultures. Geographic (rural versus urban), economic (poor versus middle class), racial, and ethnic differences among parents began to be studied. Social address investigations peered into a range of childrearing practices, including practices regarding infant feeding, sleeping, toilet training, and disciplining. One such example of cultural differences in parental practices concerns sleeping with children, known as *co-sleeping* (see Photo 3.3). Different sleeping practices are described in Box 3.3.

Photo 3.3 Co-sleeping is a controversial practice in some subcultures in the United States.

Source: © iStockphoto.com/msderrick

Box 3.3 Sleeping With Babies: Cultural Differences in Co-Sleeping

Should parents sleep with their infants and young children (a practice known as *co-sleeping* or *bed-sharing* and even *room-sharing*)? Co-sleeping is a controversial topic and whether a parent engages in it is influenced by many considerations, including cultural practices, family characteristics (economic status and ethnicity), and infant-parent biology (what makes babies happy) as well as scientific and public health information. Pediatricians recommend against it, citing a wide range of problems. Among their arguments is that co-sleeping can interfere with autonomy development, as it establishes a habit that is difficult to break; it is associated with disrupted sleep problems; it may frighten or confuse children who inadvertently wake up and witness adult intercourse; it can contribute to marital problems; and it even can be fatal in those rare cases when a deeply sleeping adult rolls over and suffocates an infant.

On the other hand, many parents enjoy the practice of co-sleeping for several reasons, including offering convenience, especially for breastfeeding; providing warmth and comfort to an infant; and accommodating for a lack of space in the home (Goldberg & Keller, 2007). Surveys reveal that co-sleeping is commonly practiced both in the United States and around the world. Rates of co-sleeping depend on many variables, including age of child, gender, and definition of co-sleeping (such as full

(Continued)

(Continued)

co-sleeping or partial co-sleeping, which involves only part of the night). In general, in the United States, 42% of parents sleep with their infants at two weeks of age, but this number drops to 27% at 12 months (Hauck, Signore, Fein, & Raju, 2008). It is more commonly practiced with infants and young children, by single mothers, in African American homes, and in immigrant families. Rates of co-sleeping are higher in many other countries. For example, more than 80% of Swedish infants and 88% of Korean children sleep with their parents (Yang & Hahn, 2002).

Because of the risk of accidental suffocation and other causes of sudden, unexpected infant death, the American Academy of Pediatrics (2011) has a series of recommendations for safe infant sleeping environments. Foremost, it recommends room-sharing rather than bed-sharing and always putting the infant to sleep on his or her back (i.e., Back to Sleep campaign).

Contemporary examples of the social address approach to research can be found in cross-cultural efforts to better understand determinants of child rearing. For example, parent researchers have carefully studied mothers and children in a number of countries, as will be discussed in Chapter 13. The contemporary work illustrates the social address approach but goes beyond the traditional approach of simply identifying group differences. Research now is directed at identifying the processes that account for the associations. Additionally, causal relations between culturally regulated childrearing practices and developmental outcomes have been investigated. One prominent example is in the area of academic achievement. Studies comparing families from different racial/ethnic groups in the United States as well as in other countries are attempting to understand what role parents play in cultural differences in their children's academic performance (e.g., Quintana et al., 2006).

The social address approach is a useful first step in documenting differences between groups of parents. Moreover, Chapter 13 will address research on the general cultural differences in parenting, research that relies heavily upon the social address approach. However, evidence is accumulating that there is considerable variation *within* cultural groups that typically goes ignored when focusing on between-group variation.

Ecological Momentary Assessment

You scratch my back, I'll scratch yours.

In sharp contrast to the macro, static, and generalized view of parenting depicted in the social address approach, the **ecological momentary assessment approach** (e.g., Shiffman, Stone, & Hufford, 2008; Trull & Ebner-Priemer, 2009) adopts a micro-analytic perspective to examine behavior as it occurs naturally (hence *ecological*). This approach allows for examining interactional processes that may occur so quickly between parents and children that most people are not aware of them. Consequently, understanding those processes requires careful observation (**micro-analytic observations**).

The key question this approach asks is this: How is ongoing behavior regulated, modified, or influenced by one or both members of the parent-child dyad? To address that question, researchers study subtle parent and child actions such as looking, smiling, vocalizations, head movements, and pauses between actions as they occur naturally. These actions form the behavioral menu for interactions and relationships. Some of the early work in this approach focused on how mothers modulate (or control) their infants' attention (e.g., Brazelton, Koslowski, & Main, 1974). In one analysis of mother-infant interaction, the great majority of behaviors of interest lasted from 0.3 to 1.0 second (Stern, 1977).

Certain qualities of relationships can be identified by closely observing parent-child interactions. One central quality is **dyadic synchrony** (Harrist & Waugh, 2002). **Synchrony** refers to actions of one person that are coordinated with and supportive of ongoing actions of another. *Dyadic synchrony* refers to what is considered the ideal type of interaction between a parent and child (usually infants). Such back-and-forth exchanges are mutually regulated, reciprocal, and harmonious. It has been described poetically as "the dance" between parent and infant. Through repeatedly engaging in synchronous interactions, infants begin to learn about the nature of social relationships and such features as **turn-taking** in conversation and complementarity (healthy interdependence) in relationships. **Positive synchrony** occurs then two individuals are engaged in an interaction, the interactions are harmonious and reciprocal, and there is shared effect.

The ecological momentary assessment approach is illustrated in a study of the interactions between mothers, fathers, and their five-month-old first-born infants (Gordon & Feldman, 2008). The investigators documented the second-by-second affect and behavior of the family members in three situations: the mother-infant dyad, the father-infant dyad, and the mother-father-infant triad. They found that both mothers and fathers engaged in similar interactions, though fathers took longer to display positive emotion to their infants than did mothers and did not vocalize as much. When the family was interacting together, the mother and father engaged in co-parenting by, for example, the father gazing at the infant while the mother was vocalizing to the infant. The authors concluded that by the first half of the first year, the mother-father-infant triad has learned how to interact together or in synchrony.

The ecological momentary assessment approach has been particularly helpful in revealing how parents go about disciplining their children. Holden, Williamson, and Holland (2014) had 33 mothers audio-record, for up to six nights, their home interactions with their preschool-age children. When coding those recordings, 41 incidents of spanking or slapping were heard. When those incidents were analyzed, it was found that parents were hitting their children on average within 30 seconds after the conflict began and mostly for trivial reasons (such as turning the pages of a book too quickly). The ecological momentary assessment approach was invaluable in this study, as it demanded moment-by-moment tracking of interactional stimulus and response. These results would not have been observed using another, more global approach.

As such studies illustrate, this approach can provide unique and valuable information about specific parenting behaviors as well as reveal insights to understanding the nature and quality of parent-child relationships. However, the ecological momentary assessment approach is limited by the types of questions it can answer as well as by its exclusive focus on ongoing interactions. To address other questions, different approaches are needed.

Parent Cognition

> *You know, we have spent a lot of time thinking about why our daughter keeps sucking her thumb, despite all the things we've tried and the fact that she's now getting teased by peers. . . . We just can't figure it out.*

Many research approaches, such as child effects and the ecological momentary assessment, rely on observing and interpreting the actions of parents and children. Although systematic observation is the best way to document the behaviors that parents engage in, observations do not reveal what is going on inside parents' heads. That question comes under the purview of the *parent cognition approach* (also known as the **social cognition approach**), which seeks to understand what and how parents are *thinking* about their children and their child rearing. The parent cognition approach did not crystallize until the mid-1980s, when several reviews and books appeared on the topic. To date, a number of different parent cognition constructs have been investigated, 10 of which are listed and defined in Table 3.3.

Our behavior is, in part, a function of our perceptions. Recall the Puritan American parent who was taught that infants have a sinful nature and that any willfulness in a child should be broken. That parent would *perceive* and *act* differently from another parent who

Table 3.3 Types and Definitions of Parental Cognitions

Attitude: A predisposition, reaction to, or affective evaluation of the supposed facts about children or parenting.
Attributions: An assessment of the cause of a child's or parent's behavior.
Beliefs (Knowledge): Mental acceptance of and conviction in the truth or validity of something related to child rearing.
Decision-Making Ability: The cognitive process of reaching a childrearing decision.
Expectations: The anticipation that something will or should happen, such as pertaining to the child's capabilities.
Goals: The purpose of a behavior or endeavor; the objective. For example, parenting goals can be child-centered, parent-centered, or intended for socialization.
Metaparenting: Evaluative reflections on child rearing, usually occurring in the absence of children. Includes anticipating, accessing, problem solving, ruminating, and reflecting.
Perceptions: Recognition and interpretation of child sensory stimuli.
Problem-Solving Ability: Thought processes involved in dealing with and solving a childrearing problem.
Self-Perception: An awareness of the parent's own characteristics; self-knowledge.

subscribed to John Locke's more neutral assumptions about the nature of children (see Chapter 1). The Locke-influenced parent would perceive an infant as a blank slate, neither good nor bad. Perceptions—and the assumptions that those perceptions may trigger—have powerful effects on behavior.

A dramatic example of the impact of parental perceptions has been shown in the area of children's gender. The mere labeling of a newborn as a boy or a girl can elicit very different thoughts about the infant. In one of the first studies to demonstrate this effect, parents were asked to describe their **neonate** (Rubin, Provenzano, & Luria, 1974). Fathers in particular were more likely to enlist stereotypic terms. They described their newborn sons as *big*, *strong*, and *hardy*. The fathers of girls used adjectives such as *fine-featured*, *quiet*, *calm*, and *delicate*. Subsequent studies pursued the extent to which perceptions of the child's gender affected parents' behavior. A review of these studies concluded that gender labeling does elicit sex-stereotyped responses, but the adults' behavior was also influenced by factors other than the child's sex, such as the child's characteristics (e.g., attractiveness), the child's behavior, and whether the adult had a traditional sex-role orientation (Stern & Karraker, 1989).

Parents have their own perceptions of their children, and these perceptions can begin even prenatally—as soon as they hear "It's a girl!" or "It's a boy!" The parent cognition approach has been used to study parents' perceptions of prematurity, attractiveness, temperament, and behavior problems. Investigators have also examined parents' appraisals of their child's functioning, their assessments of their child's abilities, and their awareness of their youth's behavior and social preferences, such as sexual orientation (e.g., D'Augelli, Grossman, & Starks, 2005). In general, this work demonstrates that parental perceptions contain both objective and subjective components and are affected by multiple variables, including the amount of time spent with a child, a parent's memory, and a parent's personality (e.g., Kurdek, 2003).

Another type of perception that mothers and fathers have is their feelings concerning their own child rearing. Researchers have investigated two closely related types of parental self-perceptions: feelings of self-efficacy and feelings of competence as a parent. Parents who believe they are effective as parents and have the ability to manage their children typically are more competent in their parenting abilities (Coleman & Karraker, 1998). Parents who feel they are effective typically have children who are better adjusted (Jones & Prinz, 2005). Two additional types of self-perceptions are related to competence and self-efficacy: feelings of stress and satisfaction experienced in the parenting role (Deater-Deckard, 2004; Puff & Renk, 2014). As you might guess, these findings might best be evaluated by considering more than one research approach. Proponents of a bidirectional or transactional research approach could well argue that "easy" or more compliant children cause their parents to feel more competent. Which came first? The chicken or the egg?

Attributions about children's behavior are another important parent cognition variable. Parents assess children's behavior and then make causal attributions about the behavior (Bugental & Happaney, 2002; Lansford et al., 2011). Why does a child act in a certain way? Is a parent of a well-behaved child a more effective parent, or did he just "luck out" with an easy child? Parents differ in their attributions about the relative roles of nature and nurture in development, the degree to which parents can influence their own children, the ingredients involved in school success, and the factors by which their own behavior is determined (Miller, 1995). Mothers who attribute negative intentions to normal infant behaviors are more likely to maltreat the child (Berlin, Dodge, & Reznick, 2013). Attributions also differ between mothers and fathers and across racial/ethnic groups (Lansford et al., 2011). Parents' attributions and perceptions—rightly or wrongly—affect their behavior, as described in Box 3.4.

Box 3.4 Attributions About Child Misbehavior—and Its Effects

Why did the child act that way? Was the misbehavior intentional, accidental, or simply situational? In an effort to test the effects of different types of attribution on emotion and behavior, Amy Smith Slep and Susan O'Leary (1998) experimentally manipulated mothers' attributions about their 2- to 3½-year-old children. Mother-child dyads were randomly assigned to one of two conditions: a *child responsible* or *child not responsible* for misbehavior. In the child-responsible condition, mothers were instructed that children often misbehave to get their own way or to get attention. In the other condition, mothers were told that children misbehave because of their age or their inability to regulate their own behavior. Thus mothers were primed to make certain types of attributions. The mothers were then videotaped while interacting with their children in a room filled with tempting but off-limits toys.

The results of the study indicated that mothers in the child-responsible condition were overreactive in disciplining their children and tended to feel angrier than the other mothers. In addition, the children in the child-responsible condition exhibited much more negative emotion than children in the other condition, indicating they were responding to the mothers' negative affect. This study provides compelling evidence that parental attributions can indeed have a powerful effect on parent-child interactions and emotion.

Though parental perceptions and attributions are significant, the preponderance of research into parental cognition has focused on documenting beliefs (knowledge and ideas) about children and child rearing. A recent example is the study of mothers' knowledge about what their children think about discipline (Davidov, Grusec, & Wolfe, 2012). Investigations into parental beliefs can be categorized into four domains: content, quality, sources, and effects (Goodnow & Collins, 1990). The *content* of beliefs includes ideas about the nature of physical, motoric, and cognitive development of children and ideas about how parents influence this development. The *quality* of beliefs refers to the structure, intensity, and accuracy of the beliefs. The *sources* of beliefs include family members or authority figures, personal experience, parenting books, Internet, or culture. Many cross-cultural studies have compared parental attitudes and beliefs across ethnic groups and countries. Such culturally derived beliefs have been labeled parental **ethnotheories** (Harkness & Super, 2006). Finally, the *effects* of beliefs have received the least attention. However, there is some evidence that mothers who have more knowledge about child rearing had children who were more socially competent (Benasich & Brooks-Gunn, 1996).

Parental attitudes, defined as *dispositions*, *reactions*, or *affective evaluations*, have been studied for more than 75 years [Preview Question]. Parents hold many **attitudes** about child rearing—such as whether to breastfeed, to spank, and how much screen time a child should have. Our attitudes develop from multiple sources, including from our own parents and experiences. For example, mothers who were reared by harsh parents developed negative attitudes about life, had unrealistic developmental expectations about their children, and were likely to have negative attitudes about their own children (Daggett, O'Brien, Zanolli, & Peyton, 2000). In a remarkable longitudinal study of the effects of parental attitudes, parents' attitudes about authority (assessed during their transition to parenthood) accurately predicted their own children's conservative or progressive attitudes *seventeen* years later (Fraley, Griffin, Belsky, & Roisman, 2012).

A fifth domain studied in parental cognition is the process of problem solving and **decision making**. Dealing with problems, from the most insignificant to the very momentous, is part of the parenting experience. Part II of this book will address many of the common types of problems parents typically experience and some of the decisions they make. Relatively few studies have explored parental problem solving or decision making. The research that has been conducted has found mixed results with regard to that cognitive process. One study did find that parents who maltreat their children are worse at problem solving than non-abusive parents (Hansen, Pallotta, Christopher, Conaway, & Lunquist, 1995). However, an intervention study that taught problem solving to parents did not help them become more effective in treating their child's obesity (Epstein, Paluch, Gordy, Saelens, & Ernst, 2000). We all learn by experience; one study demonstrated that experiencing a common problem with infants does improve at least one particular type of problem-solving ability. Parents of infants were found to better diagnose why an infant was crying than individuals without that caregiving experience (Holden, 1988; see Box 3.5 and Figure 3.1).

Box 3.5 How Experience With Children Can Improve Problem-Solving Ability

The question is universal to all parents of infants: Why is the baby crying? One study, adopting an information-processing technique, was designed to reveal how different levels of previous experience with infants affected an adult's problem-solving process. A computer simulation offered participants bits of information in order to figure out why a baby was crying. Twenty-five types of information were available, including information about the cry (how long the baby had been crying), the baby (age and temperament), the setting (where the baby was), the time (time since the last feeding), and the baby's parents (their mood and age). The task required participants to sequentially acquire information until they thought they knew which of nine possible answers was correct. The goal was to arrive at the correct hypothesis most quickly by asking for the least amount of information.

Results revealed that mothers were the best solvers of this problem. They chose about eight pieces of information before selecting a hypothesis—which was almost always correct. Fathers generally

(Continued)

(Continued)

needed a little more information; on average, they used 10 pieces of information before selecting the correct hypothesis. When nonparents were compared with parents, some interesting results emerged. Women who were not mothers but had babysitting experience performed similarly to the mothers. But the group of participants who stood out was those inexperienced males who were not fathers. Not only did non-fathers need more information (13 pieces on average) than the other groups, they also made about three guesses before arriving at the correct answer. This high rate of incorrect guessing revealed their limited problem-solving ability in this domain, because they did not have the experience with infants to know what information to select or how to rule out various causes. The graph below depicts the performances of the different groups.

Figure 3.1 The Influence of Experience in Determining Why a Baby Is Crying

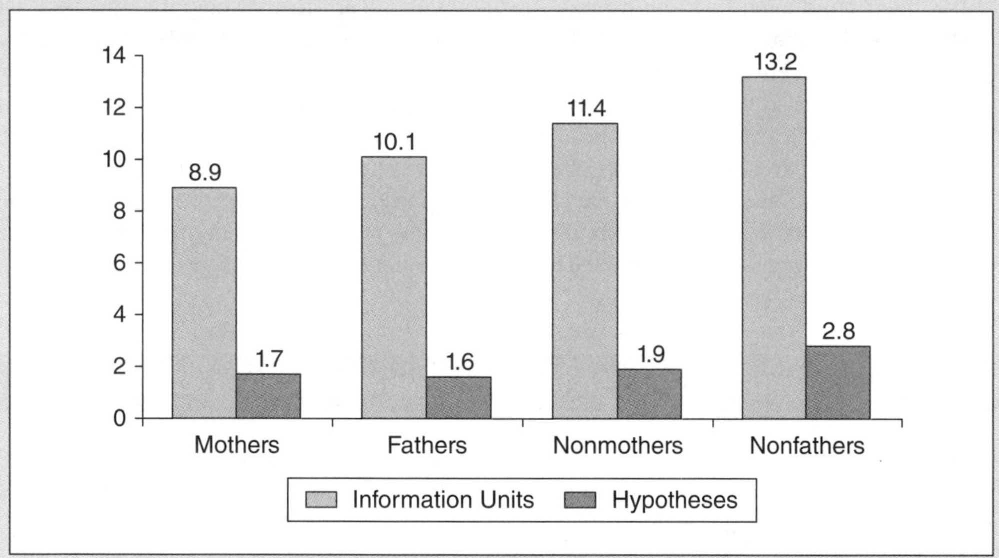

Source: Holden, 1988.

The newest construct in parental cognition is labeled **metaparenting**. Metaparenting refers to the evaluative process parents engage in about their children or their child rearing. Metaparenting usually occurs when the children aren't around, either before or after interactions (Holden & Hawk, 2003). Effective parents anticipate their children's needs and behavior, they plan in advance, they assess how their children are developing, they efficiently solve common childrearing problems, and they reflect about the quality of their

with the children. If children and adoptive parents actually share similar characteristics (and there is evidence that they do), then *that* correlation should be included in statistical modeling (Plomin, DeFries, McClearn, & McGuffin, 2001). A final confound of this method would be the possibility that the child's *in utero* environment (e.g., nutritional deficiency) affected his or her development (DiLalla, 2002). In cases such as this, an apparently significant difference between adopted children and either biological or adoptive parents might be attributed to a third factor—what happened to them before they were born.

Recall from the last chapter that a key concept in the behavioral genetics approach is that of shared and nonshared environments. *Shared environments* refer to the characteristics of experience that are similar for both children (such as being parented the same way or living in the same home and neighborhood). *Nonshared environments* refer to a child's unique experiences (such as different treatment by parents, separate friends, and different teachers). By separating out shared and nonshared environments, scientists can better understand the extent to which the environment influences traits.

A good example of what can be learned from this approach is found in Kirby Deater-Deckard and Kenneth Dodge's (1997) review of genetic and parenting influences on antisocial behavior. They determined that while there is some evidence for genetic influences, stronger evidence indicates childrearing practices (in particular, harsh physical discipline) were related to childhood aggression and delinquency. Although the magnitude of the relation depended on several variables (culture, gender, the quality of the parent-child relationship), it was clear that the environment played a stronger role than did genetic inheritance.

However, one cannot assume a polarized, all-or-nothing, nature-or-nurture view of behavioral genetics. That would be like saying that weather consists either of temperature *or* precipitation. In fact, it is an intricate process that produces either a sunny day or a violent storm. So it is with genes and the environment. Much of the current work into genetics and family, then, focuses on gene-environment interactions (Rutter, Moffitt, & Caspi, 2005).

Although the behavioral genetics approach has been criticized on various methodological and statistical grounds (e.g., Gottlieb, 2003), it is changing to keep abreast of new findings in biology and genetics. The approach provides a healthy antidote to an extreme emphasis on social/environmental effects by reminding us that genetic inheritance does play an important role in behavioral outcomes.

Large Datasets

The newest approach to parenting research relies on using large **datasets** to investigate parent-child relationships. Large datasets that include thousands of individuals offer several advantages over other approaches. First, if the dataset is longitudinal, then the temporal (what came first) relations between variables can be assessed. For example, do children with difficult temperaments elicit a different quality of parenting than a child with an easy temperament? Second, in real life, individuals and families have many characteristics. These characteristics can relate to each other in various ways (e.g., additive, interactive, compensatory), and only with a large sample can relations between variables be tested. A third benefit of large datasets is they allow for testing whether findings are consistent across different families and individuals, such as those differing by age, sex, race/ethnicity, or some other background characteristic. By using datasets with samples in the thousands, more of the complexity in family life can be analyzed [Preview Question].

The hallmark of this approach is that it relies on advanced statistical methods to investigate relations between parental behavior and child outcomes. Statistical analysis techniques such as HLM (hierarchical linear models), SEM (structural equation models), and MLM (multivariate linear models) are utilized to better understand the relations between multiple variables. This information is gathered by researchers, usually through surveys or interviews. Most large datasets are longitudinal, so questions about development over time can be investigated and linked to hundreds of variables (e.g., education level, cultural or ethnic group, religious involvement, and stress; see Table 3.4 for a brief description of 10 of these datasets).

Collecting longitudinal datasets is expensive and complicated, as researchers must diligently maintain contact with the group members and might spend years following them through their life changes. The National Children's Study, mentioned in Chapter 1, is the largest study ever conducted of children's health. This prospective study of 100,000 individuals will follow them from birth until age 21. Once that dataset is complete, just like others, it will be made available to researchers for additional analyses. In this way, many investigators can use the extensive information gathered to study any number of questions, including the role of parents in their children's development. Examples of 10 large datasets are listed in Table 3.4.

Large datasets are used to examine a wide variety of questions. For example, the approach can evaluate which parenting variables best predict healthy child adjustment (Anderson,

Table 3.4 Large Datasets Focusing on the Family

Name of Dataset and Website	Sample Size	Description
Early Childhood Longitudinal Study (ECLS) http://nces.ed.gov/ECLS (3 different cohorts)	Birth cohort = 10,700	A nationally representative study following children from birth through 8th grade. A wide range of family, school, and community variables are collected.
Fragile Families and Child Wellbeing Study (FF) http://www.fragilefamilies.princeton.edu	5,000 children (75% born to unmarried parents)	Follows children born between 1998 and 2000 to at-risk parents in twenty large U.S. cities.
Head Start Family and Child Experiences Survey (FACES) http://www.acf.hhs.gov/programs/opre/research/project/head-start-family-and-child-experiences-survey-faces	3,500	A nationally representative longitudinal study on the characteristics, experiences, and outcomes of Head Start children and their families. Four cohorts have been studied: 1997, 2000, 2003, and 2006.

Name of Dataset and Website	Sample Size	Description
Longitudinal Study of Child Abuse and Neglect (LONGSCAN) http://www.iprc.unc.edu/longscan	1,354 children abused or at risk for abuse	A six-site project concerning the etiology and impact of child maltreatment. Comprehensive assessments of children, their parents, and their teachers occur every two years, from ages 4 through 18 years.
NICHD Study of Early Child Care (SECC) http://secc.rti.org	Began with 1,364 infants and their families	Focuses on how variations in child care are related to children's development. Follows infants through adolescence from 10 locations around the country.
National Children's Study (NCS) http://www.nationalchildrensstudy.gov	100,000 birth to age 21 in 25 states	Examines the development of a variety of health problems including autism, learning disabilities, birth defects, diabetes, asthma, and obesity. Began in 2009.
National Longitudinal Study of Adolescent Health (Add Health) http://www.cpc.unc.edu/projects/addhealth	90,000 adolescents	A nationally representative sample of adolescents in Grades 7 to 12 in the United States during the 1994–1995 school year, through ages 24 to 32. Focuses on how social environments and behaviors in adolescence are linked to health and achievement outcomes in young adulthood.
National Longitudinal Survey of Youth (NLSY79) http://www.bls.gov/nls/nlsy79.htm	12,686 14-to 22-year-olds	A nationally representative sample first surveyed in 1979. These individuals were interviewed annually through 1994 and are currently interviewed on a biennial basis.
National Survey of Children's Health (NSCH) http://www.cdc.gov/nchs/slaits/nsch.htm	102,353 children	Examines the physical and emotional health of children ages 0 to 17 in a nationally representative sample of families.
Panel Study of Income Dynamics, Child Supplement http://psidonline.isr.umich.edu	7,000 families	Begun in 1968, a longitudinal study of a representative sample of U.S. individuals and the families, focusing on dynamic aspects of economic and demographic behavior along with sociological and psychological measures.

Hetherington, Reiss, & Howe, 1994). It is also used to test how well predicted relationships among variables fit within different ethnic or racial groups. For example, Shumow and Lomax (2002) tested the role of parental efficacy perceptions as they related to other parenting variables and adolescent adjustment. Another example of this approach to parenting involved a study of a parenting intervention program. Changes in parenting effectiveness were found to depend on the initial level of the child's behavior problems as well as initial levels of maternal criticism of their children (Reid, Webster-Stratton, & Baydar, 2004).

Structural equation modeling is a good statistical technique to use with large datasets in order to analyze psychological variables or constructs (such as a mother's warmth toward a child or a father's controlling behavior) that are assessed by multiple people (such as two parents and a child) or multiple instruments (such as an interview of a parent and responses to different questionnaires). Structural equation modeling is a broad data-analytic framework that has a number of strengths for testing hypotheses with nonexperimental designs (Tomarken & Waller, 2005). With the technique, one can investigate how well different variables interrelate to form models of psychological processes. Second, it allows for using multiple measures of a construct from more than one informant (e.g., parent, child, and teacher). Third, it can simultaneously evaluate multiple models rather than having to sequentially test them.

An example of a large database study examined the role of poverty, parenting, and self-control in predicting substance use in emerging adults, using the Panel Study of Income Dynamics (Lee, McClernon, Kollins, Prybol, & Fuemmeler, 2013). Using structural equation modeling, they found that poverty was associated with an increased likelihood of smoking. This was especially the case with adolescents who had poorer self-control. Positive parenting was associated with greater self-control. Figure 3.2 illustrates the relationships.

Another key strength of using large datasets is that they allow for greater precision in evaluating how different variables work in conjunction with each other. In particular, investigators can test how a particular variable works as a **moderator** or as a **mediator** of relations between variables. When one variable influences the strength or direction of a relation

Figure 3.2 Structural Equation Model Linking Poverty to Smoking

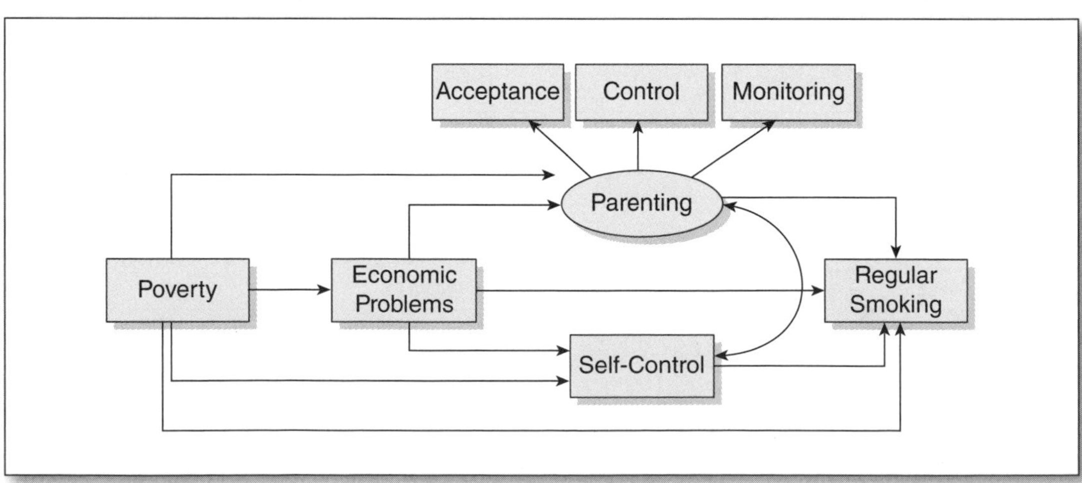

Source: Lee et al., 2013.

between two other variables, it is called a *moderator*. A moderator variable may be socioeconomic status or culture; a child's age, sex, or temperament; or any number of other variables. For example, it has been found that child temperament moderates parent behavior in promoting the development of conscience. Children with bold, exploratory temperaments benefit in their moral development from parents who are responsive and warm. In contrast, the moral development of shy or fearful children profits more from gentle and calm childrearing techniques (Kochanska, 1997). Thus the type of temperament moderates or influences the conditions under which the relation between parenting and conscience development will occur. Another example concerned the effects of dangerous neighborhoods on parenting (Ceballo & McLoyd, 2002). When African American mothers received emotional support from family and friends, they were more likely to be nurturant with their children if the neighborhood they lived in was not dangerous. However, in crime-ridden neighborhoods, the link between emotional support and nurturance was weakened.

In contrast, a *mediator* is a variable that explains how or why two variables are related. A mediator can be thought of as a link in a causal chain; without that link, there would be no significant relation between the variables. For example, it has been found that children's appraisals of the threat and self-blame associated with their parents' marital conflict mediates their adjustment (Grych, Harold, & Miles, 2003). Another example was found in the relations between a mother's avoidant attachment style and whether she felt close to her infant (Sierau, Jungmann, & Herzberg, 2013). Mothers who enjoyed a good relationship with their partners (the mediator) felt closer to their infants despite their negative attachment style than mothers who did not have good partner relationships. Moderators and mediators are shown in Figure 3.3.

Figure 3.3 Moderator and Mediator Variables

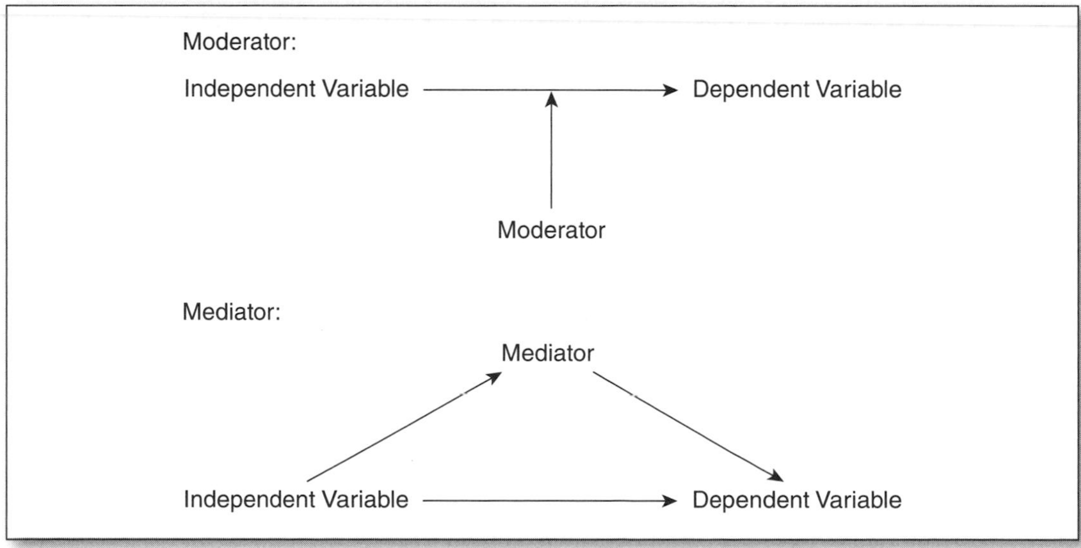

COMPARING APPROACHES

The approaches we've discussed are not the only types of approaches used to study parent-child relationships. For example, using physiological measures such as salivary cortisol to assess maternal stress levels (Hibel, Mercado, & Trumbell, 2012) is another approach. Nevertheless, the eight distinct perspectives described above are the most common ways that researchers currently investigate parent-child relationships. Some of the approaches are **complementary** (such as social address and parent cognition) and together provide a richer understanding of parents than if used alone. Other approaches, however, (such as parental traits and child effect) are fundamentally incompatible.

The approaches can be compared on five key questions:

1. What is the primary question asked by the approach?
2. What assumptions are made by the approach about the determinants of parental behavior?
3. At what level of specificity does each analyze parental behavior?
4. What assumption is made about the direction of parent-child influence?
5. What is the time frame for analysis of causal relations?

As can be seem in Table 3.5, each approach focuses on a different central question. For example, the parenting traits approach addresses the question of how individual differences in parenting affect children's development. In contrast, the ecological momentary assessment approach focuses on how the parent and child modulate each other's ongoing behavior. Different still, the child effects approach identifies the child characteristics that modify or jointly interact with parental behavior, and the behavioral genetics approach addresses the nature-nurture question.

Similarly, each approach takes a different view of the etiology of parental behavior. The social learning approach assumes that parenting is determined by previous social experiences; in particular, the feedback that parents receive from their own actions determines their subsequent behavior. In contrast, the social address approach takes the orientation that beliefs or practices of the larger cultural group form the central basis of parenting. The parent cognition approach views parents' own thinking as the major determinant of their behavior.

The approaches also differ on the level with which they examine parents. The ecological momentary assessment approach consists of detailed analyses of a small segment of behavior, whereas the parenting traits and large dataset approaches make generalizations about typical behavioral patterns. The parent cognition and social learning approaches take the middle of the road, typically focusing on the adjustments or changes that parents are capable of making in the course of parenting.

Assumptions about the direction of influence constitute a fourth dimension of comparison across the approaches. Parenting traits, social learning, social address, parent cognition, and behavioral genetics all assume that a parent has more influence on the child than vice versa. The child effects approach holds the opposite view, and the ecological momentary assessment approach assumes a bidirectional influence.

Table 3.5 Comparing Approaches

Approach	Primary Question	Level of Analysis	Determinants of Parental Behavior	Direction of Influence	Time Frame for Causal Relations
Parenting Traits	How do variations in parent characteristics affect children's development?	Global and aggregated	Stable, core traits	P → C	Long term
Child Effects	In what ways do children affect their parents' behavior?	Specific and nonaggregated	Children's characteristics and behavior	C → P or bidirectional	Immediate or short term
Social Learning	How do parents shape their children's behavior?	Some global and aggregated; other specific	Experience, authorities, behavior learning principles	Predominantly P → C	Immediate and short term
Social Address	How do families differ across social locations or cultures?	Global and aggregated	Beliefs and practices of the social group	P → C	Long term
Ecological Momentary Assessment	How are parent-child interactions structured and regulated?	Specific and nonaggregated	Proximate events and experiences	Bidirectional	Immediate
Parent Cognition	How is parental thinking related to parenting?	Specific and nonaggregated	Parents' beliefs and appraisals	P → C	Immediate and short term
Behavioral Genetics	What is the relation between the parents' genes and child's outcomes?	Specific	Genes	P → C	Short and long term
Large Datasets	What are the relations between variables?	Global and aggregated	Multiple influences	Multiple and bidirectional	Intermediate to long term

A fifth dimension on which the approaches can be compared is the time frame implicated for causal relations. Some approaches (such as social address and parenting traits) assume that parental influence occurs only after years of interactions. In contrast, ecological momentary assessment focuses on the present and looks at effects over a time span of only minutes or even seconds. Large datasets include a wide range of time frames but are likely to contain data collected annually or semiannually.

One problem of having multiple approaches is that it can make for an empirical picture of parent-child relationships that is sometimes disjointed. One way to try to integrate the approaches is by developing what has been called the *Person-Process-Context* model of development. Such a model includes the recognition of the individual characteristics of both the parent and the child and can mediate the impact of a particular process (such as attachment or discipline) in a particular context. This model reflects a merging of the parenting traits, child effects, and social address approaches. Rather than conceptualizing parenting as having a consistent effect on children, this model recognizes that parental influence may be a dynamic interaction of parent and child variables as well as the result of a particular context.

CHAPTER SUMMARY

Eight distinct approaches to studying parent-child relationships have been identified. Each approach has a unique orientation and focus to the investigation of parent-child relationships. These eight major approaches provide a rich and complex arena from which researchers can pick and choose to study parenting and parent child relations. No single approach can adequately address all the key questions associated with parenting. It is beneficial to entertain multiple and sometimes competing approaches, which can address different questions as well as provide a check-and-balance system to research. Each of the eight approaches identified here has particular strengths and limitations. Together, they uniquely function to help reveal the fundamental and transient, the enduring and transitional nature of parenting.

Naturally, such an assortment of research approaches to the clearly dynamic and complex questions of parenting can lead to controversy and debate. One major controversy has been raised based on findings from the behavioral genetics approach: Do parents even affect their children's development at all? That question is the focus of the next chapter.

THOUGHT QUESTIONS

- Give an example of a way in which a singular parenting trait or characteristic might affect parenting. What are the limitations to characterizing parenting with just one adjective?
- If you have siblings, what aspects of your environment were shared and nonshared? Were you treated differently from your siblings? If so, what approach does that illustrate?
- Which of the approaches to researching parents makes the most sense to you, and why?
- Frame a question about parents you would like to investigate. What would be the best research approach to use, and why? What would be its strengths and limitations?

CHAPTER GLOSSARY

assortative mating Refers to the practice of individuals seeking out and then having children with other individuals who are similar (in positive assortative mating) or dissimilar (negative assortative mating) to themselves in one or more characteristics, such as appearance or intelligence.

attention-deficit/hyperactivity disorder (ADHD) A condition (more commonly found in males) characterized by inattention, impulsivity, and hyperactivity.

attitudes Positive or negative evaluations of beliefs.

attributions Assessments of the cause of a behavior.

authoritarian A parenting trait characterized by strict control, low levels of communication, and low levels of warmth.

authoritative A parenting trait characterized by warm, open communication but also firm control.

behavioral genetics approach One of the approaches to the study of parenting that focuses on studying the role of genetics and the environment to understand the source of human characteristics.

child effects and transactions approach An approach to the study of parenting that focuses on how children's characteristics influence or interact with parental characteristics or behavior to change behavior.

complementarity When one person's acts complete another's.

datasets Information gathered by researchers, usually through surveys, interviews, or observations about parents, children, the context, and so on.

decision making The cognitive processes involved in reaching a decision.

differential susceptibility The hypothesis that only the children with certain characteristics will respond to particular types of parenting.

direction of effect This refers to the issue of who is influencing whom.

dizygotic twins Twins that do not share an identical genotype. Also known as *fraternal twins*.

dyadic synchrony Parent-child interactions that are mutually regulated, reciprocal, and harmonious.

ecological momentary assessment approach An approach that closely examines ongoing, moment-to-moment behavior in parent-child interactions in settings where it normally occurs.

ethnotheories The theories and beliefs that underlie the values and practices of members of a particular culture.

helicopter parent A term used in the popular press to refer to parents who are overly involved in the lives of their children and hover over them, both figuratively and literally.

large datasets approach The newest approach to parenting that typically uses large datasets, multiple variables, and advanced statistical analytic techniques to investigate questions about child rearing.

mediator A variable that explains how or why other variables are associated.

metaparenting The thoughts parents have about their children or their child rearing before or after interactions.

micro-analytic observations Careful observations of ongoing parent-child interactions, typically completed by making video or digital recordings for later analysis.

moderator A variable that affects the strength or direction of a relation between two other variables: a predictor (independent) variable and an outcome (dependent) variable.

monozygotic twins Twins that have the same genotype. Also called *identical twins*.

neonate An infant from birth through four weeks of age.

parental traits approach Characterizing parents on the basis of one or two qualities or characteristics.

permissive A parenting trait characterized by parents who are warm and loving but fail to control or expect mature behavior from their children.

positive synchrony When the interactions in families are harmonious, reciprocal, responsive, interconnected, and engaged, and when there is a shared affect.

sensitivity Synonymous with *sensitive parenting* (see Chapter 2 for more information).

social address approach An approach to the study of parenting that compares parents from different locations or "addresses." These might include different cultures, geographic locals, religious backgrounds, racial or ethnic groups, or socioeconomic status groups.

social cognition approach An approach to studying parents that focuses on various types of parental social cognitive processes (e.g., attitudes, beliefs, and problem solving) as they relate to children.

synchrony When both individuals attend to the same thing, are responsive to each other, and (perhaps) may share emotions.

turn-taking Alternating actions between individuals during an interaction.

CHAPTER 4

How Important Are Parents?

Chapter Preview: True or False?

- Studies of children raised without parents have provided clear-cut empirical evidence of the effects of neglect.
- The strength of the parent-child attachment at 12 months determines the child's behavior in adolescence and adulthood.
- Some researchers have argued that peers have a bigger effect on children than do parents.

The question might seem ludicrous at first: Does parenting really matter? Contrary to the fanciful accounts of Tarzan the Ape Man or of Romulus and Remus, the first mythical kings of Rome, gorillas and wolves just do not cut it. Every child needs an adult to provide care, safety, and other basic needs.

But to what extent do the actions of parents—their techniques, habits, and styles—truly influence a child's development and life outcomes? What power, if any, does a parent have to determine the course of a child's temperament, personality, and significant life choices? This is the question of parental influence.

Recall from Chapter 2 that the psychologist John B. Watson considered parents to have almost limitless ability to determine what their children developed into—be it a banker or a beggar. He believed that simply by controlling the environment, parents could mold children in various ways. Of course, the paramount importance Watson gave to *nurture* is an extreme view. At the other end of the continuum of influence lies the biological authority of genetic material, commonly referred to as *nature*. Some behavioral geneticists (and others) believe that parental influence is limited to the parents' genetic material passed on to the child.

HISTORICAL EVIDENCE ABOUT PARENTAL INFLUENCE

Throughout much of history, how parents rear their children has been assumed to be of fundamental importance. Many examples in the first three chapters support the importance of parental nurture during the younger years. Early philosophers never doubted it. Freud and many subsequent psychologists developed various theories about the ways that parents influence their children. Indeed, as Chapter 3 illustrates, multiple scientific approaches have been developed to examine and document how child rearing influences children.

Other evidence of widely held assumptions about parental influence includes sayings and folk theories concerning development. The lore of many countries contain some variation on the proverb "like father, like son; like mother, like daughter," including "The son of a swan is a good swimmer" (Egypt) and "From such a stick comes such a splinter" (Spain). The British poet William Wordsworth (1770–1850) phrased the idea as "The child is father of the man." A much older adage, attributed to the Roman poet Virgil (70–19 BCE), more explicitly suggests the role of nurture: "As the twig is bent, the tree inclines."

In our contemporary society, many serious social problems have, at least in part, been associated with problematic childrearing practices. Substance abuse, high school failure, poverty, delinquency, crime, and teenage pregnancy are just some of the problems many people assume are direct a consequence of poor parenting (e.g., Westerman, 1994). The antidote to those problems and other social woes, according to some individuals, is improved parenting. Pediatrician T. Berry Brazelton even went so far as to argue that effective nurturing during the first three years of life protects children against the lure of tobacco when they become adolescents (Brazelton, 1998).

To what extent do parents influence their children's development? How do parents influence their children? Research addressing those questions will be discussed in this chapter. The body of evidence begins with what are called **experiments of nature**. Animal studies also were influential in efforts to understand parental influence. Subsequently, research into parent-child attachment, parenting styles, and specific childrearing techniques has informed the question.

Experiments of Nature

Experiments of nature, for our purposes, refer to incidents in which children have been raised without parents or deprived of a normal environment because of an unusual set of circumstances, not as a result of planned scientific inquiry. Sometimes these cases result from intentional abusive parenting (see Box 4.1), but not always. The best-known examples of these natural experiments come from reports of "feral children"—children supposedly raised by animals in the absence of parents, language, and culture (see http://www.feral-children.com). Fewer than 100 cases of such children have been reported throughout history. After a careful analysis of each case, however, most of the supposed feral children were, in fact, abandoned children who were already mentally ill, in some way handicapped, or survivors of abuse (Clarke & Clarke, 1976; Newton, 2002). Somehow these children, such as the "wild boy of Aveyron," who was discovered in France in 1799 (Itard, 1962), managed to survive in the wild. Because there was no information about the state of the boy of Aveyron before his wilderness experience nor about the duration or quality of that experience, it is impossible to draw any useful scientific conclusions [Preview Question].

Box 4.1 A Girl Named Genie

Perhaps the best-documented example of the effects of isolation on a child comes from the sad case of Genie. She was discovered in 1970 after having been raised in a closet and isolated from social interaction. Her isolation began in her second year of life and continued until she was 13 years old. Her abusive and mentally ill father (who also abused his wife) strapped Genie to a potty chair for much of that time. When she and her blind, helpless mother finally escaped, Genie weighed just 59 pounds and was mute.

During the next few years, she showed remarkable development, as described by the linguist who worked with her (Curtis, 1977). Genie eventually learned to talk and developed some of the sensory, motor, and social skills she was missing, but she was unable to fully recover from her long-term neglect. One of the most obvious deficits she had concerned her syntax—how she put words together. Although she developed a large vocabulary, she was never able to master the rules of grammar.

A fascinating history of the case can be found in a book titled *Genie: A Scientific Tragedy* by Russ Rymer (1993). In the book, Rymer raised serious ethical questions about whether the team of therapists and scientists who studied and worked with Genie were more interested in furthering their careers than in providing the best psychological help.

This kind of abuse is rare but continues even today. A shocking but all-too-similar case of **child maltreatment** was discovered in Texas in 2001. An eight-year-old girl was discovered after being locked in a closet for six years. When rescued, she weighed less than 26 pounds—comparable to the weight of a normal two-year-old child (Farwell, 2013).

A better source of experiments of nature concerning the effects of not having parents comes from children raised in orphanages and residential institutions. In the 1940s, the alarm sounded that children deprived of mothers were developing abnormally and were at risk for a variety of emotional, cognitive, and health problems. Psychiatrist René Spitz (1945) described the children as being *starved of affect* (referring to the children's need for loving care) and the resulting problem as *hospitalism*. He recognized that those children were deprived not just of love but of social interaction and cognitive stimulation.

Although studies of children in institutions have been riddled with methodological problems (Pinneau, 1955), the research provided sufficient evidence to confirm the obvious: The absence of loving and frequent social contact early in life is deleterious to healthy development. The investigations into institutional deprivation had the positive effect of shuttering many institutions in Western Europe and America. Unfortunately, less affluent countries could not afford alternative care and continued the practice of orphanages. It is estimated that there are about 1.5 million children being raised in public care (orphanages or group homes) in Central and Eastern Europe alone (Nelson, 2007).

When Westerners began adopting children from Romanian, Russian, and Chinese orphanages in the late 20th century, some of the children continued to show signs of the poor conditions they were raised in. Common problems included impaired social competence and behavior problems as well as delays in physical and cognitive development (Smyke et al., 2007). More than half of the children studied in the Bucharest Early Intervention Project, a study of orphans in Romanian institutions, had some type of diagnosable psychological disorder (Zeanah, Egger, & Smyke, 2009). Other problems among these children can include **failure to thrive** (when otherwise normal children show stunted growth patterns) and difficulties forming relationships (Block & Krebs, 2005; Rutter et al., 2007). Notice the relatively few child care workers and the sterile environment in the photo of the orphanage in Photo 4.1.

As the review of the well-being of children who grew up in institutions, foster care, and adoptive homes makes clear, parenting and positive family environments do matter. The data reveal a **dose-response relationship** of parenting (Schoenmaker, Juffer, van IJzendoorn, & Bakermans-Kranenburg, 2014). That is, the sooner and the more positive parenting that a child receives outside of an institution, the more likely he or she is to experience positive outcomes.

Animal Studies

Other evidence about the importance of parents and the effects of early experience are extrapolated from animal studies. One of the first and most provocative psychologists to use animals to address questions about human development was the American-trained Chinese researcher Zing-Yang Kuo (1898–1970). Kuo investigated such fundamental questions as the nature of animal instincts, the role of the environment in development, and the relation between nature and nurture. A number of his animal studies challenged the prevailing views about the nature of human development by demonstrating that animals could be trained to behave in ways that appeared "unnatural" or even anti-instinctual. For example, he trained rats to rear cats and he modified the fighting, eating, and sexual behavior of pugnacious chow dogs (Kuo, 1967). Through his manipulations of the environment, Kuo created extraordinary demonstrations of the variability of behavior and the role that experience can play in subsequent behavior.

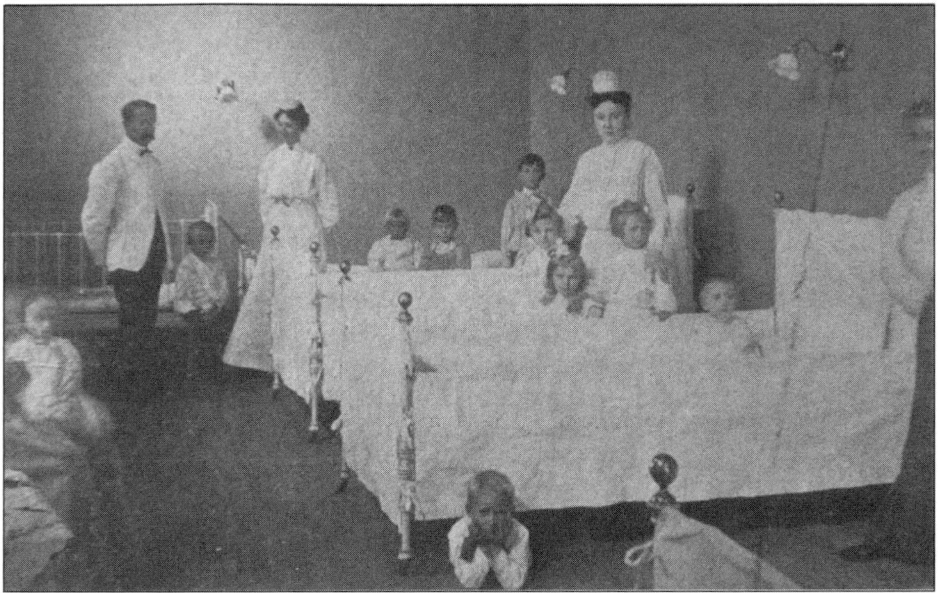

Photo 4.1 A postcard of a room in an orphanage from the first half of the 20th century.

Konrad Lorenz (1903–1989) was another influential animal behavior scientist (**ethologist**). Along with others, Lorenz founded the field of **ethology** (the study of behavior in animals' natural habitats). Lorenz is best remembered for studying the phenomenon of **imprinting**. This concept refers to rapid learning—usually very early in life—that is apparently independent of behavioral consequences. Lorenz famously got a gaggle of goslings to follow him because the incubated baby geese imprinted on the first moving object they saw at about 36 hours after hatching.

Imprinting in geese provided evidence for the idea of irreversible **critical periods** in development. This refers to time periods early in life when an organism is particularly susceptible or vulnerable to experiences or substances. Subsequent research in embryology has documented many critical periods for the development of organs. If a developing embryo or fetus is exposed to certain substances *in utero* (such as alcohol, drugs, or certain medications), this can cause irreversible negative effects. If a period is *sensitive,* though, rather than *critical*, the effects may be reversible (Bornstein, 1989). Borrowed from both ethology and biology, the concepts of imprinting and critical and sensitive developmental periods have influenced subsequent thinking about the importance of parents early in a child's life.

A psychologist who studied animals as a way of better understanding parent-child relationships was Harry Harlow, first introduced in Box 2.1. Harlow used rhesus monkeys to challenge contemporary views about why the young seek out their parents. Harlow did not subscribe to the learning theory view that children love their mothers mainly because mothers are the source of nourishment. At the University of Wisconsin, Harlow and his colleagues developed experimental apparatuses to investigate various questions about the nature of love, the role of early experience, and animal intelligence.

Harlow studied, among other questions, the effects of raising rhesus monkeys in isolation. Harlow discovered that without mothers, baby monkeys developed extreme pathological behavior, including **stereotyped behaviors** (repetitive or ritualistic movement, postures, or utterances) and antisocial behavior. When these monkeys became adults, they showed abnormal sexual behavior (Harlow, Dodsworth, & Harlow, 1965).

Subsequent investigations have documented the dramatic effects of early social deprivation in a variety of species, including humans. For example, socially deprived children were found to experience deleterious neurobiological effects (Fries, Shirtcliff, & Pollak, 2008). Such studies served to highlight the importance of early parent-child relationships. Animal studies reflect an indirect source of evidence about human development and are limited by issues of generalizability to humans. Still, they have played a prominent role in helping scientists develop and conceptualize parental impact on children's development (Clarke-Stewart, 1988). Experiments of nature and animal research, then, provided preliminary evidence and set the stage for investigations into the effects of childrearing environments on children's development.

ASSOCIATIONS BETWEEN PARENTING AND CHILDREN'S OUTCOMES

The once-prevailing view that parents had a one-way or **unidirectional effect** on children was clear in the words of a psychologist who wrote, "Recent psychological studies indicate that personality is very largely a product of the interactions between parents and child" (Symonds, 1949, p. 3). Investigators typically assumed that when a parent behavior related to a child behavior, it was because the parent's behavior had directly impacted that of the child. However, virtually all of the findings purportedly showing parental effects on children reveal not causes but *correlations* between parental characteristics (behavior) and child outcomes. Very few experimental studies, where families are randomly assigned to conditions, have ever been conducted (see Cummings, 1995). And it is only through using true experiments that we can confidently talk about causality. So it is more accurate to describe the results of such research as reflecting *associations* between characteristics of parents and children.

The literature on parent-child associations is voluminous; a thorough review could fill several books. Reviews of the literature published can be found in various places, such as the *Handbook of Psychology: Developmental Psychology* (Lerner, Easterbrooks, & Mistry, 2013). Other useful sources include the *Handbook of Parenting* (Bornstein, 2002), and *Social Development: Relationships in Infancy, Childhood, and Adolescence* (Underwood & Rosen, 2011). As these sources reveal, there is now a vast amount of research into parent-child relationships.

Rather than attempt to provide a comprehensive review of the research linking parenting to children's outcomes, this chapter provides a representative sampling of some of the work on the topic. The research cited has relied on a variety of theories (Chapter 2) and reflects work from all eight approaches to the study of parents (Chapter 3). Many of the other chapters in the book also include research that links parenting to children's positive as well as negative development.

Research findings into the associations between parenting and children's characteristics and behavior can be grouped into positive outcomes, negative outcomes, and no apparent associations. However, views about what are positive, substantive, and empirically verifiable outcomes in children change over time. For example, children's resistance to temptation in laboratory settings (tested by leaving a child alone in a laboratory room with an appealing but prohibited toy) was a prominent outcome measure used in 1960s research. Then, it was considered a key index of the child's ability to delay gratification and evidence of a developing conscience. That outcome variable has been discarded in favor of more ecologically valid and direct indices of children's functioning, such as mothers' reports about children's guilt and remorse after misbehavior (Kochanska, 2002). Currently, commonly measured child outcomes associated with parenting include general competence, peer relations, internalization, **prosocial behavior**, cognitive development, and school achievement. We will use the outcomes of *competence* or *well-being* as examples as we consider the study of beneficial associations between parenting and child outcomes.

Competence refers to being able to make use of environmental and personal resources to achieve positive personal development. Parenting has been related to children's general competence chiefly through three areas of investigation: parent-child attachment, parenting styles (also called *parenting patterns*), and specific parenting behaviors.

Parent-Child Attachment

According to attachment theory, infants who are securely attached at 12 months of age will develop a positive working model of themselves and others. They will then carry these ideas into new relationships, such as with teachers and peers. Many studies have found support for the theory: Children securely attached to their mothers at 12 or 18 months of age are indeed more compliant, enthusiastic, persistent, cooperative, and better at problem solving than are insecurely attached children (Thompson, 2006). The evidence, though, is not always clear-cut [Preview Question]. For example, the predictive validity of the association is not always strong. In one study, although securely attached preschool-age girls were more socially competent than insecurely attached girls on several different indices—such as teacher and peer ratings—the relation did not hold for boys (LaFreniere & Sroufe, 1985). In another example, using a modification of the Strange Situation procedure for older children (see Table 2.1), it was found that six-year-old boys who were classified as insecurely attached were less well liked by peers and rated as less competent by teachers. However, no comparable associations held for girls (Cohn, 1990).

There are several explanations for these mixed results. First, relationships are dynamic and changeable. A child who is securely attached at one age may subsequently develop more insecure attachment owing to his or her parents' divorce, a move to a new town, or some other stressful experience, particularly if the event took place in early childhood (Fraley & Heffernan, 2013; Pianta, Sroufe, & Egeland, 1989).

Another reason for mixed results can be due to the fact that children may have a different *quality* of attachments with their mothers and fathers. Children's attachment to their parents is often of similar quality, but not always. For example, in a meta-analytic review of attachment classifications between mothers and fathers, 69% of children had the same secure

Photo 4.2 A father cares for his two toddlers in Yemen, Southwest Asia.

Source: Photograph by J. P. Bell

(50%) or insecure (19%) classification with both their mother and father (see Photo 4.2). The remaining 31% of the children were securely attached with one parent but not the other (Fox, Kimmerly, & Schafer, 1991). Recent evidence indicates that as long as you are attached securely to one parent, you will have the benefits of a secure attachment. However, children who are insecurely attached with both mothers and fathers are more likely to have more behavior problems in middle childhood than securely attached children or children with mixed attachments (Kochanska & Kim, 2013).

Rather than making predictions about children's outcomes based solely on their attachment classification at 12 months of age, researchers are currently focusing on individuals' internal working models (see Chapter 2). These mental models concerning how people act developed from an individual's previous history of close relationships and provide a representation of both the self and others (Bretherton & Munholland, 2008). Using a carefully designed interview (the Adult Attachment Interview [AAI]) or questionnaires to assess current attachment styles (Crowell, Fraley, & Shaver, 2008), a number of developmental and social psychologists are finding links between how people think about their early attachment relations and how they currently function. In adults, representations of others have frequently been studied using the conceptual framework developed by Kim Bartholomew (1990) and others (e.g., Feeney, 2008). Bartholomew created a 2-by-2 matrix to diagram the four possibilities of how we view ourselves and others (see Table 4.1).

Table 4.1 Classification Scheme of Attachment-Based Representations of Self and Others

	View of Self	
View of Others	**Positive**	**Negative**
Positive	Secure	Preoccupied
Negative	Dismissing	Fearful

Source: From Bartholomew, 1990. Reprinted with permission of SAGE Publications.

Adults who have a positive view of self and others are considered to have a **secure attachment style**. However, people who have a negative view of self and a positive view of others are considered to have a **preoccupied attachment style**. These individuals would be uncomfortable having someone else accept them for who they are. They may feel they could not live up to others' expectations. They would not understand how someone else could love them and thus would undermine the other person's loving efforts, which would only serve to confirm their low expectations. Individuals whose view of others is negative but view of self is positive would be classified as having a **dismissing attachment style**. These people would be likely to negate other people's feelings and inflate the importance of their own. Finally, negative views of both the self and others define a **fearful attachment style**. These individuals do not think they are worthy of being loved nor are other people worthy of loving. Consequently, they are fearful of forming relationships.

These four adult attachment classifications relate to both interpersonal competence as well as childhood recollections. Persons who hold secure representations of attachment with their parents are comfortable with intimacy as well as with autonomy. These individuals value their attachment experiences and are able to provide an objective and balanced description of their childhood—one that may include negative experiences as well as positive ones. Preoccupied, dismissing, and fearful individuals all experience relationship problems. Preoccupied adults provide confused or incoherent accounts of their childhood attachment relationships. They may express anger or passivity in recalling their childhood. People characterized as dismissing may have difficulty in recalling their own histories and may devalue their childhood relationships. These individuals' recollections suggest a desire to distance themselves from the emotionally charged childhood relationships. Such individuals may idealize, denigrate, or be unable to recall their early experiences. Fearful individuals are likely to report negative or traumatic childhood experiences.

Individuals classified into these categories have been found to have systematic personality and behavioral differences. Many of the findings are reviewed in the second edition of the *Handbook of Attachment* (Cassidy & Shaver, 2008). The results from a variety of studies highlight the importance of working models. For example, results from prospective mothers' adult attachment interview conducted during pregnancy accurately predicted the Strange Situation attachment classifications of their 12-month-old infants in 75% of the cases (Fonagy, Steele, & Steele, 1991). Mothers who expressed autonomous views of their own relationships were likely to develop a secure attachment with their infants, but women who were dismissing or preoccupied were likely to have an insecure attachment. Many more examples can be found in the quality of dating relationships among college students. For instance, along the lines of the theory, students with secure representations have better-quality romantic relationships than students with other types of internal representations (e.g., Feeney, 2008).

Parenting Styles

A different way used to link parenting with subsequent child competence can be found in the parenting traits research approach. Since the 1950s, a number of investigators have found connections between parenting style and various child behaviors. The most careful and prominent work along these lines was conducted by Diana Baumrind (1971). In a longitudinal sample of children and their parents, Baumrind found evidence indicating that different childrearing patterns were associated with particular outcomes in children. Authoritative parenting—characterized by warm, open communication but also firm limits—was correlated with a variety of positive outcomes in children at different ages. Children of these parents were more competent, as exhibited by greater social responsibility (including cooperative behavior and friendliness toward peers) and independence. Baumrind wrote that the outcome associated with the authoritative pattern "is uniformly positive for both sexes at all ages studied, unlike any other child rearing pattern" (1983, p. 138). That conclusion still holds, more than 40 years later (Larzelere, Morris, & Harrist, 2013).

The two other major patterns of child rearing were associated with lower levels of child competence. Authoritarian parents discouraged independence, the questioning of parental authority, and displays of affection. When a child misbehaved, authoritarian parents tended to resort to harsh punishment. Their children were less independent, less assertive, and less achievement-oriented than were the children of authoritative parents. The third major category of parents—permissive—was warm and loving but failed to control or expect mature behavior from their children. Children in these families were neither independent nor achievement oriented.

Despite researchers' enthusiasm for using Baumrind's typology of parents, the effects are not as robust as is commonly thought. A close reading of her work indicates that the associations between parenting types and child outcomes are complex. For example, some of the associations differ based on the gender of the child. Furthermore, Catherine Lewis (1981) pointed out that the data could be interpreted in a different way. She argued that the direction of effect could be opposite from Baumrind's interpretation: Competent children may *elicit* authoritative child rearing from their parents. Indeed, a parent does not need to use harsh discipline with an easy, compliant child. Thus Lewis argued for child effects on parents. Although Baumrind (1983) took issue with that interpretation, it is likely that the competence of both parents and children is the product of a reciprocal process.

Many studies concerning associations between parents and the functioning of their children—from preschoolers through adolescents—have adopted Baumrind's parenting classification scheme. For instance, the typology proved its usefulness in accounting for relations between parenting characteristics and adolescent behavior in a study of some 4,000 families. Based on self-reports and school records of teenagers, youth from authoritative families were found to be the best adjusted. This assessment tapped a variety of indices, including psychosocial development (self-reliance, work orientation, self-esteem, and personal competence), problem behaviors (substance use, delinquency, and antisocial behavior), psychological distress (anxiety and depression), and school achievement. Children from neglectful homes fared the worst (Lamborn, Mounts, Steinberg, & Dornbusch, 1991). In a follow-up study with 2,353 of the adolescents one year later, the results were replicated and extended (Steinberg, Mounts, Lamborn, & Dornbusch, 1994). Differences in adjustment (such as levels of delinquency or academic competence) that were associated with parenting style were maintained or had even widened.

These studies helped to spark a renewed enthusiasm for the parenting traits and the investigation of multiple related themes (Morris, Cui, & Steinberg, 2013). A central focus has been on unpacking different traits to better understand the components involved in child competence. For instance, a large number of studies have focused on the studying the nature of parental control and how it relates to child behavior (see review by Bugental & Grusec, 2006). Other work has focused on better understanding child effects on parenting styles, including the contributions of genetics and gene-environment interactions to child behavior and well-being (e.g., Bakermans-Kranenburg & van IJzendoorn, 2006).

Specific Parenting Behaviors

A third approach intended to link child rearing with child competence focused on correlates of *particular* parenting practices. One example of this work was a cross-cultural study that found, in both North America and Egypt, maternal vocal stimulation to be positively related to toddler behavioral competence (Wachs et al., 1993). Another study found that sensitive mothers, those who engaged in mutually responsive orientation with their toddlers, have children that are more likely to develop a conscience (Kochanska, 2002). In fact, there are dozens of other examples that could be included. Reviews of the research on the topic indicate that some of the other parental practices commonly associated with competence and well-being in children include appropriate involvement, **behavioral control**, empathic responsiveness, warmth, effective problem solving, **monitoring**, flexibility, and, increasingly, positive parenting techniques (Crouter & Head, 2002; Grusec & Davidov, 2007). Many more examples of specific parenting behaviors linked to child well-being will be provided in subsequent chapters.

THE BEHAVIORAL GENETICS CHALLENGE

The problem with all the studies mentioned above, according to the perspective of behavioral genetics, is that they do not take into account of the role of genes. For example, consider the parent whose genotype predisposes him to have an aggressive personality. Given that children share about 50% of each parents' genes, a child of such a parent may inherit the genes that contribute to aggressive behavior. According to the original behavioral genetics viewpoint, it does not matter how the parent behaves toward the child. The fact that the child carries those genes means that child is destined to be aggressive.

The more recent behavioral genetic view is more nuanced, focusing on gene-environment interactions and seeking to understand the role of the environment. That is, a child may have a genetic makeup that provides a proclivity toward certain response patterns, but it takes an environment to either bring out that proclivity or protect against it. One example of this interaction between genes and the environment—labeled the **diathesis-stress model**—has been recognized in clinical psychology to account for the emergence of some psychiatric disorders such as depression and schizophrenia. This model assumes that there is a genetic predisposition toward the problem but that the expression of the problem only occurs when combined with particular kinds of environmental stressors or individual characteristics (e.g., Reinelt et al., 2013).

David Rowe, in a book titled *The Limits of Family Influence* (1994), reviewed the evidence about genetic influences on children's outcomes. Based on twin and adoption studies, he argued that the evidence for childrearing effects on intelligence, personality variables, and various behaviors (such as delinquency and smoking) was modest at best. Instead, the correlations between monozygotic (identical) twins indicate a strong genetic influence on such behaviors as inattentiveness and hyperactivity (see Table 4.2). Rowe concluded that specific parenting practices or patterns do not appear to have much effect on children's outcomes. As he carefully worded it, "Variation in rearing is a weak source of trait variation" (p. 223).

Table 4.2 Some Human Behavioral Genetics Data Regarding Correlations Between Siblings

Characteristic	Mean *r*	Social Relation	Number of Pairs
Extraversion	.43	MZ twins	116
	.23	Siblings	177
Inattentiveness/ Hyperactivity	.62 .23	MZ twins DZ twins	64 98
IQ	.86	MZ twins	4,672
	.72	MZ twins, reared apart	65
	.60	DZ twins	5,533
	.47	Siblings	26,473

Source: Adapted from Rowe, 1994.

Note: A correlation of less than .30 is considered small, .30 to .50 is moderate, and above .50 is large.

Another psychologist who used the behavioral genetic approach was Sandra Scarr. She joined in the budding controversy over parental influence through a provocative statement in her presidential address at the Society for Research in Child Development, published in 1992:

> Ordinary differences between families have little effect on children's development, unless the family is outside of a normal, developmental range. . . . Children's outcomes do not depend on whether parents take children to the ball game or to a museum so much as they depend on genetic transmission, on plentiful opportunities, and on having a good enough environment that supports children's development to become themselves. (Scarr, 1992, p. 15)

A few years later, Judith Rich Harris (1995) contended that much of what has been attributed to parental nurture is genetic in origin. She developed her arguments in a popular book titled *The Nurture Assumption* (Harris, 1998). The book received considerable attention, and articles about her theory appeared in magazines and newspapers around the country. Although she relied on behavioral genetics data as a starting point, she distanced herself from that approach by arguing that the environment *does* play an important role in development—but the environmental influences do not come from parents but from peers [Preview Question]. She has proposed the theory of group socialization, which will be discussed in Chapter 10.

The next year, psychologist David Cohen (1999) published his perspective on parental influence, which was also based on a behavioral genetics argument. He contended that parents had little impact on their children, except perhaps in the domain of sociability. But in contrast to Harris, he did not believe that peers held particularly long-term influence. Peers may hold sway during the adolescent stage but their influence decreases once individuals move into adulthood. He concluded that parents cannot take responsibility for their children's successes but neither should they be held in blame if the child goes astray.

Taken together, this behavioral-genetics–inspired assault on the role of childrearing behavior and the environment has attracted a considerable amount of attention from the media and stirred up a controversy among psychologists and other scientists. Most current analyses recognize the interactions between genes and the environment. For example, individuals who have a genetic propensity for violence are much more likely to engage in violence if they live in poverty or in a violent neighborhood (Barnes & Jacobs, 2013; Simons et al., 2011). In a very different area of inquiry, childhood obesity is believed to result from the interaction of genetic, family, and environmental **risk factors** (Stang & Loth, 2011).

A NEW PERSPECTIVE ON HOW PARENTS MATTER

Parental nurturance—with its thousands of reprimands, reinforcements, reminders, and lectures, and its tens of thousands of hours of attention—is not without power. But at least some of the behavioral genetics argument is correct: Childrearing practices alone do not have the ability to strictly mold a child the way John B. Watson envisioned. Variations in child rearing from one parent to another appear to have limited effect in terms of modifying core components of a child's personality. However, only more research—using newer and better methods and concepts—can answer the question concerning the extent of parental nurturance. So the controversy about parental nurturance continues, in part because of different approaches used to support the opposing views.

Child rearing is a multidimensional, multi-activity endeavor. As was listed in Table 1.1, effective parenting involves many roles and functions. Parents must feed, clothe, and protect their children. They also stimulate, educate, and discipline them, as Bradley (2007) itemized. However, another type of role that was not listed because it has been largely ignored by researchers is that of *guiding* a child's development. Parental guidance can have a profound effect on how a child develops and functions as an adult. And its investigation could provide a rapprochement between the researchers, parents, and others who believe that parental nurturance plays a fundamental role in children's development and those who just as strongly argue that child rearing has little impact on children.

The trajectory model proposed by Holden (2010) hypothesizes that parents guide their children's development in three basic ways. First, parents *establish* trajectories, determining the direction that the children's development will take. Second, parents *mediate* these

Photo 4.3 Parents help guide a child down a slide—and through childhood.

Source: Photograph by J. P. Bell

trajectories, exerting a powerful influence on how children perceive, react to, and understand their environment and experiences. Third, parents *modify the speed* at which children have experiences that may promote their development. Parental actions can then result in either accelerating or slowing down that development (see Photo 4.3).

Establishing Trajectories

To visualize what is meant by *trajectories*, imagine a trail through the woods. Now picture a parent guiding a child on that trail. The scenery is always changing; thus one must adjust one's speed, exertion, and direction in order to stay on the path. The concept is helpful, because children are constantly changing as they grow. Of course, in reality, children do not travel just one path; they develop simultaneously on multiple trajectories. Parents determine how children develop through selecting the environments that children are exposed to, thereby influencing the direction of their personal development.

Parents are the ones who usually set the child's feet on a path, although there certainly are exceptions to this (coaches, teachers, or even the child herself). Parents might "put up fences" to attempt to block entrance to other, less desirable paths. This is a simple picture of what is meant by parental establishment of trajectories.

We can discover hints as to the types of trajectories a child is on by looking at the environment within his or her home. Some homes have lots of books, magazines, and other types of reading materials. Other homes have musical instruments around, and music is always playing. Sports equipment can be found in some homes, while religious objects—such as crosses, menorahs, or the Qur'an—may be displayed in others.

Those objects may indicate possible trajectories that a child could be on, but even better evidence can be gathered by observing parental behavior. What activities do the parents engage in? Which of these activities include their children, and how? Some focus their children's time and attention on schoolwork, but others orient their children into competitive games and sports or perhaps musical expression—or a busy combination of all of the above. By selecting environments, activities, and social interactions, parents are guiding development.

Whether or not parents are aware that they are thinking about their child rearing in this way, they do guide their children along certain paths and not others. The establishment of trajectories is not always a conscious decision. Parents are likely influenced by culture, socioeconomic status, goals, values, resources, and their own parenting history. Moreover, the choice of trajectories may also be influenced by other family members, particularly by siblings' needs and activities. Although each influence is important, we know the most about parental *goals* for their children. A study on parental values and goals in Midwestern middle-class American families provides some examples (Dunn, Kinney, & Hofferth, 2003). The most commonly mentioned goal of parents for their children was "happiness." This was further delineated into physical health, financial stability, and specific child attributes such as social competence. Those goals and others were compiled into a list by Ted Dix and Sylvia Branca (2003) that can be found in Table 4.3. Depending on the parental goal—and the parents' views about how to obtain that goal—different trajectories may be promoted.

Table 4.3 Examples of Parental Socialization Goals

Parents desire for their children to	
Survive; be healthy and safe	Be loyal to family
Be obedient	Be independent
Follow family routines	Be happy
Display proper manners	Be a moral person
Be socially competent	Be economically self-sufficient; get a good job
Do well in school	
Respect • parents • elders • property • cultural traditions, customs	

Source: Dix & Branca, 2003. Reprinted with permission of SAGE Publications.

Parents establish and promote trajectories in a variety of ways, but the most obvious is in the decisions they make—large and small—that affect their children's lives. When purchasing a home, parents may consider features such as the quality of the school district, safety of the neighborhood, presence of other children, and accessibility of parks. As children grow, so do the number of decisions parents make regarding trajectories. New pathways can be launched in various domains such as music, athletics, and religion. Social pathways are likely influenced by the number of social agents the child is exposed to as well as the quality of the social interactions. This includes siblings, peers, extended family, neighbors, teachers, coaches, and other adults. As the family grows, the parents' attention to their other children with their own (possibly competing) trajectories undoubtedly impacts every child in the family in various ways. Some parents initiate an educational trajectory even before their child is born—by registering their unborn child in a particular day care, purchasing prenatal stimulation equipment, or equipping the nursery with materials designed to promote cognitive development.

As the child develops, the parents' provision of experiences becomes increasingly intentional. By the time a child is in elementary school, parents engage in what Furstenberg (1993) called *promotive* strategies, designed to foster the child's talents and opportunities. These strategies may involve encouraging the child; engaging in parent-child collaborative activities; or creating new pathways through such activities as music lessons, after-school programs (such as Boy Scouts or Girl Scouts), summer camps, and religious youth-group events. In a study of inner-city children and their parents, Furstenberg and his colleagues found that almost all (95%) of the parents reported engaging in some activity to promote development of a child's talent or skill (Furstenberg, Cook, Eccles, Elder, & Sameroff, 1999). These actions ranged from investigating opportunities and encouraging participation to volunteering as a coach or even transferring to a more favorable school.

According to college students, mothers and fathers engage in both guidance and, to a lesser degree, pressure to develop along various trajectories (Holden, Bayan, Baruah, & Holland, 2013). Fifteen common trajectories were reported on, ranging from education and family closeness to peer relations, sports, religion, and music. Family closeness and educational success were the two trajectories that both mothers and fathers were most likely to promote for both genders. At the bottom of the list were environmental consciousness, art, music, and politics. Figure 4.1 displays some of the results.

Figure 4.1 Parental Guidance on Eight Trajectories

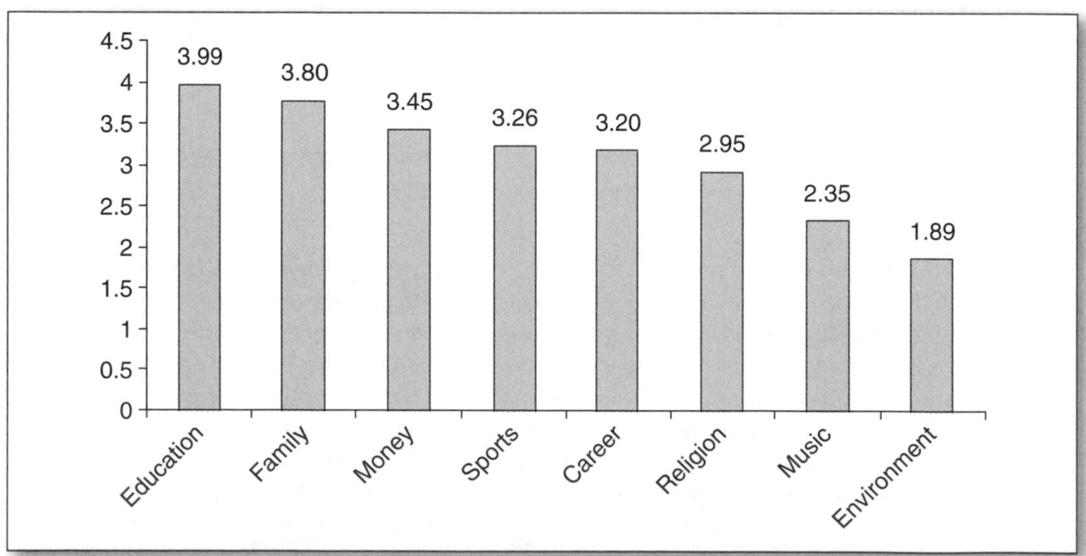

Parents also guide their children toward particular pathways by direct instruction. In a study of Mexican American and European American parents, more than 90% reported intentionally teaching their children how to behave appropriately as well as how not to misbehave (Azmitia, Cooper, Garcia, & Dunbar, 1996). Some parents explicitly warn about negative role models (e.g., gang members) and what happens to them in an effort to educate their children about positive developmental trajectories.

Just as parents instruct their children about positive pathways, they also proactively initiate these pathways in an attempt to avoid potentially negative outcomes. They regulate their children's circumstances and experiences in the hopes of protecting them from potentially hazardous individuals or settings—such as negative peer influence, substance use, early sexual activity, emotionally upsetting experiences, and violence. Furstenberg et al. (1999) labeled these protective and instructive behaviors parental *preventive strategies*.

One preventive strategy adopted by some parents is to homeschool a child in order to buffer that child from negative influences in the school system (see Box 4.2). Goodnow (1997) dubbed this type of practice, whereby parents seek to shield their children from negative influences for some period of time, "*cocooning*." By forestalling exposure to perceived negative influences, parents hope their children will develop resiliency through the internalization of parental values. This shielding of a child from potential negative social influences includes curbing a child's exposure to those influences or to alternative values. It may also involve restricting behavior that conflicts with parental values (Goodnow, 1997).

Box 4.2 Homeschooling as Protection

An increasingly common preventive strategy in contemporary American society in the domain of parenting and education is homeschooling. There are more than 1.5 million children homeschooled in the United States, and that number increases each year (National Center for Education Statistics, 2014). There are many parental motivations for homeschooling: safety, limiting exposure to drugs or negative peer pressure, the desire to provide religious or moral training, and, foremost, the quality of education (Ice & Hoover-Dempsey, 2011; Isenberg, 2007).

Independent of parental reasons, the evidence indicates that students can thrive academically at home. But how well students learn is best predicted by the level of education his or her parent received (Collom, 2005). Presumably, parents who are better educated are able to teach their children better at home than other parents.

Starting a child down a pathway is not enough, however, to keep the child on course. Parents must attend to their children, encourage them, provide **parental support**, and usually provide them material help (such as by purchasing athletic equipment or chauffeuring them to events). Leibham and her colleagues (Leibham, Alexander, Johnson, Neitzel, & Reis-Henrie, 2005) found that children who continued to pursue particular interests across a one-year time span (from four to five years old) had parents who, compared with parents of children who did not have sustained interests, provided more materials (such as corresponding books and objects) in the home and believed in academic stimulation as well as the importance of curiosity. Consider what parents of world-class athletes, musicians, or mathematicians have to do in order to develop their children's talents. As Feldman and Piirto (2002) summarized, it is well established that parents, after first recognizing unusual talent in their children, must invest at least 10 years of "sustained, coordinated, and effective support . . . to have a chance at fulfilling its promise" (p. 205) for these children who develop exceptional ability.

Mediating Trajectories

Not all parents, of course, have the time, money, or know-how to make the choices they would like for their children. For example, parental employment may preclude moving to a more preferable location. Or a family may not have the financial resources to move out of the inner city. Nevertheless, these parents still have the ability to mediate trajectories by interpreting their child's experience and sense of reality. They can do this in three ways: *Pre-arming* prepares children mentally and emotionally for what is coming; *concurrent mediation* helps children make sense of their world in the midst of an experience; and *debriefing* can help after the experience is over.

Pre-arming

Imagine (or remember) that while you were in grade school, you moved to a new city or state. Moving is stressful for anyone, but it can be particularly painful for children leaving a close group of friends. Many other experiences, both positive and negative, have the potential to derail a child's developmental course: the birth of a sibling, a parent's divorce or remarriage, a serious illness, an unexpected financial windfall, natural disasters, peer problems, exposure to violence, or racism. Even positive changes can affect developmental trajectories due to the stress and general repercussions they evoke. Bradley (2007) called these "developmentally challenging circumstances" (p. 99). By preparing the child for these types of experiences, parents can influence how the child will perceive and react. Pre-arming helps to prepare children for changing situations, so the technique has also been called **parental inoculation**.

Pre-arming may prove a particularly important technique when parents must counteract stereotypes or cultural pressures in contexts not amenable to change. African American parents engage in **race socialization** in order to prepare their children for hostility, prejudice, and discrimination (Lesane-Brown, 2006; see Photo 4.4). This includes teaching specific strategies, denigrating the threatening group, and discussing the potential for discrimination. Similarly, in one study, parents prepared their daughters for anticipated gender discrimination in sports by providing special encouragement (Fredricks & Eccles, 2004).

Another pre-arming strategy is to draw attention to potential dangers. Mothers living in dangerous neighborhoods rehearse with their children the dangers that destroyed the lives of people they know (Ardelt & Eccles, 2001). Anecdotal parental reports indicate that another pre-arming technique related to times when parents cannot be directly monitoring

Photo 4.4 Minority parents educate their children in race socialization.

Source: © David Sacks/Digital Vision/Thinkstock

their children is to provide simple rules or what could be called *mantras*. These sayings are given to children to help them deal with problematic situations. "Make good decisions," "Don't talk to strangers," and "Remember who you are and what you stand for" are three examples.

Concurrent Mediation

The second way parents mediate children's experience is by helping a child interpret a situation while (or shortly after) the child is experiencing it. Here, the parent attempts to modify the child's perceptions and reactions to an event in order to mediate a negative experience or influence—such as exposure to inappropriate media, discrimination, **bullying**, teasing, or trauma. Concurrent mediation is most often designed to counteract negative experiences but sometimes highlights or reinforces a positive behavior or experience.

Power (2004) reviewed the strategies parents used to influence their children's appraisal of stress. As parents model their own emotional reactions to a situation, they also may coach their child on how to react. Such coaching includes drawing attention to relevant stimuli, seeking out appropriate information, encouraging logical thinking, helping to understand cause and effect, and encouraging perspective taking.

Most research into concurrent mediation has focused on parental reactions to media influence. For instance, parents practice mediation in order to interpret objectionable televised content (e.g., Austin, Bolls, Fujioka, & Engelbertson, 1999). This practice consists of watching TV with their children and then discussing the content (Nathanson, 2001). Parents praise actions they value when they see an actor engage in them; they point out why the behaviors of other actors are wrong and should be avoided. In this way, parents can help to shape children's reactions to what they see and help them advance along the path of prosocial development.

Debriefing

A third type of trajectory mediation is *debriefing*, or attempting to influence how a child perceives or thinks about an experience after the event is over. Here, the parent may be counteracting a damaging experience or a negative message directed at the child. Researchers have rarely investigated this type of mediation, and when they have, it has been conducted following traumatic events (Stallard & Salter, 2003). So the best evidence about parents engaging in debriefing comes from the child sexual abuse literature, looking at the behavior of non-abusive parents. Following disclosure of abuse, parents who are sympathetic, take the child's accusations seriously, and are responsive have children who are better able to cope with the abuse than are children whose parents deny the abuse, invalidate its damage, or take no action against it (Elliott & Carnes, 2001).

Parents can also serve a debriefing function by nonjudgmentally encouraging children to express their feelings. This enables children to process the emotions associated with a difficult situation. Debriefing helps to explain the finding that mothers who are more aware and communicative about their adolescents' problems had teens who were functioning better (Hartos, Eitel, Haynie, & Simons-Morton, 2000). In this way, parents attempt to repair damage done to their child and reroute them onto a positive trajectory.

Modifying the Speed

In addition to directing and supporting developmental pathways and mediating the experiences children have while traveling them, parents also affect their children's development by influencing the speed at which a child progresses on a certain trajectory. Parents can encourage *acceleration* or *deceleration* on a pathway. Parents are not the only family members who influence the speed of a child's progress along a developmental path. From the family system perspective, competition between siblings can encourage more rapid skill development in healthy ways—for example, learning how to play soccer better so you can play with your older sister and her friends. Similarly, sibling competition could play a role in accelerating the development of antisocial behaviors, as when a younger sibling joins a gang in order to "keep up" with his older brother.

Acceleration

American parents are often eager to speed up their children's development. It is not difficult to find examples of this: expectant mothers "training" their fetuses, infants enrolled in cognitive-enrichment day cares, parents reading to infants to enhance later literacy skills, and toddlers participating in organized sports (Clarke-Stewart, 1998; Whitehurst & Lonigan,

1998; see also Photo 4.5). Some parents promote early independence in their children by separating themselves from their infants. Another indication is the abundance of commercial products available to purportedly speed up child development, ranging from prenatal devices to computer programs. This interest in acceleration is not a recent phenomenon; more than 50 years ago, Jean Piaget recognized this national preoccupation and dubbed it the "American Question" (Niemark, 1975, p. 584).

Elkind (2001) characterized children who are pressured to grow up too soon and too fast as "hurried children" (p. 3). He argued that parents have increasingly been overstructuring their children's leisure-activity time. Parents fast-track their children for multiple reasons. They may do this to give their children a head start in the competitive world, provide peer interactions in the absence of same-age peers, guard children's safety, promote a child's self-esteem, or feel their own pride in the child's accomplishments. The effect on the child, according to Elkind, is stress and burnout at an early age. However, a review of the evidence does not find overscheduling to be a majority phenomenon in the United States, though it certainly is common. Hofferth, Kinney, and Dunn (2006) determined that 23.9% of a sample of 315 nine-year-old to 12-year-old children could be classified as "hurried." These children were involved in either three (or more) activities each week or two activities for four or more hours on two days per week.

Photo 4.5 Children participating in sports while their parents look on.

Source: © Ableimages/Photodisc/Thinkstock

Deceleration

Alternatively, some parents may seek to slow down their children's development—at least, in some trajectories. The motive may be to protect a child from having to grow up too quickly, to give the child a competitive advantage, to allow a delayed child a more level playing field with peers, or to maintain control over a child rather than allow the appropriate autonomy.

Parents use several techniques to decelerate development. **Overprotection** occurs when parents make all the decisions for the child (Parker, 1983) and refuse or delay giving the child increasing and age-appropriate autonomy. Other parents may seek to protect and prolong the stage of cognitive "innocence" by promoting fantasy beliefs such as Santa Claus or the Tooth Fairy (Woolley, 1995) beyond the usual time.

Another type of deceleration technique is to delay certain types of social involvement. Keeping a toddler away from peers or not allowing an older child to participate in extracurricular activities serves to delay normal socialization experiences. But one increasingly popular method today is to delay school entry—also known as *academic redshirting*. By waiting a year before enrolling in kindergarten or the first grade, a child gains the benefits of a year of physical, cognitive, and social maturity. Existing research results are conflicting as to whether this helps children in the long run. This "gift of time" does not ensure academic success, although it has often found to be an advantage in sports achievement (Graue, Kroeger, & Brown, 2002; March, 2005).

TRAJECTORIES AND DEVELOPMENT

Parents who actively and appropriately guide their children's trajectories provide an influence on children's outcomes. Such a view is in line with work that increasingly recognizes the goal-directed nature of child rearing (e.g., Dix & Branca, 2003; Hastings & Grusec, 1998). The following examples from two trajectories—healthy physical development and social competence—illustrate parents' role in promoting positive developmental trajectories.

Healthy Physical Development

Throughout infancy, childhood, and adolescence, parents engage in a variety of actions to promote their children's health and safety. Most mentally sound parents desire their children to be healthy. However, some parents are more successful than others at accomplishing this goal. Good health is promoted through a variety of actions, including modifying the environment, modeling good habits, instructing, creating rules, reinforcing, and punishing (Tinsley, Markey, Ericksen, Ortiz, & Kwasman, 2002). For example, new parents safeguard their infants by "childproofing" the home; they structure and plan activities to avoid dangers (Holden, 1985). They also make decisions and rules about whether to allow their toddlers to engage in certain behaviors based on beliefs about safety and perceptions of the child's abilities. In middle childhood, parents engage in various forms of socialization to prevent childhood injury. These include lecturing, disciplining, changing the environment, modifying rules, and/or imposing restrictions. And it pays off; parents who closely monitor their children have children with fewer accidents and injuries than parents who do not (Crouter & Head, 2002).

Promoting healthy eating patterns is another example of parents guiding a healthy developmental trajectory. Consequently, increasing evidence has documented various ways that parents can prevent or contribute to children's obesity (Patrick & Nicklas, 2005). For example, Hays, Power, and Olvera (2001) found that those immigrant Mexican American mothers who discussed healthy eating practices with their children (four to eight years old) had children who were more knowledgeable and aware of the related health issues. It is increasingly clear that obesity prevention requires concerted parental efforts: modeling sensible eating habits, purchasing proper foods, controlling (in appropriate ways) children's eating practices, educating children about nutrition, and monitoring children's eating actions from infancy through adolescence.

As will be discussed in Chapter 10, the preadolescent and adolescent years pose a variety of new potential health and safety hazards: cigarette smoking, automobile driving, alcohol and drug use, and precocious or risky sexual activity. There is evidence that the parent's role is important for successfully navigating this challenging developmental period. Parents who were concerned about the health consequences of adolescent cigarette smoking were more active in combating it by discussing the topic, discouraging its use, and monitoring and controlling their children. These techniques were successful for nonsmoking parents but less so for parents who smoked (Chassin et al., 2005), highlighting the dominant role of behavioral modeling in shaping trajectories. With regard to driving, adolescents who reported that their parents engaged in more controlling and monitoring of behavior reported less risky driving behaviors and traffic violations (Hartos et al., 2000). Teenagers who perceived parental disapproval or other negative consequences for drinking alcohol were less likely to drink alcohol or **binge drink**, engage in premarital sex, or become pregnant (Resnick et al., 1997). Parental monitoring decreases the likelihood—or delays the onset—of drug use both in middle childhood and adolescence (Crouter & Head, 2002). Conversely, parents who were unaware of their children's involvement with alcohol (Beck, 1990) or attempts at suicide (Walker, Moreau, & Weissman, 1990) had children with more emotional problems. Parental reasoning, modeling, and disapproval of health-harming substances are part of what has been proposed as *risk socialization* (Miller-Day, 2002), a concept tantamount to keeping children on a safe and healthy trajectory.

Box 4.3 A Fundamental Parental Dilemma

How far should parents go to support and guide their children? Should parents put helmets ("Baby no Bump") on their children to protect them from falls? What about monitor their teenagers' driving habits and whereabouts with GPS devices? How about alcohol? Should parents provide alcohol to their high school children to prepare them for drinking at college? These are just a few of the dilemmas that some parents face and deliberate about as they try to guide their children on healthy trajectories. How far should a parent go to protect and guide their children versus letting their children develop on their own?

Competent Social Relationships

A second trajectory that parents commonly value and promote in their offspring is social competence. A variety of childrearing behaviors have been linked to this goal, with both indirect and direct effects (Ladd & Pettit, 2002). The road to social competence begins in infancy, when the origins of social interactions (**reciprocity**, turn-taking, and synchrony) first appear (Harrist & Waugh, 2002).

Parental sensitivity—leading to secure attachment—is linked to social competence, although the concept and evidence is somewhat ambiguous (Shin, Park, Ryu, & Seomun, 2008; Thompson, 1998). The data are much clearer about the *direct* influences that parents have in promoting social competence in their children. By designing, mediating, supervising, and monitoring their children's peer relationships, many parents are actively guiding this trajectory (Ladd & Pettit, 2002). In a review of over 50 years of work on monitoring and peer relations, Crouter and Head (2002) found that the practice of parental monitoring was positively associated with social competence in children. Monitoring is increasingly being recognized, though, as a *bilateral variable* (reflecting the bidirectional parent-child relationship) due to the fundamental role of disclosure: A parent cannot monitor what a child successfully disguises (Stattin & Kerr, 2000). Monitoring parents faced with the problem of an undisclosing youth must determine ways to promote communication.

For minority-group parents, the task of maintaining a positive social trajectory is even more challenging. Parents need to prepare their children to be successful in mainstream culture while maintaining their children's own sense of self and their cultural heritage (Hughes, 2003; Johnson, 2005). Investigations into racial socialization revealed that parents pre-arm their children in preparation for potential discrimination by first promoting racial/cultural pride and ethnic history. Messages encouraging mistrust of members of the majority group are delayed until early adolescence (Johnson, 2005). There are a variety of other racial coping skills that parents may teach or model, ranging from inoculation of racist ideas to conflict avoidance (Garcia Coll et al., 1996; Johnson, 2005).

CHAPTER SUMMARY

The ways that parents may influence children is a fascinating topic that is attracting increased attention. Researchers from various theoretical orientations have made valuable contributions to understanding the role of nature and nurture in development. The different perspectives—including attachment, parenting traits, and human behavioral genetics—have each contributed pieces of understanding to the puzzle of development.

As researchers gain a better understanding of children's development, it is clear that the model promoted by early researchers of a direct parental effect (P → C) is no longer tenable. The equation linking how children are parented and how they develop is considerably more complex. For example, particular parent and child characteristics may interact with each other, resulting in different effects. Mediators and moderators are also operating. In addition, it is clear that children affect parents and vice versa. The characteristics of both parents and children shape experiences; some have described this as a *transactional principle* of influence. Nevertheless, the argument advanced by Harris (1998) and a few other individuals to, in essence, throw parents out of the equation is unsupported by the preponderance of the evidence.

In addition to the established approaches for understanding how parents influence their children, another way of thinking about parents' role in development is to consider them as guides of their children's developmental trajectories. This view does not negate other important influences on children's trajectories, such as child effects, peers and other individuals, resources, or culture. However, it reframes the question of how parents may be influencing their children in important ways.

THOUGHT QUESTIONS

- In what ways do you think your parents have influenced you?
- Why would twins be more similar in personality or intelligence than non-twin siblings? What about identical twins?
- Why do children and youth "fall off" positive developmental trajectories?
- What characteristics of children make them more resilient so they remain on positive trajectories despite problems around them?

CHAPTER GLOSSARY

behavioral control Parental actions designed to control, manage, or regulate a child.

binge drink To consume alcoholic beverages with the primary goal of getting drunk. It is usually defined as consuming five or more drinks on the same occasion.

bullying Repeated negative actions perpetrated over time by a more dominant child/youth to another child/youth.

child maltreatment The physical abuse, sexual abuse, neglect, or psychological mistreatment of a child.

critical periods Limited periods of time, usually early in life, in which an event can occur that can have a transformative effect on the organism.

diathesis-stress model A model concerning genes and the environment that assumes that the presence of a genetic predisposition to having a problem only results in the phenotypic expression of the problem when the individual is exposed to particular kinds of environmental stressors.

dismissing attachment style A pattern of relating to others in adulthood guided by a negative view of others but a positive view of oneself.

dose-response relationship The amount or extent of the dose affects the magnitude of the response.

ethologist A scientist who studies the behavior of animals in their natural habitat.

ethology The study of behavior in its natural habitat from an evolutionary perspective.

experiments of nature When an abnormal situation occurs in the absence of scientific manipulation and provides information about development.

failure to thrive A problem, beginning in infancy, when a child shows little weight gain and physical growth due to inadequate nutrition.

fearful attachment style A relational style in adults characterized by a negative self-image as well as a distrust of others.

imprinting A concept referring to rapid learning—usually very early in life—that is apparently independent of behavioral consequences.

monitoring Parental knowledge of children's whereabouts and whom they are with. This requires disclosure and communication on the part of the child.

overprotection When a parent engages in inappropriate care and behavior that reflects a denial of the child's autonomy.

parental inoculation When a parent in some way prepares a child for an upcoming potentially difficult or troubling experience.

parental nurturance Parenting behavior that provides essential care to the child, including feeding, sheltering, bathing, and protecting.

parental support A parenting dimension that includes being involved, loving, emotionally available, and responsive.

preoccupied attachment style A style of relating to others in adulthood that is characterized by a negative view of the self but a positive view of others.

prosocial behavior Behavior that is intended to benefit others, such as helping, sharing, and comforting.

race socialization The training and guidance minority parents give to their children to help them deal with racism, prejudice, and living as a minority group member.

reciprocity When acts are supportive of each other and become similar.

risk factors Characteristics, variables, and/or conditions that could adversely affect the individual.

secure attachment style In adults, it reflects a healthy style of relating to others and is characterized by a positive view of oneself and others.

stereotyped behaviors Abnormal behavior characterized by repeatedly engaging in repetitive, similar behavior without an obvious goal or function.

unidirectional effect The once-prevailing view that parents influenced their children but their children did not influence them.

CHAPTER 5

Determinants of Parenting

Chapter Preview: True or False?

- Research has found more than 30 variables that influence parenting behavior.
- The parent's personality is not considered to be a key determinant of child rearing.
- Parents' behavior toward their children at home is affected by employment variables, even just a bad day at work.

Individuals rear their children in different ways. Picture one father who frequently bellows demands at his children in contrast to another who patiently and gently makes requests. Consider the contrasts between one mother who is constantly controlling and intrusive while her neighbor is sensitive and child centered. We are reminded of such differences when we read about certain celebrity parents whose poor parenting practices make the evening news. Why do parents act the way they do? Where does it come from? What influences their behavior? This chapter addresses those questions.

CATEGORIES OF DETERMINANTS

For more than 50 years, parenting researchers have investigated why parents behave the way they do. The first extensive assessment of the topic was conducted by Lois Stolz (1967), who concluded that parent behavior can be influenced by many variables and pressures, only some of which win out and determine childrearing behavior. To provide some organization to these many variables, Harmon and Brim (1980) used four basic categories of influences on parenting behavior. These influences are called *determinants*:

1. *General cultural factors,* such as nationality and socioeconomic status
2. *Individual factors,* such as characteristics of the parent and unconscious influences
3. *Interpersonal factors,* such as child behavior and family structure
4. *Setting,* such as the home or a park

A Mid-Level Model

A short time after Harmon and Brim published their classification scheme, Jay Belsky (1984) proposed a model depicting how some of these determinants work together. The model provided the framework for many subsequent studies. Belsky identified three central categories of influence:

1. *Parental psychological resources,* such as developmental history and personality
2. *Child characteristics,* such as gender and behavior
3. *Contextual sources of stress and social support,* such as marital relations, social networks, and work relationships

These three sets of influences combine to determine how a parent interacts with a child. It begins with a parent's developmental history. Based on his or her childhood experiences and genetic makeup, the parent's personality emerges. That personality influences three different types of variables: marital relations, work, and social network (or family and friends). In turn, each of those three variables, along with the child's characteristics, has a role in affecting parenting behavior. Note in Belsky's original model (reproduced in Figure 5.1) that some arrows go one way (unidirectional) but others are two way (bidirectional).

Of all the determinants identified, Belsky and his colleagues believed that *personality* played the most important role in parenting behavior (Belsky & Barends, 2002). A psychologically stable and emotionally strong parent can better withstand the stresses, for instance, of a temperamentally challenging or handicapped child. Such individuals can also better deal with contextual pressures—such as marital disharmony or financial burdens—than can

Figure 5.1 A Model of the Determinants of Parenting

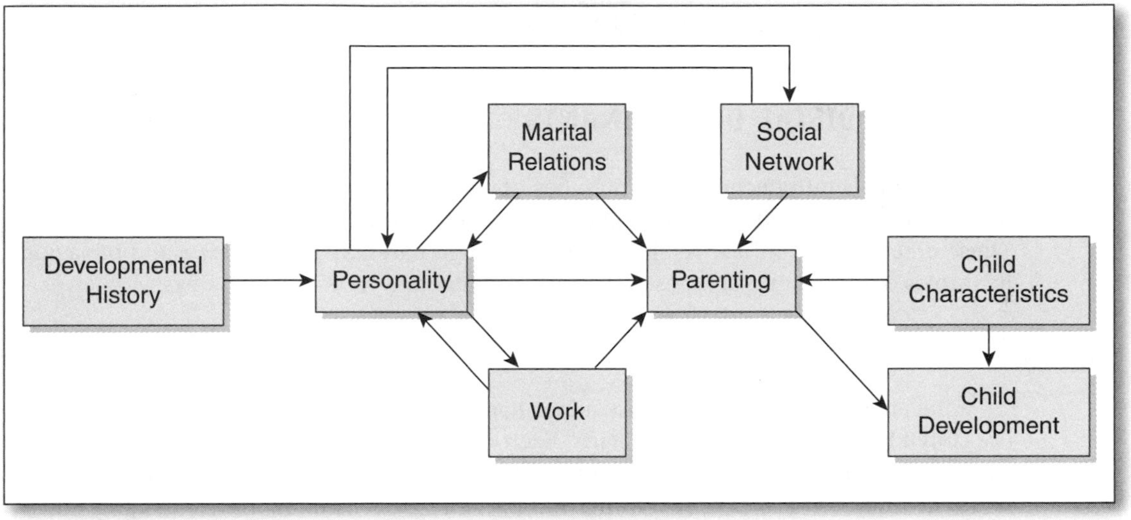

Source: Belsky, 1984.

other individuals. In fact, all the other determinants are mediated through a parent's personality and individual psychological functioning. For example, picture two parents in a troubled marital relationship, characterized by frequent arguments and considerable hostility. The parents would likely feel distressed, irritable, and even depressed. This could, in turn, lead to impatience with their children, inconsistency in discipline, harsh parenting, or being emotionally unavailable as a parent (Vondra, Sysko, & Belsky, 2005). However, a parent with a stable emotional and psychological base would be more likely to stay engaged in parenting, control his or her temper, and perhaps even assist the child in coping with the home's hostile tone.

Social support and resources are another important determinant that can mediate the impact of stressors. Social supports include parents, other children, grandparents, and other relatives, friends, and neighbors. Resources can include financial assets, social and emotional support, and material goods. If one parent faced with a challenging child has a spouse who is an actively involved and effective co-parent, then the parent will be less stressed than would similar parents with less spousal support. Hence, "the parenting system is buffered against threats to its integrity that could derive from any single weakness in any single source" (Belsky, 1984, p. 91).

Although one could argue that Belsky's model fails to take into account all the ways that these determinants mutually influence each other, the model does nicely organize three key **determinants of parenting** and their interrelations. However, the model ignores a number of other determinants on child rearing. Some of the missing influences are immediate or **proximal**. For example, there are situational influences: Was the parent at home or in a crowded theater? Was the interaction in the middle of the night or outside on a beautiful day? Transient parental qualities—such as mood or illness—can also influence parenting.

The model is also missing some more **distal** or distant determinants, such as the parent's cultural background or socioeconomic status (SES). Belsky's model, then, can be described as **mid-level determinants**: It effectively captures some of the key influences on parenting somewhere between proximal and distal levels.

CULTURAL AND DISTAL DETERMINANTS

Child rearing is influenced by several types of cultural or distal variables. These variables have been investigated primarily under the headings of SES, religion, and race/ethnicity. These determinants influence child rearing through parental goals, values, and behavior. Examples of the first three types of distal determinants will be provided next.

Culture

Think about a child being reared in a Brazilian *favela* (slum), an American Indian reservation in Oklahoma, or a suburb in Paris. Each child experiences a dramatically different culture. The *cultural context* can be defined as the way of life shared by its members (Ogbu, 1988). It reflects the social, economic, and psychological adaptation of a people. When related to child rearing, culture involves many aspects of the environment. It includes the setting; methods of care; material products (toys, clothing, media); and parental values, goals, and beliefs as well as norms and expectations for acceptable behavior in children. It also prescribes general rules of parenting conduct (Weisner, 2011).

Cultural anthropologists were the first to note similarities and differences in parents from various countries. They also realized that differing cultures could provide a type of "experiment of nature" and help reveal how parental behavior was related to children's development (Whiting & Child, 1953). Cross-cultural childrearing studies are now widespread, although the majority of studies outside of North America come from Western Europe, Australia, China, and Japan.

Conducting cross-cultural research is difficult and expensive. It often requires overcoming language or dialect barriers. Moreover, cultural constructs do not always transfer smoothly across cultures. Just try comparing a typical elementary school in Tokyo—with its strict academic structure—to one of the "Waldkindergartens" in Germany, where children spend most of the day in a forest, encouraged to learn about their world mainly through unbridled exploration. Both of these settings are *schools*, but the realities within them are worlds apart. These types of issues must be considered when analyzing and comparing cultures. But despite the challenges, psychologists are increasingly applying cross-cultural research as a way of examining both the universals of parenting and how parents differ across cultures (Bornstein & Cheah, 2006).

Usually, researchers define a parent's culture by the country where the parent dwells (or from which he or she immigrated), but sometimes it is broken down more precisely. For example, two investigators examined parental values in rural Cameroon by comparing parents who were Muslim, Christian, or adherents to the indigenous African religion (Nsamenang & Lamb, 1995). In most cases, however, when parents are compared in cross-cultural studies, it is usually where one sample from one country is compared with a sample from a second country. Both samples of parents are assumed to be representative of that culture—a big assumption.

Exploring cultural differences in mother-infant relationships is one of the most popular topics of cross-cultural research; it is thought that impressions from a culture are stamped early in a child's development (see Photo 5.1). One such study searched for cultural differences in maternal behavior toward five-month-old infants in three countries: the United States, France, and Japan (Bornstein et al., 1992). Forty naturally occurring, five-minute mother-infant interactions were recorded on video. Researchers then conducted a micro-analysis of the behavior to compare mothers' responsiveness to their infants. Overall, they found very few differences in maternal or infant behavior. However, one cultural difference occurred in maternal responses to their infants' looking. Japanese mothers were significantly more responsive when their infants were looking at other people than were either the American or French mothers. Presumably, this maternal involvement and encouragement in social looking is a reflection of the Japanese beliefs about and emphasis on close interpersonal relationships.

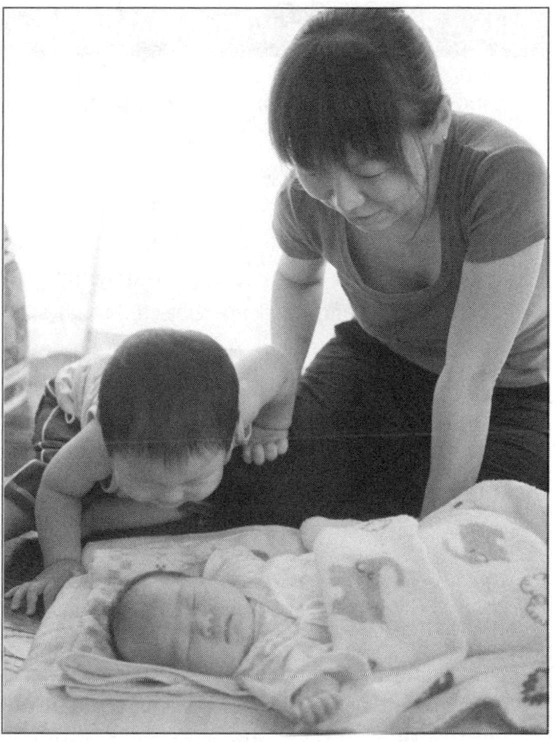

Photo 5.1 An Asian mother and child examine their new family member.

Source: © Eri Morita/Taxi Japan/Getty Images

Cultural differences in parenting between Japan and North America can be isolated more readily *after* infancy, when differences emerge in the standards for acceptable child behavior and child independence. The two competing cultural values—**independence versus interdependence**—are in sharp contrast when comparing child rearing in Japan and in the United States. In Japan, socialization practices are designed to promote interdependence between individuals. In the United States, however, we encourage independence at an early age. Japanese interdependence is fostered by such practices as constant and close physical relationships (also called **skinship**), co-sleeping, co-bathing, and punishment based on separation (such as locking a misbehaving child out of the house) rather than on the use of authority and physical force, a common practice in North America. As illustrated by these childrearing practices, culture promotes differences in adult values and behavior. See Box 5.1 for a description of what we in the Western world would consider unusual and even abusive feeding practices by parents of girls in an African country.

Box 5.1 A Place Where Obesity in Girls Is Prized

In most homes in the United States, parents do not seek to "fatten up" their daughters for marriage. But in the sub-Saharan West African country of Mauritania (as well as some other West African countries), obesity in women is valued as a sign of wealth—and health. In turn, obese young women are more likely to get married. Consequently, some parents force their daughters, beginning as young as five years old, to drink each day up to five gallons of camel's or cow's milk. This practice is called *gavage* (the term also used for force-feeding geese in order to obtain *foie gras*) (Popenoe, 2004). Girls who resist or get sick are subjected to physical punishment, forced to drink their own vomit, and sometimes even tortured. A 2001 survey found that two in five women in Mauritania were overweight—a surprisingly high rate for a poor country, where the annual **per capita income** is $2,100 (Central Intelligence Agency, 2014). The government is currently trying to combat the practice through a health education program to inform the women about the dangers associated with obesity, including type 2 diabetes, strokes, sleep apnea, and mental health problems.

Socioeconomic Status

Subordinate to culture but also a potent determinant of behavior is the SES of the parent. Formerly called *social class*, SES is a multifaceted variable that reflects the distribution of resources, power, and influence within a society (Hill & Witherspoon, 2011). SES is most often determined by income (or poverty) level, education level, and employment status, occupation, or occupational prestige. Scales used to measure these factors are formed and parents are grouped, often arbitrarily, into SES levels. Occupations that received high scores included doctors, lawyers, and business executives. Occupations at the other end of the scale, considered *low status*, included convenience store attendants and child care workers (see Bornstein & Bradley, 2003).

Typically, studies have contrasted parents of lower and middle SES on a range of behavioral variables, including warmth, breastfeeding habits, toilet training practices, and disciplinary techniques. One of the most common findings is that parents from a lower SES background (see Photo 5.2) are more likely to use physical punishment or **coercive discipline** in comparison to middle-class parents, who rely more on noncoercive discipline such as reasoning or guilt.

What accounts for the relation between SES and parent behavior? One plausible explanation has been around for a long time. Melvin Kohn (1979) theorized that parental occupation and general life situations lead parents to hold particular childrearing values. Specifically, parents from higher social classes occupy jobs where responsibility, self-direction, initiative, and independence are valued and rewarded. Those parents, in turn, are likely to value and promote similar goals in their children by encouraging, for instance, autonomy, responsibility, and creativity. On the other hand, parents from a lower SES, who have relatively little freedom or responsibility in their jobs, are more likely to value conformity to external authority. Obedience and the ability to stick to the rules are more likely

Photo 5.2 Living in the inner city.

Source: © iStockphoto.com/track5

to pay off in blue-collar or manual labor occupations, so such parents might strongly emphasize obedience to parents, self-control, getting along with others, and acting as a boy or girl "should."

Kohn's pioneering model reflects the way requirements or demands of one's life situation affect childrearing values, which in turn modify childrearing practices. This can be diagrammed as follows:

socioeconomic status → values → childrearing values → parenting behavior

Parenting behavior, according to Kohn, is thereby strongly influenced by SES. Support for links between SES and parental values have been found in eight countries (Kohn, Naoi, Shoenbach, Schooler, & Slomczynski, 1990). This work has been extended by Lareau (e.g., Weininger & Lareau, 2009), who differentiates two SES-influenced approaches to parenting. Higher-SES parents facilitate their children's development through *concerted cultivation* or promoted skills and abilities by providing additional resources not typically available to children of lower-SES families (e.g., tutoring, music lessons). In contrast, lower-SES parents adopt a *natural growth* approach to child rearing. Here, while conformity to external authority is valued, these parents provide free time and open schedules to allow their children to develop naturally. Subsequent investigations have largely confirmed that these two parenting approaches are influenced by SES (e.g., Bush & Peterson, 2013).

Religion

Religious beliefs for those who adhere to a particular faith practices can have a powerful effect on child rearing (Holden & Williamson, 2014). Religion not only influences parents' beliefs and practices but it also has a potent impact on the law, cultural institutions, cultural norms, transmission of moral values, regulation of sexuality, and interpersonal orientations (Browning, Green, & Witte, 2006). Recall from Chapter 1 the Puritan ministers' admonitions to parents about the need to use strict discipline. Children were perceived as born with a propensity to sin, and parents were instructed by their ministers to break the will of children in order to socialize them into faithful adults (Greven, 1977). In contrast, both Confucianism and Islam espouse the view (also promulgated by the Catholic Jean-Jacques Rousseau in 1762) that children are inherently good (Husain, 1979; Stewart et al., 1999).

Studies of parenting practices often focus on differences among religious groups. This is not surprising, given the prevalence of religiously based childrearing articles and manuals. In the United States, bookstores are stocked with dozens of Christian parenting books, including best sellers like James Dobson's *Dare to Discipline* books (Dobson, 1992), which have sold more than 3.5 million copies. *Hadassah Magazine* frequently publishes articles that inform and prescribe practices for Jewish parents. Similarly, childrearing manuals based on the Qur'an (or Koran) are readily available for Muslims (Husain, 1979; Sabiruddin, 1990; see Photo 5.3). Childrearing advice can even be found stemming from Buddhism. In line with the Buddhist orientation toward selflessness and living-in-the-present is the concept of **mindful parenting**. This refers to a moment-to-moment, nonjudgmental awareness by which parents reach beyond their automatic thoughts and feelings to remain intentional in their child rearing and grounded in the present moment (Kabat-Zinn & Kabat-Zinn, 1997). When translated to parenting, *mindfulness* means listening with full attention, a nonjudgmental acceptance of self and child, being emotionally aware, regulating behavior before responding, and having compassion for both the child and oneself (Duncan, Coatsworth, & Greenberg, 2009). Mindful parents have been found to experience less **childrearing stress** and depressive symptoms (Beer, Ward, & Moar, 2013).

Photo 5.3 The influence of religion starts early. Here, a young boy reads the Qur'an in a mosque in Yemen.

Source: Photograph by J. P. Bell

Fundamentally, religion is about what is to be valued in life. Several cross-cultural studies have examined relations between religion or **religiosity** (how faithfully religion is practiced) and adult values. A meta-analytic review of research across cultures and religious groups determined that religious people shared the values of kindness, tradition, and conformity, while they disdained hedonism (Saroglu, Delpierre, & Dernelle, 2004). In analyzing 63 societies, Inglehart and Baker (2000) discovered that adults who described themselves as religious were more likely to value tradition, obedience, respect for authority, and religious faith in their children over independence and self-determination.

All three of the world's great deistic religions (Christianity, Judaism, and Islam) emphasize the family and encourage parents to devote considerable time and attention to their children. It follows, then, that religious parents (compared to nonreligious parents) would hold different values, allocate time differently, and be more likely to involve their children in social networks associated with a religious community. Links between religious beliefs and parenting have been made in multiple areas. For example, religious parents are more likely to be more involved and affectionate with their children; provide more supervision, guidance, and firmer discipline; and model better behavior (e.g., health promoting, coping) and less likely to maltreat their children than nonreligious parents (Holden & Williamson, 2014).

One popular topic of inquiry is how religion can influence attitudes about child discipline. In particular, Christian denominations in the United States and Holland that espouse literalist interpretations of the Bible have been studied. Many conservative Protestants accept as God's literal intention such statements as "Do not withhold discipline from a child; if you punish him with the rod, he will not die" (Proverbs 23:13, New International Version). These parents report more positive attitudes toward (and more frequent use of) physical punishment than do other Christians or adherents of other religions (de Roos, Iedema, & Miedema, 2004; Gershoff, Miller, & Holden, 1999). Children reared by conservative Protestants are less likely to show some of the behavior problems associated with corporal punishment—so long as their parents stopped spanking them during the preschool period (Ellison, Musick, & Holden, 2011).

It should be pointed out that the relation between religion and parenting can be bidirectional; the onset of fatherhood can prompt more religious involvement in men (Palkovitz & Palm, 1998).

CONTEXTUAL DETERMINANTS

Contextual determinants refer to those features of the environment that influence child rearing. Four variables provide particularly good illustrations of how context can influence parenting: parental employment, stress, social support, and neighborhoods.

Parental Employment

Outside-the-home parental employment or unemployment can have a variety of obvious as well as subtle influences on parenting. But parental employment as a variable is not dichotomous. It in fact represents a complex constellation of variables. The objective features of the job (such as the type of job and the number of hours spent at work) must, of course, be considered. But so must a host of other related variables such as financial need and resources, a person's career orientation versus family orientation, and a person's subjective feelings about the job (how fulfilling or stressful he or she finds it). Despite the complexity of this determinant, psychologists have documented that the "long arm of the job" influences a parent's values, psychological and physical well-being, daily moods, and availability for involvement in parenting activities (Crouter & McHale, 2005) [Preview Question]. In turn, depending on many variables, including the type and quality of the job, maternal ethnicity and SES, and the child's developmental level, maternal employment can have either positive or negative effects on child outcomes (Bush & Peterson, 2013).

Prompting much of the attention to this topic is the dramatic increase in the proportion of young mothers who work outside the home. In 1960, only 18% of mothers with children under age six worked outside the home. By 1987, the proportion had climbed to about 57%. By 2012, 65% of mothers with young children worked outside the home (Bureau of Labor Statistics, 2013). This remarkable social change in the way families lead their lives, graphed in Figure 5.2, has resulted in a number of consequences for child rearing.

Figure 5.2 Changes in Maternal Employment Levels From 1961 to 2012

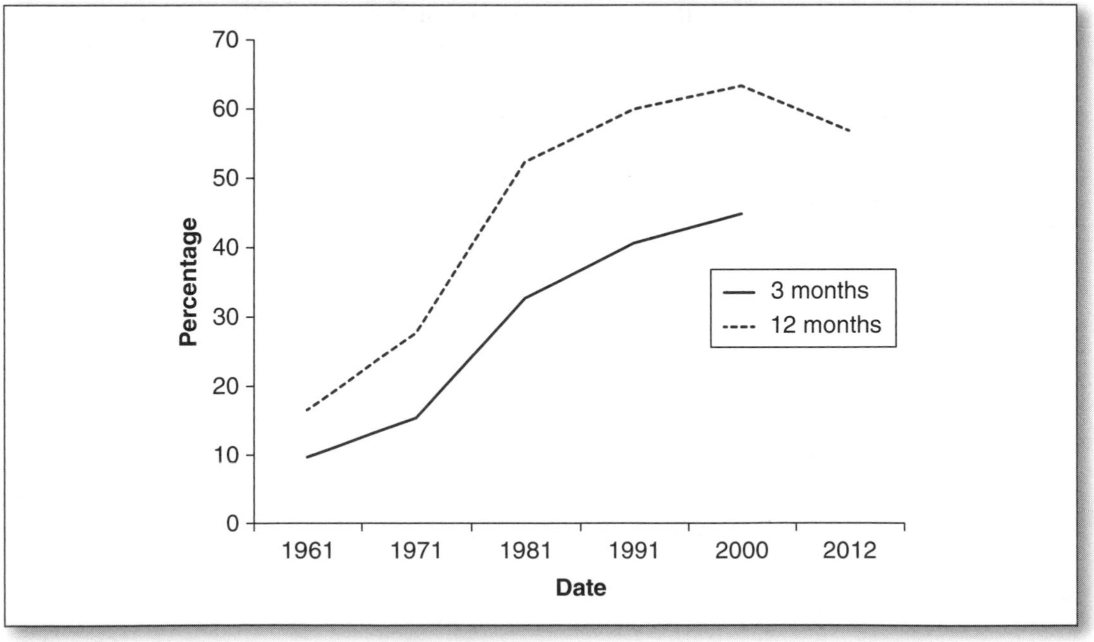

Source: Laughlin, 2011; Bureau of Labor Statistics, 2013.

Note: Data are of first-time mothers working outside the home after three months. Data for 2012 at the three-month mark were unavailable.

One important change has been an increased reliance on day care and other forms of child care. Another effect of maternal employment is the impact on paternal involvement. Families are dynamic entities; husbands are affected by their wives' employment. In general, husbands of working wives are more involved in child care and household work than are those in families with single-earner fathers (Gottfried, Gottfried, & Bathurst, 2002). However, time spent in child care is not divided equally between parents. Several different studies, including investigations from a variety of industrialized nations, have found major discrepancies between the number of hours worked by mothers and fathers. Research in the late 1980s found that fathers, on average, worked 50 hours a week in combined employment and household tasks, whereas mothers worked 80 to 90 hours per week at the same tasks (e.g., Scarr, Phillips, & McCartney, 1989). The workload inequity between employed mothers and fathers is especially pronounced when the children are under age three. By the time the child becomes a preschooler, the trend is for more role balance, although mothers continue to provide more care (Gottfried et al., 2002).

Box 5.2 He Said, She Said: Mothers' Versus Fathers' Reports of Father Involvement

To what extent are fathers involved in child rearing? It depends on whom you ask. Fathers report spending significantly more time (18% more) engaged in 11 child care activities than mothers report. The most frequent activities done at least five days a week according to fathers were "telling the child you appreciate something they did," "putting the child to bed," and "playing inside with the child." The biggest discrepancies were in reports of "assisting the child with eating," "putting the child to bed," and "letting the child help you with chores." In each case, fathers reported doing it at least one day per week more than mothers reported (Mikelson, 2008).

One variable that plays an important influence in the relation between work and parenting is **childrearing commitment**. The amount of time and energy parents commit to their multiple roles (parent, spouse, and worker) has implications for parental behavior, stress, and perceptions of children. A study investigating some of the relations between parenting and working illustrate one aspect of this issue. Ellen Greenberger and her colleagues found mothers to be just as committed to their employment work as fathers were, and they shared a similar level of job satisfaction. However, mothers experienced more stress than fathers did as they attempted to balance the demands of parenting along with work (Greenberger, Goldberg, Hamill, O'Neil, & Payne, 1989). This is not at all surprising, given the fact that mothers continue to shoulder a majority of household and childrearing tasks in addition to their paid employment.

For good or ill, maternal employment affects a mother's emotional state. On the positive side, it can impact her general satisfaction and morale by providing mental stimulation, building self-esteem, and offering a break from child care and home chores. Also, maternal employment serves as a buffer from the stress of marital difficulties or a difficult or challenged child. For one or more of these reasons, maternal employment can potentially enhance the quality of parenting during the time the mother is home, particularly if the woman enjoys her job and exercises some responsibility in it (Gottfried et al., 2002). However, many mothers feel conflicted about their work and being separated from their children. The extent of this conflict depends not only on whether or not the mother is employed but also on her preferences (whether she wants to be employed), the extent of her anxiety over separation from her child, and the degree to which she is invested in her maternal role (e.g., Hock, DeMeis, & McBride, 1988).

In addition to causing guilt and anxiety for some mothers about being away from their young children, employment can add considerable stress to a mother's life. Indeed, there is evidence that under some circumstances, a mother's emotional state, childrearing practices, and perceptions of children may be negatively affected by her employment. However, most studies have found that maternal employment may actually have a positive impact on parenting and it is *not* a risk factor for children (Crouter & McHale, 2005).

Stress

Another general contextual factor that can dramatically influence parenting is stress. Stress on parents comes in a variety of manifestations, both positive and negative. Even such apparently positive events as a major job promotion, the birth of another child, or an economic windfall are experienced as stressful because they trigger changes in the family system. Major life stressors include natural disasters, serious illness or injuries, death, separation or divorce, moving, and change in employment. A second group of stressors, those related to everyday occurrences, has also received considerable research attention. There are four main classes of these proximate stressors:

1. Marital or relationship stressors
2. Work or financial stressors
3. Personal characteristics
4. Child-related stressors

Parenting stress refers to the fourth category of stressors and refers to "the experience of distress or discomfort that results from demands associated with the role of parenting" (Hayes & Watson, 2013, p. 629).

Parenting stress is a function of individual child characteristics (e.g., challenging temperament, developmental disabilities), parent characteristics (e.g., age, attributions about the child's behavior), and situations (e.g., premature birth, living in a violent neighborhood) (Crnic & Low, 2002). Some of these stressors reflect acute situations; others are chronic. When two or more stressors team up, they likely have an **additive effect** on parents (Deater-Deckard, 2004).

Stress is not benign, as it can have a powerful negative influence on parental functioning. Stressed parents are less nurturant, supportive, patient, and involved. Instead, they are likely to be irritable, negative, punitive, and withdrawn (Crnic & Low, 2002; Deater-Deckard, 2004). In turn, children's functioning can be negatively affected.

Social Support

Social support, or assistance from other people, helps to counteract the effects of stress. There is someone to turn to when life is challenging, when the unexpected happened, or when a crisis arises. A socially supported person feels cared for, loved, and valued. Social support can come from a variety of individuals including relatives, friends, neighbors, and fellow members of a faith-based organization. Usually, the principal support for a parent is the partner or spouse, and this support (an example of positive co-parenting) manifests in emotional comfort and instrumental assistance (McHale et al., 2002). Instrumental assistance can be in form of babysitting, running errands, or providing food or clothing.

A number of studies have indicated that support from a social network can mitigate the effects of stress and promote positive parenting. For example, not surprisingly, Dutch parents of children diagnosed with cancer reacted with high levels of distress (Hoekstra-Weebers, Jaspers, Kamps, & Klip, 2001). Those fathers (but not mothers in this sample) who received more social support experienced less distress. Support was also found to have a positive effect in a very different sample of poor African American single mothers. Mothers who received more support were found to engage in more nurturant parenting, although this relation weakened in high-crime neighborhoods (Ceballo & McLoyd, 2002).

Neighborhood

It is not hard to see how a person's residence can influence his or her parenting behavior. Look at the photograph of urban high-rise apartment buildings (see Photo 5.1). How might child rearing be affected by living in such apartments in contrast to other environments, such as suburbia or rural environments?

Urban poverty is the most problematic neighborhood characteristic. Being raised in a poor, inner-city neighborhood is associated with a wide range of negative outcomes for children: crime, health problems, academic failure, substance abuse, and teen pregnancy. The atmosphere has been described as a "war zone" and a toxic atmosphere for children to grow up in (Garbarino, Kostelny, & Barry, 1997). It is not surprising that parenting in high-crime neighborhoods is characterized by a distrust of nonfamilial individuals, an encouragement of children's early independence and self-reliance, an emphasis on aggressive play, and an early withdrawal of emotional support (Halpern, 1990). Some observers have argued that these patterns result from the behavior of stressed, powerless mothers whose own needs are not being met, which renders them unable to provide consistent, supportive, nonpunitive parenting. An alternative explanation, articulated by anthropologist John Ogbu (1988), views the childrearing behavior as an adaptive response to the dangers of the environment that maximizes the likelihood of survival and the success of the children.

Photo 5.4 Urban high-rise apartments created neighborhoods with high concentrations of low-income families.

Source: ©iStockphoto.com/Terraxplorer

More recent work on the topic of parenting in the inner city has documented some of the difficulties and consequences of living in such dangerous and low-income environments (Ceballo & McLoyd, 2002). Some parents respond to living in such contexts with depression and harsh child punishment, but others are active and strategic in their childrearing efforts (Burton & Jarrett, 2000). Parents who are successful in helping their children live in low-income environments engage in actions to prevent various problematic child outcomes that they observe around them, such as dropping out of school, getting pregnant, or experimenting with drugs. Thus the inner city represents a unique context that elicits different types of parenting behaviors, depending on the particular parent. It provides a clear example of how the living context can determine childrearing behavior.

STABLE CHARACTERISTICS DETERMINANTS

Yet another group of determinants on child rearing are variables that reflect stable characteristics of the parent, child, or the family. Examples of these will be briefly reviewed next.

Stable Parent Characteristics

There are several stable attributes of parents. The four central characteristics related to child rearing are gender, prior experiences, social cognitions (attitudes and beliefs), and personality.

Gender

Do mothers and fathers parent differently? This question has been the topic of much speculation and research. The answer is not simple, in part due to the social trends that result in changes in parenting roles and levels of involvement with children (Cabrera, Tamis-LeMonda, Bradley, Hofferth, & Lamb, 2000). For example, maternal employment and father absence due to divorce are two societal changes with clear implications that result in modification of both mothering and fathering (see Photo 5.5).

One reliable difference between mothers and fathers in most families concerns involvement in child care. For example, paternal involvement, despite having increased significantly over the past three decades, still lags well behind maternal involvement. Fathers are estimated to spend 67% as much time as mothers during the weekdays in child-related activities (Cabrera et al., 2000). Involvement changes dramatically, of course, when fathers are single parents. See Box 5.3 for a description of single fathers who assume the role of primary caregiver.

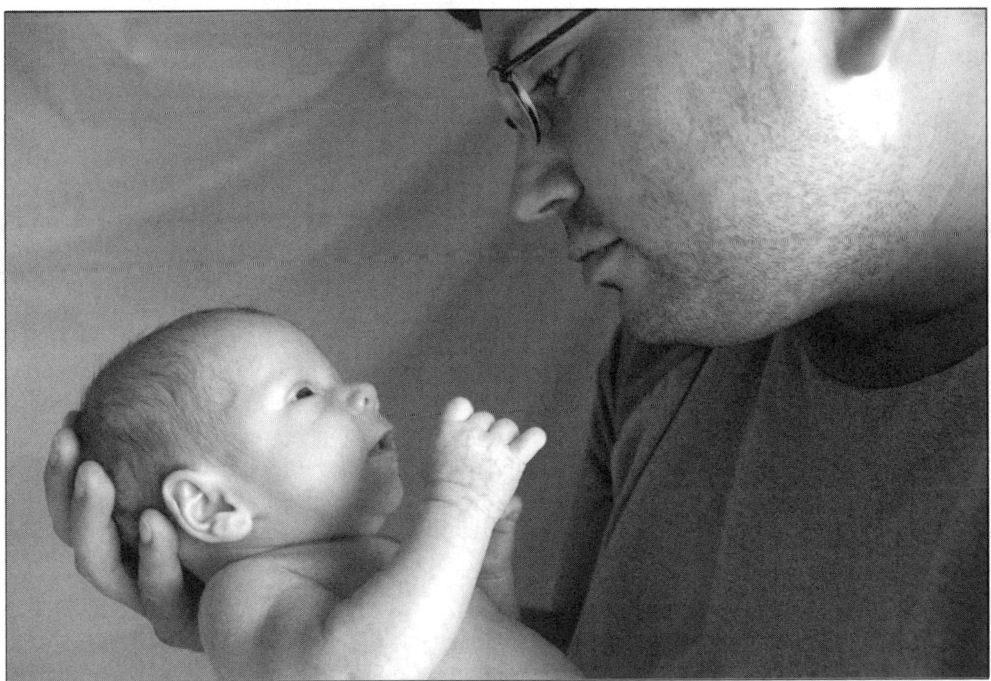

Photo 5.5 A father lovingly gazes at his infant son.

Source: Photograph by J. P. Bell

Box 5.3 Fathers as Single Parents

Census information from 2006 indicates there are 2.5 million single fathers raising one or more children in the United States (U.S. Census Bureau, 2008). These father-headed homes represent almost 20% of single-parent homes. Men assume this role for various reasons. Many are divorced fathers, some are widowed, others were never married, and some of the fathers include gay men. How do these men fare as primary caregiving parents? Despite the increasing attention being devoted to the role of fathers in development (Cabrera et al., 2000; Lamb, 2010), research on fathers as single parents is largely missing (Russell, 1999).

Why is this? In part, single fathers who are the primary caregivers are difficult to study because they are relatively rare and, like all single parents, they are extremely busy. Their schedules do not allow much time to participate in research. When studies are conducted with these men, they often consist of very small samples. In two of the more recent empirical efforts into this topic, only twenty single fathers were included in one study (Hilton & Desrochers, 2000) and ten in another (Coles, 2002).

Available evidence indicates that men can certainly be competent fathers, but to understand their effects, it is necessary to look at the specific features of their caregiving and their situation. Information is needed about the nature and extent of their involvement, the quality of their child care and child rearing, the stress and support they receive, and, in general, their life situation (such as the reason for being a single parent and their employment status). Indeed, these are the same types of variables needed to understand how single fathers—or any type of parent—may influence their children's development.

Mothers and fathers also differ in certain behaviors and attitudes. Using the ecological momentary assessment approach, researchers in several countries have observed fathers interacting with their children differently from mothers. Fathers tend to engage in verbal or didactic play less than mothers do; they are more physically stimulating and rough in their play. Mothers, compared to fathers, tend to be more responsive to variations in their children's play; they are more likely to enforce rules and communicate and play peekaboo-type games (Lamb & Tamis-LeMonda, 2004). Mothers and fathers also differ in their childrearing attitudes (Holden & Buck, 2002). For example, mothers place greater importance on expressive issues such as emotions, intimacy, and the child's enjoyment, in contrast to fathers, who place greater value in self-control, achievement, and responsibility. However, there are many aspects of child rearing where mothers and fathers do not differ (Lamb, 2004).

Prior Experiences

At least three types of prior experiences are particularly relevant as parenting determinants: experiences from the parent's own childhood, nonparenting experiences with other children, and previous parenting experiences.

A powerful influence on future parental behavior comes from "ghosts in the nursery" (Fraiberg, 1987) or experiences with one's own parents. From a social learning theory perspective, a number of studies have found similarities between two generations of individuals in terms of the disciplinary practices they use or prefer (Holden & Zambarano, 1992). Using Bowlby and Ainsworth's attachment theory, a number of investigators are discovering links between a mother's perception of her own early attachment experience and her relationship with her child (Bretherton & Munholland, 2008). For example, as mentioned in the last chapter, mothers' representations of attachment with their own mothers subsequently predicted attachment classification when their infants were 12 months old in 75% of the cases (Fonagy, Steele, & Steele, 1991). In another study, mothers' internal working models were associated with the quality of their parenting as well as with their toddlers' and preschoolers' adjustment (Eiden, Teti, & Corns, 1995). Those studies provide strong evidence for the consideration of internal working models as a determinant of parenting.

A second type of prior experience comes from babysitting or otherwise interacting with other children. In most cultures, girls are exposed to many more childcare experiences than boys are. This experiential discrepancy may well account for why females, compared to males, are generally considered more adept at child rearing. Presumably, extensive babysitting experience contributes to greater competency as a parent (Fogel & Melson, 1986). There is some supporting evidence: Recall from Box 3.4 that individuals with more childcare experience (either through parenthood or babysitting) solved a childrearing problem more efficiently and accurately than did those without such experiences (Holden, 1988).

Prior experiences can also result from on-the-job training or learning based on raising the firstborn child. Whiteman, McHale, and Crouter (2003) examined parental reports of behavior and the quality of interactions with firstborn teenagers and—several years later—with second-born teenagers at the same age. Parents appeared to have learned from their experiences with their firstborn child and had become more effective parents. They had greater knowledge of the second-born child's needs and lower rates of conflict.

Social Cognitions

As described in Chapter 3, parental social cognition has been shown to affect parental behavior. Some types of social cognitions are relatively stable, such as certain attributions and attitudes. If a father has an unrealistic expectation about when children are capable of toilet training, he is likely to become frustrated and angry when his child continues to have "accidents." Mothers who have positive beliefs and attitudes about breastfeeding or reading to young children are likely to engage in these beneficial behaviors.

Social cognitions are important because they can be closely linked to behavior and emotions. The best predictor of spanking practices, according to a study by Holden, Coleman, and Schmidt (1995), was a positive attitude about spanking. As would be expected, the mothers who viewed spanking as an effective technique for stopping misbehavior were most likely to engage in it. The advertisement reproduced in Photo 5.6 exemplifies the idea that some parents believe paddling is a useful educational tool.

Parental mood is also affected by social cognition. Specifically, parents' beliefs about the degree to which they can control a child's behavior (parental self-efficacy) affect parental emotion. Mothers who believed they had little power in influencing the behavior of a child were likely to be unassertive and irritable when interacting with children. Such parents, when interacting or anticipating future interactions with children, actually showed measurable increases in bodily stress, such as increased sweating, heart rate, and cortisol levels (e.g., Bugental & Cortez, 1988; Martorell & Bugental, 2006). These effects are particularly strong with children who have challenging temperaments.

Parental social cognitions are important, not just because they influence behavior but because they provide the most readily accessible avenue for *changing* parental behavior. As proximal influences, they may supersede more distal ones such as culture and SES.

Photo 5.6 Shingles can also be used for childrearing purposes, according to this old advertisement.

Personality

Recall from earlier in this chapter that Jay Belsky placed parental personality at the top of the list in his model of parenting determinants. He argued that parental maturity and psychological well-being were fundamental ingredients for effective parental functioning (Belsky & Barends, 2002). Thus parental personality is considered by many to be a key determinant of child rearing [Preview Question].

Studies have indeed linked personality to parenting cognitions and behavior, though the relations are not necessarily simple. Marc Bornstein and his colleagues (Bornstein, Hahn, & Haynes, 2011) found that the five-factor model of personality (openness, neuroticism, extraversion, agreeableness, and conscientiousness) related to 35% of maternal cognitions and 10% of the childrearing behavior assessed. Another researcher, Grazyna Kochanska, and her colleagues discovered a good example of how personality can affect parenting. Parents who had memories of unhappy and unstable childhoods were likely to engage in **power assertion** (Kochanska, Aksan, Penney, & Boldt, 2007). However, that relation was moderated by certain personality characteristics, such as optimism and trust. Thus personality characteristics can compensate for negative experiences and result in positive parenting practices.

Various other specific personality characteristics, such as patience and calmness, have been proposed to influence parenting. However, one personality attribute that has received much attention is the capacity for **empathy** (e.g., Psychogiou, Daley, Thompson, & Sonuga-Barke, 2008). This refers to a parent's ability to experience events from the child's point of view and therefore understand better what an infant or young child might be feeling. Not surprisingly, parents judged to be higher in empathy levels are more involved, nurturant, and positive toward their children than those considered lower in empathy. Empathy in parents is described in more detail in Box 5.4.

Box 5.4 The Power of Empathy

Empathy, or lack thereof, can greatly influence how parents react to a particular misbehavior or annoying characteristic in a child. Consider children who throw a noisy tantrum when they cannot get a toy to work as they want it to. Parents with empathy will be able to consider the situation from the child's perspective before deciding on an appropriate action. The parent might consider the child's physical needs (Is the child tired?), emotional needs (Does the child need help to properly deal with his or her frustration?), or personal desires (Is there something I can help the child achieve?). However, a parent without empathy at the time—whether due to a lack of skill or overwhelming personal needs—will likely have one thought: How do I shut the child up?! Parents' empathic concerns about their children represent a necessary and key attribute of positive parenting. College students who viewed their parents as empathetic had higher self-esteem and were less likely to report symptoms of depression or to exploit others (Trumpeter, Watson, O'Leary, & Weathington, 2008).

Other Parenting Characteristics

There are several other types of stable parental characteristics that have received research attention, such as intelligence and parental age. There are no clear consistent findings about how intelligence (at least in the normal range) affects child rearing. However, studies of parent age have received sustained attention. Two separate age-of-parent questions have been investigated. One concerns the quality of child care provided by adolescent parents, a topic further discussed in Chapter 12. For example, adolescent mothers are more likely to engage in harsh discipline than older mothers (Lee, 2009). The other question is whether older parents (usually those in their 30s and 40s) of young children differ in their parenting from younger parents. The effects of age on parenting are of interest in part due to the increasingly common trend for women to wait longer to bear children. The mean age of women in the United States for having their first child is now 25.1 years (U.S. Census Bureau, 2012).

Studies examining how individuals behave when they become parents at different ages have had conflicting results. That may be because the answer depends on the particular childrearing domain. For example, warmth and taking care of the physical needs of the child have relatively few age-of-mother effects. However, other parenting behaviors, such as maternal speech, structuring the environment, and use of corporal punishment have been found to be related to age. Adolescent mothers and emerging adult mothers (19 to 25 years) were less likely to talk to their children and structure the environment but more likely to spank than older mothers (Bornstein, Putnick, Suwalsky, & Gini, 2006; Lewin, Mitchell, & Ronzio, 2013).

Stable Child Characteristics

Research has shown that the characteristics of children can be prime determinants of how their parents behave toward them. The best documented characteristics are the child's age, the child's gender, the child's temperament, and the child's birth order.

Child's Age

Age of the child is the single most powerful influence on parental behavior. This is likely because with aging comes changes in a child's physical size, cognitive and linguistic ability, emotional maturity, and social skills. In response to their children's changing characteristics, parents show affection, communicate, discipline, and provide care in very different ways (see Bornstein, 2002). The role of age in parenting will be examined in some detail in the second part of this book.

Child's Gender

The first question asked after the birth of a child is "Is it a boy or a girl?" The answer to that question will have a profound effect on his or her development. Whether the child is a boy or girl influences parental behavior in various ways. First, fertility decisions are often based on sex. Mothers may bear more children until the desired son or daughter is born. Also, parents who had wanted a child of the opposite sex were more likely to perceive problems with their child and to spend less time playing with him or her compared with parents who were pleased with the gender of their child (Stattin & Klackenberg-Larsson, 1991).

To what extent do parents treat boys and girls differently? Many observational studies have found that certain aspects of parental behavior appear to be influenced by the sex of the child. Recall from Chapter 3 that parental perceptions of newborns and young children were dramatically affected simply by the label of *girl* or *boy*. Given the large number of studies in this area, two researchers (Lytton & Romney, 1991) set out to conduct a systematic review. The meta-analytic review of 172 studies, concerning whether parents systematically treat boys and girls differently, arrived at a surprising conclusion: Gender effects are not as pervasive as commonly believed. In fact, there were few significant findings. The strongest gender effects appeared to be in parental expectations or early perceptions about boys and girls, but most differences in parental treatment decreased with children's age. The authors concluded that when all the evidence is taken together, there are few robust, consistent differences in how boys and girls are treated by their parents.

More recent reviewers have identified other parental behaviors that appear to be influenced by the child's gender from the early childhood years through adolescence (e.g., Leaper, 2002; Leaper & Bigler, 2011). For example, early autonomy is encouraged in boys but not in girls. Boys are more likely to be encouraged to play, explore, and achieve more, whereas girls are encouraged to help their mothers around the house and focus on interpersonal relationships. There is also evidence of parenting differences in such areas as affectionate behavior, emotion talk and expressiveness, gender-typed play, household chores, and explicitly or implicitly supporting gender stereotypes.

Child's Temperament

The child's temperament is arguably the second most important determinant of parental behavior. *Temperament* refers to the biologically rooted behavioral style of the child. It helps define how emotionally expressive the child is and how the child responds to changes in his or her environment. Models of temperament are likely to include variables such as the child's activity level, emotions, ability to self-regulate, and social behavior. However, there is considerable disagreement about exactly which traits are the core components of temperament (Zentner & Bates, 2008).

As many researchers recognize, it is not the child's temperament itself that is most important for his or her early development but rather how the child's parents *relate* to it (Putnam, Sanson, & Rothbart, 2002). One parent might label a quiet, introverted child as "good" because the child does not interrupt. Another may call the same child "rude" because the child will not address strangers. Now, imagine describing the same child as "thoughtful and perceptive" or "prefers to listen" or even "courageous" when he or she does speak up. You can see how a particular child can be exposed to very different parenting based on how that parent perceives and reacts to the child's temperament.

Indeed, a parent's interpretation of and interaction with a child's temperament can have a profound effect on the child's self-perception and development. How well parental actions relate to a children's temperament has been called *matching*, *congruence*, or **goodness of fit**. Sometimes a child fits like a glove into his or her family. When this is not the case, significant parental effort may be required in order to relate well to a child with an extremely shy or challenging temperament.

Children who are perceived by their parents as difficult to manage are likely to elicit less positive and responsive caregiving from mothers than are those perceived as easygoing. Several different studies have shown that parents of challenging children are more likely to be negative and use punitive techniques, whereas parents of easygoing children appear more authoritative and responsive (e.g., Combs-Orme & Cain, 2008; Putnam et al., 2002). A recent Finnish study of mothers and their six-year-old children shows that other variables can affect how a child's temperament is responded to. The researchers found that maternal well-being mediated the relationship between a child's challenging temperament and parenting (Laukkanen, Ojansuu, Tolvanen, Alatupa, & Aunola, 2014). Mothers who were psychologically healthy were able to be more affectionate and less negative with challenging children compared with mothers who had depressive symptoms and low self-esteem.

Child's Birth Order

Since the 1950s, investigators have explored ways in which parenting and, in turn, children may be affected by birth order. It continues to be a question that has fascinated people (Marini & Kurtz, 2011; Rodgers, 2014). Among the typical findings is that firstborn infants receive more care, attention, and affection than do later-born infants, because first-time parents have more enthusiasm and energy to devote to the child. However, firstborn children also were reported to receive more pressure for achievement, presumably because the parents hold higher expectations for them than for later-born children (Lasko, 1954; Rothbart, 1971).

More recent investigations into the topic have shown that the influence of birth order on parenting is more complicated than traditionally thought. At least three other variables also come into play: the child's gender, the spacing (time between births) of the children, and the family size. In perhaps the most careful observational study conducted to date on this topic, 193 mothers were observed interacting with their three-month-old babies (Lewis & Kreitzberg, 1979). As predicted, the firstborn children generally received more maternal attention than did the later-born children. The spacing between the children also had a significant effect: Both closely and widely spaced children received more attention than did moderately spaced (1.5 to 3.5 years) children. The authors concluded that the spacing of their children modified mothers' perceptions and thus the attention devoted to the children.

Of course, there are other child characteristics besides age, gender, temperament, and birth order that can be determinants of parenting behavior. As will be discussed in a subsequent chapter, premature babies or children with developmental disabilities (such as **autism**) are two examples of such child characteristics. Parents of children with disabilities are more likely to experience distress, disruptions in normal family functioning (mealtimes, sleep schedules, social life), marital difficulties, and even psychiatric problems than are parents of children without disabilities (Hayes & Watson, 2013; Yirmiya & Shaked, 2005). In sum, stable child characteristics and other differences among children represent a basic determinant of parental behavior.

Stable Family Characteristics

Two stable family characteristics have frequently been found to influence parenting: family structure and marital relations.

Family Structure

The primary variable of family structure is whether it is a single- or two-parent family. In 2008, 40.6% of all births in the United States were to unmarried women (U.S. Census Bureau, 2012). About 30 years earlier, that percentage was 18.4. These 12.9 million single parents—81% of them women (U.S. Census Bureau, 2012)—differ from married parents in some of their parenting behavior. In part as a result of the increased stress and pressure of limited time, unmarried single parents (compared to married parents) tend to spend less time with their children and engage in less supervision and monitoring. Because single parents must deal with all aspects of parenting by themselves, they are at risk for high stress, exhaustion, and depression. There is some evidence that single mothers have more psychiatric symptoms (e.g., depression, anxiety) than married mothers (Schleider, Chorpita, & Weisz, 2014). They also exhibit a diminished level of parenting with regard to the time and attention they are able to devote to their offspring (Weinraub, Horvath, & Gringlas, 2002). Single parents will be discussed further in Chapter 11.

A second key family structure variable is the number of children in the home. Given that there is only so much time and energy parents can devote to children, it comes as no surprise that family size has been associated with differences in parental behavior. Family structure, in terms of number of children, can influence parenting practices. The average American mother now has two children, with the fertility rate at 2.06 (Henry J. Kaiser Family Foundation, 2013). See Figure 5.3 for the fertility rate of women in 10 different countries. There is only limited evidence that family size influences parental disciplinary practices. For example, in larger families (four or more children), it was found that discipline tends to be more punitive and authoritarian than in smaller families (Wagner, Schubert, & Schubert, 1985).

Figure 5.3 Number of Children Born per Woman in Ten Countries

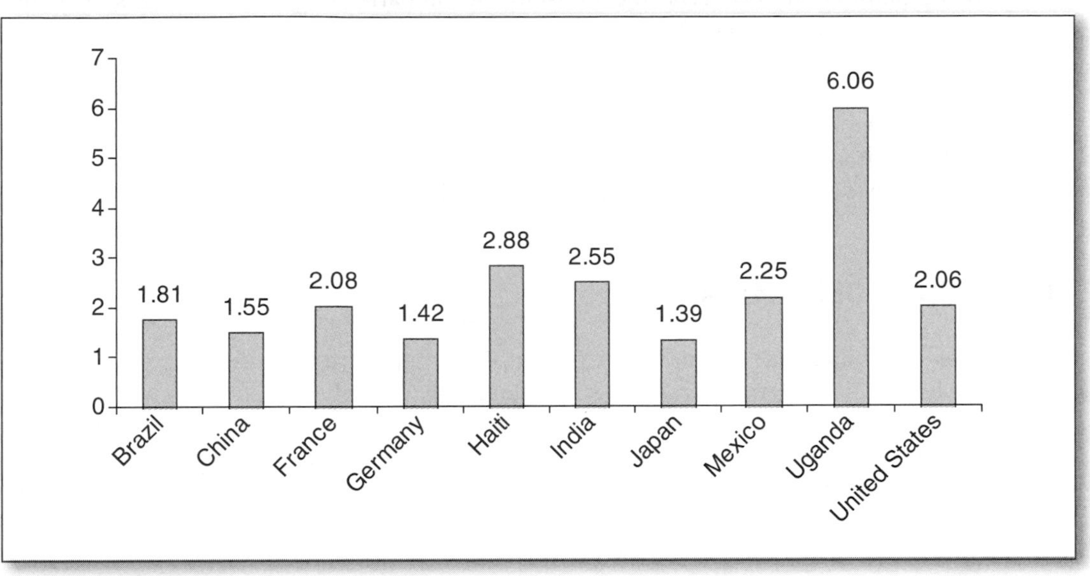

Marital Relations

How the quality of the marital relationship affects child rearing provides a clear example of systemic interactions described by family systems theory. Here, there are reciprocal relations between functioning in the spousal and parental subsystems. Close, supportive, and thereby satisfying marital relationships were found to be associated with sensitive and positive parenting as well as more positive attitudes and perceptions about children (Grych, 2002; Kwok, Cheng, Chow, & Ling, 2013). On the other hand, conflict between spouses can result in negative parenting and child adjustment problems. Rhoades (2008) reviewed a meta-analysis of 71 studies and found that children and youth who experience interparental conflict are likely to show physiological, behavioral, self-esteem, and relational problems.

Parents experiencing discordant marriages (compared with those in happy marriages) exhibit less consistent practices and less effective childrearing practices. It is likely that parents in unhappy marriages are less emotionally available and less involved with their children (Easterbrooks & Emde, 1988). Marital discord may manifest itself in disagreements over childrearing practices. Consequently, parents in discordant relationships tend to be more negative in disciplinary practices than nondiscordant parents. In addition, the interspousal conflict may spill over, bringing on parent-child conflict and, in turn, child adjustment problems (Coln, Jordan, & Mercer, 2013; Grych, 2002).

Such a negative spillover into parenting can be dramatically seen in homes of battered women. Men who physically abuse their wives are frequently irritable. According to one study, almost all of the battered women reported that they argued with their husbands at least every few days. In contrast, only 16% of women in a comparison group reported a similar rate of arguments. It is likely that at least some of these marital arguments spilled over into the father's interactions with his children. Violent men reportedly got angry at their children every few days, in contrast to the comparison fathers' rate of less than once a week (Holden & Ritchie, 1991).

An alternative to the **spillover hypothesis** is the **compensatory hypothesis**. Here, a parent who fails to find love and warmth in a marital relationship may seek to meet those needs in her relationship with her child. According to the hypothesis, the child may in this way be **buffered** from the ill effects of the marital discord. However, to date, there is little research evidence to support this hypothesis (Erel & Burman, 1995; Grych, 2002).

SITUATIONAL DETERMINANTS

Does the immediate situation that parents find themselves in affect their childrearing behavior? The evidence is that it certainly does. As will be shown, parenting is much more flexible, fluid, and changeable than many researchers have recognized. Parenting is, in fact, a dynamic process. Indeed, effective and competent parents must adapt their behavior to the situation by taking into account a change of setting, a swing of mood, or an undesired child behavior. These situational determinants can be grouped into context, transient parent characteristics, and transient child characteristics.

Context

Relatively few studies have examined the role of context in parent-child relationships. But context is very important in determining childrearing behavior. Parents take the context into account when interacting with their children. Ask parents how they react when their children misbehave, and they are likely to respond, "It depends on the situation." The central features of a context for parents are the setting (location) where the interaction takes place, the presence of others, and the time.

The most obvious contextual variable is the setting or environment that a parent is in. Parenting occurs most often in the home but also in the car, at the supermarket, on vacation, and in numerous other locales. Observational studies that compared parental behavior across two or more settings (such as the home, a laboratory, or a park) arrived at similar conclusions: Parental behavior can show considerable variation across different settings (Bradley, 2002; Holden & Miller, 1999; Miller, Shim, & Holden, 1998). Even within a particular setting, childrearing behavior is affected by ongoing activity in that setting. If a mother is multitasking, her parenting will change considerably. A child's raucous laughter might delight a mother playing hide-and-seek but irritate the same mother trying to make a phone call.

A second contextual variable that can influence dyadic interactions is the presence of additional individuals. The presence of another child or a second parent can modify parental behavior. This type of second-order effect was explained under family systems theory. The presence of many people in a home (i.e., crowding) can also affect child rearing. Parents in crowded homes tend to talk in less-complex sentences to their children than parents who live in uncrowded homes (Evans, Maxwell, & Hart, 1999). Related to crowded homes is chaos. Children in chaotic homes exhibit more problems than other children (Evans & Wachs, 2010). Items from a family chaos scale are listed in Table 5.1.

A final contextual variable that has received some research attention is the time at which the interaction occurs—both the time of day and the time of year. During the summer months, parental involvement and monitoring can change systematically in relation to a parent's work status (Crouter & McHale, 1993). The time of day that interactions occur is also likely to influence behaviors. If parents are in a hurry or tired, they are likely to behave differently than they would otherwise. Fatigue on the part of parents and children may account for the finding that mothers are twice as likely to spank their children in the evening as in the morning (Holden et al., 1995).

Transient Parent Characteristics

Two types of parent characteristics that influence parenting can be considered transient because they are likely to change within a short period of time: thoughts and emotions. As described earlier, parental social cognitions can provide *stable* influences on behavior, as in the case of attitudes and beliefs. Thoughts can also, however, have *transient* effects, as is the case with short-term goals, which can change minute by minute. The particular goal that a parent has in mind is potentially a strong influence on that parent's behavior. For instance, parents often enter situations with either child-centered, parent-centered, or socialization goals in mind (Dix & Branca, 2003). Child-centered goals are oriented around the child's needs rather than the parent's. Socialization goals focus on long-term development; examples of them were listed in Table 4.3.

Closely linked to goals are emotions. Positive or negative emotions are aroused when parental goals are either met or frustrated, respectively (Dix, 1991). These emotions are

Table 5.1 Items From the Confusion, Hubbub, and Order Scale (CHAOS)

1. You can't hear yourself think in our home.
2. There is very little commotion in our home. (reverse scored)
3. It's a real zoo in our home.
4. We are usually able to stay on top of things. (reverse scored)
5. There is usually a television turned on somewhere in our home.
6. The atmosphere in our house is calm. (reverse scored)
7. We almost always seem to be rushed.
8. We can usually find things when we need them. (reverse scored)

Source: Matheny, Wachs, Ludwig, & Phillips, 1995.

essential for effective parenting because they help to organize the parent's sensitive and responsive childrearing behaviors. However, when emotions are too strong, too weak, or inappropriately matched to the child's behavior, they serve to undermine effective parenting.

Several empirical studies have documented linkages among parental cognitions, emotions, and behavior. To give one example, mothers' attachment classification with their own mothers, as assessed by the Adult Attachment Interview (AAI), is related to how they parent their two-year-old children. For example, preoccupied mothers exhibit angry and intrusive caregiving. In contrast, dismissing mothers—those who had depressed symptoms—were less warm and responsive than secure mothers (Adam, Gunnar, & Tanaka, 2004).

Transient Child Characteristics

Parental behavior can also be influenced by a child's rapidly changing emotions and behavior. We know that children are more susceptible than parents to changes in their physiological or emotional states. This is why we can have compassion for a screaming toddler who has just dropped his or her ice cream cone. For a two-year-old, that is as serious as totaling a new car. Effective parents are able to take into account these changes in their children—whether it is toddler frustration or teenage angst—when doling out consequences.

The best way to study how transient child characteristics influence parental behavior is through the child effects and transactions approach. Studies examining parental responses to changes in a child's behavior have shown that when a child misbehaves, the *type* of misdeed is a powerful determinant (Grusec & Kuczynski, 1980). However, the mother's attitude and the child's gender are also important determinants of responses (Hastings & Rubin, 1999).

INTERRELATIONS AMONG DETERMINANTS

As must be clear to the reader by now, parental behavior is multiply determined. Characteristics of the parent, the child, and the context all contribute to why parents do what they do. Unfortunately, the more than thirty influences on parenting that have been identified in the research literature cannot be clearly demarcated like the components of a chemical reaction.

Different contexts can affect each other, as the ecological model proposes. What happens in the work environment can be brought home and affect the quality of parenting, as Jennifer Matjasko and Amy Feldman (2006) found. They investigated whether there was evidence of how the context of work could spill over to child rearing once the parent was home. They found evidence that both mothers and fathers can bring emotional experiences from the workplace to the home [Preview Question]. When mothers reported being happy, angry, or anxious at work, they also reported feeling similar emotions at home. Fathers, on the other hand, reported only bringing feelings of anxiety home with them.

The different determinants of parenting can also influence each other in several ways. Most commonly, the variables can have additive, moderating, or mediating effects. In addition, they can work together by interacting or compensating. Each of these interrelations between variables will be explained next.

Additive effects (also called *cumulative effects*) result from variables combining to form a stronger influence on behavior than any of the variables has on its own. A parent with an explosive temper plus a temperamentally difficult child is a dangerous combination. Add to this equation a loss of the parent's employment and the risk of abusive parenting is considerably higher than it would be if only one or even two of these variables were present. Sometimes these potentially problematic variables are called *risk factors*. The more risk factors affecting parental behavior, the greater the likelihood of a poor childrearing environment. In a study of risk factors, Kristi Hannan and Tom Luster (1991) assessed six potentially detrimental influences on child rearing in 602 families with one-year-old children: three contextual factors (absence of a partner, three or more children, and low income); two maternal characteristics (low IQ score and adolescent mother); and one child characteristic (difficult temperament). The risk factors present in each family were then added together to form a **risk index**. Each family was also assessed on the HOME (Home Observation for the Measurement of the Environment) scale, which rated the quality of the home environment. The results revealed a strong relation between risk index and low HOME score. Only 22% of families with one risk factor had low HOME scores, in contrast to 88% of those families with all six risk factors.

Recall from Chapter 3 the discussion of *moderating* and *mediating* variables. For parenting, the most important moderating variable is the marital relationship. Supportive spouses can reduce the effects of stress by providing assistance, advice, and encouragement to their mate. A loving marital relationship can moderate the negative parental effects of financial hardship (Simons, Lorenz, Conger, & Wu, 1992) and even of a parent's psychologically painful childhood. For example, supportive spouses provide encouragement, promote healing, and suggest positive childrearing behaviors rather than allowing their partners to engage in the negative childrearing behavior that they experienced in childhood.

A mediating variable affects the strength of another variable, sometimes negating it completely. For example, economic hardship can certainly influence a parent's behavior. But as a determinant, economic problems are mediated by feelings of economic strain. If a parent fails to recognize his or her financial problems, ignores them, or is surrounded by others content in the same situation, it is unlikely that economic hardship will have much influence on his or her parenting. But when the financial problems are recognized and experienced in the form of strain or worry, parenting will likely be negatively impacted (Simons et al., 1992). Thus, in this case, parental awareness, attitude, and even the neighborhood context mediate the strength of economic hardship as a determinant of child rearing.

Generally, the single most important mediator of child rearing is parental cognition. If parents can revise or reframe their thinking, then parental behavior can be changed. For example, mothers with irritable infants provided less supportive care if they believed (true or not) that responsive care would reinforce the demandingness of their infants. Thus maternal beliefs mediated the extent to which infant irritability was predictive of maternal sensitivity (Crockenberg & McCluskey, 1986). Faulty cognitions (including attributions, expectations, and problem solving) are a key determinant of why some parents maltreat their children (Seng & Prinz, 2008).

A fourth way that parenting determinants can relate to one another is through their **interaction**. Interactions occur when one parenting variable impacts a second parenting variable. A common interaction found in parent-child relationships is between the gender of the parent (a parent characteristic) and the gender of the child (a child characteristic). Fathers, for example, are sometimes observed to behave differently toward their sons than toward their daughters (Russell & Saebel, 1997). Another example of an interaction with parent gender is that children disclose more personal and emotional experiences to their mothers than to their fathers (Smetana, Metzger, Gettman, & Campione-Barr, 2006).

Finally, determinants can relate through **compensation**. If one positive variable is strong enough, it can compensate for the presence of a negative one. For example, the features that are perceived to make babies cute and adorable to parents help to compensate for the incredible amount of work required to rear a child. A second example concerns stress. As described above, parental stress can be a powerful negative influence on child rearing. However, high levels of social support could compensate for the stress so that parenting would not be adversely affected.

CHAPTER SUMMARY

This chapter addressed the question "What determines how a particular parent behaves?" The simple answer is that there are a lot of determinants. More than thirty variables can influence parenting behavior. These variables range from proud cultural traditions to fleeting thoughts and emotions that we might not even notice—if a researcher was not observing them. Four categories were used to organize these determinants. The most general type of variable was that of cultural and distal variables such as socioeconomic status and religious beliefs. The second category concerned contextual variables. These influences included parental employment status, stress, social support, and the neighborhood where the family resides. Stable characteristics of the parents, children, and family formed the third category. This group of variables included such considerations as parental gender and personality, child age and temperament, and family size and structure. The final category consisted of situational variables that are prone to change rapidly—such as the context of the interaction or the parent's mood.

When trying to chart out the relations between these variables, the task quickly becomes overwhelmingly complex. The determinants of parenting can relate to each other in at least five ways. The simplest relation is when two or more variables have similar and therefore additive effects. However, other variables may moderate, mediate, interact with, or compensate with or for another variable. Just how particular determinants relate depend on which variables are being examined.

THOUGHT QUESTIONS

- What were the major influences on your parents' childrearing behavior?
- Select two or three determinants. How do they interrelate? Is one more powerful than another?

- Parental beliefs about child rearing are susceptible to change. What are some ways of modifying parental beliefs?
- What are some of the implications of knowing the different influences on parenting?

CHAPTER GLOSSARY

additive effect When two or more variables combine to form a stronger influence on behavior than any of the variables has on its own. Also called *cumulative effects*.

autism Also known as *autism spectrum disorder* (*ASD*), it is a type of pervasive developmental disorder with a neurological basis. Although the severity of the disorder varies, symptoms appear in the first two years of life and typically involve severe impairment in communications and social relationships.

buffered When one variable protects against the potential adverse effects of another. Also called a *protective factor*.

childrearing commitment The extent to which a parent is dedicated to the child and his or her well-being.

childrearing stress The experience of distress or discomfort due to child rearing.

coercive discipline When a parent forces a child to comply or behave in a desired way.

compensation When a positive variable is strong enough to overcome the presence of a negative variable.

compensatory hypothesis One variable can compensate or counteract the negative effects of another variable. For example, one parent may attempt to compensate for an acrimonious marital relationship by devoting extra attention and warmth to a child.

determinants of parenting Variables that influence a parent's childrearing behavior or beliefs.

distal Distant.

empathy Experiencing how someone else feels or perceives a situation. With regard to parenting, this refers to a parent's ability to experience events from the child's point of view.

goodness of fit The quality of the match between a child's characteristics (i.e., temperament) and the parenting. Also called *matching* or *congruence*.

independence versus interdependence Two different cultural orientations concerning the individual. Cultures that value independence promote individual autonomy. In contrast, other cultures value a sense of togetherness and group membership.

interaction When two variables have a nonadditive effect on each other in statistical analyses.

mid-level determinants Influences on parenting that are between immediate, situational, and distal or cultural determinants. Examples include stable parent and child characteristics and marital relations.

mindful parenting A parent's nonjudgmental awareness of the child in the immediate context.

parenting stress Aversive psychological or physiological reactions experienced in the parenting role.

per capita income Total national income divided by the number of citizens in the country.

power assertion Parental controlling behaviors intended to show force or the threat of force.

proximal Close or immediate.

religiosity When referring to individuals, this term means the degree to which a person is religious.

risk index Cumulative risk factors present in a family.

skinship A parent-child relationship characterized by close physical contact. Often practiced in Japan.

spillover hypothesis A hypothesis that the mood or quality of interactions in one domain carry over into another domain. With regard to parents, examples include how conflictual marital relationships or stress at work spills over and affects the quality of parent-child interactions at home.

PART II

Parenting and Development

CHAPTER 6

Becoming a Parent

Chapter Preview: True or False?

- Half of all pregnancies are unintended.
- There are more than 4,000 chromosomal and genetic disorders.
- Becoming a parent is an easy and joyous transition for most families.

For most people, rearing a child is the single most important, time-consuming, and demanding activity they will ever engage in. Bringing a child into the world is a peak experience that brings joy into parents' lives. But it also produces fundamental life changes. As parenting expert Marc Bornstein observed, "By their very coming into existence, infants forever alter the sleeping, eating, and working habits of their parents; they change who parents are and how parents define themselves" (2002, p. 3).

Having a child is a momentous, life-defining occurrence. Despite this, all too often, people do not plan to become parents. In fact, about half (51%) of the 6.6 million pregnancies in the United States are unintended (Guttmacher Institute, 2013) [Preview Question]. The rates are highest among young, poor, and low-educated women (see Photo 6.1). The U.S. percentage (51%) is about double of the rate (25%) of European countries (Singh, Sedgh, & Hussain, 2010).

What accounts for such a high rate of unintended pregnancies? Most young adults report that it is very important to them to avoid pregnancy (Hayford & Guzzo, 2013). The problem is due to multiple factors, among them lack of accurate information (i.e., sex education) and the difficulty in obtaining simple and inexpensive contraception (Finer & Sonfield, 2013). It is estimated that 85% of couples who are sexually active but do not use any form of contraceptive will experience a pregnancy within a year. Those couples who do use contraceptives may also experience a pregnancy—depending on the type of contraceptive used and whether it is used according to instructions (Trussell, 2011). The least effective contraceptives (spermicides, fertility-awareness–based methods) result in unintended pregnancies about 25% of the time. In contrast, the most effective techniques (implants, intrauterine devices) have a failure rate of less than 1%. Sixty percent of unintended pregnancies result in births; 40% were terminated with abortions (Guttmacher Institute, 2013). Not surprisingly, unwanted children are at risk for a range of problems, as will be discussed later in this chapter.

The arrival of the baby signifies the onset of a major new responsibility, results in role changes, and may dredge up old psychological issues from the new parent's own childhood. Due to these and other changes, early researchers studying the transition to parenthood dubbed it a time of "crisis" (LeMasters, 1957).

Although subsequent researchers have toned down the alarmist language, there is no question that the arrival of an infant introduces fundamental changes for parents. One obvious adjustment is economic; raising a child is expensive. It is not just baby food and diapers. There are health care costs, child care and education, food, housing, transportation, and miscellaneous expenses (toys, books, personal care, entertainment). The total expense for raising a child at different ages is depicted in Figure 6.1. When all those expenses are added together and averaged across different parts of the country, the cost for a middle-income couple to have and raise a child (through age 17 years) is estimated to add up to $241,000 (Lino, 2013).

To see for yourself the different expenses associated with rearing children and how the costs change based on family structure, region of the country, and family income, go to http://www.cnpp.usda.gov/tools/CRC_Calculator/default.aspx.

Why does it cost so much to rear a child? Consider some of the expenses for an infant's first year of life. Two-parent families with an income level of $60,000 to $105,000 spend about $740 on baby clothes, $580 for health care, and $3,250 for infant care annually (Lino, 2013). The family will also need a crib, car seat, toys, and other necessities such as diapers. Then there are costs for food, housing, and transportation. Keep in mind that a high-end stroller can cost almost $1,000! Costs vary, of course, depending on multiple factors: where

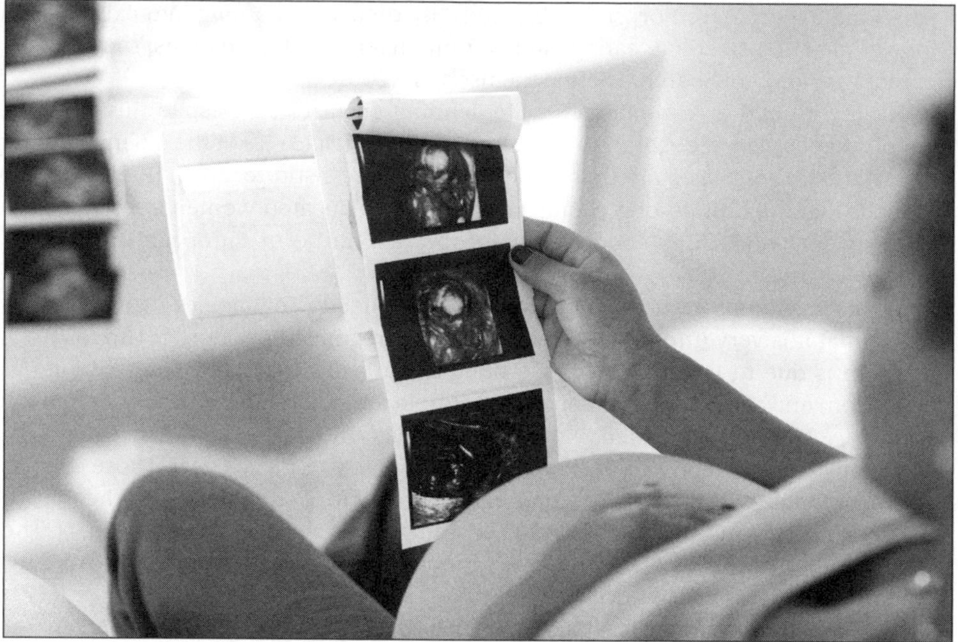

Photo 6.1 Pregnant woman.

Source: © iStockphoto.com/RuslanDashinsky

one lives, one's income, and the family structure. However, the United States Department of Agriculture estimates that the first three years of a child's life will cost parents somewhere between $18,580 and $42,000 (Lino, 2013). Some specific costs of childbirth, diapers, feeding, and day care can be found in Figure 6.1.

DECIDING TO HAVE A CHILD

Not all couples decide to have children. In the past, voluntarily childless couples were often viewed with pity or criticism. They were seen as selfish, immature, abnormal, or simply unhappy (DeOllos & Kapinus, 2002). Today, however, the choice is more accepted. And whereas many couples struggling with infertility consider themselves *childless*, an increasing number of couples are choosing this state and prefer the term *childfree*. In Germany, about 25% of married couples are, by choice, childfree. In the United States, the number is 18% (Livingston, 2010). Many motivations can lead couples to this decision. They may consider themselves too old, dislike children, seek a different lifestyle, have financial or career concerns, or view the world as too hostile a place to introduce children (Weston & Qu, 2001). One environmental group, the Voluntary Human Extinction Movement (http://www.vhemt.org), even promotes going childless because humans have polluted the earth (Weisman, 2007). They distribute bumper stickers that read "Thank You for Not Breeding" and encourage adoption instead for those who wish to fulfill their parenting desires.

Figure 6.1 Some First-Year Expenses Associated With Having a Newborn

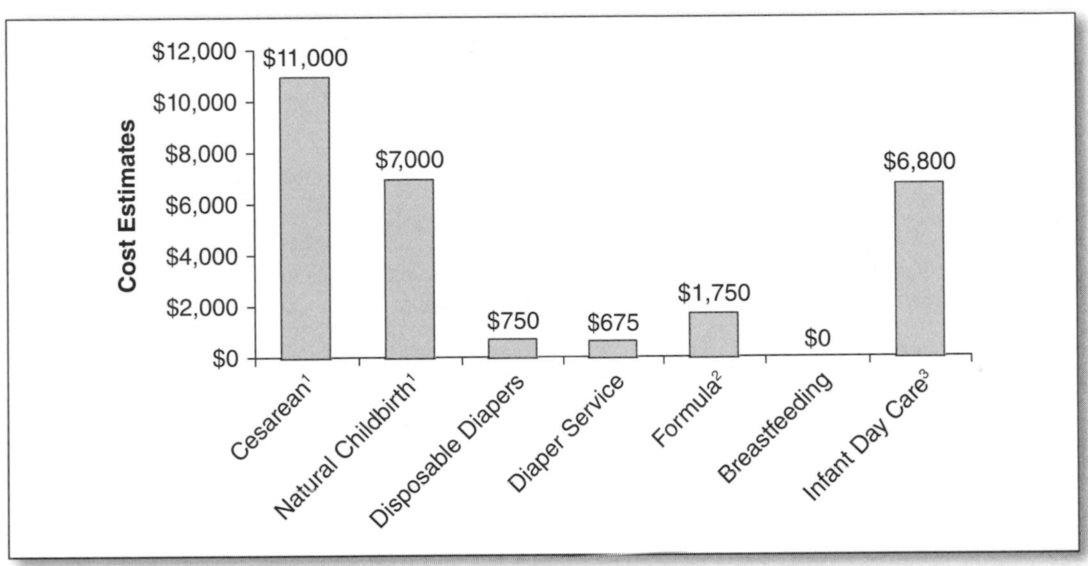

1 Ordoñez, 2007.

2 Estimates based on six to eight ounces every four to six hours at 13.5¢ per ounce.

3 Estimates based on 40 weeks at $170 per week.

Many couples, however, do have children—either through a decision, an "accident," or adoption. For parents who make the decision, they provide many different reasons. Several studies have explored parents' decision to have a child (e.g., Groat, Giordano, Cernkovich, Pugh, & Swinford, 1997; Pinquart, Stotzka, & Silbereisen, 2008). Table 6.1 lists some of the most frequently mentioned benefits and problems associated with being a parent, according to those couples.

Based on the pattern of advantages and disadvantages identified by the 600 couples studied in one study, four types of parents were identified. Surprisingly, only 30% of the couples were classified as *pro-children* (they identified many pros and few cons to becoming parents). An equal percentage of couples were labeled *anti-children* (they saw few benefits but many problems). Twenty percent of the couples equally identified both pros and cons to the idea and were classified *ambivalent*. The remaining 20% of couples apparently had not thought much about having children, because they mentioned few advantages or disadvantages. They were labeled *indifferent*. Neal and his colleagues (1989) concluded that although some couples make a careful, deliberate decision to have a child, other couples "simply experience their pregnancies as happenings, unplanned events, occurrences, or the will of God" (p. 325). Given that there are both advantages and disadvantages to having children, it is not surprising that some individuals are ambivalent about the prospect of becoming a parent (Cowan & Cowan, 2012; Pinquart et al., 2008).

Table 6.1 Adults' Views About Advantages and Disadvantages of Having Children

Advantages	Disadvantages
Allows for a full family life, important for a good marriage	Results in a drastic change in lifestyle
Offers a sense of personal accomplishment	Creates many time-consuming responsibilities
Adds excitement to life, joy of children	Increases expenses
Provides a source of love and affection, someone to care for me when old	Introduces difficulties regarding mothers' employment
Promotes a sense of immortality	Contributes to overpopulation
Other: Gives spiritual fulfillment, establishes oneself as a mature person, spousal/partner wishes, pressure from family, and fulfills sexual love	Other: creates worry and tension, makes for too much disorder, and introduces negative effects on one's health and stamina

Sources: Adapted from Groat et al., 1997; Livingston & Cohn, 2010; and Neal, Groat, & Wicks, 1989.

GETTING PREGNANT, STAYING PREGNANT, AND ENCOUNTERING PROBLEMS

Whether or not a deliberate decision was made to have a child, once a woman's egg is fertilized, she undergoes a course of dramatic and rapid change in her body and in the developing embryo and fetus. On average, pregnancies last 40 weeks from the first day of the woman's last menstrual period, though anywhere from 38 to 42 weeks is considered normal.

There are many advantages to planning a pregnancy. If a woman plans to get pregnant, she can prepare her body by adjusting such things as her weight, alcohol consumption, medication intake, and fitness level. It is also recommended to begin taking prenatal vitamins that include folic acid to avoid neural tube defects in her baby. Psychologically, it is also helpful to try to minimize stress and prepare for the changes associated with pregnancy and having a child. Men can also optimize their fertility by avoiding alcohol and tobacco and engaging in healthful eating and physical activity. Economically, unintended pregnancies cost the nation billions of dollars (Finer & Sonfield, 2013).

There are also several potential dangers to the developing embryo of an unplanned pregnancy. The principal danger is exposing the embryo to harmful substances. These substances, called **teratogens**, include drugs (including prescriptions, over-the-counter medications, alcohol, and nicotine), health factors (such as diabetes), infections (especially sexually transmitted diseases), environmental chemicals (such as herbicides), and physical agents (especially X-rays). Teratogenic effects depend on such factors as the time since conception, the type and dose of the substance, and the length of time the embryo or fetus was exposed to the substance as well as the developing child's genetic susceptibility.

Alcohol is one of the most commonly used teratogens. The problem that can result from maternal drinking during pregnancy is called Fetal Alcohol Spectrum Disorders (FASD). This disorder is estimated to occur in 1% of births (Kodituwakku & Kodituwakku, 2013). It is labeled *spectrum* because there is a continuum of permanent birth defects. One of the most severe FASDs is **Fetal Alcohol Syndrome (FAS)**. It is characterized by abnormal facial features, growth deficiencies, and problems with a child's central nervous system. Areas commonly affected by FAS include learning, memory, attention span, communication, vision, and hearing.

How much alcohol does it take to cause a FASD? There is no simple answer. Many children (60% to 70%) born to alcoholics show no signs of FAS, but they *are* likely to have some indications of damage due to alcohol. Still, there is evidence that even a single alcohol binge can damage an embryo's brain (Olney, 2000). In 2005, the then-U.S. Surgeon General, Richard H. Carmona, urged pregnant women and even women who could become pregnant to avoid any alcohol consumption.

Smoking cigarettes is another easily avoidable teratogen. In the United States, about 16.5% of women smoke, and 10.7% of pregnant women smoke during the last trimester (Centers for Disease Control and Prevention, 2014c). Cigarette smoking decreases the amount of oxygen that crosses the placenta and exposes the fetus to nicotine and carbon monoxide. This doubles the likelihood of having a low-birth-weight or preterm baby and increases the risk of pregnancy complications, including stillbirth (delivery of a dead baby) (March of Dimes, 2014).

Although not technically a teratogen, a mother's negative emotions can be damaging, too. There is some evidence that a woman's feelings about her pregnancy can have important long-term implications for both the mother and child. Negative feelings are certainly understandable. Women's bodies go through a number of dramatic changes in order to carry a fetus to term and prepare for childbirth and breastfeeding. Most obvious is the change in abdomen size and shape. A woman with a pre-pregnancy waist size of 28 inches may grow to 48 inches before delivery. If not for the pregnancy, this would be considered a bizarre and unhealthy body change. Although some women enjoy pregnancy and the changes that accompany it, other women react negatively. Weight gain is an inevitable consequence of pregnancy. Women of normal pre-pregnancy weight should gain 25 to 35 pounds (more for twins), but some women gain much more. One in five women gain more than 40 pounds, an amount considered excessive for most women (Martin, Hamilton, Ventura, Osterman, & Mathews, 2013). Then there are the hormonal changes, changes in breast size and tenderness, and sometimes dramatic emotional shifts. Women who accept their pregnancy and all the changes that it brings (whether the pregnancy was planned or not) tend to have lower levels of parenting stress later and are more likely to raise a securely attached child (Ispa, Sable, Porter, & Ciszmadia, 2007).

Although many people aspire to become parents, the path to parenthood has several potential pitfalls. Some of these are infertility, genetic defects, and maternal problems during pregnancy.

Infertility and Its Treatment

About 11% of women and 9.4% of men experience some type of infertility problem (Chandra, Copen, & Stephen, 2013). The human reproductive process is a complex system that can malfunction for many reasons—from either partner. Female fertility problems can be caused by a number of issues, including fallopian tube damage, **endometriosis** (when uterine tissue grows outside the uterus), ovulation disorders, hormonal problems, and early menopause. The most common causes of male infertility include problems in producing healthy sperm, low sperm concentrations, hormonal problems, genetic defects, impaired delivery of sperm, or overheating of the testicles (often from frequent use of hot tubs). For more information, visit the Mayo Clinic's website (http://www.mayoclinic.org).

Though few women would choose infertility, many American families are inadvertently increasing their risk for infertility by delaying childbirth beyond their peak birthing years. The average maternal age in the United States for first birth, as mentioned in the last chapter, is 25.1 years (U.S. Census Bureau, 2012). Twenty percent of mothers have their first child after the age of 35. This trend is also present in Ireland and other European countries; the average age of first-time mothers in Ireland is now 31. Some women delaying parenthood are pursuing an education or a career. Some are simply waiting for the right partner.

Delayed parenthood means increased likelihood of fertility problems. Older women ovulate less frequently, and a woman's risk for some conditions—such as endometriosis, gestational diabetes, and placental defects—increases as she ages. The attrition rate of female germ cells is startling. The number of eggs at a girl's first menstrual cycle is 300,000 to 400,000. By age 30, it's down between 39,000 to 52,000 (13% of the eggs at puberty). By age 40, women have only 3% of their initial cache of eggs—about 9,000 to 12,000 eggs—and many of these eggs will not be viable. Older fathers are more at risk for fertility problems as well (for very different reasons, as we will see below).

Older parenthood increases the risk of birth defects in children. A well-documented example is the positive association of maternal age and children born with **Down syndrome** (also called *Trisomy 21*). Although it is possible for a young mother to have a child with Down syndrome, the likelihood increases dramatically after about age 35 (Pandya, Mevada, Patel, & Suthar, 2013). Fathers' age also has been linked to increased likelihood of Down's syndrome births—when their wives are over 35 years of age (Kovac et al., 2013). Paternal age is also a risk factor for schizophrenia as a consequence of "de novo" mutations in the fathers' sperm (Jaffe, Eaton, Straub, Marenco, & Weinberger, 2013). Both maternal and paternal ages have been linked to increased likelihood of having a child with autism (Croen, Najjar, Fireman, & Grether, 2007).

Box 6.1 The "Big Lie" About Fertility

In her provocatively titled new book, *The Big Lie: Motherhood, Feminism and the Reality of the Biological Clock* (2014), Tanya Selvaratnam shares her thoughts on infertility and **in vitro fertilization (IVF)** treatments, the financial cost of reproductive medicine, and finding a work/life balance.

A woman in her 20s has a 20% to 25% chance of conceiving naturally per menstrual cycle. In her early 30s, the chance of pregnancy is 15% per cycle. After 35, the odds of pregnancy without medical intervention are at 10%. After 40, that number falls to 5%, and women over 45 have a 1% chance of conception.

The number of childless women in the United States today is growing. According to a Pew Research study (Livingston & Cohn, 2010), about 18% of women in the United States don't have children by the end of their childbearing years. In 2008, there were 1.9 million childless women between 40 and 44, compared with 580,000 in 1976.

Perhaps one of the greatest myths today is the ability of science to step in and make babies for women at virtually any age. Selvaratnam says that we see the success stories but rarely hear about the huge numbers of failed attempts. A 2011 report on **assisted reproductive technologies (ARTs)** (Centers for Disease Control and Prevention, American Society for Reproductive Medicine, & Society for Assisted Reproductive Technology, 2011) found that the single most important factor affecting the chances of a successful pregnancy through ARTs is a woman's age. Selvaratnam reports that at age 40, the chance is 18.7%; at 42, it's 10%; at 44, it's only 2.9%.

In perhaps 25% of infertility cases, sperm is the cause of the problem. Three important features of sperm are quantity, quality, and motility. Some men have difficulty in sperm production (producing fewer than 10 million sperm per milliliter of semen). When quality is the issue, a high percentage of abnormal sperm are present. But the most common problem is poor motility. Despite the presence of 150 to 300 million sperm in a normal ejaculation, for some men, the sperm are unable to navigate their way the three to four inches up the fallopian tubes to fertilize the egg.

Today, multiple medical techniques are available to assist with fertility problems. Under the title of assisted reproductive technology (ART), embryologists have developed sophisticated techniques to assist parents with serious fertility problems. Beyond the use of drugs to regulate ovulation, there are three basic techniques (Hansen, Kurinczuk, Milne, de Klerk, & Bower, 2013; Schwartz, 2003):

1. **Intrauterine insemination (IUI)** is the most common procedure. Frozen sperm from either the husband or a donor are placed by a catheter directly into the uterus. This procedure could be used if the husband's sperm count was very low or carried a genetic defect.

2. In vitro fertilization (IVF), where an egg and sperm are combined in a petri (or culture) dish, has now also become a standard procedure to deal with blocked fallopian tubes and other problems. The fertilized egg (zygote) is then transferred into the woman's uterus. Several zygotes might be transferred at once. There are several variations of this basic technique involving the manipulation of eggs and sperm. **Gamete intrafallopian transfer (GIFT)** consists of inserting eggs and sperm, by way of a laparoscope, into the woman's fallopian tube. Fertilization then takes place, and the resulting zygote(s) travels down into the uterus. **Zygote intrafallopian transfer (ZIFT)** is like GIFT, except fertilization occurs similarly to IVF, and the resulting zygote(s) is transferred to a fallopian tube. **Intracytoplasmic sperm injection (ICSI)** is one of the newest techniques. It is based on IVF but leaves even less to chance. A single healthy sperm is selected and then injected into a single female egg, using a microscopic glass needle. Once fertilization is confirmed, the zygote is inserted into the woman

for implantation. Generally four fertilized eggs are inserted, with the expectation that not all will continue to develop. However, sometimes they do!

3. Surrogacy is more ethically complicated because it involves a second woman. The particular role the woman plays could consist of contributing her eggs to the infertile couple, carrying a fertilized egg to term, or both. The sperm of the husband in the infertile couple is sometimes used to fertilize the egg through IVF procedures.

In conjunction with these techniques, if a prior pregnancy had revealed a genetic problem, **preimplantation genetic diagnosis (PGD)** is now performed by clinics around the country to identify potential genetic or chromosomal defects. Eggs are harvested and, using IVF, zygotes are formed. Each is then tested for certain genetic diseases. Typically, out of a group of six to eight zygotes, several will be chosen to implant in the mother's uterus.

ART is a new science; although developed in the 1980s, it has now resulted, worldwide, in more than 5 million babies (Hansen et al., 2013). In the United States, 1% of all births are conceived using ART. Nevertheless, the odds of successfully having a child through this technology are not high. The rates vary depending on the procedure, the particular clinic, and the characteristics of the woman's eggs and the man's sperm. Success rates (as determined by the birth of a normal child) range from 10% to 28%. There is also an increased risk of birth defects, health problems, and behavior problems with ART infants (Hansen et al., 2013; Klemetti, Sevón, Gissler, & Hemminki, 2006; Zhan et al., 2013). In addition, high-tech medical intervention is expensive. With the exception of IUI, which might only cost $300 per attempt, the average cost of an IVF attempt (or *cycle*) is $12,400 (Resolve, 2014). If none of the zygotes develop successfully, the procedure (and expense) is wasted. But some clinics are now offering a "guaranteed live birth plan"—at a cost that increases, of course, with maternal age and can surpass $30,000.

Genetic Defects

Each year, about 120,000 neonates in the United States (3% of all births) are born with a birth defect—also known as a **genetic disorder**. The most common of these are heart defects, orofacial clefts (such as cleft palate), and Down syndrome (see Table 6.2). In addition, over 1,150 rare diseases (each found in fewer than 200,000 people) affect some 25 million Americans.

Genetic defects include abnormalities at both the chromosomal and genetic levels. An incorrect number of chromosomes (either too many or too few) results in particular, and often devastating, defects. Humans normally have 22 **autosomal chromosome pairs**. They also have one pair of **sex chromosomes**; women have two X chromosomes, and men have one X and one Y. One chromosome from each pair is passed on to a child, so the child receives half from each parent. As this inheritance is taking place, however, defects in the process can arise. To determine whether a person has a chromosomal abnormality, the chromosomes are collected (through a blood sample), stained, and—to put it simply—photographed. The images are then arranged in pairs in what is called a **karyotype** (see Figure 6.2).

Table 6.2 Most Common Birth Defects and Genetic Disorders

Heart defects	1 in 100 to 200
Orofacial clefts	1 in 700 to 1,000
Down syndrome	1 in 800
Neural tube defect	1 in 1,000
Autism spectrum disorders	3.4 to 6.7 per 1,000

Sources: Center for Disease Control and Prevention (http://www.cdc.gov/ncbddd/bd/default.htm); National Down Syndrome Society (http://www.ndss.org).

Problems emerge for individuals born with abnormalities in the number or structure of their chromosomes. These abnormalities can usually be traced to preconception, when the egg or sperm was developing. The most common example of this is an extra chromosome.

Figure 6.2 A Karyotype of a Healthy Male

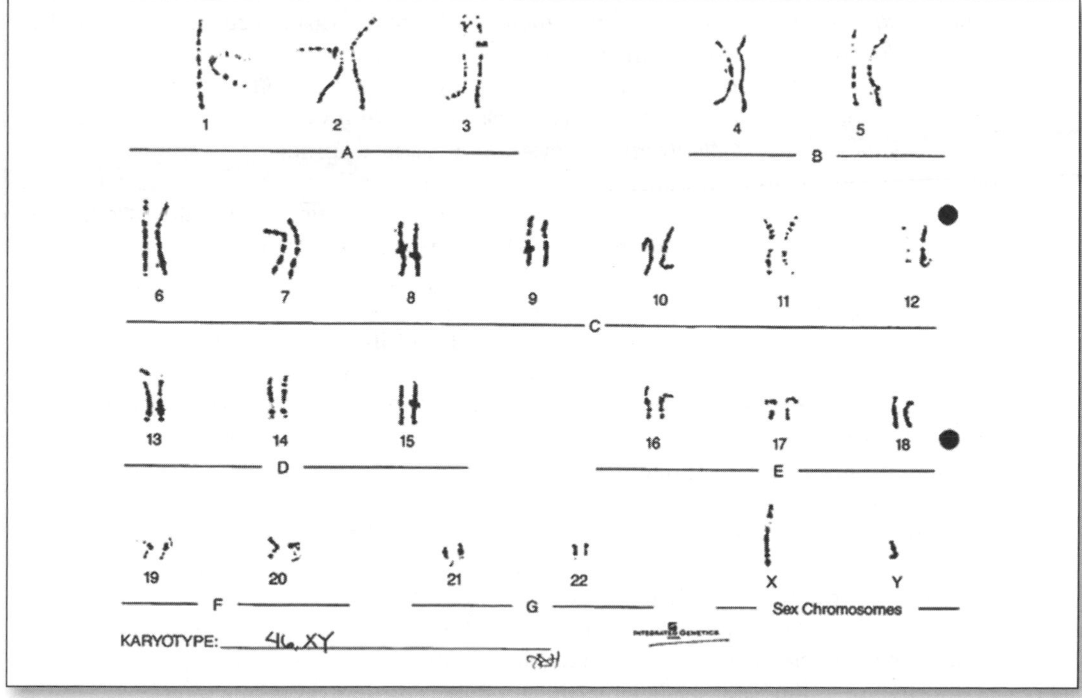

Down syndrome occurs when there is an extra 21st chromosome. The genetic abnormality results in particular facial features, some degree of mental impairment, and various health problems, such as heart defects.

When there is an extra X chromosome in males, their sex chromosome pair is a triad instead: XXY. This is known as **Klinefelter syndrome** and causes a variety of physical (e.g., small testicles) and reproductive problems (e.g., reduced fertility). Sometimes, a sex chromosome is missing, as in the case of **Turner syndrome**, where a female has only one X chromosome. This syndrome results in such physical problems as short stature and a failure of the ovaries to develop. In some cases, just a portion of a chromosome is missing, such as with ***cri du chat*** ("cry of cat") **syndrome**, where a deleted section of chromosome number 5 causes—along with other, more severe symptoms—a strange, high-pitched cry in babies.

As if this were not complicated enough, chromosomal anomalies are just the tip of the iceberg. The sheer number of individual genes in the human body presents another level of complexity. Some 20,000 to 25,000 genes (the number is still being debated) are located on our chromosomes. Made up of amino acids, our genes are the blueprints of development. The full complement of genes in individuals is known as their **genome**. In 2003, **the Human Genome Project**, after a 13-year international endeavor, successfully identified each of the genes and their chromosomal location. The project has spawned nearly endless opportunities for biologists to analyze the results, and new discoveries will likely continue indefinitely. Even a single abnormal gene can cause a birth defect. For some genetic problems, if either parent has the faulty gene, the defect can be passed on to the infant. This is called **dominant inheritance**. Examples include a form of dwarfism called achondroplasia and a connective tissue condition known as Marfan syndrome.

Other genetic diseases are only inherited when both parents pass the same abnormal gene on to their child. Examples of this **recessive inheritance** include Tay-Sachs disease (a fatal nervous system disorder) and cystic fibrosis (a disorder of the lungs and other organs). Metabolic disorders, such as **phenylketonuria (PKU)**, are usually caused by recessive genes. With **X-linked inheritance**, sons can inherit a genetic abnormality through their mother's X chromosome. Hemophilia (a blood-clotting disorder) and Duchenne muscular dystrophy (progressive muscle weakness) are examples.

Some defects are due to a combination of more than one abnormal gene—or of both genetic and environmental causes. This is called **multifactorial inheritance**. Cleft lip or cleft palate, neural tube defects (e.g., spina bifida), and some heart defects are examples. Spina bifida, for instance, can be caused by genetic factors as well as such environmental factors such as a high fever during pregnancy, a vitamin deficiency, or the mother's use of a certain drug for treating epileptic seizures (see Spina Bifida Association's website: http://www.sbaa.org).

There are more than 4,000 identified chromosomal and genetic disorders [Preview Question]. Fortunately, most are extremely rare. The March of Dimes Foundation is an excellent source of information on this topic, and they are the source of the statistics cited in this chapter unless otherwise noted. Their website (http://www.marchofdimes.com) offers statistics, detailed descriptions, and references to further information. Another useful source of information is the National Organization for Rare Disorders (http://www.rarediseases.org).

Some disorders or potential birth defects can be identified during pregnancy using simple blood tests (e.g., the recently developed cell-free fetal DNA testing), **amniocentesis**, **chorionic villus sampling (CVS)**, or **ultrasound**. When defects are identified early enough in pregnancy, prenatal surgery can be performed to repair such problems as urinary blockages or certain heart defects. However, for most disorders, no treatment is available until the fetus is delivered. Still, early detection can allow parents and physicians to prepare for the child's arrival.

Although there are few treatments available to cure birth defects, prospective parents can proactively minimize their likelihood. Women can prepare for conception by cleansing their bodies of potential teratogens—including alcohol and tobacco—several months prior to possible pregnancy. Using a barrier method of contraception for several months—rather than a birth control pill—can also allow a woman's body to purge itself of excess hormones. Men can help by improving the quality of their sperm. According to the Mayo Clinic (http://www.mayoclinic.com), men can increase their likelihood of making hardy, energetic sperm by taking multivitamins, reducing stress, getting regular exercise, and maintaining a healthy weight. Men should avoid toxins and recreational drugs, steroids, tobacco, and even hot tubs, hot baths, and saunas (the heat can lower the sperm count) for at least 70 days, as it takes this long for new sperm to complete their development cycle.

Box 6.2 Preventing Food Allergies in Children?

Food allergies are a serious problem for many people. For example, 1% to 2% of the population in many Western countries is allergic to peanuts. One of the hottest debates among allergy experts is whether a woman should eat peanut or tree nuts while pregnant. According to at least one recent prospective study, the answer is yes. The results from almost 11,000 mothers and children were clear: The more peanuts and tree nuts the mothers consumed while pregnant, the less likely her child was to develop an allergy to those nuts (Frazier, Camargo, Malspeis, Willett, & Young, 2013).

Maternal Problems During Pregnancy

Pregnant women face various health issues and potential problems during pregnancy. Three common ones will be mentioned: miscarriage, ectopic pregnancy, and psychological distress. *Miscarriages* are pregnancy losses that end before 20 weeks of gestation (after 20 weeks, pregnancy losses are called *stillbirths*). Miscarriages are very common; as many as half of all pregnancies are believed to end this way—often before the mother is aware she is pregnant. That is because most miscarriages occur early, before the 12th week. A wide range of issues—including chromosomal abnormalities, hormonal imbalances, uncontrolled diabetes, injuries to the abdomen, and substance abuse—can cause miscarriages. However, in a majority of cases, the cause is simply unknown.

Another relatively common pregnancy problem occurs when the fertilized egg implants outside the uterus, usually in the fallopian tube. This is called an *ectopic* ("out of place") or *tubal* pregnancy and occurs in about 2% of pregnancies. The embryo is unable to survive and must be removed surgically in order to protect the mother's health.

There are a number of potential sources of psychological distress for women (and men) during pregnancy. These include stress, anxiety, and depression. Stress, for example, results from strains in intimate and family relationships, financial and employment concerns, and pregnancy-related problems. How that stress and anxiety is dealt with may affect fetal growth and the risk of having a baby with a low birth weight (Dunkel Schetter, 2011). The fetus may be especially sensitive or vulnerable to the mother's psychological state, as revealed by differences in motor and mental development. Children who experienced prenatal stress have accelerated development in some domains (Sandman, Davis, & Glynn, 2012) but also more behavioral problems (Glover, 2011).

LABOR AND CHILDBIRTH

If all goes well, a pregnant woman, after about 40 weeks of pregnancy, will begin to feel frequent and regular contractions. These contractions cause the cervix to shorten and dilate in preparation for delivery. The average labor lasts 12 to 14 hours for the first baby but is often shorter for subsequent children. When the contractions are between 5 and 10 minutes apart, it is time to go to the hospital or birthing center or—for about 1% of women—to prepare for a home birth.

Vaginal childbirth is divided into three stages. Stage 1 is the labor phase. This stage lasts until the cervix dilates to about 10 centimeters. These contractions may seem like strong menstrual cramps to some women, but for others, they are shockingly painful. The comedian Bill Cosby, based on what he has observed as a veteran of five births, likened his wife's labor pain to grabbing your lower lip and pulling it over your head! Stage 2 involves pushing and delivery. This stage may take from a few minutes to a few hours. Stage 3 consists of expulsion of the placenta and lasts from 10 to 60 minutes. In all, a vaginal birth can take 12 hours or longer.

In the United States, it is common for couples to choose a childbirth method. The two most common ones are the **Bradley method of childbirth** (also called *husband-coached childbirth*) and **Lamaze**. Both approaches use classes to teach various ways of coping with the pain, such as relaxation techniques and deep-breathing exercises. The Bradley method aims to avoid the use of pain medications unless absolutely necessary, whereas the Lamaze approach is neutral on the issue. The Bradley method also involves the baby's father as birth coach and focuses on good nutrition and exercise during pregnancy.

When pain medication is needed, two types of drugs may be used: **analgesics** or **anesthesia**. Analgesics are injected or given intravenously to relieve pain without the total loss of feeling or muscle movement. Anesthesia, including spinal and epidural blocks, is given through injection and temporarily cuts off pain sensations in an area.

The epidural is a longer-lasting procedure and may involve placement of a catheter in the spinal area. This form of pain management is less likely than others to affect the baby, but it is not without risks to both mother and baby. One major disadvantage of these procedures is that they may affect motor control as well, so a woman's pushes might be less effective for birthing. The most extreme form of pain management is general anesthesia, resulting in loss of consciousness of the woman, sedation of the fetus, and additional risk to both.

The single greatest risk to a baby during delivery is experiencing a shortage of oxygen (**hypoxia**) or total lack of oxygen (**anoxia**). Depending on the degree and duration of the intrauterine hypoxia, the fetus can suffer brain damage or death. Consequently, prior to delivery, a monitor is often attached to the fetus's head to gauge the oxygen content of his or her blood and thus to monitor fetal distress. The most common cause of hypoxia is compression of the umbilical cord during delivery. This may then necessitate a **cesarean (C-section)** delivery.

C-sections involve surgically cutting the abdomen and uterus in order to birth the baby. The procedure might be recommended for many different reasons, including breech presentation (the baby's buttocks or feet leading the way down the birth canal), a birth of multiple babies, an otherwise problematic delivery, and increasingly, for convenience and reduction of childbirth stress. In 2011, almost one-third (32.8%) of the more than 4 million childbirths in the United States were C-sections (Morris, 2013). This rate reflects a 41% increase from 1996, when the percentage was 20.7%. However, the World Health Organization has stated that the rate of C-sections *should* be 10% to 15%. When the rate is below 10% or above 15%, maternal mortality increases (World Health Organization, 2012).

Women undergoing C-sections are most often given epidural anesthesia, so they are awake but do not feel any pain. Childbirth then takes only 5 to 10 minutes, but it is considered major surgery. C-sections are considerably more expensive than vaginal births (see Figure 6.1), introduce new risks to the mother (such as infection), and require more time to heal. However, the procedure does have certain advantages, such as it can be scheduled, it requires a total of 20 minutes to perform, and it lowers the risk of birth-related litigation associated with hypoxia and other birthing problems.

The rate of C-sections in the United States has increased dramatically. However convenient the operation may be, C-sections are not generally better for babies. Based on a sample of more than 5.5 million births, the neonatal mortality rate was found to be 1.77 per 1,000 live births with C-sections but only 0.62 per 1,000 with vaginal deliveries (MacDorman, Declercq, Menacker, & Malloy, 2006). Some of the mortality can be accounted for by the fact that high-risk births are typically handled with C-sections. However, vaginal births do provide at least three benefits: They release hormones in the neonate that promote healthy lung function; they physically compress the baby during labor, thereby removing fluid from the lungs; and they also prepare the mother's body for breastfeeding. Moreover, the surgical risks to both mother and baby (e.g., accidental cutting of baby, infection, and surgical complications for both mother and baby) do not occur in vaginal births.

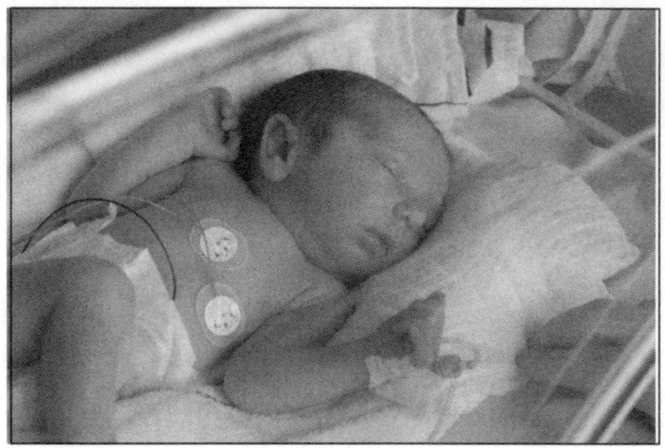

Photo 6.2a A preterm baby.

Source: © iStockphoto.com/metinkiyak

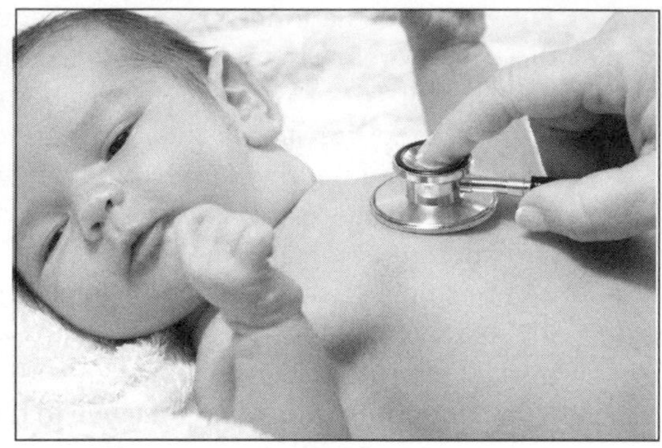

Photo 6.2b A full-term baby.

Source: © iStockphoto.com/benedamiroslav

THE PRETERM BABY

Each year, about 4 million infants are born in the United States; there were 3.95 million U.S. babies born in 2011 (Martin, Hamilton, Ventura, Osterman, & Matthews, 2013; see Photos 6.2a and 6.2b). The average neonate in the United States weighs in at 7.3 lb. (3316 g) and is about 20 in. long (Martin, Hamilton, Ventura et al., 2013). However, there is a wide variability in the weight of newborns. The heaviest newborn was delivered in Italy and tipped the scales at 22 lb. 8 oz., according to the Guinness Book of World Records (Glenday, 2006). The relative number of births of multiples (twins, triplets, etc.) has risen dramatically since 1980, largely due to a rise in fertility treatments. Still, less than 4% of births involve multiples, and 96% of the multiple births are twins. These infants are six times more likely to arrive preterm than are singletons (Martin, Hamilton, Ventura et al., 2013).

A newborn is considered *preterm* if he or she is born prior to 37 weeks of gestation. Some babies are born having a low birth weight, but they are not necessarily preterm. A baby with a low birth weight weighs less than 5.5 lb. (or 2,500 g). These infants are sometimes subdivided into *moderately low birth weight* (3.3 to 5.5 lb. or 1,500 to 2,499 g) and *very low birth weight* (less than 3.3 lbs. or 1,500 g). In 2011, 8.1% of U.S. newborn were classified as low birth weight and 1.4% as very low birth weight. However, the percent of low-birth-weight African American newborns is 13.3%, more than twice the rate of 7.1% found in non-Hispanic Whites (Martin, Hamilton, Ventura, Osterman, & Matthews, 2013).

Premature births are not just a problem in the United States: Every year, across the globe, about 15 million children are born too soon (World Health Organization, 2012). Ten countries account for 60% of the premature births. Eight of those countries, including the United States, are also in the top ten most populous countries. The ten countries with the most numbers of premature births are listed in Table 6.3.

Prematurity, and particularly for those babies born with a very low birth weight, is linked to a variety of health problems, including increased morbidity. The earlier the birth, the greater the risk for long-term problems. Premature births (determined by gestational age) are related to increased risk of a variety of problems, including cognitive delays, mental disabilities, cerebral palsy, attention-deficit/hyperactivity disorder (ADHD), and school problems (Moster, Lie, & Markestad, 2008; Wolke, 1998). Whether a child experiences any of those problems depends on various factors, the most important being how early the birth occurred.

Table 6.3 The Top Ten Countries, by Rank of Premature Births

Country	Population
1. India	1,236 million
2. China	1,355 million
3. Nigeria	177 million
4. Pakistan	196 million
5. Indonesia	253 million
6. United States of America	318 million
7. Bangladesh	166 million
8. Philippines	107 million
9. Democratic Republic of Congo	77 million
10. Brazil	202 million

Sources: World Health Organization, 2012; Central Intelligence Agency, 2014.

Who is at risk for having a baby born too soon? The major risk factors for preterm delivery include being an adolescent, smoking, having a previous preterm birth or a birth of multiples, being underweight or obese, having certain medical conditions (e.g., diabetes, hypertension), and experiencing high levels of stress (Goldenberg, Culhane, Iams, & Romero, 2008; Watson, Rayner, & Forster, 2013). The annual societal economic cost (medical, educational, lost productivity) associated with preterm birth in the United States is more than $26 billion per year or $51,600 per infant born premature (Institute of Medicine, 2006). Obviously, reducing the percentage of preterm births should be not only a personal goal for families but a societal goal as well.

TRANSITIONING TO PARENTHOOD

Newborns require almost constant care. They must be fed every few hours. After feeding, they need to be burped. They cry a lot; on average, newborns cry two hours a day. Their diapers need to be frequently changed—or they will develop diaper rash and cry even more. Newborns wake up every few hours during the night to be fed. When not sleeping or eating, they need stimulation or they will get bored—and cry. Once entertained, they need time to wind down or they will get overstimulated and—you guessed it—cry. As gratifying and joyful as parenthood is, it also represents a major life change that is stressful and, for most parents, exhausting [Preview Question].

Consider just some of the many other time-related adjustments that must be made. Overnight, the entire focus and structure of the parents' routine changes and becomes centered on the newborn. Significant sleep disruptions occur because the newborn is waking every few hours for feeding (Medina, Lederhos, & Lillis, 2009). Many new mothers stop working outside the home, whether for a few weeks, months, or many years. In the United States, few employers provide paid maternity leave. So most families with newborns face a decrease in family income. To make up for that lost income, some fathers opt to work longer hours or take on a second job. Sometimes new mothers do not have the choice but must return to work within weeks after childbirth. Achieving a balance between work and home represents a considerable challenge for both parents.

This does not mean the mothers who are at home are not working. Some studies find that new mothers spend the equivalent of 80 hours or more working in the home. The amount of time spent with children is most directly a function of parental employment status. For example, parents who do not work outside the home spend an average of 63.8 hours with children versus 49.4 hours for those who work part-time and 36.5 hours for those working full-time (Milkie, Mattingly, Nomaguchi, Bianchi, & Robinson, 2004).

The arrival of a newborn is not simply a time management challenge for the parents. It affects all individuals in the family. With the newborn the focus of attention, family roles need to be adjusted and renegotiated, and the newborn's siblings are likely to feel ignored. Given all the disruptions and changes, it should not be a surprise that the majority of couples report an increase in marital conflict and a decline in feelings of love (Holmes, Sasaki, & Hazen, 2013). How couples cope with the transition is affected by many considerations, such as prior expectations, the infant's temperament, maternal depressive symptoms, and the quality of co-parenting (Flykt et al., 2011; Rodriguez & Adamsons, 2012; Schoppe-Sullivan & Mangelsdorf, 2013).

Another set of adjustments concerns personal identity. Suddenly, the wife and husband have new labels: mother and father. In a longitudinal study of 96 couples who became parents (Cowan & Cowan, 1992, 2012), participants were asked during pregnancy to identify their different identities and what proportion each identity occupied. Common identities for the women included partner/lover, worker, friend, daughter, and mother. Figure 6.3 shows the decline both parents experienced in their identity as partner/lover from before the baby was born to six months after birth. As is evident, the partner/lover aspect of identity can easily get squeezed out by the ongoing demands and needs of the newest member of the family.

With the decreased time and energy devoted to their partners, new parents are likely to report a decline in marital satisfaction. For example, one investigation into the topic replicated the common finding that marital satisfaction decreases after the birth of a child in comparison to couples who did not have a child (Lawrence, Rothman, Cobb, Rothman, & Bradbury, 2008). This decline is shown in Figure 6.4. However, the decline was not so severe in couples who had planned for the child and couples with higher levels of marital satisfaction.

The decline in satisfaction is due to a variety of reasons, such as fatigue, stress, and reduced intimacy among parents. An additional cause can be the low levels of paternal involvement in child care. The key factors that are believed to drive fathers' involvement in child care are

Figure 6.3 Role Changes With the Onset of Parenthood

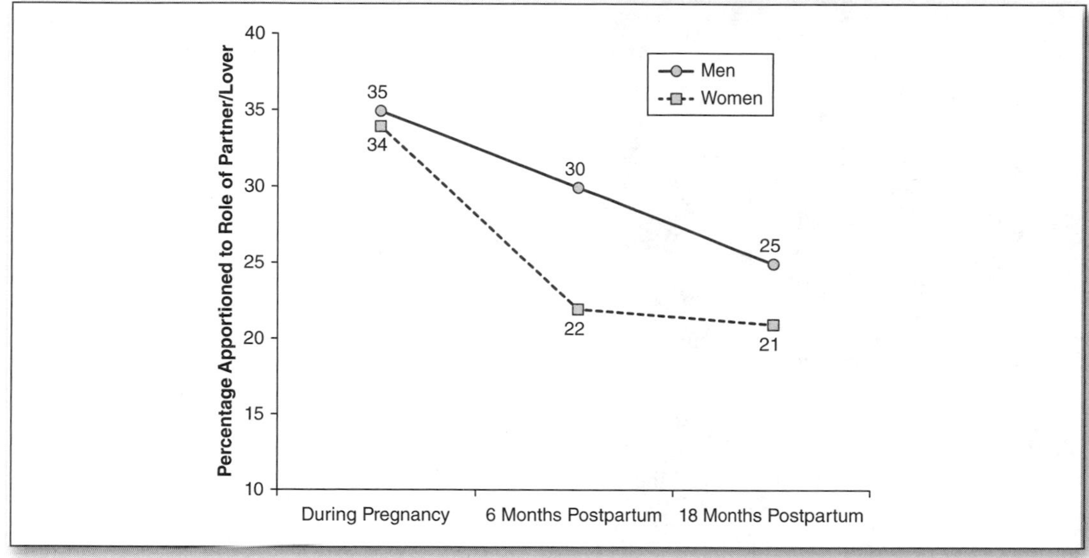

Source: Based on Cowan & Cowan, 1992.

Figure 6.4 Decline in Marital Satisfaction

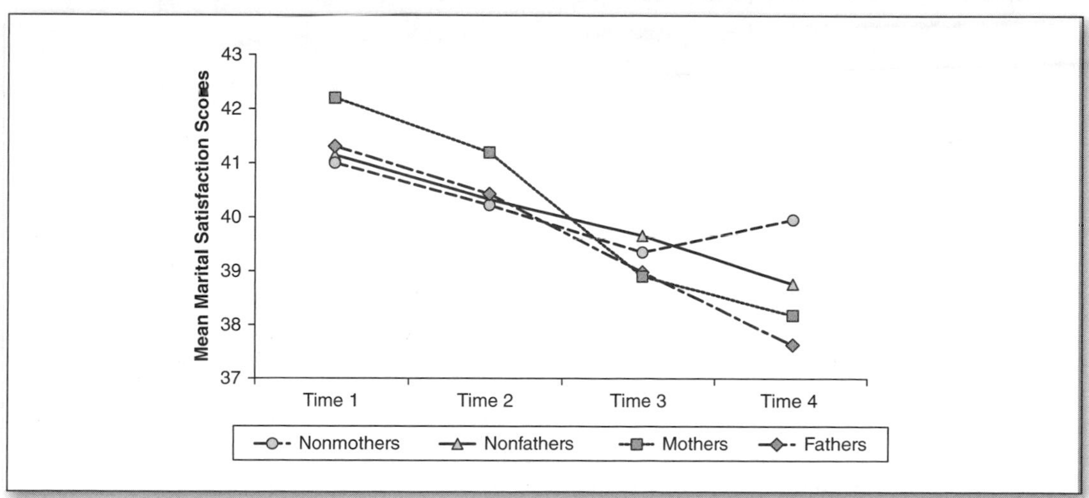

Source: Based on Lawrence et al., 2008.

Notes: Time 1 = 3 months after marriage; Time 2 = 1 month pre-birth*; Time 3 = 6 months post-birth*; Time 4 = 12 months post-birth*

*For couples who did not have children, a comparable duration in time was used for this assessment.

Photo 6.3 Fathers changed diapers even in 1631, as depicted in this painting by Adriaen Brouwer titled *Smell*.

Source: bpk, Berlin/Bildarchiv Preussischer Kulturbesitz/Art Resource, NY

motivation, skills (and self-confidence), and the marital relationship, along with social supports (Pleck & Masciadrelli, 2004). Paternal motivation can be influenced by a variety of considerations: the child's gender (some fathers are more motivated to interact with sons than daughters), whether they have a biological relationship to the child, the extent to which their own father was involved, whether fatherhood is tied to their identity, and, of course, their beliefs. Some men may model their own father's involvement level, whether high or low (see Photo 6.3). Other men may be unhappy with their own father's lack of involvement and seek to compensate.

Mothers can also play a key role in paternal involvement. If necessary, some mothers are happy to teach their husbands some of the childcare skills, such as changing diapers—a skill they may have already learned while babysitting during adolescence. However, some mothers are reluctant to let their husbands engage in any childcare responsibilities. These "gatekeeper" mothers tend to have traditional conceptions of family roles, set rigid standards for father involvement, and regard child care as exclusively their role. In one study, 20% of mothers were classified as gatekeepers (Allen & Hawkins, 1999).

PARENTING THE NEWBORN

In their role as parents of a newborn, mothers and fathers must perform a variety of mundane recurrent tasks, including feeding, clothing, diapering, comforting, and stimulating. These tasks require learning caregiving techniques that work with that particular child, often through trial and error. Fortunately, newborns are forgiving. They are also quick to inform parents about caregiving mistakes and when their needs are not being met. For first-time parents, it is a gradual process of learning about how to care for an infant as well as understanding that particular infant's needs and personality.

In contrast to a gradual learning process, two pediatricians proposed a provocative idea in the late 1970s about the importance of the time right after birth of a newborn. Their idea was that there existed a critical but short period of time right after childbirth when parents fall in love with their baby. Their idea and research investigations into it are described in Box 6.3.

Box 6.3 The Fiction of Mother-Infant Bonding at Birth

As important as it is to begin to form a loving relationship with a newborn child, two pediatricians got carried away with the idea.

In 1972, Marshall Klaus and John Kennell, along with colleagues, published an experimental study in the prestigious *New England Journal of Medicine.* They argued that there was a sensitive period of development shortly after birth when the mother was uniquely open for **bonding** with her new infant. If the mother did not have the opportunity to bond with the newborn—perhaps the neonate was premature and had to be placed in an incubator—then they argued the mother would not be able to bond with the child. To support their theory, they conducted an experimental study with 28 low-income, unmarried, **primiparous** (first-time) mothers. Half the mothers were randomly assigned to the experimental group, where they were given their newborn right after birth for an hour plus an additional five hours of contact on each of the next three days. The other group formed a traditional care group. Their exposure to their infants was limited to every four hours, when they fed the babies. One month later, all the mothers participated in an interview and a videotaped observation of how they fed their infant.

According to Klaus and colleagues, support for their hypotheses was found. On two of the interview questions, the mothers in the extended contact group were more likely to respond in the bonded way. Two of the 25 coded behaviors from the extended contact group provided evidence of more face-to-face gazing and more time touching the baby. The study and concept received a great deal of attention and resulted in changes to hospital postpartum procedures. No longer were babies whisked away to the newborn ward. Instead, healthy newborns were kept with their parents until discharge, usually about one day after birth. However, the original study contained a number of serious methodological problems (Lamb, 1982), and other researchers were largely unable to replicate the results (Grossman, Thane, & Grossman, 1981). In a book examining the bonding research, Eyer (1992) concluded that the concept is "scientific fiction."

Although bonding, *per se*, has not proven to be a valid construct, the development of a bond between the mother and newborn, as well as father and newborn, is an important postpartum task. The development of that close, loving relationship is promoted by parental sensitivity and, for mothers, breastfeeding. Another key postpartum task is to develop effective co-parenting between partners. One example of a hurdle to the successful accomplishment of these tasks will be described—the problem of **postpartum depression**.

Parental Sensitivity

The process of effectively performing common childrearing tasks is captured by the construct of sensitivity (also called *responsivity*), as was mentioned in Chapter 3. Both John Bowlby and Mary Ainsworth recognized the importance of this quality of parenting in their attachment theory. Sensitive parenting requires attunement to the infant child's cues and quick and appropriate responses. Sensitivity can be readily observed when an infant becomes distressed due to a need (such as hunger) or perhaps a fear. Three key indicators of a parent's sensitivity are how rapidly the parent responds, the dependability of the parent's response, and how successful the parent is at comforting the child. Being a sensitive caregiver requires attentiveness, empathy, correct interpretation of the infant's cues, and nonintrusiveness combined with emotional availability (Biringen & Robinson, 1991). Sensitive parents are able to quickly relieve their children's anxiety and fears by offering emotional comfort. They also respond to their infants in a flexible and balanced way so, for example, the parent is not overbearing or perhaps frightening to the infant (Solomon & George, 2008).

Breastfeeding

Whether or not to breastfeed a newborn is one of the first decisions a mother must make. On the face of it, it is not a difficult choice. Breastfeeding an infant has a number of advantages. It requires close contact with the newborn and thus promotes the development of the mother-child relationship. The American Academy of Pediatrics issued a policy statement in 2012 endorsing the practice:

> [B]reastfeeding and the use of human milk confer unique nutritional and nonnutrional benefits to the infant and the mother and, in turn, optimize infant, child, and adult health as well as child growth and development. Recently, published evidence-based studies have confirmed and quantitated the risks of not breastfeeding. Thus, infant feeding should not be considered a lifestyle choice but rather as a basic health issue. (p. 837)

Breast milk helps protect against infectious diseases that cause such problems as diarrhea, **otitis media** (inflammation of the middle ear), and respiratory infections. In this way, it reduces the risk of infant death. It also decreases the likelihood the child will develop diabetes, obesity, or asthma. Mothers themselves also benefit from breastfeeding because it costs nothing (other than the cost of a little more food for the mother), helps them lose excess weight more readily, and reduces the risk of certain types of cancer. Breastfeeding also releases oxytocin and prolactin, hormones that relax the mother and make her feel more nurturing toward her baby (see Photo 6.4).

Despite its obvious advantages, a surprisingly large number of mothers do not breastfeed their infants. In the United States, 77% of newborns are breastfed right after birth. That percentage drops to 49% by 6 months of age and 27% at 12 months (Centers for Disease Control and Prevention, 2013). The American Academy of Pediatrics (2012) recommends exclusive breastfeeding for about 6 months and then continuing breastfeeding, along with introducing solid food, for another 12 months or longer, "as mutually desired by mother and infant" (p. 832).

There are a variety of reasons that some mothers choose not to breastfeed. As many as 80% of mothers experience problems, at least initially (Bergmann et al., 2014). Some of the difficulties experienced include insufficient milk supply, breast pain, embarrassing leakage of milk, or **mastitis** (inflammation of the breasts, most commonly caused by blocked milk ducts). Other mothers find it unpleasant, difficult, time consuming, or too inconvenient, as it requires feeding young infants every three to four hours during the daytime (Schwartz et al., 2002; Taylor, Risica, & Cabral, 2003).

Given that the advantages of breastfeeding far outweigh the disadvantages, the United States Department of Health and Human Services has made it a goal by 2020 to increase the percent of breastfed babies to 60% at six months of age, and 34% at 12 months (American Academy of Pediatrics, 2012). However, that goal may be lofty. The most difficult to convince will be adolescent mothers, lower-income or less-educated mothers, and African American mothers. All these groups of women have significantly lower rates of breastfeeding than do other mothers (Centers for Disease Control and Prevention, 2013). Mothers of unintended births are also less likely to breastfeed (Gipson, Koenig, & Hindin, 2008).

Co-Parenting

In contrast to practices in some countries and traditional parenting in the United States these days, fathers are encouraged to be equally involved in child care with mothers. *Co-parenting*, a concept which recognizes the dynamic nature of family interactions, refers to the extent to which parents work together in their roles as parents (Feinberg, 2002). There are various components to this concept, such as providing support, resolving childrearing disagreements, dividing duties, and managing interaction patterns. During the transition to

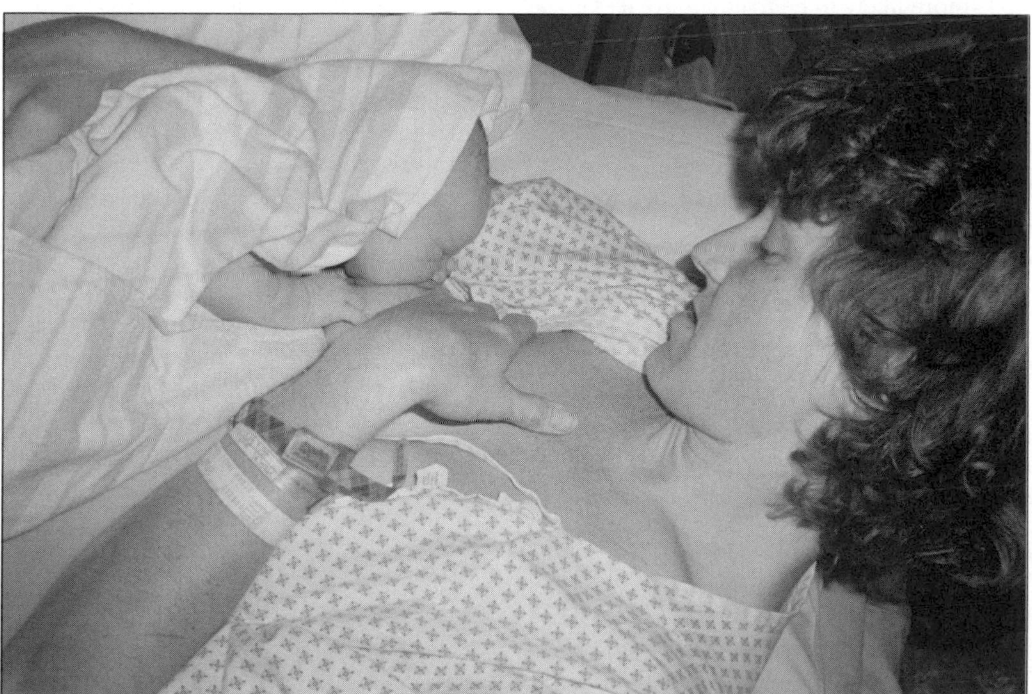

Photo 6.4 A mother in the hospital, learning how to breastfeed her newborn daughter.

Source: Photograph by G. W. Holden

parenthood, these new co-parenting behaviors need to be developed. Couples that had high-quality marital interactions before their child was born were likely to show more supportive co-parenting when their infant was 3.5 months old than couples who did not experience positive marital interactions (Schoppe-Sullivan & Mangelsdorf, 2013). Co-parenting is not only beneficial to the parent-child relationship—supportive co-parenting is also associated with couple satisfaction (McHale & Lindahl, 2011).

Postpartum Depression

Between 12% to 40% of all births (even including those of healthy babies) are accompanied by an unwelcome complication: postpartum depression in the mothers and in fathers (deMontigny, Girard, Lacharité, Dubeau, & Devault, 2013; Field, 2010). This condition is more serious and persistent than "baby blues," a feeling of letdown that subsides in a few days. The "baby blues" are experienced by a majority of new mothers (and probably many fathers, too). Postpartum depression, which can occur anytime during the first year of a baby's life, lasts two weeks or longer and is accompanied by symptoms such as sadness, insomnia, lack of interest, feelings of guilt, low energy, changes in appetite, restlessness, mood swings, and (in more extreme cases) thoughts of suicide. Mothers of unintended children are more at risk for depression (Gipson et al., 2008).

The condition can be dangerous for the baby. Mothers suffering from this syndrome are more likely to be irritable, are less engaged, provide less warmth, and play less frequently than other mothers (Lovejoy, Graczyk, O'Hare, & Neuman, 2000). The mothers may either be passive or more intrusive, are less likely to breastfeed, and are more likely to use harsh punishment (Field, 2010). Infants of depressed mothers are less likely to develop a secure attachment and more likely to have a disorganized attachment (Martins & Gaffan, 2000).

In rare cases, mothers suffer from **postpartum psychosis**, characterized by the loss of ability to discern what is real and what is not. In such a case, the mother may experience delusions, hallucinations, mental disturbances, and have obsessive thoughts about the baby. These mothers are at risk for injuring or even killing their babies (Huysman, 2003). One such mother (Andrea Yates) drowned her five children in a bathtub in 2001.

Fortunately, with appropriate medical care, postpartum depression and psychosis can be treated. The two most common treatment techniques are involvement in support groups and the use of antidepressants. Selective serotonin reuptake inhibitors—marketed under such names as Zoloft, Paxil, and Prozac—have proven to be generally effective treatments (Wisner, Parry, & Piontek, 2002). There are also behavioral interventions, such as teaching mothers to massage their infants. This approach has been shown to be effective in two studies (Field, 2010).

THE PROBLEM OF INFANT MORTALITY

As the theologian Dietrick Bonhoeffer, who died in a Nazi concentration camp, once observed, "The test of the morality of a society is what it does for its children." One of the measures of that test is how often newborn children die. Recall from Chapter 1 that in 17th-century New England, the rate of infant mortality ranged from 10% to 33%. Today, infant death rates are calculated not per hundred but per thousand—indicative of the dramatic decrease in infant deaths achieved over the past 400 years.

The year 2004 was a landmark year for the United States, because that year, the infant mortality rate declined to its lowest level on record: 6.78 per 1,000 live births (U.S. Census Bureau, 2008). The rate has continued to drop, and as of 2013, is now at 6.14 per 1,000 live births (Centers for Disease Control and Prevention, 2014a). The rate has dropped precipitously over the years due to improved health and medical care. For example, in 1900, the rate was 100 deaths per 1,000 births but declined to 47 deaths per 1,000 by 1940. However, there are glaring racial differences. The infant mortality rate for African American women (in 2007) was 13.3 per 1,000 births, about double the overall U.S. rate of 6.8 per 1,000 birth, and 4.6 for Hispanic women (Mathews & Macdorman, 2011). About half of the infants who died were born very early (less than 32 weeks of gestation) and the leading causes of death were low birth weight, congenital malformations, and sudden infant death syndrome.

The death of a baby or a developing fetus due to ectopic pregnancy, miscarriage, stillbirth, or infant death is recognized as a traumatic life event and the source of prolonged grief as well as symptoms of post-traumatic stress (Kersting et al., 2013). The loss can be overwhelming for the bereaved parents, who can show a wide range of physical, emotional, and social reactions such as depression, anxiety, weight loss, and isolation. As devastating as the loss may be for parents, if they experience a caring and supporting network of family members and friends and medical personnel, the parents are likely to cope better and show **resilience** (Lang & Carr, 2013).

Surprisingly, the United States does not compare very favorably with the infant mortality rates of many other countries, although the United States is the richest nation in the world in terms of per capita income. According to Central Intelligence Agency estimates, the United States had an infant mortality rate of 6.17 in 2014. There were 173 countries with higher rates, such as Afghanistan, which led all nations with 117.23 deaths per 1,000 live births. However, 50 countries reported lower rates of infant mortality. All the European nations have lower rates than the United States, whose rate was three times higher than that of the city-state with the lowest rate—Monaco. See Figure 6.5 for the infant mortality rates from a sample of countries, including the United States.

Why does the United States have such a relatively high rate of infant mortality? The causes are well known: poverty, lack of education, lifestyle choices (drinking, smoking), and a lack of prenatal care, often due to a lack of health insurance. There is also evidence that the gender of the child and whether or not the child was planned are risk factors (Gipson et al., 2008).

The solutions are clear, but they are difficult to implement. Foremost, all pregnant women need prenatal care, including four important services:

1. Screening and treatment for medical conditions such as diabetes, human immunodeficiency virus (HIV), and obesity
2. Managing of chronic health conditions, including an update of vaccinations and a review of current medications that could be teratogens
3. Identifying and intervening with any behavioral risk factors—such as smoking, alcohol use, and poor nutrition
4. Prescribing prenatal vitamins with folic acid in order to prevent neural tube defects and other problems

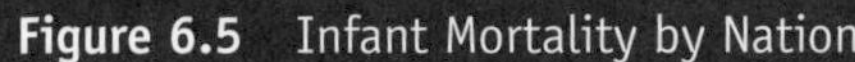

Figure 6.5 Infant Mortality by Nation

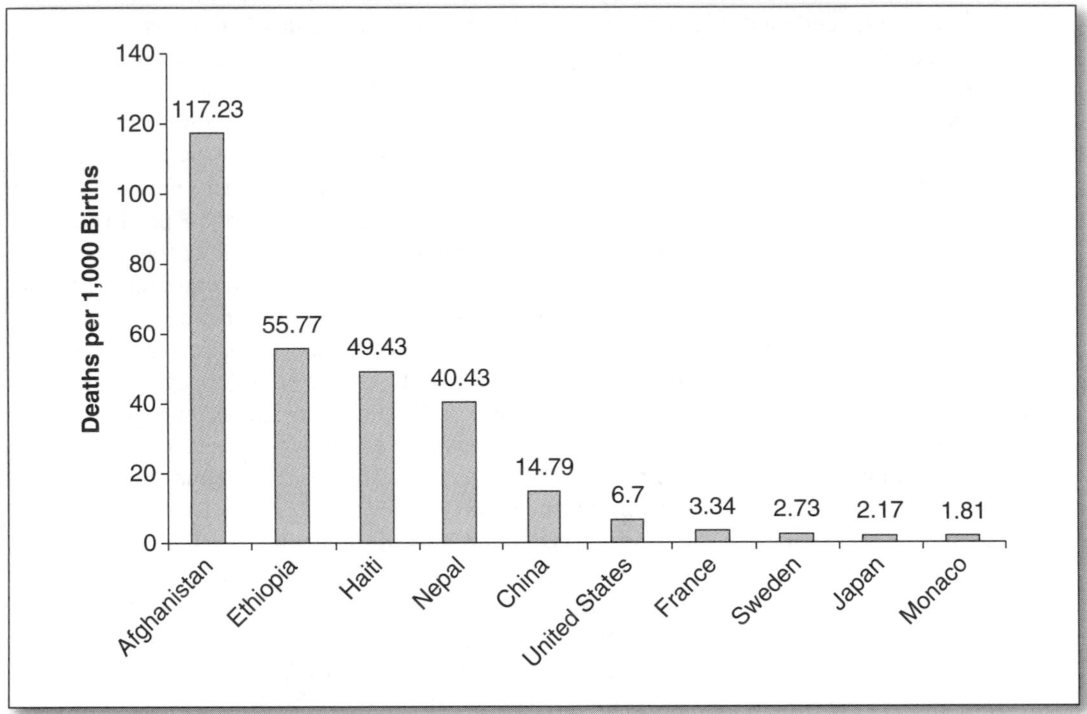

Source: Central Intelligence Agency, 2014.

Most American pregnant women (84%) receive prenatal care during their first trimester (U.S. Department of Health and Human Services, 2008). Another 12.5% begin care during their second trimester. However, 3.6% of women receive late or no care. African American women are more than twice as likely as non-Hispanic White women to receive late or no prenatal care. In addition, being an adolescent, being unmarried, and having low educational attainment are other risk factors for receiving late or no prenatal care. Women in this last group are the most likely to experience infant mortality.

In addition to ending poverty, providing prenatal health care, and increasing education, another strategy designed to reduce infant mortality is to introduce national newborn-screening standards, as recommended by the American College of Medical Genetics (ACMG). The ACMG claims that 29 conditions should be screened for, because with early identification can come early treatment that may avoid potentially serious or fatal health problems. The recommended tests are for certain genetic, metabolic, hormonal, and functional (e.g., hearing) conditions. Except for the hearing assessment, the tests are conducted on a few drops of blood taken from the newborn's heel. Opponents to the screening standards fear the consequences of a loss of privacy and unfair labeling of children, especially in the case of false-positive results.

You can find a reminder of the importance of newborn screening in a mundane place—the diet soda can. Most cans of diet soda (those containing aspartame) have a warning in small print: Contains phenylalanine. A small number of children (1 in 13,500 to 19,000) are born with the genetic disorder PKU. Children with this disorder cannot metabolize phenylalanine due to a missing enzyme. So for them, too much phenylalanine can result in brain damage. However, through a carefully controlled diet, the appropriate level of phenylalanine in the blood can be maintained and infants can develop into healthy children and adults. Currently, all states screen for PKU, but as of 2008, only 11 states (Alaska, Delaware, Iowa, Maryland, Minnesota, Mississippi, New Mexico, New York, Rhode Island, Virginia, and Wyoming) and the District of Columbia screen their newborns for all 29 conditions as recommended by the ACMG.

Preventable Illnesses

Despite the efficacy and availability of preventive health care through childhood vaccinations, parents only immunized about 81% of their children against seven major diseases (polio, measles, tetanus, diphtheria, pertussis [or whooping cough], Haemophilus influenza type B, and hepatitis B) in 2004. It has been estimated that routine childhood immunizations for these seven diseases result not just in saved lives but in savings for society of up to $43 billion (Zhou et al., 2005).

ETHICAL ISSUES

Dramatic and rapid changes in medical technology have given many previously infertile couples the ability to have biological children. However, the advent of reproductive technology has also raised a number of unprecedented ethical and moral questions. Here are just five of the many thorny questions that individuals and society are now or will soon be dealing with:

Genetic Testing

Should people know their genetic profile? Knowing one's genetic profile can lead to early detection and better treatment of hereditary disorders. It can help in making major life decisions, such as what type of occupation to pursue. For example, if you knew you carried genes linked to the early onset of Alzheimer's disease (with symptoms appearing as early as age 30), you probably would not want to go to graduate school. Couples can use their combined genetic profiles to predict what illnesses their children might face and take steps to prepare for or avoid certain outcomes.

But the very presence of this genetic information has its dangers. It could be disseminated, violating an individual's privacy. What if your employer found out that you have the gene for a late-onset debilitating illness? What if your insurance company discovered your hidden abnormality? The potential for discrimination is very real. Consequently, Congress has been debating the topic for years. Finally, in May 2008, the

Genetic Information Nondiscrimination Act (GINA) was signed into law. The law is intended to allow Americans to take advantage of genetic information and treatments without the fear of their genome being used against them.

Designer Babies

Should parents be allowed to select the features and characteristics they want in a child, including known defects? Sperm banks now let prospective parents select features they desire in the child. To increase your chances of a blond child, select a blond-haired donor. But is any feature acceptable to select? According to an article in the *New York Times,* in 3% of cases, parents have selected embryos with a genetic defect. These parents, including deaf and short-stature individuals, desire a child who shares their disability (Sanghavi, 2006).

Cloning

Should parents be allowed to clone themselves or someone else? Cloning technology is improving rapidly; many believe it will not be long before it is possible to clone a human. Are there any circumstances that would merit a human cloning? What if an only child died in an accident and the parents were too old to have another? Or consider this scenario: A world-class athlete and his nonathletic, petite wife desire a child as gifted as his father. Would not cloning be a much more efficient route than fertilization?

Prenatal Screening

Should anyone be allowed to fertility services—even if they might not provide adequate child rearing? What if a pedophile wants help having his own child? The Ethics Committee of the American Society for Reproductive Medicine (2013) recommends that fertility programs withhold services if there are reasonable grounds for suspecting that the prospective parent would not provide adequate child rearing to the offspring. On the other hand, how well can we predict the quality of parenting? Where should we draw the line between the interests of the infertile couple (or individual) and the future welfare of the offspring?

Age Discrimination

Is it an individual's right to bear children at any age? Medical procedures now enable women to bear children into their 60s; the oldest recorded woman to bear a child was 70 (see Box 6.4). Even without medical intervention, some men continue to father babies as septuagenarians. This practice of circumventing nature raises various ethical questions: When is an individual too old to parent? Is it morally wrong to impose on a child a parent who will have serious physical limitations due to aging or who will likely die before the child reaches adulthood? Or is it a greater offense to set age-related restrictions on prospective parents?

Box 6.4 Too Old to Parent?

A lot of attention has been devoted to the problem of teenage parenthood. It is now well known that many problems can occur for both parent and child when young teenagers have children. But what about child bearing and child rearing at the other end of the age spectrum? When is a parent too old to be a new parent? The new record was apparently set by a 70-year-old woman from Mumbai, India, thanks to IVF. She and her 75-year-old retired farmer husband were desperate to have a male heir. So they spent their life savings and took out a loan to fund IVF procedures. The septuagenarian mother delivered, by an emergency C-section, a healthy boy and girl. Imagine these twins' first day of kindergarten—with a 75-year-old mom. Or picture the mother as an 88-year-old, dropping off her teenagers for their first day of college. The former Senator Strom Thurmond from South Carolina, who lived from 1902 to 2003, topped that. He fathered four children with his much younger wife, beginning when he was 68 years old. According to the Guinness Book of World Records, the oldest man to father a child was 92 years and 10 months. These unusual cases raise the question, should there be age limits on medically assisted pregnancies?

CHAPTER SUMMARY

Parenthood represents a major life change as well as a long-term financial commitment; however, many individuals find themselves on the road to parenthood without much forethought. Other couples seek to have children but encounter various medical problems either in trying to get pregnant or during pregnancy. Medical advances made by embryologists in the area of assisted reproductive technology have resulted in a variety of techniques that give hope to many infertile couples. Genetic defects, present in 3% of childbirths, are another hazard for prospective parents.

Typically, after 38 weeks of pregnancy, the woman goes into labor and delivers the newborn. Children who are born premature are at risk for a variety of problems. The arrival of the newborn results in many adjustments for the parents in the areas of finances, roles, stress levels, and marital satisfaction. Couples who plan ahead and have good relationships experience less of a decrease in marital satisfaction.

Caring for the physical needs of the newborn is the central task for new parents. Sensitive caring promotes the development of secure attachment with the child. However, postpartum depression afflicts some new mothers and fathers. The variability in rates of infant mortality around the world highlights the degree to which different societies have developed policies and cultural practices that are hospitable for the healthy development of newborns. Society is also increasingly being confronted with ethical issues created by medical advances intended to help infertile couples. Several questions are raised about who should become parents and what procedures should they be allowed to use.

THOUGHT QUESTIONS

- At some point in your life, do you want to have children? If so, why? What do you see as the benefits and drawbacks?
- What role (if any) should the government play in addressing social health issues such as the high incidence of premature infants or the overuse of cesarean section in childbirth?
- Do you think couples wanting to have a child should routinely be genetically screened to identify potential problems? What are the pros and cons of such an idea?
- How can positive parenting behaviors of newborns, such as breastfeeding and sensitively responding to infant cues, be promoted in new mothers?
- What role should the government play in addressing some of the ethical issues raised by artificial reproductive techniques?

CHAPTER GLOSSARY

amniocentesis A prenatal test for chromosomal abnormalities conducted after the 15th week of pregnancy.

analgesics Childbirth pain medication that is injected or given intravenously to relieve pain without the total loss of feeling or muscle movement.

anesthesia Childbirth pain medication that includes spinal and epidural blocks; it is given intravenously and temporarily stops all feeling in an area.

anoxia Deprivation of oxygen; a severe form of hypoxia.

assisted reproductive technology (ART) Methods developed by embryologists to achieve pregnancy by artificial or partially artificial techniques.

autosomal chromosome pairs Humans normally have 22 autosomal chromosome pairs.

bonding A concept proposed by two pediatricians, asserting that the parent needs to be in physical contact with the newborn shortly after birth in order to develop a love for the infant.

Bradley method of childbirth Designed to promote natural and healthy childbirth without medication or surgery. Classes focus on nutrition, relaxation, and breathing exercises and instructing fathers as labor coaches. Also called *husband-coached childbirth*.

cesarean (C-section) A form of childbirth where a surgical incision is made in the woman's abdomen and uterus in order to remove the fetus.

chorionic villus sampling (CVS) A prenatal test for genetic abnormalities performed between the 10th and 12th weeks of pregnancy.

***cri du chat* syndrome** A chromosomal defect whereby a deleted section of chromosome 5 causes—along with other, more severe symptoms—a strange, high-pitched cry in babies.

dominant inheritance Occurs when, if either parent has a faulty gene, the defect can still be passed on to the infant.

Down syndrome Also known as *Trisomy 21*, this chromosomal abnormality occurs when there is an extra 21st chromosome. These children have genetic abnormalities, particular facial features, mental impairment, and various health problems.

endometriosis A medical problem in women that occurs when uterine tissue grows outside the uterus.

Fetal Alcohol Syndrome (FAS) A disorder found in children of mothers who have ingested alcohol during pregnancy. Depending on the severity, it can result in growth deficiencies, craniofacial abnormalities, and damage to the central nervous system.

gamete intrafallopian transfer (GIFT) Eggs and sperm are inserted by way of a laparoscope into the woman's fallopian tube.

genetic disorder Disorders caused by abnormalities in genes or chromosomes.

genome The entire hereditary information, encoded in DNA, found in an organism.

Human Genome Project A 13-year international endeavor that identified each gene and its chromosomal location.

hypoxia A problem that occurs when the fetus experiences an oxygen deficit, as in the birthing process.

intracytoplasmic sperm injection (ICSI) A single healthy sperm is selected and then injected into a single female egg using a microscopic glass needle. Once fertilization is confirmed, the zygote is inserted into the woman for implantation.

intrauterine insemination (IUI) A procedure in which sperm are placed by a catheter directly into the woman's uterus.

in vitro fertilization (IVF) An egg and sperm are combined in a culture dish. The fertilized egg (zygote) is then transferred into the woman's uterus.

karyotype The full complement of chromosomes in an individual.

Klinefelter syndrome An extra X chromosome is present, creating a male with three sex chromosomes (XXY). This syndrome is associated with a variety of physical (e.g., small testicles) and reproductive problems (e.g., reduced fertility).

Lamaze A popular method of childbirth. Prenatal classes provide instruction on relaxation and breathing techniques to deal with labor pains.

mastitis An inflammation of the breasts most commonly caused by blocked milk ducts.

multifactorial inheritance Defects are due to a combination of more than one abnormal gene—or of both genetic and environmental causes. Examples include cleft lip, schizophrenia, and neural tube defects.

otitis media A painful inflammation (caused by infection) of the middle ear that frequently occurs in infants and young children, typically after experiencing the common cold.

phenylketonuria (PKU) An autosomal recessive genetic disorder resulting in a buildup of phenylalanine due to an enzyme deficiency. If untreated, it can result in neurological damage.

postpartum depression A condition occurring in mothers during the first year of their child's life, characterized by persistent feelings of sadness, low energy, and other problems.

postpartum psychosis Much less common but more serious than postpartum depression, this mental illness may be characterized by hallucinations, delusions, feelings of anxiety and agitation, and suicidal or homicidal thoughts.

preimplantation genetic diagnosis (PGD) Procedures used on embryos prior to implantation to screen for potential genetic or chromosomal defects.

primiparous Refers to a woman who has given birth only one time.

recessive inheritance When both parents carry the same abnormal gene and pass it on to their child.

resilience Positive adaptation in the face of adversity.

sex chromosomes The 23rd pair of chromosomes that determine the child's gender. Males have an X and a Y chromosome; females have two X chromosomes.

teratogens Harmful substances that can damage a developing embryo or fetus. These include drugs, health factors, infections, environmental chemicals, and physical agents.

Turner syndrome A chromosomal abnormality that occurs when a female is missing part or all of one X chromosome. It results in physical abnormalities, health problems, and cognitive disabilities.

ultrasound A machine that uses high-frequency sound waves to construct an image, such as an image of a fetus.

X-linked inheritance When a genetic abnormality is inherited through a mother's X chromosome.

zygote intrafallopian transfer (ZIFT) Like GIFT, except fertilization occurs similarly to IVF, and the resulting zygote(s) is transferred to a fallopian tube.

CHAPTER 7

Parenting Infants and Toddlers

Chapter Preview: True or False?

- Healthy infants cry an average of one hour a day.
- Parental warmth is not an individual trait; it is a *relational* construct.
- Parents discipline toddlers up to 20 times an hour.

In the first three years of life, children change dramatically—more so than during any other span of just 1,095 days. On average, height increases 60% from an average of 20 in. (51 cm) at birth to 33 in. (84 cm), and weight increases almost fivefold from an average of 7.5 lb. (3.4 kg) to 33 lb. (15 kg). During this period, children learn to communicate through language, begin developing a self-concept, discover ways to regulate their emotions, and become increasingly competent in social interactions. This chapter covers parenting as it relates to some of the many changes that take place in infants (birth to 12 months old) and toddlers (one to three years old).

PARENTING INFANTS

Recall that Bradley's first task for parents is keeping the child healthy and safe. Parents establish a healthy trajectory by providing appropriate nutrition, ensuring adequate sleep, and taking the infant to well-baby doctor visits. Breastfeeding has frequently been shown to provide a protective effect for infants by its immunizing ability, resulting in fewer incidents and shorter durations of acute respiratory infections and diarrhea (e.g., López-Alarcón, Villalpando, & Fajardo, 1997). Breastfeeding promotes the attachment relationship (Jansen, de Weerth, & Riksen-Walraven, 2008). Closely related to breastfeeding is affectionately touching the infant. Touching an infant is linked to various positive outcomes, while touch deprivation can have negative effects on development (Field, 2010).

Parents also need to begin the practice of taking the infant to well-baby visits. These trips to the pediatrician begin at one month of age. They help monitor the infant's physical and motor development as well as give the opportunity to regularly immunize the infant on schedule (see http://www.cdc.gov/vaccines/parents/infants-toddlers.html). There has been a great deal of recent controversy over possible unintended negative side effects of immunization. See Box 7.1 for a discussion of the myth regarding the role of vaccines in causing autism spectrum disorders.

Box 7.1 The Vaccine-Autism Controversy

In 1998, a British physician named Andrew Wakefield and his colleagues published a paper reporting that within one month of receiving the measles-mumps-rubella (MMR) vaccine, 12 children (12 to 24 months) began to show signs of autism or other problems. He subsequently published a second paper purporting to provide more evidence of the link. Many parents of children with autism embraced this newest proposed cause of autism and began campaigns to change or eliminate child vaccination laws. However, since that time, more than 20 epidemiologic studies have tested that hypothesis—and found no evidence in support of several possible explanations of a link (Gerber & Offit, 2009). Close examination of the studies by Wakefield show a variety of critical flaws. However, damage has been done to the reputation of the risks of childhood immunizations, contributing to the problem of undervaccination (Feemster & Offit, 2013). Currently, only about 68.4% of children in the United States receive all their vaccinations (America's Health Rankings, 2014). A fascinating account of this controversy can be found in *Autism's False Prophets: Bad Science, Risky Medicine, and the Search for a Cure* by Paul Offit (2008).

Daily Routines, Sleep, and Infant Crying

In addition to providing basic health and safety measures, establishing healthy infant development trajectories is done by creating daily routines. An infant is not born as a *tabula rasa* or blank slate, as Aristotle and John Locke believed. Rather, infants are equipped with a variety of behavioral systems ready to be activated. These systems include reflexes (e.g., sucking and grasping), sensory abilities (e.g., orienting to sound), and crying. Babies sleep, eat, fuss, and cry, and—fortunately for parents—also smile, vocalize, and engage in self-play. Social smiling emerges at about three months of age, as do more advanced vocalizations. By 6 to 10 months of age, infants typically begin to crawl. At about 12 months, they begin to walk and speak words, and their infancy gives way to toddlerhood.

The amount of time spent in these basic behaviors changes markedly as the infant grows. Newborns spend more time sleeping than any other single activity. Sixty-five percent of a newborn's day is spent sleeping (averaging 16–17 hours), but that decreases to 57% by the end of the first year (see Photo 7.1). However, the number of hours a baby sleeps is affected by both genetic and environmental factors (Touchette et al., 2013). Gradually, stretches of nighttime sleeping lengthen. For instance, a sample of Dutch parents reported that from midnight to 6:00 A.M., two-week-old newborns sleep 4.9 hours, but one-year-old infants sleep almost all 6 hours (Meijer & van den Wittenboer, 2007). See Figure 7.1 for changes in the time spent sleeping over the first year.

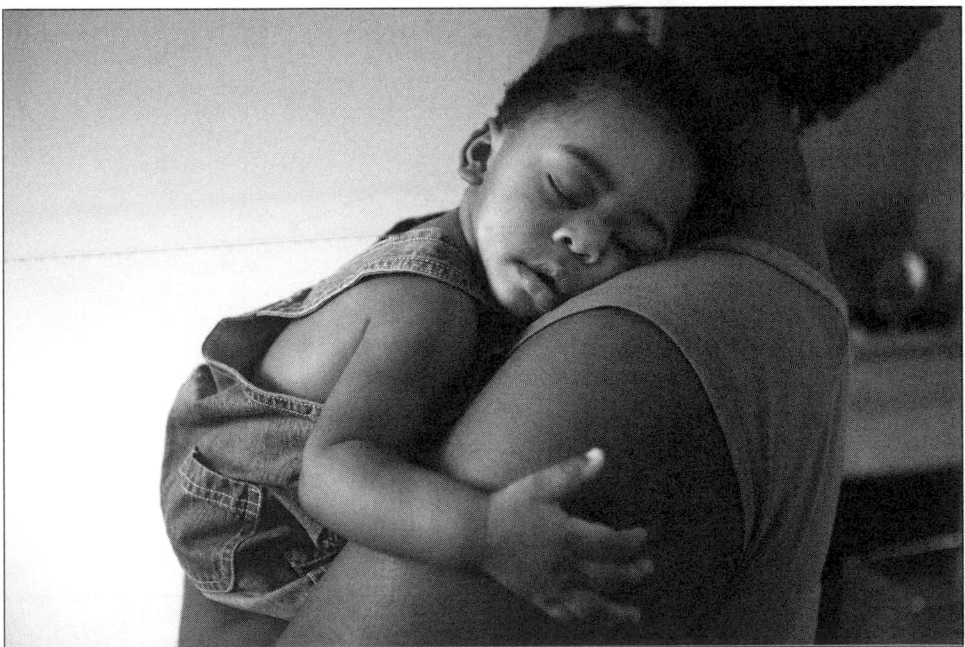

Photo 7.1 A parent and an infant.

Source: Rayes/Digital Vision/Thinkstock

Figure 7.1 Change in Sleeping Time During the First Year

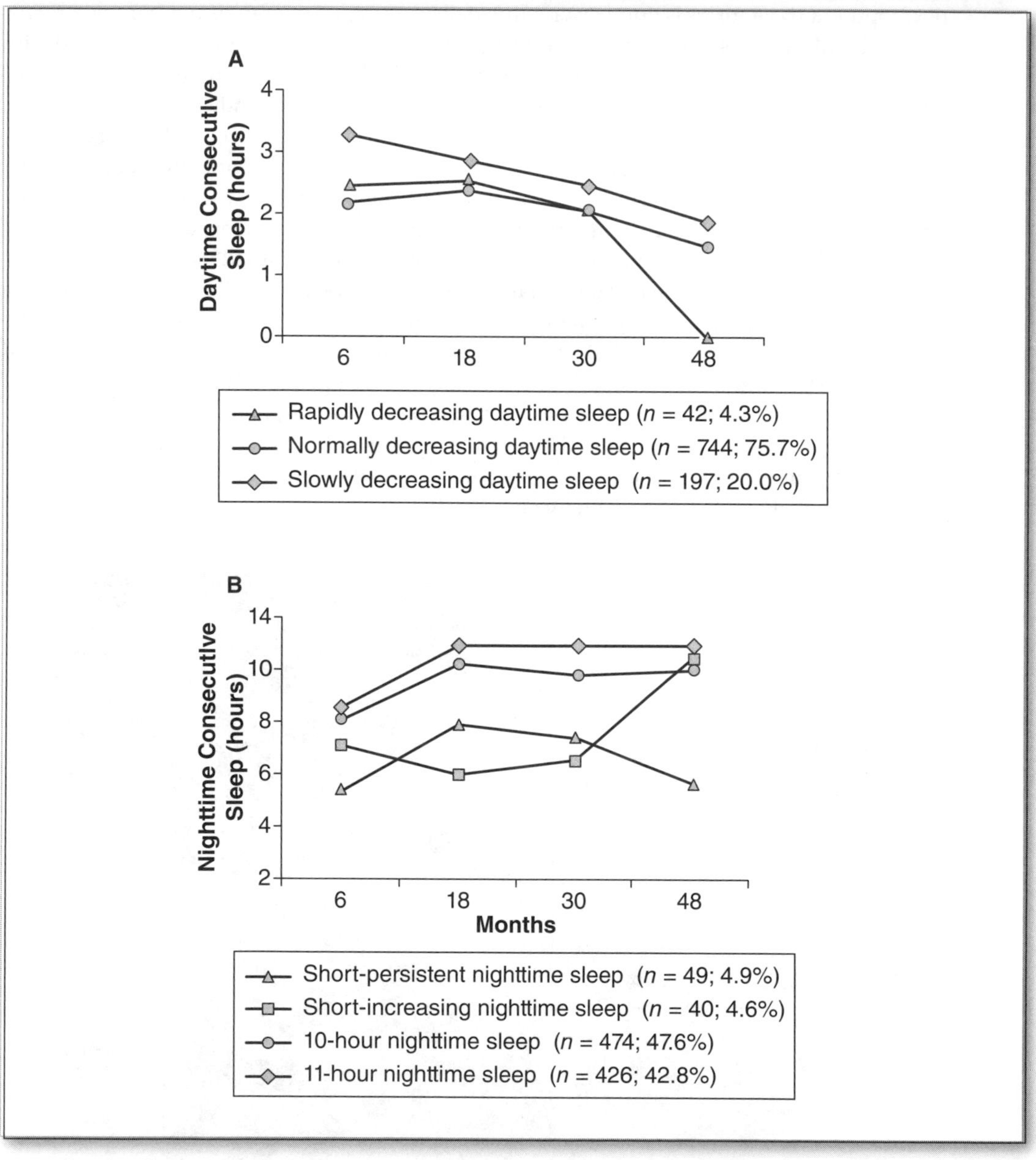

Source: Based on Touchette et al., 2013.

When awake, infants spend time in different states of alertness. Some of the time, they are *quiet alert* and spend their time gazing at the environment. Other times, they are in an *active alert* state as they engage in more movement and respond positively to stimulation from caregivers. Infants also fuss and cry. Crying peaks at six weeks of age, when it goes on for about two hours a day, according to a Danish study of 133 newborns (Alvarez, 2004) [Preview Question]. The evening time is when 40% of the fussing and crying occurs. Crying spells decrease over time, and by the beginning of the fourth month of life, the total duration of crying averages half as long as during its peak. Of course, there is wide variability across children in the amount of infant crying.

Some newborns and infants engage in excessive amounts of crying; such infants are often described as *colicky*. This term generally means that though healthy, a baby frequently cries or even screams for long periods of time without an apparent reason. Imagine a baby crying for three hours a day, three days a week or more, for weeks on end! Colicky symptoms emerge within two weeks of birth and subside by four to five months. The cause is thought to be some type of gastrointestinal problem, sometimes linked to the use of cow's milk. In these cases, substituting breast milk for infant formula is the best solution available, though it is not always effective (Lucassen et al., 1998). The latest strategy to prevent or treat colic is to give the infant oral probiotics (microbes such as bacteria and yeast). However, a meta-analysis of 12 trials of this procedure found ambiguous results. In 6 trials, crying was indeed reduced, but in the other 6, it was not (Sung et al., 2013).

Hearing an infant cry is unpleasant. From an evolutionary perspective, highly noxious cries have been selected because they are so good at eliciting a caregiver's response (Green, Gustafson, Irwin, Kalinowski, & Wood, 1995; Murray, 1979). Infant crying also affects family functioning; marital satisfaction is lower when parents hear a lot of crying (Meijer & van den Wittenboer, 2007).

In fact, excessive infant crying can incite frustrated caregivers to shake the baby, resulting in **shaken baby syndrome**. Shaking an infant is very dangerous, as it can cause brain injuries that can result (depending on the severity) in learning and physical disabilities, blindness, seizures, and death (Altimier, 2008). To educate parents about excessive crying, the *Period of Purple Crying* concept was created (see http://www.dontshake.org). Purple is an acronym: P (peak age of crying is at two months), U (unexpected), R (resists soothing), P (pain-like face), L (long lasting—up to five hours at a time), and E (most likely to occur in the afternoon or evening). This acronym helps parents recognize the normalcy of their baby's crying, and even to prepare for periods of excessive crying, for example, in the evening during dinner time.

Parents need to learn how to comfort crying babies. This includes checking to see if the baby is hungry, tired, or needs changing; walking with the baby or providing rhythmic motions or sounds; massaging the baby; or providing visual stimulation. With practice, parents become more efficient and accurate at determining why a baby is crying (Holden, 1988) and resolving the infant's (and their own) distress. This ability to efficiently problem solve has implications for sensitive parenting—and forming attachments.

Brain Development

A neonate is born with all the brain cells (**neurons**) that he or she will ever have. But brain development is a complex set of processes that begin within a few weeks of conception and continue until early adulthood (Jabès & Nelson, 2014). The size of the brain almost triples during the first five years of life, so it will grow from about one-quarter to almost three-quarters of its adult weight of 2¼ pounds. Three key neurological processes are involved in brain development: **neurogenesis**, **synaptogenesis**, and **myelination**.

Neurogenesis happens in the womb. It involves the formation of neurons (the brain cells used to process information) and **glia** (cells that provide structural support and metabolic sustenance for neurons). The rate of creation of neurons is hard to fathom: an average of 250,000 *per minute* over the nine months of gestation, for a total of about 100 *billion* neurons. Synaptogenesis is the process of forming **synapses** (connections) between these neurons, and it occurs mostly after birth. It is almost impossible to comprehend how rapidly synapses are formed to create the 1,000 trillion synapses present in a three-year-old child. This means that 1.8 million synapses are created *per second* between 2 months of gestation and 24 months of age. Along with the growth of synapses is the proliferation of **dendrites** or the branches of the neurons that allow for synaptic communication (see Figure 7.2). Most of this dendritic growth (more than 80%) occurs after the baby is born (Casey, Tottenham, Liston, & Durston, 2005; Jabès & Nelson, 2014).

During the first two years after birth, dendrites become fully extended, and synapses reach their maximum density (Eliot, 1999). As healthy development continues, there are

Figure 7.2 Diagram of a Brain Cell Showing Synapses and Dendrites

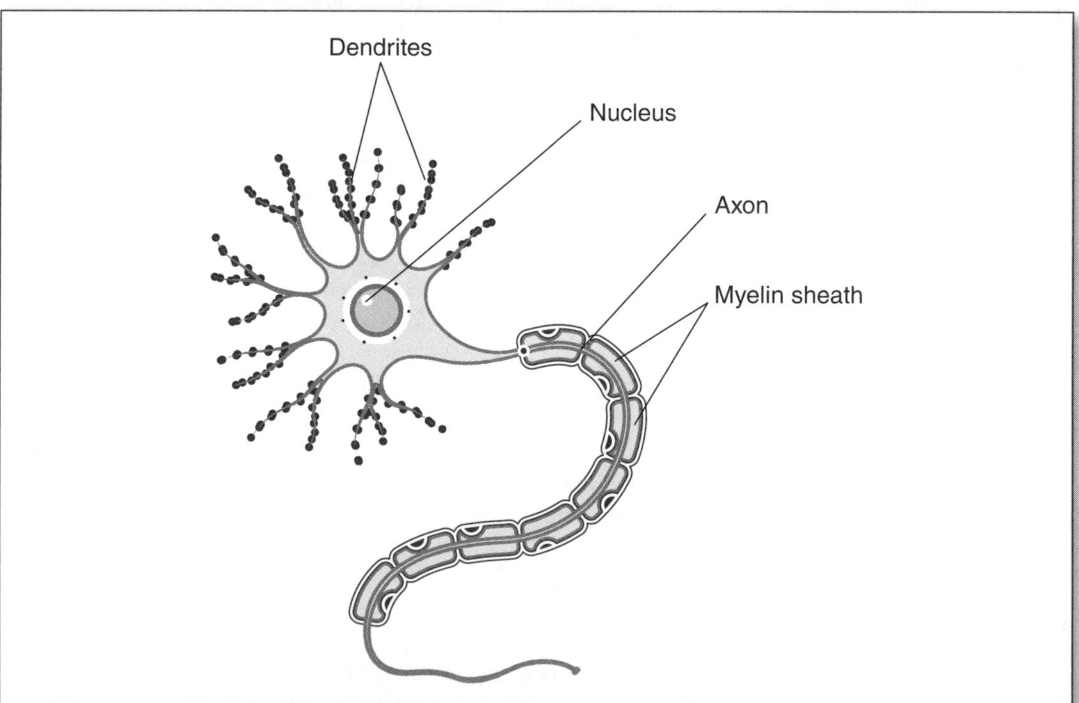

Source: Garrett, B. (2009). *Brain and behavior: An introduction to biological psychology* (2nd Ed.). Thousand Oaks: Sage.

far too many synapses for the brain to use. Consequently, the process of **synaptic pruning** must occur. This process begins at about two years of age and continues into adolescence. Synapses that are not utilized are lost—some 20 billion *per day.* Hence, the saying "use or lose it" is very applicable in this instance. This elimination of excess synapses makes brain processes more efficient, as the brain's electrical impulses have relatively fewer branches through which to navigate.

Through the process of myelination, a part of our neurons called **axons** are sheathed by **myelin** (a fatty, insulating substance) so they will conduct electrical impulses. Myelin sheathing begins in the brain in the ninth month of gestation, shows considerable growth over the first two years of life, and continues at a slower pace at least through adolescence. This process is essential for healthy functioning of the body. When demyelination occurs, such as in the case of multiple sclerosis, individuals suffer a variety of problems, including a loss of dexterity and difficulties in coordinating movements as well as visual and cognitive impairments.

The brain is also developing in other ways. A key area for early childhood is the **limbic system**. This set of brain structures (including the amygdala, hippocampus, cingulate gyrus, hypothalamus, and other parts) support various functions, including emotion, attachment, long-term memory, and behavior. Myelination in the limbic system occurs slowly, and many of its areas are not myelinated until at least nine months of age. The neurological immaturity of this system in infancy provides a biological explanation for why we do not remember events from our infancy.

As neurologist Martin Teicher (2002) wrote, "Our brains are sculpted by our early experiences" (p. 68). The dramatic neurological development that occurs in the first few years of life both helps to explain some child behavior and has implications for parenting behavior. For example, there is now evidence, based on a prospective study, that middle school children with larger hippocampus volume had mothers who were more nurturing when the children were young (Luby et al., 2012). The hippocampus is involved in the formation of new memories as well as learning and emotion. Table 7.1 provides examples of how knowledge of neurological development can inform how we rear young children.

There is increasing evidence that the relationship between parenting and brain functioning is bidirectional. Just as the quality of parenting affects infant brain growth, engaging in parental care affects neural and hormonal (e.g., oxytocin) functioning in women (Rilling, 2013). Increases in gray matter have been found in postpartum mothers (Kim et al., 2010). These increases are thought to correspond to improved functioning in the relevant area. The neuroplasticity of parental brains has also been shown when mothers view pictures of their own children versus pictures of other children (e.g., Bornstein, Arterberry, & Mash, 2013; Leibenluft, Gobbini, Harrison, & Haxby, 2004). These studies reveal that mothers' (and presumably fathers') brains are changed as a result of having children.

Promoting Healthy Brain and Cognitive Development

How do parents promote brain development? Providing appropriate levels of stimulation for the infant is one key. Recall the problems with children raised in institutions, discussed in Chapter 4. Stimulating an infant's brain occurs through all the senses. Parents should create an enriching environment for an infant, but this does not necessarily mean buying lots of gadgets or toys. Table 7.1 lists some of the activities parents should engage in to promote an infant and toddler's brain and cognitive development, beginning in the prenatal period.

Table 7.1 Rearing Smarter Children Based on Brain Research

Period	Some Recommended Actions
Prenatal	Take prenatal vitamins & stay healthy (eat well, exercise).
	Mothers should gain 15 to 30 lbs., eating an extra 300 calories a day.
	Minimize stress.
Infancy	Breastfeed for the first year.
	Engage in happy, loving interactions; avoid conflicts.
	Introduce variety in daily experience.
	Provide appropriate stimulation; avoid overstimulation.
Toddlerhood	Continue to provide good nutrition.
	Provide vitamin/mineral supplements if needed.
	Engage in a variety of daily experiences; arrange peer interactions.
	Provide appropriate stimulation; avoid overstimulation.
	Read to your toddler. Expose your child to music and/or a second language.
	Engage in mutually enjoyable activities.

Sources: Eliot, 1999; Medina, 2010.

Although parents can do much to ensure their infant's cognitive development, they should not be fooled by gimmicks that are advertised as shortcuts to making a child smart. Box 7.2 describes the one of the latest ploys.

Box 7.2 Do Infants Learn From Baby Videos?

Many parents want to give their infant every possible advantage to succeed academically. An industry has sprung up to capitalize on this desire. An early effort was dubbed *the Mozart effect.* Based on one study, it was shown that intellectual performance in college students could be enhanced by listening to a Mozart sonata (Rauscher, Shaw, & Ky, 1993). That finding was extrapolated to the extent that a state governor distributed Mozart CDs to all parents of newborns, with the hope that this would raise the children's intelligence. Subsequent studies did not replicate that effect (Bangerter & Heath, 2004). The next attempt to commercially market infant stimulation arrived in the form of the Baby Einstein videos. These videos, designed for children 12 months and older, promise to expand a child's vocabulary. But do they? In the most rigorous experimental study to date, Judy DeLoache and her colleagues (DeLoache et al., 2010) tracked word learning in 12- to 18-month-old children for a month. Children who watched the video at least five times a week for a month did not show any improved performance over the control group.

In fact, we do not yet know the long-term implications of young infants and children being exposed to "screen time" of various sorts. It is likely that a large amount of exposure to video screens and other technology affects brain development in some (as yet unknown) way. One of the major problems with using phones, computers, tablets, and television screen to entertain or even educate infants is that this practice often leaves little time for some of the most important developmental activities: talking and nonverbal exchange, interactive play, gross motor play, physical affection, and so on. The American Academy of Pediatrics (http://www.aap.org/en-us/advocacy-and-policy/aap-health-initiatives/pages/media-and-children.aspx) recommends that children under the age of two years not be exposed to *any* video, tablet, phone, or other visual technology product.

Forming Attachments

Besides feeding and responding to crying, parents engage in a variety of other nurturant caregiving actions that include sheltering, bathing, and protecting. Social behaviors help to regulate the infant's emotions as parents manage and monitor the infant's social interactions. These actions include a wide variety of visual, verbal, affective, and physical behaviors. For example, singing to the baby, playing peekaboo, tickling, and making funny faces fall into this category of caregiving behaviors.

Through **social caregiving**, infants begin learning fundamental principles of social interaction. These principles include turn-taking (alternating turns in an interaction), synchrony (when both individuals attend to the same thing, are responsive to each other, and perhaps may share emotions), reciprocity (when the acts are supportive of each other and become similar), and complementarity (when one person's acts complete or respond to the other's) (Harrist & Waugh, 2002). Comforting an upset baby through rocking and patting illustrates a complementary and synchronous interaction. Playing peekaboo with an infant—a common parental activity observed in a wide range of countries, including Iran, South Africa, Russia, and Brazil (Fernald & O'Neill, 1993)—introduces an infant to turn-taking, synchrony, and complementarity.

Through social interactions, infants also learn about the rudiments of love. Recall that both Freud and Erikson viewed the mother-infant relationship as the foundation for all subsequent relationships. Erikson (1993) saw the mother-infant relationship as the source for establishing the milestone of basic trust in others. According to attachment theory, babies learn whether other people can be trusted to care for them, protect them, and respond to their needs (e.g., Bowlby, 1969, 1988; Cassidy, Jones, & Shaver, 2013). These experiences provide children with a feeling of security (or insecurity) and, in turn, a sense (or lack) of self-worth.

Over the course of the first year of life, the quality of the interactions between parent and child leads to a complex relationship that could be considered a "partnership" (Bowlby, 1988, p. 268). This process is thought to occur in four developmental phases. See Table 7.2 for a description of the characteristics of each phase and associated age period (Marvin & Britner, 2008).

As introduced in Chapter 2, the quality of this parent-child partnership of attachment has been extensively studied from the perspective of attachment theory with the use of the Strange Situation procedure. Caregiving practices, especially sensitive parenting practices, have been linked to the formation of secure attachments (Dykas & Cassidy, 2013).

Mothers observed to be responsive and successful in addressing their infant's needs were more likely to have children classified as securely attached. In contrast, mothers who did not respond promptly or had more difficulty in comforting their babies were more likely to have infants classified as insecurely attached (either avoidant or resistant). In typical North American samples from the community, 62% of the sample will be classified as secure, 15% as insecure-avoidant, 9% insecure-resistant, and 15% insecure disorganized (van IJzendoorn, Schuengel, & Bakermans-Kranenburg, 1999). However, those percentages change when different countries are sampled or when a high-risk sample or clinical sample is assessed, such as demonstrated with depressed mothers (Martins & Gaffan, 2000).

Although attachment researchers have focused on parental sensitivity, a related characteristic encompassing a broader array of behavior and described with several synonyms is warmth, affection, acceptance, or love. Warmth has long been recognized and found to be the

Table 7.2 The Four Phases of the Development of Attachment

Phase	Key Features	Approximate Age
Phase 1	Behavior is reflexive and infant seeks contact indiscriminately	Birth to 10 weeks
Phase 2	Learning to discriminate people based on physical characteristics	10 weeks to 6 months
Phase 3	Infants become clearly attached to caregivers	6 months to 30 months
Phase 4	Infants learn to cope with separation from attachment figures	30 months

Source: Marvin & Britner, 2008.

most fundamental dimension of effective parenting (e.g., Khaleque, 2013; Maccoby & Martin, 1983). Researchers have measured it by various indices, including physical affection, acceptance of the child, giving approval for good behavior, playful joking, sharing mutually rewarding activities, and responding to the child in a positive and accepting way (Russell & Russell, 1989). As Laible and Thompson (2007) observed, parental warmth is better thought of as a dyadic or relational construct [Preview Question]. This means it is not solely a variable that resides within the parent, but it reflects the quality of the relationship. Warmth in the parent-child relationship has a number of benefits. It promotes a sense in children that they are loved and respected. In turn, children are more likely to trust that the parent has good intentions. A warm relationship also promotes children's cooperation, because it enhances their motivation to comply (Grusec, Goodnow, & Kuczynski, 2000).

One consequence of a warm parent-infant relationship and strong feelings of love for the infant is **parental separation anxiety**, a parent's unpleasant emotional state of concern and apprehension about leaving a child. The anxiety is characterized by feelings of guilt, worry, and sadness (Hock, DeMeis, & McBride, 1988). Both mothers and fathers experience separation anxiety, although mothers experience more anxiety related to work-related separations (Hock & Lutz, 1998). In a study using Belsky's (1984) model of the determinants of parenting (discussed in Chapter 5), Hsu (2004) found that separation anxiety in primiparous (first-time) mothers was multiply determined. Mothers who were not generally anxious, were happy with their marriage and their social support network, and had temperamentally easy children tended to experience more separation anxiety than did other mothers. Presumably mothers with more challenging children found some respite when they had time away from their infants.

Box 7.3 Attachment in Children With Autism Spectrum Disorder

The normal attachment process can be severely compromised in infants who have or may develop autism, now called autism spectrum disorder (ASD) in the latest *Diagnostic and Statistical Manual of Mental Disorders* (*DSM-V*), the American Psychiatric Association's (2013) diagnostic manual. ASD is a serious disorder characterized by communication problems, impaired social interactions, and repetitive behaviors. The severity ranges from individuals who can function well enough to go to college to individuals unable to care for themselves. Latest statistics from the Centers for Disease Control indicate the **prevalence** rate may be as high as 1 child in 88 (Baio, 2012). This rate has nearly doubled since 2007, something that may be attributable to better detection by teachers and doctors or (more perniciously) by some unknown environmental factor. Although many children are not diagnosed with the disability until they are toddlers, preschoolers, or even later, early indicators in infants include not smiling or showing joy at 6 months, not being able to engage in reciprocal social exchanges at 9 months, and not babbling or responding to his or her name at 12 months. The social deficits result in delayed attachments and fewer secure attachments, especially in the children who are more impaired (Rutgers, Bakermans-Kranenburg, van IJzendoorn, & van Berckelaer-Onnes, 2004).

Infant Temperament and Infant Effects

As previously described, the arrival of a newborn generally transforms a household. This is especially true for firstborn children. Suddenly, the focus of attention is the newborn; daily activities are structured around him or her. This change—how the newborn affects the behavior of those around him—is an example of a *child effect* (in this case, an infant effect), and its influence can be powerful. Simply looking at an infant, according to ethologist Konrad Lorenz (Lorenz & Kickert, 1981), can bring on a child effect. Lorenz argued that features of babies (such as a large forehead, big eyes, and a small nose) elicit, on a subconscious level, nurturant reactions from those around.

Although facial features may prompt initial reactions, behavior is a more powerful stimulus. Shortly after birth, behavioral differences in infants become apparent. Some neonates are fussy and irritable; others are mostly happy. Some infants develop regular patterns of behavior; others are less predictable. These types of differences between newborns illustrate the notion of *temperament*.

There are several competing views about what the behavioral ingredients of temperament are. Pediatricians Thomas and Chess (and their colleagues) developed the first systematic view of temperament (e.g., Thomas, Chess, Birch, & Hertzig, 1963). Based on a longitudinal study with extensive interviews of 22 parents, they distilled key child-behavior characteristics that appeared to be stable individual differences over time. They proposed that temperament consisted of nine characteristics, including activity level, adaptability, mood, and distractibility. These characteristics could then be reduced into clusters forming three categories: (1) *difficult* (negative mood, low adaptability, high intensity, and low rhythmicity); (2) *easy* (the opposite of the difficult child); and (3) *slow to warm up* (initially, the child may react more like a difficult child).

Although this pioneering work set the stage for subsequent studies, the nine characteristics and three categories have not held up to scientific scrutiny. For example, there is overlap among the nine characteristics. Subsequent studies using **factor analysis** (a statistical procedure used to identify common factors or variables by analyzing patterns of correlations) determined five behavioral factors rather than nine (Putnam, Sanson, & Rothbart, 2002). Another problem found has been Thomas and Chess's simplistic and potentially problematic labeling of a child as *difficult*. Most children could be considered difficult *or* easy, depending on the age of the child, the particular situation, or the subjective perceptions of the rater (Bates, 1989; Putnam et al., 2002). In addition, labeling a child as difficult has the danger of becoming a self-fulfilling prophecy.

Today, temperament is considered to reflect the physiologically based differences between infants in activity level and reactivity, attention, and emotionality (Rothbart & Bates, 2006). These differences are relatively stable across situations and time (Cummings, Braungart-Rieker, & Du Rocher Schudlich, 2013). That is not to say these characteristics are immutable.

An infant's temperament affects the quality of parenting as well as the parents themselves. Parents of fearful, distressed, or sad infants report more stress, depressive symptoms, and lower levels of parenting efficacy than other parents. In contrast, parents of infants with positive temperaments believed they were more efficacious as parents (Solmeyer & Feinberg, 2011).

Investigations into **negative emotionality** have been partly fruitful in linking infants' temperamental qualities to subsequent behavior problems. For example, irritable infants develop into angry, noncompliant two-year-old children, but only if their mothers are angry and punitive (Crockenberg, 1987). Based on such findings, Belsky, Hsieh, and Crnic (1998) found support for the differential susceptibility hypothesis, first introduced in Chapter 3. The idea is that young children who rate high on negative emotionality are more influenced by parenting practices than are other young children.

The relation between child temperament and parenting practices has received considerable research attention, and most of the evidence indicates that temperament does indeed affect parenting. However, parenting likely interacts with different aspects of temperament in a variety of ways (Bates & Pettit, 2007). Perhaps it is easiest to capture that idea with one of Thomas and Chess's early constructs relating to temperament and parenting. The pediatricians argued that a child's temperament always needs to be considered when determining appropriate parenting behavior (e.g., Thomas & Chess, 1977). They proposed the construct of *goodness of fit* to capture the interaction between the child's temperament and the parent's childrearing behavior. So one style of parenting would not be appropriate for all children. Instead, parents need to modify their behavior in order to provide a good fit with a child's characteristics. For instance, a fearful infant in a situation with unfamiliar people would need to be treated very differently from a sociable child in the same setting. A poor fit between infant temperament and parenting style could lead to behavior problems later as a toddler.

As infants grow into toddlerhood, the relations between temperament, parenting, and children's behavior become more complex. A child's temperament influences the parent and the parent influences the child's developing temperament. Thus there are bidirectional (or transactional) effects. Perhaps the best example is that parents of extremely shy children will modify their encouragement of independence with that child (Rubin, Nelson, Hastings, & Asendorpf, 1999). As a recent review of the parenting and temperament literature makes clear, there is evidence for both bidirectional and interactive effects of temperament and parenting in such areas as frustration, fear, self-regulation, and impulsivity (Kiff, Lengua, & Zalewski, 2011).

Role Sharing and Working Parents

Generally, mothers are the primary infant caregivers. Nevertheless, fathers are increasingly involved in child care (Jones & Mosher, 2013). Today, over 90% of fathers of young children eat meals with their children, play with them, and bathe or change their diapers on a daily basis. Sixty percent of fathers read to their young children. However, this does not mean that fathers devote the same amount of time to child care as mothers. To examine the role that fathers play in infant care, a time **diary study** was conducted of 182 dual-wage earner, middle-class U.S. families (Kotila, Schoppe-Sullivan, & Kamp Dush, 2013). Infant care was classified into three categories: routine child care (e.g., dressing, feeding, changing diapers), positive engagement (soothing, holding, playing with the child), and responsibility (organizing, planning, obtaining medical care, driving). Data were collected at two age points: when the infants were three months old and nine months old. The amount of time mothers and fathers spent in infant care activities are listed in Table 7.3.

Table 7.3 Time Spent by Mothers and Fathers in Infant Care Activities

	3 months		9 months	
	Mothers	**Fathers**	**Mothers**	**Fathers**
Child care	150	43	108	43
Positive engagement	82	59	106	73
Responsibility	39	29	36	23

Note: The numbers indicate the minutes per day spent on each activity.

The minutes indicate that in every activity at both time points, mothers devoted much more time to infant care. Nevertheless, fathers were spending a significant amount of time engaging in parenting activities. At three months, mothers spent twice as much time interacting with their infants as did fathers. Six months later, fathers were spending more time with their infants than before, and mothers slightly less. In this study, both parents worked full time outside the home. Although the amount of time was not equal, which may be an ideal proportion in some families, this study revealed that a considerable amount of co-parenting was occurring in contemporary American families.

Engaging in constructive co-parenting is beneficial to all the family members. Parents experience more satisfaction both in the childrearing domain and in their marital relationships (Holland & McElwain, 2013). However, when parents argue about how to raise their infants and then one parent undermines the other, there is less satisfaction, fewer feelings of parental efficacy, and more stress and depressive symptoms in the parents (Solmeyer & Feinberg, 2011).

Few people like to hear others argue. That is especially true with children when they overhear their parents having a conflict. There is now evidence that even infants can be negatively affected by verbal conflicts between parents. In a provocative study, Graham, Fisher, and Pfeifer (2013) used an fMRI (functional magnetic resonance imaging) machine to scan the brains of 6- to 12-month-olds infants when they were sleeping. Recordings were played of nonsense sentences spoken in very angry, mildly angry, neutral, and happy voices by an adult male. Mothers who reported more interparental conflict had infants who greater neural reactions to the angry voice relative to the neutral voice. These results indicate that marital conflict as an environmental stressor may be linked to brain functioning in infants.

Maternal Employment and Infant Well-Being

In 59% of U.S. families with children, both parents are employed in the labor force (Bureau of Labor Statistics, 2013). In contrast to some other countries, maternity leave in the United States is most often limited to three months without pay (Hofferth & Curtin, 2006). Consequently, more than half of mothers of infants (57%) return to work in the first year—and about one-third of those women are working within three months of giving birth (Bureau of Labor Statistics, 2013). Returning to work poses a variety of challenges to mothers, such as alternative child care, breastfeeding, and emotional costs.

Mothers who returned to work by the time their infant was three months old reported elevated stress levels, more depressive symptoms, and slightly more health problems than mothers who stayed at home (Chatterji, Markowtiz, & Brooks-Gunn, 2013). Not surprisingly, mothers who do return to work are much less likely to continue to breastfeed their infants (Kimbro, 2006). That decision, in turn, can result in negative health effects on the infant (Dieterich, Felice, O'Sullivan, & Rasmussen, 2013).

Despite the fewer hours employed mothers spend with their child, evidence indicates the quality of parenting is not affected. Based on a time diary study of more than 1,000 mothers, it was found that employed mothers tend to make up the time lost during the week by interacting more with their infants on the weekends than unemployed mothers (Huston & Rosenkrantz Aronson, 2005).

Infant Care

Many families during the first year and more during the second year of a child's life have to find alternative care because either both parents are working or the family has only one parent. There are several types of infant and child care available, including center-based care (e.g., for-profit commercial care centers such as Kindercare, church-based care, or university child care centers), family day care (in-home care), or relative care (e.g., a grandparent).

Finding alternative child care is a necessity for many families where both parents are employed. If the care is high quality, it can also provide a socially and cognitively stimulating environment for an infant or preschooler. Quality depends on such variables as the child care provider–to-child ratio, the child care provider's training and commitment, the physical environment, the cleanliness and safety, the availability of stimulating toys, the planned activities, and disciplinary practices (Japel, Tremblay, & Côté, 2005). The problem is that there is a dearth of high-quality, affordable day care. High-quality day care is expensive: The average annual cost for full-time infant care in a center is more than $16,400 per year in Massachusetts (Child Care Aware of America, 2013).

Photo 7.2 A young toddler at play.

Source: Photograph by J. P. Bell

Given the number of children in day care centers, many studies have examined how attendance may impact infants, toddlers, and preschoolers' development. Child care centers can be a source of stress and illness to children. A review of nine studies of infants through preschoolers found children in child care centers have higher stress levels (assessed by measuring cortisol levels) than children in at-home care (Vermeer & van IJzendoorn, 2006). Children who receive center-based care are also more likely to get sick than children who stay at home (Reves et al., 1993). There will be more discussion of the research on the effects of child care center, including attachment and behavior problems, in the next chapter.

PARENTING TODDLERS

Toddlerhood typically refers to the span of life from 12 to 36 months. Toddlers are rapidly developing in many areas. They start to use words to communicate. They are beginning to walk, to regulate their increasingly differentiated emotions, to engage in goal-directed activities, to express their independence, to learn about their gender, and to form a self-concept (e.g., Edwards & Liu, 2002, see Photo 7.2). All these changes in a child's physical, cognitive, emotional, and social abilities mean that parents need to add new behaviors to their parenting repertoire. The parenting tasks identified by Bradley (2007) expand as toddlers require more structuring, stimulating, monitoring, and disciplining.

Intentional Socialization

As defined in Chapter 1, *socialization* refers to processes whereby children are taught skills, values, and behavior necessary for competent functioning (e.g., Maccoby, 2007). It is a process that begins at birth but becomes more intentional as children grow and begin to assert their autonomy (e.g., "No!", "I want to do that by myself").

Socialization takes a number of forms in a variety of domains on multiple trajectories (Holden, 2010). Parents work to socialize their children into conforming to behavior they consider appropriate, but they also target such areas as emotions, gender, and prosocial behavior. For example, emotional socialization begins in infancy as parents learn to cope with infant crying. How parents respond to crying is linked to their beliefs. Although some parents adopt an infant's perspective to the cries ("My baby is crying because he/she is distressed and in need of something"), many other parents may think about the crying from an adult perspective ("I want to stop the crying because it bothers me," or "If I respond to the crying, my baby will get spoiled"). Mothers are more likely to take the infant's perspective, while fathers take the adult perspective (Leerkes, Parade, & Burney, 2010).

As has become clear from the child effects literature, socialization is not a unidirectional process from parent to child; it is bidirectional. This bidirectional process begins at birth: Infants are not just socialized by parents, they also socialize the parent. The infant teaches the parent which feeding, nurturing, and stimulating behaviors work—and which do not.

At the core of socialization are the goals that parents have for their children. Some of these socialization goals vary across cultures, as will be discussed in a later chapter. The contrast between Eastern socialization goals and practices with Western ones is especially pronounced. Asian cultures generally value cooperation and close-group affiliation much more than do Western cultures and the United States in particular. Japanese mothers, for example, promote these values by maintaining close physical contact and developing a relationship based on interdependence. Consequently, many Japanese infants, toddlers, and preschoolers are almost always in direct physical or visual contact with their mother when they are awake. In contrast, U.S. parents rear their children to become independent, autonomous, and instrumental (Rothbaum & Trommsdorff, 2007). In America, it is commonplace for parents to enroll their infants or toddlers in day care or to hire sitters, a practice that promotes, at an early age, experiencing separations from parents.

In addition to prosocial behavior and broad cultural values, parents have many other types of goals for their children (Hastings & Grusec, 1998; Richman & Mandara, 2013). Basic parental childrearing goals include having their children get a good education; develop into healthy, happy, and independent adults; and earn a good living. Parents work to achieve these goals through a variety of socialization processes. Some of the socialization comes about through intentional and direct instruction. However, children carefully observe those around them and may simply model their parents' behavior, as is described in Box 7.4.

Box 7.4 Young Children "Buying" Cigarettes and Alcohol!

That could be the headline of one study that investigated the consumer behavior of children age two to six in a miniature store. One hundred and twenty children were told to shop for a Barbie or Ken doll in a store stocked with 73 different miniature products. Children "purchased" (actually, all objects were free) an average of 17 items. A majority (61%) of the children "bought" beer or wine and 28% "bought" cigarettes. If parents smoked, children were four times more likely to "buy" cigarettes. Children who watched PG-13 or even R-rated movies were five times more likely to "buy" alcohol. One four-year-old girl mimicked what she had heard: "I need this for my man. A man needs cigarettes." On the other hand, one preschooler pointed to the cigarettes and said, "I'm definitely not going to buy those; they can kill you." This demonstration of social learning would not surprise Albert Bandura, who recognized the powerful role that modeling plays in development as it shapes our expectations as well as what we think is normal. The bottom line: Parents need to watch what they are doing; children sure are.

Source: Dalton et al., 2005.

A particularly salient way during the toddler years that parents encourage behaviors they want to see and discourage other behaviors is through discipline.

Discipline

Discipline is defined as training in order to act in accordance with rules. When a toddler engages in a behavior that a parent does not approve of, the parent responds with corrective discipline in an effort to teach the child how to behave. Children need *a lot* of training—that is the nature of the developmental process, which has been evolutionarily adapted to so that children can adapt to the requirements of the culture they find themselves born into. As early as when infants are five months of age, parents are making efforts to discipline them (Ahl, Fausto-Sterling, García-Coll, & Seifer, 2013). Although these efforts most often consist of prohibitions (e.g., "No!", "Don't!"), mothers also use **distraction** and even reasoning to change the infant's behavior. A small percentage of parents begin using harsh corporal discipline (e.g., slapping and spanking) well before infants are able to regulate their behavior. As many as 10% of parents slap or spank their 6- or 10-month-old infants (Combs-Orme & Cain, 2008; MacKenzie, Nicklas, Brooks-Gunn, & Waldfogel, 2011)!

By the time a child is two years old, they are frequently "misbehaving." Toddlers touch things they are not supposed to. They draw on the walls. They push and hit other children. In fact, toddlerhood is when most children engage in their highest rate of aggression (Tremblay, 2006). They tease pets. They knock over glasses of milk. They have potty training accidents. The list could go on and on. Young children engage in misbehavior anywhere from 3.5 to 20 times an hour (Dix, 1991) [Preview Question]. If you take a toddler to the supermarket, the frequency of misdeeds increases to about *once every 45 seconds* (Holden, 1983)!

Although dealing with misbehavior can be frustrating and tiresome for parents, it is through disobedience that toddlers begin to learn how to be self-assertive and test boundaries (Dix, Stewart, Gershoff, & Day, 2007). Also, children's prefrontal cortex (and hence their self-regulatory abilities) are developing slowly. In time, they will gain the neurological ability to control their behavior.

Effective parents of toddlers work strategically to avoid some of the conflicts. This has been called *proactive* or *preemptive* parenting (Dowling, Smith Slep, & O'Leary, 2009; Holden & West, 1989; Pettit, Bates, & Dodge, 1997). Recall that in the supermarket, this involved such actions as engaging the child's attention, avoiding problematic aisles, and providing objects for the toddler to play with.

If unable to avoid the conflict, parents use a variety of techniques to try to shape their child's behavior. Depending on the age, they might reason with, lecture to, negotiate, or attempt to persuade the child to behave in some way. With younger children, diverting attention from a tempting object to something else is often effective. Ignoring behaviors, and thereby avoiding reinforcing them, can be a useful approach. Time out, or the removal of the child from an ongoing activity, is often advocated by parenting experts. The standard time out procedure is to put the child in a quiet corner of a room without any objects for one minute per child's age in years. Older children respond well to withdrawal of privileges, such as putting away a toy or eliminating watching television for several nights.

Generally, if one or several of those disciplinary techniques are not effective in stopping the misbehavior, parents may threaten or yell in anger. Many parents also resort to the use of some type of corporal punishment. This may consist of slapping a hand or, in rare cases, a face. Spanking on the buttocks is a common disciplinary practice in the United States.

Figure 7.3 depicts the percentage of mothers who reported using four different disciplinary techniques from infancy through toddlerhood.

Why do toddlers misbehave? As noted, toddlers do not have the self-control abilities of older children. Another source of misbehavior is unrealistic expectations of the parent. A third cause is inappropriate parenting. Tamara Del Vecchio and Susan O'Leary (2006) found that mothers who engaged in either permissive and/or overreactive discipline had toddlers who became more aggressive to the mother during 30-minute observations. Another problematic parenting technique is that of being too intrusive. This consists of frequent physical and/or verbal directives that limit a toddler's activities. Mothers who engage in intrusive parenting of toddlers have children who are less able to express themselves, less able to control their behavior, or perform less well on an intelligence test at 36 months (Clincy & Mills-Koonce, 2013).

During the toddler years, parents also begin using **psychological control**. This type of control consists of parental efforts to constrain, invalidate, and manipulate the child's psychological and emotional experiences and expression (Barber, 1996; Barber & Xia, 2013). A common approach is "love withdrawal," occurring when the parent withdraws attention and/or affection in an effort to control the child. Parents who tell the child what to do and how they should feel are engaging in this form of control. Not all parents use this technique. Some mothers and fathers of toddlers use psychological controls while others don't (Verhoeven, Junger, Van Aken, Deković, & Van Aken, 2007). One form of psychological control—shaming—is especially common in Asian cultures (Mills, 2005; Wu et al., 2002).

Figure 7.3 How Discipline Changes During the First Four Years

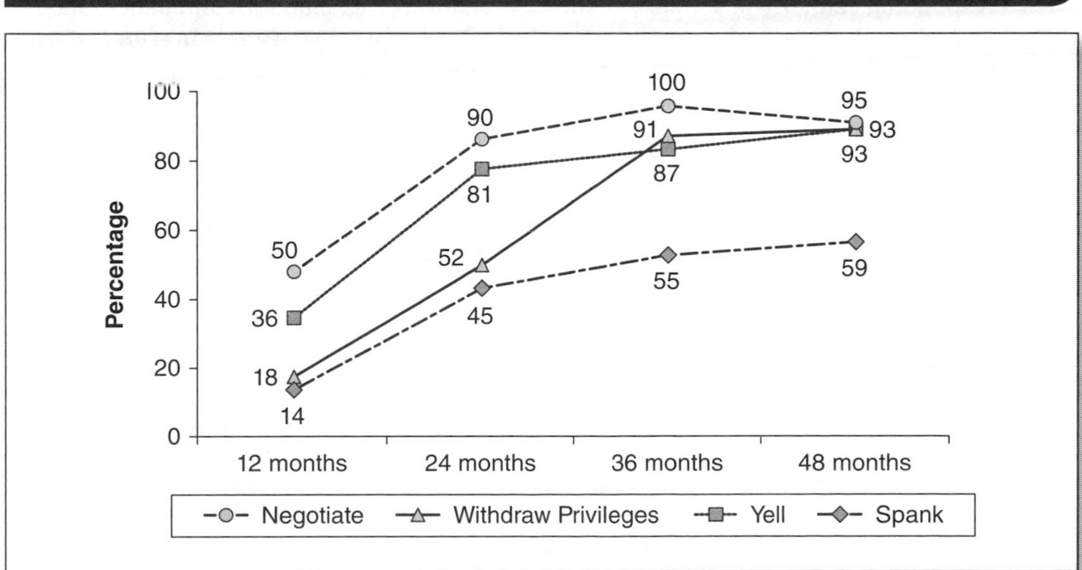

Source: Adapted from Vittrup, Holden, & Buck, 2006.

Given all these potential parenting pitfalls (being permissive, overreactive, intrusive, or psychologically controlling) how can parents discipline effectively? Grusec and Goodnow (1994) pointed out that deciding what constitutes effective discipline depends on a host of factors, including the nature of the misdeed, the nature of the child (his or her temperament and mood, for instance), and the features of the actual disciplinary response (perhaps the content of the message and how it is said). An effective parent, then, must take into account a variety of considerations before determining an appropriate response to a misdeed. There is some disagreement in the parenting literature about the extent to which power assertion is necessary. Although researchers agree that competent parents avoid unnecessary or extreme uses of power assertion—as well as arbitrary demands, unnecessary restrictions, and heavy reliance on power—some power assertion in conjunction with reasoning may be necessary to gain the child's attention or maintain control (Maccoby & Martin, 1983). Independent of the degree of power assertion they exhibit, effective parents have been observed to maintain a certain degree of warmth toward their young children while disciplining (Baumrind, 1971).

Most parents are not trained in how to use discipline effectively. Consequently, mistakes are common. The four mistakes described in Box 3.2 are inadvertently reinforce behavior they do not want to see by giving attention to it, forgetting to reward behaviors they want to see more of, overreacting (and possibly getting into a coercive bout), and giving long verbal explanations about misbehavior. Instead, parents need to train the child in a calm manner and to carefully decide which behaviors to react to. Effective discipline, then, requires a lot of patience and the ability to inhibit one's own negative emotions and behavior.

A third error is failing to practice consistent discipline. In this case, *consistent* does not mean responding in the exact same way to each and every child behavior (Grusec & Goodnow, 1994; Lytton, 1979). Rather, consistent parenting involves setting rules, responding similarly in similar situations, monitoring the child for compliance, and following up on stated consequences of misbehavior. According to Patterson (1982), the key point of consistency is giving the child the message that the parent will win a conflict and will not capitulate to the child. When parents *do* give in to a child's demands or misbehavior ("Okay, you can have a piece of candy before dinner"), they fall into a trap whereby short-term gains (such as stopping the whining) are won at the expense of reinforcing the child's difficult (and in this case, unhealthy) behavior. There is some evidence that parents who are inconsistent have children who are more likely to exhibit conduct problems and experience parent-child conflict than are the children of consistent parents (e.g., Krishnakumar & Buehler, 2000).

Providing Structure

Although disciplining a toddler is a frequent task in even the most well-run homes, how often children misbehave is a consequence, to some extent, of parental structuring. This dimension of parenting has not been examined as frequently as parental warmth or parental control, but it is an important component of parenting. *Structuring* refers to the degree to which parents provide a predictable, organized environment for a child (Slater & Power, 1987). Structure for young children is important, as it provides them with a sense of stability, predictability, and security.

Consider the homes of children raised in poverty. Many impoverished families move frequently from one home to another, and when they are in a home, it is often characterized by family turmoil, noise, chaos, a lack of schedule (such as a regular bedtime), and few regular routines (such as parental reading at bedtime). It is not hard to see the disadvantage that such settings pose for a toddler's development (Evans, 2004).

There are many ways parents can structure a child's environment. They decide when, where, and what the child eats. Some problematic eating behaviors that can be established early in life include too much snacking, relying on fast foods, eating meals alone rather than as a family, and not eating many fruits or vegetables. Increasingly, the parental establishment of healthy eating habits is being recognized as important for preventing eating problems in children—such as those contributing to child obesity (Olvera-Ezzell, Power, & Cousins, 1990).

Another example of parental structuring concerns children's sleeping practices. Parents decide where a child will sleep, what time bedtime is, and how consistently that bedtime is enforced. These decisions may be based on economic factors, family size, the availability of space, and climate (Jenni & O'Connor, 2005). In the United States, most three-month-old infants sleep in the same room as their mothers, but by 12 months, they are in their own room (Hauck, Signore, Fein, & Raju, 2008). Bed-sharing is practiced by mothers of 42% of newborns but that percent also drops off, as is indicated in Figure 7.4. The practice of bed-sharing is not recommended by pediatricians because of the danger of accidentally suffocating an infant.

Figure 7.4 Infant Sleep Locations

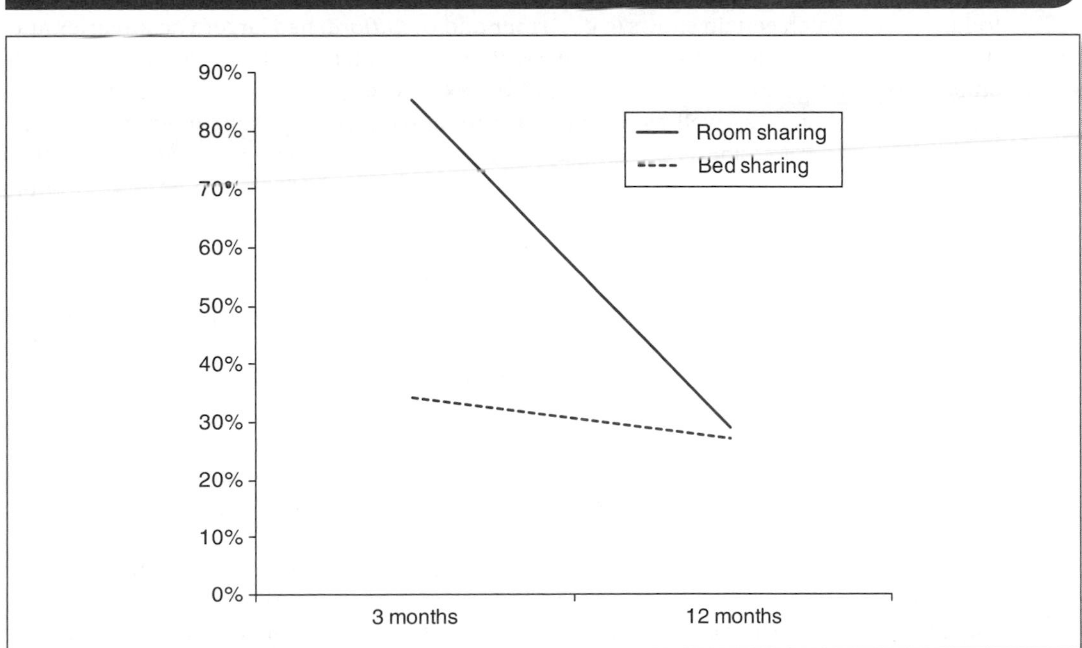

Source: Hauck et al., 2008.

Another pediatrician-recommended practice is to put infants to sleep on their back in order to reduce the likelihood of sudden infant death syndrome. About one-quarter of mothers do not put their infant to sleep on their back at 3 months, and by 12 months, that figure increases to 36% (Hauck et al., 2008).

The race/ethnicity of the family is related to sleep practices. In a study of more than 3,000 families in the United States, there were systematic variations in sleeping *location* (Milan, Snow, & Belay, 2007). A majority (57%) of Latino toddlers slept with their parent or parents, in contrast to 37% of African Americans and 23% of White families. Most of the White families (90%) had a regular bedtime for their children, as did 80% of the Latino and 79% of the African American families. The racial/ethnic groups also differed on what they emphasized during bedtime routines, with White families being more likely to read or tell a story to their toddlers, Latino families commonly giving their children bottles, and African Americans most likely to bathe their children.

Structuring also involves setting limits on children's behavior and desires that are inappropriate, dangerous, unhealthy, or incompatible with parental values, goals, or needs. One domain where there is a lot of variability in parental structuring is watching television or other electronic media. At 9 months of age, infants show interest in watching television (Linebarger & Walker, 2005). By 24 months, 90% of children are regularly watching television, DVDs, or videos for almost three hours a day, on average (Certain & Kahn, 2002; Zimmerman, Christakis, & Meltzoff, 2007). These statistics fly in the face of the American Academy of Pediatrics recommendation that children under the age of two should not be exposed to *any* screen time. Parents let their children watch television for many reasons: It is entertaining, it provides free babysitting, and they think it is educational. For example, toddlers who watch certain shows (e.g., *Arthur* and/or *Clifford*) had larger vocabularies and higher expressive language scores than toddlers who watched other shows, such as *Teletubbies* (Linebarger & Walker, 2005). However, extensive television viewing can result in parent-child conflict as well as attentional problems, passivity, consumerism, and, in some children, aggression (e.g., Christakis, Zimmerman, DiGiuseppe, & McCarty, 2004). Consequently, parents of toddlers begin to regulate and monitor the time their children spent viewing television, videos, or DVDs (or time with electronic games and computers for older children). Further discussion of the problems linked to children's exposure to electronics will be discussed in the next chapter.

In addition to structuring the daily schedule and activities of children, parents commonly structure toddlers' social interactions, because toddlers do not know how to interact with their peers in socially acceptable ways. For example, when two-year-olds play with other children, they hit their peers about once every 13 minutes (Brownlee & Bakeman, 1981). Consequently, mothers closely supervise, manage, and coach their toddlers about how they should interact with their peers (Ladd, Profilet, & Hart, 1992). By providing structure to their social interactions, mothers help their toddlers to engage in more mature interactions—illustrating Lev Vygotsky's notion of the *zone of proximal development* as a mechanism for achieving more developmentally advanced behavior (as described in Chapter 2).

Parents can also structure situations or the environment to promote positive relationships for a toddler. The observational study of mothers with their two-year-old children in the supermarket, described in Box 2.4, provides an example. Effective mothers anticipated their children's behavior and directed their children to positive activities before they misbehaved. Mothers who frequently used such proactive techniques while shopping were rewarded with children who exhibited lower rates of misbehavior (Holden, 1983). A mother's proactive management style is also associated with children who have lower rates of behavior problems (Pettit & Bates, 1989).

Structuring the environment does not just help promote positive relationships; it may help avoid serious injury or even death. As many as 25% of children are injured each year in the United States (Scheidt et al., 1995), and many of these cases require medical attention. In rare circumstances, the injuries are so severe that a child dies. Even apart from child maltreatment, children are at risk of unintentional injuries from a variety of sources. The most common ones are motor-vehicle accidents, playground injuries, falls, poisonings, residential fires, and water-related accidents. (For statistics and other information about childhood injuries, visit the website of the Centers for Disease Control: http://www.cdc.gov/injury.)

For children under age six, a majority of injuries occur in the home. Most unintended injuries could be avoided by anticipating the child's behavior and childproofing the home. Childproofing includes actions such as installing child locks on cabinets, placing covers on electric outlets, and moving breakable objects out of reach. But childproofing only prevents certain types of injuries. Caregiver supervision is also necessary. The likelihood of child injury can depend on the child's characteristics, specifically, the child's temperament. As one might expect among children age two to five years old, uninhibited and active young children were more at risk when there was low supervision. However, children high in sensation-seeking temperaments were *more* likely to get injured when being closely supervised (Morrongiello, Klemencic, & Corbett, 2008). It appears that these children injured themselves while showing off.

Emotional Regulation

Another task for parents of toddlers is to help them learn to regulate their emotions. This process begins in infancy, of course, and is closely linked to attachment (Easterbrooks, Bartlett et al., 2013). Infants and toddlers are emotionally labile. They can be happily playing one moment but upset and crying only a second later (see Photo 7.3). After a quick parent intervention, the toddlers resume their play, apparently oblivious to the prior upset. This pattern of rapid emotional changes is a reflection of their inability to regulate emotions. Another example of this occurs when toddlers fly into emotional rages, commonly called *temper tantrums*. These tantrums—though they often begin before age two—gave rise to the term, the *terrible twos*.

Although toddlers' emotions are based in neurophysiological responses to the environment, their emotional expression also results from their behavioral traits, parenting practices, and the quality of the environment as well as the parent-child relationship and the situation (Calkins, 1994; Miller, McDonough, Rosenblum, & Sameroff, 2002).

Two-year-old children do have *some* ability to regulate their emotions. When scared or distressed, they may divert their eyes or hide behind an object. By shifting their attention and thereby engaging in self-distraction, they are able to reduce the effects of the arousing stimuli. Some toddlers use self-comforting behaviors such as thumb-sucking, hair stroking, or holding a favorite blanket or object. Seeking proximity and comfort from an attachment figure is another way that infants and toddlers regulate their emotions.

Photo 7.3 A toddler crying.

Source: © Jupiterimages/Stockbyte/Thinkstock

Children learn to regulate their emotions by developing coping skills, along with the help of maturing frontal lobes (Gross, 2014). Parents help their toddlers learn to regulate their emotions in at least four ways. First, parents *model* how to deal with emotions. Some parents get angry; others manage to control their temper. Second, parents *label* emotions so the child can begin to learn to identify his or her emotional states. A third function parents can play is to explicitly *teach strategies* to manage distress, control impulses, and delay gratification. Fourth, the *emotional climate* of the family can affect this regulation process. The climate includes attachment relationship, family expressiveness of emotion, and parenting style. Parents also manage the family emotional environment so that the child's distress is limited to a manageable level. Children learn to cope with emotional upsets more easily than with major emotional distress. This managing of the environment is particularly important when one is raising an extremely shy child (Calkins & Mackler, 2011; Morris, Silk, Steinberg, Myers, & Robinson, 2007).

Parents model emotional regulation. If parents exhibit controlled, modulated behavior, then their children observe this and learn that that is how adults behave. Parents also influence the development of regulation by their interactive style, such as acknowledging and supporting the child's emotions. Finally, disciplinary practices have been related to regulation. For example, parents who are overprotective and controlling may inadvertently promote social withdrawal in their toddler when the child interacts with his or her peers (Calkins, 1994).

Talk about emotions with toddlers is not just good for their emotional regulation, it can also help in the development of their prosocial (or helping others) behavior. Celia Brownell and her colleagues (2013) conducted two observation studies with toddlers. They discovered that parents who asked their children to reflect on and talk about emotions in a picture book had children who helped and shared more quickly and more often with an adult confederate who appeared to be in need. So parents who are talking about others' emotions also are promoting their toddlers' caring about other people and responding to their needs.

Promoting Cognitive Development

During toddlerhood, parents promote their children's cognitive development in many ways. Parents provide objects to play with and read bedtime stories to their children. But foremost, they talk to their children. In a landmark study, Hart and Risley (1995) found significant socioeconomic differences in the extent to which parents talked to their infants. Children of parents on welfare heard about 600 words per hour. In contrast, children from **affluent families** heard 2,100 words. That means by the time a child is three years old, a poor child will have heard 30 million fewer words than the child of a professional couple. No wonder the word-rich children had higher IQs and did better in school. In a controlled study, using a short-term longitudinal design, Weisleder and Fernald (2013) found that toddlers who heard more words had larger expressive vocabularies about five months later.

Considering that cognitive development encompasses a much broader spectrum of behavior than just linguistic skills, we might look at ways in which parents support their toddler's sensorimotor skills more generally. Allowing plenty of time for active play (walking, running, and tumbling) will help the toddler fine-tune his or her gross motor skills and prepare him or her for more sophisticated motor learning, such as learning to ride a bicycle or play a skilled sport. Parents often feel they do not have the time to engage in such play with their children; they should be encouraged to consider this an important part of a child's healthy development.

The world of imagination also begins to open up for older toddlers, who enjoy "make believe" play, role playing, and dressing up as different sorts of characters or people. Children of this age can have a fairly elaborate "relationship" with a stuffed toy or doll and invite adults to enter in to this kind of imaginative play.

Engaging the young child in the visual arts (play with clay, finger painting, rudimentary drawing) as well as with music (rhythm games, simple instruments, singing, making different kinds of noises) also promotes brain development, which will later serve them well in academic endeavors and in more advanced fine motor skills.

CHAPTER SUMMARY

Infancy, or the first year of life, is a time of dramatic change for both the child and the parent. The infant brain is developing and changing in several ways. Parents of infants deal with basic caregiving tasks, such as quieting crying babies. A key developmental process that occurs during the first year of life is forming the parent-child attachment relationship. Individual differences in children's behavior become very apparent early in life, and this is referred to as their *temperament*. Temperaments are one obvious example of child effects—how the child impacts the parenting behavior.

As the child moves into the toddler period of development, child rearing shifts from its early focus on basic caregiving to beginning to socialize children in directions influenced by parental goals. Discipline becomes an increasingly frequent activity for parents as children begin striving for autonomy. A variety of techniques are used to discipline children. Parents also engage in structuring the environment in order to promote some goals, such as peer friendships, but also to curtail certain activities, such as too much television viewing. Finally, parents must devote considerable effort to helping the child learn to regulate emotions and promote cognitive development.

THOUGHT QUESTIONS

- Does learning that an infant's brain is going through significant changes alter how you think about a young child? In what ways?
- Reflect on your internal working models of yourself and others. Do you have one or multiple models? How trustworthy are other people? How lovable are you?
- What are some ways to help prepare individuals for the challenges of parenting toddlers?
- What is your view about discipline? How early should a parent start correcting a child?

CHAPTER GLOSSARY

affluent families Families that earn greater than twice the country's median income.

axons Nerve fibers that conduct electrical impulses away from the nerve's cell body.

dendrites The branches of the neurons that allow for synaptic communication.

diary study A research procedure in which the participant records daily, in a notebook, the data of interest to the researcher.

distraction A parenting technique whereby the child's attention is strategically shifted from one source to another.

factor analysis A statistical procedure used to identify a reduced set of common factors or variables by analyzing patterns of correlations among a larger set of variables.

glia Cells that provide structural support and metabolic sustenance for neurons.

limbic system A group of brain structures (including the amygdala, hippocampus, cingulate gyrus, hypothalamus, and other parts) that support various functions, including emotion, attachment, long-term memory, and behavior.

myelin A white, fatty substance that grows around the axons of a neuron in order to allow for electrical conductivity.

myelination The process in which axons are sheathed by myelin so they will conduct electrical impulses.

negative emotionality When a child's emotional state is characterized by negative affect, such as irritability and anger.

neurogenesis The formation of neurons and glia in the fetus.

neurons Cells that specialize in conducting nerve impulses.

parental separation anxiety A parent's unpleasant emotional state of concern and apprehension about leaving a child.

prevalence The proportion of the population experiencing an illness or having a condition.

psychological control A type of control that consists of parental efforts to constrain, invalidate, and manipulate the child's psychological and emotional experience.

shaken baby syndrome A form of physical child abuse whereby an infant is repeatedly shaken. The whiplash causes bleeding in the brain, which in turn can result in such problems as visual impairments, permanent neurological damage, or death.

social caregiving Parent caregiving behavior that focuses on an infant's or child's interpersonal interactions.

synapses Connections between neurons.

synaptic pruning The process in which synapses that are not utilized are lost.

synaptogenesis The process of forming synapses between neurons. It occurs mostly after birth.

CHAPTER 8

Parenting Preschoolers

Chapter Preview: True or False?

- In contrast to fathers, mothers are usually more inflexible about gender stereotypic behavior in their young children.
- Preschoolers who are spanked are more likely to be aggressive than those who are not spanked.
- One-half of three-year-olds have a television in their bedroom.

PARENTING A PRESCHOOLER

Although *preschool* is a broad and somewhat hard to define category, for the duration of this chapter, we will be considering children age three through six years as "preschool" age. This period is one of rapidly shifting physical, developmental, and social change. Along with many of the developmental changes during this phase of childhood come particular parenting challenges. During this phase, parents are most concerned with children's social and emotional development, and questions frequently arise as to how best to discipline children and impart socially appropriate behaviors.

In some ways, parenting gets easier when children reach preschool age. Most preschoolers are toilet trained (having mastered the skill by 36 months), so there is no longer the need to deal with diapers. Preschoolers generally don't have difficulties in falling asleep and will sleep through the night unless they experience nightmares (e.g., Milan, Snow, & Belay, 2007). Emotional regulation also improves as preschoolers grow increasingly competent at language use. Because they can better express their feelings, needs, and wants, as children approach the age of six, they have fewer emotional outbursts and physical displays of emotion (otherwise known as *fits* or *tantrums*). Five-year-old children understand at least 4,000 words and use about 2,500 words. Compare this to their understanding of 300 to 500 words and use of 300 words just two years earlier.

Continuing to strengthen the attachment bond by engaging in positive, cooperative interactions is now recognized as an important quality of the parent-child relationship that promotes healthy development in the preschool years (Kochanska, Aksan, Prisco, & Adams, 2008; Laible & Thompson, 2000). Several areas of socialization become particularly prominent in the preschool stage. These include gender identity and prosocial development. Children's developing sense of autonomy at this age often poses a challenge for parents. With increasing bids for independence come discipline problems. Other common issues parents face are the use of day care and the preparation of their children for school entry. Let's consider each of those topics.

Gender Identity

One of most notable developments during the preschool period concerns the child's understanding of self. In particular, marked change occurs in the domain of gender identity. Although toddlers have learned to label themselves as *boys* or *girls*, during the preschool period, children develop better understanding of what the label means (see Photos 8.1a and 8.1b). In particular, preschoolers understand that gender is stable (boys develop into men, for instance, and girls into women) and consistent (maleness and femaleness do not change across situations or due to personal wishes). Along with gender identity comes knowledge about gender-stereotyped activities and toys. Even before turning three years old, children exert pressure on their peers to conform; by the preschool period, the pressure becomes explicit. Preschool-age boys and girls criticize their male peers for engaging in girl-typed activities such as dress-up or doll play (Leaper & Friedman, 2007). Preschoolers often express rigid beliefs and behavior in the areas of gender-typed appearance (e.g., girls wearing clothes with feminine colors, fabric, patterns, jewelry), gender-typed dress-up and play (vehicles, guns, kitchen, soft toys; see Photo 8.1a and 8.1b, for example), and sex segregation (percentage of same-sex children the child plays with). To date, most of the research into such gender typing in preschoolers has involved White, middle-class populations. A recent longitudinal study sought to expand this study into racial ethnic populations and, indeed, found very similar gender-stereotyped trajectories in young children. The researchers concluded that from age

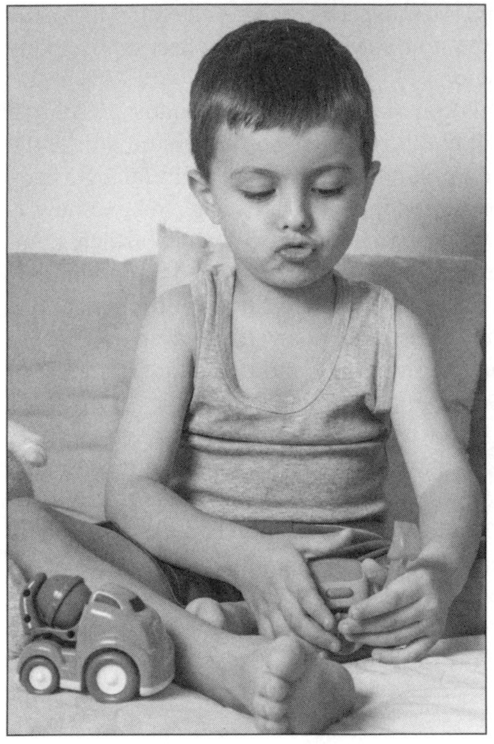

Photo 8.1a Preschool boy in sex-typed activities.

Source: © iStockphoto.com/solevnikola

Photo 8.1b Preschool girl in sex-typed activities.

Source: © iStockphoto.com/ktaylorg

three to five, children's rigidity about gender-divided roles evidenced itself in the areas of dress-up play, gender-typed play, and sex segregation. However, they found that gender-typed appearance (observed clothing, accessories, and hairstyles) decreased in rigidity over the two-year observation period, suggesting growing flexibility in this area (Halim, Ruble, Tamis-LeMonda, & Shrout, 2013).

Parents actively promote **gender socialization** in several ways. First, they label their child as a boy or a girl, so the child can learn gender identity. Then, depending on the child's cultural surroundings, the parent can use examples of women and men to explain gender constancy. They might point out that a woman with short hair is still a woman, and a man with a ponytail is still a man. Parents also help their children's gender socialization by teaching their children about male and female genitals (Bem, 1989).

Parents clothe their children differently, decorate their rooms differently, and equip their play areas differently. Boys have more vehicles, animals, and toys that promote **spatial-temporal** awareness. In contrast, girls' rooms have more dolls, floral furnishings, and ruffles. Some of these differences, of course, can be attributed to child effects; some girls just like dolls and ask for them. But it is also likely that most parents, as the gatekeepers of what goes into a child's room, support sex-typed rooms.

Parents also harbor different expectations and perceptions of their children based simply on the child's sex (Leaper, 2013). Common gender-stereotyped expectations are that boys are aggressive and girls are better at reading. Parents are more likely to have stereotyped expectations for sons, and fathers tend to have more stereotyped role ideas than do mothers (McHale, Crouter, & Whiteman, 2003) [Preview Question].

A second way parents encourage acquisition of gender roles is through modeling gender-based division of labor and assigning household chores based on gender. Although fathers' involvement with child care and housework has increased in the past 50 years, mothers continue to handle most of the domestic duties. Division of household chores tends to be gender stereotyped, even today. Fathers and sons are more likely to take out the garbage and mow the lawn, whereas mothers and daughters generally do the cooking, cleaning, laundry, and child care (McHale et al., 2003).

Parents also encourage different behavior in their sons and daughters through **differential socialization** practices. These differences in how sons and daughters are socialized tend to be subtle. The meta-analytic review by Hugh Lytton and David Romney (1991) found relatively few parenting differences as a consequence of their children's sex. Out of 19 behaviors (such as warmth, encouragement of dependency, and use of physical punishment), the only behavior that consistently differed based on children's sex was the encouragement of gender-typed activities. A significant difference found in studies from other Western countries was that boys received more physical punishment than girls. However, subsequent research has revealed further socialization differences, such as how parents talk to their sons and daughters (Leaper, Anderson, & Sanders, 1998) and the extent parents encourage autonomy in boys versus girls (Leaper, 2002).

Along with promoting certain gender differences, parents enforce gender conformity. This is especially true with parents of boys (Leaper, 2013), and boys are especially sensitive to their father's disapproval of cross-gender-typed play (Leaper & Friedman, 2007). Pressure for gender conformity is more likely to come from parents with traditional gender attitudes than from parents with more egalitarian attitudes (Fagot, Leinbach, & O'Boyle, 1992). One father, in an extreme example that made the national press, went to pick up his preschooler at a day care center and found his son laughing and playing—while wearing a dress. The father was furious that his six-year-old son had been allowed to wear a dress. He immediately withdrew his son from the center and filed a complaint with the state (Respers, 1996).

Before we start ascribing ultimate power to socialization, we must remember that parents still only play a limited role in a child's gender development. Parental actions work in concert with biology, peers, other adults (such as teachers), and the children themselves. For example, by the age of five, Chilean preschool children already held clear stereotypical expectations that girls would not like or do well in math (del Río & Strasser, 2013). When parents try to force a gender assignment on a child in conflict with the child's biological sex (XX or XY sex chromosomes), the effort is destined to fail, as was the case with a boy who was raised as a girl after suffering a botched circumcision procedure. His case is described in Box 8.1.

Box 8.1 The Boy Who Was Reared as a Girl

Due to urinary problems, six-month-old Bruce needed to be circumcised. In a horrific case of medical malpractice, the physician accidentally cauterized the boy's penis, so much so that it looked like a little burned string. Upon the advice of the famous John Hopkins University sex researcher John Money, Bruce's parents decided to have him castrated, surgically reconstructed to appear female, and then raise him as Brenda. The parents began socializing Brenda as a girl, never mentioning his early trauma to him. They started putting him in dresses, furnishing his room with dolls, and, when he got older, enrolling him in Girl Scouts. Despite the parents' best efforts, Brenda resisted it all. He hated wearing dresses, played with his brother's trucks and Tinkertoys, and put on his brother's clothes. He was anything but a content girl. His behavior and interests were obviously masculine. Nevertheless, under the guidance of Dr. Money, his parents kept trying. When he turned 12, he was injected with sex hormones. Despite his new breast development, he continued to resist developing a female identity. He not only experienced peer problems (partly due to being ridiculed by his classmates), but he began developing serious emotional problems as well. Psychotherapy was not successful. Finally, when Brenda was 14 years old, he was told about his medical history. He immediately wanted to revert to appearing as and being treated as a male. He took a new name, David, and soon began testosterone injections. About a year later, he underwent surgery again—this time to create a rudimentary penis and testicles. David was much happier in his new masculine identity than Brenda ever was. When he turned 21 years old, he even got married and appeared to be adjusting well to being a male, according to the book *As Nature Made Him: The Boy Who Was Raised as a Girl* (Colapinto, 2000). However, his hardships were not over. As an adult, he experienced depression, the death of his identical twin brother, failed investments, unemployment, and marital separation. His problems ended when he committed suicide in 2004—at age 38.

Autonomy

As Erikson (1993) recognized, a basic conflict toddlers and preschoolers experience is the desire for personal control and a sense of independence. Success leads to feelings of confidence and a sense of purpose; failure can result in doubt, shame, and guilt. Bowlby (1988) also saw a conflict over two intrinsic motivations: to become independent and competent and to retreat to the security of a loving and protective parent. The development of autonomy is a gradual process that begins at birth and is fueled by ever-increasing experiences of separation from a caregiver. By the time they are toddlers, young children exhibit a powerful motivation to do things for themselves and thereby master their own environment.

How do parents contribute to the development of autonomy? They do so by granting children a sense of control over their little worlds (St. Peters, Fitch, Huston, Wright, & Eakins, 1991). The ways parents do this are highly dependent on their children's ages. For the parents of infants, this means responding quickly to their child's cry so that these children learn their environment is responsive to them. Later, giving choices to a child, such as what to wear or eat, is a primary way to offering the child a sense of control. As children get older, families might make more decisions democratically and allow children to solve many of their own problems. This leads to a sense of psychological control and autonomy (e.g., Steinberg, Elmer, & Mounts, 1989).

A challenge for parents is to know when to reduce control and offer greater autonomy to their children. Baumrind's (1989) trait typology reflects the very different approaches to child independence that some parents take. Authoritarian parents are reluctant to allow their children choices and instead maintain a strict, controlling household. In contrast, permissive parents let their children become largely autonomous at an early age and provide little, if any, control. Authoritative parents achieve the correct balance for rearing competent children, according to Baumrind (1989; 2013). These parents provide firm control yet also discuss and negotiate with the child. These children are most likely to develop into competent adults. However, as Lewis (1981) pointed out, more competent children are also more likely to elicit more authoritative parenting. Thus child effects can be a major determinant of a child's level of autonomy.

Another trait studied by researchers of child autonomy is overprotection. Parents who are highly overprotective refuse to give any autonomy to their children. Overprotection may be appropriate in the case of a child with certain disabilities. But the trait has been recognized as characteristic of some parent-child relationships for more than 70 years, and it is linked to a variety of behavioral and mental health problems (Holmbeck et al., 2002).

How do parents support the development of autonomy? This is achieved through the use of gentle, nonintrusive control and by providing appropriate choices. Picture a parent giving the following choice: "Would you like to wear the red shirt today or the blue one?" Parents provide safe options that help the child begin to make their own decisions rather than insisting that all decisions be made by them (Grusec, 2011). In this way, children are given guidance but also receive the message that they can make decisions about themselves and those choices will be accepted by the parent.

Emotion Regulation and Self-Control

Emotion regulation—the ability to control and regulate one's own emotions—is one key aspect of self-control or self-regulation. The process begins in infancy, but in the preschool years, most children show dramatic improvements in their regulatory abilities. Children who are unable to regulate their emotions are at risk for developing two general types of behavior problems: **internalizing** (e.g., anxiety, depression) and **externalizing** (aggression and acting out) (Calkins, Howse, & Philippot, 2004).

One common example of emotion dysregulation are children who engage in temper tantrums. These are common in toddlers and preschoolers, with prevalence estimates ranging from 50% to 91% of all children (Giesbrecht, Miller, & Müller, 2010). The tantrums, typically lasting three to four minutes, consist of kicking, screaming, crying, hitting, and stiffening of the body (Potegal & Davidson, 2003). In some children, one or more tantrums can occur as frequently as once a day (see Figure 8.1). Preschoolers who have more temper tantrums are temperamentally emotionally reactive and have limited ability to regulate their anger and sadness (Giesbrecht et al., 2010).

Figure 8.1 Charting Temper Tantrums in a Preschool Boy

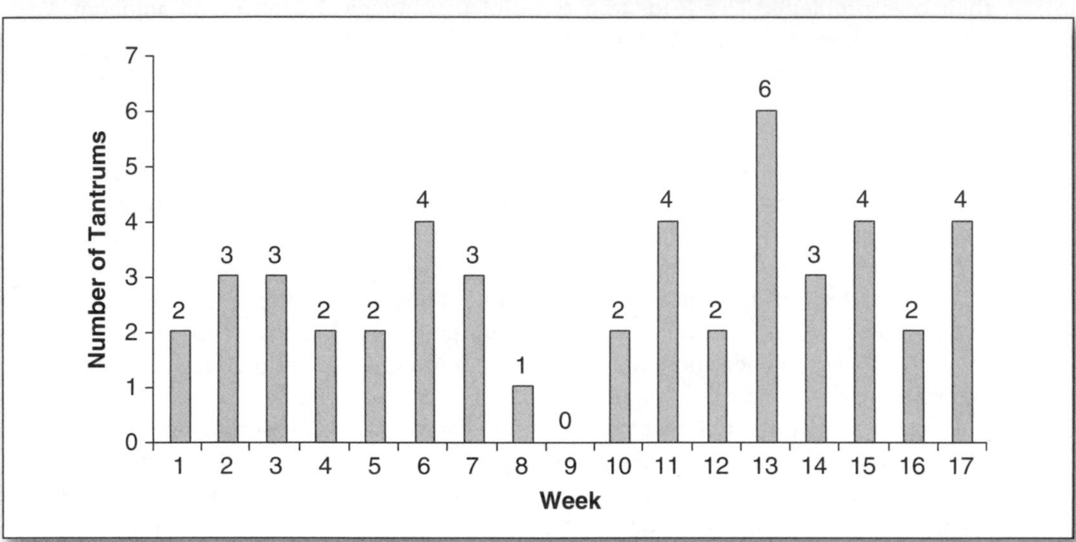

Parents help their children develop emotion regulation in several ways. Parents who are good at emotion socialization provide direct didactic instruction about emotions, model how to identify and deal with emotions, react to children's emotional expression, and discuss emotion-related topics (Eisenberg, Cumberland, & Spinrad, 1998; Zeman, Cassano, Perry-Parrish, & Stegall, 2006).

Being able to control impulses is key goal of parents' socialization efforts. There is increasing evidence that parents play a key role in this process. For example, mothers who were more sensitive to their infants and provided autonomy support had toddlers who had developed **executive functioning**—the cognitive processes enabling inhibitory control, resistance to distraction, problem solving, and goal-directed behavior (Bernier, Carlson, & Whipple, 2010). Parents also influence the development of emotion regulation in several other ways, according to Amanda Morris and her colleagues (Morris, Silk, Steinberg, Myers, & Robinson, 2007). Parents model emotion regulation. For example, in some families, parents yell at children and children yell back at parents. Parental practices that are directly related to emotions and emotion management also affect regulation. Third, characteristics of the family, such as attachment relationship, parenting style, and marital relationship, also impact a child's ability to regulate their emotions.

Researchers investigate self-control using a variety of experimental tasks, such as instructing a preschooler not to touch the candy but then leaving him or her alone in the room. These **effortful control** tasks are the most recent ways that researchers investigate self-regulation. Here, the task requires a child to suppress a predominant response and instead perform a subdominant action, such as waiting to retrieve a gift from a bag or walking on a line as slowly as possible. Preschoolers better at certain effortful control tasks show fewer behavior problems and better academic performance (Kim, Nordling, Yoon, Boldt, & Kochanska, 2013).

Executive functioning is closely related to self-regulation, though there is probably a bidirectional relation between the two (Blair & Ursache, 2011). Emotion regulation (and in turn, self-regulation) is a key ability for not just for school readiness (Ursache, Blair, & Raver, 2012) but is predictive of adult well-being: Self-control at age five was positively related to adult health and wealth and negatively related to criminality (Moffitt et al., 2011).

Prosocial Development

The development of *prosocial behavior*—loosely defined as actions considered beneficial to other people or society as a whole—is a high priority for many parents. Prosocial behaviors—such as helping, sharing, caring—emerge in the second year of life (Brownell, Svetlova, Anderson, Nichols, & Drummond, 2013). However, prosocial acts are often at odds with preschoolers' behavior. They hit and bite peers and siblings, they are self-centered, and they do not control their impulses. However, at times, preschoolers do engage in prosocial behaviors. Closely linked to prosocial behavior is empathy—being able to understand and vicariously experience what someone else is feeling. Children who empathize with others are more likely to act in prosocial ways (Taylor, Eisenberg, Spinrad, Eggum, & Sulik, 2013).

Parents promote prosocial behavior and empathy in several ways. By talking about emotions and helping their children to understand their own feelings and those of others, parents engage in emotional socialization (Katz, Maliken, & Stettler, 2012). They might verbalize empathetic concern: "I feel sad for you that your toy broke" or "I can see that you're feeling angry." Parents also both model and verbally reinforce acts of kindness. When toddlers or preschoolers cause another person distress, parents use **affective reprimands** to help their children understand the problem with their behavior. First, they raise the child's discomfort level by changing their own tone of voice. Then the parent gives a reprimand and explanation about the behavior: "Oh, Taylor. Look what you did! You hurt Sally when you pushed her down."

Alternatively, some parents mistakenly shame a child by telling the child he or she is a bad person or withdrawing their love. This disciplinary approach does not promote caring in children but rather the avoidance of adults (Barrett, Zahn-Waxler, & Cole, 1993). Preschool children who are shamed by parents are likely to develop a bias toward negative self-attributions when they get older. Depending on their gender and temperament, they may also be prone to reacting more to shame in middle childhood (Mills, Arbeau, Lall, & De Jaeger, 2010).

Parenting style (authoritarian vs. authoritative) may play a strong role in the early development of empathy in young children. Children as young as age two begin to evidence at least rudimentary concern for others in distress, as indicated by their facial expression, verbal responses, and even behavioral responses. A one-year longitudinal study of toddlers from age one to two showed increasing expressions of concern for mothers in distress and also toward some unfamiliar persons (Zahn-Waxler, Radke-Yarrow, Wagner, & Chapman, 1992). A more recent study looking into how early elementary-age children with behavior problems behave in response to others in distress suggested that mothers who were overly strict and who did not tend to reason with their children (i.e., authoritarian) were likely to impede their children's prosocial development (Hastings, Zahn-Waxler, Robinson, Usher, & Bridges, 2000).

Being empathic and prosocial is a key indicator that the child is on a healthy developmental trajectory. One of the most widely used questionnaires to assess that strength as well as problems of children ages 4 to 16 years is the 25-item Strengths and Difficulties Questionnaire developed Robert Goodman (e.g., Goodman, 1997; see Table 8.1). It can be completed in five minutes by parents or teachers and has been translated into more than 70 languages.

Corporal Punishment

Along with an increased desire for autonomy, preschoolers frequently violate standards of behavior. They might refuse to comply with parental requests, answering with a stubborn "No!" They test limits and sometimes even break rules just to see what will happen. At the same time preschool-age children are testing limits, parents are expecting more mature behavior out of them. Children's bids for autonomy coupled with their lack of behavioral control create a perfect storm for misbehavior in the preschool years. Not surprisingly, then, parental use of discipline peaks when children are three to six years old (Straus & Stewart, 1999; Vittrup, Holden, & Buck, 2006).

Parents of preschoolers use a variety of disciplinary techniques. When disciplining three-year-olds, the most common methods mothers report using (in order of frequency) include reasoning, diverting attention, negotiating, threatening, time out, ignoring, yelling, withdrawing privileges, and spanking (Regalado, Sareen, Inkelas, Wissow, & Halfon, 2004;

Table 8.1 Items From the Strengths and Difficulties Questionnaire

	Not True	Somewhat True	Certainly True
Considerate of other people's feelings			
Restless, overactive, cannot stay still for long			
Shares readily with other children			
Often loses temper			
Many worries or often seems worried			
Helpful if someone is hurt, upset, or feeling ill			
Often fights with other children or bullies them			
Often unhappy, depressed, or tearful			
Kind to younger children			
Often lies or cheats			

Source: Goodman, 1997.

Vittrup et al., 2006). As children get older, reasoning, yelling, and denying privileges are techniques particularly relied on (Lansford, Wager, Bates, Dodge, & Pettit, 2012).

Spanking is a commonly used but also controversial disciplinary practice in the United States (Straus, Douglas, & Medeiros, 2014; see Photo 8.2). As the primary method of corporal (also called *physical*) punishment (alongside slapping, grabbing, and holding), spanking falls under the heading of *coercive discipline*, whereby a parent forces a child through punishment to behave in some way. Coercive discipline also includes verbal techniques (such as threatening the child) and certain types of psychological techniques (such as shaming).

Advocates for spanking young children believe that parents need, in their disciplinary arsenal, the threat of using physical force to get children to comply (Baumrind, 2012). Some proponents cite Proverbs in the Bible as their justification. Five proverbs concern the use of the "rod of correction" (e.g., Prov. 22:15: "Folly is bound up in the heart of a child, but the rod of discipline will drive it far from him," New International Version). As mentioned in Chapter 1, those proverbs have been echoed in some childrearing manuals with conservative Christian orientations (e.g., Dobson, 1992) that continue advocating the benefits of corporal punishment (Rankin, 2005).

On the other hand, warnings about problems with spanking can be found as early as 1693 in John Locke's well-known childrearing manual, *Some Thoughts Concerning Education*. In it, Locke recommended that, "Children should only seldom be corrected by blows" (1693/1996, p. 118). Jean-Jacques Rousseau, in his book *Emile* (1762/1956), even more forcefully argued against it by warning of some of the dangers associated with its use.

What does research tell us about this controversy? In 2002, Elizabeth Gershoff published a comprehensive review of the research. She found 88 studies that had addressed the effects of spanking on children or adults. She evaluated 11 different developmental outcomes and found that there was only one positive outcome associated with spanking: that of immediate compliance. Not surprisingly, a child who is spanked will comply quickly with the parent's wishes. In contrast, significant effects were found on all 10 negative outcomes reviewed. Figure 8.2 depicts some of Gershoff's findings concerning the magnitude of the associations (effect sizes) between spanking and six different child behaviors. As the chart makes clear, spanking is associated with one outcome that parents seek—immediate compliance. However, it also is linked to three unintended negative consequences, including greater aggression, increased delinquent behavior, and a greater risk of physical child abuse

Photo 8.2 A father spanking his son.

Source: © 2009 Jupiterimages Corporation

[Preview Question]. In addition, children who are more frequently spanked exhibit lower levels of moral internalization and poorer mental health adjustment.

Parents spank or slap their children for a range of misdeeds, from trivial (picking the nose) to behaviors viewed as moral transgressions (ironically, hitting someone else) (e.g., Holden, Williamson, & Holland, 2014). However, as can be seen in Figure 8.2, aggression is the most common outcome associated with spanking. At first glance, it appears odd that the very reason many parents spank backfires. However, when thinking about it from a social cognitive approach, it makes sense. Children observe that when their parent gets frustrated or angry with them, the parent hits. So children model this behavior. Spanking also has other unintended consequences, such as being associated with mental health problems (anxiety, depression) and, in rare cases, child abuse (when the intensity of spanking escalates out of control).

Although some parents spank in an angry, emotional outburst, most parents who spank do so intentionally in an effort to eliminate misbehavior and under the belief that it will result in long-term positive outcomes. Why does spanking result in these unintended consequences? It can best be understood if one considers the entire process of spanking. A spank is intended to create pain. The child's body reacts physiologically to that pain as the child's initial reaction focuses on that pain. Next, the child has some initial cognitive reactions to the spank (e.g., "I was just hit. I do not like being hit. That makes me angry/sad" [Buck, Vittrup, & Holden, 2007]). As time passes, the child likely thinks more about it, such as when a parent reviews the misbehavior. More often than not, the child's secondary processing of the event

Figure 8.2 Mean Effect Sizes of Associations Between Spanking and Child Behaviors

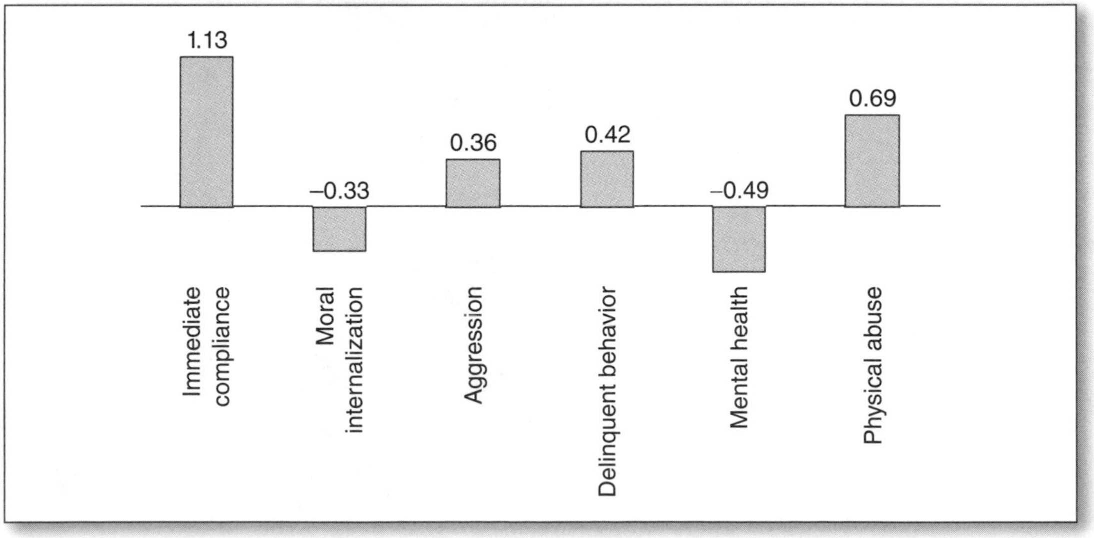

Source: Gershoff, 2002.

Note: Numbers indicate the *d* values or mean effect sizes of the associations.

is not likely to include what the parent wants the child to think about. Instead, the child may be focusing on the negative emotion that emerged. The point here is that parents spank from *their* perspective; they do not think about or understand the disciplinary experience from the child's perspective. Through this lens, it is easier to understand why spanking does not promote positive parent-child relationships.

Spanking is a controversial topic among parents—and even some researchers. Although most researchers accept the preponderance of studies indicate problems associated with spanking, a few investigators point out that there are some significant limitations to the available research (Larzelere & Baumrind, 2010). Specifically, they point out several shortcomings of the research. For example, studies that find problem behaviors (e.g., child aggression, depression) are correlational, not experimental. Second, the effects, although significant, are not sizable enough to warrant a conclusion that it is always a harmful practice. A recent meta-analysis on the topic found the effect sizes to be very small, suggesting that many children are not affected by spanking (Ferguson, 2013). Another limitation is that early research failed to control for child difficultness. The argument was that spanking could be a *reaction* to the child's difficult behavior (a child effect) rather than a *cause* of it. Recent research does take children's temperament into account and continues to find negative outcomes (e.g., Lansford et al., 2012). A fourth problem is that some studies into the effects of spanking may include parents who engage in much more severe harsh punishment, and the child is actually affected by those harsher punishments rather than the spanking. A final issue is that of moderators and mediators. Some investigators argue that variables such as maternal warmth or the normativeness of spanking will affect children's outcomes. Mediator and moderator studies are now appearing in the literature. For example, Lee, Altschul, and Gershoff (2013) tested whether maternal warmth would moderate the link between spanking and aggression at age five. Based on a study of more than 3,000 mothers and children, they determined that maternal warmth did help to ameliorate the negative impact of spanking.

Positive Discipline

Over the past twenty years, a new approach to discipline is being advocated by many parent educators and is being studied by researchers. The approach comes under the title of *positive discipline* but is also called *positive parenting*, *attachment parenting*, or *nonviolent parenting*. Advocates (e.g., Durrant, 2013; Nelsen, 2006) propose a different orientation to the traditional parent-child relationship. Rather than viewing themselves as the boss and the child as someone who needs to comply, the positive parenting approach is an extension of the authoritative approach. Parents still need to provide firm guidance, but it can be done (in theory) without disciplining a child in traditional, coercive ways. At the heart of approach is to get the parent and child to adopt a cooperative relationship orientation. Rather than the parent as the controlling person, both parent and child are regarded as individuals with, at times, competing interests, goals, and desires. The task is to figure out how to resolve the inevitable conflicts—without the parent exerting heavy-handed control.

Researchers are investigating this approach to discipline in several ways. Kochanska (2002) proposed that a mutually responsive orientation involving cooperation and positive affection not only elicits good behavior from the child but also promotes the development of conscience. This begins in infancy, and the context of these interchanges necessarily takes new shape as the child grows. For example, as the child becomes more verbal, the interchanges focus on discussions of events and ideas. Nevertheless, the quality of positive affect and reciprocal, open interchanges are maintained. Intervention programs are being designed to educate parents about this approach (Juffer, Bakermans-Kranenburg, & van IJzendoorn, 2008).

CONTEMPORARY ISSUES

Preschoolers With ADHD

Engaging in positive parenting can be especially challenging with one subgroup of preschoolers. Those are the children who can't seem to sit still; have a very short attention span; are impulsive in their behavior; perform poorly on pre-academic skills; and have deficits in their memory, planning, and self-control (Murray, 2010). Some of these children are expelled from preschool for frequent aggressive behavior. These children, who pose a serious challenge for their parents to deal with, are likely to be diagnosed with attention-deficit/hyperactivity disorder (ADHD). Estimates of the prevalence of the neurodevelopmental disorder range from a low of 0.5% to a high of 11% of the population of children, depending on the referral source, diagnostic criteria, and diagnostic instrument used (Ghuman & Ghuman, 2013; Hinshaw & Scheffler, 2014). See Box 8.2 for a discussion of the increasing rates of ADHD diagnosis.

Box 8.2 Why Is ADHD Increasing?

The rate of ADHD has doubled in 20 years. In the early 1990s, the rate was estimated to be fewer than 5% of school-age children. By 2013, the Centers for Disease Control and Prevention reported that 11% of children age 4 to 17 years had received the diagnosis. There are many possible explanations, including changes in diagnosis procedures, greater awareness of the problem, pharmaceutical industry promotions, and attention in the media. A more subtle cause is changes in schools and school policies. Psychologist Steven Hinshaw noticed some dramatic regional differences. More than 15.5% of children in North Carolina were diagnosed as ADHD in 2007 in contrast to the 6.2% rate in California. The best apparent explanation for the differences between states are the schools, school policies, and test scores. Some school districts push parents to diagnose and medicate their children so the children can be provided more services and/or not be counted in the district's test score average (Hinshaw & Scheffler, 2014).

Parents of preschoolers with ADHD have high rates of depression and stress (Baker, Neece, Fenning, Crnic, & Blacher, 2010). How do parents deal with this disorder? The two most common types of interventions are giving medication and training the parents and children. The most common intervention is also a highly controversial one. It involves, ironically, giving the children stimulant medication to calm them down. Children as young as two years old are medicated with such drugs as Adderall, Concerta, Ritalin, or Vyvanse. The central concern is how these drugs may affect the developing brain. At the present time, we do not know.

We do know that for many children, the medication works. Treatment studies find that, at least for the preschoolers who can tolerate the medication, it is effective in changing their behavior (Ghuman & Ghuman, 2013). Many parents report dramatic behavioral changes after their children have been on the medication for a short time. A slower but safer treatment option is to take a parent training program, such as Triple P Positive Parenting program or the Incredible Years. These programs can also effectively change the children's behavior (Murray, 2010).

Child Care and School Readiness

For many parents, finding good, affordable care is an essential part of early childhood. When both parents work outside the home or when a working parent is single, alternative child care is not optional. In fact, 61% of children younger than age five are in some type of non-parental childcare arrangement (Laughlin, 2013). The most common form of child care is *relative care*, such as a grandparent or other relative. Alternatively, children are placed in a variety of nonrelative care arrangements, including child care centers, Head Start centers, or care in a provider's home.

The onset, intensity, and duration of child care experiences vary widely. Some infants are enrolled in care centers within weeks of their birth and spend 40 or more hours per week there. Other children may not go to a child center until the summer before kindergarten. The type of child care also varies widely. About half of children in day care go to an individual's home; the others go to a center. Child care centers vary widely, but in contrast to home care, they are likely to be licensed by the state. Varieties of child care centers include university-sponsored facilities, national chains with local franchises, church-based child-development centers, and inner-city storefronts modified to serve as centers.

Since the 1960s, when mothers of young children started entering the workforce in large numbers, a variety of concerns have been raised about the effects of non-parental care on children's development. Child care centers have received the most scrutiny, including a major longitudinal study sponsored by the National Institute of Child Health and Human Development (NICHD). This study, described in Box 8.3, was designed to answer concerns about the effects of child care. The evidence revealed that the best kinds of non-parental care were safe, clean, stimulating environments with low group sizes, low child-adult ratios, and caregivers who did not hold authoritarian childrearing beliefs (Belsky et al., 2007). Good, quality child care is associated with some cognitive-linguistic benefits. However, independent of the quality of the center, if children log in a lot of hours at a center, they were more likely to develop elevated levels of problem behaviors, such as aggression and disobedience (Belsky, 2006).

Box 8.3 Are Child Care Centers Bad for Children?

At least since the 1970s, the effect of child care centers on children has been debated. Due to social realities such as maternal employment, divorce, and single parenthood, day care is a necessity for many families. Due to cultural fantasies about mothers and beliefs that are unsubstantiated by research, it is commonly thought that putting an infant in day care places that child at risk. Some critics fear that day care deprives children of developing a healthy, secure attachment with their mothers during the critical early years of life. Despite the fact that almost 10 million American children under age five are in day care, there is a national ambivalence about child care centers (Belsky et al., 2007).

To provide a comprehensive assessment of the effects of child care experiences, beginning in 1991, the government funded a major longitudinal study involving more than 1,300 families recruited from 10 sites around the country. The NICHD Study of Early Child Care and Youth Development tracked those families for 15 years in a carefully designed, **multi-method study** that included home observations, parent-child interaction tasks, child cognitive assessments, and teacher reports.

What has been learned? It is difficult to reduce the complex findings into a few sentences. However, it is clear that day care experiences *per se* do not have strong negative effects on children's development, as assessed through the end of Grade 6. In fact, parenting (e.g., sensitivity and quality of home environment) was found to be a stronger and more consistent predictor of children's later development than early child care experience. The largest effects associated with day care were that children who attended higher-quality day care tended to have higher vocabulary scores, and children who spent more time in day care were likely to have more externalizing problems. Somewhat surprisingly, systematic effects of the day care experience on the quality of parent-child attachment, the original concern that prompted the research, were not found (Belsky et al., 2007).

Some children are enrolled in early child care centers as training for kindergarten. Helping to prepare low-income children for school was the intent behind Headstart, the U.S. government program begun in 1965. In the United States, children typically enroll in kindergarten in the autumn after the child has turned age five, but there is considerable latitude given to parents in their enrollment decisions. Although some parents automatically enroll their child in kindergarten around the time of the fifth birthday, others consider their child's school readiness. This evaluation may lead some parents to wait a year before enrolling the child in school, with the hope that another year of maturation will be of benefit. This academic *redshirting* may have a short-term effect on children's performance in school, but it does not appear to last (Stipek, 2002).

There is indeed some empirical evidence to support the idea that early intervention (in the form of sending children to preschool) will have a positive effect for low socioeconomic status (SES) children. In a meta-analysis of 16 randomly controlled trials, it was found that enrolling economically disadvantaged children into early education intervention programs raised their IQ by more than four points. The more educationally complex the intervention is, the greater the effect on IQ. Children in centers that had strong education components successfully raised children's IQ points by more than seven points (Protzko, Aronson, & Blair, 2013).

School readiness requires a confluence of developmental processes. On the surface, children need to know their colors, shapes, letters, and numbers in order to be considered ready to enroll in kindergarten. But as Clancy Blair (2002; Ursache et al., 2012) explicated, readiness requires a combination of neurobiological maturation, emotional regulation, communication skills, and social competence.

Parents prepare their preschoolers for school by promoting emotion regulation and social competence. Others also engage in specific educational actions related to school readiness. Parents who value education are actively involved in educational activities with their children (reading books, watching educational television shows such as *Sesame Street*). Parents who have high expectations for the child's academic achievement are more likely to see their children make a successful transition to school (Hill, 2001). Whether a child is ready for school is also related to parental stress, income, and material hardship and varies according to race/ethnicity (e.g., Baker & Iruka, 2013; Brown, Ackerman, & Moore, 2013). Marital conflict can also undermine school readiness (Cabrera, Scott, Fagan, Steward-Streng, & Chien, 2012). Preschoolers from low-income families who moved three or more times in their childhood were less prepared for school, due to attentional and behavior problems (Ziol-Guest & McKenna, 2014).

Media Use

Electronics are now ubiquitous throughout the world, even the world of children. Television, videos, computers, and the Internet all powerfully appeal to children as well as adults. In fact, electronic screens have now infiltrated every stage of a child's development. Infants as young as three months old are exposed to 2.6 hours of TV or videos a day (Thompson, Adair, & Bentley, 2013). The amount an infant watches is a function of many factors, including parental attitudes, infant age, presence of siblings, and SES (Barr, Danziger, Hilliard, Andolina, & Ruskis, 2010). As many as 90% of parents report that their children who are younger than age two engage in screen viewing (Zimmerman, Christakis, & Meltzoff, 2007). By age three, about one-third of children have a TV in their bedroom, and many have their own iPads or computers (see Photo 8.3) [Preview Question]. Four- to five-year-olds are logging in close to four hours a day watching some type of electronic screen (Bleakley, Piotrowski, Hennessy, & Jordan, 2013; Tandon, Zhou, Lozano, & Christakis, 2011). Although electronics are excellent for capturing children's attention and there can be benefits to viewing some educational shows, many concerns about children's use of technology have been raised and some developmental problems have been documented.

Watching television or videos can benefit children in some domains, but more often, it is linked to problems (Thakkar, Garrison, & Christakis, 2006). Although the evidence is mixed, screen viewing can result in more aggression and self-regulation problems in children (see Table 8.2). Recent investigations into TV viewing indicate that fast-paced television can have an immediate, negative impact on executive function in four-year-olds (Lillard & Peterson, 2011) and it negatively affects school readiness by decreasing vocabulary. In a longitudinal study of almost 2,000 children, the more television viewing they did as toddlers, the worse they functioned in kindergarten (Pagani, Fitzpatrick, & Barnett, 2013). Yet another concern is the link between screen time and obesity.

Photo 8.3 A preschooler using an iPad.

Source: © iStockphoto.com/ARSELA

Pediatricians have long been concerned about media use in children. In 1999, the American Academy of Pediatrics issued a policy statement. They urged parents to avoid all television viewing for children under age two, given there are no known benefits (at least for infants)

Table 8.2 Children's Problems Associated With TV Viewing

Domain	Results	Comments
Learning/Racial attitudes	Positive effect	
Prosocial behavior	No effect	
Imaginative play	Mixed results	Depends on the type of program
Aggression	Mostly no effects but some negative findings	Depends on the type of program
Self-regulation	Mostly no effect but some negative findings	Depends on the type of program

Source: Based on review by Thakkar et al., 2006.

(Council on Communications and Media, 2011). After age two, they recommend no more than two hours per day of quality programming (Committee on Public Education, 2001). They also warn against leaving the TV on (*background TV*), especially during mealtimes.

Are parents concerned? For the most part, parents do not express a lot of concern about their children's screen time. Parents of preschoolers point out the many advantages of screen viewing (entertainment, educational tool, babysitter, bedtime coping device, family bonding time) and do not mention potential problems associated with viewing time (reduced family interactions, sedentary, unhealthy eating habits). When parents do state concerns, it is with the violent or sexual content of media (He, Irwin, Sangster Bouck, Tucker, & Pollett, 2005).

Childhood Obesity

Childhood obesity is considered to be one of the most serious public health challenges of this century. Just in the United States, the annual direct medical cost of adult obesity is estimated to be $147 billion, with another $14.3 billion spent on childhood obesity (Hodges, Smith, Tidwell, & Berry, 2013). In the 1970s, only 5% of children ages two to five years old were obese (see Photo 8.4). Today, the rate is 12.5% (Centers for Disease Control and Prevention, 2013). The rate is significantly higher among African American (1 in 5) and Hispanic (1 in 6) preschoolers. Worldwide, it is estimated that there are more than 40 million obese children (World Health Organization, 2014b).

Obesity is determined by one's body mass index (BMI), which, for children and teenagers, uses age, sex, height, and weight in the calculation (http://apps.nccd.cdc.gov/dnpabmi/). If the BMI of the individual is at or above the 95th percentile of other children of that same age and sex, then the child is classified as *obese*. If the preschooler is calculated to be at the 85th to 94th percentile, then the child is said to be *overweight*. A longitudinal study found that one-third of overweight preschoolers became obese by the eighth grade (Cunningham, Kramer, & Narayan, 2014).

Childhood obesity is a serious health problem for children; obese children are five times as likely to grow into overweight or obese adults. Adult obesity can result in multiple physical (asthma, type 2 diabetes, high blood pressure, high cholesterol, sleep problems) and psychological problems (e.g., anxiety, depression, low self-esteem) (e.g., Jansen et al., 2013).

How concerned are parents with their overweight preschoolers? One study found that in a sample of low-income mothers, overweight children only became a problem when the children were teased (Jain, Chamberlin, Carter, Powers, & Whitaker, 2001). Mothers believed weight was an inherited tendency. If the child was active and had a healthy diet and did not have any limitations with their physical activities, then the mothers believed child was not overweight. Further, they found it emotionally difficult to deny food to children who requested it, even if they had just eaten. They also pointed out that other family members were likely to undermine their efforts at controlling the child's diet.

For concerned parents, there are many things they can do. Foremost, they should be good role models by eating healthy meals and snacks. Parents need to serve fruits and vegetables and other nutritious foods for meals and snacks. Water, not soda or fruit juices,

Photo 8.4 An overweight child.

Source: © iStockphoto.com/fatihhoca

should be the beverage of choice. Parents can promote an active lifestyle by limiting screen time and engaging in physical activities themselves and with their children. Finally, parents should support and encourage preschoolers to be physically active every day. Children two years of age and older should engage in 30 minutes of activity per day and preschoolers should not be sedentary for more than 60 minutes at a time (Hodges et al., 2013).

Physical activity is not just useful for burning calories. It contributes to cognitive development and social skills learning and enhances psychological well-being in children. Play serves many functions for children. They develop interests, learn how to make decisions, follow rules, more effectively regulate their emotions, make friends, and experience joy (Gray, 2011). For preschoolers, physical play generally means rough-and-tumble play, running, climbing, sliding, and jumping. Around the age of five years, children may begin playing organized sports, such as youth soccer. Those activities and many other expressions of the way preschoolers play (dramatic play, imaginative play, and constructive play) form an important foundation for child well-being (Van Gils, 2014). Physical play also gets children outdoors and fosters an appreciation for nature and the environment. However, over the past 50 years, children's outdoor free play has seen a steep decline, in part because of parents' fear of child predators (Family Kids and Youth, 2010). That threat is just one of many potential hazards that serve to add stress to families of preschoolers.

Stress and Child Behavior Problems

Evidence is building that young children exposed to multiple forms of stressors in their environment are negatively affected. Unfortunately, in most societies, there are many forms of potential stressors. Each year, millions of children are exposed to natural disasters, war, and terrorism (Masten & Narayan, 2012). But there are many other forms of stress. For example, in a study linking childhood stress to adult health outcomes, 96 types of acute and chronic stressors were investigated (Bower, Crosswell, & Slavich, 2013). In the United States, common sources of stress for preschoolers include harsh punishment, maltreatment, and other forms of inappropriate parenting (depression, neglect), exposure to marital conflict or intimate partner violence, community violence, poverty, or exposure to some other type of trauma, such as a dog bite or car accident (Foster & Brooks-Gunn, 2009; Grasso, Ford, & Briggs-Gowan, 2013). In countries at war (e.g., Iraq, Syria) or countries where terrorists frequently engage in violent acts (e.g., Afghanistan), children are frequently exposed to life-threatening stressors.

Children react physiologically to these types of experiences. Stress triggers hypothalamus-pituitary-adrenal (HPA) axis activity, which produce glucocorticoids (e.g., cortisol) and other hormones (adrenaline). These hormones are then responded to by brain receptors. In turn, the hormones can regulate gene expression (Lupien, McEwen, Gunnar, & Heim, 2009). Based on animal research, exposure to stress early in life alters gene expression and induces neural structural changes as well as modifications in brain connectivity (Blair & Raver, 2012). Put in simpler terms, children who experience early stressors may show a variety of effects, including a greater reactivity to stimuli and fearful responses. Figure 8.3 illustrates the links from childhood adversity to self-regulation, the absence of which can lead to behavior problems. The intervening variables of stress, parenting, genes, and the brain are also included.

Figure 8.3 A Model of the Relations Between Adversity and Self-Regulation, With Intervening Variables

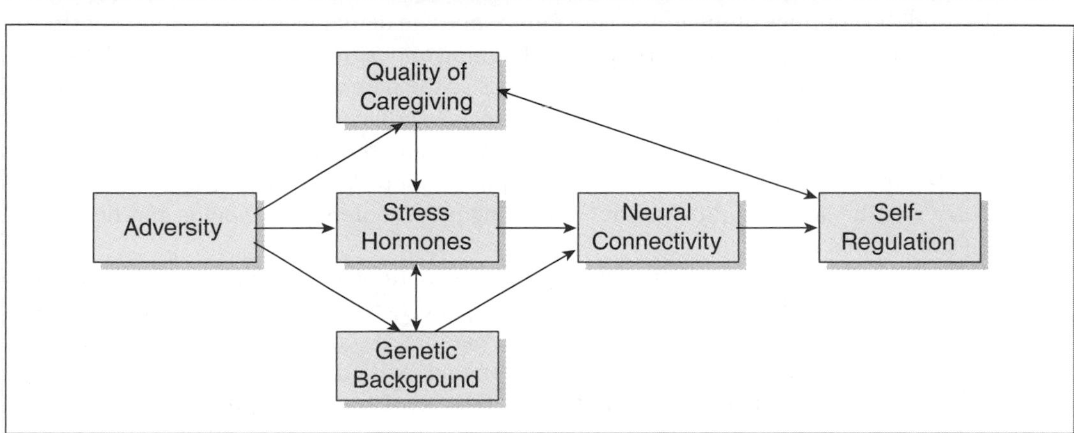

Source: Blair & Raver, 2012.

Young children exposed to adversity are likely to exhibit impaired self-regulatory abilities and behavior problems. How common are behavior problems? According to one government report using a large dataset of at least 9,000 parents, 7% of children had emotional or behavioral problems (Pastor, Reuben, & Duran, 2012). However, those data were based on parental reports to a survey and it is likely that the actual incidence rate of children's behavior problems may be significantly higher. For example, in a community sample of 541 three-year-old children, using parental interviews, as many as 20% of the children had an anxiety disorder (Dougherty et al., 2013). The children who had experienced stressful life events during the previous six months or who had mothers who had an anxiety disorder themselves were especially likely to have problems.

Of course, not all preschool behavior problems are due to stress. Problems can result from genetic disabilities, physical problems, or temperamental issues. But with regard to stress-related behavior problems, parents of preschoolers can play multiple roles. They may have a causal role, unwittingly exposing children to worries and concerns far beyond their years. Of course, there are many stressful life events beyond parental control (e.g. death, natural disasters, serious health problems), and parents cannot shield children from some of life's harsh realities. However, they can protect their children from some of the effects of stress by the manner in which they themselves cope and by intentionally shielding children and helping children understand what is going on in an age-appropriate manner. Parents can represent a major protective or coping resource for the child, assuming that the parent provides appropriate support (Foster & Brooks-Gunn, 2009; Masten & Narayan, 2012). Parents can also seek professional help early on, whether it involves getting parent education, counseling, or enrolling in an intervention project (e.g., Charach et al., 2013).

CHAPTER SUMMARY

When the toddler grows into a preschooler, gender identity and prosocial development emerge as two key domains of development. The preschooler's world begins to stretch beyond the confines of the immediate family, and the demands for behavioral control, an increased social repertoire, and expanded learning opportunities abound. This phase presents many parenting questions and challenges as the parent negotiates the child's emerging sense of independence with the need for socially appropriate teaching and self-control. Parents are also concerned about school readiness and the emergence of beginning skills for their children. Development during the preschool period sets the stage for the child's entry into the larger world of school. Preparing preschoolers for school is another central task of parents at this age.

The preschool years are a time when children continue to seek greater autonomy, with the consequence of an increase in parental discipline. In the United States, there are a plethora of attitudes about what constitutes good parental disciplinary technique. Even today, many parents in the United States rely on spanking, particularly with young children. The research evidence, although it has limitations, indicates that physical punishment of children is a problematic practice that is associated with a number of negative behavior problems. Parents need positive and effective alternatives to deal with the practical challenges they face with their preschoolers. Finally, even though the preschool years might be thought of as carefree, some children begin to exhibit problematic behavior during this stage of life (e.g., attentional difficulties, behavior problems, stress, and obesity)—problems that may continue well beyond the preschool years.

THOUGHT QUESTIONS

- The research evidence shows very early differentiation in stereotypic gender roles and behaviors. To what extent do you think these behaviors are intentionally socialized? How could you go about studying this question?
- Spanking is a controversial disciplinary practice. The research evidence overwhelmingly indicates the practice is associated with unintended consequences. Does that information influence your attitudes about spanking? Why or why not?
- What do you think of the idea of positive discipline? How could parents be encouraged to try it out?

CHAPTER GLOSSARY

affective reprimands Disciplinary responses that involve raising children's discomfort levels about the effects of their behavior and then providing an explanation about why it was wrong.

differential socialization A term referring to how parents may rear children differently due to the child's biological sex or other individual differences in the child.

effortful control The ability to regulate one's cognitive, emotional, and behavioral responses to external stimuli.

executive functioning A set of cognitive abilities that control and regulate other abilities, thoughts, and behaviors.

externalizing Problem behaviors that are directed outward (toward other people), such as noncompliance or aggression.

gender socialization The processes by which a child is taught to be a girl or a boy, as defined by the culture.

internalizing Problem behaviors that are directed inward, such as depression or anxiety.

multi-method study A study that uses more than two or more methods, such as observations, questionnaires, and interviews.

spatial-temporal Activities that involve space and time.

CHAPTER 9

Parenting During the Middle Childhood Years

Chapter Preview: True or False?

- Later-born children may be more likely to be rebellious, according to one theory.
- Ten percent of middle school children have a diagnosable disorder.
- Parents who spend more time helping their children with homework have children with better grades.

Middle childhood, the developmental period beginning at age 5 or 6 and continuing through age 12, is in some ways similar to the preschool period, as parents continue to socialize children in the same domains. According to parents of fifth graders, the key socialization issues they deal with are self-care/independence, household rules, manners/politeness, prosocial behavior, and curtailing aggression (Power & Shanks, 1989). Sounds a lot like the toddler years! Still, many parents find that child rearing gets easier during the middle childhood period. Less time is needed for basic child care, such as feeding and cleaning. More importantly, with children's increasing maturation, cognitive abilities, and abilities to self-regulate, this time period is characterized by an increase in the cooperative parent-child relationship.

However, this six- or seven-year period is also characterized by considerable change in the child's physical, cognitive, emotional, and social development. It also is the developmental stage where the child transitions from the safety of the home to the challenges of the outside world (Grusec, Chaparro, Johnston, & Sherman, 2013). Erikson (1993) claimed the task of this period of childhood was that of developing a sense of industry. Piaget observed children moving into the *concrete operations* stage, when children's cognition develops into being governed by principles of logical (though not abstract) reasoning.

Researchers have typically focused on three dimensions of parenting during middle childhood (Kuppens, Grietens, Onghena, & Michiels, 2009). The first dimension is *support*, including involvement, warmth, acceptance, emotional availability, and responsiveness. *Behavioral control,* or actions designed to control, manage, or regulate children's behavior, is the second dimension. A third dimension is *psychological control*, where the parent attempts to manipulate the child's thoughts, emotions, and feelings (Barber, 1996). As we shall see, support is clearly a beneficial attribute of parents but psychological control is not. The effects of behavioral control depend on how it is administered.

The number of potential social influences on the child also expands dramatically with the advent of school attendance, the appeal of peers, and the enticing world outside of the home. These changes require multiple adjustments and alterations in childrearing practices. There might also be major changes in the family. One common family change during this age period is the birth of another child.

PARENTS AND WITHIN-FAMILY INTERACTIONS

Birth Order and Siblings

By the time the firstborn child in a family has turned five, a majority of families (72%) will have a second child (U.S. Census Bureau, 2012). Does birth order impact the child? How does that second (or third) child affect the family? These and other related questions have been topics of speculation and research since 1874, when Sir Francis Galton (1822–1911) published his article "On Men of Science, Their Nature and Their Nurture." He discovered that many of the eminent English scientists were firstborns. Since that time, a considerable amount of research attention has been devoted to looking at birth order, siblings, and twins—in part, by behavioral geneticists to better investigate the *nature-nurture controversy*, a phrase used by Galton. As he recognized, "The interaction of nature and circumstance [nurture] is very close, and it is impossible to separate them with precision" (1883/1911, p. 131).

The most commonly investigated birth-order question is whether birth order is related to intelligence. Some researchers, such as Robert Zajonc, were convinced that family dynamics associated with birth order could account for differences in intelligence, and there have been more than 1,000 studies examining the relations of birth order to intelligence and

Photo 9.1 Whether—and if so, how—birth order influences behavior continues to be debated and investigated.

Source: © The New Yorker Collection 2006 Drew Dernavich from cartoonbank .com.

academic achievement (Sulloway, 1996). The topic continues to generate attention and controversy. If birth order does affect a child's intelligence, it is meager at best (Rodgers, 2001, 2014).

An alternative theory designed to account for birth-order effects is the **resource dilution model**, where the family is viewed as a conduit that dispenses resources to the children and, in turn, affects their academic achievement and cognitive development. Thus the amount of resources available to a child depends on the family income, the number of children, and their spacing. With the arrival of new siblings, older children experience the diminished resource of their parents' time and attention. Consequently, they may feel jealous (see Photo 9.1). Although this theory has fared better than Zajonc's **confluence theory** (based on the idea that intelligence becomes diluted with more children in the family) in empirical tests, it has also been critiqued on various grounds, including the methodology used to test the theory (Steelman, Powell, Werum, & Carter, 2002).

A different family dynamic as a consequence of birth order can be found in Frank Sulloway's book, *Born to Rebel* (1996). Taking an evolutionary theory approach, Sulloway argued that because of competitive tendencies, later-born children are more likely than firstborns to be reformers or creative thinkers who reject the *status quo*. To support his argument, Sulloway identified numerous revolutionary thinkers and activists throughout history, analyzing their birth order and family dynamics, including their parent-child relationships. A discussion of his thesis can be found in Box 9.1.

Box 9.1 Is Birth Order Linked to Rebelliousness?

In *Born to Rebel* (1996), Frank Sulloway developed a unique explanation for why some children become revolutionary thinkers. He took the perspectives of role theory and evolutionary psychology in an effort to understand how the family structure can influence individuals' thinking. His thesis was that birth order, in conjunction with certain other family dynamics, strongly influences the intellectual rebelliousness of the individual. The essence of his thesis is that firstborn children, as the eldest, identify with their parents and authority and thus enjoy their relative power and superiority over their siblings. Therefore, they seek to maintain the status quo. In contrast, later-born children are more likely to generate or support revolutionary ideas [Preview Question]. Prime examples include Nicolaus Copernicus (1473–1543), who was the youngest of four children, and Charles Darwin (1809–1882), the fifth of six children. However, it is not just birth order that Sulloway believes impacts rebelliousness. Sulloway identified more than 12 variables that appear to promote or inhibit the revolutionary tendency, including gender and the age difference between siblings. Parents also can influence the dynamics by how much conflict they have with their children.

Sulloway investigated the lives of more than 6,500 people and made a case that rebellious individuals or creative thinkers, such as Vladimir Lenin (a third-born) and Martin Luther King Jr. (a second-born), are more likely to be later-born than firstborn. However, as Sulloway acknowledged, not all revolutionary thinkers were later-borns (Galileo, Martin Luther, and Albert Einstein are prominent exceptions). He accounts for these apparent anomalies by other variables. Sulloway's thesis has not been supported by empirical work (e.g., Cundiff, 2013) but still, for our purposes, illustrates a provocative role theory approach to understanding development.

The bottom line is that the birth-order research has failed to come up with robust effects based simply on the order that a child was born into a family. There are far too many variables that influence family interactions and how children develop. The spacing between births; children's gender, genotype, and temperament; the total number of children in the family; and demographic factors such as family income and education are each an important influence on family dynamics.

On the other hand, it is now well known that parents react differently to differences in their children (*child effects*). One of those differences is birth order. Firstborn children are introduced into an environment that is different from that of second-born children. Parents have been observed to be more present, responsive, stimulating, and affectionate to their firstborn infants than to later-born children (e.g., Keller & Zach, 2002). Several other observational studies have also found birth-order effects on parental speech and behavior (e.g., Lewis & Kreitzberg, 1979; Minnett, Vandell, & Santrock, 1983; Oshima-Takane, Goodz, & Derevensky, 1996).

A more potent influence, though, on the quality of parenting of siblings is child temperament (Furman & Lanthier, 2002; Lengua, 2006). Almost as soon as the second child is born, parents are known to remark about the differences between their children's temperaments (Plomin & Daniels, 1987). These parental opinions may reflect a combination of objective differences and subjective perceptions. Indeed, there is the *tendency* of parents to think about siblings as different or contrasting. Both parents (as well as siblings) seek to promote differences between siblings in order to help the children develop their own areas of accomplishment and self-esteem. In turn, parents act differently toward their children based on these real or perceived differences. Although child characteristics can be a strong influence on parental behavior in discipline, these effects do not have an equally uniform influence on all parenting behavior. In areas where a parent holds strong values, beliefs, or goals, child effects are less influential (Holden & Miller, 1999).

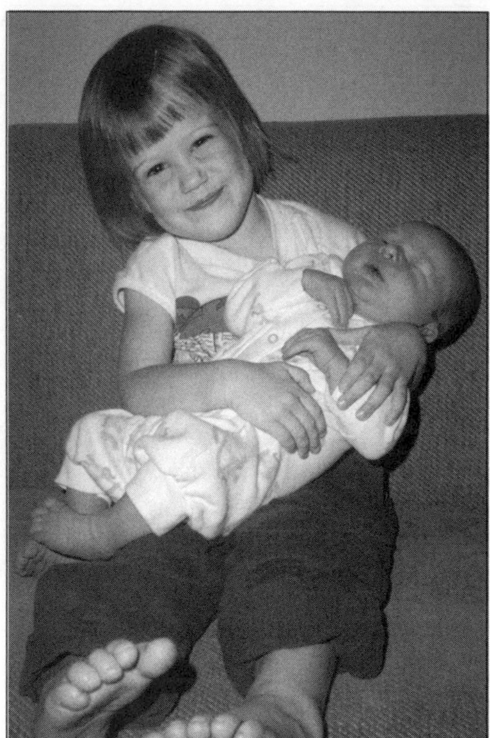

Photo 9.2 A proud three-year-old girl holds her infant brother.

Source: Photograph by G. W. Holden

A common occurrence that follows the birth of a second child is conflict between siblings. Known as **sibling rivalry**, this form of intra-family conflict is common in preschoolers and often continues at least through high school and sometimes well into adulthood (Feinberg et al., 2013; Tucker, Finkelhor, Shattuck, & Turner, 2013). Siblings often enjoy teasing or picking on their younger brothers or sisters. However, sibling conflict can turn dangerous when physical aggression crosses over into sibling abuse, particularly if an older child is teasing a younger one (Kiselica & Morrill-Richards, 2007).

There are several competing explanations as to why siblings engage in conflict. From an *evolutionary* perspective, siblings compete over scarce resources—parental attention, love, and material goods (e.g., Bjorklund & Jordan, 2013). By being stronger, smarter, or more talented than the sibling, the child should then receive more parental resources, according to this theory. In contrast, a *social interaction* perspective would pinpoint the cause of the conflict as young children living in close proximity but lacking the maturity or social skills to get along. A third explanation is that much of the conflict is generated by a *child's reaction* to perceived differential parental treatment, something children regard as unjust and worthy of retaliation against the favored child (Brody & Flor, 1998; Kowal, Krull, & Kramer, 2006). The problems in sibling relations caused by perceived favoritism may even continue into adulthood. Tension between siblings continues in adulthood when parents show favoritism (Gilligan, Suitor, Kim, & Pillemer, 2013).

Sibling relationship quality is linked to children's well-being. In a meta-analysis of 34 studies, children who enjoyed warmer sibling relationships had fewer behavior problems than other children. Alternatively, where there was significant sibling conflict, the children were more at risk for internalizing or externalizing problems (Buist, Deković, & Prinzie, 2013). Photo 9.2 clearly captures the warmth of an older sibling as she holds her infant brother.

Much of the research on sibling rivalry has focused on conflict between toddlers and preschoolers. One study that examined parenting and sibling conflict in middle childhood investigated parents' beliefs and behaviors (Perozynski & Kramer, 1999). Parents were interviewed about what they thought were the most effective ways to intervene. Common intervention techniques included parental control strategies (tell them to stop, warn they would be punished), child-centered strategies (help children use words to express their feelings), and passive nonintervention (ignore the conflict, let the children work it out). Both mothers and fathers believed that the parental control and child-centered strategies were most effective. However, when home audio recordings were analyzed, passive nonintervention techniques were the ones most commonly used.

Sibling rivalry can be exacerbated when children detect differential treatment. Indeed, children carefully monitor their parents' behavior to detect anything unfair or inequitable. If one child believes he or she is treated unfairly because a sibling is favored, then that affects the child's adjustment (McHale, Updegraff, Jackson-Newsom, Tucker, & Crouter, 2000). By middle childhood, children are well aware of differential treatment but often recognize the differences as justifiable, realizing a parent must take into account considerations such as age differences, personal attributes, and individual needs (Kowal et al., 2006). Children's perception of the fairness of differential parental treatment makes a difference: Children who view it as fair have higher self-esteem and lower levels of problems than do other children (Kowal, Kramer, Krull, & Crick, 2002).

Fights between siblings are often noxious, tiresome, and frustrating to parents and are among the most common challenges parents face (Kramer & Baron, 1995). Fortunately, in most families, sibling fighting wanes over time. Sibling conflicts are also recognized to be developmentally important in terms of educating children about such things as cooperation, negotiation, modeling, teaching, and empathy (Brody, Kim, Murry, & Brown, 2003; Feinberg et al., 2013). By the time both siblings reach middle childhood, their relationships typically become more positive, egalitarian, supportive, and companionable (Grusec et al., 2013). However, the quality of their relationship also depends on such variables as the siblings' gender and age differences. Parents of school-age children report that they typically try to help their children negotiate the conflict or teach them how to solve problems as opposed to ignoring the conflict or even approving of the aggression (Tucker & Kazura, 2013). To help parents and siblings deal with conflict, an intervention program (Siblings Are Special) has recently been tested. The 12-session program did promote positive sibling relationships and parental problem-solving strategies, but even so, it did not reduce the frequency of sibling conflict (Feinberg et al., 2013).

Twins—two siblings born at about the same time—occur in approximately 3.3% of births in the United States (Martin, Hamilton, Osterman, Curtin, & Mathews, 2013). Raising twins presents additional challenges not faced by parents of singletons. Although twins generally engage in less sibling conflict than do non-twin siblings, parents of twins do not have it easy. Imagine every childrearing task times two! Not surprisingly, in a study of Australian mothers of twins, most of the women reported they were exhausted and had no time for themselves. About one-third of the mothers revealed they were depressed (Segal, 2000).

As indicated by the research on parenting siblings, parents of twins modify their behavior to suit each child's temperament while trying to be fair (Lytton & Gallagher, 2002). Whether they like it or not, when there are twins in the family, fathers are more involved in the child care, compared with fathers of singletons (Segal, 2000).

In the next section, we turn to the research on paternal influences on children. Before we do, we should recognize that the inclusion of this lengthy review of father effects is in no way intended to undermine or diminish the very important role that mothers play in children's development. For millennia, mothers have had the single biggest influence on child rearing, often to the literal exclusion of fathers. Over the past 30 years, research included fathers in an attempt to elucidate a relatively recent social shift: the growing paternal role in caring for and affecting child outcomes (e.g., Lamb, 2010; Marsiglio & Roy, 2012).

Fathers' Involvement and Influence

Do fathers have a unique role in a child's development, or is their primary function to support mothers? The Greek philosopher Aristotle once pondered those questions, and an increasingly large body of evidence is now available from researchers to provide answers. The state of knowledge about fathers has expanded dramatically from those early investigations that focused on the effects of a father's absence (see Lamb & Tamis-LeMonda, 2004). That early work addressed children's welfare when fathers were away due to work, war, or divorce. The conclusion from that work was that the presence or absence of fathers did not have uniform effects on children.

Since the 1980s, a basic research question concerns the quantity and nature of fathers' involvement in child rearing. Identity theory (e.g., DeGarmo, 2010) indicates that the more important the identity (i.e., fathering) is to the man, the more likely he will be to engage in it. In a national sample of more than 930 men, the importance of fatherhood was either "high" or "very high" to most of the fathers sampled (Tichenor, McQuillan, Greil, Contreras, & Shreffler, 2011). The men who rated fatherhood as more important were more likely to be fathers, espouse greater religiosity, and also value career and leisure.

Although men report valuing fatherhood, they engage in less child care and interact less frequently with their children than their wives or partners. Using daily diaries, surveys, and micro-analytic observations, researchers have found largely consistent results in infancy (Lang et al., 2014), preschool (Schoppe-Sullivan, Kotila, Jia, Lang, & Bower, 2013), and middle childhood (Bianchi, Robinson, & Milkie, 2006) with regard to child care. Most fathers engage in far fewer caregiving tasks and spend much less time with children than do mothers. Based on results from a study where parents kept daily diaries of their activities, researchers learned that mothers spend twice as much time doing housework and child care as fathers do. When parents were simply asked to report on how much time they spend in child care, mothers of school-age children reported an average of 3.84 hours of direct contact with their children on a weekday and 7.25 hours on the weekend. Fathers reported 3.1 hours on a weekday and 5.72 hours on a weekend (Renk et al., 2003).

However, one specific area where fathers engage in more behavior than mothers is in what is known as *rough and tumble* play. This physical play, common in early childhood but which may continue into middle childhood, consists of wrestling, jumping on each other, tumbling and grappling—actions that might be considered aggressive in different contexts (Pellegrini & Smith, 1998). The play is rough and intense but at the same time, fun and exciting. Because mothers rarely engage in this form of play, it is thought to reflect a unique contribution to the child's development. Exactly what it may mean for children's development is not agreed upon, but speculation and some evidence indicates it is linked to improved self-regulation of emotion and behavior (Flanders et al., 2010; Paquette, 2004; Pellegrini & Smith, 1998).

Given the marked differences in paternal and maternal involvement with children, several investigators have taken a parental traits approach to classifying different types of fathers. Russell and Radojevic (1992) identified five types:

1. Uninterested and unavailable
2. Traditional
3. Assistant parent
4. Co-parent
5. Primary-care parent

The limitation with this classification scheme is that it fails to capture the multidimensional nature of paternal involvement. Involvement consists of more than a measure of direct contact. It matters how often and in what ways the father interacts with the child, his availability, and his role in childcare decisions and responsibilities (Cabrera, Tamis-LeMonda, Bradley, Hofferth, & Lamb, 2000). Other roles fathers play include providing financial support and supporting the mother—something now investigated under the label of *co-parenting*.

Does paternal involvement make a difference for children? The evidence indicates that it does. For example, in a study of 855 six-year-old children at risk for abuse or neglect, simply the presence of a father figure was associated with better cognitive performance and a feeling of self-competence in children (Dubowitz, Black, Cox, & Kerr, 2001). The more support experienced from a father or father figure, the more the children felt competent and the less they felt depressed. That finding replicated the results from many other studies that demonstrate the positive effects of father involvement. Involved and supportive fathers have children who are more successful and have fewer problems than the children of less-involved fathers (Lamb & Tamis-LeMonda, 2004).

How *do* fathers interact with their children, and what is the quality of that relationship? A common finding is that fathers tend to play more with their children, while mothers are more likely to provide care. For example, in a multi-method study of parents with children ages six or seven, fathers played more with their children than did their mothers (Russell & Russell, 1989). Mothers spent more time reading to their children, helping them with schoolwork or crafts, and caregiving (dealing with bedtime, clothing, health needs, and daily school needs). No differences were found between parents in levels of responsiveness or negativity.

Is the paternal relationship important for child development? Very much so, it seems. Increasing evidence from around the world shows that if a child feels loved and supported by the father—regardless of the child's relationship with the mother—that child will function better and have fewer problems. In contrast, it is often the case that feeling unloved or rejected by a father is associated with a number of child problems (Khaleque & Rohner, 2002).

From a young age, children begin to differentiate between their parents. Box 9.2 lists the categories of adjectives that children in elementary school used when nominating their fathers and mothers for a parenting award. Notice that for fathers, the most commonly used adjective was *love*.

Box 9.2 "Dad Loves Me": How Children Describe Their Parents

Researchers conducted a content analysis of more than 3,000 essays by elementary school children who nominated their mother or father for the Parent of the Year award. Here are the top six descriptors used to nominate their mothers and fathers:

Mothers	Fathers
Nice to me	Loves me
Cooks for me	Takes me places
Helps with my homework	Plays with me
The best	Makes time for me
Buys me things	Supports me by working
Cares for me when I'm sick	Does sports with me

Source: Milkie, Simon, & Powell, 1997.

Although mothers and fathers treat their sons and daughters similarly, as was discussed in the last chapter, there is evidence that the gender of the child does interact with the gender of the parent. In particular, fathers spend more time and are more involved with their sons than their daughters, especially when the children are school age (Raley & Bianchi, 2006). Child effects can account for some of this difference: Boys tend to seek out their fathers and to engage in activities their fathers enjoy. However, evidence of unmarried fathers' partiality for their sons has also been found in the Fragile Families study, where the fathers are more likely to have maintained contact with their sons than their daughters one year after childbirth (Lundberg, McLanahan, & Rose, 2007).

Paternal roles have changed dramatically over the past 50 years, as have notions of what makes an ideal father. Today, a good father is generally defined as someone who is a good provider, involved and nurturing with his children, and an equal partner in the parenting tasks with his wife, though this view varies across cultures (Seward & Stanley-Stevens, 2014). This view reflects a major change over the past 50 years or so, when the traditional father's key roles consisted of being the financial provider and household disciplinarian. As will be discussed next, disciplining middle-school-age children is a role not limited to fathers or mothers.

Discipline and Problem Behavior

Parents' disciplinary practices undergo various modifications during the middle school years. One illustration comes from the dramatic decrease in the percentage of parents who continue to spank their children. Before middle childhood starts, as many as 90% of parents report that they sometimes spank their children. However, by the end of this period, only about 30% of parents are using the technique (Straus & Stewart, 1999). Other disciplinary practices have long since lost their usefulness by middle childhood. Distraction, for instance, is ineffective, given that children's attention span and ability to sustain efforts are considerably longer. Time outs are no longer effective for punishment, either. Instead, parents are more apt to talk and explain, deny privileges, yell, scold or raise their voices, or spank (Lansford et al., 2012). Parents of school-age children are also likely to appeal to a sense of humor, to remind the child of personal responsibility, and to use psychological control techniques, such as shame or guilt (Collins, Madsen, & Susman-Stillman, 2002).

In general, the nature of disciplinary practices shifts during this time from parental regulation to mutual co-regulation and then to self-regulation by the child. This shift represents a power transfer, as parents gradually allow the child more autonomy. This is enhanced by encouraging children to take on more responsibility, develop independent ideas and opinions, and actively participate in family decision making (Kunz & Grych, 2013). That is not to say parents relinquish their supervisory control, but effective parents must modify how they manage their children during this age period.

As this shift suggests, effective parenting at later ages is not simply a matter of how well parents punish. Rather, it is a consequence of a two-step process of internalization, as described by Joan Grusec and Jacqueline Goodnow (1994). First, the child must clearly understand the parents' behavioral expectations and standards. Second, the child needs to accept those standards and behave accordingly. When behavior is deviant, the behavioral standards must be backed up with consequences.

Long before consequences are necessary, however, parents can do a lot to increase the likelihood of a child accepting their behavioral standards. First, they can be responsive to the child's needs. Second, they should make sure that the children consider the standards—and the consequences—fair and legitimate. This sense of fairness can be much more readily achieved if children have a positive relationship with their parents. One index of relationship quality is the presence of *positive synchrony*, first discussed in Chapter 3. Although it has mostly been studied in parent-infant interactions, it is also important when children are older (Harrist & Waugh, 2002; Thomassin & Suveg, 2014). For example, in a study of 122 low-income families, mothers and their 10-year-old sons were observed while discussing a topic of conflict. Positive synchrony was coded when the interactions were harmonious, reciprocal, responsive, interconnected, engaged, and when there was a shared affect (such as when both mother and son laughed). In families with higher levels of positive synchrony compared to other families, boys were less likely to get into trouble (Criss, Shaw, & Ingoldsby, 2003).

Having a good, quality relationship also helps parents with another aspect of effectively managing their children during the middle childhood years: monitoring. Because children are becoming increasingly oriented toward activities outside the family, parents must monitor their children from a distance. Recall from Chapter 4 that *monitoring* refers to parental awareness of the child's whereabouts and activities as well as who is with the child and, more generally, how the child is developing. As children get older, this monitoring takes new forms: the day's school performance and homework status, what the child is reading, who the child is talking with on the phone or chatting with on the Internet, what the child purchases, and so on (Crouter & Head, 2002).

Monitoring can be conducted in various ways. An authoritarian father can monitor his adolescent daughter by severely limiting her freedom. In contrast, a warm and nurturing mother may engage in monitoring through having frequent open conversations with her son. Monitoring can be conducted in very different ways—and with differing effectiveness. Like many parenting processes, monitoring is a relationship variable, as it reflects qualities of both the parent and the child. To be effective monitors, parents must be involved, interested in the child's welfare, and motivated to keep tabs on the child. But as Stattin and Kerr (2000) point out, effective monitoring also requires disclosure on the part of the child. A mother cannot be a good monitor if the child is secretive and refuses to reveal what he or she has been doing! Thankfully, in parent-child dyads where there is good communication and a good relationship, children tend to disclose what is really going on.

There is evidence for a negative association between monitoring and child behavior problems. Parents who reported monitoring their preadolescent children more (as indexed by their knowledge of the child's daily experiences) had sons with higher school grades and, in dual-earner families, fewer behavior problems (Crouter & Head, 2002). Besides effective monitoring, other attributes of positive parental discipline during the middle childhood period include guidance, responsiveness, approval, use of positive reinforcement, and consistency (e.g., Pettit, Bates, & Dodge, 1997).

Children's Behavior Problems

As children develop, it is necessary that they regulate themselves more. This is not an easy process for middle-school-age children. Though they are seeking autonomy and competence, they continue to experience difficulty controlling their own behavior. From a neurological perspective, the prefrontal cortex (involved in self-regulation and inhibition) is not fully developed. Preadolescent children continue to be motivated by self-centered goals, and they lack the more sophisticated social and communicative skills of well-adjusted adults.

Consequently, children in this age group exhibit various behaviors that their parents do not like, are concerned about, or consider problematic. Most commonly, children do not behave as they are asked (such as, "Go outside and play" or "Go to sleep"); they do things parents do not want done (create messes); and they have conflicts with others (perhaps teasing or fighting with siblings and peers). Dealing with these common problems is intrinsic to everyday child rearing.

The nature and extent of a child's difficult behavior creates a revealing barometer for how well a child is functioning. Even when children are unable to identify and verbalize the cause of their problem, their behavior belies the fact they are experiencing it. When multiple severe problems **co-occur**, they form disorders. Autism, characterized by social interaction and communication problems and repetitive, stereotyped behavior (see Chapter 5), is an example of a disorder. Autism and other disorders such as attention-deficit/hyperactivity disorder (ADHD) have an early onset (appearing in the first five years of life). Other disorders, including depression and anxiety, generally emerge during adolescence (Zahn-Waxler, Shirtcliff, & Marceau, 2008). The early-onset disorders have a male preponderance; the later ones show a female preponderance.

The most widely used instrument for documenting children's problems is the Child Behavior Checklist (CBCL), a paper-and-pencil survey developed by Thomas Achenbach (1991). There are several different versions of the instrument (one for parents of toddlers, one for teachers, and one for youth), but the one most commonly used is designed for parents of children ages 4 to 18 years. That survey contains 115 problem behaviors that children could exhibit. Some of the problems are health related, such as headaches, asthma, or allergies. Many of them are social (e.g., "physically attacks people," "gets teased a lot," "demands a lot of attention"). Also included are problems with emotions (e.g., "cries a lot," "shy or timid"), sleep (e.g., "nightmares"), and habits (e.g., "thumb-sucking"). Each problem is responded to on a three-point scale: "not true," "somewhat or sometimes true," or "very true or often true." The particular problems that children exhibit depend on a variety of factors, including the child's age, temperament, and gender; who is reporting on the problem (parent, child, or teacher); and the actual source of the problem.

Children's behavior problems are often categorized into two groups or **broad-band factors**. Problem behaviors that are directed outward, toward other people, are called *externalizing behaviors*. During middle childhood, common externalizing problems include disobedience, anger, fighting, frustration, and screaming. Other problem behaviors are directed inwardly and are labeled *internalizing behaviors*. Common internalizing problems include fear, nervousness, sadness, inhibition, and withdrawal. Table 9.1 lists 22 common internalizing and externalizing problems.

When the number or frequency of behavior problems reaches a certain level, the child is classified as having problems at the clinical level. In one study, the prevalence of serious psychiatric disorders in children between the ages of 9 and 13

Table 9.1 Common Types of Child Behavior Problems During Middle Childhood

Internalizing Problems	Externalizing Problems
Anxious • Worry, self-doubt • Fears • Nightmares	Aggressive • Hits others • Cruel to others • Lies, cheats
Depressed • Lonely • Sad Social Withdrawal • Feels persecuted • Likes to be alone	Hyperactive • Cannot concentrate • Easily distracted • Excessive movement • Impulsive
Uncommunicative • Will not talk • Stares blankly	Delinquent • Destroys others' things • Steals at home
Obsessive-Compulsive • Obsessions • Excessive talk	
Somatic Complaints • Overtired • Stomach problems	

Sources: Achenbach, 1991; Harrison, Vannest, Davis, & Reynolds, 2012.

over a three-year period was found to be 37% (Costello, Mustillo, Erkanli, Keeler, & Angold, 2003). Such children should receive professional assessment and treatment in order to address the underlying issues. In the United States, 13.1% of children ages eight to 15 have a diagnosable disorder, according to the National Health and Nutrition Examination Survey (NHANES) National Youth Fitness Survey (Centers for Disease Control and Prevention, 2013) [Preview Question].

Although most studies into children's behavior problems have been conducted in North America, the CBCL has been translated into many languages, and there are now many published investigations of children's behavior problems around the world. Box 9.3 describes some of that research.

Box 9.3 Child Behavior Problems Around the World

How similar are the behavior problems of children from different countries? Researchers have translated the CBCL, the Teacher Report Form, and the Youth Self-Report into more than 80 languages and used it in more than 67 societies (Achenbach, 2008). The results, based on more than 115,000 assessments of school-age children, were surprising. The types of problems experienced by American children and youth, as captured by the eight-syndrome model, are strikingly similar to patterns across many countries including Iran, Ethiopia, the People's Republic of China, and Lebanon. Differences *were* found, however, in the total number of problems. For example, according to 31,000 teacher reports in 21 countries/societies, children in Puerto Rico, Thailand, and Jamaica had almost three times as many problems as children in Japan, Finland, and China.

Not surprisingly, the classification of a child's problems is related to his or her environment. Clinical psychologist John Weisz and his colleagues (Weisz, Sigman, Weiss, & Mosk, 1993) compared rates of behavior problems in 11- to 15-year-old children who lived in Kenya, Thailand, and the United States. The Embu Kenyan children and the U.S. children had the highest total problem scores, though their patterns of problems differed. Embu children, who are raised with a strict emphasis on compliance and obedience, had more *internalizing* or overcontrolled problems (e.g., fears, feeling guilty, bodily complaints). The U.S. children had more *externalizing* or undercontrolled problems (e.g., arguing, disobedience at home, and cruelty to others). Those data support the view that the environment children are raised in plays a key role in not only the number of behavior problems but also what forms these problems take.

One childhood disorder that comprises multiple problems on the CBCL is ADHD, a problem mentioned in earlier chapters as well. There are varying estimates of the prevalence of ADHD. According to the National Survey of Children's Health, 11% of children and youth between 4 and 11 years received an ADHD diagnosis in 2011–2012 (Hindshaw & Sheffler, 2014). But according to the American Psychiatric Association (2013), the prevalence is about 5%, with boys being diagnosed about twice as often as girls.

It is not a problem unique to the United States; based on 30 studies from non-U.S. samples, the prevalence is even higher in some other countries (Hinshaw & Scheffler, 2013). The disorder is typically characterized by impulsivity, hyperactivity, and inattention, but there are multiple subtypes of the disorder (such as ADHD/Inattentive, ADHD/Combined Inattention and Impulsivity).

The most common cause of this externalizing problem appears to be a congenital problem (caused by problems in pregnancy or delivery) or a genetic predisposition to act in ways that are stressful, demanding, and intrusive to other family members. Children with ADHD evoke negative reactions from other family members and are often a disruptive influence on the family. Parents of children with ADHD are more likely to engage in inconsistent, harsh, and reactive discipline. ADHD sometimes co-occurs with other problems, such as *conduct disorder* (CD), a serious problem of persistent and repeated violations of social rules and the rights of others. To date, most of the research has been on boys during the elementary years, but ADHD has also been diagnosed in preschoolers, adolescents, and adults. The diagnosis is controversial because it can be easily misdiagnosed, exposing children to unneeded medication, which is the most common treatment. How long does ADHD last? For some children, symptoms disappear by ages eight to 10. However, for other children, symptoms continue into adulthood (Hinshaw & Scheffler, 2013).

Depending on the severity of the symptoms, a child with ADHD can be considered a child with special needs. Parents who have a child with behavior problems or special needs (as will be considered further in Chapter 12), face a variety of stressors and challenges. One articulate mother of a special needs child described some of her feelings, stresses, experiences, and wishes in an open letter, excerpted in Box 9.4.

Box 9.4 An Open Letter From a Mother With a Special Needs Child

To Whom It May Concern,

I am the parent of a special needs child. I was overwhelmed, confused, heartbroken, and struggling to unravel the complexities before me.

I was in survival mode to keep my family intact and to give my child the best quality of life possible.

I was presented with parental decisions that have torn me apart and kept me up more nights than I can possibly remember.

I had spent most days of the week at therapy and doctors' appointments and most nights up researching treatments and medication options.

I was forced into isolation at times due to the stigma and misconceptions that are epidemic in our society.

I became proficient at prioritizing my life and learning to let the little things go, to look at others with compassion instead of tabloid material, and to turn a blind eye to the stares or ignorant comments.

(Continued)

(Continued)

I did the best I could. I survived.

I am one of the lucky ones, my child has blossomed and has exceeded all our expectations.

I have now become strong, I have become confident and I have become a fierce advocate for parents of special needs children. The growth did not come without much pain and many tears, but it came.

So I ask you, please the next time you see a parent struggling with a raging child, a child terrified to go into school, a child making odd movements or sounds, a child that seems to be in a world of their own . . . be kind. Give a smile of recognition for what that parent is going through. Ask if there is anything you can do to help, give them a pat on the hand, or offer for them to go ahead of you in line.

The next time your child comes home telling you how Johnny or Susie is so weird, take the time to teach about differences. Take the time to talk about compassion, acceptance, and special needs. Please remember that your child learns from you. Be a role model, mirror respect, and discourage gossip.

The next time you see an out-of-control child do not assume it is bad parenting. Understand that many of these disorders have an organic basis, are biological and are real illnesses. When you hear the words mental illness, take out the "mental" and remember "illness."

Know that it is this generation that can stomp the stigma and create a world of acceptance.

The next time other parents are talking about "Those Kids," be our heroes, stand up for us.

The next time you see a special needs child know they are not just special in their needs but in their brilliance as well.

Take the time to meet our children. Take the time to know us.

Source: Marianne Russo, http://thelifeunexpected.com/archives/1705.

The specific cause (or *etiology*) of a child's behavior problems depends on a variety of factors. A large number of research studies have determined that problems can originate with the child, the parent, the parent-child relationship, or the larger environmental context. Bronfenbrenner's ecological systems theory is a useful way of organizing the different causes of problems.

The source of a problem *may* be a child's genotype, as is apparently often the case with ADHD, but other problems appear to be caused by poor parenting. And problems can occur due to faulty parent-child interactions, not just child maltreatment (to be discussed in Chapter 14). In particular, a meta-analytic review of parenting and children's externalizing problems found that parents who provided more acceptance, approval, warmth, guidance, and synchrony—and who displayed an absence of coercive control—had children with fewer externalizing behavior problems (Rothbaum & Weisz, 1994). These associations were stronger during the elementary school years than in the preschool period. However, warmth and acceptance is not always associated with healthy child development. One study found that mothers who were high in affection but also high in psychological control had children with more internalizing and externalizing problems (Aunola & Nurmi, 2005).

By using psychological control in the middle childhood years, the mothers appear to be giving guilt-inducing communications in an effort to manipulate the children and increase dependence.

There is increasing evidence that problems in the microsystem (such as marital conflict, parental stress, single parenthood, and low socioeconomic status) are associated with more childhood problems (Pettit et al., 1997). Mesosystem instability such as poverty, community violence, or living in a war zone also can be contributing factors. See Table 9.2 for a list of the many variables that have been linked to child behavior problems. These variables can be grouped into four categories of variables: child characteristics, parenting or parent-child relationships, family variables, and environment and social contexts.

The 27 variables listed in Table 9.2 are not exhaustive of all the potential negative influences on children's behavior. For example, fathers who work long hours are more likely to

Table 9.2 Variables Associated With Children's Behavior Problems

Child Characteristics	Family Variables
Biological/risk vulnerability	Single-parent family
Temperamental difficultness	Marital discord
Emotion-regulation problems	Parental psychological disorder
Cognitive delays	Stress
Deficits in social skills	Substance abuse
	Family violence
Parenting or Parent-Child Relationship	**Environmental and Social Contexts**
Insensitive/unresponsive	Low education level
Unavailable	Unemployment
Lack of warmth	Poor quality of child care
Insecure attachment	Poverty
Limited social/cognitive stimulation	Neighborhood disadvantage
Harsh, inflexible control	Natural disasters
Reliance on corporal punishment	Social unrest and war
Lax control strategies	
Inappropriate expectations	

Source: Based on Campbell, 2002.

have children with externalizing problems. Australian fathers who worked 55 hours per week or more had school-age children who had higher levels of externalizing problems than did children from other families (Johnson, Li, Kendall, Strazdins, & Jacoby, 2013). In a study of almost 500 seventh graders (13 years old), those exposed to various forms of violence (community, peer victimization) had more sleep problems and lower grade point averages (GPAs) (Lepore & Kliewer, 2013).

A good illustration of some of the variables associated with children's outcomes can be found in the research on children's reactions to marital conflict.

Marital Conflict

One well-documented source of a child's behavior problems, especially in the middle childhood years, is marital conflict. Recall from Chapter 6 that the transition to parenthood, for most parents, is joyful but challenging. Given the many adjustments that must be made—the time demands, sleep deprivation, and added pressures—it is no wonder that couples are stressed. Couples who are able to negotiate their new roles required in their transition to parenthood exhibit good co-parenting. This includes such dimensions as agreeing in parenting decisions, working together, supporting the parenting of each other, and dividing labor (Feinberg, Brown, & Kan, 2012). It also means not undermining the other parent and limiting the child's exposure to marital conflict.

For many couples, the additional stress means more marital conflict as they argue over such topics as lack of time spent together, too much time devoted to work, how money is spent, frequency of sex, time spent with relatives, and child rearing. Not surprisingly, couples who do not have good communication patterns tend to have a greater decrease in marital satisfaction than other couples.

The effects of marital conflict are not limited to a decreased satisfaction with the marriage. There is a sizable body of literature indicating that children are negatively affected by exposure to marital conflict. It is upsetting to witness intense negative emotions; it is particularly distressing if these negative emotions are coming from one's parents. Exposure to marital conflict can directly lead to problems in multiple ways (Coln, Jordan, & Mercer, 2013; Wilson & Gottman, 2002). One mechanism is that children might model some of the negative behavior they observe, assuming that aggressive behavior is a legitimate way to deal with problems. Second, marital conflict threatens children's sense of emotional security. This idea refers to a theory developed by Patrick Davies and Mark Cummings (1994), previously mentioned in Chapter 2. According to their theory, when children are exposed to marital conflict—either directly (such as by overhearing the fights) or indirectly (such as seeing the aftermath of the acrimonious relationship)—they begin to feel insecure about their own well-being. This occurs because they jump to the conclusion that the marital arguments must mean their parents are going to get divorced.

Children can also be affected by marital arguments when the conflict spills over into the parent-child relationship. Following an argument with a spouse, parents are more likely to be irritable with their children and engage in negative (such as harsh or authoritarian) parenting practices and use shame or other psychological control techniques. Alternatively, parents may become withdrawn and unavailable. Either way, the children are negatively affected, as revealed by an increase in internalizing or externalizing problems (Coln et al.,

2013; Zimet & Jacob, 2002). In a study that included middle childhood children, Buehler and Gerard (2002) found that marital conflict was linked to child maladjustment through harsh parenting and decreased involvement. There were also direct links between marital conflict and child problems, suggesting that direct exposure to the conflict was its own source of problems, apart from any changes in parenting quality. The more the children are exposed to the conflict, the more *sensitized* they become to it and show increases in negative emotions and problematic thoughts (self-blame) (Goeke-Morey, Papp, & Cummings, 2013).

A key variable that influences how children are affected by marital conflict is the way the child *thinks* about the conflict. A cognitive-contextual model that captures this internal process was developed by John Grych and Frank Fincham (1990). According to this model, children initially evaluate their parents' quarrels by the perceived negativity, level of threat, and relevance to themselves. Based on that assessment, children then make causal attributions (e.g., "My parents are arguing over my behavior; I caused it"). Children then *respond* to the conflict based on these assessments. Marital conflict can be distinguished in four dimensions: frequency, intensity, content, and resolution, as depicted in Figure 9.1.

Figure 9.1 A Cognitive-Contextual Framework for Understanding Children's Responses to Marital Conflicts

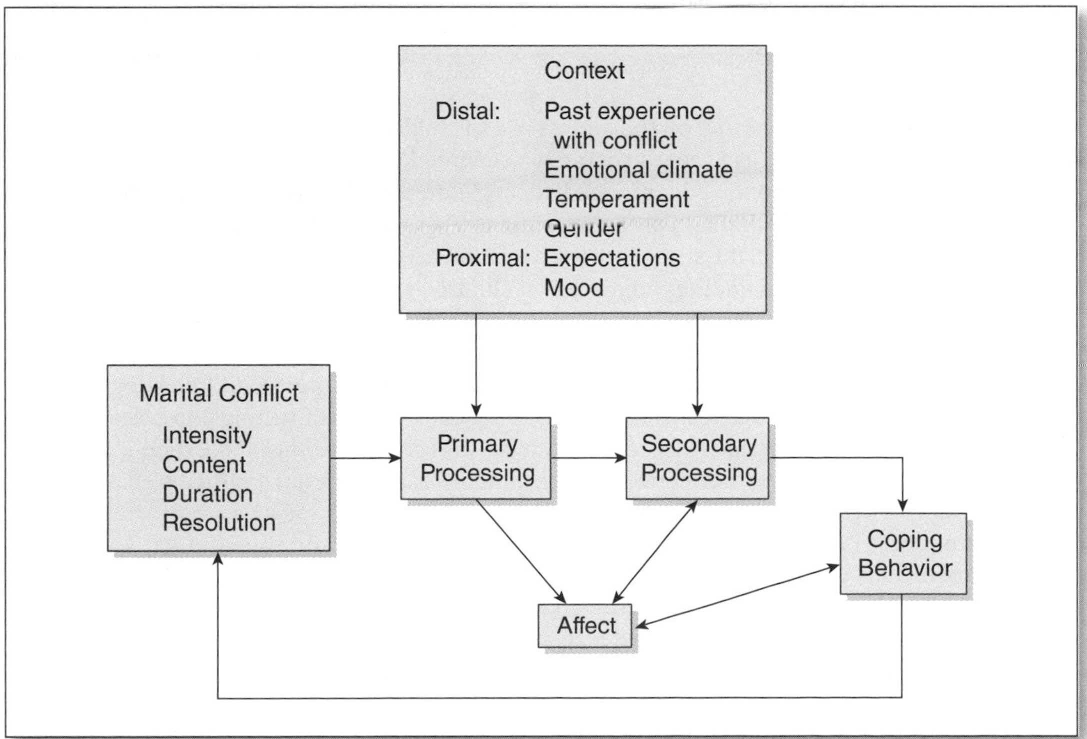

Source: Grych & Fincham, 1990.

The Grych and Fincham model helped to guide Patricia Kerig's (1998) investigation of how middle childhood children reacted to marital conflict. She wondered whether children's appraisals of marital conflict mediated or moderated their adjustment. If the perceptions *mediated* the conflict, then how the children perceived their parents' fights would directly influence the link between exposure to the conflict and the children's adjustment, as is illustrated below:

Exposure to Conflict → Child's Appraisal → Child's Adjustment

However, if children's perceptions were *moderators* of the relations, then those appraisals could influence the degree or direction of the relations between two variables, but they would not be causally related to the two variables. The figure below reflects a moderational model of marital conflict and child adjustment:

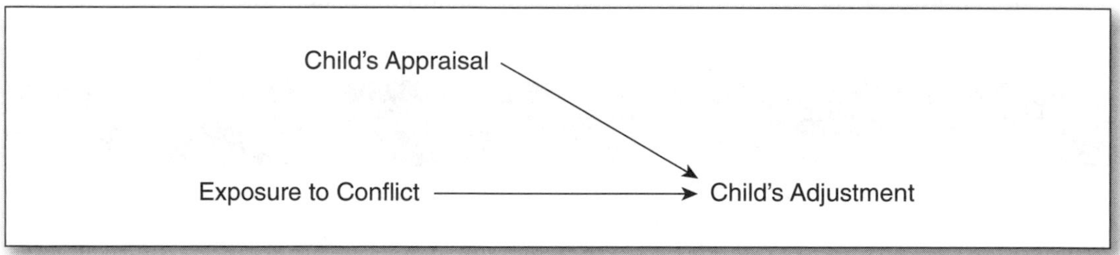

Kerig based her research on the reports of 174 children ages 7 to 11, and she determined that a moderating model more accurately accounted for the data. Furthermore, she concluded that marital conflict does indeed affect children's behavioral adjustments. Although a child's appraisal of marital conflict can intensify or reduce the effects of that conflict on the child's adjustment, the straightforward relation between the conflict and the maladjustment still exists. This finding indicates that children's appraisals influence the severity of their own reaction but cannot *protect* children from the negative effects of interpersonal conflict in the home.

There are, however, some variables that *can* help to protect children—for instance, whether the conflict was resolved. Also, was the conflict free of yelling, intense anger, verbal or physical aggression, threats, withdrawal, and child blaming? If so, then it likely will have fewer negative consequences for the child. A "safer" marital conflict is characterized by mutual respect, positive communication, and resolution (or at least progress toward resolution). When parents can amicably agree to disagree and the conflict is viewed as constructive, children show few ill effects (Cummings, Goeke-Morey, & Graham, 2002).

Next, we turn to the body of research looking into effects of divorce on children. As we will see, much of the research evidence indicates the potential for negative consequences on children's adjustment and well-being. Much of the negative impact of divorce is related to the sharp decrease in economic resources. However, there certainly are mitigating factors, and children (as we will see) are often surprisingly resilient. There are clear situations, however, for which divorce may actually prove *beneficial* to children: when there is domestic violence of any sort, child maltreatment, extreme psychiatric problems in a parent, or serious substance abuse problems in a parent. A release from a climate of abuse, violence, criminal behavior, or extremely erratic parental behavior is often a relief to children and may be related to improved child outcomes in the long run. That said, the research shows that "good enough" partnerships with two parents who are involved and loving with the child generally provide the best childrearing environment for most children.

Marital Dissolution and Its Aftermath

Sometimes marital conflicts or problems cannot be resolved, and the consequence is dissolution of the union. Each year, there are approximately 2.1 million marriages in the United States and 850,000 divorces (Centers for Disease Control and Prevention, 2014c). About half of divorces involve children, affecting 1.5 million children each year (Arkowitz & Lilienfeld, 2013). Most (90%) children will stay with their biological mother. However, about half of divorced individuals remarry within four years (Greene, Anderson, Hetherington, Forgatch, & DeGarmo, 2003). Consequently, the children will then become members of a stepfamily (also known as *blended* or *reconstituted* families).

Divorce and its aftermath is a long-term process that involves many changes and adjustments. Among the types of changes that may occur are the

- place of residence,
- daily routine,
- schools and peers,
- family financial situation,
- increased negative emotions,
- quality of parenting, and
- relationship with custodial and noncustodial parents and extended family.

For example, childrearing practices as well as the quality of the parent-child relationships have been found to change, with relationship deterioration a common finding (Kalmijn, 2013). It is not hard to understand that when mothers experience a financial decline, as is common, their parenting behavior can be negatively affected (Hetherington & Stanley-Hagan, 2002). Post-divorce, mothers are often more stressed and less likely to discipline and monitor their children effectively. Nonresidential fathers' childrearing behavior has also been found to change following divorce. They are less likely to communicate openly with their children as well as less likely to show affection or praise (Amato, 2000).

Just how well a child weathers these and other changes depends on many variables, including the child's age and gender; the amount of stress and level of acrimony between the divorcing parents; the degree of consistency and continuity in the child's life; and whether both parents are accessible, involved with the child, and cooperative with each

Photo 9.3 Some of the many changes associated with divorce.

Source: © The New Yorker Collection 2001 Christopher Weyant from cartoonbank.com. All Rights Reserved.

other (Hetherington & Stanley-Hagan, 2002; see Photo 9.3). Some 20% to 25% of children who experience parental divorce react with high levels of behavior problems, in comparison to 10% of children in non-divorcing families (Greene et al., 2003).

Although divorce and its aftermath is a difficult experience for the individuals involved, the research evidence indicates that many problems will dissipate, particularly if the mother's remarriage is a positive one or if the child is *resilient*—defined as being capable of adapting positively in the face of adversity (Goldstein & Brooks, 2013). However, some children who appear to be less resilient can continue to show lingering problems many years post-divorce. There is a linear relation between the number of parental separations/divorces in childhood and negative partner relations, partner adjustment problems, and interpartner violence later in life (Fergusson, McLeod, & Horwood, 2013). An important task for parents is to monitor their children's adjustment and seek professional help when the children exhibit severe, numerous, or persistent problems.

PARENTS AND EXTERNAL INFLUENCES

As children grow, an increasing amount of time is spent with people other than their parents. Time spent with these other individuals—and the activities they engage in—represent an inevitable influence on development. During the middle childhood years, five topics take on an increasing significance: peers, aggression and bullying, school, electronic media, and sports. Each topic will be considered next.

Peers

A child's interest in peers begins in infancy. As early as six months of age, a baby will smile at, vocalize for, gesture to, or even reach out to touch other infants. At 18 months, toddlers are highly attentive to peers. By the time they are preschool age, children engage with peers in complex social play (Rubin, Bukowski, & Parker, 1998; see Photo 9.4).

Photo 9.4 The peer group becomes increasingly important to children during the middle childhood years. Nevertheless, parents continue to play a role in managing and monitoring contacts with peers.

Source: ©iStockphoto.com/CEFutcher

As children move into the middle childhood years, the quality of peer interactions becomes increasingly sophisticated and significant to the children. Friendships are developed, and peer groups are established. Both individual and group relationships are important influences on children's development in ways that the parent-child relationship cannot be. For example, although parents may tell their children they are the best at everything they do, it is through social comparisons with peers that children learn about their true strengths and weaknesses. Peers provide pressure to conform and critical feedback either directly (by teasing or telling the child) or indirectly (by association or lack thereof). Relationships with peers are qualitatively different from relationships with parents due to the power equality shared by peers. (Remember saying, "You are not the boss of me!" and how good it felt?) Peer relationships are therefore classified as *horizontal,* versus the *vertical* relationship with one's more powerful parents. This experience with horizontal relations provides a unique staging area for later development. By dealing with equal-status peers, children learn to exercise influence in a different way. In turn, these interactions influence children's social and emotional well-being, self-concept, and self-esteem (Harter, 2006).

Parents are not idle bystanders in peer-relation processes. Rather, they play multiple roles in children's peer relationships and the development of social competence. In early childhood, this means adopting certain social roles on the child's behalf, such as being a social broker (to find friends), a gatekeeper (to exclude undesirable peers), a police officer (to intervene during conflicts), and a social coach (to improve the child's quality of interaction). Each role played by the parent helps the child become more competent in interacting with peers (Ladd & Pettit, 2002). In middle childhood, the key domains in which parents socialize their children are in reciprocity (through engaging in an egalitarian relationship), guided learning (teaching about the rules and values of the social group), group participation (engaging children in multiple types of groups), control (disciplining and modifying the child's behavior), and protection (being empathetic and providing a secure base for the child) (Grusec et al., 2013).

During middle childhood, monitoring peer relations gains prominence. Mothers also work with their children to respond to problematic peer interactions characterized by arguing, teasing, or bullying. Parents can have an indirect influence on their children's peer relationships, too. For example, there is some evidence that if there is a history of a secure parent-child attachment relationship, children are more apt to have competent social relations with peers (Thompson, 2006).

Aggression and Bullying

Aggression occurs when the aggressor intends to harm someone and that person then feels hurt. These negative actions may consist of physical aggression or **relational aggression**. Physical aggression includes such actions as pinching, slapping, hitting, punching, kicking, and beating up others. They are behaviors intended to cause physical pain to another person. In contrast, relational (or social) aggression harms others' friendships and social status through excluding, gossiping, and manipulating friendships (Underwood, 2011).

Physical aggression begins in toddlerhood (Tremblay et al., 1999), but for most children, it has decreased by the time of middle childhood. In contrast, relational aggression appears to peak and then wane during this period, although at least six different aggression trajectories have been identified (Underwood, Beron, & Rosen, 2009).

Bullying is defined as exposure, repeatedly and over time, to negative actions on the part of one or more other peers (Olweus & Breivik, 2014). Bullying typically involves a power differential and the creation of intimidation and fear in the victims. Bullying often occurs in the school setting (Marini, Spear, & Bombay, 1999). However, it has now expanded through the Internet with the advent of cyberbullying (Kowalski & Limber, 2013). In the United States, somewhere between 20% and 34% of children report being bullied (Eaton et al., 2012; Kowalski & Limber, 2013). Seventeen percent of students report being a bully and 8% say they engage in the practice at least twice a month (Kowalski & Limber, 2013). Data from 40 countries indicate that bullying is also an international problem, with 26% of 11- to 15-year-old children being affected (Craig et al., 2009).

Investigations into bullying identify three categories of participants: victims, bullies, and bully/victims. In a study of more than 4,000 middle school students (Haynie et al., 2001), 30.9% reported being bullied at least three times in the past year and 7.4% revealed that they had bullied at least three times. More than half of the bullies also reported they had also been bullied. It was this last group of bully/victims that were most likely to have behavior, emotional, and school problems.

Bullying is not a harmless rite-of-passage developmental experience. Rather it represents a significant threat to children's well-being (Olweus, 2014). It is tricky to identify outcomes of bullying because the victims have often been selected because they are shy, withdrawn, isolated, or physically weak (Wolke, Copeland, Angold, & Costello, 2013). Prospective studies discovered that peer victimization leads to social alienation and, sometimes, to deviant peer affiliation (Rudolph et al., 2014). Bullying victims are likely to show physical health problems (head and stomach aches), emotional or psychological problems (anxiety, depression, self-esteem deficits), and a negative impact on their school (school absences or poor school performance) (Kowalski & Limber, 2013; Reijntjes, Kamphuis, Prinzie, & Telch, 2010). There are also continuing risks for health-related, emotional, and social problems when victims become adults (Wolke et al., 2013). Being a victim, a bully, or a bully/victim is also associated with a high rate of suicidal thinking or even suicide attempts (Borowsky, Taliaferro, & McMorris, 2013).

How is parenting related to bullying? In a meta-analysis of 70 studies, it was found that both victims of bullying and bully/victims were more likely to be exposed to negative parenting (e.g., abusive, neglectful, or maladaptive parenting) than other children. In addition, high parental involvement, support, supervision, good communication, and having a warm and loving relationship were protective factors against bullying (Lereya, Samara, & Wolke, 2013). Those findings closely parallel the results of a meta-analysis of 48 studies examining the relations between parenting and relational aggression in the middle childhood years (Kawabata, Alink, Tseng, van IJzendoorn, & Crick, 2011).

Box 9.5 What's a Parent to Do?

As indicated by the research, bullying represents a serious threat to children and adolescents. Parents (or friends) should not be passive bystanders. Parents need to monitor their children to detect signs of mistreatment. Sometimes a child will not be forthcoming about their school experiences, and it requires gentle probing by parents. Once the child opens up about the experience, then parents can discuss potential actions, such as avoiding the bully, moving in groups, and encouraging the child to be assertive (see http://stopbullying.gov). Parents should also consider talking with school authorities to let them know where and when the bullying occurs.

Let us not forget that bullies (who are often victims themselves) have parents. Those parents (and, in fact, all parents) should take an active role in teaching children not to bully and to model respectful behavior. Oftentimes, the bullying behavior co-occurs with other problematic behavior (delinquency, poor school performance, drug or substance abuse) and is a clear indication that the child needs professional help.

School

With the exception of the more than 1.5 million children who are homeschooled in the United States (National Center for Education Statistics, 2014), a child in middle childhood spends most of his structured time in school. Schools provide a new setting for children to achieve a number of important developmental milestones, including academic success, responsive and warm relationships with teachers, and positive peer relationships (Wentzel & Looney, 2007).

Parents directly and indirectly influence a child's cognitive and school achievement through their general parental beliefs (i.e., expectations about child achievement) and behavior (such as a strong work ethic) as well as a number of specific behaviors (such as teaching strategies) (Davis-Kean, 2005; Wigfield, Eccles, Schiefele, Roeser, & Davis-Kean, 2006). Parents select the school district to live in or the particular school to attend. They arrange opportunities for a child to develop skills, provide lessons and activities outside of school, purchase educational tools, and expose children to relevant conversation and topics (Gauvain & Perez, 2005). Once the child is enrolled in school, parents talk with teachers, volunteer in classrooms, join parent-teacher associations, help with homework, and attend performances and athletic events.

By being involved—as well as setting high expectations, modeling, encouraging, and instructing—parents help promote school success with their children. The most direct way that parents are involved with their children's schooling is through homework (Hoover-Dempsey et al., 2001). However, the total amount of time spent in helping homework assistance does not correlate with achievement. In fact, a cross-culture study found the opposite was true. In China, Japan, and the United States, the more time mothers spent helping their elementary-school-age child with homework, the lower the child's grade was (Chen & Stevenson, 1989) [Preview Question]. The explanation was that the children who were doing less well in school received the most amount of time from parents in completing their assignments; thus a child effect was driving parental behavior.

An alternative explanation was not investigated: The parents who spent the most time were not *effectively* instructing their children. If parents are adept at tutoring, then children may perform better at school, as was found in a *longitudinal* study. Mothers who were observed to engage in the *scaffolding* of children's math problems as a tutoring strategy had children who performed better academically in the fourth grade (Mattanah, Pratt, Cowan, & Cowan, 2005). However, one mistake parents sometimes inadvertently make is to praise children. According the research by Carol Dweck, parents can hamper their children's academic success by labeling them as smart (Mueller & Dweck, 1998; see Box 9.6).

Box 9.6 Warning: Do Not Tell Children They Are Smart!

Well, at least that is the implication of research by Carol Dweck of Stanford University. For many years, she has studied children's motivation and achievement. Conventional wisdom is that parents should praise children for good performance by telling them they are smart. However, in a series of studies, she and her colleague (Mueller & Dweck, 1998) discovered that with fifth graders, this is a bad idea for at least two reasons. By attributing good performance to intelligence, children are likely to have the goal of getting high grades rather than the goal of learning or being challenged. Second, when children get a low grade, they then might decide that they actually are *not* smart after all. What is a parent to do? Praise the *effort* that went into earning the good grade.

If children learn the important lesson that hard work is needed for success, they will then be prone to work harder in the future to achieve their goals.

Investigators in Europe extended Dweck's work by examining the effects of inflated praise (e.g., "You did an incredibly good job!"). The researchers collected evidence showing that inflated praise, often given by adults to children with low self-esteem, may actually backfire. Such children may not feel they will be able to do such a good job in the future and thus are less likely to try new challenges (Brummelman, Thomaes, Orobio de Castro, Overbeek, & Bushman, 2014).

A good education is widely viewed by parents as a prerequisite for successful and satisfying employment (Dunn, Kinney, & Hofferth, 2003). Consequently, parents engage in a variety of activities to promote this goal. For example, parents begin reading to their children in infancy and then engage in other literacy-based practices such as shared reading (e.g., Deckner, Adamson, & Bakeman, 2006). What many parents don't realize is that although familiarity with letters and numbers may be important, a child's self-regulation, the product of the brain's executive functions is a much more important predictor of school success (Blair & Ursache, 2011).

Once parents have enrolled their children in school, they work to ensure their success. What had previously been labeled *parental school involvement* has evolved into a multidimensional construct of a complex array of parental actions, including monitoring the child, helping with homework, creating positive peer networks, and being involved with the school. Not all parents are equally involved in their children's schools. Parents who are more educated, have higher socioeconomic status, have more time available, and, most importantly, perceive their child's school as providing opportunities to participate are more active (Stacer & Perrucci, 2013).

There is strong evidence that parental involvement in education promotes positive development in preschool, middle childhood, and adolescence (e.g., Fan & Chen, 2001; Hill & Taylor, 2004). In a meta-analysis of 50 studies of parent involvement in middle school, Nancy Hill and Diana Tyson (2009) found that parent involvement was related to school achievement. They identified academic socialization as a particularly powerful parental behavior, in contrast to parental help with homework. Academic socialization involves communicating expectations and the value of education, fostering high academic aspirations in the child, discussing learning strategies, and planning for future educational endeavors. These behaviors serve to scaffold not just children's school-related cognitive abilities but also their developing autonomy and independence. Active parental involvement promotes not only academic achievement but also emotional functioning (Wang & Sheikh-Khalil, 2013).

Electronic Media

Seemingly at earlier and earlier ages, children are drawn to electronic media (including television, videos, and electronic games as well as computer and Internet use). In a survey of over 1,000 parents, it was found that by 3 months of age, 40% of infants were regularly watching TV, DVDs, or videos (Zimmerman, Christakis, & Meltzoff, 2007). At 24 months, 90% of the children were regular viewers, and they averaged 1.5 hours per day. By the time children have reached the middle childhood years, they are watching TV for more than three hours per day and spending another three hours in media use.

Electronic media are now ubiquitous. Three-quarters of all children have TV sets in their bedrooms. In many American homes, the TV is on "most of the time." In a majority of homes, it is on during meals (Rideout, Roberts, & Foehr, 2005; Vandewater, Park, Huang, & Wartella, 2005). Television provides children with many benefits, such as information, relaxation, entertainment, and education. There is evidence that TV viewing of racially diverse programs can positively affect children's racial attitudes (Vittrup & Holden, 2011). Television and the Internet can promote self-expression, identity creation, creativity, and imaginative play (Kalmus, Siibak, & Blinka, 2014). For parents, it is often a free babysitter, though one with some hidden "costs," as we will see.

Most parents are concerned about the effects of electronic media on their children, but these worries are often a function of the child's age and gender (Sorbring, 2014). Concerns include exposure to inappropriate content (e.g., pornography), lack of physical activity, sleep deprivation, falling prey to advertising and cyberbullying as well as exposure to strangers on the Internet (Kalmus et al., 2014; Lenhart, Rainie, & Lewis, 2001). Frequent depictions of violence and sex on television and in movies and electronic games may affect children's sense of what is normal and acceptable. Depictions of violence are glamorized, and the effects of the violence are not displayed. With frequent depictions of violence, children become desensitized to it (Funk, Baldacci, Pasold, & Baumgardner, 2004). Television advertising has repeatedly been shown to promote materialism and family conflict (e.g., when parents deny a purchase request) (Buijzen & Valkenburg, 2003). Food advertisements are thought to be particularly pernicious for children, as they encourage overeating. Relatively new threats come through access to the Internet: pornography, sexual solicitations, and even cyberbullying—characterized by online threats, rumors, or offensive language (Mitchell, Finkelhor, & Wolak, 2003). Last, electronic media use is a passive activity that can rob children of healthier alternatives such as reading, playing outdoors, developing talents, and spending time interacting with family or peers. In a study of electronic screen use of 10- to 12-year-old children in Iceland, it was found that screen time was associated with various mental health issues. Specifically, the more time a child spent in front of a screen, whether it be TV or video viewing, playing computer games, or some other media use, they were more likely to have sleep problems, feel sad, and have little interest in doing things (Yang, Helgason, Sigfusdottir, & Kristjansson, 2013).

Parents play a significant role in a child's exposure to electronic media—at least in the home. They decide how early in life the child will begin to watch or use media, the types of media and their locations in the home, and how much time per day the child is exposed to the media. Parents can also watch (co-view) or play the media along with the child, turning a potentially solitary activity into an opportunity for fun interaction. If children are allowed to have televisions or computers in their rooms, then the ability of parents to limit and control media use is greatly reduced.

Parents can certainly set rules for the use of electronics, but only about half of all parents set limitations on TV viewing, and only about 20% of them bother to enforce the rules, according to children (Rideout et al., 2005). One example of the wide range in parental limit setting was found in a study of mothers and their third to sixth graders. Almost one-third (29%) of the mothers had only a few rules about TV viewing. A second group of mothers (27%) had a handful of rules restricting its use. A third group, consisting of 25% of the mothers, had many rules regarding time use, the content, and required their children to ask permission prior to viewing shows. The remaining mothers (19%) gave their children considerable leeway in their use of media, so long as the children had finished their homework and chores (St. Peters et al., 1991). About half of all parents use TV ratings to inform their decisions about what their children can view, but only about 15% of parents make use of V-chip technology that allows blocking of shows with violent content. Parents can also mediate TV content by co-viewing and discussing it.

What do pediatricians say about television? The American Academy of Pediatrics (2001) recommends that middle school children watch no more than two hours of *quality* programming per day—and that televisions be kept out of bedrooms. That appears to be good advice because subsequent research found that television and video game exposure is linked to attention problems in middle childhood (Swing, Gentile, Anderson, & Walsh, 2010). Because all of this technology is now so readily available on smartphones or tablet devices, it becomes increasingly more difficult for parents to monitor their children's media use with these small portable devices. Indeed, it is common to see even very young children (toddlers and preschoolers) engaging with smartphones in the grocery cart, at restaurants, or in other public places. Children of the elementary school age may well have their own personal smartphones.

Sports

Many parents enthusiastically support involvement in sports, for many reasons. They desire their children to learn physical skills, be physically active, learn team behavior, and compete. By the time children are eight or nine years old, the majority of U.S. children are involved in some type of sports (Ommundsen, Løndal, & Loland, 2014). According to an ESPN study, the five most popular organized sports for 11-year-old youth are basketball (played by 20% of 11-year-olds), baseball (12%), soccer (10%), football (6%), and volleyball (5%) (Kelley & Carchia, 2013; see Photo 9.5). In general, participation in sports and other extracurricular activities is associated with increased likelihood of child well-being and decreased incidence of problems (Eccles, Barber, Stone, & Hunt, 2003; Ommundsen et al., 2014).

However, the benefits from youth sports involvement can be undermined by parents who push the child too fast and too hard. Some parents see childhood sports as the avenue to a college scholarship and perhaps professional stardom. However, they are likely unaware of the time commitment required in becoming an expert or at least highly accomplished. It takes about 10,000 hours of practice to become an expert at an activity (Ericsson, 2006; Ericsson & Lehmann, 1996). For male athletes making a national team, it takes on average 11 years of involvement with almost 6,000 practice hours, and for female athletes on the field hockey team, it was more than 3,500 practice hours (Baker, Côté, & Abernethy, 2003).

To date, there are no shortcuts for developing the increased efficacy of synaptic inputs required for expertise (Miall, 2013). The message for parents is clear: It takes a major time (and money) commitment for children to become experts. In the vast majority of cases, children do not develop into world-class athletes. When parents push a child to specialize in a

Photo 9.5 Middle-school-age children play soccer while their parents watch.

Source: © iStockphoto.com/dennysb

sport too soon and press them to overtrain, the potential benefits of sports involvement are lost and the risk of injury is increased (Jayanthi, Pinkham, Dugas, Patrick, & LaBella, 2013).

CHAPTER SUMMARY

In some ways, parenting a child during the middle childhood period represents a period of calm after the preschool years, before the storms of adolescence hit. However, many changes are going on in most families. One such change, if it has not already happened, is the arrival of a second or third child. Birth order and sibling interaction have been discussed. The degree to which fathers are involved with children varies widely, though paternal involvement is generally associated with better childhood behavior. During this age period, disciplinary practices are modified in line with the child's increasing autonomy. A number of child behavior problems can emerge during this time period. One of the sources of those problems is marital conflict. How a child perceives the marital conflict affects the child's response to it. When the conflict leads to marital dissolution, a variety of changes follow. These changes commonly include modifications in parenting, living situation, and finances. Many children in turn respond to these stressful transitions by exhibiting behavior problems.

Middle childhood is also a time when influences outside the family become increasingly attractive and influential. In particular, peers, aggression and bullying, school, electronic media, and sports are primary centers of attention for children during this age period. Parents are not passive bystanders to these external influences. Rather, the ways in which parents manage their children's peer relations and sports participation, are involved in their children's school and homework, and supervise media exposure are linked to children's developmental outcomes.

THOUGHT QUESTIONS

- What is your theory of how birth order affects personality and behavior?
- What are some of the ways parents can effectively address children's behavior problems? What are ineffective ways?
- Consider the roles of peers during middle childhood. In what domains are they most influential? What role do parents play in peer influence during this time?
- What do you see as the benefits and hazards of electronic media?

CHAPTER GLOSSARY

broad-band factors When a group of problems are combined to form a large category.

confluence theory A theory about how birth order and family size affect a child's intellectual attainment.

co-occur When two or more problems occur at the same time.

relational aggression Engaging in intentional hurtful behavior by excluding, gossiping, and manipulating friendships.

resource dilution model A theory about birth order effects that views the family as having a finite amount of resources (e.g., parental time, energy, and money); the presence of siblings necessarily dilutes the available resources for a child.

sibling rivalry Competition and conflict between siblings.

CHAPTER 10

Parenting Adolescents

Chapter Preview: True or False?

- Adolescence is a time of substantial neurological changes.
- Parent-child conflict peaks during adolescence.
- Twenty-five percent of adolescents think about suicide.

The adolescent years have been described in colorful ways. G. Stanley Hall, one of the fathers of American psychology and a pioneer of research into adolescence, called it a time of "heightened storm and stress" (1904, vol. 1, p. xiii). It has also been referred to as the *tumultuous* and *awkward years*. As youth grow into the adolescent years, the interpersonal equilibrium established with parents is often disrupted. It is a developmental stage that can be characterized by mood changes and risky behavior. Some researchers differentiate adolescence into three developmental periods: early adolescence (10–13 years), middle adolescence (14–17), and late adolescence (18 to early 20s) (Smetana, Campione-Barr, & Metzger, 2006). In this chapter, we will focus mostly on middle adolescence.

Many parents approach the adolescent years with trepidation, perhaps inspired by autobiographic memories, stereotypes, and misinformation. Common stereotypes describe teens as being difficult, oppositional, and moody due to "raging hormones," among other things. For all these reasons, parents are wary of the adolescent years. To be sure, adolescence is a time of change, but it does not necessarily result in rebellious youth. Although some parents erroneously believe their childrearing duties are over once adolescence hits, the evidence indicates that in certain ways, this time period is especially important for parent-child relationships. Parents need to be responsive to the many types of changes that are going on with the adolescent, including physical, cognitive, self-concept, and social.

DEVELOPMENTAL CHANGES IN ADOLESCENCE

The core task for the adolescent is identity formation, whereby the individual negotiates the transition between the safety of childhood and the complex, boundless world of adulthood (e.g., Erikson, 1993; Schwartz, Donnellan, Ravert, Luyckx, & Zamboanga, 2013). During late adolescence and early adulthood, individuals embark on their life paths, whether they are engaged in such activities as pursuing education, beginning full-time employment, establishing a family, or joining the military (see Photo 10.1). This identity formation process occurs among a sea of changes: physical, neurological, and cognitive as well as social.

Physical and Hormonal Changes

In several ways, parents' relations with their adolescents are linked to developmental changes. The most obvious indicator of development is the physical transformation associated with puberty. Puberty has long been regarded as the hallmark of adolescence (Susman & Dorn, 2012). In actuality, the surge in sex hormones that precipitates puberty occurs in middle-childhood years (see Box 10.1). Physical changes include emergence of pubic hair, changes in body shape and fat distribution, and breast development and the onset of menstruation in females. The median age of onset of menarche in girls in the United States is now 12.4 years (with the mean age being younger for African American and Latino girls than for White girls) (Chumlea et al., 2003). Breast development can begin as early as age seven in girls and even earlier for African American girls (Biro et al., 2010). Physical changes in males include emergence of body, facial, and pubic hair; growth of muscle; and change in voice, body shape, and testicular size and function. Boys go through puberty about 18 to 24 months later than girls (Patton & Viner, 2007).

Photo 10.1 Homework time for a teenager

Source: © iStockphoto.com/bowdenimages

Box 10.1 Raging Adolescent Hormones?

Parents are quick to attribute adolescent mood swings to raging hormones. But what is the evidence that the swings are due to endocrine changes? Surprisingly, the evidence that hormones are responsible for dramatic mood swings is weak. Instead, research reviews indicate that biology does indeed contribute to emotional volatility and negative moods, but the relation is complex. Hormone levels interact with other variables, including the brain, peers, parents, and situational factors, rather than simply and directly influencing behavior (Peper & Dahl, 2013). For example, Pennsylvania State University researchers tested whether testosterone levels in children and adolescents from 6 to 18 years old were linked to two types of behavior: taking risks (e.g., doing something dangerous for the thrill, damaging property, skipping school, or getting drunk) and depression (Booth, Johnson, Granger, Crouter, & McHale, 2003). They used quick, noninvasive saliva tests for testosterone. They found little evidence for direct effects of testosterone on behavior. Instead, the investigators determined that the quality of parent-child relationships moderated the negative effects of testosterone. That is, in families with good parent-child relationships, children high in testosterone did not engage in risk-taking behavior or experience depression. However, in families with poorer-quality parent-child relationships, there was evidence of testosterone-related adjustment problems. This study provides supporting evidence for the ecological model of development because the social context (i.e., quality of relationship with parents) moderates how hormones are expressed.

Many factors influence the onset of puberty, including genes, culture, socioeconomic status (SES), diet, exercise, and stress (Ellis, 2004). A provocative prediction based in evolutionary theory was proposed by Jay Belsky, Larry Steinberg, and Patricia Draper in 1991. They hypothesized that the home environment—and, particularly, parenting behavior—would influence the onset of puberty. Families characterized by stress and harsh parenting should have daughters who attained puberty earlier in contrast to warm and emotionally supportive family environments. In a recent test of that prediction, Belsky and his colleagues (Belsky, Houts, & Fearon, 2010) found that adolescent females who had insecure attachments as infants tended to have earlier onset and completion of menarche than girls with secure attachments.

The timing of physical maturation has many more repercussions on teenagers than simply their bodies. It influences boys' and girls' psychological well-being (i.e., self-esteem) and, conversely, the onset of emotional problems (i.e., depression). For example, adolescents who think they look older than their peers can experience emotional distress (Resnick et al., 1997). However, gender plays a determining role. Boys who mature early and thereby grow taller and heavier are at a distinct advantage for playing many sports. Consequently, early maturing boys can receive a positive psychological impact from their physical changes, though many early maturing boys do show psychosocial adjustment and behavioral problems (Mensah et al., 2013). Early maturing girls, who generally are heavier than late maturing girls, are at risk for experiencing emotional problems. A recent study of more than 11,000 girls found that early menarche was associated with being friends with deviant peers and engaging in more aggression (Mrug et al., 2014). However, early maturing children were also likely to have exhibited problems as preschoolers and middle-schoolers (Mensah et al., 2013).

Neurological and Cognitive Changes

During the period of puberty, adolescents are also undergoing substantial neurological and cognitive changes [Preview Question]. As one neurologist described it, "Brain structure goes through explosive changes during the teen years" (Giedd, 2004, p. 83). With the advent of the noninvasive magnetic resonance imaging (MRI) and functional magnetic resonance imaging (fMRI) techniques, detailed images of the adolescent brain and brain functioning are now available. The adolescent brain undergoes several types of changes (see Figure 10.1). Neurodevelopmental changes in adolescence are variable and can be grouped into three major categories of change: (1) *adolescent nonspecific*, referring to brain development that begins in early childhood and continues relatively evenly through young adulthood; (2) *adolescent emergent*, meaning brain development that happens at adolescence and levels off; and (3) *adolescent specific*, where brain development peaks at adolescence and then drops off (Casey, 2013).

There is both structural and functional remodeling of the limbic and cortical regions of the brain during adolescence (Eiland & Romeo, 2013). For example, brain scans indicate that in two locations on the cortex (prefrontal cortex and parietal lobe) there is a linear increase in white matter (containing myelinated axon cells) responsible for neural communication. In addition, there is a decrease in gray matter (consisting of the cell bodies of neurons and dendrites). These brain changes are significant: They relate to

Figure 10.1 Neurodevelopmental Changes in Adolescence

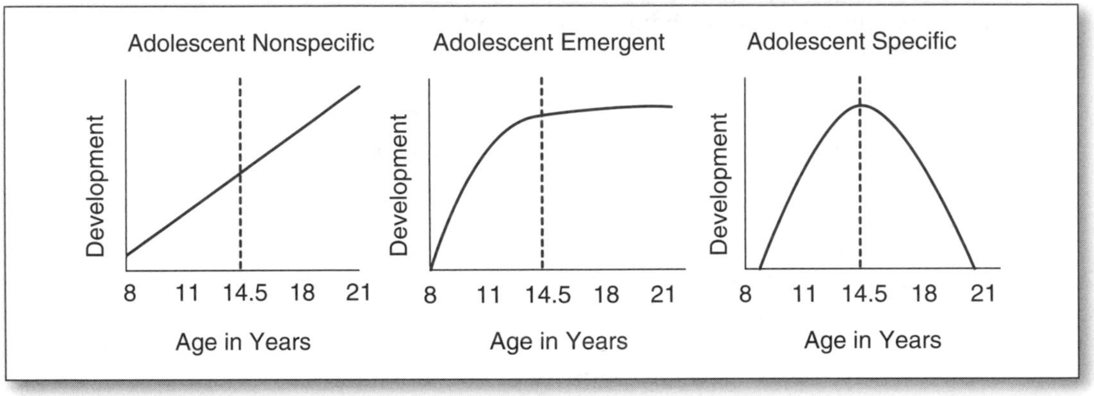

Source: Casey, 2013, p. 81.

behavioral variations in such key areas as self-control, sensitivity to social evaluation, and decision making (e.g., Albert, Chein, & Steinberg, 2013; Casey & Caudle, 2013; Somerville, 2013).

Many of the neurological changes that occur during adolescence are thought to underlie increases in what is called *executive function*—the capacity to control and coordinate thoughts and behavior. The prefrontal cortex is also associated with controlling impulses, weighing potential consequences of decisions, prioritizing, and strategizing. The prefrontal cortex is also involved in self-awareness and perspective taking, the latter ability underlying the capacity for empathy. There is also evidence for development in the brain's emotion processing and cognitive appraisal (the limbic and frontal cortical areas) related to engaging in risky or reckless behavior—an all-too-common feature of adolescent behavior that parents fear. Changing adolescent brains may also be at risk for the effects of stress. In Eiland and Romeo's (2013) review of the data, they concluded that the adolescent brain may be particularly sensitive to stress-induced neurobehavioral dysfunction, negatively impacting adolescent mental health.

Other developing brain structures have implications for adolescent behavior. The medial prefrontal cortex (MPFC) and the striatum are both continuing to develop during the adolescent period. The striatum, a part of the brain associated with risk taking and reward, gradually matures over the adolescence (Albert et al., 2013; Casey & Caudle, 2013). A recent fMRI study of adolescents found them to be more self-conscious than other age groups about their images being projected to peers. Markers of neurophysiological response included both autonomic nervous system peak activation and brain activity in the MPFC and the striatum (Somerville et al., 2013).

Adolescent cognitive abilities become more sophisticated during this phase of development, resulting in thinking that is more abstract, multidimensional, and relativistic. The cognitive developmental theorist Jean Piaget recognized this change, positing what he called the *formal operations* stage of cognition. Teens view rules, whether set by parents or others in authority positions, as social conventions: subjective and arbitrary. Thus parental requests to do chores or clean up messy rooms—a common source of conflict with adolescents—are often regarded by teens as unnecessary. For their part, parents often get upset when teenagers challenge their rules, requests, or values.

Despite improving cognitive sophistication, teens' reasoning abilities are not necessarily adultlike. Teen thinking can be characterized by egocentrism, which is linked to two characteristics of adolescent cognition. First is their heightened sense of self-consciousness—dubbed the **imaginary audience**. Because teens (often erroneously) believe others are watching and thinking about them, then they must be a special person. Second, is the teenage belief in what has been called their **personal fable**—the belief that what they experience is unique to them (e.g., Goossens, Beyers, Emmen, & Van Aken, 2002). These reasoning processes can feed into the belief of invincibility; problems other teens have (e.g., pregnancy, car wrecks) cannot happen to them (Sanders, 2013).

Cognitive changes also contribute to changes in identity. Adolescence brings an increased desire for independence and responsibility—as well as newfound access to money. Consequently, many teens work for pay. Twenty-eight percent of high school students work during their high school years (Davis, 2012). Typically, they find part-time jobs as sales clerks, cashiers, waiters, janitors, or child care providers. Employment provides a variety of benefits, including spending money or money for the family, interpersonal and occupation-specific skills, arenas to develop discipline and responsibility, and opportunities to enhance self-confidence. But hazards also exist in terms of the time work takes away from school and extracurricular activities. In addition, the working teen may experience increased stress and time pressure and be exposed to the possibility of job-related injuries (Resnick et al., 1997).

Another manifestation of the adolescent desire for independence from parents is expressed in hair length, clothing, tattoos or body piercings, or substance abuse. Some teens may be experimenting with autonomy and discovering themselves, while others may engage in behaviors directly intended to challenge parental control. From the parents' perspective, these behavioral expressions, whatever the source, are often perceived as rejections of parental values, the family's way of life, and authority (Steinberg, 2001).

Social Changes

In addition to physical and neurological/cognitive changes, a third area of rapid development is in social relationships. Given that adolescents seek distance and autonomy from their parents as they form their identities, they gravitate toward peers. By the time adolescence arrives, teens are spending about 40% of their nonschool hours engaged in homework, chores, or paid work. The rest of the time they are watching TV, surfing the Internet, socializing, or engaging in sports or structured activities. All told, adolescents may spend about 7.5 hours a day using electronic devices, much of it in communication with peers (Rideout, Foehr, & Roberts, 2010; see Photo 10.2).

Photo 10.2 A mother surveilling her teen.

Source: © iStockphoto.com/MachineHeadz

Along with an increasing orientation toward peers comes a change in emotional distance from parents. This distance is commonly thought to give rise to increases in conflicts with parents. Indeed, adolescent-parent conflict is common over such mundane issues as refusing to pick up rooms, resisting chores, fighting with siblings, and failing to complete homework (Smetana, Daddis, & Chuang, 2003). However, contrary to stereotypes, conflicts with parents are not the highest during adolescence [Preview Question]. A systematic review of the literature found the rate of conflict actually decreases significantly from pre- or early adolescence (10 to 12 years) to middle adolescence (13 to 16 years), although the intensity increases slightly (Laursen, Coy, & Collins, 1998). Furthermore, only a small proportion of adolescents (ranging from 5% to 15%, depending on the sample) have highly conflicted relationships with their parents and engage in extremely rebellious behavior (Smetana, Campione-Barr et al., 2006).

Adolescence is marked by the increasing time spent with and the growing importance of peers. Recreational, athletic, academic, and social activities are spent with youth of roughly the same age. Peers hold an immediate and powerful attraction. Friends become emotional confidants, provide advice, and serve as models of behavior and attitude (Wentzel & Caldwell, 1997). On the other hand, peers can be negative influences. It is most often friends who introduce teens to tobacco, alcohol and drugs, sex, and violence.

A Theory About Peer Influence

One controversial view that recognizes the important role that peers can have on adolescents is the group socialization theory. According to the theory (mentioned in Chapters 2 and 4), it is peers who are the most important social-environmental influence on teens' development, not parents. The theory stemmed from a mother's observation of her adolescent daughters. One daughter had a relatively smooth adolescence, but her younger daughter experienced considerable turmoil and rebelliousness. The fact that her younger teen was adopted prompted the mother to think about development from a behavioral genetics perspective. The mother was Judith Rich Harris, a former Harvard psychology graduate student who became a writer of developmental textbooks. In an effort to provide a theoretical answer to what made her daughters behave so differently, she integrated research from behavioral genetics, anthropology, and sociology as well as social and evolutionary psychology. Her solution was *group socialization theory* (Harris, 1995, 1998).

At the heart of Harris's theory is a strong social-environmental perspective—but not from parents. Although parents may be important determinants of behavior inside the family home, Harris believes that once a child is out of the confines of the home, it is peers who become the dominant developmental influence (Harris, 1998). According to Harris, parents, with the exception of providing genes, have little or no effect on the psychological characteristics that children will have as adults, including personality, emotional regulation, behavior, or cognitions. Recall from Chapter 2 that human behavioral genetics research indicates heritability from parent to child accounts for 30% to 60% of the variance in personality characteristics; the rest of the environmental influence comes either from a shared (common to all the children in the home) or unshared (unique to that child) home environment. Harris argued that the shared and unshared environment has little importance in the face of peers: That is, peers trump parents. She believes the influence of peers has been underestimated, along with other nonfamilial agents, such as the movies and television.

Harris does not refute the studies that find that parent-adolescent behavior is correlated; she just reinterprets them. Studies that link harsh parenting to delinquent adolescent behavior can be interpreted as revealing a genetic predisposition toward aggressive behavior. Further, the associations between parent and child are revealing child effects rather than parent effects. So Harris believes parents *react* to their adolescents' aggression and acting out with harsh punishment ("tough love") rather than negatively influencing them to act out because of harsh rules and regulations (Harris, 1998).

As might be expected, Harris's theory has elicited strong reactions from the research community. Steven Pinker, a well-known Harvard University psychologist, gushed that "it will come to be seen as a turning point in the history of psychology" (Pinker, 1998, p. xiii). However, many developmental psychologists (and parents) rejected Harris's theory on various grounds (see Box 10.2). The jury is still out, but most psychologists believe that parents continue to influence their adolescents' behavior and development in many ways. However, part of Harris's theory is undoubtedly accurate: Sometimes peer groups do lead other youth off their positive developmental trajectories and onto negative paths.

Box 10.2 Evaluating the Group Socialization Theory

Harris's controversial book (1998) attracted a lot of attention from the popular media and researchers. Not surprisingly, many developmental psychologists found her theory to be highly inaccurate by discounting the crucial roles that parents play in promoting positive development. Some researchers also pointed out the potentially dangerous implications of her comments: If parents do not matter in how their children turn out, then it follows that it does not matter how parents rear their children. To date, there has not been much empirical support for her theory (cf. Loehlin, 1997), but many critiques (e.g., Collins, Maccoby, Steinberg, Hetherington, & Bornstein, 2000; Gottlieb, 2003; Maccoby, 2000; Vandell, 2000). The following reasons stand out among the critiques:

- Her research review was incomplete or too simplified.
- Pertinent research on siblings, teachers, and friendships is ignored.
- Behavioral genetics research is limited by its assumptions and computations.
- Gene-environment interactions were not examined.
- Parental influence over peer group exposure was not considered; parents affect the choice of and access to peers.
- Parents influence the behaviors, attitudes, and decisions of their children in particular domains that peers do not.
- Harris focused only on adolescent outcomes and failed to take a longer life-span developmental perspective.

As we have seen, adolescence is a time of many changes, including physical, cognitive, and social. Some of the behaviors that adolescents engage in that are risky and problematic—and that Harris thought were so revealing of peer influence—will be considered next. Following a short discussion of eight types of problems, we will then consider what parents should do to avoid the problems or effectively deal with them.

PROBLEMS FOR ADOLESCENTS AND THEIR PARENTS

What are some of the potential pitfalls of adolescence that parents fear? Some problems may be short-lived, such as experimentation with cigarettes or marijuana. However, sometimes those behaviors become habit forming or lead to serious problems or consequences. Parents are especially fearful of more long-term or even fatal consequences of their teens' behavior. Given the particular combination of emerging adult drivers, risk-taking behavior, and poor judgment, adolescents are a particular risk for death from preventable causes (accident, homicide, and suicide). The teen death rate (for 15- to

19-year-olds) is 49 per 100,000. Only about a quarter of these deaths are due to illness (cancer and heart disease). About three-fourths of adolescent deaths come from car accidents, homicides, and suicides, with car fatalities accounting for three times as many deaths as the other two causes (Annie E. Casey Foundation, 2014). Other, nonfatal problems include drug and substance abuse, exposure to violence, pregnancy, and dropping out of high school; some of these troubles will be described in more detail below. The list is not exhaustive. For example, teens are also susceptible to other problems, including gang involvement, gambling, and materialism.

Automobile Accidents

One of the developmental milestones in adolescence is becoming eligible to obtain a driver's license, in most states at age 16. Automobile driving promotes autonomy, independence, and responsibility. However, it is also dangerous: Car accidents involving teenagers are the most common cause of death for individuals between the ages of 16 and 19. In 2010, every day, seven teens died from motor vehicle crashes, resulting in 2,700 deaths. Another 282,000 teens sustained nonfatal injuries (Centers for Disease Control and Prevention, 2014b). Investigations into teen car accidents determined that two risk factors were (1) driving with two or more friends in the car and (2) driving at night. Why do adolescents get into accidents? In a nutshell, teens do not have driving experience; they underestimate hazardous driving situations, fail to recognize dangerous conditions, and may not wear seatbelts. They also tailgate, drive too fast, and are distracted by talking on a cell phone or even typing text messages. Another cause of automobile accidents is alcohol. In a study of 17,000 high school seniors, 28% reported that within the past 14 days, they drove or rode with a driver who was under the influence of alcohol, marijuana, or some other illicit drug (O'Malley & Johnston, 2013). Drinking is implicated as a cause in 20% of fatal car crashes involving adolescent males (Centers for Disease Control and Prevention, Vital Signs, 2012). Thus adolescents engage in a variety of risky driving practices. One effective solution has been to institute **graduated driver licensing laws**, as described in Box 10.3.

Box 10.3 Promoting Safer Teenage Drivers With Graduated Driver Licensing Laws

One effective way to combat the fact that novice drivers have higher crash rates is through graduated driver licensing (GDL) laws. These laws consist of differentiating drivers into the "Learner Stage" and then "Intermediate Stage" before giving the driver full privileges. Common components of the law include restrictions on nighttime driving and the number of passengers and banning all cell phone use. All 50 states and many countries have enacted one or more component of these types of laws. The laws were based on research into the factors that increased or decreased the risk of crashes among teenagers. GDL laws are successful: They have reduced automobile accidents by teen drivers by 20% to 40% (Shope, 2007).

Sexual Initiation, Contraception Use, and Pregnancy

Premarital sexual intercourse among older adolescents is widespread. By the age of 19 years, 71% of U.S. youth will have had sexual intercourse (Guttmacher Institute, 2013). Sexual activity is also common among younger teens; 33% of 16-year-olds have had sex (see Figure 10.2). Early sexual debut is associated with various problems for the teenager. Initiation at early ages is associated with multiple partners and unprotected intercourse.

In turn, sex without contraceptives can result in two types of serious problems: sexually transmitted infections (STIs) and pregnancies (see Photo 10.3).

Each year, 750,000 female teens age 15 to 19 years old become pregnant; two-thirds of these young women are to 18 and 19 years old (68 per 1,000 teenage females). The teen pregnancy rate has declined substantially from 1990, when the rate peaked at 117 per 1,000 teenage females. The decline is primarily due to improved contraceptive use and, to a lesser extent, the decision to delay sexual activity (Guttmacher Institute, 2013). Nevertheless, it is estimated that nationally, the cost of teen childbearing to taxpayers is estimated to be more than $9.4 billion. To see statistics on teen pregnancy and costs per state, visit the National Campaign to Prevent Teen and Unplanned Pregnancy's website (http://thenationalcampaign.org/).

Figure 10.2 Age by Which First Sexual Intercourse Experienced

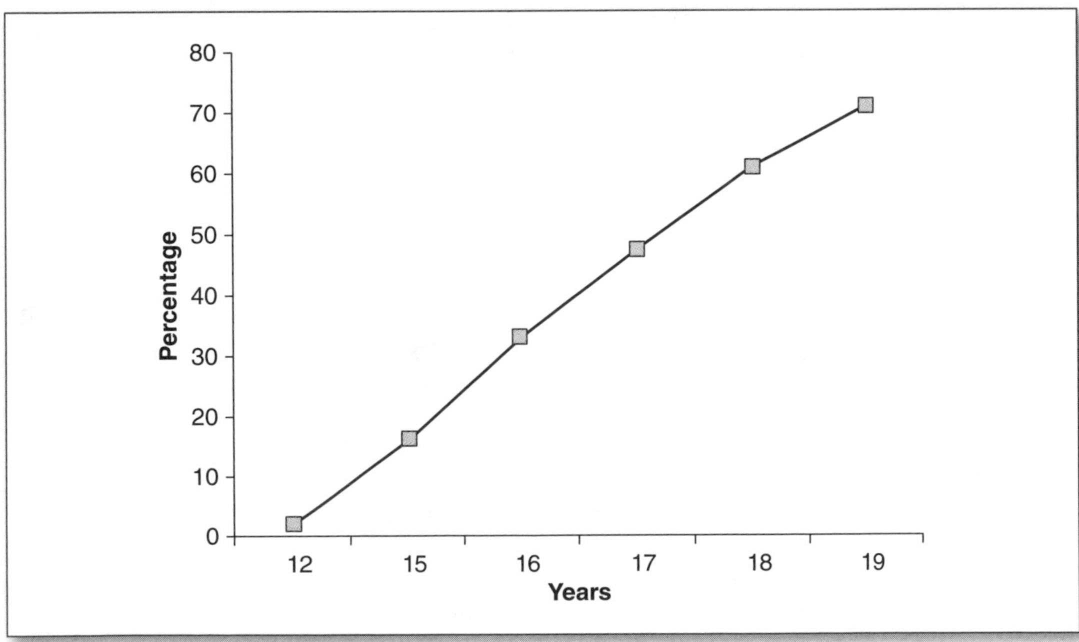

Source: Guttmacher Institute, 2013.

Photo 10.3 Teenage pregnancy and parenthood is one of the potential pitfalls of adolescence.

Source: © iStockphoto.com/ArtisticCaptures

Electronic Media Problems

Adolescents seek excitement, arousal, and intense stimulation (Dahl, 2004). Consequently, electronic media (including cell phones, tablet devices, Internet, and TV) is a dominant focus of teen attention. According to the Pew Internet Survey of 800 nationally representative teens, most adolescents (93%) go online, more than 80% of 16-year-olds have cell phones, about 80% own an iPod (or MP3 player) as well as a gaming device, and 82% use online social networks (Lenhart, Purcell, Smith, & Zickuhr, 2010). In terms of time, teens spend more than 11 hours a day using a variety of media (Rideout et al., 2010).

Although television viewing and the electronic media in general can have positive effects on youth, too much screen time is a problem. For instance, although gaming may enhance hand-eye coordination, a common concern from parents is that time spent in front of the screens means time cannot be spent in active activities. Video gamers spent 30% less time reading and 34% less time doing homework than non-gamers and 9% less time interacting with parents or friends (Cummings & Vandewater, 2007). Watching a lot (e.g., 5 hours) of television each day is also associated with such problems as early sexual initiation (Collins et al., 2004) and obesity (Koplan, Liverman, & Kraak, 2005). A high degree of screen time is also associated with more pervasive problems, such as sleep loss, consumerism, substance use, and violence (e.g., Council on Communications and Media, 2013).

Teen texting can pose another problem. Youth send an average of 60 messages a day (Lenhart, 2012). According to a study that analyzed the content of teen messages, the most common type of messaging was positive or neutral. However, 14% were negative (negative comments about others or groups), another 2% were about sex, and less than one percent of messages were about physical or social aggression and substance use (Underwood, Ehrenreich, More, Solis, & Brinkley, 2014). The negative talk was not inconsequential—the senders of those messages were more likely to report internalizing problems, anxious depression, and somatic (physical) complaints. In addition, teens who text about antisocial topics were found to subsequently engage in more rule-breaking and aggressive behavior than teens who did not (Ehrenreich, Underwood, & Ackerman, 2014).

Eating Problems and Body Dissatisfaction

There are two common types of adolescent eating problems: eating too much and eating too little. Eating too much, in conjunction with a lack of activity, results in obesity. Child and adolescent obesity is a widespread problem in the United States and worldwide (e.g., Hughes, Sherriff, Lawlor, Ness, & Reilly, 2011). In the United States, according to a national study with more than 9,000 children and adolescents, 31.8% of children age 2 to 19 years are overweight and 16.9% are obese as defined by a body mass index (BMI) at or above the 95th percentile (Ogden, Carroll, Kit, & Flegal, 2014). Hispanic boys had the highest percent of obesity (24%) and Asian girls had the lowest (5.6%). The good news is that this rate, though high, has not significantly increased over the past eight years. Want to find out your own BMI? See Box 10.4 for how to calculate your own BMI.

Obesity is a complex problem involving family lifestyle patterns, family and peer dynamics, and child variables (e.g., self-control, emotional problems) (Harrist et al., 2012). The problem typically begins early in life and develops into a habit. Eating high-calorie and super-sized foods in front of TV screens has become the norm. As many as 22.8% of children age two through five years are overweight (Ogden et al., 2014). By middle childhood, the rate is one in three children. In a low-income inner-city sample, the rate was found to be even higher (Robbins et al., 2007). Studied over a two-year period, 29% of three- to seven-year-old children were found to be overweight, and an additional 19% were at risk of being overweight (Robbins et al., 2007).

Box 10.4 Your BMI Index—and What It Means

To calculate your own BMI (for individuals 20 years old and older), divide your weight (in pounds) by your height (in inches, squared). Then multiply by a conversion factor of 703. Alternatively, BMI calculators can be found online (e.g., http://www.nhlbi.nih.gov/guidelines/obesity/BMI/bmicalc.htm). To simplify classification into categories, the Centers for Disease Control and Prevention now uses the same index values for both men and women:

Category	BMI
Obese	> 30
Overweight	25.0–29.9
Normal	18.5–24.9
Underweight	< 18.5

To calculate the BMI of children and adolescents, the calculations also take into account age and gender (e.g., http://apps.nccd.cdc.gov/dnpabmi/Calculator.aspx). The BMI can then be used to determine the category of the individual, as listed below:

Category	BMI	Percentile
Obese	> 29.9	> 195th
Overweight	24.9–29.9	85th to 95th
Normal	18.5–24.9	5th to <85th
Underweight	< 18.5	< 5th

Obesity in children is associated with a variety of health problems as well as life adjustments. Some of the health problems include juvenile (type 1) diabetes, liver failure, heart disease, and a variety of other health problems, even some resulting in death.

The opposite type of eating problem evidences itself in the exaggerated desire to be thin. In our culture, the female ideal of extreme thinness is promoted in teen magazines, on television, and in the movies. Teenagers (nearly always girls) with these kinds of disorders typically engage in one of three eating patterns as identified in the fifth edition of the *Diagnostic and Statistical Manual of Mental Disorders* (*DSM-V*): (1) *anorexia nervosa*: severely limiting food intake such that it is not enough to sustain one's weight; (2) *bulimia nervosa*: binge eating followed by efforts to minimize the effects of overeating by vomiting, exercise, or fasting, or (3) *binge eating disorder*: binge eating without the efforts to minimize the effects. By age 20, 13.1% of females will have experienced one type of eating disorder (Stice, Marti, & Rohde, 2013). Males also experience eating disorders, but at significantly lower rates (Hudson, Hiripi, Pope, & Kessler, 2007).

Eating disorders, often **comorbid** with other mental health problems, put the adolescent female at risk for a variety of health and psychological problems. In the process of starving their bodies, teenage girls can delay their normal pubertal development, negatively affect their self-concept and self-esteem, and even cause irreversible organ damage.

According to researcher in Australia, a key variable related to the role of obesity and teen emotional well-being is the role of body dissatisfaction. Being overweight does not necessarily negatively impact a teen's emotional well-being. It only negatively impacts their well-being when they have high levels of body dissatisfaction. In those cases, the teen may experience psychological distress and their self-esteem may be seriously compromised (Mond, van den Berg, Boutelle, Hannan, & Neumark-Sztainer, 2011).

School Dropouts

In 2011, 7% of teenagers age 16 to 24 dropped out of high school and have not subsequently earned a general educational development (GED) certificate (U.S. Department of Education, 2013). However, there is great racial disparity in the percentages of dropouts: Hispanic/Latinos have a 14% rate, Blacks have a 7% rate, and Whites have a 5% rate. Although the 2011 rate is down from the 12% rate of 1990, it means more than 1.3 million teenagers are committing "economic suicide" because they have at least temporarily closed the door on their educational future and getting a job that pays well.

Teens who drop out from high school will earn about $2,100,000 less in their lifetime than their peers who get a diploma (Amos, 2008) and a net benefit to taxpayers of $127,000 per graduate. If the dropout rate could be cut in half, it would result in a $90 billion financial benefit per year, according to two economists (Levin & Rouse, 2012). In addition to the obvious financial negatives, dropping out of school is associated with a variety of lifestyle problems. Those who leave high school prior to graduation are more likely to consume drugs, commit crimes, be incarcerated, and have health problems than those who do not (Belfield & Levin, 2007). Thus, dropping out of high school has significant repercussions for the teen as well as society.

Substance Use and Abuse

Teens commonly use three types of problematic substances: cigarettes, alcohol, and illegal drugs (primarily marijuana). Prevalence rates are estimated based on results from the Monitoring the Future study that surveyed 46,500 high school students (Johnston, O'Malley, Bachman, & Schulenberg, 2011). When surveyed, it was found that about 20% of high school seniors smoked cigarettes within the past 30 days. The percentage of high school seniors smoking has declined steadily since 1997, when 38% of seniors had smoked. Though cigarette smoking may be on the wane, other types of nicotine ingestion are on the rise. E-cigarettes are gaining popularity with teens and may even serve to promote traditional cigarette smoking (Dutra & Glantz, 2014).

Teen alcohol use is a larger problem than tobacco for various reasons. It is more widely used: The national survey mentioned above determined that 16.6% of teenagers (12 to 17 years old) had used alcohol in the past month, and when they drank, they consumed an average of 4.5 alcoholic drinks. This is called *binge drinking*, typically defined as consuming five or more alcoholic drinks in a short period of time. By the time they are high school seniors, 22% of high school seniors reported binge drinking during the past 30 days (Johnston et al., 2011). Drinking alcohol may be fun and provide a good, momentary escape from problems, but it has potentially serious effects. It is associated with a variety of problems, including violence, unprotected sexual intercourse, multiple sexual partners, alcohol dependency, and suicide attempts.

Alcohol use among college students is even more of a problem. On average, 63.7% of 18- to 22-year-old college students reported alcohol use in the past month. Of those, 43.6% engaged in binge drinking. A smaller percentage (15.3%) of these students also reported they drank heavily (binge drinking on five or more days in the past month) (Substance Abuse and Mental Health Services Administration [SAMHSA], 2008). Excessive college drinking is not just linked to academic problems; it is also a cause of health problems, injuries and accidents, unsafe sex, date rape, and, in rare cases, death (Hingson, Heeren, Winter, & Wechsler, 2005).

Other drugs are not consumed as frequently as alcohol. Almost half (48%) of high school seniors report using some form of illegal drugs in the past 12 months. Most of that illicit drug use is marijuana. However, about 18% of seniors report using cocaine, inhalants, hallucinogens, heroin, or prescription-type medications to get high (Johnston et al., 2011). Access to drugs often comes from peers at school: 25% of students are exposed to illegal drugs at school (Dinkes, Cataldi, Lin-Kelly, & Snyder, 2007).

Mental Health Problems

Most adult psychiatric disorders have their origins in childhood or adolescence; up to 50% begin in adolescence (Belfer, 2008). Mental health problems are surprisingly prevalent in adolescence. More than one-quarter (26.8%) of American youth 12 to 17 years of age received some type of mental health treatment in 2007 (SAMHSA, 2008), although all were not diagnosed with a disorder. Mental health problems that begin in adolescence are more likely to involve females, in contrast to childhood-onset disorders (e.g., autism, attention-deficit/hyperactivity disorder [ADHD]), where there is a preponderance of males (Zahn-Waxler, Shirtcliff, & Marceau, 2008).

Depression is the most common mental health problem evidenced in adolescence. Almost 2 million youth (8.1% of teens) experience a major depressive episode each year (Substance Abuse and Mental Health Services Administration, 2012). The disorder is characterized by either a depressed mood (manifest as extreme irritability and/or prolonged sadness) or an extended loss of interest or the inability to take pleasure in activities. Indicators of depression include chronic problems with eating, sleeping, cognitive performance, and emotional well-being.

Depression is a particularly serious adolescent-onset disorder. Females become depressed almost three times as frequently as males (Office of Applied Studies, 2009). Depression is a complex disorder because it is multi-determined: It can be caused by genetic, biological, familial, and extrafamilial factors or a combination. Depression does not just affect behavior, but it can be debilitating and leads to the development of suicidal ideation (thoughts) and suicide attempts. In one study, 25% of adolescents reported they had thought about suicide at some time (33% of girls and 18% of boys), and 13% of girls and 6% of boys made suicide attempts (Eisenberg, Olson, Neumark-Sztainer, Story, & Bearinger, 2004) [Preview Question].

When a large sample of high school students reported on their emotional health in the past year, the rates were considerably lower but nevertheless alarming: 5.1% of female and 2.0% of male adolescents disclosed suicide attempts (Borowsky, Ireland, & Resnick, 2001). Suicidal thoughts and attempts are clear and alarming calls for help. Box 10.5 describes actions you can take in responding to an adolescent or friend who expresses suicidal thoughts.

Box 10.5 "I Wish I Were Dead": Responding to a Friend's Suicidal Thoughts

How would you respond to a friend who is despondent and wants to die? Sometimes it is obvious because the individual will say something like, "I want to die" or "I'm going to shoot myself." In other cases, it is subtle. There may be indirect statements, including, "I'm causing all the problems in the family" or "My friends don't need me; all I do is cause trouble." You may see indications that your friend has engaged in cutting or other forms of self-injury. Alternatively, you may just notice behavioral changes, such as chronic sadness, frequent crying, high levels of anxiety, withdrawal from people, decline in grades, or preoccupation with death or Heaven.

Your first response should be to take the threat extremely seriously. Suicidal comments are cries for help when someone feels overwhelmed by burdens. Show concern, provide comfort, and listen in a calm, sympathetic way. Be nonjudgmental and patient. It is a good idea to treat the matter with extreme caution; your friend might be in imminent danger. A safe response would be to call the National Suicide Prevention Lifeline (800-SUICIDE or 800-273-TALK). If the individual is not in immediate danger, you still need to get your friend to see a physician, college counselor, or mental health care professional as soon as possible.

Source: American Psychological Association, 2014.

Data from Canada provide a slightly different picture of the patterns of mental illness in youth. Although the reported incidence of mental health disorders in youth is lower than that estimated in the United States, the type of disorders seen are also different. A total of 15% of the 937,000 children and youth living in British Columbia were estimated to have a mental health problem (Waddell & Shepherd, 2002). In that sample, anxiety disorders were the most common, followed by conduct disorder (CD), ADHD, and depression. Anxiety disorders include reactions to a specific trauma (posttraumatic stress disorder [PTSD]), generalized anxiety, social phobias, obsessive-compulsive disorder, and panic disorders. CD refers to persistent and repeated violations of social rules and the rights of others. It often involves aggression toward others, animal abuse, theft or property destruction, deceitfulness, impulsive behavior, and a lack of empathy. The problem is two to four times more common in boys than girls (Moffitt, Caspi, Rutter, & Silva, 2001).

Not all children with CD have the same types of symptoms or show the same pathway. For some children with CD, it begins by age ten and continues into adulthood. For others, it is limited to adolescence, as individuals gradually cease involvement in delinquent behavior by late adolescence (Moffitt, 1993). Early onset CD has been linked to poor parenting and parental antisocial behavior as well as neurological deficits (Moffitt, 1993). The types of problems and their prevalence in one province of Canada can be found in Table 10.1.

Table 10.1 Prevalence of Mental Disorders in Children and Youth in British Columbia, Canada

Disorder	Estimated Prevalence (%)	Estimated Number of Children/Teens Affected
Anxiety disorders	6.5	60,900
CD	3.3	30,900
ADHD	3.3	30,900
Depression	2.1	19,700
Substance abuse	.8	7,500
Pervasive developmental disorder (e.g., autism spectrum disorder)	.3	2,800
Obsessive-compulsive disorder	.2	1,900
Schizophrenia	.1	900
Tourette's disorder	.1	900
Eating disorders	.1	900
Bipolar disorder	< .1	< 900
Total (any disorder)	**15**	**140,500**

Source: Waddell & Shepherd, 2002.

Youth Violence and Delinquency

Youth violence is a serious and pervasive problem in the United States. During adolescence, violence is perpetrated and experienced in many ways: bullying and school fights, date violence and rape, robbery, theft, drug dealing, and even homicide. These problems occur in every setting, but all too often, even schools are not safe environments. Bullying continues to be a pervasive problem in schools, as discussed in the last chapter. In a nationally representative sample of 20,000 students in the United States, 16% reported they had been bullied at some time in school (Limber, Olweus, & Luxenberg, 2013). In addition to violence, the presence of drugs and weapons in high schools is also high. Twenty-five percent of students reported being exposed to illegal drugs at schools, and 10% of male students revealed they had been threatened or injured with a weapon on school property in the past year (Dinkes et al., 2007; see Photo 10.4).

With the advent of adolescence comes dating. By the eighth and ninth grades, many adolescents have begun dating. And with dating, in a startlingly high number of cases, comes violence. Determining prevalence rates of violent behavior is difficult due to variations across studies on different dimensions (physical, psychological/emotional, sexual, stalking), including definitions of violence, the time period of the violent act (past year, lifetime), the sample characteristics, and the methodology (interview versus questionnaire, retrospective versus prospective). A recent nationally representative sample of 2,203 tenth-graders revealed that 35% reported being a victim of dating violence and 31% reported perpetrating either physical or verbal violence toward their dates (Haynie et al., 2013).

When an adolescent persists in violent or antisocial behavior, he or she is labeled a *delinquent*. But delinquency does not begin in adolescence; its roots are sometimes evident as early as toddlerhood. Therefore, it is useful to examine developmental trajectories when analyzing the origins of delinquent youth. There is currently considerable debate in the research literature about the nature of the developmental pathways leading to violence in adolescence (Loeber & Stouthamer-Loeber, 1998; Tremblay et al., 2004).

The evidence clearly indicates that there is not just one pathway toward delinquency. There are several pathways that reflect differences in when the aggression began (early versus late onset), whether the violence is reactive or proactive, and the nature of the violence or aggression (e.g., breaking parental rules, truancy, physical fights, shoplifting, property damage, burglary, drug dealing, or weapons use) (e.g., Barker, Tremblay, Nagin, Vitaro, & Lacourse, 2006). One set of pathways was proposed by researchers who have extensively studied adolescent aggression (Kelley, Loeber, Keenan, & DeLamatre, 1997). The most common pathway

Photo 10.4 Aggression is a common problem during the adolescent years.

Source: © iStockphoto.com/P_Wei P_Wei

is that of **authority conflict**. It also begins the earliest and has its roots in stubborn behavior in toddlers and preschoolers. That obstinacy then leads to defiance and disobedience before morphing into adolescent authority avoidance acts, such as breaking parental rules by staying out late, truancy, and running away from home.

A second pathway is **overt aggression**. The onset of this behavior comes later than the authority conflict pathway. It begins with minor aggression, such as bullying. As the youth gets older, aggression is expressed as physical fighting, either individually or in gangs. Finally, the aggression escalates into serious violence, including rapes. The third pathway, also emerging later than the authority conflict, can be called **covert aggression**. It begins with minor dishonest behavior, such as shoplifting and frequent lying. As these youth get older, they engage in property damage, such as breaking objects or setting fires. As an adolescent, the severity of the actions can escalate into drug dealing and engaging in such behaviors as fraud, burglary, and theft. Although the causes of these three different delinquent pathways are not entirely understood, it is likely that the roles parents play in them may be different.

HOW PARENTS HELP TEENS NAVIGATE ADOLESCENCE

How do parents help their children survive the adolescent years? Effective parenting of adolescents requires a balance between maintaining some oversight and control while encouraging independence and responsibility in preparation for adulthood. Although some parents may disengage when their children become teenagers, the evidence is that effective parents continue to play an important role in helping their youth successfully navigate the hazards of adolescence. The research into parenting and adolescent well-being has implicated certain parenting processes.

Diana Baumrind (1991, 2005) was one of the first researchers to examine links between the quality of child rearing and adolescent competence using longitudinal data. She recognized that in early adolescence, firm guidance and sustained emotional support are important qualities in parents. However, adolescents differentiate between legitimate and illegitimate authority and seek greater control over decisions that affect them. Privacy and secrecy issues also begin to surface. Baumrind found that parents who were authoritative and used appropriate control techniques (exerting reasonable control, being warm and supportive, communicating openly, and encouraging independence) had children who had the highest levels of competence, were socially responsible, and had good relationships with their parents.

Subsequent studies on much larger samples confirmed that parents with an authoritative style of child rearing have adolescents who are better adjusted in terms of academic achievement and psychosocial development. Their teens also exhibit fewer behavior problems, including smoking and mental health problems, than others whose parents' childrearing style is different (e.g., Mewse, Eiser, Slater, & Lea, 2004; Steinberg & Morris, 2001). This relation held across ethnic groups and SES levels, although authoritative parenting was reported less frequently in ethnic minorities and poor families (Knight, Virdin, & Roosa, 1994; Mason, Cauce, Gonzales, & Hiraga, 1996). The association is also present in juvenile delinquents: Authoritative parenting was associated with relatively more psychosocial maturity, greater academic competence, and less internalizing and externalizing problems than juveniles with other types of parents (Steinberg, Blatt-Eisengart, & Cauffman, 2006).

What are the ingredients or parenting skills involved in authoritative parenting at this age? Five key qualities of effective parent-child relationships with teenagers include the following:

- Staying connected via warm, positive relationships
- Maintaining open communications
- Supporting autonomy development
- Monitoring and being knowledgeable
- Using appropriate control techniques

Staying Connected via Positive, Warm Relationships

Having a warm, loving, and positive relationship (sometimes called *involved*, *accepting*, *supportive*, *close*, *connected*, and *caring* relationships) is the single most important quality of the parent-teen relationship (Luthar & Latendresse, 2005; Roth & Brooks-Gunn, 2000). This characteristic is commonly found when investigators examine why some teens avoid succumbing to problems. For example, positive relationships are associated with various adolescent behaviors, including better educational outcomes, fewer mental health problems, delayed onset of sexual activity, fewer sexual partners, and increased likelihood of using contraceptives (McNeely et al., 2002; Miller, Benson, & Galbraith, 2001; Resnick et al., 1997).

Conversely, a lack of closeness increases the influence of peers on teens' sexual activity and externalizing behavior problems (Gerard, Krishnakumar, & Buehler, 2006; Miller et al., 2001). Even controlling for other influences, such as deviant peer associations, poor-quality parent-teen relationships still predicted more externalizing behavior in teens and parental unhappiness (Buehler, 2006).

Open Communication

Having a good relationship facilitates a second key ingredient of effective parenting: open communication. This means that both the parent and the child are comfortable in communicating their views to each other about topics such as school grades, money, household rules, and peers (McElhaney & Allen, 2001). Maintaining good communications during adolescence is a challenge because teenagers increasingly believe that they should not disclose to their parents information from certain domains, such as dating or substance use (Smetana, Metzger, Gettman, & Campione-Barr, 2006). Teenagers are more likely to disclose to mothers than to fathers, and girls are more likely to confide than boys.

Talking about sex with adolescents provides a great example of the awkwardness of the developmental stage. Parents recognize it is important to prepare their teens to deal with sex but they often have reservations about talking about the topic (as do their teens with them). Parents find talking to their children about sex threatening and challenging due to embarrassment, difficulty in explaining, fear about knowing the correct answers to questions, or an inability to find the right moment for "the talk" (Jaccard, Dittus, & Gordon, 2000; Mauras, Grolnick, & Friendly, 2013). In many cases, "the talk" occurs after daughters have initiated sex or the mother is concerned about her daughter's behavior (Averett & Estelle, 2013). However awkward, mothers who clearly expressed their disapproval of teen sexual activity had daughters who engaged in later sexual initiation (McNeely et al., 2002).

Despite the difficulty in communication, the importance of open and frequent discussions can be paramount for youth safety. Parents who talked with their teens more frequently about safe driving had children with more positive attitudes toward driving safety (Yang, Campo et al., 2013).

Box 10.6 Tips for Talking With Teens

Many parents find it difficult to talk with their children about sensitive topics such as sex, alcohol and drugs, and violence. The Office of Adolescent Health, part of the U.S. Department of Health & Human Services, has some tips (http://www.hhs.gov/ash/oah/resources-and-publications/info/parents).

The tips include the following:

- Choose a good moment; car rides can provide a good opportunity.
- Be a good listener; accept the teen's feelings.
- Be positive, give praise.
- Discuss calmly and honestly.
- Negotiate; respect the teen's need for autonomy and privacy.
- Don't lecture, nag, or use guilt—It doesn't work.
- Use humor. Lighten it up!
- Sometimes the teen is not in the mood to talk. Accept that. Try again later.

Another important topic that merits open communication concerns alcohol and drugs. The messages parents give about the topic show the variability in parental communication practices. For instance, in a study assessing adolescents' perceptions of their parents' messages about substance use, the most common parental messages were to tell the child to use his or her own judgment (79%) or to inform the youth about the dangers of substances (42%). Less common was providing indirect messages that hinted about parental expectations or wishes (29%). About one-fifth of parents took a hard line and said they would not tolerate it (22.6%) or would threaten punishment (18%). According to the students, only a small percentage of parents (8.8%) never brought up the topic (Miller-Day, 2008).

One way to maintain relationships and communication is by having family meals (Fiese, 2006). In the National Survey of Children's Health from 2007, almost 92,000 parents or guardians were interviewed (http://www.cdc.gov/nchs/slaits/nsch.htm#2007nsch). Sixty-nine percent of families with children 12 to 18 years of age shared a meal on four or more days each week, and 33% of teens' families shared daily meals. Rates did not differ greatly between ethnic groups and social classes. Typically lasting about 20 minutes, dinnertime allows parents to connect with their children, address problems, and make plans. Adolescents report that about 50% of mealtime (three hours per week) is spent talking to parents (Offer, 2013). That time, at least in well-functioning families, provides an opportunity for open communication, emotional support, and feelings of respect, all qualities that promote teen well-being (Fiese, Foley, & Spagnola, 2006). Frequency of family meals with adolescents is inversely related to early sexual activity, substance use, poor school performance, and depression (Fulkerson et al., 2006).

Monitoring/Knowledge

Having a good relationship and good communication with a teenager is important—but not enough. Parents need to continue to monitor their teenagers, particularly in the early teenage years. This monitoring or supervision from a distance requires knowledge—what the teen is doing, with whom, and when. However, that knowledge can only be acquired from parent-child involvement and communication. A teenager needs to disclose information in order for the parent to monitor and make judgments about the child's activities and friends.

Parental monitoring of youth is associated with fewer problems in adolescence, including early onset of sexual activity (McNeely et al., 2002), delinquency (Hoeve et al., 2009), and smoking (Dick et al., 2007). For some variables, such as school misconduct and alcohol use, a linear relationship has been found: The more monitoring knowledge the parent has, the better the child behaves. But for other variables, there appears to be a curvilinear relation between monitoring knowledge and its effectiveness. This effect was found in the relation between behavioral supervision of grades and grade point average (GPA). Moderate levels of supervision facilitated the highest GPAs in adolescents, whereas too little or too much was associated with lower GPAs (Kurdek, Fine, & Sinclair, 1995). These data indicate that problems can emerge when a parent engages in too much monitoring. The issue of when monitoring goes too far is discussed in Box 10.7.

Box 10.7 My Mother, the Narc!

Monitoring knowledge is a good thing. But when does monitoring a teenager go too far? What if a parent suspects his or her teenager of doing drugs or driving too fast or drinking and driving? In the old days, a parent might rifle through the child's drawers or clothes, looking for evidence. Today, many parents use home drug-testing kits and GPS devices to monitor their teen's behavior. For only $15 to $25, a parent can purchase a home drug-testing kit. Planting a GPS device in a car is a bit more expensive ($139 to $280) but provides highly accurate information about their teen's driving characteristics (accelerations and speed) and whereabouts. The dilemma is, should a parent be trusting or monitoring? A parent should not be naïve about common adolescent temptations. But on the other hand, if a parent does not trust or respect the adolescent but instead treats him or her like a potential criminal, the teen is likely to be resentful, develop a hostile relationship with the parent, and perhaps act out.

Appropriate Limits

The essence of the teenage years involves teens developing their own identity and some independence from parents. Parents need to engage in autonomy granting by respecting their child's emerging individuality, allowing the teen some privacy, encouraging their children to think independently and express their views, and then being receptive to those statements and tolerating differences (Barber, Xia, Olsen, McNeely, & Bose, 2012; Kunz & Grych, 2013).

Although most studies find that supporting a teen's autonomy is associated with better-quality parent-child relationships and child well-being (Smetana, Campione-Barr et al., 2006), there are at least two qualifications to that. First, in early and middle adolescence (but not in late adolescence), parental involvement in decision making is linked to better child adjustment (Smetana, Campione-Barr, & Daddis, 2004). Second, in high-risk families (low income and living in a dangerous neighborhood), giving the youth full autonomy is not necessarily a good thing (McElhaney & Allen, 2001).

Appropriate control during adolescence consists of providing support and allowing for the development of autonomy while sometimes setting limits. This means providing consistent boundaries for behavior and using age-appropriate discipline. Appropriate disciplining may take the form of teaching the adolescent to assume the natural consequences of behavior (e.g., they pay for the speeding ticket), limit setting (e.g., early curfew in response to staying out too late), and removal of privileges (e.g., car use). These kinds of actions reflect behavioral control, in contrast to psychological control. Psychological control consists of intrusive and manipulative verbalizations designed to change how the teen is thinking about things or blaming the child for other family members' problems.

Ineffective disciplinary practices during the adolescent years include inconsistent discipline, corporal punishment, and psychological control. Each practice has been associated with teen problems. For example, psychological control (e.g., such as using guilt, shaming, or threatening to withdraw love) has been linked to internalizing (e.g., depression) and externalizing (e.g., delinquency) problems, in contrast to positive outcomes associated with behavioral control, such as increased social initiative and fewer externalizing problems (Barber, Stolz, & Olsen, 2005; Hoeve et al., 2009).

A subtle distinction in rearing an adolescent concerns the difference between psychological control and a failure to grant autonomy. Although some parents may be reluctant to grant autonomy, perhaps due to fears about the youth's well-being, their behavior reflects a different goal than the parents who use psychological control. Parents who use psychological control wield their authority to put down a child, maintain power over the child, or make the child feel badly. Not surprisingly, a study that separated out this difference found that psychological control was linked to teen depression, anxiety, and low self-esteem. These results provide a sharp contrast to those in which parents grant autonomy to their teens (Silk, Morris, Kanaya, & Steinberg, 2003). Examples of psychological control and autonomy granting can be found in Table 10.2.

Table 10.2 Examples of Items That Differentiate Psychological Control From Autonomy Granting

Psychological Control	Autonomy Granting
• When I get a poor grade, my parents make me feel guilty.	• When I get a good grade, my parents give me more freedom to make my own decisions.
• My parents tell me their ideas are correct and I should not correct them.	• My parents emphasize that it is important to get my ideas across even if others do not like it.
• My parents answer my arguments with something like, "You'll know better when you grow up."	• My parents say that you should always look at both sides of the issue.
• My parents say that I should give in on arguments rather than make people angry.	• My parents emphasize that every member of the family should have some say in family decisions.

Source: Silk et al., 2003.

It may sound unusual, but some parents of teenagers continue to use corporal punishment with adolescents. This practice (as when used with younger children) is linked to internalizing and externalizing problems in teens (e.g., Turner & Muller, 2004). Other parents use frequent criticism of their teenagers. Criticizing is problematic because it undermines a close relationship and has been associated with adolescent problems, including eating disorders (Luthar & Latendresse, 2005). Alternative strategies to managing adolescents, such as those discussed above, are likely to be much more effective in promoting positive and healthy behavior.

Other Ways Parents Influence Their Teenagers

Several other parental practices have been linked to positive development. As mentioned above, mothers who disapproved strongly of teen sexual activity had daughters (but not sons) who engaged in later sexual initiation (McNeely et al., 2002). Strict discipline has also been found to be associated with delayed sex initiation (Forste & Haas, 2002).

Parents influence their teens in other ways as well. They serve as role models. Parents' own substance use is a key predictor of their children's use of cigarettes (e.g., Scal, Ireland, & Borowsky, 2003). They also model eating practices, physical activity, dieting, and body esteem (Gattario, Frisén, & Anderson-Fye, 2014). Parents who provide encouragement for a healthful diet, control the food that is in the home, and give information about nutrition have children with better eating practices (Patrick & Nicklas, 2005). By modeling charitable giving and volunteering, parents are more likely to have children who follow suit (Ottoni-Wilhelm, Estell, & Perdue, 2014).

Parents also have an indirect influence by the friends they keep, the quality of relationships, the rules they create, and the activities they engage in. For example, parents influence their children's weight through rules concerning television viewing and other electronic media, physical activity, and consumerism (Krishnamoorthy, Hart, & Jelalian, 2006).

Limits of Parental Influence on Teens

Parental behavior and parent-child relationships have a strong influence on teen behavior. However, all parenting does not affect children in the same way or to the same extent. Examples to support that point come from the work in gene-environment research. Just as some children may be more vulnerable to adverse environmental experiences than others, as Jay Belsky and Michael Pluess (2009) capture in their "differential susceptibility" framework, it may also be the case that some children benefit more from positive environments and positive parenting (Pluess & Belsky, 2013).

An illustration to support this "vantage susceptibility" hypothesis can be found in a study of parenting, genes, and youth age 9 to 15 years. Hankin and colleagues (2011) found that youth who had a particular variant of a serotonin transporter gene (5-HTTLPR short allele) *and* experienced positive/supportive parenting were more likely to have positive affect than other children.

Another limitation of parental influence is due to the fact that parents are just one of several potential influences. Particular characteristics of the adolescent (i.e., temperament, intelligence, behavior) and other individuals (e.g., peers, teachers, coaches, mentors, religious leaders) as well as the context (neighborhood, school) also influence the teen's behavior and well-being (Žukauskienė, 2014). For example, teen externalizing behavior problems often *elicit* parental negativity rather than cause it—an example of child effects on parenting (Marceau et al., 2013). With regard to sexual activity, the adolescent's values, intentions, self-restraint, alcohol/drug use, and depression as well as whether he or she is involved in a steady dating relationship are all variables that can affect whether parents influence the teen's sexual activity (Miller et al., 2001).

Adolescent behavior is determined not just by the self, as self-determination theory posits, but the many different agents, developmental assets, and **protective factors** and risks as well, as the ecological model reminds us (e.g., Zhou et al., 2012). Problematic adolescent behavior could emerge from such sources as genetic susceptibility, temperamental predispositions, negative incidents (e.g., trauma or some failure), or exposure to certain experiences. For example, violence on television, films, and video games contribute to teen violence, at least with some individuals (Huesmann & Taylor, 2006).

Nevertheless, parents are the preeminent guides of their adolescents through these potentially turbulent years (Holden, 2010). Researchers have identified two effective ways that parents guide teens: by encouraging and by supporting involvement in extracurricular and religious activities. These actions are considered protective factors because they decrease the likelihood of risky behavior. Extracurricular activities and involvement in organized religion have also been found to protect adolescents against delinquency, drug use, and early sexual activity (e.g., Holden & Williamson, 2014; Pearce & Haynie, 2004).

CHAPTER SUMMARY

Adolescence can be a difficult stage of life—for both teens and their parents. Teens are going through many physical changes and are struggling with identity formation. Beneath the surface of their skulls, their brains are also going through changes. These changes result in storm and stress for some teenagers and can be manifested in a variety of potential problems. Some problems reflect risk-taking behavior, such as automobile accidents, smoking, binge drinking, and unprotected sexual activity. Other problems include school failure, eating disorders, mental health problems, and violence.

The evidence reveals that parents continue to play an important role in guiding their adolescents' development. Through authoritative parenting and maintaining positive relationships, parents can continue to influence their children's development. Other key attributes of parenting success during this age period include maintaining good communication patterns, effectively monitoring the teen, and using appropriate control techniques. During this developmental period, parents need to modify their parenting to grant increasing autonomy to their teenagers. Parents must also deal with other sources of influences, such as the peer group. Although this chapter has focused on the many challenges and potential problems that adolescents face, it should be remembered that a majority of teens experience few or no major problems during these tumultuous years. Their parents deserve at least some of the credit.

THOUGHT QUESTIONS

- In what ways can parents, mentors, and educators use findings from adolescent brain research to modify expectations or help guide adolescents more effectively?
- How well can you predict which teenagers will become rebellious? What personal and family characteristics contribute to or reduce the likelihood of that?
- Although the chapter delineates clear differences between parental psychological control versus granting autonomy, what are some examples of parental behavior in which this distinction becomes blurred?
- In what ways can parents exhibit trust while still monitoring their adolescents?

CHAPTER GLOSSARY

authority conflict When an adolescent is disobedient and defiant to figures of authority.

comorbid Two or more disorders in an individual.

covert aggression One pathway of adolescent aggression that begins with minor dishonesty but escalates into more serious acts such as theft.

graduated driver licensing laws Laws that gradually remove restrictions on adolescent drivers, such as number of passengers.

imaginary audience Adolescents' heightened sense of self-consciousness.

overt aggression One type of aggressive adolescent pattern of behavior that begins with minor aggressive acts and then escalates into serious violence.

personal fable The belief in some adolescents that what they experience is unique to them.

protective factors Conditions or circumstances that promote healthy behavior and well-being.

PART III

Contemporary Issues

CHAPTER 11

Parenting in Nontraditional Families

Single Parents
Adolescent Mothers
ART Families
Adoptive Parents
Gay and Lesbian Parents
Blended/Stepparent Families
Grandparents as Parents
Foster Parents
Parenting Emergent Adults

Chapter Preview: True or False?

- In the United States today, more than 40% of children are born to single mothers.
- Teenage pregnancy rates in the United States are higher than any other country in the world.
- The evidence is clear that children raised by gay or lesbian parents have many more problems than those reared by heterosexual parents.

Much of the research described in the prior chapters comes from investigations of traditional American families. For the most part, the term *traditional family* refers to a two-parent family with a mother and father, usually around 30 to 40 years old, raising their biological children. However, only 59% of children live with their two biological parents married to each other (see Figure 11.1). Another aspect of the traditional view is that the mother stays home to rear the children while the father earns the family income. Mothers today more typically work outside the home. America's working mothers are now the primary breadwinners in a record 40% of households with children—a milestone in the changing face of modern families, up from just 11% in 1965 (Parker & Wang, 2013; for more information, see

Figure 11.1 Family Structures in the United States

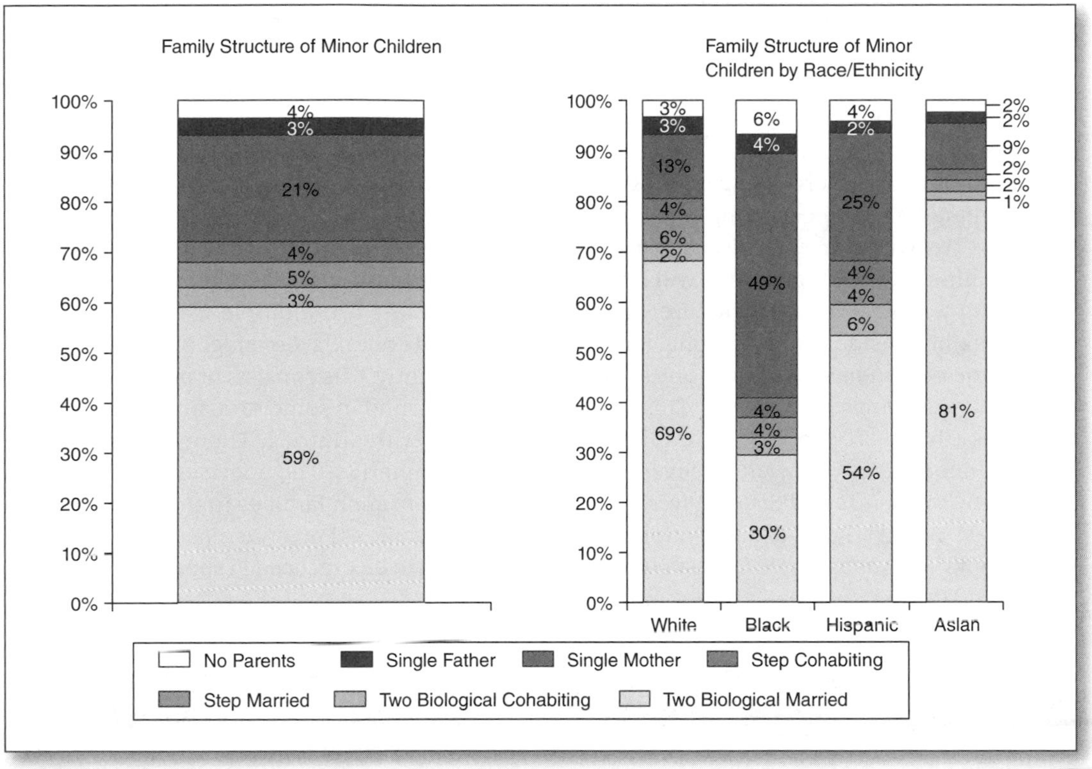

Source: Payne, 2013.

also http://www.pewsocialtrends.org/2013/05/29/breadwinner-moms/). Sixty-five percent of married mothers with school-age (or younger) children work outside the home. Furthermore, more than half a million men (3.5% of married couples with children) report that they stay at home and are the primary caregiver to their children (Morin, 2013). As we can see from these statistics, the traditional American family as we have thought of it is rapidly moving toward becoming a minority.

Both in the United States and around the world, parenting occurs in many different manifestations. Many of these families are culturally diverse, as will be discussed in Chapter 13. But increasingly, there is great diversity in other variables, such as the age of parents, the number of parents in a household, the sexual orientation of the parents, or the biological heritage of the child. These kinds of **nontraditional families** are the topic of this chapter. A child may start out in a traditional family but then transition into a different situation, reflecting a very common dynamic in contemporary family life. To paraphrase Ross Parke's (2013) book title on the topic, *Future Families: Diverse Forms, Rich Possibilities*, families contain diverse forms and rich possibilities.

It is important to keep in mind that, along with nontraditional family structures, there are often concomitant variables and commonly occurring social situations. Single-parent families typically have lower incomes than two-parent families. Children born outside of marriage are usually born to younger, less healthy, and less educated parents than those born in a marriage (Wildsmith, Steward-Streng, & Manlove, 2011). They are also likely to experience more instability in their lives because their parents are more prone to split up and move into new relationships. Children in gay or lesbian families may experience social stigma or discrimination. The list goes on. Consequently, some of the effects found in the research literature—on parenting or the children—may not be due to the family structure but rather to co-occurring variables.

We will start the discussion of nontraditional families with an unusual example. Although most Americans will reflexively think of a mother and a father when considering a typical family structure, around the world, there are multiple forms of what we might consider nontraditional family structures and contexts. Consider **polygamy** (when one person has more than one spouse). Most frequently, this consists of **polygyny** (a man having two or more wives). This family structure is found in some African countries (such as Ghana, Congo, and Tanzania) and Middle Eastern countries. Though illegal in the United States, it's even discovered occasionally in America. The television reality shows *My Five Wives* and *Sister Wives* provide a glimpse into such families in the United States. See Box 11.1 for a description of polygynous families. Polyandry (a woman having multiple husbands) is far less common but continues to be practiced in some areas in China and the upper Himalayan region of Nepal.

Box 11.1 One Father but Multiple Mothers: Polygynous Families

Although outlawed in the United States, polygamy is legal in more than 850 societies around the world (Elbedour, Onwuegbuzie, Caridine, & Abu-Saad, 2002). The most common form of polygamy is *polygyny*—when a man marries two or more women. This form of nontraditional family structure in the United States made news in the summer of 2008, when officials raided the home of a small religious sect in west Texas. Four hundred and forty children were removed from their parents due to suspicion of child abuse. It turned out that polygyny was being practiced there.

How are children affected by this type of family structure? As reviewed by Elbedour and his colleagues (2002), the research indicates that all is not well in families with multiple wives. A number of potential factors put children's healthy development at risk. First, polygamous marriages are more likely to be characterized by marital tension and conflict. There is often jealousy among the wives, who are frequently unhappy. The wives also often feel helpless to leave their situation, because they are unemployed. Wives in polygamous compared to monogamous marriages are also more likely to report mental health problems, particularly for the first wives (Al-Krenawi, 2013). Children in polygynous families are more likely to be exposed to marital violence and father absences than are children in two-parent families (Elbedour et al., 2002). In sum, the available research indicates that this is family structure is not recommended for a happy family life.

SINGLE PARENTS

In U.S. society, the most common nontraditional family structure is single parenthood. Twenty-eight percent of children are living in single-parent families, and most (87%) live with their mothers. Although there are exceptions, this state usually occurs for one of three reasons: The parent was never married, the parent has been separated or divorced from the spouse, or the spouse has died. Generally, single parents are mothers. In the United States, 24% of children lived with only their mothers, whereas about 4% lived with only their fathers (Vespa, Lewis, & Kreider, 2013). Race plays a big role in this statistic: 21% of White children lived with a single mother, compared to 55% of African American children (Vespa et al., 2013). Divorce often leads to single parenthood; 16% to 35% of marriages end within the first 10 years (when children are likely to be born). The least common cause of single parenthood is death of a parent, most likely the father. Only 1.7% of single parents are widowed.

One of the most dramatic structural shifts over time in U.S. families has been the number of unmarried women who become mothers. In 2003, more than one-third of births in the United States were to unmarried women. That added up to more than 1 million babies born in a single year (Martin, Kochanek, Strobino, Guyer, & MacDorman, 2005). And these numbers have increased. By 2012, the percentage of babies born to single women rose to

Figure 11.2 Percentage of All Children (and by Racial/Ethnic Group) Living in Single-Parent Homes

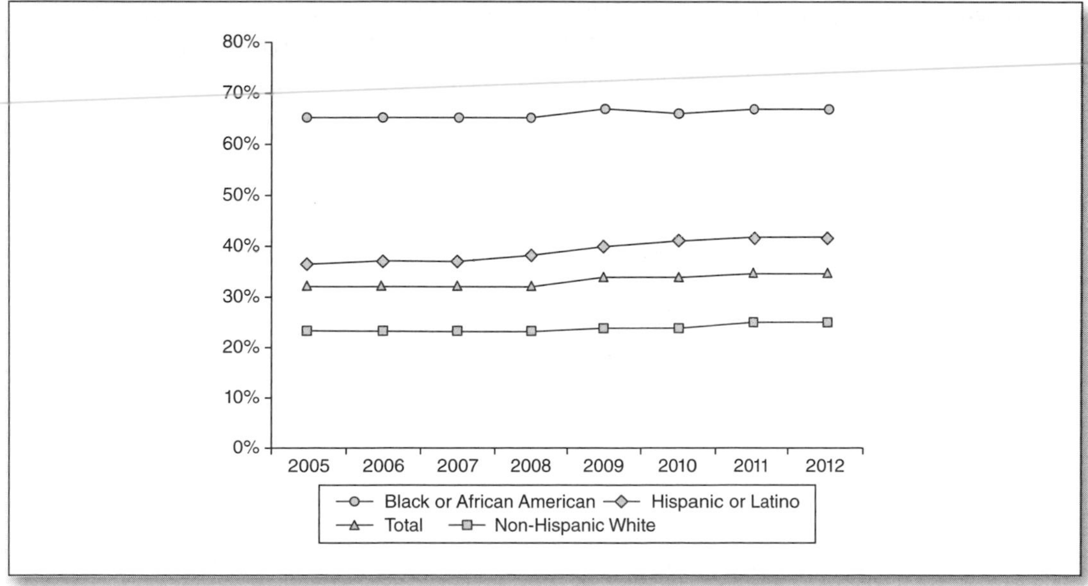

Source: The Annie E. Casey Foundation, KIDS COUNT Data Center, http://datacenter.kidscount.org.

40.7%, resulting in 1,609,619 live births to unmarried women (Martin, Hamilton, Osterman, Curtin, & Mathews, 2013) [Preview Question]. It is increasingly common for single women to decide to have children. In 1960, the percentage of children living in single-parent households was 9.1%. Forty years later, this had risen to 26.7% (Federal Interagency Forum on Child and Family Statistics, 2008). In terms of numbers, there are now 8.6 million single-mother and another 2.7 million single-father households (Pew Research, 2013). The number of African American single-parent homes is especially high. Figure 11.2 depicts the ethnic/racial group differences.

Unmarried mothers are a diverse group. The main subgroups consist of adolescent single women, older single women, and unmarried women living with a partner (Weinraub, Horvath, & Gringlas, 2002). The reasons an unmarried mother is single can affect both the quality of parenting and how children are influenced. Consider the single successful professional woman who deliberately chooses to have a baby in her late 30s. Contrast that situation with the unintended pregnancy of a 15-year-old adolescent with no source of income. In addition, single parenthood is not a static attribute of mothers. Many single parents are *legally* single but are supported by a partner; women are often in long-term relationships but choose not to marry (see Box 11.2). Some are single for a finite amount of time and then choose to marry or remarry. Many children being raised in single-parent families spend 20% of their time in the presence of their mother and her cohabiting partner (Bumpass & Raley, 1995).

Box 11.2 No Need to Marry?

It has already happened in northern Europe and Scandinavia. Increasingly in the United States, parents of children are choosing not to get married. Unmarried partner households have increased by 70%, and over a 10-year period, there has been nearly a 100% increase in the number of children living with their unwed parents. Today, 52% of nonmarital births are to cohabiting couples, compared to 29% of nonmarital births in the early 1980s (Wildsmith et al., 2011). An estimated 4.3 million children were being raised in such families in 1999. According to another estimate, two-fifths of all children will spend part of their childhood living with cohabiting parents (statistics cited by Manning & Brown, 2006).

Why don't the parents marry? For lots of reasons. A common reason is financial. By not marrying, costly weddings are avoided (which average anywhere from $14,000 to $43,000, according to a search of "cost of wedding" sites on the Internet). Some couples put off marriage until it is the "right time." As one mother told a reporter, "We want to be a little more established. We want to be a little more with the money" (Sege, 2007). Still other cohabiting couples choose not to marry due to their belief that marriage is oppressive to women, but cohabitation is progressive.

Based on demographic information, two types of concerns have been raised about unwed families. The first is the instability of the partner relationships. In the Fragile Families and Child Wellbeing study, one year after birth, 48% of fathers were living away from their children. That percent rose to 63% at five years (Carlson, McLanahan, & Brooks-Gunn, 2008).The other concern about unwed parents is they tend to be less educated and have lower income than married parents. About one-fifth (23%) of children living in households with cohabiting biological parents are raised in poverty (Smock, 2000).

The diversity of single-motherhood situations makes it difficult to summarize how single motherhood affects children. The caregiving quality of single mothers covers the entire range from neglectful and abusive to exemplary parenting. However, due to the nature of a single-parent family's structure, single mothers commonly experience excessive demands on their time and, consequently, high levels of stress. Variations in the amount of stress (and the amount of support, which can mitigate stress) influence parental interactions.

Stress for a single mother comes from many sources, including financial problems, troubled relationships, the never-ending demands of parenting, and a lack of time for rest or other self-care tasks. The relation between single parenthood and financial stress is well documented: 43% of children living with single mothers are in households at or below the poverty level. Compare this to only 8% of children being raised in homes with married biological parents (Manning & Brown, 2006). Poverty often means living in low-income neighborhoods, an environment highly stressful in itself (Kotchick, Dorsey, & Heller, 2005).

Social supports can compensate for the effects of stress; recall Belsky's model of the determinants of parenting (presented in Chapter 5). Social support includes material and financial help—such as diapers, babysitting, and money. Social support also consists of having someone to talk with about the children, such as a spouse or a friend. Supportive friends provide a mixture of sympathetic listening to frustrations, assistance in solving problems, and encouraging comments (Crnic & Low, 2002).

Interestingly, *feelings of satisfaction* with social support are more important than the *actual amount* of social support received. Each mother has different needs and expectations about what constitutes adequate support. One mother may need to talk only once a week to a friend in order to feel supported. Another mother would like a relative or friend to sit with her baby each day. Social support provides a powerful moderator (or *buffer*) of the adverse effects of stress on mothers. This was empirically demonstrated in a study of low-income African American single mothers and their children. Those mothers who experienced neighborhood stress (violence, gangs, crowding, drug use) had greater psychological distress (anxiety, depression) and were, in turn, less positive in their parenting practices (less monitoring, more lax or inconsistent discipline) than were other mothers. Perceived support from family, friends, and neighbors lessened the negative impact of the neighborhood stress on the mothers (Kotchick et al., 2005). The number of stressors is also linked to children's psychosocial adjustment (as shown in Figure 11.3). The more risk factors (neighborhood problems, poverty) a single mother experienced, the more likely her children were to have internalizing problems (Jones, Forehand, Brody, & Armistead, 2002). These data illustrate what is called a **cumulative risk model**.

One of the most dramatic trends over the past 50 years is the increase in single-father-headed households. In 1960, there were fewer than 300,000, but by 2011, the number had grown to 2.7 million, a ninefold increase (Livingston, 2013). Consequently, single fathers make up 24% of the single-parent households. These men tend to be younger, less educated, and less affluent than their married counterparts. About one-quarter of the men are living at or below the poverty line. A majority of these men (59%) are not cohabiting.

Although single fatherhood is most often the result of divorce, in some cases, it is due to maternal death, with cancer being the leading cause. More than 100,000 children live with widowed fathers in the United States, and how well the fathers cope with the loss and their emotional availability to their children is closely linked to the children's mental health

Figure 11.3 Number of Maternal Risk Factors and Their Children's Internalizing Problems

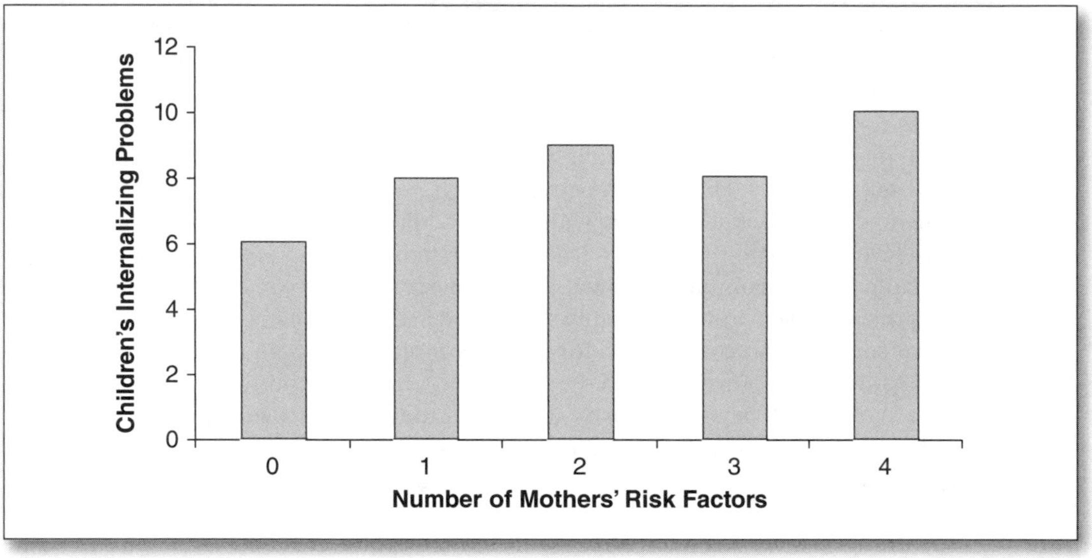

Source: Jones et al., 2002.

(Yopp & Rosenstein, 2012). Single fathers spend similar time as single mothers in many respects, except for providing child care to children five and under. In those cases, fathers spend less time in physical care and housework but more time in play and eating with their children (Hook & Chalasani, 2008). Whatever the cause of single fatherhood, it is not surprising that these fathers are more likely to be depressed and report lower happiness than married fathers (Shapiro & Lambert, 1999; von der Lippe, Rattay, & Domanska, 2013).

How do children in single-parent families turn out? The short answer is not as well as children from two-parent households. For example, based on four nationally representative longitudinal studies with a total of more than 20,000 participants, Sarah McLanahan and Gary Sandefur (1994) concluded that, on average, children who grow up in families with one biological parent do not do as well as children who have been raised by both biological parents. The problematic outcomes included being more likely to drop out of high school, to have a child before they were 20, or to be unemployed. Those results are partially due to the decreased economic resources in single-parent families but are also probably due to decreased parental involvement and supervision and lower aspirational levels, along the negative effects of residential mobility. In a more recent review of 47 studies, father absence was found to negatively affect children's socioemotional well-being, particularly if the father absence occurs during early childhood. This negative effect was stronger for boys than for girls (McLanahan, Tach, & Schneider, 2013).

The finding that children of single parents are more at risk for problems is supported by a new large-scale study by Mark Regnerus (2012a) called the New Family Structure Study (NFSS). It is a nationally representative investigation of nearly 3000 young adults (ages 19 to 39). These individuals, reared in seven different family structures (e.g., intact, with both biological parents; single parent; adopted by strangers; stepfamily) were assessed in telephone interviews on 40 outcome variables (e.g., educational attainment, income, depression, substance use, etc.). Regnerus compared the reports of 919 adults who had lived with both parents for their first 18 years, with 816 adults who had lived with a single parent. He found that those from single-parent homes had significant differences from two-parent homes on 62.5% of the outcomes. For example, adults from single-parent families reported they were more likely to be receiving public assistance, to be in therapy, to have relationship problems, and to use marijuana. Moreover, these adults were less likely to feel close to their biological parent and to attain as much education as adults who grew up in two-biological-parent households.

These studies do not mean that all children from single-parent homes will experience problems. The research focuses on the *averages* across all the participants in a group. Given the variability within each group, it should be recognized that many children in single-parent families do *better* than children in two-parent households. How children fare depends much more on the quality of parenting and other variables, than simply on one versus two parents at homes, as we examine below.

Box 11.3 Overcoming Exceptional Odds: The Story of Sonia Sotomayor

Although it is true that many children from single-parent homes will suffer economic hardship with all its accompanying stresses, simply being reared in a single-parent home does not destine one to failure. The President of the United States, Barak Obama, was reared by a single mother early in his life, as was, for a time, President Bill Clinton. Both these presidents were helped by their maternal grandparents, and both had stepfathers for at least part of their childhood. Supreme Court Justice Sonia Sotomayor, in her recent memoir, *My Beloved World* (2013), wrote poignantly of a number of challenging family circumstances that she ultimately overcame (see Photo 11.1). Sotomayor was diagnosed with diabetes as a very young child and had to give herself insulin injections from the age of eight. Though her parents were married, her father was an alcoholic who had difficulty keeping employment. The family was poor, living in public housing in a dangerous neighborhood in the Bronx borough of New York City. Both of her parents were Puerto Rican immigrants. Sonia did not learn English until she was in school. Early on, she struggled with reading and writing in English. Her father died when she was only nine, and Sonia's mother raised her and her younger brother alone on an income of less than $5,000 per year.

Justice Sotomayor credits her mother with much of her success: instilling a respect for learning; sacrificing mightily so that Sonia and her brother could attend Catholic schools; and providing a role model of dedication, hard work, and sacrifice. Sotomayor's loving connections with extended family members also undoubtedly played a role in her positive adjustment, as did her will to succeed in order to give back to her Puerto Rican community. Her native intelligence, drive, and incredible work ethic also played a key role in her overcoming considerable economic, linguistic, academic, and social odds. She stands as an inspirational role model for many young persons who wish to succeed and is a living testament to the power of will over circumstance.

Photo 11.1 Justice Sonia Sotomayor.

Source: Collection of the Supreme Court of the United States, Steve Petteway/Wikipedia

ADOLESCENT MOTHERS

Each year in the United States, about 750,000 adolescent females become pregnant, according to the Guttmacher Institute (Kost & Henshaw, 2013; see Photo 11.2). Most (82%) of those pregnancies are unintended. More than half (59%) of the pregnancies of 15- to 19-year-olds and 43% of the pregnancies of girls younger than 15 are carried to term. The other pregnancies end in abortion (29%) or miscarriage/stillbirth (14%). Births to teenage mothers total 11% of the babies born each year. The good news is that fewer babies are being born to U.S. teenagers now than ever reported, with a rate of 29.4 per 1,000 teenage females (Martin et al., 2013).

See Box 11.4 for a discussion of the rates of teen pregnancy in the United States in comparison to those of other developed countries.

Box 11.4 Teenage Pregnancy and Childbearing Rates in the United States Compared to Other Developed Countries

How do teenagers in the United States compare with teens in other developed countries on issues related to teen sexuality and childbearing? Not very well, according to reports issued by the Guttmacher Institute, a leading organization specializing in the study of sexual and reproductive health issues. What the institute has found is that teen sexual activity is generally similar across developed countries: By age 18, more than 60% of women in Sweden, Great Britain, and the United States report having had sexual intercourse. Canadian and French women report percentages in the 50% range. But by age 20, more than 80% of women in four of the five countries (not Canada) have been sexually active (Boonstra, 2002; Guttmacher Institute, 2014).

Although the U.S. rate of sexual activity is comparable to other countries, the United States leads *all countries in the world* in rate of teen pregnancy [Preview Question]. U.S. teen pregnancy rates are almost twice as high as those in England and Canada and eight times as high as those in the Netherlands and Japan. The United States also has high rates of sexually transmitted infections (STIs) compared with Canada and Western Europe. The United States also has one of the highest rates of abortions among developed nations. A final problem associated with U.S. sexual activity in teens is the birthrate for mothers ages 15 to 17 years (which is more than 20 per 1,000 teens). This rate is two to four times higher than many European countries.

The primary reason for the high U.S. teen rates of STIs, abortions, pregnancies, and childbearing is a lower rate of contraceptive use. Countries performing better in these areas are characterized by social acceptance of adolescent sexual relations. Those countries also provide comprehensive sex education and easy access to contraceptives.

Just as single mothers form a heterogeneous group, so too do adolescent mothers. The married 19-year-old young woman is classified as an adolescent. So is the single 13-year-old eighth grader. Most teen parents reside with their own parents, but others may live alone or with their boyfriends. Teen mothers come from all economic backgrounds. Some (at least 20%) adolescent mothers have a second child while they are teens (Beers & Hollo, 2009). So the wide variability of this group should be kept in mind. Typically, however, when teen mothers are studied, the label refers to young women living without a partner in a socioeconomically disadvantaged situation.

What contributes to adolescent pregnancies? A number of prominent risk factors have been identified: living in poor neighborhoods, experiencing school problems or failure, failing to use contraceptives, positive expectations about being a parent, and having few or low aspirations for the future. In addition, adolescent mothers are more likely than their peers to have a relative or friend who was also an adolescent parent *and* to have unrealistic thoughts about how easy it is to be a parent (Barr, Simons, Simons, Gibbons, & Gerrard, 2013; Coley & Chase-Lansdale, 1998; Moore & Brooks-Gunn, 2002).

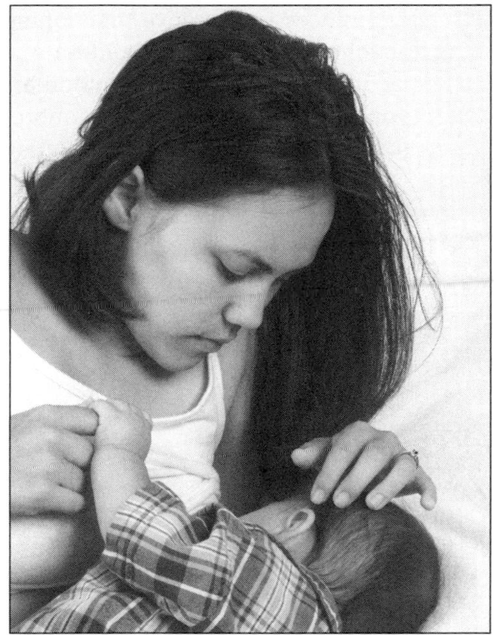

Photo 11.2 A teen mother and child.

Source: © iStockphoto.com/mocker_bat

Do adolescents make adequate parents? In many ways, teenage mothers *can* be good parents. When observed by researchers, adolescent mothers are often competent caregivers who are just as warm and responsive as older mothers are. Teen mothers also demonstrate that they can discipline reasonably. However, some researchers have found that adolescent mothers are less likely to talk to and cognitively stimulate their infants (Moore & Brooks-Gunn, 2002). More importantly, many teenagers experience the pregnancy and parenthood as a crisis. Not only are teenagers unprepared for being a parent, but their own phase of development conflicts with early parenthood as well. For example, the typical adolescent tasks of identity formation and role experimentation are not easily accomplished at the same time as assuming the parental role. Adolescent egocentrism may interfere with forming an attachment with and developing empathy for the newborn (Beers & Hollo, 2009).

Parenting is a 24/7 task with few shortcuts; infants require constant attention, planning, problem solving, sleep disruptions, patience, and giving of oneself. Most teenagers are unprepared to provide these sacrifices. In addition to a lack of personal maturity necessary for effective parenting, the teenage parent often faces an unstable family life, stress, low earnings or reliance on public assistance, relationship problems (including marital disruption if she is married), additional births, and poor health outcomes (such as depression) during and after pregnancy (Furstenberg, 2003). Often, teen mothers have experienced some type of abuse in their childhood (Meyers & Battistoni, 2003). Each of these conditions puts a child at risk when born to an adolescent.

How well adjusted *are* the children of adolescent mothers? Whether children's outcomes are negatively affected by their mother's age appears to be a function of multiple factors, including the mother's intelligence, her self-esteem, the amount of adversity she faces, and the presence of mental health problems (Weed, Keogh, & Borkowski, 2006). The most commonly found differences between children of teen mothers and those of older mothers are differences in cognitive functioning and psychosocial problems (such as behavior and attachment problems). Children of adolescent mothers have more school problems later (as indicated by grade repetition and truancy, for example), engage in sexual activity at younger ages, and experience more externalizing behavior problems than other children (Levine, Emery, & Pollack, 2007; Moore & Brooks-Gunn, 2002).

When thinking about teen parenthood from a family systems perspective, several questions emerge: What role does the biological father play? How about the grandparents or siblings of the adolescent mother? The stress and problems associated with motherhood vary greatly depending on how these individuals react to and either support or undermine the new mother. For example, maternal grandmothers typically play an integral role in the quality and functioning of the new family (Beers & Hollo, 2009).

ART FAMILIES

Assisted reproductive technology (ART), with its first successful birth in 1978, now makes it possible for individuals with fertility problems, gay or lesbian couples, and individuals without partners the opportunity to become parents. More than 176,000 ART *cycles* or attempts at pregnancy were performed at 456 clinics in the United States in 2012. The attempts were successful in 51,294 cases, resulting in 65,179 births (Centers for Disease Control, 2014c). Worldwide, more than 4.5 million have been born with the help of these technologies (Golombok, Blake, Casey, Roman, & Jadva, 2013). These various technologies (described in Chapter 6) raise multiple complex ethical and legal issues (Fronek & Crawshaw, 2014).

Some parenting differences have been found in couples who have experienced fertility problems. Women conceiving through ART are more anxious about the pregnancy (McMahon et al., 2013). When a baby finally arrives, they are likely to be even more elated and more protective than other parents (Zhan et al., 2013). Many of them are also older parents. Maternal age is often a cause of infertility, although—surprisingly—many women are unaware of the relationship between age and infertility (MacDougall, Beyene, & Nachtigall, 2013).

There is no evidence that the type of ART method used has any impact on parenting. In a longitudinal study that compared mothers who became parents by egg donation, donor insemination, surrogacy, and natural conception, there were no systematic differences found in maternal positivity, negativity, or distress. However, those mothers who did not tell their child about their biological origins had higher levels of distress (Golombok et al., 2013).

ART families can themselves be affected by the technology in at least two ways. First, it makes them poorer. The cost of a single cycle, depending on the procedure, can cost up to $73,000 (Parke, 2013). Second, parenting can be affected through child effects—if the child is born with a disability or serious behavior problems, for instance. According to a new meta-analysis of 45 studies, there is a 30% increased risk of birth defects in ART infants (Hansen, Kurinczuk, Milne, de Klerk, & Bower, 2013). ART children are also somewhat more likely than others to have behavior problems (Carson et al., 2013; Zhan et al., 2013). However, the biological relatedness of the child to the parent, at least in terms of ART families, does not impact child adjustment (Golombok et al., 2013).

ADOPTIVE PARENTS

Each year in the United States, about 500,000 women seek to adopt a child, and more than 136,000 families successfully adopt (Child Welfare Information Gateway, 2011; see Photo 11.3). There are a variety of types of adoption, including domestic, international, foster care or special needs, transracial, and kinship (for instance, stepparent) adoptions. Most adoptions come through one of two sources: a private agency or a state child welfare agency. Adoptions through private agencies typically involve infants. Children adopted through a child welfare agency are generally older than infants. For example, 46% of international private-agency adoptions in 2001 were infants compared to 2% of those from child welfare agencies (U.S. Department of Health and Human Services, 2001). Most parents (more than 80%) who adopt an infant do so because they are unable to have a biological child. In contrast, only about half of the parents who adopt from foster care (child welfare) cite infertility as their reason for adoption (Berry, Barth, & Needell, 1996). Some parents adopt for altruistic reasons completely separate from issues of fertility. Table 11.1 displays the total number of adoptions in the U.S. as well as the top seven countries from which American parents adopted children in 2013. Some of these international figures reflect an 18% drop from the prior year due to new regulations in some countries.

In cases where an adoption is prompted by fertility problems, the processes underlying the transition to parenthood differ from those of biological families. The transition to parenthood for adoptive families depends on such characteristics as expectations, preparation, social support, and letting go of the biological parenthood identity (Brodzinsky & Pinderhughes, 2002). One unusual feature of adoptive parents is that they have to be certified as fit to be parents. In contrast to biological parents, adoptive parents are intensely scrutinized before gaining the approval and endorsement needed to become parents. This evaluation,

Table 11.1 Total Adoptions in the United States and Top Seven Countries for International Adoptions in 2013

United States	136,000
China	2,306
Ethiopia	993
Ukraine	438
Haiti	388
Congo	313
Uganda	276
Russia	250

Source: Intercountry Adoption, Bureau of Consular Affairs, U.S. Department of State (http://adoption.state.gov/about_us/statistics.php).

although stressful, helps to prepare them for parenthood. That screening procedure, along with their positive expectations about parenthood, contributes to reports of positive experiences with their adoptive children (Levy-Shiff, Goldshmidt, & Har-Even, 1991).

Adopting a child raises several unique concerns typically not present with a biological child. Questions must be addressed about the genetic makeup, prenatal environment, and early experiences of the child. Adopted children, particularly those from foster care systems, are more at risk for genetically based psychological problems (Brodzinsky & Pinderhughes, 2002). They also may have experienced prenatal difficulties, such as inadequate nutrition or exposure to teratogens. Once born, the infant may have experienced malnourishment or maltreatment. This is one reason why many adoptive parents are understandably drawn to newborns.

Consider the early experiences of children adopted from developing countries, where overcrowding, inadequate staff, and little stimulation are the norm. Romanian orphans in particular were known to experience severe deprivation. Twenty to thirty infants were kept in cribs in a sterile room with little sensory stimulation. Due to poor caretaker-to-child ratios (one caregiver for 10 to 20 infants), children were left in their cribs, without toys, for 20 hours per day. The children rarely interacted with adults. In one investigation, 46 of these orphans, who had spent an average of 18 months in a Romanian orphanage and were subsequently adopted by Canadian parents, were compared to other Canadian children (Fisher, Ames, Chisholm, & Savoie, 1997). Many differences were found. The Romanian children had a larger total number of problems as well as more internalizing problems, eating problems, medical problems, stereotyped behavior problems, and relationship problems with peers and siblings.

A prominent aspect of the early experiences of an adoptive child is the attachment process, both before and after the adoption. In adoptions, the attachment process is potentially complicated due to parents' difficulties accepting the child as their own, unresolved fertility

Photo 11.3 Parents with adoptive child from another country.

Source: Don Mason/Blend Images/Getty Images

considerations, lack of family support, or disappointment when the child does not meet parental expectations (Brodzinsky & Pinderhughes, 2002). In addition, when children are adopted past the early infancy period, their prior attachment experiences (or lack thereof) are risk factors for attachment problems. See Box 11.5 for a description of the problem of **reactive attachment disorder (RAD)**.

Box 11.5 Reactive Attachment Disorder

Orphanages and institutions have been raising children in the United States since the 18th century (Mintz, 2004). Today, few children are raised in institutional care in the United States, but the practice continues to be common in developing nations, such as Romania. Although many children who come from institutions are physically and mentally healthy, some exhibit serious problems with forming new relationships and show extensive deficits in social interaction skills (Fox, Nelson, & Zeanah, 2013).

(Continued)

(Continued)

RAD refers to a syndrome concerning the inappropriate development of attachment relationships that can begin in infancy and appears prior to age five. It may take one of two forms: inhibited/emotionally withdrawn or indiscriminant/disinhibited (where children are unselective in their attachment behavior). The children may also be hypervigilant or ambivalent in their responses (frozen watchfulness, resistance to comfort, etc.). Children with RAD do not have a preferred adult as a source of comfort when distressed, they don't respond to comforting when offered, they don't show social or emotional reciprocity, and they have difficulties with emotional regulation.

This disorder, according to the *Diagnostic and Statistical Manual of Mental Disorders (DSM-V;* American Psychiatric Association, 2013), is a result of serious neglect or repeated changes in caregivers that precluded forming a stable, secure attachment. It occurs most often in children who have been maltreated (Kay & Green, 2013; Zeanah et al., 2004).

What is the prognosis for a child with RAD? Indiscriminant attachment behavior can last for years, and some children have persistent and serious developmental problems into the teen years and beyond (Kay & Green, 2013). Parenting a child with RAD is a very challenging and stressful task characterized by an unstable relationship (Follan & McNamara, 2013). Fortunately, most children with RAD who are adopted into good homes are able to develop attachments, many of which develop into secure ones (e.g., O'Connor & Zeanah, 2003).

Another common issue associated with adoptions concerns the child's identity. Beginning in the late preschool or early grade school years, children begin to differentiate biological from adoptive status. Adopted children are curious about their birth mothers and families. Some parents, however, fear that talking about the adoption may confuse the child or negatively affect his or her self-esteem, so they are secretive about the child's biological status. Investigations into the question, however, find just the opposite. Adoptive families who promote openness in communication about the adoption do not confuse children or lower their self-esteem. Rather, children who had contact with their birth mothers were more satisfied and well-adjusted than other adopted youth (Grotevant, McRoy, Wrobel, & Ayers-Lopez, 2013). During adolescence, a child's need for identity is especially pronounced, and parents must negotiate the challenges with care. The issues can be even more complex with special needs, transracial, and international adoptions (Brodzinsky & Pinderhughes, 2002; Leslie, Smith, Hrapczynski, & Riley, 2013).

The type and severity of problems that adopted children have are linked to the type of adoptive group. For example, children adopted from the child welfare system tend to have higher rates of school problems than do children adopted as infants, children adopted internationally, or children adopted within their birth families (Howard, Smith, & Ryan, 2004). The severity of the problems is often increased when the child has experienced abuse, neglect, or multiple primary caregivers. Of all nontraditional groups studied in the Regnerus (2012a) New Family Structures Study, adopted children most resembled the children from biologically intact families; they differed on only 17.5% of the outcome variables.

Adoption serves a vital function for adults who want to be parents, and it provides a dramatic and powerful intervention for many adoptees. A meta-analysis of 62 studies including more than 17,000 adopted children found that adoption significantly improved a child's intelligence scores and school performance compared with siblings or peers who remained in orphanages or in deprived environments (van IJzendoorn & Juffer, 2005). So although adopted children do not score as high on school performance or IQ tests as their nonbiologically related siblings or peers raised in biological families, they perform *much* higher than their biological siblings and peers left behind in subpar environments.

GAY AND LESBIAN PARENTS

Since the early 1980s, another type of nontraditional family structure has been investigated: one where both parents are the same gender (see Photo 11.4). According to a Gallup Poll of more than 120,000 interviews, 3.4% of Americans identify themselves as lesbian, gay, bisexual, or transsexual (Gates & Newport, 2012). It is estimated that 16% of same-sex couples have children under the age of 18 years (Gates, 2012). Gays, bisexuals, or lesbians (sometimes called *lesbigay* parents) become mothers and fathers in various ways. Some bore children in previous heterosexual marriages and continue to rear them either as a single parent or with a same-sex partner. Others become parents through ARTs (such as donor insemination) or adoption. Empirical studies, gradually accumulating on this topic, address two central questions: Do gay/lesbian parents differ from heterosexual parents in their parenting? What are the effects on children of having gay/lesbian parents?

Given the low percentage of gay/lesbian parents, it is difficult to collect samples. Most of the research on this topic could be characterized as limited by small (sometimes less than 10 families per group), convenient, and nonrepresentative samples. Among those samples, the evidence is consistent: There are few significant differences in the reported parenting practices, beliefs, or attitudes of gay/lesbian parents compared to traditional parents (Golombok et al., 2013; Patterson, 2004; Tasker, 2005). When differences *are* found, studies often find more positive functioning in gay-father families (Golombok et al., 2013) or that gay/lesbian parents are more likely than heterosexual parents to share childcare tasks more evenly (Farr & Patterson, 2013). Some investigations reveal benefits of same-sex parenting. Compared to heterosexual parents, lesbian mothers showed more awareness of their children, perhaps because of their concern about raising a child in a nontraditional environment (Flaks, Ficher, Masterpasqua, & Joseph, 1995) and were observed to engage in more supportive co-parenting than gay or heterosexual couples (Farr & Patterson, 2013).

How do children of gay/lesbian parents fare when they grow up? Do these children become homosexuals themselves? On most of the variables investigated, children of homosexual parents are largely indistinguishable from their heterosexual peers; they appear to be typically developing children and youth. In general, studies do not find negative effects from this nontraditional parenting on the children's psychological well-being as assessed by anxiety and self-esteem, behavior problems, alcohol and drug use, school grades, and sexual behavior and preferences (Farr & Paterson, 2013; Golombok et al., 2013;

Photo 11.4 A nontraditional family.

Patterson, 2002; Perrin & Committee on Psychosocial Aspects of Child and Family Health, 2002; Wainright, Russell, & Patterson, 2004).

That is not to say that there are no effects from being reared by same-sex parents. Not surprisingly, one difference uncovered is that children with gay/lesbian parents are more open to same-sex relationships. However, children raised in these nontraditional families often face antigay prejudice, teasing, and harassment from peers (Gartrell, Deck, Rodas, Peyser, & Banks, 2005). It is likely that these children develop coping skills, just like children from other nontraditional families or minority groups.

Other findings reveal that this particular type of nontraditional family may face certain hardships. For instance, these families are more likely to report receiving less social support from family members than do heterosexual parents (Kurdek, 2004). In a meta-analytic review, Stacey and Biblarz (2001), after reviewing 21 studies on the topic, concluded that researchers have downplayed findings regarding children's gender interests and sexual preferences. They also identified significant methodological weaknesses of the research conducted to date, including the nonrepresentative samples used, ambiguity in definitions of sexual orientation, and the lack of developmental research on these children. The investigators argued that future researchers should avoid these problems.

Many of those problems were remedied in the large study of alternative family structures by Mark Regnerus (2012a) mentioned previously. Regnerus compared the outcomes of young adults who were reared by lesbian mothers or gay fathers with those reared by intact biological parents. In contrast to previous studies, he found a number of differences. In fact, the adult children of the lesbian mothers differed from the biological families on 62.5% of the variables examined (e.g., educational attainment, depression, physical health, quality of current relationship); adult children from gay families differed from biological families on 25% of the variables. The study can be faulted for not accounting for the frequency of family transitions or other possible determinants of adjustment problems. Not surprisingly, the study elicited considerable criticism (Regnerus, 2012b) despite its strong methodology (Amato, 2012).

In sum, there is conflicting evidence regarding the specific effects of children being reared by homosexual parents [Preview Question]. More research is needed to carefully identify what processes may account for possible effects on children raised in this nontraditional parent environment.

Box 11.6 Military Parents: A Case of Occupation Affecting the Family

Today, there are more than 1.4 million members of the military, with many more in military-connected employment. Fifty-six percent of them are married and almost 44% in active duty have children (U.S. Department of Defense, 2012). Being a parent in the military poses a variety of challenges for families, including frequent moves, high levels of stress and conflict due to the long deployments, disruptions to family roles and routines, extended duty hours, possible trauma from the deployments, and the threat of injury or death (e.g., Paley, Lester, & Mogil, 2013; Park, 2011).

Not surprisingly, military family members are at risk for various problems. When military parents were compared with civilians, two studies reported higher rates of child maltreatment, two studies found lower rates, and two studies had mixed findings (Rentz et al., 2006). Military children report higher rates of emotional problems than representative nonmilitary children (Chandra et al., 2010). Nevertheless, from attachment and family systems theoretical perspectives, despite the challenges, a number of strengths can be identified in well-functioning military families (Riggs & Riggs, 2011). For example, parents who are adept at navigating the separation-reunion transitions and adopt positive approaches to the frequent changes are likely to have more resilient children (Milburn & Lightfoot, 2013). In fact, military-connected youth function better than other children in some domains such as self-regulation and academic performance (Easterbrooks, Ginsburg, & Lerner, 2013).

BLENDED/STEPPARENT FAMILIES

Over the past decade, there were more than 2 million marriages each year in the United States. However, each year also had more than 840,000 divorces (Tejada-Vera & Sutton, 2010). Remarriages represent about 29% of existing marriages and 38% of new marriages (Whitton, Stanley, Markman, & Johnson, 2013). Approximately 9% of children in the United States live in a family with a stepparent, who is most often a stepfather (Payne, 2013).

Due to the relationship dynamics, stepfamilies represent an especially heterogeneous nontraditional structure. Consider the relationship in just a three-person family, where the child is living with the biological mother. The couple may or may not be married. There are stepfather-child and biological mother-child relationships. The quality of these relationships can depend on the gender of the child, the child's age and temperament, the child's acceptance of the stepfather, and the quality of the stepfather-biological mother relationship. The quality of the relationship with the stepfather can depend on the degree of hostility toward the former spouse or the child's relationship with the biological father. Or if the biological parent is dead, there are other issues to deal with (Coleman, Ganong, & Russell, 2013).

Nevertheless, reviews of the research into the parenting of stepparents (e.g., Coleman, Ganong, & Leon, 2006; Coleman et al., 2013; Hetherington & Stanley-Hagan, 2002) indicate that children in stepfamilies experience more problems than children in two-biological-parent homes. Children living with a stepparent may have problems due to various issues, such as disruption of relationship with the noncustodial parent and multiple transitions as well as the quality of relationships with new family members (Dunn, Davies, O'Connor, & Sturgess, 2000). Not surprisingly, the evidence is that children in stepfamilies are likely to experience adjustment problems, especially in the first few years after the remarriage. However, problems can persist. In the Regnerus (2012a) study of the well-being of young adults from different family structures, he found that children raised in stepfamilies differed from those raised in intact biological families on 60% of the variables assessed.

At the same time, there is evidence that the quality of parenting in cases of divorce does affect the well-being and resilience of children. Such variables as being involved, providing warmth, monitoring, supervising, disciplining, and helping with the child's emotional adjustment have been shown to be affected by divorce and, in turn, relate to children's behavior problems and well-being (Coleman et al., 2013; Lansford, 2009).

GRANDPARENTS AS PARENTS

Grandparents are the first alternative as surrogate parents of children (see Photo 11.5). According to the Pew Research Center, 7.7 million children in the United States live with a grandparent, the most common type of next-of-kin that children live with. Of those, the primary caregiver for about 2 million children is a grandparent (Livingston, 2013). Grandparents are not just older parents; in as many as one-third of cases, the grandparent-headed families are below the poverty line (U.S. Census Bureau, 2013). This nontraditional family situation occurs for multiple reasons, including financial problems, incarceration, illness, maltreatment, substance abuse, or death of the child's parent.

Grandparents have both strengths and challenges when being a parent the second time around. They have more wisdom and knowledge, time, and gratitude—though less energy, more problems with discipline, and being faced with a generation gap (Dunifon, 2013). They also may have dual roles to negotiate as well as their own identity issues and feelings of resentment at having to be a parent again at this later stage in life (Backhouse & Graham, 2012).

Typically, grandparents-as-parents are found to be highly committed to the well-being of their grandchild and their parenting is in the normal range (Kirby & Sanders, 2013). However, different parenting styles of grandparents depend on the age and personality of the grandparent. Older individuals (more than 65 years) tend to adopt a formal parenting role compared with the "fun-seeker" grandparents who are younger and maintain informal and playful relations with their grandchildren. A second group of younger grandparents can be characterized as having benevolent but distant relationships (see review by Thomas, Sperry, & Yarbrough, 2000). Involved grandparents can serve as positive influences on children's lives. In one study of European American single mothers, living with both a single mother and grandmother was associated with positive child development. In particular, children who also lived with a grandmother received more cognitive stimulation and had higher reading scores compared to children in homes with just a single mother (Dunifon & Kowaleski-Jones, 2007).

Photo 11.5 In the United States, 5% of children are being raised by their grandmothers or grandparents.

Source: Jack Hollingsworth/Photodisc/Thinkstock

Although caring for grandchildren is good for the children and can be rewarding for the grandparent, it is also taxing. Grandparents who are surrogate parents react with anger and resentment at their adult child for putting them in this situation (Glass & Huneycutt, 2002). Not surprisingly, they are more likely to report mental health problems (e.g., depression) than non-caregiver grandparents (Fuller-Thomson & Minkler, 2000; Thomas et al., 2000). Financial strains and physical problems are other difficulties commonly experienced by grandparents who are surrogate parents (Thomas et al., 2000).

FOSTER PARENTS

There are almost 400,000 children in foster care in the United States because their parents provide an unsafe environment or cannot provide for them. About one-quarter of them are in relatives' homes (Child Welfare Information Gateway, 2013). Foster parents are temporary parents; the long-term goal for more than half of the children is to reunify them with their biological parents. Being in foster care means a disruption in caregiving, transitions into a new environment, and, in many cases, a history of maltreatment. Thus being a foster parent requires not just the normal parenting ability but extraordinary abilities to provide nurturing and responsive care along with skills in dealing with attachment and behavior problems

(Dozier, Albus, Fisher, & Sepulveda, 2002). Foster parents also have the added burden of frequent contacts with state agencies, social workers, and other child welfare individuals (Rhodes, Orme, & Buehler, 2001).

Many well-meaning parents are not up to this challenge, and 30% to 50% of foster parents quit each year. This is due to many reasons, including high levels of stress, financial burden, lack of preparedness for the challenges, or dissatisfaction with caseworkers. Other factors also contribute to foster parents' situation: moving, change in employment, health, or family situations (e.g., problems coping with the foster parents' own biological children) (Rhodes et al., 2001; Rodger, Cummings, & Leschied, 2006; Serbinski & Shlonsky, 2014). Another common problem is sibling conflict between maltreated children in the foster homes. Physical aggression between siblings was reported in 82% of the foster homes samples (Linares et al., 2014).

What are the key caregiving qualities needed to foster parent vulnerable children? According to Mary Dozier and her colleagues (Dozier, Zeanah, & Bernard, 2013) four qualities are essential: love (or nurturance), synchrony to the child so he or she can develop better self-regulatory skills, stability of care, and commitment. Foster mothers who were more committed to the foster child had previously fostered fewer children, were fostering younger children, and took more delight in the child. Parents who showed more commitment were more likely to still have the foster child at least two years after placement (Dozier & Lindhiem, 2006).

PARENTING EMERGENT ADULTS

One of the newest nontraditional family structures in the United States is for adult children to continue to live with their parents or perhaps return after graduating from college. Living with what Jeffrey Arnett (2000) labeled *emergent* adults (ages 18 to 29 years) poses various novel problems for parents. For one, the young adults often don't consider themselves as adults (Nelson et al., 2007). Consequently, that results in a dilemma for parents. How should the child/adult be treated? To what extent, if any, should the child continue to be parented? If living at home, should they live under the same rules that they did as adolescents?

To date, most of the research into parenting emergent adults has not separated out families where the children have returned home from other families. What studies are available indicate that parents of the young adults remain highly involved. Parents frequently offer practical advice as well as emotional and financial support (Fingerman, Cheng, Tighe, Birditt, & Zarit, 2012). After collecting data from more than 400 parents of emerging adults, three parenting patterns emerged: uninvolved, controlling-indulgent, and authoritative (Nelson, Padilla-Walker, Christensen, Evans, & Carroll, 2011). It is easy to predict which type of parenting would be most effective and satisfying to the emerging adult.

CHAPTER SUMMARY

There are many kinds of nontraditional family structures and characteristics, and each nontraditional family has unique issues that characterize its functioning. Nine types of nontraditional families have been discussed: single parents, adolescent mothers, adoptive parents, ART parents, gay/lesbian parents, stepparents, grandparents as parents, foster parents, and parenting emerging adults. There are other types of nontraditional families, such as children living in group homes and commuter families (where one parent works—and may live at—a different location from the rest of the family), but those family forms are much less common than those covered here.

It should be kept in mind that it is difficult to make broad generalizations about the groups because they are heterogeneous, and parenting as well as child adjustment depends on many considerations. The research evidence generally indicates that the structure of the family, the sexual orientation of the parents, and the biological status of the children are not nearly as important as how the family members interact. It is the within-family processes (e.g., quality of parenting), factors external to the family, and transitions that are responsible for positive or negative effects on children. Nevertheless, there is some evidence indicating that children in nontraditional homes *are* at risk for greater number of behavioral problems than children from two-biological-parent homes, all other things being equal. More extensive research, with better group definitions, will continue to enhance our understanding of the many factors that play into parenting outcomes and help parents from all sorts of family structures better cope with the many challenges of parenting well.

THOUGHT QUESTIONS

- Are the labels *traditional* and *nontraditional* still meaningful in today's society? Why or why not?
- What are some of the different ways you could classify or group the nine nontraditional family structures discussed in this chapter?
- In what ways might the political debate about the legal definition of marriage (between a man and a woman—or not) affect children in nontraditional families?
- For children living in nontraditional families, what are some of possible effects on children not discussed? What role might stigmatization play?

CHAPTER GLOSSARY

cumulative risk model A model depicting the accumulation of separate risks or problems; when multiple risk factors add up to create negative effects on a child.

nontraditional family Any family structure that does not contain two heterosexual biological parents.

polygamy When one adult has more than one spouse.

polygyny When a man has two or more wives.

reactive attachment disorder (RAD) A syndrome of developmentally inappropriate behavior with regard to interpersonal relationships.

CHAPTER 12

Parents at Risk

Chapter Preview: True or False?

- Children in affluent families have fewer problems than poor children do.
- Childhood experiences affect health in adulthood.
- Unloving mothers drive their children to become autistic.

Child rearing is, at times, demanding, tiring, and stressful. Even under the best of circumstances, parenting is challenging. These challenges become much more difficult in the face of various contextual factors or individual parent/child circumstances. In those situations, parents are at risk for engaging in defective child rearing or worse—maltreatment. This chapter addresses seven variables associated with potentially problematic parenting. Three of the variables concern the context: parenting in poor families, parenting in homeless families, and parenting in affluent families. The next four variables are problems in the parent: violent intimate partner relationships, a history of adverse childhood experiences, mental health problems, and substance abuse. Finally, we consider parents who are rearing children with serious disabilities, such as children with autism spectrum disorder (ASD).

ECONOMIC FACTORS

Socioeconomic status (SES) is considered one of the most important determinants of parenting (Chapter 5), and it's one of the most widely studied constructs in social science (Bradley & Corwyn, 2002). SES is not easily quantified, but it's commonly determined on the basis of parental occupation, highest educational degree obtained, and income. It is a convenient variable that serves as a proxy to represent very different physical and social environmental experiences for children. Differences in SES are closely linked to variations in three types of resources that affect children's development:

- financial capital (money);
- human capital (the availability, involvement, and motivation of other people to promote a child's development); and
- social capital (access and connections to others in the community, including providers of medical care).

But SES is not just linked to resources; it is also associated with parenting in at least three ways: social cognition, traits, and behaviors (Bornstein & Bradley, 2003). Studies regarding parental social cognition have identified SES effects in variables such as values, expectations, and self-perceptions. Recall from Chapter 5 Kohn's theory that lower-SES parents value conformity in their children in contrast to higher-SES parents, who value self-directedness. SES differences are also found in mothers' expectations and self-perceptions. Mothers from higher-SES groups, compared with lower-SES mothers, tend to have higher expectations about their infants and children. Lower-SES mothers perceive less control over their children's outcomes than do higher-SES mothers (Brody, Flor, & Gibson, 1999; Elder, Eccles, Ardelt, & Lord, 1995).

A trait approach to parenting reveals further differences linked to SES. Higher-SES parents engage in more authoritative parenting; those of low SES are more likely to be either authoritarian or permissive (Glasgow, Dornbusch, Troyer, Steinberg, & Ritter, 1997).

What about SES and specific parenting behaviors? Differences attributable to SES have been found in such areas as verbal interaction, discipline, control, and management. For example, mothers in higher-SES families, compared with lower-SES mothers, talk to their children more often and with speech characterized by more variety, syntactic complexity (how words are put together), and questions (Hoff-Ginsburg, 1998). The behavioral differences attributable to SES are sometimes more subtle and limited to particular areas. A study that compared the experiences of African American infants in low-, middle-, and high-SES homes is described in Box 12.1.

Box 12.1 Babies' Experiences in Different SES Groups

How does SES affect infants? One study compared the experiences of three- to four-month-old African American infants from three SES groups: low (most families had an annual income of less than $10,000), middle (most incomes in the $35,000 to $55,000 range), and upper (average income above $80,000) groups. The researchers (Fouts, Roopnarine, & Lamb, 2007) observed infants for 12 hours over four days to examine 16 different behaviors, including social interactions, sleeping, smiling, vocalizing, self-play, fussing, and crying.

Although all the infants slept and were vocalized to for similar amounts of time, higher-SES infants differed from the middle- and lower-SES infants in several ways. They vocalized and fussed less but engaged in more self-play. They also received more verbal affection and soothing responses. Lower-SES infants interacted more with relatives. It is clear that the lower-SES infants did not experience social deprivation, although they were experiencing a different social environment than the other children. How differences like these subsequently translate into different child outcomes remains to be seen.

A more dramatic and commonly found SES difference concerns the use of physical punishment as a socialization tool. As far back as 1936, researchers discovered that lower-SES parents more frequently report they use physical punishment to discipline their children than do higher-SES parents (Gecas, 1979). More than 70 years later, studies continue to find large SES effects in the use of physical punishment (Gershoff, 2002). What accounts for this difference? According to research by Ellen Pinderhughes and her colleagues (Pinderhughes, Dodge, Bates, Pettit, & Zelli, 2000), the answer lies in a combination of the parents' stress levels, perceptions of their children, and cognitive-emotional processes such as parental beliefs about the utility of physical force to resolve conflict. Based on structural equation modeling, it was found that lower-SES parents disciplined in a more reactive way—in part as a consequence of their stress levels—compared with higher-SES parents.

Another way of considering SES effects on parenting is to examine child rearing at the two extremes of SES—those living in poverty and those residing in affluence.

Parents With Low Incomes

If one had to choose one risk factor with the greatest likelihood for negative effects on parenting and children's development, it would be low income, also investigated as *poverty* or *low SES* (Bradley & Corwyn, 2002). When a family has inadequate financial resources to meet its daily needs, its members live in poverty, and this condition brings with it a variety of problems. How is poverty status determined? The U.S. Census Bureau measures poverty by family income, adjusting the figure depending on family size and composition as well as current inflation. For 2014, the poverty threshold for a two-parent family with two children was set at $23,850. Currently, about 23% of U.S. children are being raised in poverty, though that rate varies greatly depending on race/ethnicity and region of the country. Table 12.1 reveals how the rates of child poverty differ by child race/ethnicity.

Photo 12.1 A child living in a low-income area.

Source: iStockphoto.com/BrandyTaylor

What are the ramifications of living in poverty? First, it means living in a poor-quality physical environment (see Photo 12.1). Children in poverty live in toxic environments—both literally and figuratively. Many are raised in poor urban neighborhoods (labeled *war zones*; Garbarino, Kostelny, & Dubrow, 1991), exposed to toxins such as lead paint or polluted air and water. These residential areas are often plagued by crime, drugs, and violent gang-related activity. In a multiethnic sample of poor fourth and fifth graders in Detroit, 89% of the children regularly heard gunfire, 66% had seen someone mugged, and 25% had witnessed a stabbing or shooting. Many of the children had themselves been victimized: 65% reported being assaulted, 44% had been threatened, 26% had been chased by gangs, 24% had been mugged, and 21% had been at home when the place was burglarized (Ceballo, Dahl, Aretakis, & Ramirez, 2001).

Poverty also means crowded and noisy living spaces; frequently changing housing situations; unemployment or low-paying jobs; underfunded, poor-quality day cares and schools; and—for minority members especially—discrimination. Children who are first- or second-generation Americans often face language hurdles as well.

The evidence is very clear that low income is interrelated with multiple negative contextual and interpersonal characteristics. Poor families have less financial and social capital to invest in their children. Higher incomes allow parents to live in better neighborhoods and provide more cognitively stimulating material (toys, books, computers), better nutrition, and

Table 12.1 Child Poverty Rate in the United States, 2012

Race	Percent
American Indian	37
Asian and Pacific Islander	15
Black or African American	40
Hispanic or Latino	34
Non-Hispanic White	14
Two or More Races	24
Total	23

Source: The Annie E. Casey Foundation, KIDS COUNT Data Center, www.kidscount.org.

better health care. In addition, higher-income parents often have more time to devote to child rearing and engaging the child in social relationships with others. In contrast, poor families tend to live in noisier, more dangerous, and more chaotic environments as well as experience more family turmoil and violence (Evans & Cassells, 2013; Evans & Wachs, 2010). Such families are also more likely to be made up of single parents or members of a minority or immigrant group and have low educational achievement (Huston & Bentley, 2010).

Not all parenting is adversely affected by living in low-income urban neighborhoods. Some parents respond to this dangerous environment in a variety of ways to try to counteract or at least buffer their children from some of the potentially damaging experiences (Burton & Jarrett, 2000). Reactions by some parents include heightened commitment to their role as a parent, modifying their parenting practices to protect their children, and seeking out resources and opportunities for their children.

The effects of poverty reach beyond the environment to permeate the quality of parenting. The impact of poverty on parenting has been most extensively documented using the HOME (Home Observation for Measurement of the Environment) assessment, developed by Robert Bradley and Bettye Caldwell (1984). This instrument consists of both a parent interview and observations of the home and parent-child interactions during the interview. The nine subscales of the preschool version of the HOME are listed in Table 12.2.

Researchers using the HOME instrument have documented that poverty affects at least all the parenting tasks identified by Bradley (2007), first presented in Chapter 1:

- Ensuring safety and sustenance
- Simulating and instructing
- Giving socioemotional support
- Monitoring and surveillance
- Structuring
- Providing social connectedness

Table 12.2 The Home Inventory (Preschool Version): Examples of Subscale Items

I. Learning Stimulation
• Child has toys that teach color, size, or shape. • Family buys and reads a daily newspaper.
II. Language Stimulation
• Child is encouraged to learn the alphabet. • Mother uses correct grammar and pronunciation.
III. Physical Environment
• Building appears safe. • House is reasonably clean and minimally cluttered.
IV. Warmth and Acceptance
• Parent praises child's qualities twice during visit. • Parent caresses, kisses, or cuddles child during visit.
V. Academic Stimulation
• Child is encouraged to learn colors. • Child is encouraged to learn to read a few words.
VI. Modeling
• Parent introduces visitor to child. • Child can express negative feelings without reprisal.
VII. Variety in Experience
• Child is taken on outings by family member at least every other week. • Child eats at least one meal per day with mother and father.
VIII. Physical Punishment
• Parent does not scold or derogate child more than once. • Parent neither slaps nor spanks child during visit.

Source: Bradley & Caldwell, 1984.

Poverty interferes with or degrades these parenting tasks. Several researchers have described how poverty affects many dimensions of family life and creates widespread environmental inequities for children (e.g., Evans, 2004). Children in poverty are likely to face more family conflict and turmoil, unstable and chaotic households, and separation from loved ones. These children also receive less social support, and their more-authoritarian parents provide less warmth, cognitive stimulation, and responsive parenting. Economic hardship, of course, diminishes a parent's capacity for supportive, consistent, and involved caregiving, in part because it results in depression (McLoyd, Jayaratne, Ceballo, & Borquez, 1994). Children raised in poverty watch more TV, are read to less often, and have less access to books or computers. No wonder these children are prone to many more problems than their more fortunate peers! Vonnie McLoyd (1990) developed a model of how poverty affects parenting and, in turn, children. Her model, as tested by Nievar and Luster (2006)—with some adaptations—is found in Figure 12.1.

Low-income parents are chronically stressed and, on average, have more health and emotional problems than their higher-income peers. In terms of their parenting, they tend to be less warm, less responsive, and less talkative to their children. They are more likely to engage in harsh discipline (i.e., corporal punishment) and neglectful parenting (Bøe et al., 2013; Bradley & Corwyn, 2002; Evans & Kim, 2013; Kang, 2013).

The well-being of children in poor families is at risk for a variety of health and behavioral problems. These children have more self-regulatory deficits, attentional problems, maladaptive coping skills (i.e., withdrawal and avoidance), behavior problems, and school failure than their higher-income peers (Brooks-Gunn, Duncan, & Maritato, 1997; Evans & Kim, 2013). Many of these problems co-occur. Poor children are 1.3 to 6.8 times as likely to have learning or behavior problems, to become a teen parent, or to be a victim of child maltreatment (Brooks-Gunn, Duncan, & Aber, 1997). Finally, these children are also at risk for neglect and maltreatment, as will be discussed in more detail in Chapter 14. Many of the problems closely linked to poverty are listed in Table 12.3.

Despite the collective wealth of the United States, the fact that almost *one child out of four* is being raised in poverty is a troubling statistic. When thinking about minority children, that rate goes up to about one child in three. Indeed, it is difficult for many of us to imagine how a family of four can live on $23,850 a year. It is even harder to imagine how one-fifth of the world's population (1 billion people) can survive on less than $1 a day. See Box 12.2 for a brief description of these families.

Figure 12.1 Model of How Poverty Affects Parenting

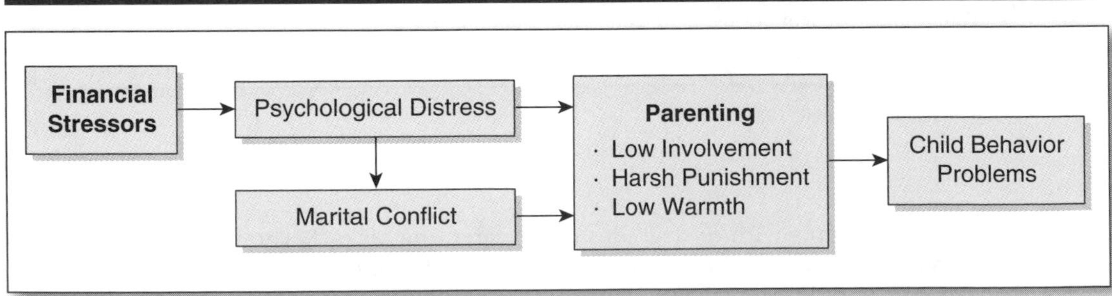

Source: Based on Nievar & Luster, 2006.

Table 12.3 Problems Associated With Poverty for Children and Youth

Physical Health	Social and Emotional Adjustment
Premature birth	Problems with self-regulation
Birth defects	Low effectance motivation
Malnutrition	Anxiety disorders
Obesity	Aggression, delinquency
Asthma	Relationship difficulties
Increased blood lead levels	
Competence and Achievement	
Attention difficulties (e.g., attention-deficit/hyperactivity disorder [ADHD])	
Mental retardation	
Learning disabilities	
Poor grades and dropping out	
Lower college attendance	

Box 12.2 Surviving on $1 a Day?

According to the World Bank, about 1 billion people live on less than $1 a day. Another 1.5 billion people live on $2 a day. The extremely poor typically live in families of 6 to 12 people. What are the ramifications for parenting and children's development in such extreme poverty?

These parents spend their time trying to survive and eke out an existence. They survive by subsistence farming or working as laborers. According to two professors at the Massachusetts Institute of Technology, the extreme poor *do* manage to make it without spending all of their money on subsistence food (Banerjee & Duflo, 2007). They spend 56% to 78% of their income on food, 4% to 8% on alcohol and tobacco, and 10% on festival or family events (such as weddings and funerals). Less than 1% is spent for entertainment. They have little to spend on their children's education (an average of 2%), and children help out instead by working as laborers or perhaps selling goods.

Families living in extreme poverty face many hardships. They deal with hunger and malnutrition. Their access to health services, clean water, and sanitation is often nonexistent. The educational opportunities for the children are inadequate and underfunded. What's more, these families are particularly vulnerable to economic problems, natural disasters, and crime. The only good news is that there are about half as many of these families now as there were 30 years ago.

Parents Who Are Homeless

An extreme case of economic instability is seen in the homeless population in the United States. On any single night in America, 36% of the homeless (more than 222,000 individuals) constitute homeless *families*. Fifty-eight percent of these individuals are children. Half of the families are living temporarily in shelters (Henry, Cortes, & Morris, 2013). These mother-headed families are rarely found on the street. Rather, they live temporarily in homeless shelters or with extended family or friends. And their homelessness is relatively short-lived. Most of these families (87%) are homeless for fewer than five months. The mothers in these homeless families exhibit a multitude of risk factors. Many are young, minority, jobless, have multiple children, and have been abandoned by the father of their children. In addition, many are survivors of unhappy childhoods and/or intimate partner violence. Many struggle with substance abuse problems, and more than a third have serious mental health problems (Hinton & Cassel, 2013; Monn et al., 2013).

Homeless families are at risk for a variety of problems, both for parents and for children. Mothers report high rates of stress, depression, and use of harsh and inconsistent discipline (e.g., Holtrop, McNeil, & McWey, 2014). However, homeless mothers are not always found to have high levels of problems. Ann Easterbrooks and Christine Graham (1999) compared 55 homeless mothers and children with 57 low-income (not homeless) mothers and children. They assessed maternal mental health, attachment relations, reported parenting practices, and stressors. Surprisingly, the homeless mothers did not differ reliably from the low-income mothers on any of the variables. That does not mean that either group was faring well. Both groups of mothers evidenced a number of problems and problematic behaviors.

Indeed, most studies of homeless children find high rates of problems due to cumulative risks that cascade. These children tend to have poor health, behavior problems, educational delays, and poor academic performance. There is evidence that the longer the children are living as homeless, the more internalizing symptoms (such as depression, anxiety, and social withdrawal) they show (Buckner, Bassuk, Weinreb, & Brooks, 1999; Monn et al., 2013). Nevertheless, there is striking variability within the homeless population. Some homeless children show remarkable resilience despite the risks (Masten, 2011). One source of resilience is the quality of the child rearing. High-quality parenting (warm, responsive, consistent discipline, appropriate structure, and positive expectations for the child) can protect the child against some of the negative effects of unstable living situations (Herbers et al., 2011).

Parents With High Incomes

At the other end of the SES continuum are *affluent families*, technically defined as families earning greater than twice the country's median income (the median income in the United States in 2013 was $51,017). Although material resources are not a problem with these families, and children of affluent families are assumed to be low risk, the evidence indicates this is not an accurate perception. A review of the limited literature (Luthar, 2003) identified some of the adjustment problems of children from these wealthy families. They included anxiety, depression, and substance use (cigarettes, alcohol, marijuana, and other drugs). Other researchers have also found that children in affluent families are at risk for emotional problems (Csikszentmihalyi & Schneider, 2000) [Preview Question].

Privileged children are believed to be at risk for several reasons: They may experience unusually high achievement pressure, they may be more isolated from their parents (literally and emotionally), and their parents may devote less time to them (see Box 12.3). Children of affluent families perceive their parents as emotionally and physically unavailable—to the same extent as youth raised in poverty. They may lack after-school supervision, which is associated with externalizing problems (Luthar & Latendresse, 2005). High-profile parents may also be reluctant to seek professional help in their efforts to maintain a veneer of well-being. Finally, children of affluence often have more than adequate money to spend on illegal drugs and alcohol (Lund & Dearing, 2013; Luthar & Latendresse, 2005).

Another potential cause of youth problems in affluent families is the parents' excessive focus on acquiring possessions (*materialism*). According to Tim Kasser (2002), who has studied these families,

- they value money, work, and possessions;
- they model consumerism (by their shopping habits and responses to advertisements);
- they devote energy to making money and purchasing items rather than to family time; and
- they reinforce valued child behavior with gifts or money.

Materialism and consumerism are associated with unhappiness because the desire for more and more possessions forces us into a more frantic pace of life, causing stress, strain, and neglected relationships (Kasser, 2002). Think about the parents-as-guides model of child rearing. What materialistic parents are doing—either intentionally or otherwise—is shaping their children's values in, perceptions of, and orientation toward the external world. Happiness becomes linked to acquiring fashionable clothes, the latest cell phone, the lightest and fastest computer, and the biggest and most luxurious car.

What research is available does indeed indicate that children and youth from affluent families are at risk for several types of problems. The most commonly documented problems are anxiety, unhappiness and depression, and somatic problems (insomnia, gastrointestinal disturbance) as well as delinquency and substance abuse (Elgar et al., 2013; Luthar, 2003). Other outcomes associated with affluence are the development of overly materialistic values to the neglect of more prosocial values (Kasser, Ryan, Zax, & Sameroff, 1995). Parents, as well as peers, can directly influence the development of materialism by modeling, reinforcement, and communicating consumption attitudes. Alternatively, there may be some mediating influences on the development of materialism, according to Chaplin and John (2010). Youth with positive self-perceptions are less materialistic, so parents who are supportive of their children and promote healthy and realistic self-esteem will have adolescents who are less consumer oriented.

Box 12.3 Workaholic Parents

Affluent families tend to have one or more parents who are workaholics (or who have a "work addiction"). Workaholism not only negatively affects the parent, who may be working 12-hour days or 100 hours in a week, but it also affects the family system. Family problems include high levels of marital unhappiness and divorce as well as relational and psychological problems (depression, anxiety, obsessive-compulsive tendencies) in the children (Chamberlin & Zhang, 2009; Robinson, Flowers, & Carroll, 2001). Children of workaholic parents resent the lack of physical and emotional availability of the parent. Another type of problem created by the parents' absence is **parentification** of the child, when the child is put into the role of an adult in the family. Older children are sometimes put in the position of providing child care for a younger child or emotional support for a parent. When this occurs, the child carries the burden of inappropriate responsibility (Robinson & Carroll, 1999). Youth who perceive parentification as unfair are likely to exhibit mental health symptoms (Jankowski, Hooper, Sandage, & Hannah, 2013).

PARENT CONTEXT

Parents in Violent Intimate Partner Relationships

It is estimated that 6% of American children are exposed to violence between their parents or a parent and a partner (Hamby, Finkelhor, Turner, & Ormrod, 2011). In most of these homes, the father is the major perpetrator of the violence, although it is not unusual for the violence to be bidirectional as mothers attempt to defend themselves (Holden, 2003). Fathers who are violent toward their partners are also likely to be authoritarian, angry, controlling, and verbally abusive (Bancroft & Silverman, 2002; Edleson & Williams, 2007). However, not all fathers who engage in violence with their partners are poor parents. For example, in a study comparing 56 interpersonally violent men in a battering intervention program with 39 comparison fathers from the community, only 18% of the violent men were at risk for maltreating their children compared with 3% of the community fathers. However, the violent men who were at risk for child maltreatment differed significantly from the other men on half of the variables assessed. These fathers reported more stress, anger, substance abuse problems, and psychological problems as well as behavior problems in their children than the men who were not at risk for maltreatment (Holden, Barker, Appel, & Hazlewood, 2010).

Mothers living with violent men are also at risk for problematic parenting, often because they are overwhelmed by stress and trying to cope with a violent partner (Radford & Hester, 2001). Mothers who are more traumatized and have poorer psychological functioning are more likely to show poor parenting practices, such as less warmth and more frequent verbal or physical harsh punishment (Holmes, 2013; Levendosky & Graham-Bermann, 2001).

Children living in families where there is intimate partner abuse are at high risk for problems. Many factors contribute to this: the trauma of seeing their parents fight, problematic parenting, and other commonly co-occurring problems (e.g., poverty, child maltreatment, mental health and substance abuse problems). In a meta-analysis of 60 studies of preschool- through adolescent-age children, those exposed to intimate partner violence were significantly more likely to have internalizing, externalizing, and trauma symptoms than other children. Boys were especially at risk for exhibiting externalizing problems (Evans, Davies, & DiLillo, 2008).

Parents With Adverse Childhood History

The majority of Americans and the vast majority of college students are reared in families and communities that are stable and nonviolent. However, many children are not so fortunate. Consider the true case of a child, whom we will call "Donnie." Donnie was raised in an inner-city apartment in a poor neighborhood of a major city. Drug dealing and gang violence was rampant. He lived with his unemployed mother and three siblings in a small, noisy apartment. But the worst part of his childhood was his mother. She was a drug addict and prostitute. If she had a boyfriend, he was likely to be abusive to her. Donnie was born addicted to heroin. His mother's child rearing consisted primarily of yelling, name-calling, and hitting with objects—there were never any expressions of love or affection. At age 6, Donnie was sexually abused by a neighbor. He was also subjected to abuse from siblings, including an older brother who eventually went to prison. Donnie finally escaped that toxic environment when he was 15 because he was arrested for selling drugs. A juvenile correction home became his safe house.

Although Donnie represents an extreme case, being raised in unfavorable environments is not. To investigate the effects of childhood environments on adult functioning, the Adverse Childhood Experiences (ACE) study was conducted. More than 17,000 adults who enrolled in a health maintenance organization in California participated by reporting on the number of adverse circumstances they experienced as well as their current mental and physical health. Information about three types of adverse conditions was collected: abuse, neglect, and household dysfunction.

Many different dependent variables have been examined from this extensive study. The consistent finding is that adverse childhood experiences impact mental health (e.g., depression), physical health (e.g., liver disease, health-related quality of life), and behavior (e.g., early initiation of sexual activity and smoking, substance abuse) [Preview Question]. Furthermore, it has been repeatedly found that the greater the exposure to adversities, the greater the risk for problems (Felitti et al., 1998). To put it differently, there is often a dose-response relationship between the number of adversities and individual's well-being. Donnie's ACE score was 10. See Box 12.4 to calculate your ACE score.

Box 12.4 Calculate Your Own ACE Score

While you were growing up, during your first 18 years of life

1. Did a parent or other adult in the household often or very often . . .

   Swear at you, insult you, put you down, or humiliate you? Or act in a way that made you afraid that you might be physically hurt?

2. Did a parent or other adult in the household often or very often . . .

   Push, grab, slap, or throw something at you? Or ever hit you so hard that you had marks or were injured?

3. Did an adult or person at least five years older than you ever . . .

   Touch or fondle you or have you touch their body in a sexual way? Or attempt or actually have oral, anal, or vaginal intercourse with you?

4. Did you often or very often feel that . . .

   No one in your family loved you or thought you were important or special? Or your family didn't look out for each other, feel close to each other, or support each other?

5. Did you often or very often feel that you didn't have enough to eat, had to wear dirty clothes, and had no one to protect you? Or your parents were too drunk or high to take care of you or take you to the doctor if you needed it?
6. Were your parents ever separated or divorced?
7. Was your mother or stepmother

   often or very often pushed, grabbed, slapped, or had something thrown at her? Or sometimes, often, or very often kicked, bitten, hit with a fist, or hit with something hard?

8. Did you live with anyone who was a problem drinker or alcoholic or who used street drugs?
9. Was a household member depressed or mentally ill, or did a household member attempt suicide?
10. Did a household member go to prison?

Total score is the total number of "yes" answers.

Source: http://acestudy.org/ace_score

How is parenting affected by having adverse childhood experiences? What are the chances that Donnie will make a nurturing father? Although to date, the ACE study researchers have not investigated parenting as an outcome, other researchers have. For example, Chung and colleagues used the ACE variables to test for effects on parenting. They discovered that if mothers had an ACE score of two or more, they were more likely to spank their infant (Chung et al., 2009). Other investigators find that childhood maltreatment is a significant risk for future abuse, as will be discussed in Chapter 14.

Of course, there are many other adverse childhood conditions or experiences that cause trauma and jeopardize the child's well-being and future child rearing. Death of a parent; living in a war zone; or experiencing an environmental disaster such as a hurricane, flood, or tornado are just three examples. Each situation can be traumatic for the child and result in lasting effects for different reasons. The continuing legacy of childhood experiences could be accounted for by a variety of underlying mechanisms, including physiological and neurological, social, emotional, and cognitive (Leen-Feldner et al., 2013; Shonkoff et al., 2012).

On the other hand, childhood is not necessarily destiny. Yes, there is much evidence for intergenerational transmission of maladaptive parenting practices after childhood maltreatment (e.g., Conger, Schofield, & Neppl, 2012) as well as in such areas as attachment, positive parenting, and harsh punishment (Conger, Belsky, & Capaldi, 2009; Serbin & Karp, 2004; van IJzendoorn, 1992). However, there are also many cases of discontinuity when parents do not repeat the same pattern of behavior they were exposed to as children. For example, if a parent, reared in a family with harsh punishment, had a spouse who engaged in loving and supportive child rearing, then the intergenerational transmission can be disrupted (Conger et al., 2012).

Parents With Serious Mental Illness

A mother in Houston, Texas, made headlines in 2001 after drowning her five young children in a bathtub. From the time of the birth of her fourth child, Andrea Yates had suffered from postpartum depression, but medication had successfully controlled the problem. When her fifth child was born, she relapsed into severe depression, and the antidepressant drugs were ineffective. Her defense lawyers argued that she was both depressed and psychotic. Before the killings, she said, she heard voices telling her to kill her children to save their souls. In 2006, she was tried for murder, acquitted by reason of insanity, and committed to a state mental hospital.

Fortunately, it is unusual for mentally ill parents to murder their children. However, serious mental illness in adults is not rare: It is estimated that 4% to 7% of American adults have at least one episode of a diagnosable mental illness over the course of a year (U.S. Department of Health and Human Services, 1999). About 40% of adults will experience a diagnosable disorder during their lifetime. Some mental health problems, such as postpartum depression, are generally short-lived for many individuals (as mentioned in Chapter 6). However, other serious psychological problems can be chronic. In addition, certain problems affect a significant portion of society. It is estimated that more than 9% of children (more than 6 million) in the United States live with a parent who has abused or been dependent on alcohol or an illicit drug (Substance Abuse and Mental Health Services Administration, 2004).

There are six commonly studied categories of mental health problems in parents:

- Depression
- Anxiety
- Schizophrenia
- Bipolar disorder
- Antisocial personality disorder
- Alcohol or substance abuse

To date, we have an incomplete understanding of how mental illness affects parenting and children's development. Part of the reason is that research into mental disorders and parenting has focused mostly on mothers. One notable exception is a meta-analytic review of 28 studies examining the effects of depression on fathers' parenting (Wilson & Durbin, 2010). They found that depressed fathers engaged in fewer positive and more negative parenting behaviors.

Part of the reason for the focus on mothers is that they are typically the primary caregivers. But there is also a long history of **mother blaming**. Mothers have been accused of causing a variety of problems in their children. Autism—according to male psychiatrists in the 1950s—was the result of cold and unloving mothers. The etiology of childhood schizophrenia was also thought to be due to aberrant maternal behavior called *schizophrenogenic* parenting. These and other examples of mother blaming (see Box 12.5) are due to an orientation or cultural view that a mother has primary responsibility for the growth, development, and behavior of her children (Caplan & Hall-McCorquodale, 1985).

Box 12.5 It's the Mother's Fault!

There is a long history of blaming women for a diverse assortment of childbearing or childrearing issues. King Henry VIII had his wife, Anne Boleyn, executed because she had failed to bear him a son. A more benign attack on mothers has come from those psychiatrists and psychologists who accused mothers of causing a variety of problems in children. "Refrigerator mothers" were thought to cause autism through their cold and aloof behavior. "Schizophrenogenic mothers" elicited schizophrenia in their children. A mother who was "close-binding" and intimate with her son while being dominant and minimizing to her husband was the "classic pattern" for causing homosexuality (Bieber et al., 1962). The list of blamable offenses goes on and on and includes epilepsy, asthma, ADHD, and transgendered children (Caplan & Hall-McCorquodale, 1985; Johnson & Benson, 2014; Singh, 2004).

Subsequent research has refuted all those extreme environmental, Watsonian contentions [Preview Question]. When differences in maternal behavior *are* found, they can readily be explained by child effects. For example, children with ASD typically have severe communication problems, avoid eye contact, resist affection, and struggle with reciprocal interactions. It is no wonder that their mothers' behavior differs dramatically from mothers of typical children! Interestingly, fathers have rarely been accused of causing these types of problems.

When considering how mental health problems affect parenting and children's development, the environmental context needs to be considered; psychological problems do not occur in a vacuum. When a parent has a serious mental illness, there are often other problems in the family. For example, individuals with a mental illness often abuse alcohol or drugs and have strained interpersonal relationships. In addition, poverty and violence are found in many of these families. Thus there are two types of multiple problems in these individuals: co-occurrence (two or more problems in the family) and comorbidity (two or more disorders in the individual). For example, parents who are alcoholic are also likely to have other forms of mental illness and to live in a dysfunctional family. Mental health problems can be both a cause and a consequence of homelessness (Chambers et al., 2013). Thus it is often difficult to sort out exactly which effects can be attributed to particular problems. For research purposes, however, certain statistical procedures (such as partial correlations, covariance, and structural equation modeling) can be used to control for multiple problems.

How is child rearing affected by a parent's serious mental illness? The answer depends on such considerations as the type of mental health problem, the severity of it, and whether the problem is chronic or acute (with short episodes) (Zahn-Waxler, Duggal, & Gruber, 2002). Mental health problems impede effective parenting in multiple ways. Mentally ill individuals typically cannot provide the warmth, emotional nurturance, reciprocal interactions, structure and stimulation, appropriate supervision, and discipline that young children need. In addition, when the children get older, mentally ill parents may have difficulty granting increasing autonomy to the child. Mothers with mental illness also report more stress, less social support, and less nurturance than other mothers (Oyserman, Bybee, & Mowbray, 2002).

The mental health problem that has attracted the most attention is depression in mothers. The problem is not uncommon; about one-third of women experience depression at some point in their lives. It is also a highly recurrent condition; more than 80% experience more than one depressive bout. Depression affects parenting in various ways. Ted Dix and Leah Meunier (2008), based on 152 studies, identified 13 potential regulatory processes that may be involved when a parent is depressed and thus serve to undermine effective parenting. For example, depressed parents can be less child focused, less attentive, more negative, and more prone to use coercive parenting. A review of 46 observational studies of depressed mothers determined that depressed mothers are significantly more likely than nondepressed mothers to be irritable, negative and to be disengaged or withdrawn from their infants or children. Their disciplinary practices tend to be lax, inconsistent, and ineffective (Lovejoy, Graczyk, O'Hare, & Neuman, 2000). On the other hand, some depressed mothers engage in a different pattern of behavior—that of being highly intrusive and overstimulating their infants (Field, Hernandez-Reif, & Diego, 2006).

Why are children affected when parents have a mental illness? It is impossible to isolate any single cause because multiple processes are at work. Children of mentally ill parents can be affected by genetics and biology; parenting processes (e.g., attachment, child discipline, and modeling); cognitive processes; family interactions; and family characteristics, such as a low income and a lack of social resources (Elgar, McGrath, Waschbusch, Stewart, & Curtis, 2004; Goodman & Gotlib, 1999). If the mentally ill individual is unable to parent adequately, a child's needs go unmet. The child's behavior is then affected, and this in turn leads to more problems for the ill parent.

Living with a mentally ill parent certainly represents a risk for children's development. When a mother has chronic depression, her children are not just at risk for depression and other mental health problems but also for behavioral, emotional, cognitive, academic, and health problems (Downey & Coyne, 1990). Part of the task for a child living in this situation is to understand the fact that the parent is ill. This challenge is captured in the true story presented in Box 12.6.

Box 12.6 Reared by a Mentally Ill Mother

Raven had lived with just her mother since she was two, after her parents had divorced. Raven's mother experienced delusions and hallucinations and acted out in ways that were unusual and unexplainable to the child. But Raven believed in her mother, to whom she had a strong attachment; she had never had another caregiver. Raven didn't recognize that her mother had a mental illness. The mother kept her illness hidden, and it was years before she received an accurate diagnosis and treatment.

At school, Raven began to exhibit behaviors that concerned her teachers. She shared her "special powers" with friends, but the friends began to withdraw from her, saying she was "strange" and "weird." They began to avoid her and to make fun of the stories she told. Raven often played alone, and spoke intently to her imaginary friends, the only consistent friends she had ever had. Academically, she was struggling; her reading and writing levels were years behind. The other children noticed this as well, and it was another excuse to tease and belittle her. At times, the young girl was oblivious to the teasing and bullying; at other times, she was very aware that she was being ostracized.

The school situation prompted an investigation by the Ministry for Children and Families, and Raven was removed from her mother's care. Shortly after being placed in her father's care, Raven came into the Kids in Control group.

It became clear almost immediately that she had been affected by her mother's illness. She described unusual situations that she and her mother had experienced. She talked about special powers she had and how she could use her powers. She talked about being afraid of certain people and how the "bad men" were trying to hurt her and her mother. Many of the disturbing stories were obviously a result of things her mother had said to her.

In an unusual twist of circumstances, I happened to be assigned to work with Raven in a family outreach program. My initial assessment of her concluded that she had experienced trauma while in her mother's care. She had normalized the incidents, believing that all young people had the same experiences growing up. One of the goals of Kids in Control is to help children recognize that they are not responsible for their parent's illness. Raven had, in effect, been her mother's caregiver since a very early age. She truly believed the frightening stories her mother had told her. Affected by the years of fear that had been instilled in her, Raven was afraid to meet or trust new people. And she had difficulty understanding that many of the things her mother had said to her were false and the result of delusions. Somehow the two had survived, depending on one another, and not letting anyone into their lives.

Raven attended the Kids in Control program twice over two years. She gradually learned about mental illness and finally came to her own conclusion that her mother had been in need of medical attention for a very long time. She came to recognize that much of what she had learned about the world from her mother was false.

Source: Originally appeared as a web-only article in *Visions: BC's Mental Health and Addictions Journal,* 2007, vol. 3, no 3. Reproduced with permission of the author and the BC Partners for Mental Health and Addictions Information.

Despite the associations found between parental mental health problems and children's problems, the likelihood that a child of mentally ill parents will develop problems is not high. According to a meta-analysis of 134 different samples of mentally ill parents and children (Connell & Goodman, 2002), the likelihood of children having behavior problems was small. The average effect size (a statistic that can be interpreted similarly to a correlation) is 0.17 for mothers and 0.16 for fathers. These associations vary by the age of the children and the parents' type of mental health problem, but they indicate that it is far from inevitable that a child will develop a serious problem. Given the multiple challenges these children face, it is remarkable how many of them appear to be resilient as they weather their difficult childhood circumstances.

Box 12.7 How Incarceration Impacts Parenting

The United States boasts the highest rate of incarceration in the world with 1.6 million prisoners (Population Reference Bureau, 2014). About 90% are men and many of those men are fathers. This forced family disruption has multiple implications for parenting. When the incarcerated parent goes to prison, the parent at home must transition into the role of the single parent. While in prison, it is difficult to maintain relations with children. Nevertheless, fathers who have maintained regular contact with their children prior to release and have good family support are more likely to have positive relations with their children (Visher & Travis, 2011). If it is the mother in jail, in many cases, the child's grandmother steps in to become the parent. Once released from prison, parents have to transition back into their previous roles. With all the other readjustment problems they face (e.g., employment, reestablishing relationships, etc.), this transition is often difficult and requires effective co-parenting (see Poehlmann & Eddy, 2013).

Parents With Substance Abuse Problems

Closely related to parents who have mental disorders are parents who abuse substances. Often, the two problems are co-occurring. It is estimated that about 9% to 14% of children in the United States have a parent with an alcohol or illicit drug problem (Child Welfare Information Gateway, 2009; ICF International, 2009; Suchman, Pajulo, & Mayes, 2013). Illicit drugs include marijuana, cocaine, methamphetamine (crystal meth), hallucinogens (LSD, ecstasy), inhalants, and heroin.

Parents with substance abuse problems are characterized by cycles of relapse and recovery. During recovery periods, the parent may have minimal, if any, childrearing deficiencies. However, during a relapse, there can be many negative effects. Some of these effects are direct ones on the quality of parenting, and others may be indirect effects on the home (e.g., more chaotic), the child (e.g., unfed), or interactions with others (more partner conflict) (Keller, Cummings, Davies, & Mitchell, 2008). To start, a baby born to a substance-abusing mother is likely to have physical, cognitive, and/or behavioral impairments. As the children grow, they are at risk for attachment problems as well as child maltreatment. Parents who are preoccupied with drugs or frequently high are unlikely to provide the warmth or responsiveness to a child but instead rely on harsh discipline (Barnard & McKegancy, 2004). Parents with substance abuse problems are likely to exhibit negative emotions as well as have difficulty controlling their emotions (Conners-Burrow et al., 2013; Haller & Chassin, 2011). Other problems found in substance-abusing fathers who also engaged in intimate partner violence included negative parenting and poor co-parenting relationships (Stover, Easton, & McMahon, 2013).

Children of alcoholic parents are more likely to develop alcohol and drug problems, internalizing problems (such as depression), externalizing behavior problems (such as lack of control), and mental health problems (such as anxiety). They also tend to have lower academic achievement than other children (Chassin, Pitts, DeLucia, & Todd, 1999). There is evidence that these problems persist well into adulthood, as the children continue to be at risk for such difficulties as substance abuse, depression, anxiety, aggression, low self-esteem, distress, and problematic intimate relationships (Harter, 2006).

Parents of Children With Special Needs

In Chapter 6, we discussed chromosomal abnormalities in children, but this is just one type of serious developmental difficulty some children have. Trauma during the birthing process can produce brain damage and lead to severe mental disabilities. Some children appear to be typical newborns at birth but—within a year or two—show signs of a pervasive developmental disorder, such as ASD. Other children may be born with or experience a problem and consequently develop a sensory (blindness, deafness) or physical disability. Approximately 15% of all children in the United States have a developmental disability, such as ASD, attention deficit disorder, a sensory disability, or a developmental delay (Boyle et al., 2011). See Figure 12.2 for a depiction of the estimated prevalence of eight types of childhood disabilities.

Developmental problems vary on many dimensions, including the degree of mental and physical impairment, the age of onset, and whether other problems are comorbid.

Figure 12.2 Prevalence of Eight Types of Child Disabilities in the United States

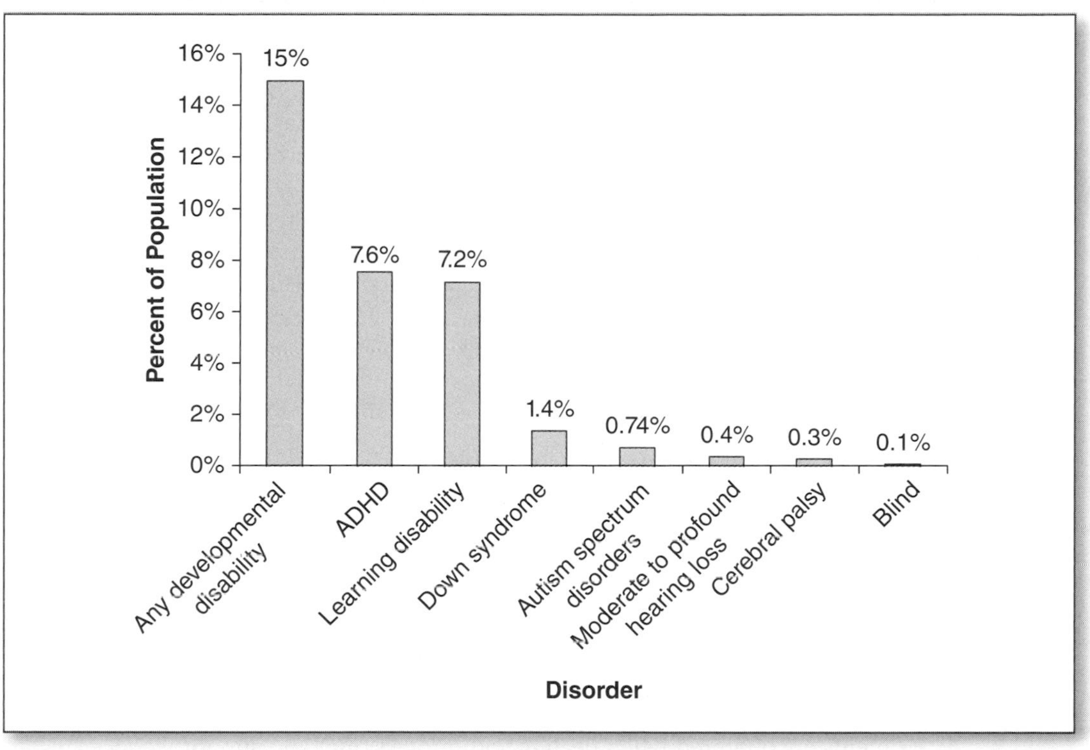

Source: All percentages come from Boyle et al., 2011, except for cerebral palsy (http://www.cdc.gov/features/dscerebralpalsy/index.html).

Consider autism, a disorder characterized by impaired social relations; problems with verbal and nonverbal communication; and the presence of repetitive and stereotyped patterns of behavior, interests, or activities. Children with autism generally do not act like other children; they are likely to engage in disruptive behaviors and to have emotional and thought problems. However, the *Diagnostic and Statistical Manual of Mental Disorders* (*DSM-V*) (American Psychiatric Association, 2013) uses the diagnosis *autism spectrum disorder* to label the problem because the severity of the condition can range from extremely severe to relatively mild (as is the case with Asperger's syndrome). Some individuals diagnosed with ASD function well in society. Four notable examples are Matt Savage, jazz pianist; Courtney Love, singer; Dr. Temple Grandin, university professor and designer of humane livestock-handling facilities; and Dr. Vernon Smith, 2002 Nobel Laureate in economics.

Certain developmental disabilities are apparent to everyone because they are associated with particular physical characteristics present at birth—such as the facial characteristics of children with Down syndrome. However, the severity of the cognitive impairment is not known at birth and can vary from mild learning disabilities to—in rare cases—profound mental impairment. Although some individuals with Down syndrome have graduated from college, most have cognitive disabilities that limit their educational achievements. For other developmental disorders, such as ASD, the extent of the problem emerges gradually. Although subtle behavioral indicators are present in the first year of life, the disorder is typically not diagnosed until the child is about three years old. But early identification is important, because intervention provided before age three has shown a much greater positive impact than that started after age five (Woods & Wetherby, 2003).

The presence of a developmental disability comes as distressing news to parents for various reasons. It means that parents have to dramatically alter their expectations and aspirations both for their child and for their own experiences as parents. It also means more stress. Parenting children with serious developmental disorders is much more demanding for many reasons (e.g., Estes et al., 2013; Rao & Beidel, 2009; Sikora et al., 2013). Parental stress comes from many sources:

- Interaction difficulties, such as aggravation and difficulty in controlling the child
- Trying to solve challenging behavior problems
- Interference with typical family functioning and other relationships
- Feelings associated with having a child with special needs
- Financial costs associated with rearing the child
- Concerns about the child's safety and protection
- Concerns over the child's future
- Problems encountered when dealing with professional and support services

In addition to being more stressful and demanding than rearing a typical child, the task is—for many parents—less rewarding. For example, a child with autism will not reciprocate physical affection in the same way that a typical child does. It's no wonder that these parents often report high levels of stress, distress, and depression. There is evidence that the relation between maternal distress and children's behavior problems is circular: Distress leads to increased child behavior problems, which in turn lead to increased maternal distress (Estes et al., 2013). Fifteen studies have confirmed that parents of children with ASD are more stressed than parents of typically developing children (Hayes & Watson, 2013).

Although parents of children with disabilities—and especially parents of children with autism—are more at risk for having mental health problems than are parents of typically developing children (Estes et al., 2013), stress does not affect all parents in the same way. For example, parents who are resilient; have more parental self-efficacy; or have a greater network of supportive friends, family, or groups are less likely to be adversely affected (e.g., Kuhn & Carter, 2006; see Photo 12.2). Some parents are able to modify their prior expectations about their child and have a positive, affirming parenting experience, as is described in Box 12.8 by a mother of a child with Down syndrome.

Photo 12.2 Rearing a child with special needs can be stressful but also rewarding.

Source: iStockphoto.com/jarenwicklund

Box 12.8 Parenting a Child With Down Syndrome

In between the umpteen medical tests and examinations at the hospital, the idea of having a child with a disability started to sink in. I said to my husband "I don't know if I can do this." He lovingly said, "We have to." After her birth, we experienced all stages of grief. We talked to a lot of people. We did a tremendous amount of research. Our emotions went back and forth in opposition: It seemed when one of us was feeling low, the other was there to provide encouragement. We started to see a small glimpse into how our lives were forever changed.

Slowly, but very surely, a transformation began and we found that we were becoming very attached to our little girl. She cooed, she cried, she made those gaseous smiles so typical of a newborn—"Did you see that? She smiled at me!" We cuddled, cried, sang, slept, and talked to each other. She was our baby and had all the same needs as any other baby. It was then that we began to see what the future might hold. . . .

(Continued)

(Continued)

Fifteen months have now passed since the birth of our daughter. She is vivacious, stubborn, and sensitive to others. She pesters her big brother, gets into things, feeds her lunch to our dog, and whines when things aren't going her way. She loves books and musical instruments and beads—oh, the beads! She greets us in the morning with some of the best hugs we've ever received and after our normally busy days, goes to bed with a brief fight and then, often, a smile.

We can't help but notice and find awe in the aura she seems to have around her. People are drawn to her everywhere we go and she seems to touch them on the inside. . . .

Becoming a parent has a transformative effect on everyone. And since the birth of our daughter, we've been transformed to the core. It's really not an overstatement to say that we are different people today than we were before her birth. We've learned that certain things really don't matter and that other things now matter more than ever. We think about the things we used to complain about and now see them as trivial. Our priorities are much more clear and we put the needs of our family first and foremost on a daily basis.

Our lives as parents of a child with Down syndrome have just begun. Our initial fears and grief have been replaced by hope, joy, and determination. We have learned more in the past year and a half than we ever thought possible. We've read and researched about Down syndrome; about our daughter's legal rights; and about her medical care, nutrition, and therapies. We look forward to her first steps, her first words, her first day of school, her first date, to high school graduation and other schooling, and to living independently. These things will come for her, albeit more slowly. She will do things in her own time, and we know that she will do and be whatever it is she wants to be—all within her own abilities, dreams, and desires.

Source: Parham, 2005. Used with permission.

CHAPTER SUMMARY

There are many threats to successful parenting. Risks can come in many guises, including socioeconomic factors (e.g., poverty, wealth), parent characteristics (e.g., childhood experiences, mental illness), or child factors (e.g., developmental disabilities). Whether the particular risk has an influence on child rearing and, in turn, a child's development depends on many considerations, such as the type of problem, the severity of it, and the chronicity. Poverty and its many related problems are a pervasive threat to child rearing. However, most families with low incomes manage to provide "good enough" parenting despite their hardships. Strange as it may seem, wealth can also be a threat to positive child rearing. Parental history plays a large role in effecting parenting and child rearing. Parents who had adverse childhood or have mental health or substance abuse challenges are also at high risk for maladaptive parenting. Sometimes, the risk to parenting comes from healthy parents who are faced with the challenge of rearing a child with special needs, such as children with

ASD or Down syndrome. A key challenge in those cases is for parents to revise their expectations about their children and manage the high level of stress. Parents who are successful at adapting and managing can mitigate the risk and find parenting to be rewarding.

THOUGHT QUESTIONS

- Mothers have often been blamed for their children's problems. What about fathers? Do we still blame mothers when children experience problems?
- Compare and contrast the different risk factors. Which ones are more difficult to overcome?
- This chapter highlighted many problematic influences on parenting (poverty, mental illness, substance abuse, family violence). Can you think of examples of people (personally or historically) who have experienced serious problems and overcome them? What factors contributed to better outcomes?
- How do you think our culture's emphasis on perfection and high achievement negatively impacts parents of children with special needs? How can this be more positively addressed?

CHAPTER GLOSSARY

mother blaming When mothers are accused of causing problems in their children.

parentification When the child is put in the role of an adult, such as when a child is assigned to care for a younger sibling or a child becomes an emotional confidante of a parent.

CHAPTER 13

Cultural Influences on Parenting

Chapter Preview: True or False?

- The majority of Asian parents are "tiger parents" (very strict and emotionally withdrawn from their children).
- Some parents discipline their children by locking them outside the home.
- Historical trauma has had a particularly strong impact on American Indians.

Much of Chapter 11 focused on diversity in contemporary family structures. This chapter will address diversity in parenting as it is found internationally or in different minority or religious groups within the United States. Cultural variation presents a problem when considering what constitutes effective parenting. What aspects of parenting are *culture-common* and what are *culture-specific* (Bornstein, 2012)? Are some parenting practices evolutionarily selected and thus universal? Alternatively, if parents from different cultures or cultural groups rear their children differently, how does someone determine what is the best way to parent?

Culture is defined as the "distinctive patterns of beliefs and behaviors that are shared by a group of people and that regulate their daily living" (Bornstein, 2012, p. 212). Culture can be thought of as forming the niche within which parent-child relationships occur (Harkness & Super, 2006). The niche consists of three main components:

- the physical and social environment,
- customs of child rearing and child care, and
- the parent's psychology (beliefs, values, attitudes).

The physical and social environment of child rearing is perhaps the most obvious feature of cultural differences. Some children live in one-room thatched huts in a rural environment (see Photos 13.1a and13.1b). Other children occupy spacious urban mansions. In some cultures, the social environment consists of an extended family that may number more than a dozen people. In other cultures, it is not unusual to find a family size of only two people, such as within single-parent families.

The second component of the **cultural niche** concerns the customs of child rearing and child care. One custom that demonstrates cultural differences appeared in Chapter 3: co-sleeping with infants. Infants in many cultures routinely sleep in the same bed with their parents, a practice that is much less common among European Americans. Similarly, there are cultural differences around the world in breastfeeding practices. In the United States, almost 70% of American mothers breastfeed for at least a short time. However, African Americans, adolescent mothers, and mothers of lower socioeconomic status (SES) are less likely to breastfeed in the United States (Ryan, Wenjun, & Acosta, 2002). In many other countries, by contrast, the rate of breastfeeding at birth is close to 100%, as was found in migrant mothers living in the slums of Turkey (Ergenekon-Ozelci, Elmaci, Ertem, & Saka, 2006). A third example illustrating cultural differences is how infants are transported. In the United States, infants are generally held in one hand on the left side or pushed in a stroller. Infants in many African cultures are carried on a parent's back. These differences

Photo 13.1a An African mother with her children.

Source: iStockphoto.com/nini

Photo 13.1b A Cambodian family.

Source: iStockphoto.com/global_explorer

in childrearing practices are not simply intriguing cultural differences. They likely have subtle influences on a child's physical, social, and cognitive development.

The third component of the cultural niche consists of parents' attitudes, beliefs, and values, also known as *ethnotheories* (Harkness & Super, 2006). Some of these theories are based on folk wisdom and cultural beliefs, passed down over generations. For example, grandmothers in the Kurdish tribe in Israel subscribed to the belief that neonates could not see until they were 30 days old (Frankel & Roer-Bornstein, 1982). Others aspects of ethnotheories are informed by a mixture of sources that can include culture; religion; advice from relatives and friends, pediatricians, books, and magazines; and research findings.

The role of context and cultural influences figured prominently into Bronfenbrenner's ecological systems theory of development (Chapter 2). In particular, his *macrosystem* level of influence explicitly includes cultural influences (as well as those of social class and laws) on development. Cultural influences also permeate the *exosystem* (through such contexts as the workplace) and the *mesosystem* (the system linking microsystems), and they can be found in the *microsystem* (the immediate child context).

This chapter addresses three types of cultural diversity. First, we'll examine cross-cultural research concerning parenting in different countries. Next, we will consider cultural variation

Photo 13.2 A family in Yemen goes to market.

Source: Photograph by J. P. Bell

within the United States—how parenting differs across socioeconomic levels as well as among ethnic and racial groups. Third, we will survey how religion provides a cultural context for parents and children. It should be remembered throughout this discussion, there is always diversity within diversity. Although *tendencies* exist within cultural groups, considerable variation can be found in any cultural group.

PARENTING IN DIFFERENT COUNTRIES

The study of parenting in different countries is the only way to identify whether there are universals in childrearing approaches and consequences. Through a careful examination of childrearing similarities and differences, cultural effects can be revealed (Bornstein & Cheah, 2006). It is important to remember that most people reading this book live in a WEIRD society (Western, educated, industrialized, rich, and democratic). It is estimated that at least 90% of developmental psychology research is conducted in the United States. The remaining 10% comes from regions that account for 90% of the world's population (Mistry, Contreras, & Dutta, 2013).

Indeed, the vast preponderance of parenting research has been conducted in Western cultures—by Western researchers—and there are inevitable biases caused by viewing other cultures from one's own perspective. For example, the "correct" way to rear an infant, according to the Western lens, is the attachment model first articulated in England by John Bowlby and then empirically investigated by Mary Ainsworth in the United States (Chapter 2). The model has been labeled the **continuous care and contact model** of infant development because the prototypic form is to have one adult providing sensitive care to the infant (Tronick, Morelli, & Ivey, 1992).

However, some cultures engage in very different infant-rearing practices. Consider the Efe (Pygmy) tribe, which lives in the central African country of the Democratic Republic of Congo (formerly Zaire). These hunter-gatherers inhabit the tropical rain forests. Efe infants and toddlers experience a rich and intense social environment—beginning as neonates when they enjoy extensive handling by many caregivers as well as being nursed by multiple women. During infancy, they spend only about half of their waking time with their mothers. By age three, they are with their mothers less than 30% of the time (Tronick et al., 1992). Being raised by multiple caregivers appears to be a social adaptation to such problems as high rates of illness and mortality as well as the heavy workload that these mothers have in terms of gathering food. Although not all hunter-gatherer societies practice extensive multiple-caregiver rearing, it does illustrate that our Western standards for optimal infant-rearing practices are not universally held.

The study of cross-cultural views of parenting has been around since the work of the anthropologists Margaret Mead and Ruth Benedict. Benedict studied childrearing practices in several European countries, including Russia, where swaddling (wrapping infants tightly) was common, and Poland, where hardening infants was valued and practiced by letting babies cry and by beating children (recall John Locke's prescriptions for hardening infants in Chapter 1). Since that time, a wide range of cross-cultural investigations into parenting values and practices can be found, which cover such topics as micro-analytic studies of verbal interchanges between mothers and infants in Germany and Cameroon (Demuth, Keller, & Yovsi, 2012) and parenting traits in Arab countries (Dwairy, Achoui, Abouserie, & Farah, 2006).

Values

Cross-cultural studies are employed to better understand the sources and consequences of childrearing differences. The most intensively investigated example of cultural influences on child rearing lies in comparing parental values between Asian and Western countries. The beliefs of the Chinese philosopher Confucius (first mentioned in Chapter 1) but also Taoism and Buddhism underlie social norms in China, Japan, and other parts of Asia (Li & Lamb, 2013). Confucian social philosophy places high value on respecting elders, social connectedness, and harmony while putting far less emphasis upon assertiveness, self-discipline, and achievement. However, parenting styles vary even within Asian cultures. For example, Chinese fathers are more controlling than Japanese fathers, and Japanese fathers perceive themselves as emotionally closer to their children than do Korean fathers, according to a review about Asian fathering (Shwalb, Nakazawa, Yamamoto, & Hyun, 2004).

Studies comparing Asian parents' values with those of Western parents find consistent differences. Asians emphasize filial piety ("parents are always right"), respect for elders, group identification, harmony, self-discipline, and achievement. Sexuality is de-emphasized, and aggression is suppressed. The family is considered the fundamental unit of society, and there is a strict hierarchical order of human relationships. These values are, in turn, reflected in childrearing attitudes: Children are expected to show family loyalty, filial piety, and elder respect. Parents and elders are assumed to train and discipline youth in these cultural norms. Consequently, Chinese mothers are more restrictive in their childrearing attitudes and exert more control over their children than European American mothers (Chao, 1994; Ng, Pomerantz, & Deng, 2014).

Box 13.1 Are All Asian Mothers "Tiger Moms"?

In 2011, Amy Chua published a provocative book titled *Battle Hymn of the Tiger Mother*. She described how she reared her two daughters. It is a variation of an authoritarian approach: setting very high expectations for academic achievement, maintaining strict discipline, and being emotionally distant to the children. The girls were allowed little time for peers or play because they were too busy studying or practicing musical instruments. Is this a common childrearing approach in Asia or China or, like Amy Chua, a Chinese American parenting style?

The available evidence indicates that *tiger parenting* is uncommon in Asian-heritage families [Preview Question]. According to one longitudinal study (Kim, Wang, Orozco-Lapray, Shen, & Murtuza, 2013), at the first assessment time, about 28% of Asian American mothers and 18% of fathers were classified as tiger parents, based on adolescent reports. The majority of parents were classified as supportive (see Figure 13.1).

Figure 13.1 A Parenting Typology of Chinese American Mothers and Fathers

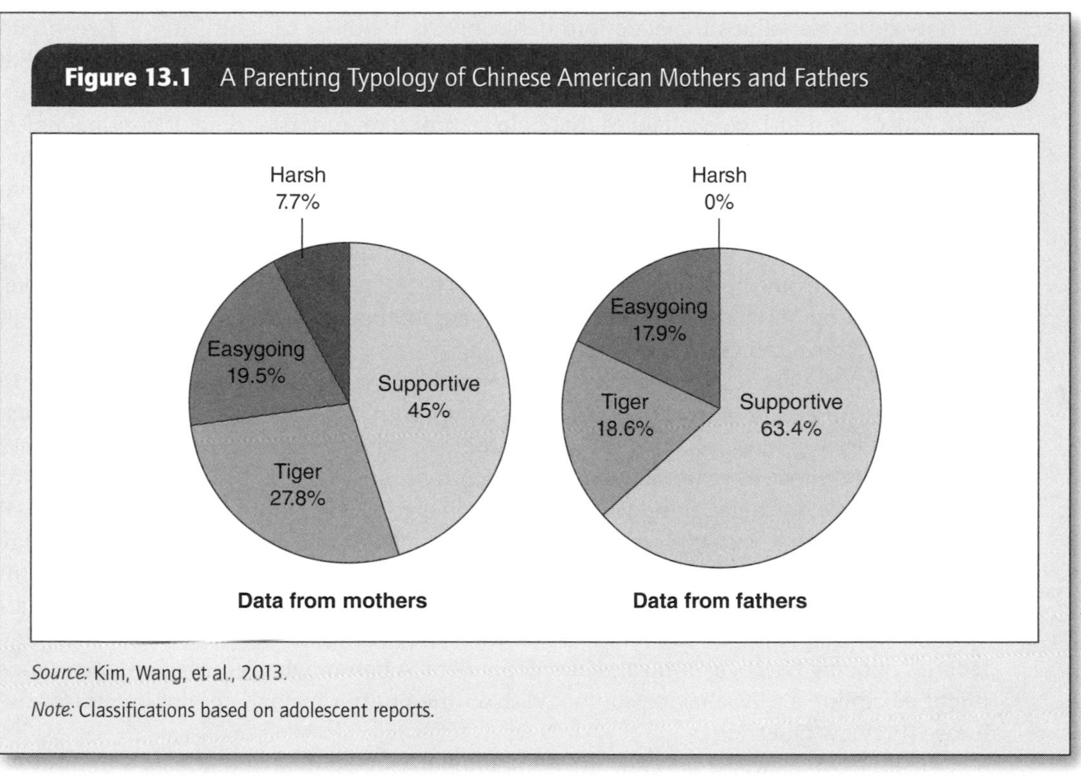

Source: Kim, Wang, et al., 2013.

Note: Classifications based on adolescent reports.

A more general cross-cultural value dichotomy concerns **individualism** versus **collectivism**. This is sometimes called *independence versus interdependence*. *Individualism* (or *independence*) emphasizes the individual's goals, with free choice held as the preeminent value. The United States is a prime example of a culture that values independence and the individual. It is not hard to think of examples of unusual individuals who stand out due to their hard work and talent, such as Supreme Court Justice Sonia Sotomayor or basketball star LeBron James. This valuing of individuality extends also to families, where the United States, as a society, values families' rights to privacy and self-determination. In cultures that value *collectivism*, personal goals are subordinate to the goals of the larger group, such as the family, employer, or community. Individuals living in collectivistic societies are defined more by group membership and position in the family than by individual characteristics or accomplishments.

These two different value systems relate directly to competing developmental goals of autonomy and relatedness. North American parents value control over their young children but they also, as the child grows older, encourage autonomy (independence), self-directiveness, personal style, and social initiative in their children as well as equality with themselves (Chen & French, 2008; Leyendecker, Lamb, Harwood, & Schölmerich, 2002). In contrast, Asian societies value interdependence and norm-based behavior, where an individual fits in rather than stands out. Japanese parents avoid confrontations with their children and will back down in the face of resistance (Rothbaum, Pott, Azuma, Miyake, & Weisz, 2000).

How do these values translate into behavior? As Heidi Keller and Patricia Greenfield (2000) described parenting in the United States and Western countries, the developmental path to independence involves dyadic attention between caregiver (mother) and infant, with lots of face-to-face exchanges that help to promote understanding of contingencies. Parents are also very involved in toy play and help children interact with objects. From these experiences, infants then learn to develop expectancies and a sense of control that fosters the development of the self as a causal agent. The infants' rudimentary sense of independence is also promoted by experiences such as being watched by babysitters, sleeping apart from the parent, and attending infant day care. As the children get older, parents promote individuality by encouraging exploration and recognizing how the children differ from siblings or peers.

In countries where interdependence is valued, the path is different. For children in Africa, Asia, and Latin America, socialization occurs with a great deal of close body contact, giving children a sense of warmth and relatedness with multiple caregivers. Child care occurs in the midst of other activities. Children then begin to learn about themselves as **coagents** (joint partners) along with their caregivers rather than being the single causal actor. Mothers also verbally emphasize relatedness ("We had fun together!" "Let's play together with these toys") instead of autonomy ("What do you want to do?" "Once you finish that activity, you can leave"). Another manifestation in cultures that promote interrelatedness is the use of uniforms in school. All these types of experiences contribute to valuing feelings of being part of a group and interdependent. A parent who values interdependence might discipline a misbehaving son not with a time out but by locking him outside of the house [Preview Question].

Consider two examples of how interdependence is promoted and affects parent-child relations. The West African Nso mothers of Cameroon carry their infants most of the day and share the same bed with all of their children; separation from infants is unimaginable. Negative signals from the infant get an immediate response with breastfeeding. Body contact and stimulation are common, in part to promote motor development so the child will be able to help with daily chores (Keller, Voelker, & Yovsi, 2005). When evaluating whether a parenting situation was pleasant or not, Central American mothers consider mutual enjoyment, child cooperation, and appropriateness of the child's behavior. In contrast, European Americans enjoyed it when they could watch the child play by him- or herself but disliked it when they felt they had to keep the child entertained (Leyendecker et al., 2002).

Another way parents can promote a sense of collectivism in their children is by engaging in a particular parenting style. As Duane Rudy and Joan Grusec (2006) found, authoritarian parenting styles are likely to promote a sense of collectivism by negating individual choice. In a study of Canadian immigrant mothers from either Europe or Asia, those from Asia did indeed endorse authoritarian parenting practices more than did the mothers with European (individualistic) heritage. A further example can be found in views about infant sleeping patterns. American mothers believe that a child's temperament is an important consideration when considering sleep practices, such as when and where to put the child to bed. In contrast, mothers from Holland do not recognize a child's individuality as an important consideration in sleep schedules (Harkness & Super, 2006).

Cultural differences can be readily recognized in *ethnotheories* of development—a parent's system of beliefs concerning the nature of an ideal child and how to socialize the child to achieve those values. Differences and similarities across cultures can be seen in childrearing values mentioned by mothers in Greece, Taiwan, and the United States (Tamis-LeMonda, Wang, Koutsouvanou, & Albright, 2002). Only three values (honesty, independence, and respect of others) were shared by about one-third or more of the mothers. Greek mothers were the most apt to value respect of elders, loyalty to family, and religion or spiritual development. Mothers from Taiwan were likely to value independence, getting along with others, good habits, and being polite. In contrast, the additional values mentioned by the most U.S. mothers were compassion, self-esteem, and sharing. See Table 13.1 for the percentage of mothers who mentioned each value.

Cross-cultural investigations also reveal that cultures change—sometimes rapidly. Thanks to the Internet and other developments, the world is becoming *flat* (that is, a level

Table 13.1 Mothers' Childrearing Values in Three Countries

	Greece	Taiwan	United States
Honesty	**79**	**50**	**63**
Respect of others/fairness	**50**	**42**	**54**
Independence	29	**46**	**33**
Respect elders	**46**	17	21
Loyalty to family	**38**	8	13
Religion/spirituality	**38**	4	8
Getting along with others	25	**42**	29
Good habits	4	**38**	13
Polite	8	**38**	25
Education/school	25	**33**	13
Curiosity	4	13	**33**
Self-esteem	13	13	**50**
Compassion/consideration	21	29	**63**
Sharing	29	17	**46**

Source: Tamis-LeMonda et al., 2002.

Note: Numbers represent percentage of mothers to mention a value. Only the values brought up by at least 30% of one group of mothers (highlighted in boldface) are included.

playing field), with increased urbanization, globalization, and ease of information flow (Friedman, 2006). In China, as the country moves to a market economy, some of its traditional values are being challenged or supplanted by Western ones. For example, the childrearing value of interdependence is in dynamic interplay with autonomy—and which one wins out appears to depend on such considerations as the particular culture, context, age of child, and state of economic change (Tamis-LeMonda et al., 2008). Another example of social change concerns arranged marriages, as is described in Box 13.2.

Box 13.2 What's Love Got to Do With It? Parents and Arranged Marriages

Traditionally, in South Asia (e.g., India, Nepal, Pakistan) and many other parts of the world (such as Africa, Asia, and the Middle East), marriage isn't necessarily about love. Instead, it is about who your parents think will be a suitable partner for you. Parents take into account such factors as reputation and wealth of the family, vocation of the groom, appearance, and religion when choosing a mate for their child. In some cases, the arranged marriages are also forced marriages. This is particularly common when it involves children. In some countries (e.g., Yemen), girls as young as eight years old become brides.

One of the ways to evaluate whether arranged marriages work is to examine the divorce rate. In India, only about 7% of marriages fail (Giridharadas, 2008). In contrast, the divorce rate in the United States is around 44% (Monthly Labor Review, 2013).

The tradition of arranged marriages is declining in favor of love marriages as a consequence of expanding educational experiences, exposure to other cultures, children enjoying greater contact with potential partners, and increased respect for a child's autonomy (Allendorf, 2013; Gangoli, McCarry, & Razak, 2009). Parents are increasingly considering their children's opinions before making a determination of partners. In some places, a potential mate is now suggested by the youth and then accepted or rejected by the parents.

Discipline

Perhaps the single most extensively investigated childrearing variable around the world is disciplinary practices. How similarly do parents from different countries discipline their children? Given the attention devoted to corporal punishment over the past decade or so, a number of studies have examined parental punitive attitudes and behavior.

Recent evidence makes clear that the majority of parents worldwide do not hold positive attitudes toward or report using corporal punishment, but rates vary widely depending on the country and sample characteristics. In one study of 34 developing countries comprising more than 166,000 mothers or primary caregivers of children ages two to 14 years, in only two countries (Syria and Sierra Leone) did the majority of respondents believe corporal punishment was necessary (Cappa & Khan, 2011). The percent of parents who had positive attitudes ranged from a low of 6% in in Albania to a high of about 92% in Syria. However, the percentages varied depending on the SES as well as whether they lived in an urban or rural environment. In a study limited to families with two- to four-year old children from 24 countries, only 29% of caregivers believed that corporal punishment was necessary for proper child rearing. However, in some African countries (Ghana, Cote d'Ivoire, Central African Republic, and Sierra Leone), more than 90% of parents reported using physical punishment (Lansford & Deater-Deckard, 2012). A third international study found somewhat higher rates. More than 14,000 mothers were interviewed in six countries (Brazil, Chile, Egypt, India, Philippines, and the United States) from 10 high-, middle-, and low-income communities. Fifty-five percent of the parents reported using corporal punishment, but in different ways. In addition to slapping and spanking, parents admitted to such violent acts as hitting their children with objects; shaking, kicking, burning, and choking their children; and even beating them up (Runyan et al., 2010).

These studies reveal that parents in different countries do show different preferences in their disciplinary practices, but there is also substantial within-country variation. In general, parents from low-income communities or countries and with less education are more likely to engage in harsh discipline (Lansford & Deater-Deckard, 2012). But roughly half of all parents do not use any violent parenting techniques such as corporal punishment or slapping.

Child maltreatment is universally harmful. For example, a meta-analysis of 43 studies from around the world determined that children who feel rejected by their parents are more likely to have psychological adjustment problems compared with children who feel loved—regardless of geographic area, culture, race, language, or gender (Khaleque & Rohner, 2002). But do variations in the frequency of corporal punishment have uniform associations across countries? To phrase it differently, if corporal punishment is common or normative in one country, are those children less affected by it? The answer appears to be yes. Two multinational studies comparing disciplinary practices and associated child behaviors found that harsh parenting (e.g., corporal punishment and yelling) was linked to child problems (e.g., aggression and anxiety). However, those associations were moderated by children's perceptions of the normativeness of the practice (Gershoff et al., 2010; Lansford et al., 2005). A related (and somewhat contradictory) finding is that in countries where corporal punishment is more common and thus condoned, those nations also have higher rates of child aggression, warfare, and interpersonal violence (Lansford & Dodge, 2008).

CULTURAL DIVERSITY AMONG NORTH AMERICAN PARENTS

The United States today is a highly diverse culture in terms of racial and ethnic minorities and immigrants from all over the globe. Native Americans, the first inhabitants of the region, were diverse in themselves, with hundreds of different tribes and multiple languages. Systematic arrivals of non-Native Americans began with the landing of the Mayflower in Plymouth, Massachusetts, in 1620. Families came in search of religious freedom or new opportunities. Slaves from Africa began arriving later. By 1697, slaves comprised 20% of the population of New York. By the early 18th century, African Americans made up almost 70% of the population of South Carolina and 40% of the population of Virginia (Mintz, 2004).

Another major source of diversity came in the form of immigrants seeking a better life. In the late 1800s, mostly European immigrants began arriving in New York and (as of 1892) were processed through Ellis Island. By 1910, 28% of all children in the United States lived in immigrant families (Hernandez, Denton, & Macartney, 2008). Latinos—from Central and South America as well as the Caribbean—have provided another major source of diversity. They now make up 14% of the nation's population. There are now 40 million immigrants living in the United States, and 10 million are illegal (Pew Hispanic Center, 2013). About 10% of them are refugees from war or from political, social, or ethnic oppression (Singer & Wilson, 2006). Today, about 23% of children in the United States are being raised in immigrant families, a rate not too different from that of 100 years ago (Hernandez et al., 2008).

Cultural diversity in American families is typically investigated in one of two ways: by examining ethnic/racial background or by examining differences of socioeconomic circumstances. Having provided the discussion about the role of SES on parenting in Chapter 11, we will not consider it separately here. Instead, we will examine parenting in different ethnic/racial groups as well as in religious groups.

Minority Groups

In what ways do minority parents—parents from nonwhite racial groups—differ in their parenting? What are the sources of those differences? Early research into ethnic and minority parenting adopted a deficit model: Minority parents were deficient in parenting when compared to White, middle-class parents. More recent work acknowledges the adaptive advantage of certain forms of parenting and does not assume that the majority racial ethnic group always adopts the best parenting style. Instead, more current work focuses on identifying *why* differences in observed parenting may be adaptive for their particular culture and how minority members are resilient in the face of a number of hardships (Bermudez & Mancini, 2013; Garcia Coll & Pachter, 2002).

Ethnic and minority families experience life differently than do families in the majority. They endure racism, prejudice, and discrimination, which leads to continued economic deprivation, geographic isolation, and stress (Cabrera & the SRCD Ethnic and Racial Issues Committee, 2013; McAdoo, 2002; Taylor & Wang, 2008). The forms the discrimination takes may not be as obvious as in the past, when African Americans had to sit in the back of the bus and drink from segregated water fountains differentiated by racial labels. But bigotry continues to be a social problem, particularly in the economic sphere.

A second variable that differentiates ethnic and minority families is the process of **acculturation**, which refers to how well the family has adapted to the norms and values of the majority society. The more acculturated minority parents become, the more their childrearing beliefs mirror those of the majority culture (Birman & Simon, 2014; Savage & Gauvain, 1998). Acculturation is a dynamic process occurring over time; it is multidimensional and bidirectional. As time passes, some aspects of cultural heritage are retained while other dimensions undergo change (Garcia Coll & Pachter, 2002; Yoshikawa, 2011).

We next consider how child rearing differs among five major minority groups in the United States: Latinos/Hispanic Americans, African Americans, Asian Americans, Native Americans, and immigrants.

Latino/Hispanic Americans

Latino/Hispanic Americans constitute the largest and most diverse minority group in the United States. About 16.9% of the nation's population is classified as Latino (U.S. Census Bureau, 2014). Technically, *Latino* refers to persons of Latin ethnic origin (typically from the Caribbean or Central American or South American countries) who speak Spanish. *Hispanic* refers to persons from Spain, Portugal, or Iberia who speak Spanish or Portuguese. However, these two terms have become interchangeable in the United States. The U.S. Census Bureau uses the term *Latino* to include individuals from many different countries (e.g., Spain, the Caribbean, Central America, and South America), counting recent immigrants as well as those families that have been living in the United States for multiple generatons. Consequently, Latinos as a group do not subscribe to uniform parenting beliefs or practices. To date, much of the Latino research participants have been mothers, although fathers are beginning to get more attention (e.g., Lee, Altschul, Shair, & Taylor, 2011; see Photo 13.3).

Commonly identified characteristics of Latino families are the values of *respeto* and *familismo* (Harwood, Leyendecker, Carlson, Asencio, & Miller, 2002). *Respeto,* or "proper demeanor," refers to maintaining appropriate relatedness to others. It is most clearly manifested in parents teaching children to respect and obey them as well as other adults (Rodriguez & Olswang, 2003). *Familismo* concerns valuing the importance of the family. This family-centered, multidimensional orientation has been related to enjoyment of family life, positive attitudes toward parents, and a large and close extended-family social network (Harwood et al., 2002).

Due to the heterogeneity of the Latino/Hispanic Americans, there is inconsistent evidence about whether these cultural groups engage in particular parenting practices. The results depend on such considerations as which particular subgroup is studied, their degree of acculturation, their SES, and the parenting variable that is being examined (Halgunseth, Ispa, & Rudy, 2006). Consequently, some studies find Latino parents more permissive while others find them to be harsher. Two examples illustrate the complexity. In a study that separated foreign-born Latino fathers from those born in the United States, it was found that the foreign-born fathers used less corporal punishment on their three-year-old children than Latinos born in the U.S. or other fathers (Lee et al., 2011). In a study of Mexican American parents, both mothers and fathers who were dealing with economic hardship and lived in dangerous neighborhoods showed less warmth to their adolescents (Gonzales et al., 2011). Although studies have begun to assess different aspects of Latino parenting (e.g., see review on parental control by Halgunseth et al., 2006), many more studies are needed to sort out the ways in which Latino/Hispanic parents may be similar to or different from other cultural subgroups.

African Americans

African Americans are the second-largest minority group in the United States, as they comprise about 13.1% of the population (U.S. Census Bureau, 2014). Although there is a considerable amount of intragroup variability among this population, several common

Photo 13.3 A Latino family praying.

Source: iStockphoto.com/IS_ImageSource

parenting features have been identified. However, these features are based on research with African American mothers. Despite the fact that 47% of these families include fathers, the men are rarely studied beyond the question of how involved they are in the family (Letiecq & Koblinsky, 2004; Roopnarine, 2004; see Photo 13.4).

The single most commonly reported characteristic of African American mothers is that they tend to assume authoritarian parenting styles (Brody & Flor, 1997; Hill, Murry, & Anderson, 2005). Gene Brody has labeled it, based on his research in the rural South, a "no-nonsense" style. The primary attributes of the trait are that the parents value respect for authority and quick compliance. In contrast to European Americans, African American mothers show lower levels of emotional support and warmth—interpreted by some researchers as an effort to toughen up their children in preparation for future hardships.

A second characteristic sometimes attributed to African American parents is a reliance on physical punishment. Indeed, a number of studies indicate that they are apt to spank their children more frequently than White parents do (e.g., Bradley, Corwyn, Burchinal, McAdoo, & Coll, 2001). However, SES is more often linked to use of corporal punishment. In a recent comparison of 585 parents, White parents reported more reasoning, denying privileges, and yelling than did African American parents, but there was no difference in the amount of spanking between the two groups (Lansford, Wager, Bates, Dodge, & Pettit, 2012). However, SES was negatively associated with use of spanking. In other studies, when individual parenting characteristics such as stress and beliefs are taken into account, some of the initial racial differences regarding discipline disappear (Pinderhughes, Dodge, Bates, Pettit, & Zelli, 2000). The disciplinary practices of African American mothers are also affected by education and depression (Bluestone & Tamis-LeMonda, 1999).

African American parents engage in one type of parenting that White parents do not. By virtue of their minority status, they are compelled to engage in race socialization in an effort to prepare their children to deal with the majority culture. This type of socialization involves verbal and nonverbal messages transmitted to children so they can develop appropriate values, attitudes, and behaviors in light of their minority status (Lesane-Brown, 2006). It includes messages about racism, group identity, intergroup interactions, and role

Photo 13.4 An African American grandfather.

Source: Cavan Images/Iconica/Getty Images

models. Race socialization is recognized as a mechanism for promoting positive development in African American youth (Evans et al., 2012).

Asian Americans

Asian Americans make up 5.1% of the U.S. population (U.S. Census Bureau, 2014). They originally came from countries such as China, Taiwan, Japan, Korea, Vietnam, Cambodia, Laos, Pakistan, Malaysia, and the Philippines. Thus Asian Americans form a diverse group and they do not adhere to one particular childrearing approach.

Nevertheless, Asian Americans have been labeled the "model minority" because of their high academic achievement and career success. These families tend to put great import on academic achievement. For example, 27% of all Americans have a college degree, but 42% of Asian Americans do. Despite their successes, a higher percentage of Asian Americans live in poverty (10%) than European Americans (8.2%). This can be accounted for by the large number of Asian immigrants, as will be discussed below. However, when Chinese parents emigrate to the United States, their values become diluted by acculturation and soon fall more in between Chinese and American mothers (e.g., Chao, 1994).

Photo 13.5 An Asian immigrant mother and her daughter work at a farmer's market.

Source: Photograph by J. P. Bell

What accounts for the academic success of Asian Americans? Asian American parents differ from other Americans on certain values. For one, they place a high value on working hard to get ahead (Chao & Tseng, 2002). Education is regarded as the route to success, so Asian American parents consider it as a key socialization goal. Consequently, they put considerable emphasis and pressure on their children to perform well in school. Parents have high expectations and make sure their children work hard to achieve those ends. This emphasis on education does not necessarily mean monitoring homework more closely than do European American parents. However, it does mean promoting an intellectual orientation in the family climate and structuring a child's daily schedule to ensure adequate time for school work. Asian American parents accomplish these goals by engaging in such activities as taking their children on educational outings (to museums, libraries) and restricting television viewing (Chao, 2000).

But this achievement orientation can come with a cost. Asian Americans experience a wide range of mental health problems (depression, anxiety, phobias, eating and learning disorders) and may have a similar need for mental health services as other groups (Hwang, Wood, & Fujimoto, 2010; Jacob, Gray, & Johnson, 2013). Asian American children and youth face such problems as high achievement pressure (from parents and themselves), a concern to maintain their family's positive image, cultural conflicts with parents, and a reluctance to seek mental health services.

Asian American families also have various strengths in line with their Asian cultural roots, such as the values of family loyalty, conformity, and social harmony. These values were highlighted in a study comparing parental goals in Chinese American, African American, Mexican American, and European American families (Suizzo, 2007). Across all four groups, the most valued goal was self-direction (considered *very* or *extremely important*), followed by kindness, tradition/conformity, and relatedness. Power and achievement had the lowest mean score across the four groups. As can be seen in Table 13.2, Chinese Americans showed evidence of acculturation because they did not differ in the goal of agency and self-direction from the European Americans or Mexican Americans, and their mean value was only somewhat below African Americans. They did however, have the highest mean score on kindness and relatedness, as one would expect based on their cultural heritage.

Table 13.2 Parental Childrearing Goals in Four Groups of U.S. Mothers

Goals	Chinese Americans	African Americans	Mexican Americans	European Americans
Tradition/ conformity	4.0	4.4	4.2	3.4
Achievement	2.7	2.7	2.8	1.9
Relatedness	3.4	3.0	2.9	3.4
Self-direction	4.5	4.8	4.6	4.5
Kindness	4.4	4.3	4.3	4.0

Source: Suizzo, 2007.

Note: $N = 343$. Numbers are mean scale scores; higher numbers indicate greater importance.

Native Americans

Ironically, American Indians and Alaska Natives—the original American parents—have been the focus of relatively little empirical childrearing research, despite comprising 1.6% of the population (U.S. Census Bureau, 2012) and numbering more than 5 million, with 566 different tribes. The legacy of Native Americans is one of considerable trauma. They faced mass genocide, pandemic disease, forced relocation, loss of their indigenous language, and disrupted families during the "boarding school era" as well as indoctrination of religious and cultural beliefs that were foreign to them (Sarche & Whitesell, 2012). Current problems of poverty and unemployment, alcohol abuse, intimate partner violence, gambling, and (among youth) delinquency and suicide compound the effects of the historical traumas (Robbins, Robbins, & Stennerson, 2013). Survivors of that historical trauma, such as Holocaust survivors from World War II, carry subtle vulnerabilities [Preview Question]. At the individual level, survivors of historical trauma are more likely to develop post-traumatic stress disorder (PTSD). At the family level, the parent-child relationship can be affected by reactions to stress or memories of the trauma or its consequences (Evans-Campbell, 2008).

Generalizing about Native American childrearing values and practices is problematic, given the large number and diversity of individual tribes in the United States. For example, the American Indians in the Ute reservation in Colorado maintain close kinship networks and value consensus and cooperation. Childrearing practices tend to be child-centered, and parents use shame rather than corporal punishment for discipline (MacPhee, Fritz, & Miller-Heyl, 1996). However, there are reports that certain American Indian parents show problematic childrearing behavior. For example, a sample of Lumbee American Indians from North Carolina was observed to provide low levels of stimulation and interaction to their premature infants (Brooks, Holditch-Davis, & Landerman, 2013). In a study of American Indian women attending a health clinic in New Mexico, 40% reported they survived at least one form of severe maltreatment in their childhood, including sexual abuse (23%), neglect (19%), or physical abuse (18%) (Duran et al., 2004).

Variations in American Indian parenting practices have been linked to children's behavior problems. In a sample of mothers of middle-school age children from a Great Lakes Indian reservation, parents with less adequate parenting skills and those experiencing financial strain had children with more behavior problems (Momper & Jackson, 2007). In contrast, close, positive parent-child relationships were found to be a protective factor against adolescent substance use on an American Indian reservation in the Northern Plains (Whitesell et al., 2014).

Immigrants

With the exception of the last group discussed, all Americans are immigrants. The distinction is that some have resided in the country longer than others. The term *immigrant* refers to an individual who is living in the United States but who was born a citizen of another country (*first-generation immigrant*) or who was born in the United States to at least one foreign-born parent (*second-generation immigrant*). At least 12.9% of Americans were born in another country (U.S. Census Bureau, 2014). There are 40.4 million immigrants are currently living in the U.S., 11 million of which are unauthorized to do so (Pew Hispanic Center, 2013).

Immigrants are, as a group, diverse. They include Latinos and Asian Americans, as we have discussed. But they arrive in the United States from many other countries as well (see Figure 13.2) and for various reasons. Most seek economic opportunity. Some, classified as *refugees*, seek a safe haven from persecution due to race, nationality, political opinion, religion, or group membership. Since 1983, 2 million refugees have settled in the United States from such areas as the former USSR, Vietnam, Yugoslavia, Laos, Cambodia, Iran, and Cuba.

Most children (79%) living with their immigrant parents were born in the United States, and about 24% of them have at least one parent who was also born here (Hernandez et al., 2008). This means that there is considerable variation among and within immigrant families as to language proficiency, economic status, education, and the extent to which they have acculturated to mainstream American culture. Some immigrants do not want to modify their language, practices, or identity and thereby resist acculturation in an effort to preserve their culture. For many parents, the conflict over cultural preservation versus acculturation is a continuing and unresolved issue in their lives (Farver, Narang, & Bhadha, 2002).

When there is a discrepancy between the parents' and children's level of acculturation, unsupportive childrearing and a sense of alienation between the parent and child is a likely consequence. In turn, the child is at risk for adjustment problems, as was found in a longitudinal study of Chinese immigrant families (Kim, Chen, Wang, Shen, & Orozco-Lapray, 2013). The resulting depression and academic problems that surfaced for the young teenagers persisted into middle adolescent years.

Figure 13.2 Country or Region of Origin of Immigrant Families Arriving in the United States (2000–2010)

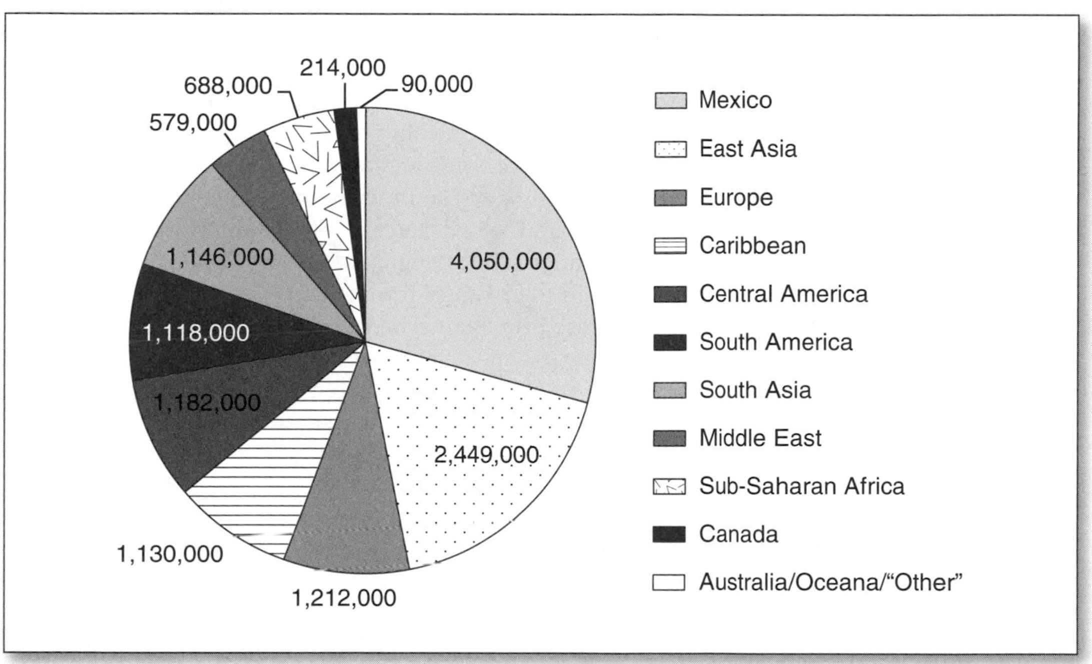

Source: Camarota, 2012.

Note: Total = 13,857,000.

Box 13.3 One Immigrant Mother's Story

Emiliana slipped into the United States from a village in Mexico when she was in her late 20s. She found her way to New York City and subsequently married and had two children. Her husband, Victor Sr., was also undocumented but found work as a cook 12 hours a day, six days a week. Emiliana's daily schedule consisted of waking up at 6 a.m., getting her children ready for day care or preschool, going to work cleaning homes, and returning home to cook dinner and care for her children before putting them to bed. She then did house work and waited for her husband to return from work so she could feed him dinner. She went to bed around 1 a.m. most days. She was committed to supporting her children's education though she speaks little English and has almost no sources of support.

Source: Yoshikawa, 2011.

Language barriers and economic stress are two central issues that immigrant families face, and these issues affect their parenting. With regard to language, comfort in conversing in the new language was found to be a key determinant of immigrant parents' involvement in their children's education (Garcia Coll & Garrido, 2000). Many immigrants experience economic hardships. Almost 20% of immigrants in the United States live in poverty compared to 13.5% of nonimmigrants (Camarota, 2012). As discussed, living in poverty or near-poverty has dramatic effects on parenting. If the parents are undocumented, they likely live in a state of anxiety about deportation, feelings of inadequacy to provide for their children, and isolation (Yoshikawa, 2011). For those and other reasons, immigrant parents whose children are born in another country are more likely than other parents to report that they are aggravated with their children, as indexed by feeling that the child was a burden, bothered them, and made them angry (Yu & Singh, 2012).

Immigrant parents carry with them their values from their home countries (as previously discussed). For example, Chinese immigrants value promoting physical closeness, family relatedness, and interdependence while de-emphasizing a child's individuality and uniqueness (Rothbaum et al., 2000). The closeness promoted among the immigrants did not extend to all domains, however. With regard to nudity in children up to the preschool years, less than one-quarter (23%) of the immigrant Chinese parents thought that children's nudity was acceptable, in contrast to most (85%) of the European American comparison group. In a study that compared immigrant and nonimmigrant Latino fathers, the immigrant fathers did less child care and were less engaged in positive activities with their infant children but reported more stress than nonimmigrant fathers (D'Angelo, Palacios, & Chase-Lansdale, 2012).

Although many studies focus on identifying their differences, there are striking similarities among groups of immigrant parents. For example, in a study comparing parents from 27 countries living in New York City, four common themes emerged. The parents, irrespective of their country of origin, valued the importance and centrality of the family, respect of parents and elders, and the importance of religion or spirituality. They also experienced the common struggle of dealing with the conflict over acculturation versus cultural preservation (McEvoy et al., 2005).

RELIGION AND PARENTING

Religion also provides a cultural context, with its values and beliefs, traditions, and rituals as well as sometimes specific prescriptions for how children should be reared. Worldwide, 80% of people claim to be a member of a religious group (Pew Research Center, 2012, see Figure 13.3).

In the United States, the majority (78.3%) of citizens consider themselves Christians. About 16.4% are nonreligious (atheist, agnostic, nonbelievers); 1.8% affiliate with Judaism; and less than 1% are adherents of Islam, Buddhism, or Hinduism. Religion is particularly important once people become parents. Most (95%) married couples and parents report a religious affiliation, and 90% want their children to have some religious training (Mahoney, Pargament, Tarakeshwar, & Swank, 2001).

Figure 13.3 Religious Affiliations Worldwide

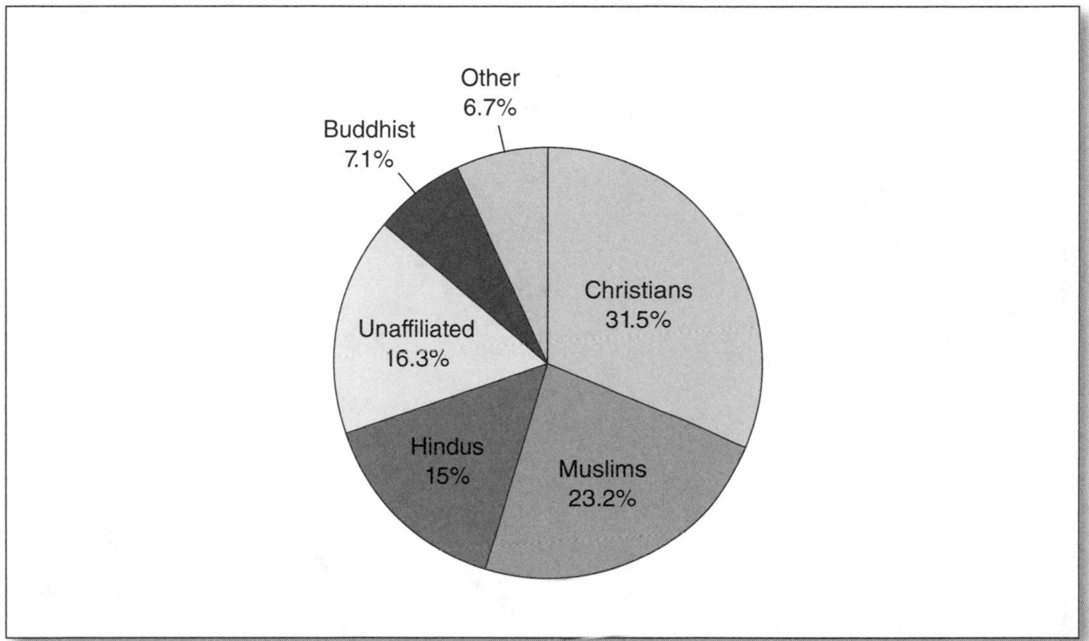

All three of the world's great deistic religions (Christianity, Judaism, and Islam) share an emphasis on the family and encourage parents to devote considerable time and attention to their children (see Photo 13.6). It follows, then, that religious parents (compared to nonreligious parents) may hold different values, allocate time differently, and involve their children in social networks associated with a religious community (Holden & Williamson, 2014; Wilcox, 2002).

Religious beliefs, like culture, provide a fundamental contextual influence on how parents think about child rearing and their children. Religions supply long-term parenting goals by specifying desirable behavior both in childhood and adulthood. Consequently, many religions and devotees responsible for interpreting the sacred texts have specific prescriptions for how to attain certain childrearing goals. Muslim women, according to one interpreter, may work outside the home "as long as it does not interfere with her first duty as a mother, the one who first trains her children in the Islamic call. So her first, holy, and most important mission is to be mother and wife" (Stewart et al., 1999, p. 751).

At their core, religions are concerned with what is to be valued in life. In a meta-analytic review of religious groups around the world, it was found that religious people shared the values of kindness, tradition, and conformity, while they disdained hedonism (Saroglu, Delpierre, & Dernelle, 2004). Similarly, an analysis of 63 societies revealed that those

Photo 13.6 American Indian family.

Source: John Lund/Marc Romanelli/Blend Images/Getty Images

adults who were more religious were also more likely to value tradition, obedience, respect for authority, and religious faith in their children rather than independence and self-determination (Inglehart & Baker, 2000).

There are many historical examples illustrating how religion shapes parenting beliefs. One illustration provided in Chapter 1 concerned the beliefs of the Puritans. Children were perceived as born with original sin, and parents were instructed by their ministers to break the will of children to socialize them into faithful adults (Greven, 1977). In contrast, both Confucianism and Islam espouse the view (one also promulgated by the Catholic Jean-Jacques Rousseau in 1762) that children are inherently good, and they emphasize the role that parents play in children's development (Stewart et al., 1999).

In contrast, a very different religious belief about the basic nature of children can be found in many African, South Asian, and Native North American cultures. For many inhabitants in those societies, children are believed to be reincarnations of ancestral spirits. Consequently, a child's personality, luck, spiritual journey, and fate are largely a consequence of that inherited spirit (Gottlieb, 2006; Mattis, Ahluwalia, Cowie, & Kirkland-Harris, 2006). Another religiously inspired conviction, one that highlights the potential pernicious role of the environment in development, can be found in parents who subscribe to a belief in the "evil eye." The curse of the evil eye occurs when someone enviously admires an infant with a direct and extended look or with lavish praise and compliments. This belief, still held in Latin America, Caribbean countries, Northern Africa, Europe, and South Asia, reveals parental assumptions about the spiritual vulnerability of children (Mattis et al., 2006).

There are many ways in which religion can affect parenting and children's development. In rare cases when the religious message becomes misguided, religion can be dangerous to a child (Greven, 1991; Heimlich, 2011). But for the great majority of parents, religion is a positive influence in their lives that, in turn, promotes children's well-being (Holden & Williamson, 2014). See Table 13.3 for some of the mechanisms that have been found linking religion, family functioning, and positive development.

Religion also relates to child rearing in a less newsworthy but more widespread way: disciplinary beliefs. A variety of studies have found religion associated with childrearing

Table 13.3 Mechanisms Linking Religion, Parenting, and Child Development

Domain	Variable
The child/youth	Provides a clear moral code for behavior
	Gives a sense of identity
	Values self-control
	Promotes character development
The parents	Greater commitment to the marriage
	More marital satisfaction
	Less conflict, aggression, divorce
Child rearing	Pregnancy is considered spiritually significant
	Greater involvement and love
	Firmer discipline
	More harmonious interactions
	More supervision
	Model healthy behaviors
	Better coping in adversity
	Reduced risk of child maltreatment
Social network	Exposure to adults who are positive role models
	Exposure to nondeviant peers
	Availability of resources

Source: Based on Holden & Williamson, 2014.

attitudes and parental responses to children's misbehavior. In particular, conservative Protestants (including Baptists, Nazarenes, and Pentecostals) believe that it is important to use physical punishment on misbehaving children. The justification can be found in five proverbs in the Old Testament, as was previously discussed in Chapters 1 and 8. However, other Christians cite teachings in the New Testament as justification for their rejection of physical punishment. Consequently, conservative Christian parents have more positive attitudes toward and make more frequent use of physical punishment than do other Christians (including Roman Catholic, mainline Presbyterian, and Methodist) or those with no religious affiliation (de Roos, Iedema, & Miedema, 2004; Ellison, 1996; Gershoff, Miller, & Holden, 1999). For example, Figure 13.4 depicts the likelihood of responding with a spank or reason in response to vignettes about children who continue to misbehave. The conservative Protestant parents were about twice as likely as the other parents to report they would respond to the child with a spank.

In Cameroon, both Christian and Muslim parents shared harsher discipline perspectives than did the parents who adhered to traditional African religions, where children are considered a divine gift and it is believed ancestors will punish those who are cruel to them

Figure 13.4 Likelihood of Spanking and Reasoning Following Continued Child Misbehavior

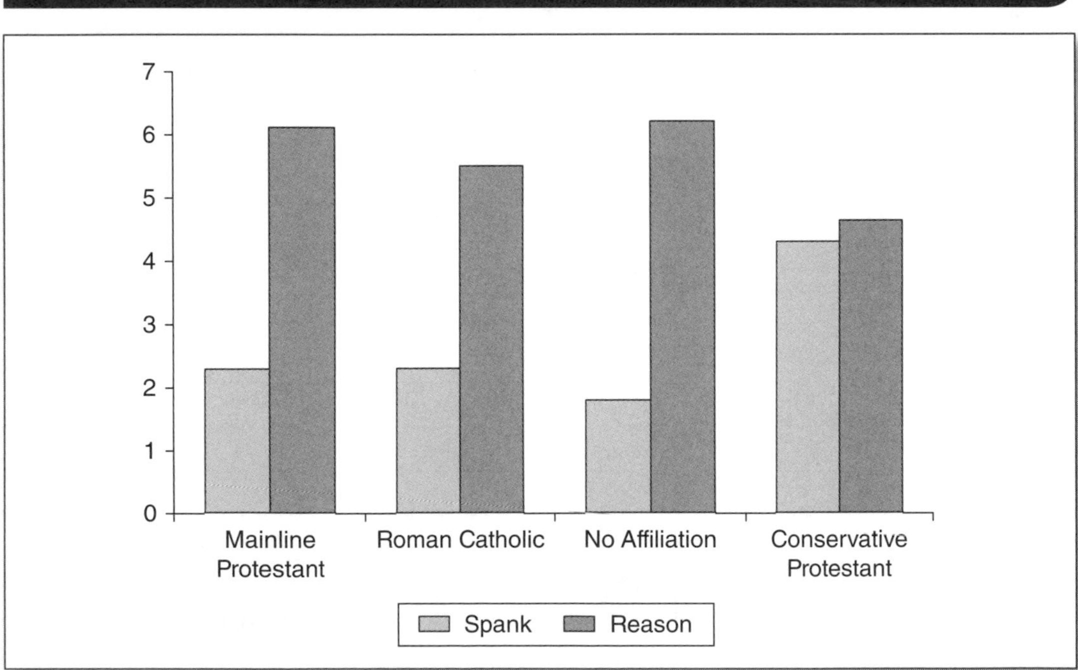

Source: Gershoff et al., 1999.

(Nsamenang & Lamb, 1995). Among Hindu, Muslim, and Christian mothers living in India, the Christian mothers had the most restrictive and punitive attitudes. Hindu mothers had the least restrictive attitudes. However, Christian mothers espoused warmer and more protective attitudes than did the Muslim mothers (Ojha & Pramanick, 1992).

Research has empirically linked religion to several other types of parenting behavior. In terms of involvement and the quality of social relationships, more religious mothers and fathers are warmer toward (giving praise, hugs, etc.) and enjoy more positive relations with their children than do less religious parents (Bartkowski & Wilcox, 2000; King & Furrow, 2004). A negative association was observed between religiosity and maternal authoritarian behavior, but religiosity was not related to father behavior (Gunnoe, Hetherington, & Reiss, 1999). Infant feeding practices have also been linked to religious involvement. In a study comparing the practices of Indian Hindu, Muslim, and Christian mothers, only about half of the Hindu mothers breastfed their infants, in contrast to 75% of the other mothers. Hindu mothers who did breastfeed were likely to wean their children earlier than did the other mothers (Ojha & Pramanick, 1992).

Religion has also been linked to at least one other area of parental behavior—coping with children's medical or developmental problems (Mahoney et al., 2001). Debra Skinner and her colleagues (Skinner, Correa, Skinner, & Bailey, 2001), in a qualitative study of Mexican and Puerto Rican parents living in the United States, found that organized religion as well as individual faith served as an important coping mechanism for parents of young children who had mental disabilities or developmental delays.

CHAPTER SUMMARY

This chapter focused on how culture influences parenting. Three categories of culture were considered: country, minority group membership, and religion. Research across different cultures and countries throughout the world shows there are culture-specific trends in parenting practices as well as some commonalities in practice and parenting values. Much more cross-cultural and comparative work remains to be done, particularly in the area of investigating families that are not WEIRD (Western, educated, industrialized, rich, and democratic).

The United States itself is populated by a rich diversity of families and individuals, with peoples from every country and every world culture living and rearing children in America. In this chapter, we examined the research into cultural diversity in some major minority groups within the United States. Latino/Hispanic American, African American, and Asian American families are the most prevalent minority groups and have some unique parenting characteristics. Added to this mix is a constant arrival of new immigrants. However, it needs to be remembered that generalizing is hazardous due to the high degree of heterogeneity within groups.

The role of religion on parenting and in families was also discussed. Religion can be a potent source of parenting beliefs and behavior, as research reveals. Religious beliefs can play a significant factor in promoting healthy adjustment in children as well as parents.

THOUGHT QUESTIONS

- What are the pros/cons of a strong emphasis on either independence or interdependence in childrearing strategies? Do you think Americans are out of balance? If so, how might parents become more balanced in their parenting strategies?
- How has your own particular cultural experience influenced your development or that of others you may know? Think of specific examples.
- Engage in a cross-cultural dialogue with someone from a different ethnic or cultural background. In what ways were your childhood experiences different and similar?
- How have your religious or agnostic beliefs informed your views about childrearing practices or children's development? What about the views of your friends with different faith beliefs?

CHAPTER GLOSSARY

acculturation How well an individual has adapted to the norms and values of the majority society.

coagents Two individuals who work together toward some action.

collectivism A cultural orientation that emphasizes the good of the larger group or society over the individual.

continuous care and contact model A view of infant care that says that one adult needs to provide sensitive care to a child for optimal development.

cultural niche The specific environment in which relationships occur. It consists of the physical and social environment, customs of child rearing and child care, and the parent's ethnotheories.

individualism A cultural orientation that emphasizes the individual's rights, goals, and free choice.

CHAPTER 14

Child Maltreatment

When Parenting Goes Awry

Chapter Preview: True or False?

- Child abuse is caused by a child-abusing personality in parents.
- Half a million children are maltreated each year in the United States.
- The United States has one of the highest rates of child maltreatment in the world.

Including the concept of child abuse in a parenting book may at first seem incongruous: Why would a parent knowingly harm a child? Many people are under the mistaken impression that parents are not likely to be perpetrators and that strangers are much more likely to abduct and harm a child. However, in the United States, child abduction by a stranger happens only about 2,400 times a year (in contrast to as many as 354,000 abductions by family members), and most of these children are returned safely (Boudreaux, Lord, & Etter, 2000). The fact is that children are targets of maltreatment, injury, or trauma from many (often familiar) sources. These may include siblings and other family members, peers, teachers, and neighbors (Finkelhor, Ormrod, & Turner, 2007). Given the time they spend with their children, parents are *by far* the group of individuals who pose the biggest threat to children's safety. As we will see, parents maltreat children for many reasons and in many ways.

Child maltreatment is the most visible and obvious indicator of dysfunctional parenting. It was once thought that child abusers were very different from other parents and were characterized by a child-abusing personality. No such personality type has been found [Preview Question]. On the basis of research conducted mostly since the 1970s, researchers now have a much better understanding of the reasons otherwise typical parents do something as abnormal as abuse their children. Parenting can be better thought of as occurring on a continuum, as is illustrated below. This chapter focuses on the far left end of that continuum.

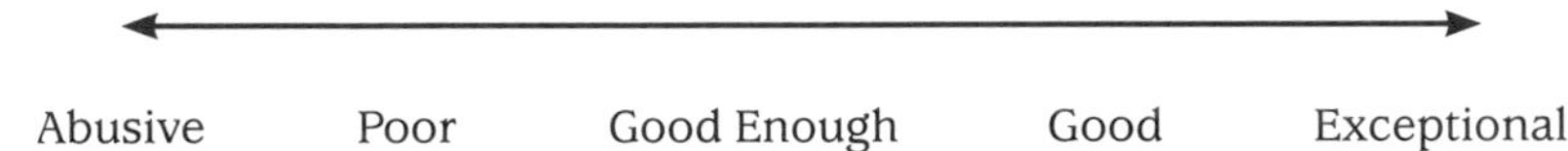

What is child abuse? The World Health Organization (2014a) defined the problem as:

> Child maltreatment is the abuse and neglect that occurs to children under 18 years of age. It includes all types of physical and/or emotional ill-treatment, sexual abuse, neglect, negligence and commercial or other exploitation, which results in actual or potential harm to the child's health, survival, development or dignity in the context of a relationship of responsibility, trust or power.

Exposure to intimate partner violence is also now recognized as a form of child maltreatment.

CHILD MALTREATMENT THROUGHOUT HISTORY

The history of parental abuse of their children is extensive. Historians and anthropologists agree that children have been maltreated since antiquity (Ariès, 1962; deMause, 1975; Sommerville, 1982). In fact, the earliest case of physical abuse of a toddler was recently unearthed in Egypt, dating back from between 50 CE to 450 CE (Wheeler, Williams, Beauchesne, & Dupras, 2013). The skeleton revealed both non-accidental head injuries and bone fractures. Societies have tolerated or even sanctioned a wide range of atrocities to children that parents—and others—have committed for thousands of years. A few examples will serve to illustrate the nature and prevalence of child maltreatment.

Infanticide, the killing of a child during the first year of life, has long been used as a method for culling out unwanted or handicapped babies, as mentioned in Chapter 1. The practice was routine in ancient Greece, Rome, Arabia, and China (Sommerville, 1982; Zigler & Hall, 1989). Both Plato and Aristotle advocated killing "defective" newborns, and the Greek physician Sonorus, in his second-century CE book, included a section titled "How to Recognize the Newborn That Is Worth Rearing" (Ruhrah, 1925, p. 6). Infanticide was often a passive act; undesired infants were abandoned in a secluded place.

Documents can be found that allude to other practices that today we would label abusive. Sonorus warned of potentially abusive women when he wrote of the need to carefully select wet nurses not just on the basis of health, age, and breast size but also on the basis of their personality. He recommended finding an even-tempered woman so she would be less likely to roughly handle or drop the baby. In 900 CE, a Persian physician named Rhazes wrote that many children who lived in the harems of Baghdad had been intentionally struck. About 800 years after that, a guidebook for physicians was published that warned that swelling in infants' heads could be due to dropping the infant or hitting it against something. The swelling is an effect of what is now labeled *shaken baby syndrome* (Photo 14.1).

Rough treatment of children and harsh punishment have also been common practices throughout history (Greven, 1991). Recall from Chapter 1 that in colonial America, hitting children was an accepted method to "drive the devil out," to "break the will," and to teach appropriate behavior.

Child sexual abuse also has a long history. In at least two societies, the legal system sanctioned what may often have been nonconsensual sexual activity, giving license to those in power to abuse the less powerful. During the Roman Republic, the doctrine of ***ius primae noctis*** gave the father of the family the right to have sexual relations with any female member of his household who was socially his inferior. Similarly, the 18th-century French doctrine of the ***droit du seigneur*** allowed the head of the household to sleep with any subordinate woman in his home.

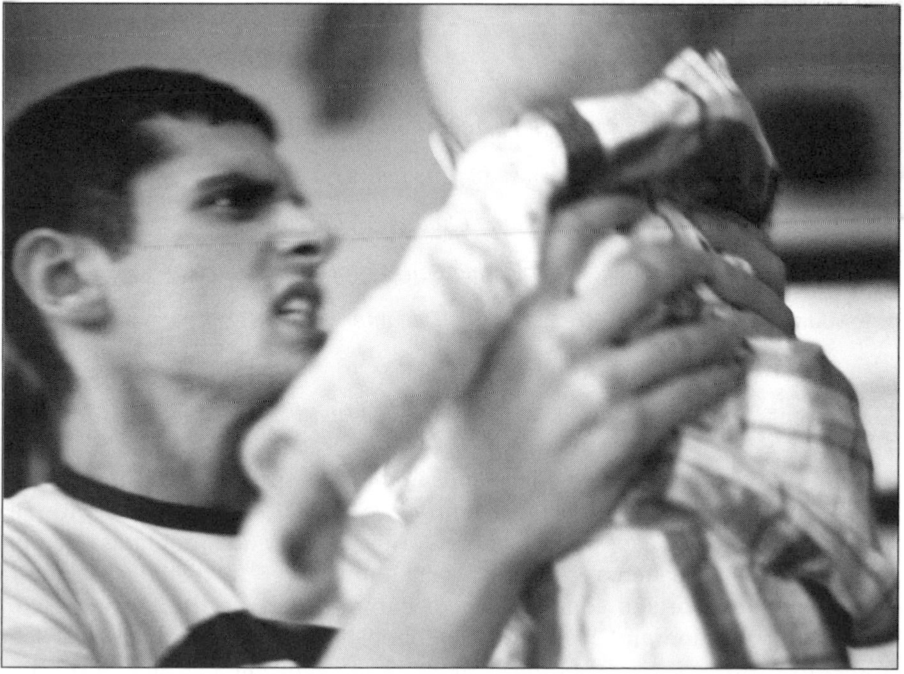

Photo 14.1 An angry and frustrated parent shakes his child. This is dangerous behavior, as it can result in shaken baby syndrome.

Source: © 2009 Jupiterimages Corporation

Child labor is yet another example of how children have been maltreated and exploited, with little to no protection from the legal system. During the Industrial Revolution in the latter part of the 18th century, children as young as five years old were forced to work in factories and other settings. In the 19th and early part of the 20th century, children in the United States labored on farms as well as in factories (sweatshops), restaurants, and mines. Child labor in textile mills attracted a lot of attention from children's rights activists because these children toiled long hours in dangerous conditions. U.S. labor and education laws have only prohibited child labor for about the past 75 years, with the passage of the Fair Labor Standards Act in 1938, which set federal standards for child labor. The practice of child labor continues even now in the form of migrant labor in the United States. In many other parts of the world, especially developing nations, child labor continues to be widely practiced.

As these examples illustrate, parents and many other individuals—including nurses and teachers—have maltreated children throughout history. More broadly speaking, cultural, religious, and economic institutions have sanctioned this maltreatment (deMause, 1975). Only since the 20th century has there been a dramatic shift toward empathy for the welfare of children and a greater awareness of the problem of child abuse.

THE MANY FACES OF CHILD MALTREATMENT

Consider the following headlines:

- *Pair Charged in Baby's Death From Heroin*
- *Man Gets 25 Years for Microwaving His Baby*
- *Woman Gets 80 Years for Holding Child in Scalding Water*
- *Man Gets Life Sentence for Injecting Son With HIV*
- *Man Pleads Guilty in Attempt to Sell Daughter, 4, for $1,500*
- *Girl Lives on Dog Food After Mother Takes Off*
- *Parents Charged in Boy's Death: 13-Year-Old Had Been Tied to Tree for 2 Nights*

Sadly, all of those headlines have appeared in newspapers, and more appear almost daily in communities around the country. We react to such stories with shock and outrage, but not long ago, people ignored or dismissed such problems. Sigmund Freud theorized that his patients' claims of sexual abuse were actually repressed fantasies. A watershed in efforts to combat abuse occurred as late as 1962, when the physician Dr. C. Henry Kempe and his colleagues published a journal article that labeled the problem of physical abuse as the *battered child syndrome* (Kempe, Silverman, Steele, Droegemueller, & Silver, 1962).

Over time, it became clear that the battering of children—what has come to be known as *physical abuse*—was just one of the more obvious forms of child maltreatment. The word *maltreatment* is preferable to the term *child abuse* because it subsumes two types of behaviors: actively doing something (commission) to injure a child and failing to do something (omission) and thereby harming a child. Both types of acts are damaging. Today, child maltreatment is classified into four categories: physical abuse, sexual abuse, neglect, and **psychological maltreatment.**

The Fourth National Incidence Study of Child Abuse and Neglect (NIS-4; Sedlak et al., 2010), using the standard of whether a child has been harmed, found that the annual incidence of maltreatment in the United States is about 1.25 million (a rate of 17.2 per 1,000) [Preview Question]. As can be seen in Figure 14.1, neglect is by far the largest category.

Figure 14.1 Types of Child Maltreatment by Percentage of Victims

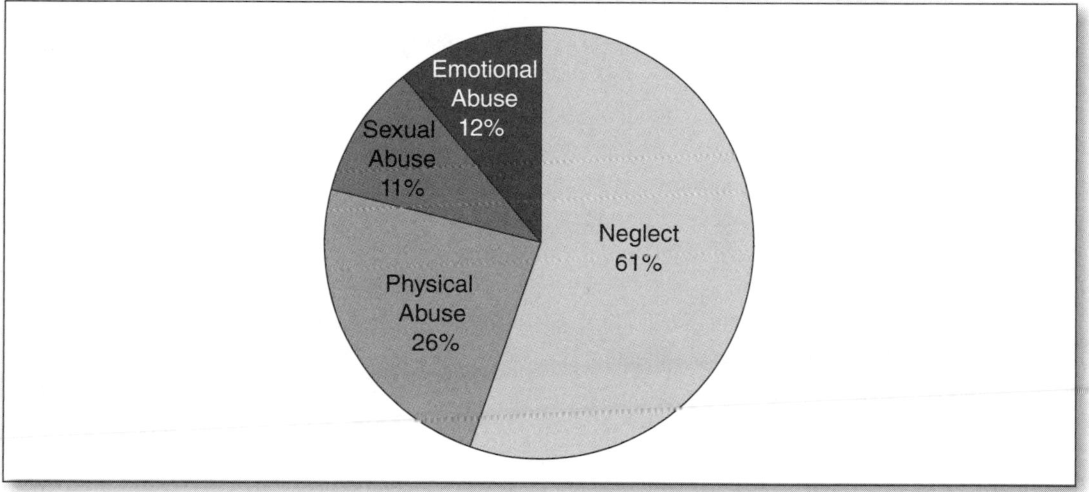

Source: Sedlak et al., 2010.

Physical Abuse

Physical abuse is the most extensively studied form of maltreatment because it is easiest to detect. It involves an act of commission, whereby a parent or other individual injures a child. Kempe and his colleagues (1962) identified bone fractures or broken bones, bruises, neurological damage, and child deaths as common outcomes of abuse. Subsequently, many other types of injuries have been added, including sprains, dislocated bones, abrasions from ropes or straps, burns (from cigarettes, appliances, or hot water), abnormal loss of hair or teeth, scars, and various internal injuries. Poisoning and suffocating a child are also examples of physical abuse. An unusual form of physical abuse, Munchausen syndrome by proxy (MSBP), is described in Box 14.1.

Box 14.1 A Strange Form of Physical Abuse: Munchausen Syndrome by Proxy

One of the more peculiar and rare forms of physical abuse is Munchausen Syndrome by Proxy (MSBP). The publication of *Sickened* (Gregory & Feldman, 2003), written by a survivor of MSBP, attracted considerable public attention to the syndrome. This disorder is named after the 18th-century German Baron, Karl Friedrich von Munchausen, known for telling wildly imaginative stories about himself. Some individuals with Munchausen syndrome intentionally make themselves sick to elicit medical attention and sympathy from others. MSBP goes a step further: An individual (usually a parent) either produces or feigns illness in another person (usually the child) in an effort to get attention and support for him- or herself. The disorder was recognized in the late 1970s by the medical community but it remains confusing and controversial (Squires & Squires, 2013). What is clear is that MSBP is rare: There are perhaps 1,200 cases per year in the United States. In most cases (95%), the perpetrator is the mother (Schreier, 2002). Typically, the mother intentionally causes an illness in her child but then either saves the child herself or rushes to the emergency room at a local hospital to procure medical help. In other cases, the mother fabricates medical symptoms but seeks medical tests and even surgery. In one case heard in a Texas courtroom, a mother of four young girls took them to the emergency room more than 150 times over a four-year period. The mother persuaded doctors that the girls needed treatment for cystic fibrosis, cerebral palsy, and seizures—illnesses they never had (Nielsen, 2008).

In some cases, the mother actually kills the child. For example, certain infant deaths originally attributed to sudden infant death syndrome (SIDS) have been reclassified as MSBP cases where mothers suffocate their children but blame it on SIDS (Firstman & Talan, 1997).

Although MSBP is difficult to detect, one group of researchers covertly videotaped suspected MSBP mothers when they were with their allegedly ill children in the hospital (Hall, Eubanks, Meyyazhagan, Kenney, & Johnson, 2000). Of the 41 mothers videotaped, 23 were determined to be MSBP mothers. The video monitoring revealed that almost three-fourths of the suspected MSBP mothers surreptitiously engaged in such actions as tampering with hospital equipment, smothering their children, or staging a disease when their children were healthy.

Physical abuse is often a reaction to a mundane event, such as when a parent becomes frustrated with an infant's cries, overreacts to a toileting accident, or improperly disciplines a disrespectful child. In some cultures, harsh or cruel punishments are not uncommon. In Yemen, for example, misbehaving boys can be shackled for weeks at a time (see Photo 14.2). The actions that lead to abuse may begin with a shake, push, or spank and escalate into behaviors that result in injury or even death. In some cases, the abuse is intentional. Much more commonly, however, the injury is unintended.

The injuries suffered by children who are physically abused are not just physical but emotional as well. Physically abused children are likely to exhibit a wide range of consequences

(Kolko, 1996; Trickett & Negriff, 2011). Internalizing (e.g., depression, anxiety) and externalizing (e.g., aggression) behavior problems are commonly found in children who have been abused. Emotional deficits (e.g., low self-esteem), insecure attachments, limitations in controlling emotions, and cognitive problems (e.g., poor school performance) are also frequent consequences of abuse.

Not all children are equally likely to be physically abused. In fact, the characteristics of victims help to reveal the dynamics of the problem. Young children and infants are more likely to be victimized than older children: 51% of those abused are five years old or younger. Physically abused children also tend to have difficult or challenging temperaments. Children who are handicapped or who have serious medical problems (such as prematurity) are at higher risk for abuse (Sullivan & Knutson, 2000). These and other examples of child risk factors can be found in Table 14.1.

Photo 14.2 In Yemen, parents can request authorities to place their misbehaving children in leg irons.

Source: Photograph by J. P. Bell

Parents are the perpetrators of physical abuse about 80.3% of the time; 88.5% of perpetrators are the biological parents. Mothers are the sole perpetrators in 36.6% of the cases, fathers act alone in 18.7%, and both mothers and fathers are involved 19.4% of the time. Mothers are more likely to be the perpetrator of abuse than fathers are, undoubtedly because they spend so much more time with their children than do fathers. Other relatives (e.g., siblings, grandparents) are implicated in 4.5% of the cases, and unmarried partners of the child's parent constitute about 2.6% of the perpetrators (U.S. Department of Health and Human Services, 2012). In the case of child abuse fatalities, one or both parents were responsible for 80% of child fatalities occurring in 2012. In these cases, mothers were the perpetrators more often than fathers. In 27.1% of the cases, mothers were the sole perpetrators, whereas fathers acted alone in 17.1% of the cases. Both parents engaged in abuse resulting in child death in 21.2% of the cases.

A parent is at heightened risk for perpetrating abuse if he or she has a serious diagnosable mental illness (such as depression, schizophrenia, or antisocial personality disorder). In such cases, the likelihood of physical abuse doubles (Walsh, MacMillan, & Jamieson, 2002). However, mental illness is not implicated in most cases of physical abuse. A large number of parental risk factors have been identified by researchers (Table 14.1), indicating the multiple-etiology nature of the problem.

Table 14.1 Risk Factors in Physical Abuse

Child Characteristics
Young age
Difficult temperament
Handicap
Illness
Parent Characteristics
Hyperreactive
Attachment problems (e.g., insecurely attached in childhood, unwanted child)
Childhood trauma (e.g., abused in childhood, exposed to marital violence)
Emotional problems (e.g., immature, jealous of child)
Mental illness (e.g., depression, antisocial)
Reliance on corporal punishment
Social cognition deficits (e.g., unreasonable attributions, unrealistic expectations, negative perceptions of child, feelings of powerlessness)
Substance abuse (e.g., alcohol, crack, methamphetamines)
Contextual Characteristics
Partner violence
Isolation or little social support
Poverty

Contributing factors can be divided into biological, cognitive-affective, and behavior characteristics (Berger, 2005; Milner & Dopke, 1997). For example, individuals who are biologically predisposed to be hyperreactive parents are more at risk to abuse than are calmer individuals. A large number of cognitive-affective variables have been linked to physical abuse. In particular, parental social-cognition problems include poor problem-solving skills, inadequate parenting knowledge, unrealistic expectations about children, hostile attributions, and feelings of powerlessness when trying to control children (e.g., Berlin, Dodge, & Reznick, 2013; Cavanagh, Dobash, & Dobash, 2007). Behavioral characteristics include a reliance on physical punishment and personal substance abuse. Children of substance-abusing parents are three times more likely to be abused than are other children (Califano, 2007).

In addition to individual difference factors, a parent's context or environment can contribute to risks. Four commonly identified factors are poverty, poor social support, having been raised in an abusive family, and experiencing partner violence. Many of these risk factors (listed in Table 14.1) can be organized into a model of physical child abuse (Tolan, Gorman-Smith, & Henry, 2006). The model begins with risk factors based on parent, child, and contextual variables. Next, when the individual then has a child, he or she does not engage in effective parenting, and so the child develops problems. Those problems then contribute to poor quality parent-child interactions, negative emotion, coercive cycles, and escalating aggression. Eventually, the negative interactions result in child abuse, as is displayed in Figure 14.2.

It is clear that there are multiple pathways to becoming a perpetrator of abuse. Some hyperreactive parents, when under stress, overreact. Other parents escalate the intensity of their actions when initial disciplinary efforts fail. Still others may have emotional or mental health problems. Many abusive behaviors are likely instigated by stress, such as marital problems or poverty, which then may elicit actions that otherwise would not occur.

The different pathways to physical abuse have been most clearly understood in the examination of a particularly tragic incident of maltreatment—when parents murder their children. These cases of filicide help reveal the different causes and motivations of severe abuse as well as how such abuse differs by parent gender (Koenen & Thompson, 2008; Stanton & Simpson, 2002). Ania Wilczynski (1997) identified seven different causes of abuse. Mothers were most likely to kill children they hadn't wanted (43% of cases) or if they themselves were mentally ill (21% of cases). In another 14% of the cases, mothers believed they were engaging in an altruistic act ("mercy killing") by ending the suffering of their ailing or handicapped child. A study that compiled 36 years of filicide data in Sweden

Figure 14.2 A Model of Physical Child Abuse

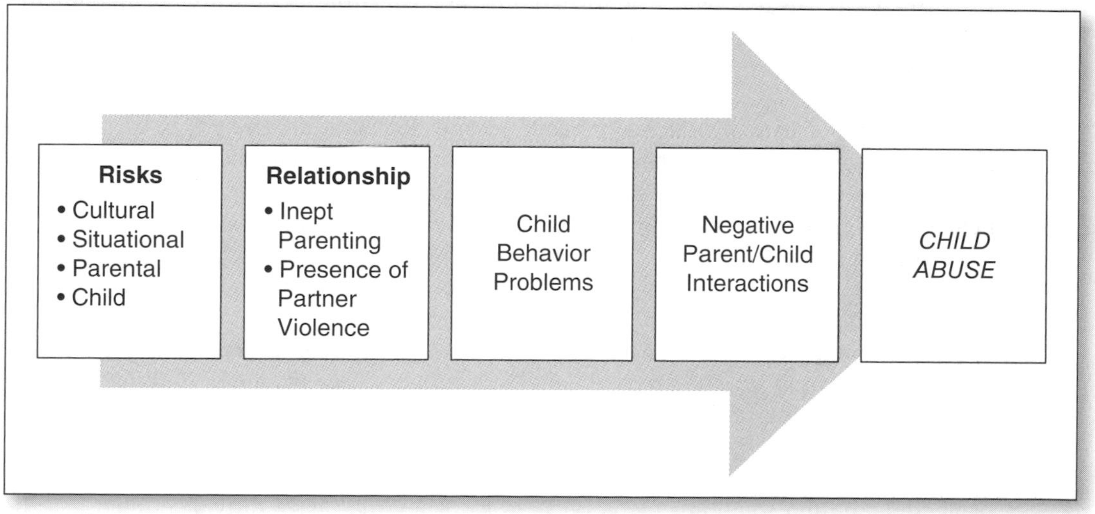

Source: Tolan, Gorman-Smith, & Henry, 2006.

found that 19.2% of the parents had a major psychiatric disorder. Other risk factors included a traumatic injury, prior suicide attempt, and prior violent crimes (Lysell, Runeson, Lichtenstein, & Langstrom, 2014).

Fathers had different pathways toward filicide than did mothers. In 30% of the cases, the fatality happened during a disciplinary episode. In another 30% of the cases, the father was retaliating against the mother in a syndrome known as the *Medea syndrome* (after the Greek tragedy by Euripides). Here, the motivation for murder is to hurt the spouse (typically in the aftermath of a separation or divorce). In contrast to mothers, 20% of the fathers had a novel motivation for murder: They were jealous of the attention the child received or they perceived the child as rejecting them. Figure 14.3 graphs these gender differences in filicide.

Neglect

In comparison to physical abuse, the omission of child care sounds benign. But it's not. Neglect concerns the failure of a caregiver to provide the physical and social ingredients for what is considered, based on community standards, the minimal care necessary for children to grow and thrive. Some of the infants raised in understaffed and underfunded orphanages in Romania are a prime example of neglect, as was mentioned in Chapter 11.

Neglect takes multiple forms. Consider the following illustrations of neglect:

- Karen and Bill were professionals who lived in a spacious home. While they were entertaining guests one evening, their two-year-old child climbed into a hot tub and drowned.
- Jacob and Michelle left their nine-year-old son in charge of his five-year-old autistic brother while they flew to Las Vegas for the weekend. (Before leaving town, they took their puppies to a dog sitter.)
- A 19-year-old boy, weighing 45 pounds, was found rummaging in a neighbor's trash can. He and his malnourished brothers had survived by eating wallboard and uncooked pancake batter. Their adoptive foster parents defended themselves by arguing that the boys had eating disorders.

Each of these examples actually occurred and depicts a different type of neglectful parenting. Signs of neglect include inadequate nutrition, tattered clothing, poor hygiene, unsafe environments, a lack of supervision, and abandonment. Medical, dental, or mental health problems, such as failure to thrive (as indicated by small stature), can also be indicators of neglect (Stowman & Donohue, 2005). Although neglectful supervision can have fatal repercussions in a matter of minutes (as in the drowning illustration), neglect generally refers to a longer-term pattern of behavior.

Physical neglect is the classic and stereotypic manifestation of a neglected child. The child lives in a filthy, unsanitary, and dangerous home, where we might find piled-up garbage, exposed wiring, broken glass, bugs or rodents, and perhaps animal feces. These conditions are classic red flags of neglect. Parents who allow their children to live in such squalid conditions may also be unlikely to take care of their children's basic needs. Physically neglected children sometimes look uncared for. They may have dirty, lice-filled hair; be

Figure 14.3 Reasons Why Parents Kill Their Children

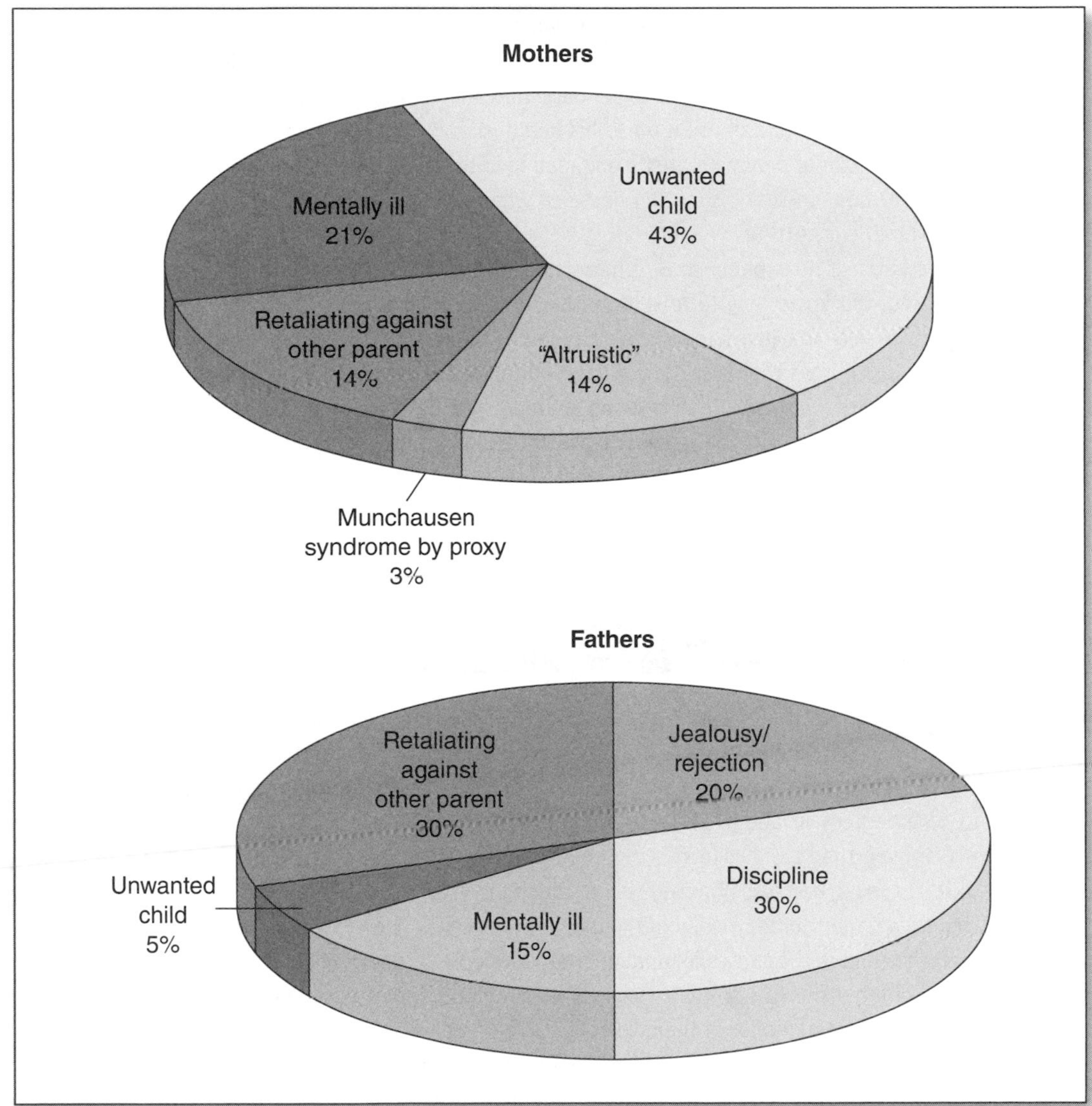

Source: Wilczynski, 1997.

dressed inappropriately for the weather; exhibit poor hygiene; and appear malnourished. They may also be left unsupervised or inappropriately put in charge of younger children. See Boxes 14.2 and 14.3 for two types of neglect cases. One was due to extreme ignorance; the other is more common but completely avoidable.

Box 14.2 The Boy Who Was Raised as a Dog

An extreme (and tragic) example of the way in which a parent's thinking process can permanently damage a child's development is described in a book by the child psychiatrist Bruce Perry (Perry & Szalavitz, 2007). Dr. Perry recounts his experience with Justin, a six-year-old child hospitalized with a severe case of pneumonia. In addition to his health problem, it was clear the boy was extremely disturbed and difficult to deal with. Justin engaged in autistic-like behavior, wore diapers, and yelled at the staff. It turned out that his mother had died when he was 11 months old and so he lived with his mother's boyfriend, Arthur.

Arthur had almost no experience with infants or children so he did not know how to rear a child. However, Arthur did know how to raise dogs. So Arthur put Justin in a dog cage beside his other dogs. Justin was fed and his diapers were changed, but he was rarely spoken to or played with. Unbelievably, Justin lived that way for five years—until he contracted pneumonia and was taken to the hospital. Despite the severe neglect Justin suffered, he moved in with a foster family and showed dramatic improvements, such that he eventually was able to attend kindergarten—when he was eight years old.

Box 14.3 Left Behind: Neglected in Hot Vehicles

Every summer, a curious tragedy occurs at least 35 times across the United States: Infants and young children die when they are left in automobiles. Everyone knows that the temperature skyrockets in cars parked in the summer sun. On a 90-degree day, the interior temperature in a closed vehicle rises to about 130 degrees in about 30 minutes (McLaren, Null, & Quinn, 2005). Children can die of heatstroke or hyperthermia in as few as 15 minutes. And in warm climates, hyperthermia can happen year-round (Duzinksi, Barczyk, Wheeler, Iyer, & Lawson, 2014).

How could a parent forget a child in the car? In some cases, the mother did not forget but intentionally left the child in the car while running errands. In other cases, parents were unaware that their children had entered the cars to play. However, most of the time, the parent unintentionally left a sleeping child in the parking lot of their workplace, which was what happened to a university professor in California. He had forgotten to drop off his sleeping infant son at the day care center on his way to work. Simply forgetting is the reason given in more than three-fourths of these cases (Breed, 2007).

Should parents whose children die in hot cars be prosecuted for child maltreatment, or have they already been punished enough by the death of their child? Fourteen states have laws prohibiting leaving a child unattended in a vehicle. Charges are filed in about 60% of the cases when a child was unintentionally left in a car. Most of the cases result in convictions, including jail time (median sentence is two years) in about half of cases (Breed, 2007).

Medical neglect refers to a failure to provide appropriate health care for a child (despite the financial ability to do so). About 1% of all child maltreatment cases involve this form of neglect (U.S. Department of Health and Human Services, 2012). The most common reasons for this form of neglect are cultural or religious beliefs, anxiety about a medical condition or intervention, and financial considerations.

Parental beliefs are the most common problem underlying medical neglect. For example, members of certain religious groups (e.g., Christian Scientists, Followers of Christ) believe that ill children must be healed through prayer alone (Heimlich, 2011). Consequently, they may refuse to seek medical attention for their sick children. In one case, a two-year-old boy was stung more than 400 times by yellow jacket bees. The parents, members of a fundamentalist Christian church, waited seven hours before seeking medical attention. By then, it was too late; the child died. In a review of 172 faith-related child fatalities that included 23 different denominations, 98% of the noncancerous but ill children would have had a good or excellent outcome if the parents had sought medical help in a timely manner (Asser & Swan, 1998). Sometimes medical neglect is caused by parents who do not know any better (such as those uneducated on dental hygiene) or who harbor mistaken beliefs (such as an exaggerated fear of immunizations).

The other two major categories of neglect are emotional/psychological and educational. Emotional neglect will be discussed later in this chapter, under "Psychological Maltreatment." **Educational neglect** refers to failing to comply with state laws requiring school attendance, failing to provide an approved home curriculum, permitting truancy without appropriate reason, or not attending to special education needs (Stowman & Donohue, 2005). To date, little research attention has been devoted to educational neglect or to the parents who engage in it.

Neglect can affect not just the physical development and well-being of children (due to malnutrition and failure to thrive) but also their emotional, cognitive, linguistic, and social functioning. Recall Box 4.1 concerning the lasting effects of extreme neglect on Genie. Neglected children tend to be apathetic and withdrawn. They exhibit low self-esteem, negative affect, and disturbed attachment and interaction patterns. Some of these behaviors may well be due to brain damage that has occurred as a direct result of inadequate love, attention, and stimulation (see Box 14.4).

Box 14.4 Maltreatment and the Brain

Recall from Chapter 7 that during the first few years of life, the human brain undergoes significant change. Much of that change is guided by how the brain is stimulated and used (Perry, 1997). Once neurological pathways are established, they are very difficult if not impossible to unlearn (like trying to unlearn riding a bike). In the case of extreme neglect, if an infant's brain does not get adequate stimulation or does not receive sufficient nurturance, it will likely suffer irreversible damage.

(Continued)

(Continued)

Similarly, when children are chronically exposed to stress and trauma, their brains are bathed in stress hormones. These hormones likely affect the brain's development in abnormal ways (Glaser, 2000). Reviews of brain development in maltreated children are revealing the ways in which brain structures can be affected (see Figure 14.4). In particular, there is evidence that the prefrontal cortex, hippocampus, amygdala, cerebellar vermis, and corpus callosum are affected by high levels of stress hormones (e.g., cortisol) (Teicher, Polcari, Anderson, Anderson, & Navalta, 2003; Weber & Reynolds, 2004). It is not surprising that these children have self-regulation, emotional, and behavioral problems. As neurologist Martin Teicher (2000) stated: "Our brains are sculpted by our early experiences. Maltreatment is a chisel that shapes a brain to contend with strife, but at the cost of deep, enduring wounds" (p. 67).

Why does neglect occur? Occasionally, parents may be unaware of it. The psychiatrist Bruce Perry (Perry & Szalavitz, 2007) recounts several cases of neglect by babysitters. In one example, a working mother hired her cousin to babysit her infant. Without the mother's knowledge, the sitter was leaving the child alone virtually all day while working at another job. When the toddler was 18 months old, the mother returned home early one day to find him alone in a dark room with no toys, music, or any other form of stimulation. Although the mother had suspected something was wrong with her son due to his developmental delays, it had never occurred to her or her pediatrician that the child, with autistic-like symptoms, was suffering from neglect. Severe lack of sensory and social stimulation will likely result in irreparable damage to a developing brain. Some of the regions affected by neglect and other forms of maltreatment are depicted in Figure 14.4.

Neglect more commonly occurs as a consequence of the parents' own developmental history, unusual beliefs, poor psychological functioning, and/or lack of coping strategies and resources. Many neglectful parents were themselves abused or neglected and may have never experienced adequate parenting. Some are addicted to substances. Their addictions divert all their resources and energy and leave them in no state to care for a child. Other parents have unusual beliefs that can result in neglect. One vegan couple (who refused to consume any animal products) was found guilty in 2007 of starving their six-week-old infant to death. Although babies at this age require breast milk or formula, the parents would feed their son only soy milk and apple juice.

Although poverty and economic stress are likely to be contributing factors to neglect, they are not sufficient to explain all cases. Almost one in five children (22% of the population) are now being raised in poverty (Jiang, Ekono, & Skinner, 2014). However, most of the 16.1 million children who live in poor families are *not* neglected. Each year, approximately 3% of children being reared in poverty are neglected (Children's Bureau, 2014).

Neglect occurs for many reasons. Gary Evans and Pilyoung Kim (2013) identified three pathways of poverty to negative outcomes in children, including neglect. The first

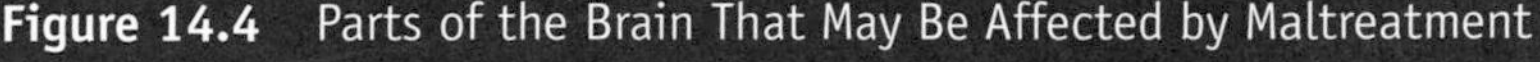

Figure 14.4 Parts of the Brain That May Be Affected by Maltreatment

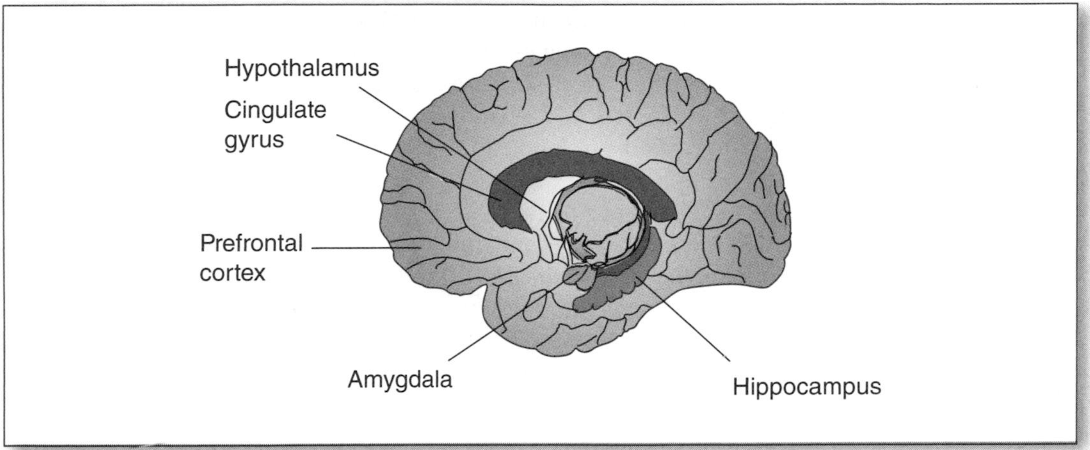

trajectory is lack of parental investment. Poor parents may not have the resources or the knowledge to provide their children with appropriate cognitive and language stimulation. Another explanation for neglect is the elevated chronic stress due to low income. Poverty puts families under extraordinary chronic stress, which can be exacerbated by substance abuse, mental health problems, or disabilities. It is not surprising that the children in low-income families are at a heightened risk for neglect as well as physical abuse.

Still, poverty level is the strongest predictor of neglect. Most of the research into neglectful parenting focuses on mothers, though fathers, of course, are equally responsible (Dubowitz, Black, Kerr, Starr, & Harrington, 2000). These mothers often live in poverty-stricken, dangerous neighborhoods that produce low morale and hopelessness. In an attempt to identify different patterns of maternal neglect, researchers studied 100 mothers, all confirmed by Child Protective Services to be neglectful. The mothers were similar in annual income, number of depressive symptoms, and amount of social support. No distinctive clusters of variables differentiated the mothers into distinct neglect groups. However, the mothers varied considerably in how well they functioned as caregivers, their sense of efficacy, their degree of inhibition, and the number of problems they were experiencing (Wilson, Kuebli, & Hughes, 2005).

Sexual Abuse

Sexual abuse of children has received sustained research attention in the United States only since the late 1970s. Given the secretive nature of the acts, the abuse usually becomes known only when the child discloses it or an alert adult recognizes some of the behavioral indicators. These include changes in habits, sudden fear of an individual, unexplained knowledge about sex, or preoccupation with genitalia. *Child sexual abuse* is commonly defined as either sexual activity between a child and a significantly older individual or a forced sexual behavior imposed by an adult. The abusive sexual behaviors vary in their degree of physical contact. A few do not involve physical contact at all, such as when a man (a flasher) unnaturally exposes his genitals to a child or when a parent lets a child view pornographic material. However, most sexual abuse actions do involve contact. These range from fondling to intercourse. In one study of a group of child survivors of sexual abuse, 62% of the children had been fondled, 38% had experienced rape, 23% had had oral-to-genital contact, 25% had been touched in the genital or anal area, and 17% had experienced attempted rape (Kellogg & Hoffman, 1997).

This form of maltreatment is heavily gendered, both for victims and perpetrators. Girls are the victims in all but about 10% of the cases (modal age is 10 years), and at least 90% of the perpetrators are male. The victim, in as many as 90% of the cases, knows the perpetrator (e.g., a father or stepfather, neighbor, teacher, brother, cousin, uncle, or grandfather). In contrast to the other forms of maltreatment discussed here, biological mothers are rarely the perpetrators of sexual abuse. For example, in a study of sexual abuse in New Zealand (Fanslow, Robinson, Crengle, & Perese, 2007), biological fathers and stepfathers committed the crime in 12% and 9% of the 457 cases analyzed; only one biological mother and two stepmothers did so (.2% of cases). Uncles were the most common male perpetrators (24%), followed by siblings or stepsiblings (14%), cousins (11%), grandfathers (9%), and acquaintances (8%).

Perpetrators of sexual abuse tend to be a heterogeneous group, so identifying a set of common characteristics is not possible. Risk factors include a childhood history of abuse (sexual, physical, or neglect), psychopathology (e.g., antisocial personality disorder), substance abuse, deviant sexual interests, low levels of involvement in caregiving of the victim during the first five years, deficits in social skills, marital dissatisfaction, and cognitive distortions (Chaffin, Letourneau, & Silovsky, 2002). Examples of cognitive distortions include these ideas: "Having sex with kids is a good way to teach them about sex," "It is better to have sex with my daughter than to commit adultery," and "Children usually outgrow any problems resulting from a sexual experience they had as a child" (McGrath, Cann, & Konopasky, 1998).

Childhood sexual abuse results in a number of immediate and long-term negative effects on the victimized child (but see Box 14.5 to read about a controversy in the research over the effects). It is common for children to experience post-traumatic stress disorder (PTSD), characterized by frequent re-experiencing of events (flashbacks, nightmares, intrusive thoughts), a numbing of affect, and persistent symptoms of increased arousal (sleep problems, poor concentration). Other common emotional consequences are depression, elevated anxiety, avoidance, and dissociation. Some children respond to their emotional agitation by engaging in tension-reducing activities, including cutting or self-mutilation, substance abuse, binge eating and purging, indiscriminant sexual behavior, or suicide attempts. In extreme cases, the child might develop dissociative identity disorder, commonly known as *multiple personality disorder* (American Psychiatric Association, 2013).

Box 14.5 The Controversy Over Effects of Sexual Abuse

The review, published in *Psychological Bulletin* (Rind, Tromovitch, & Bauserman, 1998), did not attract much attention—until the radio talk show host Dr. Laura (Schlessinger) learned about it and publicly criticized its authors. The controversy escalated from there and culminated in a U.S. congressional resolution condemning the review. The authors had made the claim that, based on a meta-analytic review of 59 studies, individuals who were sexually abused as children did not show pervasive negative effects by the time they were in college. Although some negative effects were noted on 17 of the 18 variables studies, the authors argued that the "negative effects were neither pervasive nor typically intense, and that men reacted much less negatively than women" (p. 22). The review concluded with the provocative argument that mental health workers had overstated the negative effects of sexual contact. Most controversially, the authors proposed changing terminology to value-neutral terms such as *adult-child sex* rather than *child sexual abuse*.

Many therapists, professionals, and survivors of child sexual abuse were outraged about the review. How could such an article have been published in a premier review journal? The storm generated by the controversy resulted in several research committees evaluating the review and its conclusions. A careful evaluation of the article revealed a number of subtle problems with the review and not-so-subtle problems with the authors' interpretations. For example, the reviewers included some old and poor-quality studies, did not use a consistent definition of child sexual abuse, and ignored some important negative effects (such as substance abuse and PTSD). Indeed, newer studies, compared with older research, are more likely to find negative effects. Another central problem was that the authors failed to adequately explain the limitations of the research. For instance, a key limitation was the selective nature of the sample: College students are high-functioning survivors of maltreatment. What about the many victims who did not grow up to go to college?

The fundamental conclusion of the study was patently wrong: There is no question that sexual abuse is damaging to the child (Putnam, 2003). The one positive outcome from the controversy is that the review did remind people that many survivors of abuse, despite their trauma, can recover and function well as young adults.

The nature and extent of how children respond to sexual abuse is a function of a number of factors, including the child's age and gender; the nature, duration, and severity of the abuse; the child's perceptions and attributions; the parents' post-abuse response; and whether the child received effective therapy, such as trauma-focused cognitive behavior therapy (Foster & Carson, 2013). In addition, some children are resilient and appear to recover from trauma more quickly than others (Crenshaw, 2013).

Parents, assuming they were not involved in the sexual abuse, can have several important roles in helping children recover. First, they must believe the child's disclosure. Next, they need to keep the child safely away from the perpetrator. Third, parents should obtain therapy for the child. Finally, parents can help the child minimize the likelihood of cognitive distortions, including self-blame, guilt, and dysfunctional attributions. In this way, they work to restore the child's self-esteem. Children of parents who were supportive of the child after the abuse was disclosed are better adjusted (less distress, better attachment quality with parents) than those with unsupportive parents or unaware parents (Godbout, Briere, Sabourin, & Lussier, 2014).

Psychological Maltreatment

The problem of psychological maltreatment (also called *emotional abuse*, *verbal abuse*, and *mental injury* or *deprivation*) demonstrates the obvious falsehood of the old saying, "Sticks and stones can break my bones, but words can never hurt me." Children are greatly affected by words that degrade, denigrate, or reflect parental rejection of the child. This type of language and its accompanying actions can severely injure a child's developing self-concept and feelings of self-worth. They are the essence of psychological maltreatment, defined as "a repeated pattern of caregiver behavior or extreme incident(s) that convey to children that they are worthless, flawed, unloved, unwanted, endangered, or only of value in meeting another's needs" (Hart, Brassard, Binggeli, & Davidson, 2002). Psychological maltreatment has also been called *verbal aggression* (LeRoy, Mahoney, Boxer, Gullan, & Fang, 2014).

The nature of psychological maltreatment makes it particularly difficult to document and study. Parents can readily adjust their behavior when in the presence of Child Protective Services investigators. There are no physical injuries associated with it. In addition, its consequences may not be immediately apparent. Nor are there uniform effects on children. For all these reasons, psychological maltreatment is difficult to corroborate and prosecute. It therefore comprises only 6.6% of the substantiated child maltreatment cases. However, many experts think psychological abuse is the most widespread form of maltreatment and is at the core of all forms of maltreatment (Hart et al., 2002). It often co-occurs with physical aggression (LeRoy et al., 2014).

Psychological maltreatment is expressed in a variety of ways. The seven major manifestations are degrading, denying emotional responsiveness, rejecting, terrorizing, isolating, corrupting, and exploiting. These are defined and illustrated with examples in Table 14.2. However, these expressions are not exhaustive of the ways that parents can psychologically maltreat their offspring. Other childrearing behaviors that can be abusive include excessive psychological control, showing favoritism and/or scapegoating among siblings, reversal of parent-child roles, and chaotic and incompetent parenting (Gagne & Bouchard, 2004).

Psychological maltreatment attacks children's basic developmental need for love and affection as well as their developing self-concept (Miller, 1984). Such children consequently suffer from low self-esteem and a variety of other emotional and behavioral problems. They display developmental delays and a failure to thrive as well as internalizing and externalizing problems (such as depression, anxiety, and aggression). These children may also show physical health problems as well as cognitive deficits (Hart et al., 2002).

One of the specific populations of children who are psychologically maltreated is those whose parents or parents' partners engage in intimate partner violence. Over the past quarter century, research has been accumulating about these children, and they are described in Box 14.6.

Table 14.2 Types, Definitions, and Examples of Seven Forms of Psychological Maltreatment

Type	Definition	Examples
Spurning (Degrading)	Labeling as inferior, shaming, or publicly humiliating	Name calling: "stupid," "worthless," "you're disgusting"
Denying Responsiveness	Being detached or uninvolved	Ignoring or failing to respond to a child's attempts to interact
Rejecting	Refusing bids for contact or affection	Avoiding, criticizing, or expressing hatred for the child
Terrorizing	Verbally assaulting, creating a climate of fear	Threatening injury or abandonment
Isolating	Cutting off normal social experiences	Refusing to allow any peer contact
Corrupting	Teaching socially deviant behavior	Promoting delinquency, racism, or substance abuse
Exploiting	Using the child inappropriately for parent's needs	Using the child to make money through prostitution or child labor

Box 14.6 Children Exposed to Intimate Partner Violence

Children exposed to intimate partner violence can be classified as victims of psychological maltreatment because they are terrorized by simply living in homes characterized by a climate of tension and hostility between their parents or parent figures. A recent study estimated that 15.5 million children live in families where partner violence had occurred in the past year, and 7 million of those children were exposed to *severe* partner violence (McDonald, Jouriles, Ramisetty-Mikler, Caetano, & Green, 2006). It is now well documented that children in such families show a variety of serious behavioral problems. A meta-analysis of 60 studies found strong effect sizes linking exposure to behavior problems (Evans, Davies, & DiLillo, 2008).

Why are children affected by the exposure? In addition to the terror and trauma of marital physical and psychological violence, the children suffer from disrupted parent-child relationships, a compromised neurological and physiological system, high stress levels, and problems regulating their emotions. They might also be abused themselves.

Many mothers who leave these situations report that they resolved to leave their batterer only after they became aware of how their children were being negatively affected. For instance, when these mothers observed their sons engaging in animal cruelty or mistreating their sisters, they slowly recognized that if nothing was done to break the cycle, their sons would grow up to also become batterers.

Why do parents engage in psychological maltreatment? Like all dysfunctional behavior patterns, there are many reasons. It is possible that some parents may be unaware that their actions are psychologically damaging (this may be the case with some children exposed to intimate partner violence). However, in most cases, parents are likely aware of the damage they are doing. Parents psychologically abuse their offspring for many reasons:

- Their children are unwanted.
- They dislike, disapprove of, or resent their children.
- They have a deviant childrearing belief system.
- They lack childrearing knowledge or have unrealistic expectations.
- They themselves were abused as children.
- They lack awareness of or empathy for the child.
- They are stressed and have little social support.
- They have emotional problems and mistreat their children because of their own needs.
- They are poverty stricken, so they exploit their children for financial gain.

Box 14.7 addresses one type of child psychological maltreatment that typically involves sexual and physical maltreatment—that of child trafficking.

Box 14.7 Child Trafficking

It is estimated that around the world, more than 7.8 million children are held in slavery. Most of these children are in forced labor, including 1.8 million child prostitutes, and some 300,000 children have been coerced to become child soldiers. Child slavery is a global problem: Asia and the Pacific are the regions with the highest incidence of child slaves, followed by Latin America, the Caribbean, Africa, Eastern Europe, and then the Middle East. But slavery also occurs in the United States. Boys are usually trafficked to provide labor for farms or to be involved in the drug trade. Girls are enslaved for sexual exploitation or domestic service.

Why would parents have their children enslaved? In some cases, children are abducted. The more common cause is extreme poverty. Selling or trading a child to extinguish a debt is not an uncommon practice in developing countries. When poverty is compounded by a natural disaster or an illness in the family, the parents believe they are left with no choice or other means of survival (van de Glind & Kooijmans, 2008). In Haiti, it is estimated that somewhere between 150,000 and 500,000 children work as *restaveks*, or unpaid domestic laborers, and are frequently subjected to physical and sexual abuse (Balsari, Lemery, Williams, & Nelson, 2010).

Psychological maltreatment is regarded as a form of dysfunctional parenting, and it may manifest itself more commonly than we think. Murray Straus and Carolyn Field (2003) argued that most parents in the United States engage in at least one form of psychological aggression: yelling in anger. In their sample of parents of children ages two to four years, almost all parents reported periodic or frequent yelling, screaming, or shouting at their children. In fact, after reasoning, yelling at children is often found to be the most frequent parental disciplinary response to misbehavior (e.g., Lansford, Wager, Bates, Dodge, & Pettit, 2012). Does this behavior constitute psychological abuse? Some researchers, such as sociologist Murray Straus, argue that it does because it terrorizes children. Clearly, more research is needed to investigate this ubiquitous manifestation of child maltreatment and to explore the continuum of child effects from mild to severe.

Co-Occurring Maltreatment

Ironically, one limitation of the child maltreatment research has been that it artificially categorizes child maltreatment into one of the four categories discussed above. The fact that more than one kind of maltreatment often co-occurs has frequently been overlooked in efforts to understand the different expressions of this tragedy (Appel & Holden, 1998). Investigators have been examining how individual children are multiply maltreated, also known as **poly-victimization** (Finkelhor, Ormrod, Turner, & Hamby, 2005). Using a telephone survey, children and youth or their parents reported on 48 different forms of direct or indirect victimization, such as witnessing shooting or bombing. Children and youth ages 10 to 17 years were asked the questions; for younger children, a parent was asked to report on behalf of the child. In a nationally representative sample of 2,030 respondents, the investigators determined that 38.7% of the sample had been poly-victimized (Finkelhor, Turner, Ormrod, Hamby, & Kracke, 2009). Twenty-two percent of the sample had experienced four or more forms of abuse. Other investigators also find high rates of co-occurrence of violence. Mennen, Kim, Sang, and Trickett (2010) found that 54% of a sample of 9- to 12-year-old children had experienced at least two forms of maltreatment.

Does experiencing two or more forms of child maltreatment make it worse for a child? The evidence indicates that it does. For example, a study of 8,667 adults (Edwards, Holden, Felitti, & Anda, 2003) investigated reports of childhood maltreatment and current mental health. About one-third (34.6%) of the participants reported multiple forms of maltreatment (physical abuse, sexual abuse, or exposure to intimate partner violence). The adults who revealed they were survivors of one form of childhood maltreatment reported lower levels of mental health well-being than did the adults who indicated they had not experienced any of these three types of abuse. This pattern was especially pronounced in individuals who were also exposed to severe emotional abuse. Similarly, those adults who reported all three types of maltreatment were functioning less well than those who reported two types. In sum, these data support a dose-response view of the effects of maltreatment—the stronger the dose of abuse, the worse the outcomes (see Figure 14.5).

Figure 14.5 Dose-Response Effects of Maltreatment

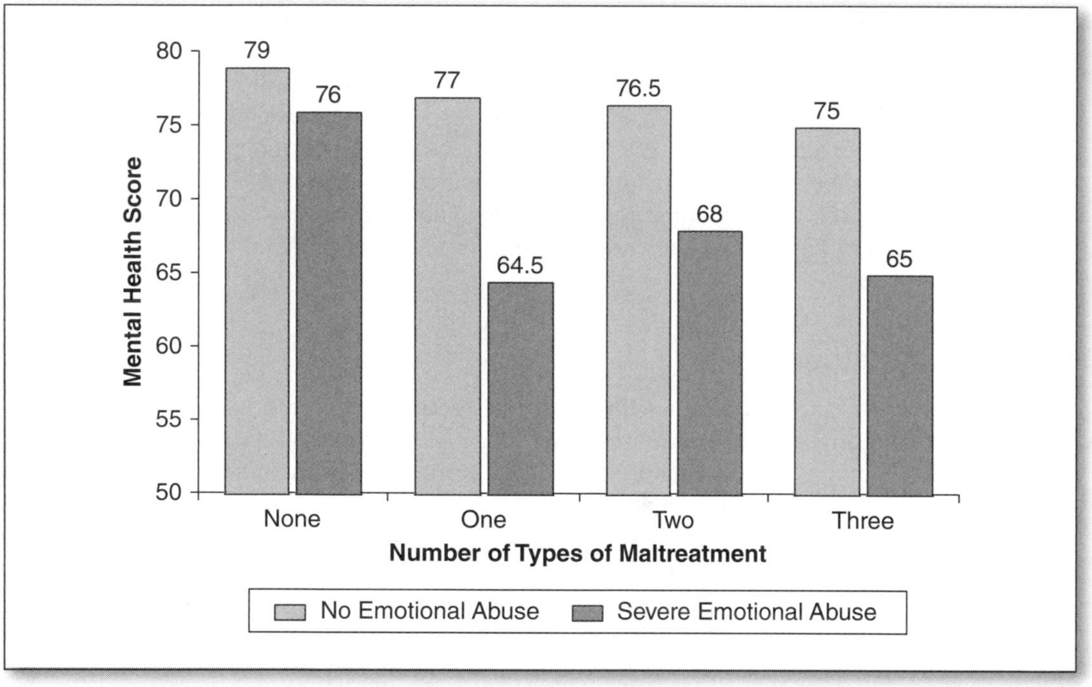

Source: Edwards et al., 2003.

MALTREATMENT ACROSS TIME AND COUNTRY

Determining the prevalence of child maltreatment is a difficult task. The United States maintains excellent statistical records about the occurrence of many different problems. But in the case of child maltreatment, the quality of statistical prevalence estimates depends on a variety of methodological considerations, including the source of the data (e.g., Child Protective Services reports, hospital records, self-reports), how maltreatment was defined and assessed, the time frame used (e.g., past month, past year, lifetime), the sample size, and the sample characteristics (including the sampling method).

The incidence rate of child maltreatment reported in the introduction of this chapter comes from the National Child Abuse and Neglect Data System (NCANDS). That organization collects official incidence reports from Child Protective Services and professionals in schools, hospitals, and other agencies to determine how widespread the problem is. However, those estimates are likely low because many forces influence which acts are recorded: budgets, political agendas, and varying definitions (Tolan et al., 2006).

Is the rate of child maltreatment changing? The rate of substantiated child maltreatment has seen declines over the past 20 years, particularly in the rates of physical and sexual abuse (Child Trends, 2013). For example, in 1994, the total number of child maltreatment cases was 1,032,000 (15.2 per thousand children), but by 2011, the number was down to 681,000 (9.1 per thousand). However, since 2007, there have been only very modest annual declines. On the other hand, there is some evidence of increasing rates of child fatalities due to abuse. Government estimates were that 1,077 children were killed as a result of abuse in 1996 versus 1,570 in 2011 (Child Trends, 2013). Part of the reason could be more accurately determining the cause of child death through committees in many states that carefully review the records of all child fatalities. These Child Fatality Review committees then make official determinations about the cause of death. However, the data do appear to illustrate a real increase in the number of child deaths.

Each year, more evidence concerning the rates of maltreatment in countries outside the United States is becoming available. Although it is difficult to compare rates across the different studies due to methodological differences, it is clear that child maltreatment is a pervasive problem in every country where it has been assessed. For example, in the study mentioned in Chapter 13, Des Runyan and his colleagues (2010) assessed harsh child discipline (kicked, choked, smothered with hand or pillow, burned/scalded or branded, beat, shook child less than two years old, hit with object) in six countries (Brazil, Chile, Egypt, India, Philippines, and the U.S. [North and South Carolina]). Based on reports from 14,239 mothers, the percent of children who received harsh discipline ranged from a low of 9.1% in one Indian urban, non-slum community to a high of 74% in an Indian rural community. Data from the United States indicated that 25% of children received harsh discipline, the same rate as Chile but lower than Egypt (46%) or the Philippines (56%).

Jennifer Lansford and Kirby Deater-Deckard (2012) analyzed an even larger sample of countries and parents. They compared reports of discipline from 30,470 families in 24 countries. Across all the countries, 16% of caregivers reported they or someone in the home had used severe physical violence on the child in the past month. That percent ranged from 1% (Belarus, Kazakhstan, and Ukraine) to a high of 40% (Mongolia and Yemen). Based on those and other studies, it is clear that physical child maltreatment is a ubiquitous international problem and the United States is not among the countries with the highest rates of child maltreatment [Preview Question].

Box 14.8 Reporting Abuse: What to Do

All states in the United States (as well as the District of Columbia, American Samoa, Guam, Northern Mariana Islands, Puerto Rico, and the U.S. Virgin Islands) have laws about who is required to report suspected cases of child maltreatment (Child Welfare Information Gateway, 2012). For example, in Texas, anyone who suspects a child is being abused, neglected, or exploited must report it to Department of Family and Protective Services (1-800-252-5400). Those who report suspected abuse "in good faith" are immune from liability and their names are kept confidential. However, you can be held liable if you do not report suspected abuse. For information about each state's reporting laws, go to the Child Welfare Information Gateway site (https://www.childwelfare.gov/systemwide/laws_policies/state/index.cfm). Regardless of statutory law, it is incumbent upon adults to protect children who are (or have been) abused. It is everyone's ethical, moral—and in some cases, legal—obligation to report suspected abuse.

PROTECTING MALTREATED CHILDREN: FOSTER PARENTS

The scope of child maltreatment is staggering. Child Protective Services personnel in the United States received 3.4 million reports of possible child maltreatment involving some 6.3 million children (U.S. Department of Health and Human Services, 2012). Credible reports are then investigated by case workers, when there are adequate staff and resources to do so. Child Protective Services investigators face the dilemma of whether to remove children from their homes (thereby protecting them from possible additional abuse but separating them from the familiarity of family) or to keep the family together under a policy called **family preservation** (which may or may not place the children at risk for continued abuse).

Based on risk assessments and other considerations, about one-fifth of child victims are removed from their home and placed in foster care. Foster care for children began in the late 1800s, but it wasn't until the 1960s that the federal government began to provide substantial funds for paying foster parents (Haugaard & Hazan, 2002). By 2012, there were almost 400,000 children in foster care (Child Welfare Information Gateway, 2013). However, the system cannot handle the demand: Many children are waiting for foster families.

Why do adults become foster parents? Sometimes the foster parent wants to help a child, who may be a relative. Often, the adult wants to do something positive for the community, likes having children around, or does it as a source of income (Wilson, Fyson, & Newstone, 2006). However, foster parenting can be extremely difficult, given the damage that has been done to many maltreated children. Foster parents need to provide all the normal parenting functions as well as several unique ones. The parents have to work closely with the social workers and, sometimes, the child's biological parents. Foster parents also need to form attachments with the child despite the recognition that the relationship is, by definition, a temporary one.

Foster parenting is a challenging task as mentioned in Chapter 11; the temporary surrogate parent of a maltreated child needs skills beyond the repertoire of "normal" parenting. A good foster parent must provide not only the basic childrearing requirements for the child but also be able to deal with the child's special needs, his or her history of maltreatment and trauma, and the changes in attachment figures and family structure (Berrick & Skivenes, 2012). There are further complexities foster parents must navigate as a result of working with the foster care bureaucracy and becoming attached to a child who will leave before long (Combs-Orme & Orme, 2014).

Not surprisingly, 30% to 50% of foster parents quit their roles. The most frequent reasons cited include inadequate agency support (40%), poor communication with foster care workers (33%), and that the children were too difficult to handle (34%) (Rhodes, Orme, & Buehler, 2001). A common problem is that foster children have high rates of disorganized attachment, poor self-regulation, and externalizing problems (Dozier, Zeanah, & Bernard, 2013). Despite the considerable stressors and challenges, many foster parents are committed to the task and delight in the child (Bernard & Dozier, 2011). Only a very small percentage of foster parents maltreat their charges. Each year, somewhere between 0.3% and 2% of children in foster care in the United States are maltreated (Biehal, 2014).

One recent development in dealing with the problem of child maltreatment is the advent of Child Advocacy Centers across the United States. These centers were created in an effort to minimize re-traumatizing a child survivor of sexual abuse and maximize the likelihood of successful prosecution of the perpetrator. See Box 14.9 for a description of these centers.

Box 14.9 Reducing Additional Trauma: Child Advocacy Centers

In 1984, Bud Cramer, a district attorney in Alabama (who subsequently became a congressman), proposed a novel idea to deal with the aftermath of the disclosure of serious child maltreatment. Rather than having a child face multiple interviews by authorities in environments that children find cold and scary (such as police stations), why not streamline the process so children would have to undergo only one interview in a child-friendly environment? A model of child advocacy centers was subsequently created. Three of the model's hallmarks are: (a) centers are located in houses designed to be child-friendly environments; (b) children undergo one interview and medical exam (if needed), which is conducted and recorded by specially trained professionals; and (c) multidisciplinary teams (law enforcement, Child Protective Services, prosecution, mental health, medical, and victim advocates) meet at the center to facilitate communication and prosecution of the perpetrators. Centers may also provide therapy and family support services.

Today, there are more than 700 such centers in the United States. These centers provide a dramatic improvement for the care of traumatized children in the wake of abuse. Formal evaluations of the efficacy of the centers are beginning to be published (see Faller & Palusci, 2007), but to date, there is no information as to whether the centers have resulted in more successful criminal prosecution of the perpetrators.

THE COSTS OF CHILD MALTREATMENT

Although the mental, social, and physical health costs of child maltreatment are obviously of paramount importance, there are also considerable financial costs associated with the problem. The costs incurred are not just for the physical and mental health problems. Rather, a comprehensive bill that includes also the costs of health care, criminal justice costs, productivity loss, welfare, and special education for nonfatal child maltreatment is estimated to be $210,012 per case (Fang, Brown, Florence, & Mercy, 2012).

Consider just the expenses borne by communities within the criminal justice system. Expenses include staffing Child Protective Services to investigate into reports of maltreatment, prosecutors to take the perpetrators to trial, judges to try the cases, foster parents to care for the children, and prisons to house the perpetrators. More than a decade ago, the costs of investigating, prosecuting, and incarcerating one offender and providing treatment the victim were estimated to add up to $144,000 per child (Becker & Hunter, 1992). Further costs accrue over the long term when abused children go untreated. They are more likely than other children to run away from home, drop out of school, become involved in prostitution, abuse drugs, or end up in prison. The total lifetime economic burden from child maltreatment (including fatalities) in just the year 2008, based on the substantiated cases of maltreated, was estimated to be $124 billion (Fang et al., 2012).

Even more concerning than the financial expenses are the costs to the survivors' mental and physical health. There is now ample evidence about the pervasive negative effects of maltreatment on individuals' functioning (Moffitt, 2013). As identified by Kendall-Tackett (2013), there are five interrelated pathways through which maltreatment affects the survivors' health: physiological (due to the body's reactions to trauma), emotional (due to trauma and depression), behavioral (as a consequence of survivors engaging in harmful behaviors such as substance abuse), cognitive (due to developing negative beliefs about oneself and others), and social (as a result of difficulties in maintaining close, healthy relationships).

One way to reduce costs is by providing effective treatments for survivors of maltreatment. Therapeutic interventions, such as one approach utilizing attachment theory and family systems theory for survivors (e.g., Karakurt & Silver, 2014) and one for family members of abused children (van Toledo & Seymour, 2013), are essential. Parenting interventions for perpetrators (e.g., Chaffin & Friedrich, 2004) are also needed so that parents do not re-abuse their child or abuse other children. However, these efforts do not address the causes of the problem. The final chapter will consider some ways to prevent child maltreatment and other problems that children face.

CHAPTER SUMMARY

This chapter began with a question: How could parents maltreat their children? It is not a new problem: There is ample evidence that children have been abused since antiquity. Although the matter has been a social concern since the second half of the 20th century, it is estimated that 1.25 million children in the United States are maltreated each year. As is now evident, the question of why parents abuse their children is complex and has many answers. Parents mistreat their children in four basic ways: physical abuse, neglect, sexual abuse, and psychological maltreatment. Each type of maltreatment has been associated with different causes, including high levels of stress and poverty, psychological problems, social cognition deficits, and adults having themselves been abused as children. Moreover, it is increasingly clear that different types of maltreatment may co-occur. The consequences of abuse range from temporary bruises to behavior problems to brain damage and death.

Although child maltreatment is a serious problem in the United States, it is even more prevalent in many other countries. One way to protect children from future abuse is to remove them from abusive parents and place them in foster care. However, there is an inadequate supply of these temporary parents and a high rate of failure, as indicated by foster parents who prematurely return the maltreated children. Child maltreatment is a significant burden to the children who experience it but maltreatment also results in a high cost to society.

THOUGHT QUESTIONS

- Why might children, even when they are abused, want to stay with their parents?
- What variables account for fluctuating rates of maltreatment over time and across nations?
- Which causes of child maltreatment are most difficult to address? Which ones are more amenable to intervention?
- How might the foster parent system be improved?

CHAPTER GLOSSARY

droit du seigneur The "right of the lord"—the medieval doctrine that the head of household could sleep with any subordinate woman in his home.

educational neglect The failure to provide the opportunities and supervision necessary to meet the child's educational needs. Examples include failing to enroll a child in school or allowing the child to frequently skip school.

family preservation A policy whereby children are kept with their abusive parents who have undergone intervention rather than being placed in foster care.

ius primae noctis The doctrine, from the Romans, that the father has the right to have sexual relations with any female member of his household who is his social inferior.

medical neglect A failure to provide timely and necessary medical treatment to a child. This includes refusing to allow a child to be immunized.

physical neglect Occurs when a child's physical needs, such as adequate clothing, shelter, and food, are not met.

poly-victimization When an individual is maltreated in two or more ways.

psychological maltreatment A repeated pattern of caregiver behavior or extreme incident(s) that conveys the message to children that they are worthless, flawed, unloved, unwanted, endangered, or only of value in meeting another's needs.

CHAPTER 15

Social Policy Issues

Chapter Preview: True or False?

- Some countries have laws limiting the number of children you can have.
- The United States is one of three countries that has not ratified the Convention on the Rights of the Child.
- According to some professionals, parents should be licensed to have children.

As the preceding chapters have made clear, many of the major contemporary problems in our society are closely linked to how well families function. A well-functioning family produces children who grow into educated, competent, healthy, and well-adjusted adults. In turn, these adults rear their own children, who also become contributing members of society. But what about those families who saddle their children with experiences that lead to **educational failure**, behavioral and mental health problems, emotional and substance abuse, violence, and unemployment? Parenting is the *single* most important variable implicated in *all* of those maladies. Not the economy. Not the peer group. Parenting. How we raise our children is clearly a social concern.

What role should society and government play in promoting certain behaviors and acting to eliminate others? Some people believe that it is the responsibility of government to take action to address social problems. Many citizens see it otherwise: Government should not infringe on the rights of individuals, which they believe is an inevitable consequence of government intervention. A recent example of health-motivated government intervention occurred in Japan. To reduce health problems associated with obesity, a national law went into effect in 2008 requiring annual waistline measurements of all adults between the ages of 40 and 74 years. Those whose waistlines exceed the government limits (33.5 inches for men, 35.4 inches for nonpregnant women) and who have a weight-related ailment must lose weight or their employer (or the local government) will be fined. Although intrusive by American standards, the new law is relatively uncomplicated compared to the many measures that have been proposed in the United States to regulate an even more influential health variable than waistlines: the dynamics of the family.

This chapter begins with a description of how American families have changed over the past half century. We'll review some of the costs associated with several social problems. The rest of the chapter addresses social policies and parenting intervention programs of the past, those of the present, and some controversial ideas for the future.

THE CHANGING AMERICAN FAMILY

The family structure has undergone dramatic changes over the past half century, particularly in developed nations. Some sociologists, such as David Popenoe (2005), have argued that these social trends reflect alarming negative changes in the family. Political groups latch onto this attitude and often bemoan "the death of the American family." Others, such as psychologist Ross Parke (2013), counter with sensitive questions and research-based answers to address this ever-changing profile of family structures. Clearly, big changes have been afoot for at least two to three generations, and it is important for policymakers and others look into these widespread changes with open minds.

What are some of the easily identifiable changes in family patterns in the past few generations? Popenoe identified four:

- Fewer number of children born
- Proportionately more unwed mothers
- Proportionately more women in the labor force with young children
- An increased divorce rate

The four factors that Popenoe pinpointed are not mutually exclusive; each impacts and is affected by the other in complex ways. The reasons for these changing trends are multifaceted: social, cultural, health and technology related, and economic. They are a consequence of personal and societal pressures and even positive trends affecting both men and women, with sometimes-dramatic consequences for families. Arguments can be made on both sides of the table about whether the above changes are a harbinger of societal "death" or a bellwether of more flexible, diverse, and ultimately more accommodating families, as suggested in Ross Parke's recent book, *Future Families* (2013). Regardless, this is an important discussion to entertain.

Let us briefly examine the four changing family trends. Currently, the childbearing rate in the United States is an average of 2.1 children per adult female, a rate much lower than the average of more than 3.5 children per mother in the late 1950s (Bongaarts & Feeney, 1998; U.S. Census Bureau, 2011). This trend reflects several social changes, including the desire for fewer children, dissatisfaction with parenthood, and a decrease in the stigma of childlessness. A second change is the dramatic increase in the number of children born to single women. As discussed in Chapter 11, currently, 40.7% of all births in the United States are to single women, up from 15% in 2002 and 5% in 1960 (Martin, Hamilton, Osterman, Curtin, & Mathews, 2013). There are distinct racial-ethnic differences in single motherhood: 28% of White women, 75% of Black women, and 51% of Latinas bore children as single mothers in 2007. The third trend Popenoe mentions is the increased percentage of mothers of young children who are gainfully employed. Whether single, married, or divorced, most mothers today are in the labor force. In 1960, only 19% of women with children under six years old worked outside the home. Today, that figure has climbed to 64.8% (Bureau of Labor Statistics, 2013). Not only are more mothers working outside the home, but they are also returning to the paid labor force sooner after childbirth than did mothers from previous generations. The fourth and final trend identified by Popenoe is the increased rate of divorce. The United States claims title to one of the highest divorce rates in the world. The likelihood that a marriage will end in divorce ranges from 43% to 66%, depending on how the statistics are computed. Each year, more than 1 million children witness the dissolution of their parents' marriage. By the time they are 16 years old, more than 40% of all children in the United States will have experienced their parents' divorce (Amato & Keith, 1991).

From a policy standpoint, it is easy to identify the economic (and other resource) pressures that may accompany these four familial cultural shifts. Typically, two parents can provide more resources for a child than can one. Two parents (who successfully co-parent) can share tasks and attend to children while simultaneously holding down commitments outside the family. Finances and attending to children represent two challenging pressures for all families. These pressures are exacerbated in single-parent families.

Although it is difficult to identify all the causes of the surge in single motherhood, many single mothers are cohabiting with their partners and may or may not plan to marry their partners at a later date. The degree to which never-married single mothers are receiving financial support from fathers is variable. No one questions that children benefit from positive paternal support: financial, emotional, and otherwise. However, the majority of fathers do not pay child support for their children. For example, one study of more than 1,000 nonresident fathers found that only 24% were making regular formal child support payments (Nepomnyaschy, 2007). The amount of child support paid depends on many factors, such as the net income of the noncustodial parent, the number of children, which parent pays health insurance, and the state of residence.

Interestingly, the average annual child support payment in 2010 was $5,150 (U.S. Census Bureau, 2012). Forcing "deadbeat" fathers to financially support their children is a difficult task, partly because some of the fathers move out of state to avoid making payments. Nevertheless, the government spends some $2 billion each year collecting $10.8 billion in child support payments for more than 3.4 million families (Wheaton & Sorensen, 1998). It is estimated that fathers owe some $105 billion in child support (Hatcher, 2007).

In addition to financial pressures on single-parent families, there are pressures on working families for the provision of child care. One effect of the increased level of maternal employment is the expanded need for alternative child care. Quality child care is expensive. The annual costs of full-time day care for one child can range from $3,000 to $16,000 or more, depending on where one lives, the age of the child, and the quality of the center, as mentioned in Chapter 7. For low-income single parents, daycare expenses can consume more than one-third of the family's income.

An extension of the need for quality supervised care of children can be seen in the need for quality after-school programming. Many elementary-age children are unsupervised after school. These "latchkey" or "self-care" children make up a substantial number: Between 2 and 4 million children are currently unsupervised after school. Generally, self-care children pass the time in unsupervised peer play or in front of the television. These children are more likely to experience emotional problems or experiment with alcohol, drugs, stealing, or sex than are children who are supervised (see Aizer, 2004). They are also more likely to suffer potentially hazardous situations. However, if the children were able to attend after-school programs, they would likely benefit from the experience. Positive academic, social, and behavioral effects have been documented in two meta-analyses of research into the efficacy of after-school programs (Granger, 2008). Quality after-school programming may, however, be a piecemeal solution to a larger problem, which touches on the interplay of public policy and children's needs. The structure of the academic year and school hours is an antiquated system that was based upon the needs of an agrarian society dating from the late 1800s. Some educators today believe that change in this system is long overdue and advocate an extended school day and year-round schooling. Such widespread change could serve both working families (who need child supervision) and youth (who need improved educational opportunities).

THE SOCIETAL COSTS OF FAMILY PROBLEMS

Over one hundred years ago, President Theodore Roosevelt was concerned for the needs of children in the United States. In a special address to Congress in 1909, he said "Each of our children represents either a potential addition to the productive capacity and the enlightened citizenship of the nation, or, if allowed to suffer from neglect, a potential addition to the destructive forces of the community." Roosevelt looked out on a nation where, he said, "child mortality rates were high, millions of children were employed, school attendance was low, poverty was widespread, and countless children dependent on the community languished in almshouses and orphanages" (Yarrow, 2009). It is fascinating to note that while the concerns we have today are often quite different than those of a hundred years ago, the need for child advocacy remains strong. Children need supportive families and a supportive community to realize their potential.

What are the societal indicators of children's well-being? Since the 1970s, a variety of indicators have been considered (Lippman, Moore, & McIntosh, 2011). Child Trends (http://www.childtrends.org) now publishes more than 100 indicators! The privately funded Annie E. Casey Foundation makes an annual assessment of child well-being in their publication, *Kids Count* (http://kidscount.org). The 2014 Data Book looks at the reporting year of 2012 and shows us a "national report card" on how well the nation, as well as individual states, are doing in terms of 16 key indices of child well-being. These sixteen indices are research derived and are often linked to poverty and/or material well-being. According to the 2014 Data Book, the five states with the best scorecard for children are (from #1–#5): Massachusetts, Vermont, Iowa, New Hampshire, and Minnesota. The five states with the worst scorecard for children are (from #46–#50): Arizona, Louisiana, Nevada, New Mexico, and Mississippi. The 16 indices appear below, in Table 15.1, along with the corresponding percentage of children in the United States.

It is clear from the statistics in Table 15.1 that while the United States is one of the wealthiest nations in the world, there are serious deficiencies for many of its children. Particularly concerning is the sheer number of children living in poverty (23% of all children in the United States) and the high percentages of underachieving children in grade school and middle school. These are the kinds of problems that can be addressed and solved with good social policies.

These challenges are not only social problems for individuals and families but constitute a significant economic drain upon society. An economic analysis of the cost of family problems to our society helps to bring into focus the scope of the maladies. Financial costs associated with four problem areas will be briefly described: births to teenagers, academic underachievement and dropouts, juvenile delinquency, and child maltreatment.

Teen Pregnancy

In 2012, 305,420 of the babies born in the United States were born to teen mothers ages 15 to19. Almost 90% of these mothers were not married (U.S. Department of Health and Human Services, 2014). More often than not, these mothers are not finished with their high school education, and they do not have secure employment. Their prospects for future education, college, and employment that will lift them above the poverty level are not good. Obviously, the financial burden to society, both in terms of their unrealized potential and in terms of the needs of their dependent children, is high.

Moreover, young adolescent mothers are also at high risk for giving birth early (DuPlessis, Bell, & Richards, 1997). Teen mothers are more likely than mothers over age 20 to give birth prematurely (before 37 completed weeks of pregnancy). Between 2003 and 2005, preterm birth rates averaged 14.5% for women under age 20 compared to 11.9% for women ages 20 to 29. Babies born prematurely face an increased risk of newborn health

Table 15.1 Key Indicators of Children's Well-Being in the United States

Economic Well-Being	
23%	Children in poverty
31%	Parents lack secure employment
38%	Living in households with high housing cost burden
8%	Teens not in school and not working
Education	
54%	Children not attending preschool
66%	Fourth graders not proficient in reading
66%	Eighth graders not proficient in math
19%	High school students not graduating on time
Health	
8%	Low-birth-weight babies
7%	Children without health insurance
26	Child and teen deaths per 100,000
6%	Teens who abuse alcohol or drugs
Family and Community	
35%	Children in single-parent families
15%	Children in families where head of household lacks high school diploma
13%	Children living in high-poverty areas
29	Teen births per 1,000

Source: Annie E. Casey Foundation, 2014.

problems, long-term disabilities, and even death (March of Dimes, 2012). Recall from Chapter 6 that premature birth occurs for many reasons; the specific cause is often unknown. However, adolescent mothers are the least likely group to obtain prenatal care (with a total cost of only $1,400) and are three times more likely to give birth to a premature infant (Hewlett, 1991). Infants with very low birth weight require one of the most expensive types of hospitalization; costs associated with a premature delivery can easily exceed $100,000, depending on the neonates' birth weight and severity of resulting medical problems (Almond, Chay, & Lee, 2005).

Low-birth-weight babies are also at higher risk for developmental delay and other developmental problems, which can make it more difficult for these children to be successful in school later on.

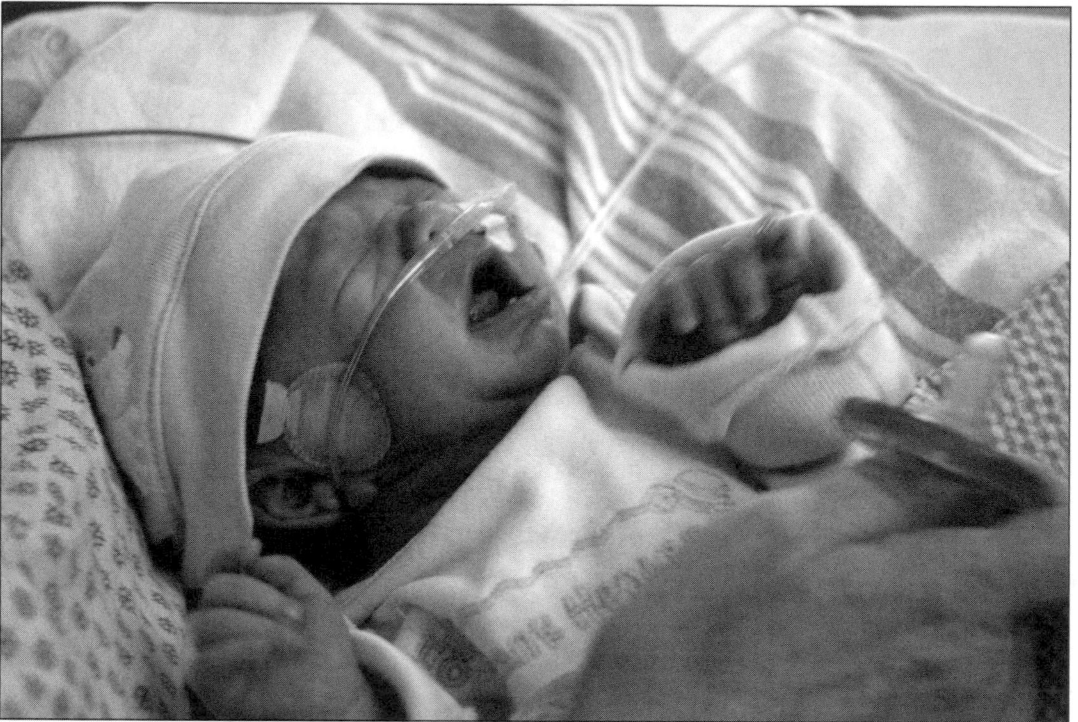

Photo 15.1 A baby boy born five weeks premature is cared for in a neonatal intensive care unit.

Source: Photograph by J. P. Bell

Underachievement and School Dropouts

The United States educational system is failing to give most children the basic skills they need to continue their education and to succeed in the workplace. In 2011, the vast majority of fourth grade children (68%) were not performing at a proficiency level in reading for their grade. Further, the majority of eighth grade children (66%) could not demonstrate basic proficiency in mathematics skills. Our failure to educate children in these basic skills is alarming—and has serious economic implications for society. Children who are failing in reading and math will struggle mightily when they get to high school—if they even continue to attend school. They are at great risk for school failure and dropout.

The costs of educational failure—that is, an adolescent dropping out of school—are high, both on individual and societal levels. In 2012, 19% of high school students were not graduating on time; 8% of all teens were not in school nor were they working (Annie E. Casey Foundation, 2014). Approximately 1.2 million high school students drop out of school each year (Julian & Kominski, 2011). Failing to complete high school means a lower income potential for that individual, as can be seen in Figure 15.1. Dropouts are also a drain on the economy. When people earn less, they pay less in tax. Quitting school is also

Figure 15.1 Who Makes How Much Money? Average Annual Income in 2012 by Educational Attainment

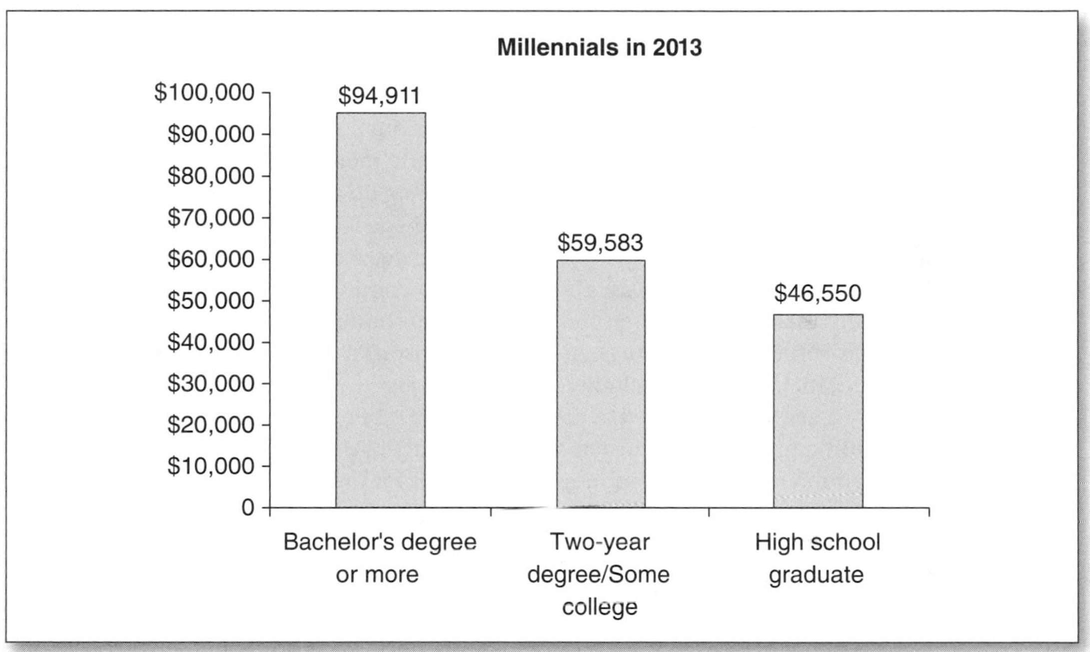

Source: Pew Research Center, 2014.

associated with teenage parenthood, crime, and time spent in (a taxpayer-supported) prison. School dropouts are more likely to require public services (such as food stamps and subsidized housing) and health care assistance. According to one analysis, each student who drops out of school costs the nation $260,000 over that individual's lifetime. That adds up to $ 3 trillion each decade (Amos, 2008)!

Although college is expensive, a recent study into the financial benefits of higher education shows it is well worth it. A typical college graduate will earn $650,000 more than the typical high school graduate over a 40-year career (Pew Research Center, 2014). However, individuals who drop out of high school almost never make it to college.

Disconnected Youth and Crime

Another major financial drain on society is caused by youth who become unneeded, disconnected from family and society. Many such youth engage in crime. When costs associated with youth crime are added up (the juvenile justice system, property damage and loss, medical and psychological expenses, etc.), the United States spends $1 trillion on crime. A significant portion of that is due to juvenile crime. It is estimated that violent youth cost society from $1.6 million to $2.3 million (Dodge, 2008). This bill results from the direct costs to the victim, court, incarceration, and treatment. So once youngsters enter a state of high risk (due often to poverty or poor parenting), they are already expensive to society, whether or not they ever end up in the juvenile justice system.

Child Maltreatment

The number of abused and neglected children in the United States is also staggering (estimated at 1.25 million) and represents another serious social health problem. The costs associated with a maltreated child include physical and mental health problems, pain and trauma, and lost productivity. One estimate, after adding up all the expenses of health care, productivity loss, welfare, criminal justice costs, and special education for nonfatal child maltreatment came to $210,012 *per child* (Fang, Brown, Florence, & Mercy, 2012). If left untreated, the costs associated with abused children continue to increase. These children are more likely than other children to run away from home, drop out of school, become involved in prostitution, abuse drugs, or end up in prison. The total lifetime economic burden from child maltreatment (including fatalities) in just the year 2008, based on 579,000 substantiated cases, was estimated to cost the nation $124 billion (Fang et al., 2012).

Society ultimately bears the burden of footing many of the financial expenses resulting from family problems. Spending money on treatment for these problems is necessary, yes. But is it also avoidable? Social policies are the best way to prevent new generations of individuals falling prey to the same harmful, expensive problems.

SOCIAL POLICY RESPONSES

Social policy refers to the principles that guide decisions or efforts to achieve desired goals (and avoid undesired results) at a group level. These policies often appear as federal, state, or local laws, but they can also be found in business policies and community standards.

Throughout history, many law and policy makers have intended to modify childbearing and childrearing practices. Emperor Augustus of Rome (ruling from 30 BCE to CE 14) introduced laws to promote family life and encourage large families. He limited parental rights to refuse consent to their children's marriage, and in an effort to increase the population, he fined childless couples (Sommerville, 1982). Another legal milestone occurred in Rome some 300 years later, when Emperor Constantine outlawed infanticide.

In 1870, Otto von Bismarck instituted Germany's first social insurance program for those who were disabled or unable to work, such as pregnant women. Since then, Western European countries have continued to lead the world in supporting the family. These countries currently provide guaranteed parental leave with pay after the birth of a child, family allowances based on the number of children in the family, national health insurance, subsidized housing for many families, and vocational and academic opportunities for all children (Kamerman & Kahn, 1989).

Compared with other Western countries, the United States has been slow and reluctant to provide assistance to families. Despite spending more on total health expenditures per capita than 12 other industrialized nations, the quality of health care provided to children in the United States ranks significantly below that of the other countries (Duderstadt, 2007).

Even more surprising is that the United States is not among the 70 countries that provide medical care and financial assistance to all pregnant women. The relatively high rate of infant mortality in the United States is likely attributable to this lack of prenatal care; 55 countries have lower rates (Central Intelligence Agency, 2014).

The United States also measures up poorly against other industrialized countries with regard to maternity leave and childcare subsidies. In a survey of 11 industrialized nations, the United States was the only one that did not provide universal, paid, job-protected maternity leave as a national policy (Waldfogel, 2001). Although the Family and Medical Leave Act of 1993 required employers to provide up to 12 weeks of leave for employees to care for a newborn, newly adopted, or fostered child or for a sick relative, mothers and fathers are not required to be paid during their leave. Some of the best companies in the United States *do* provide paid leave, however, and in 2004, California enacted a paid six-week family-leave program. Still, many other countries (169 out of 173) provide a *guaranteed* maternity leave with income. In 66 of those nations, fathers can also receive paid paternity leave (Heyman, Earle, & Hayes, 2007). Similarly, many Western countries subsidize daycare costs, but the United States does not.

Early Programs and Bills in the United States

Specifying social policy in the United States is difficult because there is no explicit national family policy. Instead, there exists a history of legislative bills, initiatives, and actions adopted at federal, state, and local levels. A study of this patchwork of social policy toward children reveals two competing orientations. On the one hand, the doctrine of ***parens patriae*** has been around since colonial days: The state is the ultimate parent of every child (Hawes, 1991). This doctrine provided the foundation for child protection laws established as early as 1735. That was the year Massachusetts passed a law providing for removal of children from neglectful parents and placing them with foster families. During the 1890s, a number of private efforts established institutions for aiding and protecting children (such as the Children's Aid Society and the Society for the Prevention of Cruelty to Children [SPCC]). Box 15.1 describes the history of the founding of the SPCC in the United States.

Box 15.1 Mary Ellen Wilson's Landmark Case and the Protection of Maltreated Children

Mary Ellen Wilson was a 10-year-old girl, neglected and physically abused by her stepmother. A community worker, Etta Wheeler, learned that the girl was being abused and investigated what legal avenues were available to help Mary Ellen. Etta soon learned that New York authorities were reluctant to intervene in family matters. She then contacted Henry Bergh, the founder of the American Society for the Prevention of Cruelty to Animals (the society was first established in England in 1824). They took the case to court.

(Continued)

(Continued)

On April 10, 1874, Mary Ellen testified:

Mamma [her stepmother] has been in the habit of whipping and beating me almost every day. She used to whip me with a twisted whip—a raw hide. The whip always left a black-and-blue mark on my body. I have now the black-and-blue marks on my head, which were made by mamma, and also a cut on the side of my forehead, which was made by a pair of scissors. She struck me with the scissors and cut me. I have no recollection of ever having been kissed by anyone—have never been kissed by mamma. I have never been taken on my mamma's lap and caressed or petted. I never dared to speak to anybody, because if I did, I would get whipped. I do not know for what I was whipped—mamma never said anything to me when she whipped me. I do not want to go back to live with mamma, because she beats me so. (Watkins, 1990, p. 502)

The case resulted in the establishment of the legal rights of children to live free from abuse and neglect. It changed the course of child protection in America and resulted in the creation of the first child protective agency in the world, the New York Society for the Prevention of Cruelty to Children (Jalongo, 2006).

Orphanages were originally established in the United States to house children whose parents had died. Subsequently, their purpose expanded to house homeless and maltreated children (Shealy, 1995). One well-known example is Boys Town, established by Father Edward Flanagan, an Irish immigrant priest. With the motto, "There are no bad boys. There is only bad environment, bad training, bad example, bad thinking," he opened his orphanage in 1917. What began as a small home for five homeless boys began filling a great need and so grew rapidly. In 1979, the programs were expanded to include girls in need, and today, this organization cares for more than 51,000 boys and girls in more than a dozen states.

In contrast to state intervention (*parens patriae*), the opposite and competing orientation is one of **noninterference**, which dates back to the Constitution. How people in power interpret the Constitution can be the determining influence on government policy toward family rights and freedoms. Not surprisingly, conflict often erupts between parents and those individuals who seek to uphold the rights of those parents' children. Despite this tension, Congress has passed much important legislation designed to protect and enhance the lives of children and families. Five federal laws stand out as particularly significant.

The Keating-Owen Bill of 1916 regulated the type and amount of work that could be required of a child. It effectively controlled some of the egregious abuses of children associated with child labor. For example, one British child-labor reformer visited some of Alabama's cotton mills in 1900. He observed children as young as six and seven years old working 12 hours a day, with only half an hour of rest (Hawes, 1991). Although the Keating-Owen Bill was declared unconstitutional two years after it became law, it set the stage for subsequent federal bills that, in conjunction with state compulsory school-attendance laws (beginning with Massachusetts in 1852 and concluding with Mississippi in 1918), resulted in a rapid decline of child labor in the United States.

A second landmark bill was the Sheppard-Towner Maternal and Infancy Protection Act of 1922, designed to reduce infant mortality. The bill created community clinics for maternal and infant hygiene in an effort to establish preventive health care habits. This act marked the first use of federal grants to aid in development and maintenance of state and local social programs. Funds were also made available through this bill to provide prenatal care for women and to hire public-health nurses to teach women about prenatal and child health.

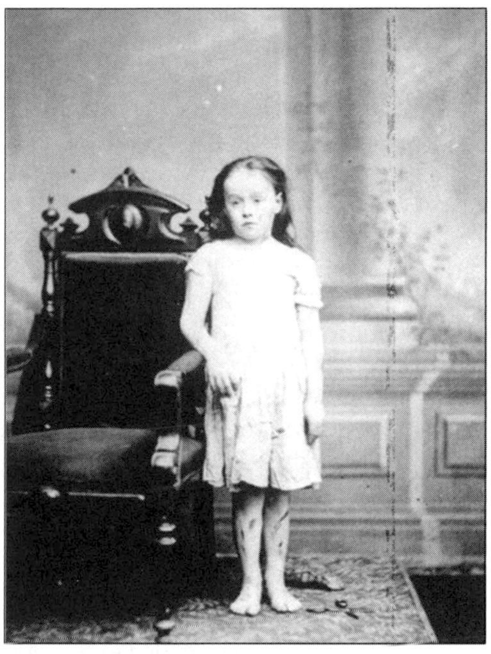

Photo 15.2 Mary Ellen Wilson.

Source: Wikimedia Commons

During the 1930s, two congressional bills helped to establish children's rights. The Social Security Act of 1935 created the Aid to Dependent Children (ADC) program, which then became Aid to Families with Dependent Children (AFDC). As part of the New Deal, it was intended to keep fatherless families together by providing payments to mothers to enable them to stay at home with their children. In addition, the act established various maternal- and child-health programs as well as other child welfare services.

A few years after that bill was passed, a new act concerning child labor was enacted. The Fair Labor Standards Act of 1938 prohibited employment of children less than 16 years old in industries that engaged in interstate commerce. In addition, children under 18 were banned from working in dangerous occupations. These two acts established two precedents for children's rights: some degree of economic security and curtailment of the employment of children and youth.

The Child Abuse Prevention and Treatment Act, passed in 1973, established the National Center on Child Abuse and Neglect (NCCAN). Federal appropriations to the center were intended to (a) develop reliable statistics about the incidence of abuse; (b) create a clearinghouse of information on abuse programs; and (c) sponsor research into the causes, identification, prevention, and treatment of child abuse. Because the act has been consistently underfunded, it has failed to live up to its promise of potentially widespread impact.

Many of these acts and other federal legislation were stimulated by a series of White House Conferences on Children. The first one was held by President Theodore Roosevelt in 1909 to plan the government's role in protecting children. It led to the establishment of the Children's Bureau in 1912. The bureau was mandated to investigate and report on issues concerning the welfare of children, such as infant mortality, illegitimacy, child labor, and juvenile delinquency. Subsequently, the bureau shifted its emphasis to public education, and it is best known for its parent education publications. In 1913, *Prenatal Care* was printed; a year later, a manual devoted to the care of infants appeared. The first two editions of *Infant Care* were based on Dr. Luther Emmett Holt's popular book (described in Chapter 1). Over time, subsequent editions of the manual (it had 12 revisions) relied on more contemporary views of child development and parenting (including Freudian concerns about infant impulses and erogenous zones). By 1921, 1.5 million copies of *Infant Care* had been distributed (Wolfenstein, 1951), and it continues to be published periodically under the title of *Child Care Bulletin*.

For many decades, the White House Conferences reconvened to monitor and examine children's status in society. These conferences have provided the impetus for the creation of a number of bills designed to help children and their families (Zigler & Muenchow, 1984). Besides establishing policy and legislation, they have served to reaffirm the rights of children to parental love and respect. They have also reiterated the goals of ending abject poverty and discrimination, providing equal educational opportunities, and promoting the freedom of all children to pursue the developmental paths they choose (Beck, 1973).

The last conference focused on child care as the single most serious problem for America's families. However, that meeting was held in 1970. Many **child advocates** have cited the subsequent failure to hold another White House Conference on Children as evidence of politicians' lack of concern for children's well-being.

Advocating Children's and Families' Rights

Social policies are tied to perceptions of children and their rights. When a nation views a child as a "subperson" having fewer rights (inherently possessed freedoms) than adults, then the social drive to protect children is reduced. Consequently, to promote the health and welfare of all children, the United Nations sponsored the creation of the Convention on the Rights of the Child. After a lengthy drafting period, it was adopted by the U.N. General Assembly in 1989. It contains 54 articles concerning the civil, political, economic, social, and cultural rights of children (see Box 15.2). Three themes underlie the articles:

1. Children's best interests should be a primary consideration in any policy.
2. Children should be provided with rights that are consistent with their developing capabilities.
3. Children's dignity should be respected.

Box 15.2 A Brief Description of Some of the Articles From the U.N. Convention on Children's Rights

Article 5: Concerns the state's duty to respect the rights and responsibilities of parents and the wider family to provide guidance appropriate to the child's developing capacities.

Article 9: Addresses children's right to (a) live with their parents unless this is incompatible with the children's best interests and (b) maintain contact with both parents if separated from one or both.

Article 12: Deals with the child's right to express an opinion, and to have that opinion taken into account, in any matter or procedure affecting the child.

Article 13: Has to do with the child's right to information and to express his or her views, unless this would violate the rights of others.

Article 14: Speaks to the child's right to freedom of thought, conscience, and religion, subject to appropriate parental guidance and national law.

Article 19: Concerns the state's obligation to (a) protect children from all forms of maltreatment by parents or others responsible for their care and (b) establish programs for prevention of abuse and treatment of victims.

Article 28: Addresses the child's right to education and the state's duty to ensure that primary education (if not more) is free and compulsory. Discipline in schools needs to respect the child's dignity.

Article 29: Indicates that education should focus on (a) developing the child's personality and talents, (b) preparing the child for active life as an adult, (c) fostering respect for basic human rights, and (d) developing respect for the child's own cultural and national values as well as those of others.

Articles 32–36: Deal with the child's rights and the state's obligation to protect children from child labor, drugs, sex, slavery, and other forms of exploitation.

Source: United Nations Office of the High Commissioner for Human Rights, 1990.

All nations that participate in the United Nations (a total of 193), with the exception of three, have ratified the Convention on the Rights of the Child. Those three countries are Somalia, South Sudan, and the United States [Preview Question]. The United States has not ratified the Convention due to opposition from two sources. Political and religious conservatives have organized themselves as vociferous opponents of the Convention because they believe aspects of it could potentially interfere with their own *individual* parental rights. Other opponents argue that the articles conflict with the U.S. Constitution (Cohen, 1996). Concerns raised by opponents include potential limits on a parent's freedom to forcibly remove a child from a religious cult, to choose corporal punishment as discipline, and to homeschool a child. Although the Convention does not explicitly deny these actions to parents, parent rights advocates fear that the Convention's language could allow for such restrictions at some point in the future.

One can reasonably assume that genuine concern for children drives at least part of the argument on both sides of the issue. Individuals who act on their concern for children refer to themselves as *child advocates*. They work to promote the rights of children—distinct from those of their parents—and they have a long history in America as catalysts for positive change. In 1897, the first National Congress of Mothers met and eventually grew into the Parent-Teacher Association (PTA). Family advocate Jane Addams opened Hull House in Chicago, the first "settlement" house for families, in 1889 in order to provide social services for the urban poor. Recall Cora Bussey Hillis, the Iowa housewife mentioned in Chapter 1, who advocated for research into children's development.

Advocates for children and families are important agents of change. For example, the advocacy group Action for Children's Television was formed in the 1960s to improve scheduling of, reduce violence in, and limit advertising during children's programming. Their work eventually culminated in the passage of the Children's Television Act of 1990, which established guidelines for children's programming, including content and quantity of advertising. It also required broadcasters to provide educational and informational programs for children (Calvert & Kotler, 2003).

Today, there are many child and parent advocacy groups that seek to inform the public and lobby for specific causes. Table 15.2 lists some of the national and international child, parent, and family advocacy groups.

Contemporary Programs to Help Families

Currently, a number of different programs provide assistance to parents and their children. Some are prophylactic and designed to reduce the likelihood of problems in at-risk families. Others provide intervention services to families already experiencing hardship. Most of the programs are intended to assist the poor. These provide nutrition assistance (such as food stamps), health care coverage (such as Medicaid), and early childhood education (see more about Head Start, below). There are also mentoring programs (such as Big Brothers Big Sisters) for children in single-parent families and other children in need. These programs facilitate one-to-one adult-child relationships for 3 million youth a year (Rhodes & DuBois, 2006).

Six of the more than 50 prevention and intervention programs operating in the United States that have been evaluated systematically are listed in Table 15.3. These programs are examples of the wide range of approaches that are targeted to help parents and their children.

Begun in 1972, Women, Infants, and Children (WIC) is an exemplary program that combats inadequate nutritional care among low-income pregnant and breastfeeding women as well as their young children up to age five. More than 7 million low-income parents in all 50 states participate in the supplemental nutritional program, which provides vouchers for high-protein foods such as milk, cheese, and beans. Nutrition education and child health checkups are also required for all participants. In 2013, the average annual cost per participant was $516 (http://www.fns.usda.gov/pd/wisummary.htm) but it is highly cost-effective because it reduces the number of low birth weights and fetal deaths, improves at-risk children's nutrition, and increases the rate of child immunizations (see http://www.fns.usda.gov/wic/about-wic-how-wic-helps).

The other widely acclaimed government prevention program is Project Head Start. Initially created in 1965, it began as a summer program for poor four- and five-year-old children to prepare them for school and help break the cycle of poverty. Very soon, it became evident that one or two summers was not enough time to prepare economically disadvantaged children for school entry. Within a few years, Head Start had expanded into

Table 15.2 Examples of National and International Advocacy Groups Concerning Parents and Children

Group	Website	Purpose
American Coalition for Fathers and Children	www.acfc.org	to promote the equal rights of all parties affected by divorce
American Family Association	www.afa.net	to alter American culture (with an emphasis on media) to reflect conservative ("traditional") family values
Autism Speaks	www.autismspeaks.org	to improve the future of individuals who struggle with autism
Children's Defense Fund	www.childrensdefense.org	to lift children out of poverty, protect them from abuse and neglect, and ensure their access to health care, quality education, and a moral and spiritual foundation
Center for Effective Discipline	www.stophitting.org	to disseminate information about the effects of physical punishment and promote alternatives to its use
Global Movement for Children	www.gmfc.org	to make the world a better place for children (worldwide association of organizations)
National Children's Advocacy Center	www.nationalcac.org	to promote and model a new way to respond to and prevent child abuse
Pacer Center	www.pacer.org	to expand opportunities and enhance quality of life for children with disabilities and their families
Parental Rights	www.parentalrights.org	to secure a constitutional amendment defending the rights of parents to direct the upbringing and education of their children
Prevent Child Abuse America	www.preventchildabuse.org	to prevent child abuse and neglect in the United States
United Nations Children's Fund (UNICEF)	www.unicef.org	to advocate and act internationally on behalf of the rights of children
U.S. Alliance to End the Hitting of Children	www.endhittingusa.org	to end of hitting of all children both in schools and at home

a year-round program, and today, it serves more than 621,000 children at 2,000 sites. Besides providing the children with a preschool education, Head Start gives meals and medical services to children. The parents are encouraged to be involved and engaged in their children's education.

Table 15.3 Examples of Evidence-Based Prevention and Intervention Programs

Program	Description
Dare to Be You	A multilevel prevention program that serves high-risk families with children two to five years old. Program objectives focus on children's developmental attainments and aspects of parenting that contribute to youth resilience to later substance abuse, including parental self-efficacy, effective child rearing, social support, and problem-solving skills.
Incredible Years	A set of three interlocking, comprehensive, and developmentally based training programs for children and their parents and teachers. These programs are guided by developmental theory on the role of multiple interacting risk and protective factors in the development of conduct problems.
Nurse-Family Partnership	A prenatal and infancy nurse home visitation program that aims to improve the health, well-being, and self-sufficiency of low-income, first-time parents and their children.
Parent-Child Interaction Therapy (PCIT)	A treatment program for young children with conduct disorders that places emphasis on improving the quality of the parent-child relationship and changing parent-child interaction patterns.
Parents as Teachers (PAT)	An early childhood family support and parent education home-visiting model. Families may enroll in Parents as Teachers beginning with pregnancy and may remain in the program until the child enters kindergarten.
The Triple P: Positive Parenting Program	A multilevel system or suite of parenting and family support strategies for families with children from birth to age 12, with extensions to families with teenagers ages 13 to 16.

Source: SAMHSA's National Registry of Evidence-Based Programs and Practices (http://nrepp.samhsa.gov/Index.aspx).

Evaluation studies of Head Start and other preschool intervention programs have determined that early intervention can indeed be successful in its efforts. Head Start graduates are more likely to be ready for school, perform better there, and exhibit higher cognitive competence compared to children who did not attend the program. It is likely that there are other positive, long-term consequences for Head Start graduates, such as increased chances of graduating from high school, becoming and staying employed, and avoiding juvenile delinquency (Zigler & Styfco, 1994). Head Start helps to set a child on a positive developmental trajectory that provides feelings of efficacy and generates successful experiences in school and elsewhere. Head Start programs also change parents. For example, Head Start parents provide more books to their children and are less likely to spank (Zhai, Waldfogel, & Brooks-Gunn, 2013). The major problem is that it is also underfunded. For every child in the program, more than three others are eligible but unable to participate due to lack of funding.

Although it is far cheaper than the alternative (remediation), early intervention is still expensive. For example, Head Start costs about $9,000 per child per year. A much more extensive intervention program (the Abecedarian program in North Carolina) begins early—when an infant is six weeks old—and costs $70,700 per child per year. A cost-benefit analysis of early childhood programs concluded that they are *all* indeed cost-effective, as they reduce the likelihood that the child will require special education classes, be retained in a grade, drop out of high school, be arrested, or smoke cigarettes as an adult (Masse & Barnett, 2002). The Child-Parent Centers in Chicago determined that for every dollar spent on early childhood programs, society saves $6 to $10. This favorable economic return exceeds most other educational interventions that begin in school-age years, such as reduced class size or youth job training (Reynolds, Temple, Robertson, & Mann, 2002).

Parent Education and Intervention

The idea that educating parents about child rearing will increase their parenting competence is a long-held belief in the United States. As early as 1815, parents were meeting together to discuss how to deal with childrearing problems (Croake & Glover, 1977). Since then, many different programs have been designed and tested to help parents function better. The programs vary considerably in terms of content (information provided), method (e.g., group instruction vs. **home visitation**), intensity (number of sessions or visits), and population served (e.g., at-risk individuals), as well as type of community where the program is offered (Cowan, Powell, & Cowan, 1998).

Responding to an ecological perspective, parenting intervention programs underwent considerable changes in the 1980s (Powell, 2005). Programs began to experiment with ways to strengthen parents' social networks, community ties, work-family relations, and other extrafamilial systems. This perspective also calls for a recognition of group and individual differences among the parents, resulting in culturally sensitive training.

The leading contemporary model of parent intervention involves the home visitation. This is a service strategy designed to identify families in need and then address those needs. The strategy has been used in the United States and Europe for more than a century, and European countries regard it as an essential part of child health programs (Shonkoff & Meisels, 2000). The model depends on the development of a positive relationship between the home visitor and the parent. The idea is that parents will change their behavior based on the information presented and the persuasive abilities of the home visitor. The parents then mediate changes in their children; home visitors typically do not interact directly with the children.

Different home visitation programs vary in focus; there are currently thousands of these programs in the United States. One of the first to be carefully evaluated is the Nurse-Family Partnership Program, which involves nurses making home visits to low-income mothers. Three large-scale, randomized-control trials have been conducted with different populations in different contexts: upstate New York; Memphis, Tennessee; and Denver, Colorado. Nurses engage in three major tasks: (a) promoting mothers' positive behavior as it related to pregnancy, children's health, and the mothers' life course; (b) helping mothers develop supportive relationships with others; and (c) linking mothers and their families to needed health and human services.

The largest home visitation program in the country is Healthy Families America (http://www.healthyfamiliesamerica.org), with more than 430 sites serving families in which the mother is a first-time parent under the age of 21. The program's major goals are to prevent child maltreatment, promote effective parenting, achieve optimal health in children, help parents become economically self-sufficient, and prevent repeated teen pregnancy. A third well-known program is Hawaii's Healthy Start, which focuses on promoting children's language and cognitive development, enhancing the quality of home environment, preventing mental health and substance abuse, encouraging educational and economic attainment, and facilitating the use of contraceptives.

Do home visitation and other parenting intervention programs work? About 27 years after the Nurse-Family Partnership program was first implemented, David Olds (2006) summarized the key results across its three sites. Although results associated with pregnancy outcomes were mixed, the program has been successful in improving the mother's life course (measured by, for instance, fewer subsequent crisis pregnancies, greater levels of employment, and reduced dependence on public assistance). It has also served to enhance the care of children, resulting in better emotional and language development and fewer cases of child maltreatment. In a meta-analysis of 60 home-visitation programs, the programs were found to have at least a modest positive effect (median effect size was .135) on a majority of the assessed child variables (cognitive and socioemotional development) and parent variables (parenting behavior and attitudes, child abuse, stress, maternal education, employment, and public assistance) (Sweet & Appelbaum, 2004).

Other meta-analyses of parent intervention programs (both home visitation and others) find somewhat stronger effects. For example, in a more focused meta-analysis of 70 intervention programs designed to enhance parental sensitivity and attachment security, programs had relatively small impact on changing behavior, with small effect sizes (e.g., .33) for modifying insensitive parenting or changing infant attachment insecurity (.20) (Bakermans-Kranenburg, van IJzendoorn, & Juffer, 2003). Intervention programs specifically designed to prevent child abuse tend to be more successful, with effect sizes in the moderate range (d = .45 to .66) (Lundahl, Nimer, & Parsons, 2006). Behavior-based programs (focusing on social contingencies, rewards, ignoring, etc.) tended to be more effective in changing perceptions but less effective than nonbehavioral-based programs (focusing on parent-child communication, authoritative parenting, child-centered cognitions, and problem solving) in changing behavior. See Figure 15.2 for a bar graph of the average effect sizes of these programs.

Designing and evaluating intervention programs for changing parents and children is a complex task. Given the variability among the features of the programs, the fact that the intervention programs are generally found to be effective is noteworthy. Further research will help to determine the most effective goals, frequency of visits, training level of home visitors, and other characteristics to enhance their efficacy. Future work needs to focus on such questions as "What are the processes involved in changing childrearing behavior?" and "For whom does a particular program work the best?" (Sandler, Schoenfelder, Wolchik, & MacKinnon, 2011).

Advances in technology offer the promise of making parent-training programs widespread and deliverable to all families in need (Forgatch, Patterson, & Gewirtz, 2013). Parenting

Figure 15.2 Effect Sizes for Changing Parental Cognitions or Behavior

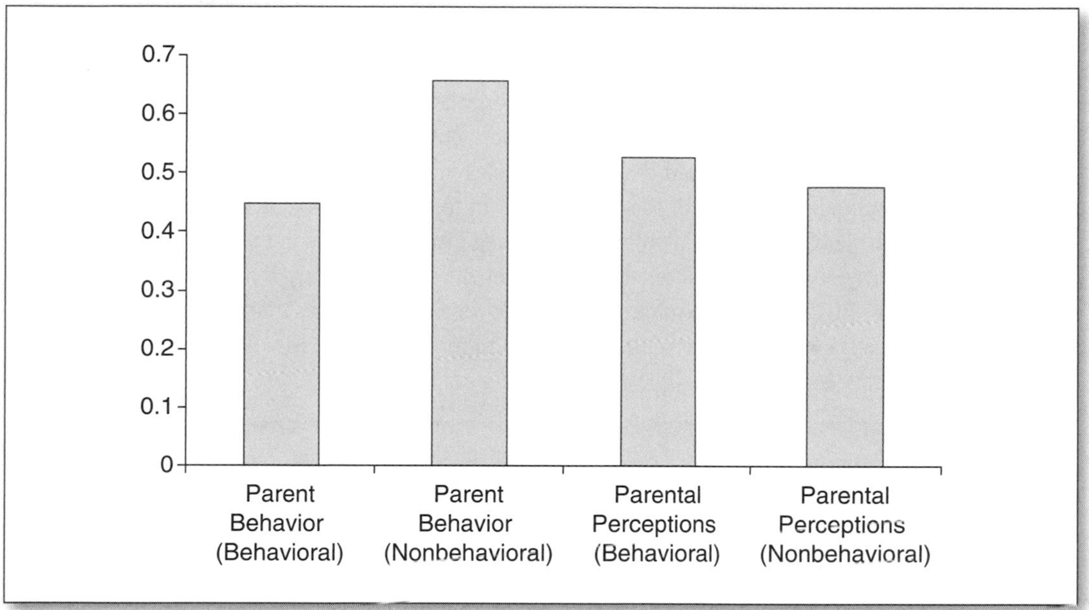

Source: Lundahl et al., 2006.

Note: Small effect size = .20; Moderate effect size = .50; Large effect size = .80.

programs are relatively inexpensive to implement (perhaps costing several hundred dollars per family) and, by preventing child behavior problems, can result in significant cost savings for the family and society (Stevens, 2014). However, to date, most communities and governments take a shortsighted approach and generally do not want to spend money on prevention. One exception is described in Box 15.3.

Box 15.3 Does Couple Relationship Building Prevent Problems?

Parenting behavior is not the only target of intervention for improving child rearing. One strategy addresses reducing the high rate of divorce and all the negative consequences that can occur from marital breakups by training low-income couples in relationship skills. Since 2005, the U.S. government has spent more than $100 million per year on these types of programs (Bartlett, 2014). To evaluate their effectiveness, the programs are being evaluated at multiple sites. One of those testing

(Continued)

(Continued)

sites is the state of Oklahoma's Family Expectations program, one of the first such programs. The intervention focused on unmarried couples expecting their first child. The theory was that if couples are taught specific relationship skills (e.g., better communication, dealing with conflicts in constructive ways, anger management, etc.), then they will experience improved family outcomes (e.g., greater happiness and couple stability, less conflict and partner abuse) as well as improved child well-being.

The 15-month evaluation showed that those couples in the program, compared with a control group, did show modest benefits of the intervention in terms of couple satisfaction and stability (Devaney & Dion, 2010). However, in other programs and after three years in the Oklahoma program, those who received the 30-hour intervention did not differ significantly from the control group (e.g., Hsueh et al., 2012). Although some sites had more positive outcomes than others, the evidence indicates that a relatively short intervention designed to teach relationship skills is not a cure-all for the many problems and stressors that low-income couples face (Bartlett, 2014).

Community Learning Centers

Across the nation, individuals and communities have developed numerous creative solutions for assisting parents and children. Such programs serve important needs, but their significance for nationwide societal change is limited by their scope. In contrast, proposals that address the nature of public schools hold considerable promise for improving the quality of life for many more parents and their children.

Calls to reform the educational system in an effort to increase literacy and competence have been many and varied. One approach was the brainchild of James Comer in the late 1960s. He sought to improve a poorly functioning inner-city school in New Haven, Connecticut, through its organization and functioning. He hoped to improve its effectiveness and raise the level of student and teacher engagement by involving faculty, students, and parents in the management of the school (Comer, 1980).

Developmental psychologist Edward Zigler, one of the founders of Head Start, has since developed a more comprehensive scheme to modify the functioning of public schools into 21st-Century Community Learning Centers. He observed that public schools, as developed in the 1900s, were falling short of meeting the needs of modern families. Although educating children is one important task, to Zigler, schools could be much more—hence the title *Community Learning Centers*. They should provide both before- and after-school programs and activities for students and be open during vacation periods. Schools should also provide day care for students' younger siblings. In addition, schools should become centers of family support in terms of information, parent education, and referral services. Table 15.4 lists the 13 activities envisioned by Zigler that could define each center (Mahoney & Zigler, 2006).

The Community Learning Center program first received government funding in 1994 for trials in certain schools in Missouri. In 2002, it was awarded $1 billion to fund programs in 6,800 schools serving more than 1 million students. The estimated cost to fully fund the school transformations across America would be $75 billion (Mahoney & Zigler, 2006).

Table 15.4 Types of Activities Provided at Community Learning Centers

Activities
• Children's daycare services
• Integrated health, social service, recreational, and cultural programs
• Summer or weekend programs in conjunction with recreation programs
• Nutrition and health programs
• Parent-skills education programs
• Literacy education programs
• Expanded library service hours
• Telecommunications and technology education programs for all ages
• Support and training for child daycare providers
• Employment counseling, training, and placement
• Services for school dropouts of any age
• Services for individuals with disabilities
• Senior citizen programs

Source: Mahoney & Zigler, 2006.

Another innovative effort to encourage low-income parents to talk more to their children is being tested out in Providence, Rhode Island. In 2013, the city won a $5 million prize to coach parents on boosting their children's language exposure in the wake of the research by Betty Hart and Todd Risley (1995) discussed in Chapter 7. The intent is to remediate the "30 million word gap" so low-income preschoolers will be more able to succeed in school (Zimmer, 2013).

CONTROVERSIAL SOCIAL POLICY IDEAS

There is no quick way to address the many challenges for parents and families that have been described in this book. Around the world, many local, state, and national governments—as well as organizations in the private sector—have developed strategies and programs to address the issues. Some social policy ideas are quite controversial. The People's Republic of China's "one-child" fertility law is a prominent example [Preview Question]. In a bold effort to reduce Chinese population growth, the 1979 federal law mandated that couples were allowed to have only one child (with some exceptions). If a second child is born, the couple is fined or taxed at a higher rate. The program was initially presented as a temporary measure, but it was in place for about 32 years. In 2013, the program was essentially dissolved with the disbanding of the organization in charge of the policy (Alcorn, 2013). The policy has resulted in a number of unintended negative consequences, most notably a sex imbalance due to sex-selective abortions and the abandonment or even murder of female neonates. In addition to this, China has seen changing family structures, a more rapidly aging population, and greater instability of marriages (Settles, Sheng, Zang, & Zhao, 2013). A recent personality study found that children born after the policy are significantly less trusting and trustworthy, less competitive and conscientious, and more risk adverse and pessimistic than children born before the policy (Cameron, Erkal, Gangadharan, & Meng, 2013).

In contrast to China's restrictive action, some Western European leaders, concerned about their declining fertility rates, have provided financial incentives to mothers so they will bear children. To make their country more family friendly, since 2007, working couples in Germany are entitled to 14 months paid leave after the birth of each child, with payments of 65% of their salary for most people. In addition, mothers receive a small maternity payment and an annual "child benefit" until the child is 18 years of age (Pidd, 2011). In certain parts of Germany, the local government provides payments to procreate: Mothers earn as much as $34,700 for every child born (Nizza, 2007). Using money (or "cash transfers") was tested as a strategy to promote improved parenting behavior in New York City. This program is described in Box 15.4.

Box 15.4 Paying Parents to Be Parents

In 2007, New York City started an experimental program for families in poverty: paying parents to do what parents should do. The Opportunity NYC program was a conditional cash transfer program modeled on a Mexican program (*Oportunidades*) first tested in 1997. Programs modeled after the Mexican one operate in 20 countries (Kelley, 2007). Opportunity NYC was designed to encourage poor parents to become more involved in their children's health and education by providing modest financial incentives. Parents could earn $4,000 to $6,000 a year by engaging in normal parenting activities: $25 for attending parent-teacher conferences, $50 for getting a library card, and $400 if their child graduates from high school. They also received money for preventive health screenings or job training or $150 a month if they keep a full-time job. In the pilot program 2,500 families participated (chosen by a lottery). The program showed some modest improvements in the lives of parents and children after one year (Miller, Riccio, & Smith, 2009) but ended in 2010.

In the United States, fertility is not our most pressing issue. Instead, our most controversial social policy ideas have addressed physical punishment of children, parental responsibility, and licensing of parents.

Banning Corporal Punishment

In an effort to protect children from physical violence, two kinds of laws banning corporal (also called *physical*) punishment have been enacted in various countries. The first type of law involves banning corporal punishment in schools. Throughout history, teachers have resorted to physical violence to discipline unruly students or even slow learners. The practice continues today, as a court case that made national news in 2004 exemplifies:

> Jessica, an 18-year-old high school senior in San Antonio, Texas, arrived on campus one morning but then walked across the street to buy a breakfast taco. When she returned, she was informed that she had broken a school rule. While being restrained by two employees, she was paddled by the interim principal. The paddling left Jessica physically injured and emotionally traumatized. She never returned to the school. (Pollard-Sacks, 2009)

Many countries have outlawed this type of school punishment. In fact, more than 225 years ago (in 1783), Poland banned corporal punishment in schools. As of 2013, more than 100 other countries have passed similar bans. In contrast, use of physical punishment in the school system is still practiced in 19 (generally southern) U.S. states; the other 31 states have enacted legislative bans. Physical punishment in the schools typically takes the form of being hit on the bottom with a paddle. In the 2006–2007 school year, more than 223,000 children received corporal punishment by school personnel. The practice is disproportionately used on minority and handicapped children (Human Rights Watch, 2009).

The second type of ban on physical punishment is considerably more controversial. Historically, parents have opposed limitations of their rights to discipline their children as they see fit (Pollard, 1983). However, to protect children from maltreatment, certain countries have restricted parental discipline by outlawing parental use of corporal punishment. This policy was first enacted in Sweden in 1979, the same year that China instituted the one-child policy. The ban, amended in 1983, reads, "Children are entitled to care, security, and a good upbringing. Children are to be treated with respect for their person and individuality and may not be subjected to corporal punishment or any other humiliating treatment."

The legislation was not an effort to criminalize parents. Rather, its major intent was to change attitudes about disciplining children. Consequently, it was accompanied by a massive public education campaign. The law was also intended to increase early identification of children at risk for abuse and promote intervention for families (Durrant, Rose-Krasnor, & Broberg, 2003).

Although the evidence is limited, what studies are available indicate that laws in Sweden and Finland have been effective in reducing corporal punishment of children by parents. In Sweden, more at-risk families have been identified, and attitudes about corporal punishment have changed (Durrant, 1999). Swedish mothers now view spanking as unnecessary, ineffective, and even harmful (Durrant et al., 2003). In Finland, 28 years after the ban was enacted, the rate of child fatalities as well as mental health problems linked to corporal punishment had decreased significantly (Österman, Björkqvist, & Wahlbeck, 2014).

The banning of all physical punishment of children, a proposition in line with the U.N. Convention on the Rights of the Child, is gradually spreading. By 2014, a total of 38 countries had banned all forms of corporal punishment. These countries, and the year their bans were enacted, are listed in Table 15.5.

Table 15.5 Nations (and the Year) That Have Banned All Corporal Punishment of Children

Brazil (2014)	Republic of Moldova (2008)	Turkmenistan (2002)
Malta (2014)	Netherlands (2007)	Bulgaria (2000)
Honduras (2013)	New Zealand (2007)	Germany (2000)
TFYR Macedonia (2013)	Portugal (2007)	Israel (2000)
South Sudan (2011)	Spain (2007)	Croatia (1999)
Albania (2010)	Togo (2007)	Latvia (1998)
Kenya (2010)	Uruguay (2007)	Denmark (1997)
Poland (2010)	Venezuela (2007)	Cyprus (1994)
Republic of Congo (2010)	Greece (2006)	Austria (1989)
Tunisia (2010)	Hungary (2005)	Norway (1987)
Costa Rica (2008)	Romania (2004)	Finland (1983)
Liechtenstein (2008)	Ukraine (2004)	Sweden (1979)
Luxembourg (2008)	Iceland (2003)	

Parent Responsibility Laws

Since the 1990s, a novel legal approach to the problem of delinquent behavior is emerging both in the United States and in other countries. It involves holding parents accountable for their children's actions. The idea is that, if parents can be charged with the crime of contributing to the delinquency of a minor, they will be motivated to be more involved with and responsible for their teenager's conduct. Generally, these responsibility laws deal with nonviolent crimes, such as drinking alcohol, driving recklessly, shoplifting, participating in gang activities, or skipping school. The laws rest on the common legal presumption that the child's delinquent behavior is a consequence of poor parenting and that the parents have not met society's parenting expectations (Pagliocca, Melton, Lyons, & Weisz, 2002). Punishments range from small fines to imprisonment.

Should parents be blamed for adolescent misconduct? For many citizens frustrated with juvenile miscreants, this sounds like a good policy. However, is it fair to hold parents accountable for actions committed by their children when the parents are unaware of the actions or unable to control their difficult children? Some psychologists do not believe it is fair. They argue parents have little influence on their children's development, particularly when children come into contact with other influences—especially peers (Cohen, 1999; Harris, 1998). Another concern with responsibility laws is their orientation to punishment rather than remediation. The laws do not help parents become more skilled or effective in controlling a teenager's behavior. The laws have also been criticized as vague, unfair (because they impose harsher penalties on parents than on children), and neglectful of parents' rights. To date, the laws have not been widely enforced, and there are no evaluation studies yet of their effectiveness (Harris, 2006; Le Sage & De Ruyter, 2008).

Licensing Parents

This book has documented that many social problems are linked to families and parenting, including behavior and mental health problems, substance abuse, obesity, crime, teenage pregnancy, poverty, and child maltreatment. The financial cost of the problems for the individuals, their families, and society is high. What is the cure? The obvious solution is to improve the quality of parenting. If parents' behavior is causally linked to or can mediate children's problems, then it follows that parenting should be improved. But how does society improve the quality of parenting? Classes offering parent education and home visitation programs are two approaches to improving parenting, but their scope is limited. A much more ambitious and controversial proposal has also been suggested: licensing individuals before they have children.

> Parents-to-be must be certified as to their competence, and a practical examination is better than a paper one. We must take an examination to obtain a license to drive a car. The child deserves no less; the good of the country demands much more. (Rheingold, 1973, p. 46)

With those words, the developmental psychologist Harriet Rheingold proposed a revolutionary idea—an idea that some people consider to be outrageous and an egregious intrusion into individual rights and family privacy. Hugh LaFollette (1980), a philosopher, took the idea of parent certification a step further by proposing that parents should be licensed to protect children from abuse and neglect. The proposal to license parents gained national attention when in 1994, the psychiatrist Jack Westerman described the idea and its rationale in a book. His proposal is simple and takes up only about five pages of his 238-page book. There are actually only three requirements for getting a license:

1. The prospective parent must be at least 18 years old.
2. The prospective parent must sign an agreement indicating that he or she agrees to care for and nurture the child while refraining from maltreating the child. The parent agrees to the financial responsibility of parenthood and the expectations of parental competence.
3. The prospective parent will complete a parenting course (although this criterion could be optional).

Jack Westerman's proposal (supplemented with ideas by Lykken, 2001) is that all parents would have to procure a parenting license prior to a baby's birth [Preview Question]. Licenses could be obtained at the time of marriage, when the individual is accepted for adoption, during pregnancy, or in the hospital immediately after childbirth. It would be handled by the authorities who issue marriage licenses and birth registrations. Prospective parents would not be judged based on their parenting beliefs or the quality of their parenting. Rather, all they would need to do is show documentation of a marriage license, proof they are of legal age, and evidence they are self-supporting. The prospective parents would then sign the agreement. According to Westerman's plan, an actual parent-education course is optional.

What happens if a parent does not obtain a license? A baby born to an unlicensed mother would be removed and put up for adoption—unless she was able to obtain a license. A single woman could have a child but would have to demonstrate to a judge that she had the resources to provide for the child's material needs. Gay and lesbian couples, in the absence of a marriage license, could obtain a parenting license through an appeal to family court. This proposal means that adolescents younger than 18 years old would have to wait to raise a child, as would unemployed or impoverished couples, until their financial circumstances improved. The death or divorce of a parent would not be grounds for removal of the child (Lykken, 2001). To read other perspectives and issues related to the idea of licensing parents, see the edited book by Peg Tittle, *Should Parents Be Licensed? Debating the Issues* (2004).

From a parent-centered perspective, the idea of having to get a license to have a child is an assault on the right to procreate. However, not everyone agrees that it is a right of all individuals to bear children. Margaret Mead (1978), late in her career as an anthropologist, thought otherwise. She argued that she did not agree with the view that every woman has an inherent right to have a child.

Photo 15.3 The goal of parenting is to rear healthy, happy, and competent individuals. Society benefits when parents are successful.

Source: © iStockphoto.com/kali9

From a child-centered perspective, parents should not have unbounded freedom to rear their children as they see fit. The British philosopher John Stuart Mill (1859/1956) put it this way:

> Causing the existence of a human being is one of the most responsible actions in the range of human life. To undertake this responsibility—to bestow a life . . . unless the being on whom it is to be bestowed will have at least the ordinary chances of a desirable existence—is a crime against that being. (p. 124)

The ultimate purpose of the proposal to license parents was not to limit the rights of adults. Rather it was to change social norms and values and to protect children. Westerman hoped that when the importance of child rearing was elevated and normative beliefs and expectations were changed, children would benefit from improved parenting. He envisioned a society where youth would not even consider becoming parents until they are reasonably mature, self-sufficient, and adequately functioning citizens committed to the childrearing task.

As indexed by the relatively low amount of money currently spent on programs and salaries, however, our society does not place great value on the work of parenting. Neither does the marketplace put much value on those who work with children, such as daycare workers and teachers. Childcare workers are among the lowest paid workers in U.S. society, with a median annual salary of $19,510 (2012 figures; Bureau of Labor Statistics, 2014). For many families, this means their salaries place them below the U.S. poverty level for a family of four. Teachers fare much better; their 2012 median salary range was $53,090 to $55,000. If children are indeed our "most precious national resource" (Rheingold, 1973), it stands to reason that the way we rear and treat them will determine our nation's future.

CHAPTER SUMMARY

Much can and needs to be done in the United States and around the world to support families in the task of rearing their young. Social policies in many Western nations are much more progressive and supportive of families than in the United States, particularly when it comes to pre- and postnatal parent support, parental leave, and child care. More progressive U.S. policies will happen only with the recognition that the foundation for a healthy and stable society lies with competent parenting. Economic pressures on families are associated with a plethora of high-risk indices such as academic underachievement, increased dropout rates, and health problems. Economics has also undoubtedly played a role in evolving social changes in the United States over the past several decades. These include such trends as an increase in single mothers, a much greater number of families in which both parents work outside the home, and a high divorce rate. All of these trends have put new stresses on child rearing.

It does little good to ignore, deny, or even fight against these continuing evolving trends. The tide of social change has turned and there is literally no going back. It can be argued that these trends bear considerable cost to society in lost productivity, a less educated workforce, and sheer economic impact. The economic consequences of such problems as premature birth, childhood obesity, school failure, juvenile delinquency, and child maltreatment cost the United States tens of billions of dollars each year.

A variety of social policies have been initiated, both in the United States and around the world. Child advocates have started many initiatives in order to promote children's rights. Some programs are aimed at preventing problems, whereas others are designed to intervene with at-risk families or address ongoing problems. Home visitation programs appear to have the most promise for changing parenting and improving the outcomes of children. Another effort to help families lies in reinventing the school system so it can better meet the needs of the families in the community. Several controversial ideas intended to combat family-related social problems have also been advanced, including banning corporal punishment, enacting parent-responsibility laws, and licensing parents.

Societies depend on parents to nurture and guide the development of children into healthy and competent adults. It is in the best interest of all societies to promote parental success. Disparities in the incidence or burden of problems that exist among families are a problem that everyone needs to address. To paraphrase the observation of the pioneering attachment theorist John Bowlby (1951), if societies are to value children, all parents must be nurtured.

THOUGHT QUESTIONS

- Some people believe the American family is in decline, as reflected by the changes in family structure. What do you think?
- Why does the United States lag behind other industrialized countries in supporting the family? How might this be changed?
- Should parents be held accountable for their adolescent's misconduct?
- Do you think licensing parents would be an effective way to address some of the social problems? What organizations would object to this proposal?

CHAPTER GLOSSARY

child advocates Individuals who campaign for or promote children's well-being.

educational failure Usually defined as when an adolescent drops out of school.

home visitation A type of parent intervention that involves visiting families in their homes, identifying their needs, and then working to address those needs.

noninterference The doctrine that the state should not interfere with the family.

parens patriae Latin for *parent of the nation*. Refers to the doctrine that the state is the ultimate guardian of all children or people with a disability.

APPENDIX

Journals That Frequently Publish Studies Pertaining to Parenting

American Journal of Orthopsychiatry

American Journal of Sociology

American Psychologist

American Sociological Review

Annual Review of Clinical Psychology

Annual Review of Psychology

Applied Developmental Psychology

Attachment & Human Development

British Journal of Developmental Psychology

Child Abuse and Neglect

Child and Family Behavior Therapy

Child: Care, Health and Development

Child Development

Child Development Perspectives

Child Maltreatment

Children and Youth Services Review

Clinical Child and Family Psychology Review

Clinical Psychology Review

Current Directions in Psychological Science

Developmental Psychology

Developmental Review

Early Child Development and Care

Early Childhood Research Quarterly

Families in Society

Family Process

Family Relations

Family Therapy

Infant Mental Health Journal

Infants and Young Children

International Journal of Behavioral Development

Journal of Abnormal Child Psychology

Journal of Adolescence

Journal of Adolescent Health

Journal of Adolescent Research

Journal of Applied Developmental Psychology

Journal of Child and Family Studies

Journal of Child Psychology and Psychiatry

Journal of Child Psychology and Psychiatry and Allied Disciplines

Journal of Child Welfare

Journal of Clinical Child Psychology

Journal of Community Psychology

Journal of Comparative Family Studies

Journal of Consulting and Clinical Psychology

Journal of Cross-Cultural Psychology

Journal of Developmental & Behavioral Pediatrics

Journal of Divorce and Remarriage

Journal of Early Adolescence

Journal of Family and Economic Issues

Journal of Family Issues

Journal of Family Psychology

Journal of Family Violence

Journal of Genetic Psychology

Journal of Interpersonal Violence

Journal of Marital and Family Therapy

Journal of Marriage and Family

Journal of Men's Studies

Journal of Pediatric Psychology

Journal of Pediatrics

Journal of Personality and Social Psychology

Journal of Research on Adolescence

Journal of Social Issues

Journal of the American Academy of Child and Adolescent Psychiatry

Journal of Youth and Adolescence

Maternal and Child Health Journal

Marriage and Family Review

Merrill-Palmer Quarterly

Monographs of the Society for Research in Child Development

Parenting: Science and Practice

Pediatrics

Personal Relationships

Psychological Bulletin

Psychology of Women Quarterly

Sex Roles

Social Development

Social Forces

Youth and Society

Glossary

acculturation How well an individual has adapted to the norms and values of the majority society.

additive effects When two or more variables combine to form a stronger influence on behavior than any of the variables has on its own. Also called *cumulative effects*.

adult-centered Thinking about children from the parent's perspective or with the parent's needs in mind.

affective reprimands Disciplinary responses that involve raising children's discomfort levels about the effects of their behavior and then providing an explanation about why it was wrong.

affluent families Families that earn greater than twice the country's median income.

altricial An organism requiring care and feeding after birth to survive.

amniocentesis A prenatal test for chromosomal abnormalities conducted after the 15th week of pregnancy.

analgesics Childbirth pain medication that is injected or given intravenously to relieve pain without the total loss of feeling or muscle movement.

anesthesia Childbirth pain medication that includes spinal and epidural blocks; it is given intravenously and temporarily stops all feeling in an area.

anoxia Deprivation of oxygen; a severe form of hypoxia.

anxious-avoidant An insecure attachment classification based on an infant's pattern of behavior, characterized by avoiding or ignoring the parent when he or she returns from a separation.

anxious-resistant An insecure attachment classification based on an infant's pattern of behavior, characterized by little exploration of the environment, wariness of unfamiliar persons, and ambivalence about the parent upon his or her return follow a separation.

assisted reproductive technology (ART) Methods developed by embryologists to achieve pregnancy by artificial or partially artificial techniques.

assortative mating Refers to the practice of individuals seeking out and then having children with other individuals who are similar (in positive assortative mating) or dissimilar (negative assortative mating) to themselves in one or more characteristics, such as appearance or intelligence.

attachment theory A theory about development that focuses on the establishment, maintenance, and consequences of affectionate bonds between parents and children.

attention-deficit/hyperactivity disorder (ADHD) A condition (more commonly found in males) characterized by inattention, impulsivity, and hyperactivity.

attitudes Positive or negative evaluations of beliefs.

attributions Assessments of the cause of a behavior.

authoritarian A parenting trait characterized by strict control, low levels of communication, and low levels of warmth.

authoritative A parenting trait characterized by warm, open communication but also firm control.

authority conflict When an adolescent is disobedient and defiant to figures of authority.

autism Also known as *autism spectrum disorder* (*ASD*), it is a type of pervasive developmental disorder with a neurological basis. Although the severity of the disorder varies, symptoms appear in the first two years of life and typically involve severe impairment in communications and social relationships.

autosomal chromosome pairs Humans normally have 22 autosomal chromosome pairs.

axons Nerve fibers that conduct electrical impulses away from the nerve's cell body.

behavioral control Parental actions designed to control, manage, or regulate a child.

behavioral genetics approach One of the approaches to the study of parenting that focuses on studying the role of genetics and the environment to understand the source of human characteristics.

behavioral genetics theory A theory that seeks to understand genetic and environmental contributions to variations in human behavior and characteristics.

beliefs Mental acceptance of and conviction in the truth or validity of something.

bidirectional Refers to the idea that dyadic behavior is influenced by both individuals.

binge drink To consume alcoholic beverages with the primary goal of getting drunk. It is usually defined as consuming five or more drinks on the same occasion.

blank slate The idea that a newborn child's mind is neither good nor bad but waiting to be written upon.

bonding A concept proposed by two pediatricians, asserting that the parent needs to be in physical contact with the newborn shortly after birth, in order to develop a love for the infant.

Bradley method of childbirth Designed to promote natural and healthy childbirth without medication or surgery. Classes focus on nutrition, relaxation, and breathing exercises and instructing fathers as labor coaches. Also called *husband-coached childbirth*.

broad-band factors When a group of problems are combined to form a large category.

buffered When one variable protects against the potential adverse effects of another. Also called a *protective factor*.

bullying Repeated negative actions over time perpetrated by a more dominant child/youth to another child/youth.

cesarean (C-section) A form of childbirth where a surgical incision is made in the woman's abdomen and uterus in order to remove the fetus.

child advocates Individuals who campaign for or promote children's well-being.

child-centered Thinking about children from the child's perspective or with the child's needs in mind.

child effects The effects a child can have on a parent as a consequence of a child characteristic or behavior.

child effects and transactions approach An approach to the study of parenting that focuses on how children's characteristics influence or interact with parental characteristics or behavior to change behavior.

child maltreatment The physical abuse, sexual abuse, neglect, or psychological mistreatment of a child.

child mortality The death of infants and children under the age of five.

childrearing commitment The extent to which a parent is dedicated to the child and his or her well-being.

childrearing stress The experience of distress or discomfort due to child rearing.

child sexual abuse A type of child abuse that occurs when a child is used for the sexual gratification of an adult or adolescent. The abuse may take a variety of forms, ranging from exposing genitals to fondling or raping a child.

chorionic villus sampling (CVS) A prenatal test for genetic abnormalities performed between the 10th and 12th weeks of pregnancy.

chronosystem This system refers to how nested systems of interactions can change over time.

classical conditioning A form of associative learning that typically involves presentations of a neutral stimulus along with a stimulus of some significance.

coagents Two individuals who work together toward some action.

coercive cycles Problematic interactions in which two individuals compete with increasing force to see who can gain control.

coercive discipline When a parent forces a child to comply or behave in a desired way.

collectivism A cultural orientation that emphasizes the good of the larger group or society over the individual.

comorbid Two or more disorders in an individual.

compensation When a positive variable is strong enough to overcome the presence of a negative variable.

compensatory hypothesis One variable can compensate or counteract the negative effects of another variable. For example, one parent may attempt to compensate for an acrimonious marital relationship by devoting extra attention and warmth to a child.

complementarity When one person's acts complete another's.

conduct disorder A group of behavioral and emotional problems in children involving difficulties in following rules or behaving in socially acceptable ways. Problematic behaviors include aggression, property destruction, lying, stealing, and truancy.

confluence theory A theory about how birth order and family size affect a child's intellectual attainment.

constructs Ideas about a psychological entity.

contingent Something, such as a behavior, that is dependent on or conditioned by something else.

continuous care and contact model A view of infant care that says that one adult needs to provide sensitive care to a child for optimal development.

control theory A narrow theory of parent-child relationships focusing on how both parents and children perceive and respond to the intensity, frequency, and situational appropriateness of behavior shown by the other.

Convention on the Rights of the Child A United Nations document designed to promote the rights of children around the world.

co-occur When two or more problems occur at the same time.

co-parenting From the family systems perspective, how well and in what ways mothers and fathers work together in their roles as parents. The term also is used to refer to the shared responsibility for a child of two parents who are separated or divorced.

covert aggression One pathway of adolescent aggression that begins with minor dishonesty but escalates into more serious acts such as theft.

***cri du chat* syndrome** A chromosomal defect whereby a deleted section of chromosome 5 causes—along with other, more severe symptoms—a strange, high-pitched cry in babies.

critical periods Limited periods of time, usually early in life, in which an event can occur that can have a transformative effect on the organism.

cultural niche The specific environment in which relationships occur. It consists of the physical and social environment, customs of child rearing and child care, and the parent's ethnotheories.

culture The way of life shared by members of a society.

cumulative risk model A model depicting the accumulation of separate risks or problems; when multiple risk factors add up to create negative effects on a child.

datasets Information gathered by researchers, usually through surveys, interviews, or observations about parents, children, the context, and so on.

decision making The cognitive processes involved in reaching a decision.

delinquent A youth who persistently engages in misdeeds such as aggression.

dendrites The branches of the neurons that allow for synaptic communication.

determinants of parenting Variables that influence a parent's childrearing behavior or beliefs.

diary study A research procedure in which the participant records, in a notebook, the data of interest to the researcher.

diathesis-stress model A model concerning genes and the environment that assumes that the presence of a genetic predisposition to having a problem only results in the phenotypic expression of the problem when the individual is exposed to particular kinds of environmental stressors.

differential socialization A term referring to how parents may rear children differently due to the child's biological sex or other individual differences in the child.

differential susceptibility The hypothesis that only the children with certain characteristics will respond to particular types of parenting.

direction of effect This refers to the issue of who is influencing whom.

discipline Training in order to produce a specific outcome or pattern of behavior. Often, this involves some type of punishment.

dismissing attachment style A pattern of relating to others in adulthood guided by a negative view of others but a positive view of oneself.

disorganized According to attachment theory, when a child shows a confused and inconsistent pattern of response to stress, he or she has a disorganized attachment style.

distal Distant.

distraction A parenting technique whereby the child's attention is strategically shifted from one source to another.

dizygotic twins Twins that do not share an identical genotype. Also known as *fraternal twins*.

dominant inheritance Occurs when, if either parent has a faulty gene, the defect can still be passed on to the infant.

dose-response relationship The amount or extent of the dose affects the magnitude of the response

Down syndrome Also known as *Trisomy 21*, this chromosomal abnormality occurs when there is an extra 21st chromosome. These children have genetic abnormalities, particular facial features, mental impairment, and various health problems.

droit du seigneur The "right of the lord"—the medieval doctrine that the head of household could sleep with any subordinate woman in his home.

dyadic synchrony Parent-child interactions that are mutually regulated, reciprocal, and harmonious.

ecological momentary assessment approach An approach that closely examines ongoing, moment-to-moment behavior in parent-child interactions in settings where it normally occurs.

ecological systems theory A theory that focuses on the interrelations of different levels of context and how they relate to child's behavior and development.

educational failure Usually defined as when an adolescent drops out of school.

educational neglect The failure to provide the opportunities and supervision necessary to meet the child's educational needs. Examples include failing to enroll a child in school or allowing the child to frequently skip school.

effortful control The ability to regulate one's cognitive, emotional, and behavioral responses to external stimuli.

emotional security theory A theory focusing on children's feelings of insecurity as a consequence of marital conflict.

emotion regulation The ability to control one's own emotions.

empathy Experiencing how someone else feels or perceives a situation. With regard to parenting, this refers to a parent's ability to experience events from the child's point of view.

endometriosis A medical problem in women that occurs when uterine tissue grows outside the uterus.

ethnotheories The theory and beliefs that underlie the values and practices of members of a particular culture.

ethologist A scientist who studies the behavior of animals in their natural habitat.

ethology The study of behavior in its natural habitat from an evolutionary perspective.

evolution A theory about the origins of plants and animals as well as processes of change.

evolutionary psychology A theory that seeks to understand human behavior and characteristics as a result of adaptive processes over tens of thousands of years.

executive functioning A set of cognitive abilities that control and regulate other abilities, thoughts, and behaviors.

exosystem The layer of context or settings in the ecological systems theory that affects children but does not directly include children (e.g., parents' workplace).

experiments of nature When an abnormal situation occurs in the absence of scientific manipulation and provides information about development.

externalizing Problem behaviors that are directed outward (toward other people), such as noncompliance or aggression.

factor analysis A statistical procedure used to identify a reduced set of common factors or variables by analyzing patterns of correlations among a larger set of variables.

failure to thrive A problem, beginning in infancy, when a child shows little weight gain and physical growth due to inadequate nutrition.

family preservation A policy whereby children are kept with their abusive parents who have undergone intervention rather than being placed in foster care.

family structure The composition of the family, including the number and gender of parents and children.

family systems theory A theory that focuses on the system of interactions, interrelations, and interconnections between family members.

fearful attachment style A relational style in adults characterized by a negative self-image as well as a distrust of others.

female genital circumcision The practice of altering female genital organs for nonmedical reasons. Also called *female genital mutilation* or *female genital cutting*.

Fetal Alcohol Syndrome (FAS) A disorder found in children of mothers who have ingested alcohol during pregnancy. Depending on the severity, it can result in growth deficiencies, craniofacial abnormalities, and damage to the central nervous system.

filicide A parent deliberately killing his or her own child.

gamete intrafallopian transfer (GIFT) Eggs and sperm are inserted by way of a laparoscope into the woman's fallopian tube.

gender socialization The processes by which a child is taught to be a girl or a boy, as defined by the culture.

gene-environment interaction The idea that a particular phenotypic expression is due to the interaction between genes and the environment.

genes Blueprints of development, comprised of a segment of DNA and made up of amino acids.

genetic disorder Disorders caused by abnormalities in genes or chromosomes.

genome The entire hereditary information, encoded in DNA, found in an organism.

genotype An individual's genetic makeup, comprised of some 20,000 to 25,000 genes.

glia Cells that provide structural support and metabolic sustenance for neurons.

goodness of fit The quality of the match between a child's characteristics (i.e., temperament) and the parenting. Also called *matching* or *congruence*.

graduated driver licensing laws Laws that gradually remove restrictions on adolescent drivers, such as number of passengers.

group socialization theory A theory of development that highlights the role that peers and peer-group processes play, particularly during adolescence.

hardening A variety of practices intended to toughen up infants in an effort to promote their survival.

helicopter parent A term used in the popular press to refer to parents who are overly involved in the lives of their children and hover over them, both figuratively and literally.

home visitation A type of parent intervention that involves visiting families in their homes, identifying their needs, and then working to address those needs.

Human Genome Project A 13-year international endeavor that identified each gene and its chromosomal location.

hunter-gatherer A society where food is procured primarily by hunting animals and gathering edible foods.

hypoxia A problem that occurs when the fetus experiences an oxygen deficit, as in the birthing process.

imaginary audience Adolescents' heightened sense of self-consciousness.

immigrant An individual born in one country but living in another.

imprinting A concept referring to rapid learning—usually very early in life—that is apparently independent of behavioral consequences.

independence versus interdependence Two different cultural orientations concerning the individual. Cultures that value independence promote individual autonomy. In contrast, other cultures value a sense of togetherness and group membership.

individualism A cultural orientation that emphasizes the individual's rights, goals, and free choice.

individuation The process of becoming an autonomous individual.

infanticide The killing of a child during the first year of life; the killing of newborns and infants.

infant mortality Child death during the first 12 months of life.

interaction When two variables have a nonadditive effect on each other in statistical analyses.

interdependence A belief system that, in contrast to independence, recognizes and values the interconnected nature of human relationships.

internalizing Problem behaviors that are directed inward, such as depression or anxiety.

internal working model Ideas and expectations about oneself and others derived from previous attachment-related experiences.

intracytoplasmic sperm injection (ICSI) A single healthy sperm is selected and then injected into a single female egg using a microscopic glass needle. Once fertilization is confirmed, the zygote is inserted into the woman for implantation.

intrauterine insemination (IUI) A procedure in which sperm are placed by a catheter directly into the woman's uterus.

in vitro fertilization (IVF) An egg and sperm are combined in a culture dish. The fertilized egg (zygote) is then transferred into the woman's uterus.

ius primae noctis The doctrine, from the Romans, that the father has the right to have sexual relations with any female member of his household who is his social inferior.

karyotype The full complement of chromosomes in an individual.

Klinefelter syndrome An extra X chromosome is present, creating a male with three sex chromosomes (XXY). This syndrome is associated with a variety of physical (e.g., small testicles) and reproductive problems (e.g., reduced fertility).

Lamaze A popular method of childbirth. Prenatal classes provide instruction on relaxation and breathing techniques to deal with labor pains

large datasets approach The newest approach to parenting that typically uses large datasets, multiple variables, and advanced statistical analytic techniques to investigate questions about child rearing.

lay theories Folk beliefs that have not been empirically verified.

limbic system A group of brain structures (including the amygdala, hippocampus, cingulate gyrus, hypothalamus, and other parts) that support various functions, including emotion, attachment, long-term memory, and behavior.

longitudinal A study that follows an individual over time and includes repeated observations or data collection points.

macrosystem The outermost level of the ecological systems theory. This level refers to the major, overarching characteristics or structures of a culture or subculture that affect children.

mastitis An inflammation of the breasts most commonly caused by blocked milk ducts.

mediator A variable that explains how or why other variables are associated.

medical neglect A failure to provide timely and necessary medical treatment to a child. This includes refusing to allow a child to be immunized.

mesosystem A layer of the ecological systems theory that refers to the system of processes or linkages taking place between two or more microsystems.

meta-analysis A type of review of research literature that involves combining and comparing the results of multiple empirical studies using a common measure, called an *effect size*.

metaparenting The thoughts parents have about their children or their child rearing before or after interactions.

micro-analytic observations Careful observations of ongoing parent-child interactions, typically completed by making video or digital recordings for later analysis.

microsystem A term in the ecological systems theory that refers to the contexts where children interact (e.g., the home, school, and playground).

mid-level determinants Influences on parenting that are between immediate, situational, and distal or cultural determinants. Examples include stable parent and child characteristics and marital relations.

mindful parenting A parent's nonjudgmental awareness of the child in the immediate context.

moderator A variable that affects the strength or direction of a relation between two other variables: a predictor (independent) variable and an outcome (dependent) variable.

monitoring Parental knowledge of children's whereabouts and whom they are with. This requires disclosure and communication on the part of the child.

monozygotic twins Twins that have the same genotype. Also called *identical twins*.

mother blaming When mothers are accused of causing problems in their children.

multifactorial inheritance Defects are due to a combination of more than one abnormal gene—or of both genetic and environmental causes. Examples include cleft lip, schizophrenia, and neural tube defects.

multi-method study A study that uses more than two or more methods, such as observations, questionnaires, and interviews.

myelin A white, fatty substance that grows around the axons of a neuron in order to allow for electrical conductivity.

myelination The process in which axons are sheathed by myelin so they will conduct electrical impulses.

nativist A view that espouses that children's genetic makeup or innate characteristics are the key determinants of development rather than the environment.

natural selection The process whereby heritable traits that are better suited for an environment will survive and other traits will become less common.

negative emotionality When a child's emotional state is characterized by negative affect, such as irritability and anger.

neonate An infant from birth through four weeks of age.

neurogenesis The formation of neurons and glia in the fetus.

neurons Cells that specialize in conducting nerve impulses.

noninterference The doctrine that the state should not interfere with the family.

nonshared environment Aspects of the environment (e.g., activities, social interactions, and friendships) that are unique to each child in a family.

nontraditional family Any family structure that does not contain two heterosexual biological parents.

novelty seeking According to attachment theory, children will seek new activities and experiences when they feel safe in their environment. Through this behavioral system, children acquire new competences.

ontogenetic Development of individuals over their life span.

operant conditioning Also known as *Skinnerian conditioning*, this refers to a form of learning where the consequences of an act modify the likelihood of its recurrence.

original sin The Christian theological concept that all children are born with sin.

otitis media A painful inflammation (caused by infection) of the middle ear that frequently occurs in infants and young children, typically after experiencing the common cold.

overprotection When a parent engages in inappropriate care and behavior that reflects a denial of the child's autonomy.

overt aggression One type of aggressive adolescent pattern of behavior that begins with minor aggressive acts and then escalates into serious violence.

parens patriae Latin for *parent of the nation*. Refers to the doctrine that the state is the ultimate guardian of all children or people with a disability.

parental acceptance-rejection theory A theory concerning children's development that is centered around the presence or absence of love between a parent and child.

parental inoculation When a parent in some way prepares a child for an upcoming potentially difficult or troubling experience.

parental investment A concept in human evolutionary theory referring to the time, energy, and resources parents devote to rearing their children.

parental nurturance Parenting behavior that provides essential care to the child, including feeding, sheltering, bathing, and protecting.

parental self-efficacy Parents who believe they can control their children typically are more competent in their parenting abilities and have children who are better adjusted.

parental separation anxiety A parent's unpleasant emotional state of concern and apprehension about leaving a child.

parental support A parenting dimension that includes being involved, loving, emotionally available, and responsive.

parental traits approach Characterizing parents on the basis of one or two qualities or characteristics.

parent effects A term that refers to changes in a child caused by a parent.

parentification When the child is put in the role of an adult, such as when a child is assigned to care for a younger sibling or a child becomes an emotional confidante of a parent.

parenting stress Aversive psychological or physiological reactions experienced in the parenting role.

patria potestas *The power of the father*—a doctrine in ancient Roman law giving authority to the father over his children, including decisions about life and death.

patriarchal The structuring of society where fathers in family units have the primary authority.

per capita income Total national income divided by the number of citizens in the country.

perceptions Recognition and interpretation of sensory stimuli.

permissive A parenting trait characterized by parents who are warm and loving but fail to control or expect mature behavior from their children.

personal fable The belief in some adolescents that what they experience is unique to them.

phenotype The physical expression or manifestation of an individual's genotype.

phenylketonuria (PKU) An autosomal recessive genetic disorder resulting in a buildup of phenylalanine due to an enzyme deficiency. If untreated, it can result in neurological damage.

phylogenetic The development of the species over time.

physical neglect Occurs when a child's physical needs, such as adequate clothing, shelter, and food, are not met.

polygamy When one adult has more than one spouse.

polygyny When a man has two or more wives.

poly-victimization When an individual is maltreated in two or more ways.

positive synchrony When the interactions in families are harmonious, reciprocal, responsive, interconnected, and engaged, and when there is a shared affect.

postpartum depression A condition occurring in mothers during the first year of their child's life, characterized by persistent feelings of sadness, low energy, and other problems.

postpartum psychosis Much less common but more serious than postpartum depression, this mental illness may be characterized by hallucinations, delusions, feelings of anxiety and agitation, and suicidal or homicidal thoughts.

power assertion Parental controlling behaviors intended to show force or the threat of force.

preimplantation genetic diagnosis (PGD) Procedures used on embryos prior to implantation to screen for potential genetic or chromosomal defects.

preoccupied attachment style A style of relating to others in adulthood that is characterized by a negative view of the self but a positive view of others.

prevalence The proportion of the population experiencing an illness or having a condition.

primiparous Refers to a woman who has given birth only one time.

problem solving Thought processes involved in dealing with a solving a problem.

prosocial behavior Behavior that is intended to benefit others, such as helping, sharing, and comforting.

protective factors Conditions or circumstances that promote healthy behavior and well-being.

proximal Close or immediate.

proximity seeking When children feel threatened or scared, they will retreat to being held by or being near the parent in an effort to regain feelings of being safe, according to attachment theory.

psychological control A type of control that consists of parental efforts to constrain, invalidate, and manipulate the child's psychological and emotional experience.

psychological maltreatment A repeated pattern of caregiver behavior or extreme incident(s) that conveys the message to children that they are worthless, flawed, unloved, unwanted, endangered, or only of value in meeting another's needs.

punishment effect From Skinner's theory of operant conditioning, a punishment is any action in response to a behavior that decreases the likelihood that the behavior will recur.

race socialization The training and guidance minority parents give to their children to help them deal with racism, prejudice, and living as a minority group member.

reactive attachment disorder (RAD) A syndrome of developmentally inappropriate behavior with regard to interpersonal relationships.

recessive inheritance When both parents carry the same abnormal gene and pass it on to their child.

reciprocity When acts are supportive of each other and become similar.

reinforcement effect According to operant conditioning principles, a reinforcement is any action that increases the likelihood that a prior behavior will recur.

relational aggression Engaging in intentional hurtful behavior by excluding, gossiping, and manipulating friendships.

religiosity When referring to individuals, this term means the degree to which a person is religious.

resilience Positive adaptation in the face of adversity.

resource dilution model A theory about birth order effects that views the family as having a finite amount of resources (e.g., parental time, energy, and money); the presence of siblings necessarily dilutes the available resources for a child.

rights Freedoms to which all humans are entitled.

risk factors Characteristics, variables, and/or conditions that could adversely affect the individual.

risk index Cumulative risk factors present in a family.

role conflict Occurs when an individual experiences conflict between two or more roles of different status. For example, many parents experience problems balancing their roles of parent and employee.

role strain Strain in roles occurs when there is tension between roles that share the same status, such as caring for a child and caring for an elderly parent.

role theory A theory from sociology that examines behavior from the perspective of the multiple socially defined categories an individual has (e.g., mother, wife, sister, and employee).

scaffolding Social interactions that support a child's behavior in a way that allows the child to exhibit more advanced behavior.

school readiness Refers to when children have the skills, knowledge, and attitudes to enable them to succeed in kindergarten.

second-order effects How individuals adjust their behavior when in the presence of a third individual.

secure attachment style In adults, it reflects a healthy style of relating to others and is characterized by a positive view of oneself and others.

securely attached A pattern of behavior from which it is inferred that infants or young children trust their parents to protect and care for them in times of need.

self-efficacy An individual's beliefs about his or her ability to affect changes in the environment.

sensitive parenting A quality of parenting (also called *responsive*) characterized by responding timely, appropriately, and reliably to the infant or child.

sensitivity Synonymous with *sensitive parenting.*

sex chromosomes The 23rd pair of chromosomes that determine the child's gender. Males have an X and a Y chromosome; females have two X chromosomes.

shaken baby syndrome A form of physical child abuse whereby an infant is repeatedly shaken. The whiplash causes bleeding in the brain, which in turn can result in such problems as visual impairments, permanent neurological damage, or death.

shaming A disciplinary technique intended to make the child feel bad, guilty, or sad.

shared environment Aspects of the environment (activities, social interactions, and friendships) experienced by two or more siblings in the same family.

sibling rivalry Competition and conflict between siblings.

skinship A parent-child relationship characterized by close physical contact. Often practiced in Japan.

social address approach An approach to the study of parenting that compares parents from different locations or "addresses." These might include different cultures, geographic locals, religious backgrounds, racial or ethnic groups, or socioeconomic status groups.

social caregiving Parent caregiving behavior that focuses on an infant's or child's interpersonal interactions.

social cognition approach An approach to studying parents that focuses on various types of parental social cognitive processes (e.g., attitudes, beliefs, and problem solving) as they relate to children.

social cognitive theory A theory of behavior that focuses on the cognitive and information-processing capacities of individuals as central influences on their social behavior.

social constructions Beliefs about children and parents that are invented or constructed by participants in a culture or society. Also known as *cultural inventions.*

socialization The processes whereby children are taught to become competent individuals.

social learning theories A collection of theories that address how children learn from their social environment.

social policies Principles that guide decisions or efforts to achieve desired goals (and avoid undesired results) concerning human needs and welfare.

social support Material, emotional, or instrumental forms of assistance provided by other people.

socioeconomic status (SES) The term used to describe the relative social position of an individual or family. Typically, it is based on income, education, and occupation.

spatial-temporal Activities that involve space and time.

spillover hypothesis A hypothesis that the mood or quality of interactions in one domain carry over into another domain. With regard to parents, examples include how conflictual marital relationships or stress at work spills over and affects the quality of parent-child interactions at home.

stage theory A type of theory based on the idea that there are discrete stages or steps and that children pass sequentially from the lower stages to the higher ones.

stereotyped behaviors Abnormal behavior characterized by repeatedly engaging in repetitive, similar behavior without an obvious goal or function.

swaddling Wrapping an infant tightly in a blanket or some type of material.

synapses Connections between neurons.

synaptic pruning The process in which synapses that are not utilized are lost.

synaptogenesis The process of forming synapses between neurons. It occurs mostly after birth.

synchrony When both individuals attend to the same thing, are responsive to each other, and (perhaps) may share emotions.

temperament Refers to the biologically based behavioral style of the child.

teratogens Harmful substances that can damage a developing embryo or fetus. These include drugs, health factors, infections, environmental chemicals, and physical agents.

transactional influence The idea that there is a continuous mutual influence of the person and environment on development. In turn, individuals change and then influence the environment around them.

trauma A physical or emotional injury.

Turner syndrome A chromosomal abnormality that occurs when a female is missing part or all of one X chromosome. It results in physical abnormalities, health problems, and cognitive disabilities.

turn-taking Alternating actions between individuals during an interaction.

ultrasound A machine that uses high-frequency sound waves to construct an image, such as an image of a fetus.

unidirectional effect The once-prevailing view that parents influenced their children but their children did not influence them.

Vygotsky's theory A theory developed by Lev Vygotsky that focused on the role of particular types of social interactions as the central influence on children's cognitive and social development.

warmth The expression of parental affection and love.

X-linked inheritance When a genetic abnormality is inherited through a mother's X chromosome.

zone of proximal development Refers to the distance between an individual's ability to do something independently and the ability of the individual to perform a task under adult (or more-advanced peer) guidance. Learning occurs when in this zone according to Vygotsky.

zygote intrafallopian transfer (ZIFT) Like GIFT, except fertilization occurs similarly to IVF, and the resulting zygote(s) is transferred to a fallopian tube.

References

Achenbach, T. M. (1991). *Manual for the Youth Self-Report and 1991 Profile*. Burlington: University of Vermont Department of Psychiatry.

Achenbach, T. M. (2008). Multicultural perspectives on developmental psychopathology. In J. J. Hudziak (Ed.), *Developmental psychopathology and wellness: Genetic and environmental influences* (pp. 23–47). Washington, DC: American Psychiatric Publishing.

Adam, E. K., Gunnar, M. R., & Tanaka, A. (2004). Adult attachment, parent emotion, and observed parenting behavior: Mediator and moderator models. *Child Development, 75,* 110–122.

Ahl, R. E., Fausto-Sterling, A., García-Coll, C., & Seifer, R. (2013). Gender and discipline in 5–12-month-old infants: A longitudinal study. *Infant Behavior and Development, 36,* 199–209.

Ainsworth, M. D. S. (1967). *Infancy in Uganda*. Baltimore, MD: Johns Hopkins.

Ainsworth, M. D. S. (1989). Attachments beyond infancy. *American Psychologist, 44,* 709–716.

Ainsworth, M. D. S., Blehar, M. C., Waters, E., & Wall, S. (1978). *Patterns of attachment*. Hillsdale, NJ: Lawrence Erlbaum Associates.

Ainsworth, M. D. S., & Bowlby, J. (1991). An ethological approach to personality development. *American Psychologist, 46,* 333–341.

Aizer, A. (2004). Home alone: Supervision after school and child behavior. *Journal of Public Economics, 88,* 1835–1848.

Albert, D., Chein, J., & Steinberg, L. (2013). The teenage brain: Peer influences on adolescent decision making. *Current Directions in Psychological Science, 22,* 114–120.

Alcorn, T. (2013). China's new leaders cut off one-child policy at the root. *The Lancet, 381,* 983.

Al-Krenawi, A. (2013). Mental health and polygamy: The Syrian case. *World Journal of Psychiatry, 3,* 1–7.

Allen, J., & Hawkins, A. (1999). Maternal gatekeeping: Mothers' beliefs and behaviors that inhibit greater father involvement in family work. *Journal of Marriage and Family, 61,* 199–212.

Allendorf, K. (2013). Schemas of marital change: From arranged marriages to eloping for love. *Journal of Marriage and Family, 75,* 453–469.

Almond, D., Chay, K. Y., & Lee, D. S. (2005). The costs of low birth weight. *Quarterly Journal of Economics, 120,* 1031–1083.

Altimier, L. (2008). Shaken baby syndrome. *The Journal of Perinatal & Neonatal Nursing, 22,* 68–76.

Alvarez, M. (2004). Caregiving and early infant crying in a Danish community. *Journal of Developmental & Behavioral Pediatrics, 25,* 91–98.

Amato, P. R. (2000). The consequences of divorce for adults and children. *Journal of Marriage and Family, 62,* 1269–1287.

Amato, P. R. (2012). The well-being of children with gay and lesbian parents. *Social Science Research, 41,* 771–774.

Amato, P. R., & Keith, B. (1991). Parental divorce and the well-being of children: A meta-analysis. *Psychological Bulletin, 110,* 26–46.

American Academy of Pediatrics. (2001). Committee on public education: Children, adolescents, and television. *Pediatrics, 107,* 423–426.

American Academy of Pediatrics. (2011). *Policy statement on SIDS and other sleep-related infant deaths: Expansion of recommendations for a safe infant sleeping environment*. Retrieved May 21, 2014, from http://pediatrics.aappublications.org/content/early/2011/10/12/peds.2011-2284.full.pdf+html

American Academy of Pediatrics. (2012). Policy statement: Breastfeeding and the use of human milk. *Pediatrics, 129,* e827–e841.

American Psychiatric Association. (2013). *Diagnostic and statistical manual of mental disorders (DSM-V)* (5th edition). Arlington, VA: American Psychiatric Publishing.

American Psychological Association. (2014). *Teen suicide is preventable*. Retrieved June 11, 2014, from http://www.apa.org/research/action/suicide.aspx

American Society for Reproductive Medicine, Ethics Committee. (2013). Child-rearing ability and the provision of fertility services: A committee opinion. *Fertility and Sterility, 100*, 50–53.

America's Health Rankings. (2014). *Immunization—Children United States*. Retrieved June 5, 2014, from http://www.americashealthrankings.org/all/immunizc

Amos, J. (2008). *Dropouts, diplomas, and dollars: U. S. high schools and the nation's economy* (pp. 1–38). Washington, DC: Alliance for Excellent Education.

Anderson, E. R., Hetherington, E. M., Reiss, D., & Howe, G. (1994). Parents' nonshared treatment of siblings and the development of social competence during adolescence. *Journal of Family Psychology, 8*, 303–320.

Annie E. Casey Foundation. (2014). *Kids Count data book: State trends in child well-being*. Baltimore, MD: Annie E. Casey Foundation.

Appel, A. E., & Holden, G. W. (1998). The co-occurrence of spouse and physical child abuse: A review and appraisal. *Journal of Family Psychology, 12*, 578–599.

Ardelt, M., & Eccles, J. S. (2001). Effects of mothers' parental efficacy beliefs and promotive parenting strategies on inner-city youth. *Journal of Family Issues, 22*, 944–972.

Ariès, P. (1962). *Centuries of childhood: A social history of family life* (R. Baldick, Trans.). New York, NY: Vintage Books.

Arkowitz, H., & Lilienfeld, S. O. (2013). Is divorce bad for children? *Scientific American Mind, 24*, 68–69.

Arnett, J. J. (2000). Emerging adulthood: A theory of development from the late teens through the twenties. *American Psychologist, 55*, 469.

Asser, S. M., & Swan, R. (1998). Child fatalities from religion-motivated medical neglect. *Pediatrics, 101*, 625–629.

Augustine. (397/1960). *Confessions* (J. K. Ryan, Trans.). New York, NY: Doubleday.

Aunola, K., & Nurmi, J-E. (2005). The role of parenting styles in children's behavior problems. *Child Development, 76*, 1144–1159.

Austin, E. W., Bolls, P., Fujioka, Y., & Engelbertson, J. (1999). How and why parents take on the tube. *Journal of Broadcasting & Electronic Media, 43*, 175–192.

Averett, S. L., & Estelle, S. M. (2013). Will daughters walk mom's talk? The effects of maternal communication about sex on the sexual behavior of female adolescents. *Review of Economics of the Household, 11*, 1–27.

Azmitia, M., Cooper, C. R., Garcia, E. E., & Dunbar, N. D. (1996). The ecology of family guidance in low-income Mexican-American and European-American families. *Social Development, 5*, 1–23.

Backhouse, J., & Graham, A. (2012). Grandparents raising grandchildren: Negotiating the complexities of role-identity conflict. *Child & Family Social Work, 17*, 306–315.

Baio, J. (2012). Prevalence of autism spectrum disorders: Autism and developmental disabilities monitoring network, 14 sites, United States, 2008. Morbidity and mortality weekly report. *Surveillance Summaries, 61*(SS03), 1–19.

Baker, J., Côté, J., & Abernethy, B. (2003). Learning from the experts: Practice activities of expert decision makers in sport. *Research Quarterly for Exercise and Sport, 74*, 342–347.

Baker, B. L., Neece, C. L., Fenning, R. M., Crnic, K. A., & Blacher, J. (2010). Mental disorders in five-year-old children with or without developmental delay: Focus on ADHD. *Journal of Clinical Child & Adolescent Psychology, 39*, 492–505.

Baker, C. E., & Iruka, I. U. (2013). Maternal psychological functioning and children's school readiness: The mediating role of home environments for African American children. *Early Childhood Research Quarterly, 28*, 509–519.

Bakermans-Kranenburg, M. J., & van IJzendoorn, M. H. (2006). Gene-environment interaction of the dopamine D4 receptor (DRD4) and observed maternal insensitivity predicting externalizing behavior in preschoolers. *Developmental Psychobiology, 48*, 406–409.

Bakermans-Kranenburg, M. J., van IJzendoorn, M. H., & Juffer, F. (2003). Less is more: Meta-analyses of sensitivity and attachment interventions in early childhood. *Psychological Bulletin, 129*, 195–215.

Baldwin, A. L., Kalhorn, J., & Breese, F. (1945). Patterns of parent behavior. *Psychological Monographs, 58*(3), i–75.

Balsari, S., Lemery, J., Williams, T. P., & Nelson, B. D. (2010). Protecting the children of Haiti. *New England Journal of Medicine, 362*, e25–29.

Bancroft, L., & Silverman, J. G. (2002). *The batterer as parent: Assessing the impact of domestic violence on family dynamics*. Thousand Oaks, CA: SAGE.

Bandura, A. (2001). Social cognitive theory: An agentic perspective. *Annual Review of Psychology, 52*, 1–26.

Bandura, A., Ross, D., & Ross, S. A. (1963). Imitation of film-mediated aggressive models. *Journal of Abnormal and Social Development, 66*, 3–11.

Banerjee, A. V., & Duflo, E. (2007). The economic lives of the poor. *Journal of Economic Perspectives, 21*, 141–167.

Bangerter, A., & Heath, C. (2004). The Mozart effect: Tracking the evolution of a scientific legend. *British Journal of Social Psychology, 43*, 605–623.

Barber, B. K. (1996). Parental psychological control: Revisiting a neglected construct. *Child Development, 67*, 3296–3319.

Barber, B. K., Stolz, H. E., & Olsen, J. A. (2005). Parental support, psychological control, and behavioral control: Assessing relevance across time, culture, and method. *Monographs of the Society for Research in Child Development, 70*(282, Serial No. 4).

Barber, B. K., & Xia, M. (2013). The centrality of control to parenting and its effects. In R. E. Larzelere, A. S. Morris, & A. W. Harrist (Eds.), *Authoritative parenting: Synthesizing nurturance and discipline for optimal child development* (pp. 61–87). Washington, DC: American Psychological Association.

Barber, B. K., Xia, M., Olsen, J. A., McNeely, C. A., & Bose, K. (2012). Feeling disrespected by parents: Refining the measurement and understanding of psychological control. *Journal of Adolescence, 35*, 273–287.

Barker, E. D., Tremblay, R. E., Nagin, D. S., Vitaro, F., & Lacourse, E. (2006). Development of male proactive and reactive physical aggression during adolescence. *Journal of Child Psychology and Psychiatry, 47*, 783–790.

Barkley, R. A., & Cunningham, C. E. (1979). Stimulant drugs and activity level in hyperactive children. *American Journal of Orthopsychiatry, 49*, 491–499.

Barnard, M., & McKeganey, N. (2004). The impact of parental problem drug use on children: What is the problem and what can be done to help? *Addiction, 99*, 552–559.

Barnes, J. C., & Jacobs, B. A. (2013). Genetic risk for violent behavior and environmental exposure to disadvantage and violent crime: The case for gene-environment interaction. *Journal of Interpersonal Violence, 28*, 92–120.

Barr, A. B., Simons, R. L., Simons, L. G., Gibbons, F. X., & Gerrard, M. (2013). Teen motherhood and pregnancy prototypes: The role of social context in changing young African American mothers' risk images and contraceptive expectations. *Journal of Youth and Adolescence, 42*, 1884–1897.

Barr, R., Danziger, C., Hilliard, M. E., Andolina, C., & Ruskis, J. (2010). Amount, content and context of infant media exposure: A parental questionnaire and diary analysis. *International Journal of Early Years Education, 18*, 107–122.

Barrett, K. C., Zahn-Waxler, C., & Cole, P. M. (1993). Avoiders vs. amenders: Implications for the investigation of guilt and shame during toddlerhood? *Cognition and Emotion, 7*, 481–505.

Bartholomew, K. (1990). Avoidance of intimacy: An attachment perspective. *Journal of Social and Personal Relationships, 7*, 147–178.

Bartkowski, J. P., & Wilcox, W. B. (2000). Conservative Protestant child discipline: The case of parental yelling. *Social Forces, 79*, 265–290.

Bartlett, T. (2014, January 31). Can tax dollars buy love? *Dallas Morning News*. Retrieved June 19, 2014, from http://www.dallasnews.com/opinion/sunday-commentary/20140131-can-tax-dollars-buy-love.ece

Bates, J. E. (1989). Concepts and measures of temperament. In G. A. Kohnstamm, J. E. Bates, & M. K. Rothbart (Eds.), *Temperament in childhood* (pp. 3–26). New York, NY: Wiley.

Bates, J. E., & Pettit, G. S. (2007). Temperament, parenting, and socialization. In J. E. Grusec & P. D. Hastings (Eds.), *Handbook of socialization* (pp. 153–180). New York, NY: Guilford.

Baumer, D. (2008). My story: Raising (and surviving) three ADHD children. *ADDitude, Spring*. Retrieved

June 16, 2014, from http://www.additudemag.com/adhd/article/3285.html

Baumrind, D. (1971). Current patterns of parental authority. *Developmental Psychology Monographs, 4*(1, Pt.2), 1–103.

Baumrind, D. (1983). Rejoinder to Lewis' reinterpretation of parental firm control effects: Are authoritative families really harmonious? *Psychological Bulletin, 94*, 132–142.

Baumrind, D. (1989). Rearing competent children. In W. Damon (Ed.), *Child development today and tomorrow* (pp. 349–378). San Francisco, CA: Jossey-Bass.

Baumrind, D. (1991). The influence of parenting style on adolescent competence and substance use. *Journal of Early Adolescence, 11*, 56–95.

Baumrind, D. (2005). Patterns of parental authority and adolescent autonomy. *New Directions for Child and Adolescent Development, 108*, 61–69.

Baumrind, D. (2012). Differentiating between confrontive and coercive kinds of parental power-assertive disciplinary practices. *Human Development, 55*, 35–51.

Baumrind, D. (2013). Authoritative parenting revisited: History and current status. In R. E. Larzelere, A. S. Morris, & A. W. Harrist (Eds.), *Authoritative parenting: Synthesizing nurturance and discipline for optimal child development* (pp. 11–34). Washington, DC: American Psychological Association.

Beck, R. (1973). The White House Conferences on Children: An historical perspective. *Harvard Educational Review, 43*, 653–668.

Beck, K. (1990). Monitoring parent concerns about teenage drinking and driving. *American Journal of Drug and Alcohol Abuse, 16*, 109–124.

Becker, J. V., & Hunter, J. A. (1992). Evaluation of treatment outcome for adult perpetrators of child sexual abuse. *Criminal Justice and Behavior, 19*, 74–92.

Beekman, D. (1977). *The mechanical baby: A popular history of the theory and practice of child raising*. Westport, CT: Lawrence Hill.

Beer, M., Ward, L., & Moar, K. (2013). The relationship between mindful parenting and distress in parents of children with an autism spectrum disorder. *Mindfulness, 4*, 102–112.

Beers, L. A. S., & Hollo, R. E. (2009). Approaching the adolescent-headed family: A review of teen parenting. *Current Problems in Pediatric and Adolescent Health Care, 39*, 216–233.

Belfer, M. L. (2008). Child and adolescent mental disorders: The magnitude of the problem across the globe. *Journal of Child Psychology and Psychiatry, 49*, 226–236.

Belfield, C. R., & Levin, H. M. (2007). *The economic losses from high school dropouts in California: California Dropout Research Project*. Santa Barbara: University of California, Santa Barbara.

Bell, R. Q. (1968). A reinterpretation of the direction of effects in studies of socialization. *Psychological Review, 75*, 81–95.

Bell, R. Q. (1979). Parent, child, and reciprocal influences. *American Psychologist, 34*, 821–826.

Bell, R. Q., & Chapman, M. (1986). Child effect in studies using experimental or brief longitudinal approaches to socialization. *Developmental Psychology, 22*, 595–603.

Belsky, J. (1984). The determinants of parenting: A process model. *Child Development, 55*, 83–96.

Belsky, J. (1997). Variation in susceptibility to environment influence: An evolutionary argument. *Psychological Inquiry, 8*, 182–186.

Belsky, J. (2006). Early child care and early child development: Major findings of the NICHD study of early child care. *European Journal of Developmental Psychology, 3*, 95–110.

Belsky, J., & Barends, N. (2002). Personality and parenting. In M. H. Bornstein (Ed.), *Handbook of parenting, vol. 3: Being and becoming a parent* (2nd ed., pp. 415–438). Mahwah, NJ: Lawrence Erlbaum Associates.

Belsky, J., Burchinal, M., McCartney, K., Vandell, D. L., Clarke-Stewart, K. A., & Owen, M. T. (2007). Are there long-term effects of early child care? *Child Development, 78*, 681–701.

Belsky, J., Houts, R. M., & Fearon, R. M. P. (2010). Infant attachment security and the timing of puberty: Testing an evolutionary hypothesis. *Psychological Science, 21*, 1195–1201.

Belsky, J., Hsieh, K-H., & Crnic, K. (1998). Mothering, fathering, and infant negativity as antecedents of boys' externalizing problems and inhibition at age 3 years: Differential susceptibility to rearing experience? *Development and Psychopathology, 10*, 301–319.

Belsky, J., & Pluess, M. (2009). Beyond diathesis stress: Differential susceptibility to environmental influences. *Psychological Bulletin, 135*, 885–908.

Belsky, J., Steinberg, L., & Draper, P. (1991). Childhood experience, interpersonal development, and reproductive strategy: An evolutionary theory of socialization. *Child Development, 62*, 647–670.

Bem, S. (1989). Genital knowledge and gender constancy in preschool children. *Child Development, 60*, 649–662.

Benasich, A. A., & Brooks-Gunn, J. (1996). Maternal attitudes and knowledge of child-rearing: Associations with family and child outcomes. *Child Development, 67*, 1186–1205.

Benedict, R. (1949). Child rearing in certain European countries. *American Journal of Orthopsychiatry, 19*, 342–350.

Berger, L. M. (2005). Income, family characteristics, and physical violence toward children. *Child Abuse and Neglect, 29*, 107–133.

Bergmann, R. L., Bergmann, K. E., von Weizsäcker, K., Berns, M., Henrich, W., & Dudenhausen, J. W. (2014). Breastfeeding is natural but not always easy: Intervention for common medical problems of breastfeeding mothers—A review of the scientific evidence. *Journal of Perinatal Medicine, 42*, 9–18.

Berlin, L. J., Dodge, K. A., & Reznick, J. S. (2013). Examining pregnant women's hostile attributions about infants as a predictor of offspring maltreatment. *JAMA Pediatrics, 167*, 549–553.

Bermudez, J. M., & Mancini, J. A. (2013). Familias fuertes: Family resilience among Latinos. In D. S. Becvar (Ed.), *Handbook of family resilience* (pp. 215–227). New York, NY: Springer.

Bernard, K., & Dozier, M. (2011). This is my baby: Foster parents' feelings of commitment and displays of delight. *Infant Mental Health Journal, 32*, 251–262.

Bernier, A., Carlson, S. M., & Whipple, N. (2010). From external regulation to self-regulation: Early parenting precursors of young children's executive functioning. *Child Development, 81*, 326–339.

Berrick, J. D., & Skivenes, M. (2012). Dimensions of high quality foster care: Parenting plus. *Children and Youth Services Review, 34*, 1956–1965.

Berry, M., Barth, R. P., & Needell, B. (1996). Preparation, support, and satisfaction of adoptive families in agency and independent adoptions. *Child and Adolescent Social Work Journal, 13*, 157–183.

Bianchi, S. M., Robinson, J. P., & Milkie, M. A. (2006). *Changing rhythms of American family life*. New York, NY: Russell Sage.

Bieber, I., Dain, H., Dince, P., Drellich, M., Grand, H., Gundlach, R., . . . Bieber, T. (1962). *Homosexuality: A psychoanalytic study*. New York, NY: Basic Books.

Biehal, N. (2014). Maltreatment in foster care: A review of the evidence. *Child Abuse Review, 23*, 48–60.

Biringen, Z., & Robinson, J. (1991). Emotional availability in mother-child interactions: A reconceptualization for research. *American Journal of Orthopsychiatry, 61*, 258–271.

Birman, D., & Simon, C. D. (2014). Acculturation research: Challenges, complexities, and possibilities. In F. T. L. Leong, L. Comas-Diaz, G. C. Nagayama Hall, V. C. Mcloyd, & J. E. Trimble (Eds.), *APA handbook of multicultural psychology, vol. 1: Theory and research* (pp. 207–230). Washington, DC: American Psychological Association.

Biro, F. M., Galvez, M. P., Greenspan, L. C., Succop, P. A., Vangeepuram, N., Pinney, S. M., . . . Wolff, M. S. (2010). Pubertal assessment method and baseline characteristics in a mixed longitudinal study of girls. *Pediatrics, 126*, e583–e590.

Bjorklund, D., & Jordan, A. C. (2013). Human parenting from an evolutionary perspective. In W. B. Wilcox & K. K. Kline (Eds.), *Gender and parenthood: Biological and social science perspectives* (pp. 61–90). New York, NY: Columbia University Press.

Blair, C. (2002). School readiness: Integrating cognition and emotion in a neurological conceptualization of children's functioning at school entry. *American Psychologist, 57*, 111–127.

Blair, C., & Raver, C. C. (2012). Child development in the context of adversity: Experiential canalization of brain and behavior. *American Psychologist, 67*, 309–318.

Blair, C., & Ursache, A. (2011). A bidirectional model of executive functions and self-regulation. In

K. D. Vohs & R. F. Baumeister (Eds.), *Handbook of self-regulation: Research, theory, and applications* (2nd ed., pp. 300–320). New York, NY: Guilford Press.

Bleakley, A., Piotrowski, J. T., Hennessy, M., & Jordan, A. (2013). Predictors of parents' intention to limit children's television viewing. *Journal of Public Health, 35*, 525–532.

Block, R. W., & Krebs, N. F. (2005). Failure to thrive as a manifestation of child neglect. *Pediatrics, 116*, 1234–1237.

Bluestone, C., & Tamis-LeMonda, C. S. (1999). Correlates of parental styles in predominantly work- and middle-class African American mothers. *Journal of Marriage and Family, 61*, 881–893.

Blum, D. (2002). *Love at Goon Park: Harry Harlow and the science of affection*. New York, NY: Berkley Books.

Bøe, T., Sivertsen, B., Heiervang, E., Goodman, R., Lundervold, A. J., & Hysing, M. (2013). Socioeconomic status and child mental health: The role of parental emotional well-being and parenting practices. *Journal of Abnormal Child Psychology, 41*, 1–11.

Bongaarts, J., & Feeney, G. (1998). On the quantum and tempo of fertility. *Population and Development Review, 24*, 271–291.

Boonstra, H. (2002). Teen pregnancy: Trends and lessons learned. *Guttmacher Report on Public Policy*. New York, NY: Guttmacher Institute.

Booth, A., Johnson, D. R., Granger, D. A., Crouter, A. C., & McHale, S. (2003). Testosterone and child and adolescent adjustment: The moderating role of parent-child relationships. *Developmental Psychology, 39*, 85–98.

Bornstein, M. H. (1989). Sensitive periods in development: Structural characteristics and causal interpretations. *Psychological Bulletin, 105*, 179–197.

Bornstein, M. H. (Ed.). (2002). *Handbook of parenting* (2nd ed.). Mahwah, NJ: Lawrence Erlbaum Associates.

Bornstein, M. H. (2012). Cultural approaches to parenting. *Parenting: Science and Practice, 12*, 212–221.

Bornstein, M. H., Arterberry, M. E., & Mash, C. (2013). Differentiated brain activity in response to faces of "own" versus "unfamiliar" babies in primipara mothers: An electrophysiological study. *Developmental Neuropsychology, 38*, 365–385.

Bornstein, M. H., & Bradley, R. H. (2003). *Socioeconomic status, parenting, and child development*. New York, NY: Routledge.

Bornstein, M. H., & Cheah, C. S. L. (2006). The place of "culture and parenting" in the ecological context perspective on developmental science. In K. H. Rubin & O. B. Chung (Eds.), *Parenting beliefs, behaviors, and parent-child relations: A cross-cultural perspective* (pp. 3–33). New York, NY: Psychology Press.

Bornstein, M. H., Hahn, C-S., & Haynes, O. M. (2011). Maternal personality, parenting cognitions, and parenting practices. *Developmental Psychology, 47*, 658–675.

Bornstein, M. H., Putnick, D. L., Suwalsky, J. T. D., & Gini, M. (2006). Maternal chronological age, prenatal and perinatal history, social support, and parenting of infants. *Child Development, 77*, 875–892.

Bornstein, M. H., Tamis-LeMonda, C. S., Tal, J., Ludemann, P., Toda, S., Rahn, C. W., . . . Vardi, D. (1992). Maternal responsiveness to infants in three societies: The United States, France, and Japan. *Child Development, 63*, 808–821.

Borowsky, I. W., Ireland, M., & Resnick, M. D. (2001). Adolescent suicide attempts: Risks and protectors. *Pediatrics, 107*, 485–493.

Borowsky, I. W., Taliaferro, L. A., & McMorris, B. J. (2013). Suicidal thinking and behavior among youth involved in verbal and social bullying: Risk and protective factors. *Journal of Adolescent Health, 53*, S4–S12.

Boudreaux, M. C., Lord, W. D., & Etter, S. E. (2000). Child abduction: An overview of current and historical perspectives. *Child Maltreatment, 5*, 63–71.

Bower, J. E., Crosswell, A. D., & Slavich, G. M. (2014). Childhood adversity and cumulative life stress: Risk factors for cancer-related fatigue. *Clinical Psychological Science, 2*, 108–115.

Bowlby, J. (1951). *Maternal care and mental health*. Geneva, Switzerland: World Health Organization.

Bowlby, J. (1969). *Attachment and loss: Vol. 1, attachment*. New York, NY: Basic Books.

Bowlby, J. (1988). *A secure base: Parent-child attachment and healthy human development*. New York, NY: Basic Books.

Boyle, C. A., Boulet, S., Schieve, L. A., Cohen, R. A., Blumberg, S. J., Yeargin-Allsopp, M., . . . Kogan, M. D. (2011). Trends in the prevalence of developmental disabilities in US children, 1997-2008. *Pediatrics, 127*, 1034–1042.

Bradley, R. H. (2002). Environment and parenting. In M. H. Bornstein (Ed.), *Handbook of parenting, vol. 2: Biology and ecology of parenting* (pp. 281–314). Mahwah, NJ: Lawrence Erlbaum Associates.

Bradley, R. H. (2007). Parenting in the breach: How parents help children cope with developmentally challenging circumstances. *Parenting: Science and Practice, 7*, 99–148.

Bradley, R. H., & Caldwell, B. M. (1984). The HOME inventory and family demographics. *Developmental Psychology, 20*, 315–320.

Bradley, R. H., & Corwyn, R. F. (2002). Socioeconomic status and child development. *Annual Review of Psychology, 53*, 371–399.

Bradley, R. H., Corwyn, R. F., Burchinal, M., McAdoo, H. P., & Coll, C. G. (2001). The home environments of children in the United States Part II: Relations with behavioral development through age thirteen. *Child Development, 72*, 1868–1886.

Brazelton, T. B. (1998, May 21). To curb teenage smoking, nurture children in their earliest years. *Boston Globe.*

Brazelton, T. B., Koslowski, B., & Main, M. (1974). The origin of reciprocity: The early mother-infant interaction. In M. Lewis & L. Rosenblum (Eds.), *The effect of the infant on its caregiver* (pp. 49–76). New York, NY: Wiley.

Breed, A. G. (2007, July 29). Kids left to die in hot cars create dilemma for judges. *Associated Press*.

Bretherton, I., & Munholland, K. A. (2008). Internal working models in attachment relationships: Elaborating a central construct in attachment theory. In J. Cassidy & P. R. Shaver (Eds.), *Handbook of attachment* (2nd ed., pp. 102–127). New York, NY: Guilford.

Brody, G. H., & Flor, D. L. (1997). Maternal psychological functioning, family processes, and child adjustment in rural, single-parent, African American families. *Developmental Psychology, 33*, 1000–1011.

Brody, G. H., & Flor, D. L. (1998). Maternal resources, parenting practices, and child competence in rural, single-parent African. *Child Development, 69*, 803–816.

Brody, G. H., Flor, D. L., & Gibson, N. M. (1999). Linking maternal efficacy beliefs, developmental goals, parenting practices, and child competence in rural single-parent African American families. *Child Development, 70*, 1197–1208.

Brody, G. H., Kim, S., Murry, V. M., & Brown, A. C. (2003). Longitudinal direct and indirect pathways linking older sibling competence to the development of young sibling competence. *Developmental Psychology, 39*, 618–628.

Brody, J. E. (1998, June 20). Final advice from Dr. Spock: Eat only all your vegetables. *The New York Times*. Retrieved May 26, 2014, from http://www.nytimes.com/1998/06/20/us/final-advice-from-dr-spock-eat-only-all-your-vegetables.html

Brodzinsky, D. M., & Pinderhughes, E. (2002). Parenting and child development in adoptive families. In M. H. Bornstein (Ed.), *Handbook of parenting, vol. 1: Children and parenting* (2nd ed., pp. 279–312). Mahwah, NJ: Lawrence Erlbaum Associates.

Bronfenbrenner, U. (1979). *The ecology of human development: Experiments by nature and design*. Cambridge, MA: Harvard University Press.

Bronfenbrenner, U., & Morris, P. (2006). The ecology of developmental processes. In W. Damon & R. Lerner (Eds.), *Handbook of child psychology* (6th ed., vol. 1, pp. 993–1028). New York, NY: Wiley.

Brooks, J. L., Holditch-Davis, D., & Landerman, L. R. (2013). Interactive behaviors of American Indian mothers and their premature infants. *Research in Nursing & Health, 36*, 591–602.

Brooks-Gunn, J., Duncan, G. J., & Aber, J. L. (Eds.). (1997). *Neighborhood poverty: Context and consequences for children* (vol. 1). New York, NY: Russell Sage.

Brooks-Gunn, J., Duncan, G. J., & Maritato, N. (1997). Poor families, poor outcomes: The well-being of children and youth. In G. J. Duncan & J. Brooks-Gunn (Eds.), *Consequences of growing up poor* (pp. 1–17). New York, NY: Russell Sage.

Brown, E. D., Ackerman, B. P., & Moore, C. A. (2013). Family adversity and inhibitory control for economically disadvantaged children: Preschool relations and associations with school readiness. *Journal of Family Psychology, 27*, 443–452.

Brownell, C. A., Svetlova, M., Anderson, R., Nichols, S. R., & Drummond, J. (2013). Socialization of early prosocial behavior: Parents' talk about emotions is associated with sharing and helping in toddlers. *Infancy, 18*, 91–119.

Browning, D. S., Green, M. C., & Witte, J., Jr. (Eds.). (2006). *Sex, marriage, and family in world religions*. New York, NY: Columbia.

Brownlee, J. R., & Bakeman, R. (1981). Hitting in toddler-peer interaction. *Child Development, 52*, 1076–1079.

Brummelman, E., Thomaes, S., Orobio de Castro, B., Overbeek, G., & Bushman, B. J. (2014). "That's not just beautiful—That's incredibly beautiful!": The adverse impact of inflated praise on children with low self-esteem. *Psychological Science, 25*, 728–735.

Buck, M. J., Vittrup, B., & Holden, G. W. (2007). "It makes me feel really sad"; The role of children's reactions to discipline in internalization. In A. Columbus (Ed.), *Advances in psychology research* (vol. 38, pp. 117–136). New York, NY: Nova Science Publishers.

Buckner, J. C., Bassuk, E. L., Weinreb, L. F., & Brooks, M. G. (1999). Homelessness and its relation to the mental health and behavior of low-income school-age children. *Developmental Psychology, 35*, 246–257.

Buehler, C. (2006). Parents and peers in relation to early adolescent problem behavior. *Journal of Marriage and Family, 68*, 109–124.

Buehler, C., Anthony, C., Krishnakumar, A., Stone, G., Gerard, J., & Pemberton, S. (1997). Interparental conflict and youth problem behaviors: A meta-analysis. *Journal of Child and Family Studies, 6*, 233–247.

Buehler, C., & Gerard, J. M. (2002). Marital conflict, ineffective parenting, and children's and adolescents' maladjustment. *Journal of Marriage and Family, 64*, 78–92.

Bugental, D. B., Blue, J., & Cruzcosa, M. (1989). Perceived control over caregiving outcomes: Implications for child abuse. *Developmental Psychology, 25*, 532–539.

Bugental, D. B., & Cortez, V. L. (1988). Physiological reactivity to responsive and unresponsive children as moderated by perceived control. *Child Development, 59*, 686–693.

Bugental, D. B., & Grusec, J. E. (2006). Socialization processes. In N. Eisenberg (Ed.), *Handbook of child psychology: Vol. 3, social, emotional, and personality development* (6th ed., pp. 366–428). Hoboken, NJ: John Wiley & Sons Inc.

Bugental, D. B., & Happaney, K. (2002). Parental attributions. In M. H. Bornstein (Ed.), *Being and becoming parents* (2nd ed., vol. 3, pp. 509–535). Mahwah, NJ: Lawrence Erlbaum Associates.

Buijzen, M., & Valkenburg, P. M. (2003). The unintended effects of television advertising: A parent-child survey. *Consumer Research, 30*, 483–503.

Buist, K. L., Deković, M., & Prinzie, P. (2013). Sibling relationship quality and psychopathology of children and adolescents: A meta-analysis. *Clinical Psychology Review, 33*, 97–106.

Bumpass, L. L., & Raley, R. K. (1955). Redefining single-parent families: Cohabitation and changing family reality. *Demography, 32*, 97–109.

Bureau of Labor Statistics. (2013). *Employment characteristics of families 2012*. Washington, DC: U.S. Department of Labor.

Bureau of Labor Statistics. (2014). Childcare workers. *Occupational Outlook Handbook*. Retrieved June 13, 2014, from http://www.bls.gov/ooh/personal-care-and-service/childcare-workers.htm

Buri, J. R. (1991). Parental Authority Questionnaire. *Journal of Personality Assessment, 57*, 110–119.

Burton, L. M., & Jarrett, R. L. (2000). In the mix, yet on the margins: The place of families in urban neighborhood and child development research. *Journal of Marriage and Family, 62*, 1114–1135.

Bush, K. R., & Peterson, G. W. (2013). Parent-child relationships in diverse contexts. In G. W. Peterson & K. R. Bush (Eds.), *Handbook of marriage and the family* (pp. 275–302). New York, NY: Springer.

Bushnell, H. (1908/2000). *Christian nurture*. Eugene, OR: Wipf & Stock Publishers.

Butterfield, F. (1995). *All God's children: The Bosket family and the American tradition of violence*. New York, NY: Alfred A. Knopf.

Cable, M. (1972). *The little darlings: A history of child rearing in America*. New York, NY: Charles Scribner's Sons.

Cabrera, N. J., Scott, M., Fagan, J., Steward-Streng, N., & Chien, N. (2012). Co-parenting and children's school readiness: A mediational model. *Family Process, 51*, 307–324.

Cabrera, N. J., & SRCD Ethic and Racial Issues Committee. (2013). Positive development of minority children. *Social Policy Report, 27*(2). Retrieved June 6, 2014, from http://www.srcd.org/sites/default/files/documents/washington/spr_272_final.pdf

Cabrera, N. J., Tamis-LeMonda, C. S., Bradley, R. H., Hofferth, S., & Lamb, M. E. (2000). Fatherhood in the twenty-first century. *Child Development, 71*, 127–136.

Cairns, R. B. (1979). *Social development: The origins and plasticity of interchanges*. San Francisco, CA: Freeman.

Califano, J., J. A. (2007). *High society: How substance abuse ravages America and what to do about it*. New York, NY: Public Affairs.

Calkins, S. D. (1994). Origins and outcomes of individual differences in emotion regulation. *Monographs of the Society for Research in Child Development, 59*(2–3), 53–72.

Calkins, S. D., Howse, R. B., & Philippot, P. (2004). Individual differences in self-regulation: Implications for childhood adjustment. In P. Philippot & R. S. Feldman (Eds.), *The regulation of emotion* (pp. 307–332). Mahwah, NJ: Lawrence Erlbaum Associates.

Calkins, S. D., & Mackler, J. S. (2011). Temperament, emotion regulation, and social development. In M. K. Underwood & L. H. Rosen (Eds.), *Social development: Relationships in infancy, childhood, and adolescence* (pp. 44–72). New York, NY: Guilford Press.

Calvert, S. L., & Kotler, J. A. (2003). Lessons from children's television: The impact of the Children's Television Act on children's learning. *Journal of Applied Developmental Psychology, 24*, 275–335.

Calvin, J. (1536/1960). *The Institutes of the Christian religion* (F. L. Battles, Trans.). Philadelphia, PA: Westminster Press.

Camarota, S. A. (2012). *Immigrants in the United States: A profile of America's foreign-born population*. Washington, DC: Center for Immigration Studies.

Cameron, L., Erkal, N., Gangadharan, L., & Meng, X. (2013). Little emperors: Behavioral impacts of China's one-child policy. *Science, 339*, 953–957.

Campbell, S. (2002). *Behavior problems in preschool children: Clinical and developmental issues* (2nd ed.). New York, NY: Guilford Press.

Caplan, P. J., & Hall-McCorquodale, I. (1985). Mother-blaming in major clinical journals. *American Journal of Orthopsychiatry, 55*, 345–353.

Cappa, C., & Khan, S. M. (2011). Understanding caregivers' attitudes towards physical punishment of children: Evidence from 34 low- and middle-income countries. *Child Abuse and Neglect, 35*, 1009–1021.

Carlson, M. J., McLanahan, S. S., & Brooks-Gunn, J. (2008). Co-parenting and nonresident fathers' involvement with young children after a nonmarital birth. *Demography, 45*, 461–488.

Carson, C., Redshaw, M., Sacker, A., Kelly, Y., Kurinczuk, J. J., & Quigley, M. A. (2013). Effects of pregnancy planning, fertility, and assisted reproductive treatment on child behavioral problems at 5 and 7 years: Evidence from the Millennium Cohort Study. *Fertility and Sterility, 99*, 456–463.

Carter, B., & McGoldrick, M. (Eds.). (2005). *The expanded family life cycle: Individual, family, and social perspectives* (3rd ed.). New York, NY: Allyn and Bacon.

Casey, B. J. (2013). The teenage brain: An overview. *Current Directions in Psychological Science, 22*, 80–81.

Casey, B. J., & Caudle, K. (2013). The teenage brain: Self-control. *Current Directions in Psychological Science, 22*, 82–87.

Casey, B. J., Tottenham, N., Liston, C., & Durston, S. (2005). Imaging the developing brain: What have we learned about cognitive development? *Trends in Cognitive Sciences, 9*, 104–110.

Cassidy, J. (2008). The nature of the child's ties. In J. Cassidy & P. R. Shaver (Eds.), *The handbook of attachment* (2nd ed., pp. 3–22). New York, NY: Guilford.

Cassidy, J., Jones, J. D., & Shaver, P. R. (2013). Contributions of attachment theory and research: A framework for future research, translation, and policy. *Development and Psychopathology, 25*, 1415–1434.

Cassidy, J., & Shaver, P. R. (Eds.). (2008). *Handbook of attachment* (2nd ed.). New York, NY: Guilford.

Cavanagh, K., Dobash, R. E., & Dobash, R. P. (2007). The murder of children by fathers in the context of child abuse. *Child Abuse and Neglect, 31*, 731–746.

Ceballo, R., Dahl, T. A., Aretakis, M. T., & Ramirez, C. (2001). Inner-city children's exposure to community violence: How much do parents know? *Journal of Marriage and Family, 63*, 927–940.

Ceballo, R., & McLoyd, V. C. (2002). Social support and parenting in poor, dangerous neighborhoods. *Child Development, 73*, 1310–1321.

Centers for Disease Control and Prevention. (2013). *Breastfeeding report card 2013*. Atlanta, GA: Author.

Centers for Disease Control and Prevention. (2014a). *Infant health*. Retrieved June 16, 2014, from http://www.cdc.gov/nchs/fastats/infant-health.htm

Centers for Disease Control and Prevention (2014b). *Injury prevention & control: Motor vehicle safety, teen drivers fact sheet*. Atlanta, GA: National Center for Injury Prevention and Control, CDC. Retrieved June 16, 2014, from http://www.cdc.gov/motorvehiclesafety/teen_drivers/teendrivers_factsheet.html

Centers for Disease Control and Prevention. (2014c). *What is assisted reproductive technology*? Atlanta, GA: Center for Disease Control and Prevention.

Centers for Disease Control and Prevention, American Society for Reproductive Medicine, & Society for Assisted Reproductive Technology. (2011). *2009 assisted reproductive technology success rates: National summary and fertility clinic reports*. Atlanta, GA: U.S. Department of Health and Human Services.

Centers for Disease Control and Prevention, Vital Signs. (2012). *Teen drinking and driving: A dangerous mix*. Atlanta, GA: National Center for Injury Prevention and Control, CDC.

Central Intelligence Agency. (2014). *The world factbook*. Retrieved May 16, 2014, from https://www.cia.gov/library/publications/the-world-factbook/

Certain, L. K., & Kahn, R. S. (2002). Prevalence, correlates, and trajectory of television viewing among infants and toddlers. *Pediatrics, 109*, 634–643.

Chaffin, M., & Friedrich, B. (2004). Evidence-based treatments in child abuse and neglect. *Children and Youth Services Review, 26*, 1097–1113.

Chaffin, M., Letourneau, E., & Silovsky, J. F. (2002). Adults, adolescents, and children who sexually abuse children: A developmental perspective. In J. E. B. Myers, L. Berliner, J. Briere, C. T. Hendrix, C. Jenny, & T. A. Reid (Eds.), *The APSAC handbook on child maltreatment* (3nd ed., pp. 205–232). Thousand Oaks, CA: SAGE.

Chamberlin, C. M., & Zhang, N. (2009). Workaholism, health, and self-acceptance. *Journal of Counseling & Development, 87*, 159–169.

Chambers, C., Chiu, S., Scott, A. N., Tolomiczenko, G., Redelmeier, D. A., Levinson, W., & Hwang, S. W. (2013). Factors associated with poor mental health status among homeless women with and without dependent children. *Community Mental Health Journal, 39*, 1–7.

Chandra, A., Copen, C. E., & Stephen, E. H. (2013). Infertility and impaired fecundity in the United States, 1982–2010: Data from the National Survey of Family Growth. *National Health Statistics Reports* (vol. 67). Retrieved May 18, 2014, from http://www.cdc.gov/nchs/data/nhsr/nhsr067.pdf

Chandra, A., Lara-Cinisomo, S., Jaycox, L. H., Tanielian, T., Burns, R. M., Ruder, T., & Han, B. (2010). Children on the homefront: The experience of children from military families. *Pediatrics, 125*, 16–25.

Chao, R. K. (1994). Beyond parental control and authoritarian parenting style: Understanding Chinese parenting through the cultural notion of training. *Child Development, 65*, 1111–1119.

Chao, R. K. (2000). The parenting of immigrant Chinese and European American mothers: Relations between parenting styles, socialization goals, and parental practices. *Journal of Applied Developmental Psychology, 21*, 233–248.

Chao, R. K., & Tseng, V. (2002). Parenting of Asians. In M. H. Bornstein (Ed.), *Handbook of parenting, vol. 4: Social conditions and applied parenting* (2nd ed., pp. 59–93). Mahwah, NJ: Lawrence Erlbaum Associates.

Chaplin, L. N., & John, D. R. (2010). Interpersonal influences on adolescent materialism: A new look at the role of parents and peers. *Journal of Consumer Psychology, 20*, 176–184.

Charach, A., Carson, P., Fox, S., Ali, M. U., Beckett, J., & Lim, C. G. (2013). Interventions for preschool children at high risk for ADHD: A comparative effectiveness review. *Pediatrics, 131*, e1584–e1604.

Chassin, L., Pitts, S. C., DeLucia, C., & Todd, M. (1999). A longitudinal study of children of alcoholics: Predicting young adult substance use disorders, anxiety, and depression. *Journal of Abnormal Psychology, 108*, 106–119.

Chassin, L., Presson, C. C., Rose, J., Sherman, S. J., Davis, M. J., & Gonzalez, J. L. (2005). Parenting style and smoking-specific parenting practices as predictors of adolescent smoking onset. *Journal of Pediatric Psychology, 30*, 333–344.

Chatterji, P., Markowitz, S., & Brooks-Gunn, J. (2013). Effects of early maternal employment on maternal health and well-being. *Journal of Population Economics, 26*, 285–301.

Chen, C., & Stevenson, H. W. (1989). Homework: A cross-cultural examination. *Child Development, 60*, 551–561.

Chen, X., & French, D. C. (2008). Children's social competence in cultural context. *Annual Review of Psychology, 59*, 591–616.

Child Care Aware of America. (2013). *Parents and the high cost of child care, 2013*. Arlington, VA: Author.

Child Welfare Information Gateway. (2009). *Parental substance use and the child welfare system*. Washington, DC: U.S. Department of Health and Human Services, Children's Bureau.

Child Welfare Information Gateway. (2011). *How many children were adopted in 2007 and 2008?* Washington, DC: U.S. Department of Health and Human Services, Children's Bureau.

Child Welfare Information Gateway. (2012). *Mandatory reporters of child abuse and neglect*. Washington, DC: U.S. Department of Health and Human Services, Children's Bureau.

Child Welfare Information Gateway. (2013). *Foster care statistics 2012*. Washington, DC: U.S. Department of Health and Human Services, Children's Bureau.

ChildTrends. (2013). *Child maltreatment: Indicators on children and youth, ChildTrends Data Bank*. Bethesda, MD: Author.

Children's Bureau. (2014). Child abuse & neglect frequently asked question #7. Retrieved June 17, 2014, from http://www.acf.hhs.gov/programs/cb/resource/can-faq7

Christakis, D. A., Zimmerman, F. J., DiGiuseppe, D. L., & McCarty, C. A. (2004). Early television exposure and subsequent attentional problems in children. *Pediatrics, 113*, 708–713.

Chua, A. (2011). *Battle hymn of the tiger mother*. New York, NY: Penguin Press.

Chumlea, W., Schubert, C., Roche, A., Kulin, H., Lee, P., Himes, J., & Sun, S. (2003). Age at menarche and racial comparisons in U.S. girls. *Pediatrics, 111*, 110–113.

Chung, E. K., Mathew, L., Rothkopf, A. C., Elo, I. T., Coyne, J. C., & Culhane, J. F. (2009). Parenting attitudes and infant spanking: The influence of childhood experiences. *Pediatrics, 124*, e278–e286.

Clarke-Stewart, A. (1998). Historical shifts and underlying themes in ideas about rearing young children in the United States: Where have we been? Where are we going? *Early Development and Parenting, 7*, 110–117.

Clarke, A. M., & Clarke, A. D. B. (1976). *Early experience: Myth and evidence*. New York, NY: Free Press.

Clarke-Stewart, K. A. (1988). Parents' effects on children's development: A decade of progress? *Journal of Applied Developmental Psychology, 9*, 41–84.

Clincy, A. R., & Mills-Koonce, W. R. (2013). Trajectories of intrusive parenting during infancy and toddlerhood as predictors of rural, low-income African American boys' school-related outcomes. *American Journal of Orthopsychiatry, 83*, 194–206.

Cohen, C. P. (1996). Monitoring the United Nations Convention on the Rights of the Child in a non-party state: The United States. In E. Verhellen (Ed.), *Monitoring children's rights* (pp. 475–490). Amsterdam, the Netherlands: Martinus Nighoff.

Cohen, D. B. (1999). *Stranger in the nest: Do parents really shape their child's personality?* New York, NY: John Wiley.

Cohn, D. A. (1990). Child-mother attachment of six-year-olds and social competence at school. *Child Development, 61*, 152–162.

Colapinto, J. (2000). *As nature made him: The boy who was raised as a girl*. New York, NY: Harper Collins.

Coleman, M., Ganong, L., & Leon, K. (2006). Divorce and post-divorce relationships. In A. L. Vangelisti & D. Perlman (Eds.), *The Cambridge handbook of personal relationships* (pp. 157–173). New York, NY: Cambridge University Press.

Coleman, M., Ganong, L., & Russell, L. T. (2013). Resilience in stepfamilies. In D. S. Becvar (Ed.), *Handbook of family resilience* (pp. 85–103). New York, NY: Springer.

Coleman, P. K., & Karraker, K. H. (1998). Self-efficacy and parenting quality: Findings and future applications. *Developmental Review, 18*, 47–85.

Coles, R. L. (2002). Black single fathers: Choosing to parent full-time. *Journal of Contemporary Ethnography, 31*, 411–439.

Coley, R. L., & Chase-Lansdale, P. L. (1998). Adolescent pregnancy and parenthood: Recent evidence and future directions. *American Psychologist, 53*, 152–166.

Collins, R. L., Elliott, M. N., Berry, S. H., Kanouse, D. E., Kunkel, D., Hunter, S. B., & Miu, A. (2004). Watching sex on television predicts adolescent initiation of sexual behavior. *Pediatrics, 114*, 280–289.

Collins, W. A., Maccoby, E.E., Steinberg, L., Hetherington, E.M., & Bornstein, M.H. (2000). Contemporary research on parenting: The case for nature and nurture. *American Psychologist, 55*, 218–232.

Collins, W. A., Madsen, S. D., & Susman-Stillman, A. (2002). Parenting during middle childhood. In M. H. Bornstein (Ed.), *Handbook of parenting, vol. 1: Children and parenting* (2nd ed., pp. 73–101). Mahwah, NJ: Lawrence Erlbaum Associates.

Collom, E. (2005). The ins and outs of homeschooling: The determinants of parental motivations and student achievement. *Education and Urban Society, 37*, 307–335.

Coln, K. L., Jordan, S. S., & Mercer, S. H. (2013). A unified model exploring parenting practices as mediators of marital conflict and children's adjustment. *Child Psychiatry & Human Development, 44*, 1–11.

Colon, A. R. (1999). *Nurturing children: A history of pediatrics*. Westport, CT: Greenwood.

Combs-Orme, T., & Cain, D. S. (2008). Predictors of mothers' use of spanking with their infants. *Child Abuse and Neglect, 32*, 649–657.

Combs-Orme, T., & Orme, J. G. (2014). Foster parenting together: Assessing foster parent applicant couples. *Children and Youth Services Review, 36*, 70–80.

Comer, J. P. (1980). *School power*. New York, NY: Free Press.

Committee on Public Education. (2001). Children, adolescents, and television. *Pediatrics, 107*, 423–426.

Conger, R. D., Belsky, J., & Capaldi, D. M. (2009). The intergenerational transmission of parenting: Closing comments for the special section. *Developmental Psychology, 45*, 1276–1283.

Conger, R. D., Schofield, T. J., & Neppl, T. K. (2012). Intergenerational continuity and discontinuity in harsh parenting. *Parenting: Science and Practice, 12*, 222–231.

Connell, A. M., & Goodman, S. H. (2002). The association between psychopathology in fathers versus mothers and children's internalizing and externalizing behavior problems: A meta-analysis. *Psychological Bulletin, 128*, 746–773.

Conners-Burrow, N. A., McKelvey, L., Pemberton, J. R., Lagory, J., Mesman, G. R., & Whiteside-Mansell, L. (2013). Moderators of the relationship between maternal substance abuse symptoms and preschool children's behavioral outcomes. *Journal of Child and Family Studies, 22*, 1120–1129.

Costello, E. J., Mustillo, S., Erkanli, A., Keeler, G., & Angold, A. (2003). Prevalence and development of psychiatric disorders in childhood and adolescence. *Archives General of Psychiatry, 60*, 837–844.

Council on Communications and Media. (2011). Media use by children younger than 2 years. *Pediatrics, 128*, 1040–1045.

Council on Communications and Media. (2013). Children, adolescents, and the media. *Pediatrics, 132*, 958–961.

Cowan, C. P., & Cowan, P. A. (1992). *When partners become parents: The big life change for couples*. New York, NY: Basic Books.

Cowan, P. A., & Cowan, C. P. (2012). Normative family transitions, normal family process, and healthy child development. In F. Walsh (Ed.), *Normal family processes: Growing diversity and complexity* (4th ed., pp. 428–451). New York, NY: Guilford Press.

Cowan, P. A., Powell, D., & Cowan, C. P. (1998). Parenting interventions: A family systems perspective. In I. E. Sigel & K. A. Renninger (Eds.), *Child psychology in practice* (5th ed., vol. 4, pp. 3–72). New York, NY: John Wiley & Sons.

Cox, M. J., & Paley, B. (2003). Understanding families as systems. *Current Directions in Psychological Science, 12*, 193–196.

Craig, W., Harel-Fisch, Y., Fogel-Grinvald, H., Dostaler, S., Hetland, J., Simons-Morton, B., . . . Due, P. (2009). A cross-national profile of bullying and victimization among adolescents in 40 countries. *International Journal of Public Health, 54*, 216–224.

Crenshaw, D. A. (2013). A resilience framework for treating severe child trauma. In S. Goldstein & R. B. Brooks (Eds.), *Handbook of resilience in children* (pp. 309–327). New York, NY: Springer.

Criss, M. M., Shaw, D. S., & Ingoldsby, E. M. (2003). Mother-son positive synchrony in middle childhood: Relation to antisocial behavior. *Social Development, 12*, 379–400.

Crnic, K., & Low, C. (2002). Everyday stress and parenting. In M. H. Bornstein (Ed.), *Handbook of parenting, vol. 5: Practical issues in parenting* (2nd ed., pp. 243–268). Mahwah, NJ: Lawrence Erlbaum Associates.

Croake, J. W., & Glover, K. E. (1977). A history and evaluation of parent education. *Family Coordinator, 26*, 151–158.

Crockenberg, S. B. (1987). Predictors and correlates of anger toward and punitive control of toddlers by adolescent mothers. *Child Development, 58*, 964–975.

Crockenberg, S. B., & McCluskey, K. (1986). Change in maternal behavior during the baby's first year of life. *Child Development, 57*, 746–753.

Croen, L. A., Najjar, D. V., Fireman, B., & Grether, J. K. (2007). Maternal and paternal age and risk of autism spectrum disorders. *Archives of Pediatrics and Adolescent Medicine, 161*, 334–340.

Crouter, A. C., & Head, M. R. (2002). Parental monitoring and knowledge of children. In M. H. Bornstein (Ed.), *Handbook of parenting, vol. 3: Being and becoming a parent* (2nd ed., pp. 461–483). Mahwah, NJ: Lawrence Erlbaum Associates.

Crouter, A. C., & McHale, S. M. (1993). Temporal rhythms in family life: Seasonal variation in the relation between parental work and family processes. *Developmental Psychology, 29*, 198–205.

Crouter, A. C., & McHale, S. M. (2005). The long arm of the job revisited: Parenting in dual-earner families. In T. Luster & L. Okagaki (Eds.), *Parenting: An ecological perspective* (2nd ed., pp. 275–296). Mahwah, NJ: Lawrence Erlbaum Associates.

Crowell, J. A., Fraley, R. C., & Shaver, P. R. (2008). Measurement of individual differences in adolescent and adult attachment. In J. Cassidy & P. R. Shaver (Eds.), *Handbook of attachment* (2nd ed., pp. 434–465). New York, NY: Guilford.

Csikszentmihalyi, M., & Schneider, B. (2000). *Becoming adult: How teenagers prepare for the world of work*. New York, NY: Basic Books.

Cummings, E. M. (1995). Usefulness of experiments for the study of the family. *Journal of Family Psychology, 9*, 175–185.

Cummings, E. M., Braungart-Rieker, J. M., & Du Rocher Schudlich, T. D. (2013). Emotion and personality development. In R. M. Lerner, M. A. Easterbrooks, & J. Mistry (Eds.), *Developmental psychology* (2nd ed., vol. 6, pp. 215–241). New York, NY: John Wiley & Sons.

Cummings, E. M., Goeke-Morey, M. C., & Graham, M. A. (2002). Interparent relations as a dimension of parenting. In J. G. Borkowski, S. L. Ramey, & M. Bristol-Power (Eds.), *Parenting and the child's world: Influences on academic, intellectual, and social-emotional development* (pp. 251–264). Mahwah, NJ: Lawrence Erlbaum Associates.

Cummings, E. M., Schermerhorn, A. C., Davies, P. T., Goeke-Morey, M. C., & Cummings, J. S. (2006). Interparental discord and child adjustment: Prospective investigations of emotional security as an explanatory mechanism. *Child Development, 77*, 132–152.

Cummings, H. M., & Vandewater, E. A. (2007). Relation of adolescent video game play to time spent in other activities. *Archives of Pediatric and Adolescent Medicine, 161*, 684–689.

Cundiff, P. R. (2013). Ordered delinquency: The "effects" of birth order on delinquency. *Personality and Social Psychology Bulletin, 39*, 1017–1029.

Cunningham, S. A., Kramer, M. R., & Narayan, K. M. V. (2014). Incidence of childhood obesity in the United States. *New England Journal of Medicine, 370*, 403–411.

Curtis, S. (1977). *Genie: A psycholinguistic study of a modern day wild child*. New York, NY: Academic Press.

Daggett, J., O'Brien, M., Zanolli, K., & Peyton, V. (2000). Parents' attitudes about children: Associations with parental life histories and child-rearing quality. *Journal of Family Psychology, 14*, 187–199.

Dahl, R. E. (2004). Adolescent brain development: A period of vulnerabilities and opportunities. *Annals of the New York Academy of Sciences, 1021*, 1–22.

Dalton, M. A., Bernhardt, A. M., Gibson, J. J., Sargent, J. D., Beach, M. L., Adachi-Mejia, A. M., . . . Hetherton, T. F. (2005). Use of cigarettes and alcohol by preschoolers while role-playing as adults: "Honey, have some smokes." *Archives of Pediatric Adolescent Medicine, 159*, 854–859.

Daly, M., & Wilson, M. I. (1996). Violence against stepchildren. *Current Directions in Psychological Science, 5*, 77–81.

Damrosch, L. (2005). *Jean-Jacques Rousseau: Restless genius*. New York, NY: Houghton Mifflin.

D'Angelo, A. V., Palacios, N. A., & Chase-Lansdale, L. (2012). Latino immigrant differences in father involvement with infants. *Fathering: A Journal of Theory, Research, & Practice About Men as Fathers, 10*, 178–212.

D'Augelli, A. R., Grossman, A. H., & Starks, M. T. (2005). Parents' awareness of lesbian, gay, and bisexual youths' sexual orientation. *Journal of Marriage and Family, 67*, 474–482.

Davidov, M., Grusec, J. E., & Wolfe, J. L. (2012). Mothers' knowledge of their children's evaluations of discipline: The role of type of discipline and misdeed, and parenting practices. *Merrill-Palmer Quarterly, 58*, 314–340.

Davies, P. T., & Cummings, E. M. (1994). Marital conflict and child adjustment: An emotional security hypothesis. *Psychological Bulletin, 116*, 387–411.

Davis, J. (2012). *School enrollment and work status: 2011, American Community Survey Briefs*. Washington, DC: U.S. Department of Commerce, U.S. Census Bureau.

Davis-Kean, P. E. (2005). The influence of parent education and family income on child achievement: The indirect role of parental expectations and the home environment. *Journal of Family Psychology, 19*, 294–304.

Dawkins, R. (1976). *The selfish gene*. New York, NY: Oxford University Press.

Deater-Deckard, K. (2004). *Parenting stress*. New Haven, CT: Yale University.

Deater-Deckard, K., & Dodge, K. A. (1997). Externalizing behavior problems and discipline revisited: Nonlinear effects and variation by culture, context, and gender. *Psychological Inquiry, 8*, 161–175.

Deci, E. L., & Ryan, R. M. (2012). Motivation, personality, and development within embedded social contexts: An overview of self-determination theory. In R. M. Ryan (Ed.), *Oxford handbook of human motivation* (pp. 85–107). New York, NY: Oxford University Press.

Deckner, D. F., Adamson, L. B., & Bakeman, R. (2006). Child and maternal contributions to shared reading: Effects on language and literacy development. *Applied Developmental Psychology, 27*, 31–41.

DeGarmo, D. S. (2010). A time varying evaluation of identity theory and father involvement for full custody, shared custody, and no custody divorced fathers. *Fathering: A Journal of Theory, Research, and Practice about Men as Fathers, 8*, 181–202.

DeGarmo, D. S., & Forgatch, M. S. (2005). Early development of delinquency within divorced families: Evaluating a randomized preventive intervention trial. *Developmental Science, 8*, 229–239.

del Río, M. F., & Strasser, K. (2013). Preschool children's beliefs about gender differences in academic skills. *Sex Roles, 68*, 231–238.

Del Vecchio, T., & O'Leary, S. G. (2006). Antecedents of toddler aggression: Dysfunctional parenting in mother-toddler dyads. *Journal of Clinical Child & Adolescent Psychology, 35*, 194–202.

DeLoache, J. S., Chiong, C., Sherman, K., Islam, N., Vanderborght, M., Troseth, G. L., . . . O'Doherty, K. (2010). Do babies learn from baby media? *Psychological Science, 21*, 1570–1574.

deMause, L. (Ed.). (1975). *The history of childhood*. New York, NY: Harper Torchbooks.

Demick, J. (2002). Stages of parental development. In M. H. Bornstein (Ed.), *Handbook of parenting. Vol. 3: Becoming and being a parent* (2nd ed., pp. 389–413). Mahwah, NJ: Lawrence Erlbaum Associates.

Demick, J. (2006). Parental development: Theory and practice. In R. L. Mosher, D. J. Youngman, & J. M. Day (Eds.), *Human development across the life span: Educational and psychological applications* (pp. 177–193). Westport, CT: Praeger.

deMontigny, F., Girard, M-E., Lacharité, C., Dubeau, D., & Devault, A. (2013). Psychosocial factors associated with paternal postnatal depression. *Journal of Affective Disorders, 150*, 44–49.

Demuth, C., Keller, H., & Yovsi, R. D. (2012). Cultural models in communication with infants: Lessons from Kikaikelaki, Cameroon and Muenster, Germany. *Journal of Early Childhood Research, 10*, 70–87.

DeOllos, I. Y., & Kapinus, C. A. (2002). Aging childless individuals and couples: Suggestions for new directions in research. *Sociological Inquiry, 72*, 72–80.

de Roos, S. A., Iedema, J., & Miedema, S. (2004). Influence of maternal denomination, God concepts, and child-rearing practices on young children's God concepts. *Journal for the Scientific Study of Religion, 43*, 519–535.

Devaney, B. L., & Dion, M. R. (2010). *15-month impacts of Oklahoma's Family Expectations program*. Princeton, NJ: Mathematica Policy Research.

Diallo, Y., Hagemann, F., Etienne, A., Gurbuzer, Y., & Mehran, F. (2010). *Global child labour developments: Measuring trends from 2004 to 2008. Statistical Information and Monitoring Programme on Child Labour (SIMPOC)*. Geneva, Switzerland: International Labour Office.

Dick, D. M., Viken, R., Purcell, S., Kaprio, J., Pulkkinen, L., & Rose, R. J. (2007). Parental monitoring moderates the importance of genetic and environmental influences on adolescent smoking. *Journal of Abnormal Psychology, 116*, 213–218.

Dieterich, C. M., Felice, J. P., O'Sullivan, E., & Rasmussen, K. M. (2013). Breastfeeding and health outcomes for the mother-infant dyad. *Pediatric Clinics of North America, 60*, 31–48.

DiLalla, L. F. (2002). Behavior genetics of aggression in children: Review and future directions. *Developmental Review, 22*, 593–622.

Dinkes, R., Cataldi, E. F., Lin-Kelly, W., & Snyder, T. D. (2007). *Indicators of school crime and safety: 2007*. Rockville, MD: National Center for Education Statistics.

Dix, T. (1991). The affective organization of parenting: Adaptive and maladaptive processes. *Psychological Bulletin, 110*, 3–25.

Dix, T., & Branca, S. H. (2003). Parenting as a goal-regulation process. In L. Kuczynski (Ed.), *Handbook of the dynamics in parent-child relations* (pp. 167–187). Thousand Oaks, CA: SAGE.

Dix, T., & Meunier, L. N. (2009). Depressive symptoms and parenting competence: An analysis of 13 regulatory processes. *Developmental Review, 29*, 45–68.

Dix, T., Stewart, A. D., Gershoff, E. T., & Day, W. H. (2007). Autonomy and children's reactions to being controlled: Evidence that both compliance and defiance may be positive markers in early development. *Child Development, 78*, 1204–1221.

Dobson, J. (1992). *The new dare to discipline*. Wheaton, IL: Tinsdale House.

Dodge, K. A. (2008). Framing public policy and prevention of chronic violence in American youths. *American Psychologist, 63*, 573–590.

Domjan, M. (2015). *The principles of learning and behavior* (7th ed.). Stanford, CT: Cengage Learning.

Dougherty, L. R., Tolep, M. R., Bufferd, S. J., Olino, T. M., Dyson, M., Traditi, J., . . . Klein, D. N. (2013). Preschool anxiety disorders: Comprehensive assessment of clinical, demographic, temperamental, familial, and life stress correlates. *Journal of Clinical Child & Adolescent Psychology, 41*, 1299–1310.

Dowling, C. B., Smith Slep, A. M., & O'Leary, S. G. (2009). Understanding preemptive parenting: Relations with toddlers' misbehavior, overreactive and lax discipline, and praise. *Journal of Clinical Child & Adolescent Psychology, 38*, 850–857.

Downey, G., & Coyne, J. C. (1990). Children of depressed parents: An integrative review. *Psychological Bulletin, 108*, 50–76.

Dozier, M., Albus, K., Fisher, P. A., & Sepulveda, S. (2002). Interventions for foster parents: Implications for developmental theory. *Development and Psychopathology, 14*, 843–860.

Dozier, M., & Lindhiem, O. (2006). This is my child: Differences among foster parents in commitment to their young children. *Child Maltreatment, 11*, 338–345.

Dozier, M., Zeanah, C. H., & Bernard, K. (2013). Infants and toddlers in foster care. *Child Development Perspectives, 7*, 166–171.

Dubowitz, H., Black, M., Cox, C. E., & Kerr, M. A. (2001). Father involvement and children's functioning at age 6 years: A multisite study. *Child Maltreatment, 6*, 300–309.

Dubowitz, H., Black, M. M., Kerr, M. A., Starr, R. H., & Harrington, D. (2000). Fathers and child neglect. *Archives of Pediatrics & Adolescent Medicine, 154*, 135–141.

Duderstadt, K. G. (2007). The importance of investing in children's health. *Journal of Pediatric Health Care, 21*, 276–278.

Duncan, L. G., Coatsworth, J. D., & Greenberg, M. T. (2009). A model of mindful parenting: Implications for parent-child relationships and prevention research. *Clinical Child and Family Psychology Review, 12*, 255–270.

Dunifon, R. (2013). The influence of grandparents on the lives of children and adolescents. *Child Development Perspectives, 7*, 55–60.

Dunifon, R., & Kowaleski-Jones, L. (2007). The influence of grandparents in single-mother families. *Journal of Marriage and Family, 69*, 465–481.

Dunkel Schetter, C. (2011). Psychological science on pregnancy: Stress processes, biopsychosocial models, and emerging research issues. *Annual Review of Psychology, 62*, 531–558.

Dunn, J., Davies, L. C., O'Connor, T. G., & Sturgess, W. (2000). Parents' and partners' life course and family experiences: Links with parent-child relationships in different family settings. *Journal of Child Psychology and Psychiatry and Allied Disciplines, 41*, 955–968.

Dunn, J., & Plomin, R. (1990). *Separate lives: Why siblings are so different*. New York, NY: Basic Books.

Dunn, J. S., Kinney, D. A., & Hofferth, S. L. (2003). Parental ideologies and children's after-school activities. *American Behavioral Scientist, 46*, 1359–1386.

DuPlessis, H. M., Bell, R., & Richards, T. (1997). Adolescent pregnancy: Understanding the impact of age and race on outcomes. *Journal of Adolescent Health, 20*, 187–197.

Duran, B., Malcoe, L. H., Sanders, M., Waitzkin, H., Skipper, B., & Yager, J. (2004). Child maltreatment prevalence and mental disorders outcomes among American Indian women in primary care. *Child Abuse and Neglect, 28*, 131–145.

Durrant, J. E. (1999). Evaluating the success of Sweden's corporal punishment ban. *Child Abuse and Neglect, 23*, 435–448.

Durrant, J. E. (2013). *Positive discipline in everyday parenting* (3rd ed.). Stockholm, Sweden: Save the Children Sweden.

Durrant, J. E., Rose-Krasnor, L., & Broberg, A. G. (2003). Physical punishment and maternal beliefs in Sweden and Canada. *Journal of Comparative Family Studies, 34*, 585–604.

Dutra, L. M., & Glantz, S. A. (2014). Electronic cigarettes and conventional cigarette use among US adolescents: A cross-sectional study. *JAMA Pediatrics*, 168.

Duzinski, S. V., Barczyk, A. N., Wheeler, T. C., Iyer, S. S., & Lawson, K. A. (2014). Threat of pediatric hyperthermia in an enclosed vehicle: A year-round study. *Injury Prevention, 20*, 220–225.

Dwairy, M., Achoui, M., Abouserie, R., & Farah, A. (2006). Parenting styles, individuation, and mental health of Arab adolescents. *Journal of Cross-Cultural Psychology, 37*, 262–272.

Dykas, M. J., & Cassidy, J. (2013). The first bond experience: The basics of infant-caregiver attachment. In C. Hazan & M. I. Campa (Eds.), *Human bonding: The science of affectional ties* (pp. 11–40). New York, NY: Guilford Press.

Easterbrooks, M. A., Bartlett, J. D., Beeghly, M., & Thompson, R. A. (2013). Social and emotional development in infancy. In R. M. Lerner, M. A. Easterbrooks, & J. Mistry (Eds.), *Developmental psychology* (2nd ed., vol. 6, pp. 91–120). New York, NY: John Wiley & Sons.

Easterbrooks, M. A., & Emde, R. N. (1988). Marital and parent-child relationships: The role of affect in the family system. In R. A. Hinde & J. Stevenson-Hinde (Eds.), *Relationships within families: Mutual influences* (pp. 83–103). New York, NY: Oxford University Press.

Easterbrooks, M. A., Ginsburg, K., & Lerner, R. M. (2013). Resilience among military youth. *Future of Children, 23*, 99–120.

Easterbrooks, M. A., & Graham, C. A. (1999). Security of attachment and parenting: Homeless and low-income housed mothers and infants. *American Journal of Orthopsychiatry, 69*, 337–346.

Eaton, D. K., Kann, L., Kinchen, S., Shanklin, S., Flint, K. H., Hawkins, J., . . . Chyen, D. (2012). Youth risk behavior surveillance—United States, 2011. *Morbidity and mortality weekly report. Surveillance summaries* (vol. 61, pp. 1–162). Washington, DC: Centers for Disease Control and Prevention.

Eccles, J. S., Barber, B. L., Stone, M., & Hunt, J. (2003). Extracurricular activities and adolescent development. *Journal of Social Issues, 59*, 865–889.

Edleson, J. L., & Williams, O. J. (Eds.). (2007). *Parenting by men who batter: New directions for assessment and intervention*. New York, NY: Oxford University Press.

Edwards, C. P., & Liu, W-L. (2002). Parenting toddlers. In M. H. Bornstein (Ed.), *Handbook of parenting, vol. 1: Children and parenting* (pp. 45–72). Mahwah, NJ: Lawrence Erlbaum Associates.

Edwards, V. J., Holden, G. W., Felitti, V. J., & Anda, R. F. (2003). Relationship between multiple forms of childhood maltreatment and adult mental health in community respondents: Results from the Adverse Childhood Experiences study. *American Journal of Psychiatry, 160*, 1453–1460.

Ehrenreich, S. E., Underwood, M. K., & Ackerman, R. A. (2014). Adolescents' text message communication and growth in antisocial behavior across the first year of high school. *Journal of Abnormal Child Psychology, 42*, 251–264.

Eibl-Eibesfeldt, I. (1970). *Ethology: The biology of behavior*. New York, NY: Holt, Rinehart, & Winston.

Eiden, R. D., Teti, D. M., & Corns, K. M. (1995). Maternal working models of attachment, marital adjustment, and the parent-child relationship. *Child Development, 66*, 1504–1518.

Eiland, L., & Romeo, R. D. (2013). Stress and the developing adolescent brain. *Neuroscience, 249*, 162–171.

Eisenberg, M. E., Olson, R. E., Neumark-Sztainer, D., Story, M., & Bearinger, L. H. (2004). Correlations between family meals and psychosocial well-being among adolescents. *Archives of Pediatric and Adolescent Medicine, 158*, 792–796.

Eisenberg, N., Cumberland, A., & Spinrad, T. L. (1998). Parental socialization of emotion. *Psychological Inquiry, 9*, 241–273.

Elbedour, S., Onwuegbuzie, A. J., Caridine, C., & Abu-Saad, H. (2002). The effect of polygamous marital structure on behavioral, emotional, and academic adjustment in children: A comprehensive review of the literature. *Clinical Child and Family Psychology Review, 5*, 255–271.

Elder, G., Eccles, J. S., Ardelt, M., & Lord, S. (1995). Inner-city parents under economic pressure: Perspectives on the strategies of parenting. *Journal of Marriage and Family, 57*, 771–784.

Elgar, F. J., De Clercq, B., Schnohr, C. W., Bird, P., Pickett, K. E., Torsheim, T., . . . Currie, C. (2013). Absolute and relative family affluence and psychosomatic symptoms in adolescents. *Social Science & Medicine, 91*, 25–31.

Elgar, F. J., McGrath, P. J., Waschbusch, D. A., Stewart, S. H., & Curtis, L. J. (2004). Mutual influences on maternal depression and child adjustment problems. *Clinical Psychology Review, 24*, 441–459.

Eliot, L. (1999). *What's going on in there? How the brain and mind develop in the first five years of life*. New York, NY: Bantam Books.

Elkind, D. (2001). *The hurried child: Growing up too fast too soon*. Cambridge, MA: Perseus.

Elliott, A. N., & Carnes, C. N. (2001). Reactions of nonoffending parents to the sexual abuse of their children: A review of the literature. *Child Maltreatment, 6*, 314–331.

Ellis, B. J. (2004). Timing of pubertal maturation in girls: An integrated life history approach. *Psychological Bulletin, 130*, 920–958.

Ellison, C. G. (1996). Conservative Protestantism and the corporal punishment of children: Clarifying the issues. *Journal for the Scientific Study of Religion, 35*, 1–16.

Ellison, C. G., Musick, M. A., & Holden, G. W. (2011). Does conservative Protestantism moderate the association between corporal punishment and child outcomes? *Journal of Marriage and Family, 73*, 946–961.

Epstein, L. H., Paluch, R. A., Gordy, C. C., Saelens, B. E., & Ernst, M. M. (2000). Problem solving in the treatment of childhood obesity. *Journal of Consulting and Clinical Psychology, 68*, 717–721.

Erel, S., & Burman, B. (1995). Interrelatedness of marital relations and parent-child relations: A meta-analytic review. *Psychological Bulletin, 118*, 108–132.

Ergenekon-Ozelci, P., Elmaci, N., Ertem, M., & Saka, G. (2006). Breastfeeding beliefs and practices among migrant mothers in slums of Diyarbakir, Turkey, 2001. *The European Journal of Public Health, 16*, 143–148.

Ericsson, K. A. (2006). The influence of experience and deliberate practice on the development of superior expert performance. *The Cambridge handbook of expertise and expert performance* (pp. 683–703). Cambridge, UK: Cambridge University Press.

Ericsson, K. A., & Lehmann, A. C. (1996). Expert and exceptional performance: Evidence of maximal adaptation to task constraints. *Annual Review of Psychology, 47*, 273–305.

Erikson, E. H. (1993). *Childhood and society*. New York, NY: W. W. Norton.

Estes, A., Olson, E., Sullivan, K., Greenson, J., Winter, J., Dawson, G., & Munson, J. (2013). Parenting-related stress and psychological distress in mothers of toddlers with autism spectrum disorders. *Brain and Development, 35*, 133–138.

Evans, A. B., Banerjee, M., Meyer, R., Aldana, A., Foust, M., & Rowley, S. (2012). Racial socialization as a mechanism for positive development among African American youth. *Child Development Perspectives, 6*, 251–257.

Evans, G. W. (2004). The environment of childhood poverty. *American Psychologist, 59*, 77–92.

Evans, G. W., & Cassells, R. C. (2013). Childhood poverty, cumulative risk exposure, and mental health in emerging adults. *Clinical Psychological Science, 2*, 286–296.

Evans, G. W., & Kim, P. (2013). Childhood poverty, chronic stress, self-regulation, and coping. *Child Development Perspectives, 7*, 43–48.

Evans, G. W., Maxwell, L. E., & Hart, B. (1999). Parental language and verbal responsiveness to children in crowded homes. *Developmental Psychology, 35*, 1020–1023.

Evans, G. W., & Wachs, T. D. (Eds.). (2010). *Chaos and its influence on children's development: An ecological perspective*. Washington, DC: American Psychological Association.

Evans, S. E., Davies, C., & DiLillo, D. (2008). Exposure to domestic violence: A meta-analysis of child and adolescent outcomes. *Aggression and Violent Behavior, 13*, 131–140.

Evans-Campbell, T. (2008). Historical trauma in American Indian/Native Alaska communities: A multilevel framework for exploring impacts on individuals, families, and communities. *Journal of Interpersonal Violence, 23*, 316–338.

Eyer, D. E. (1992). *Mother-infant bonding: A scientific fiction*. New Haven, CT: Yale University Press.

Fagot, B. I., Leinbach, M. D., & O'Boyle, C. (1992). Gender labeling, gender stereotyping, and parenting behaviors. *Developmental Psychology, 28*, 225–230.

Faller, K. C., & Palusci, V. J. (2007). Children's advocacy centers: Do they lead to positive case outcomes? *Child Abuse and Neglect, 31*, 1021–1029.

Family Kids and Youth. (2010). *Playreport*. Retrieved June 6, 2014, from http://www.kidsandyouth.com/?s=play

Fan, X., & Chen, M. (2001). Parental involvement and students' academic achievement: A meta-analysis. *Educational Psychology Review, 13*, 1–22.

Fang, X., Brown, D. S., Florence, C. S., & Mercy, J. A. (2012). The economic burden of child maltreatment in the United States and implications for prevention. *Child Abuse and Neglect, 36*, 156–165.

Fanslow, J. L., Robinson, E. M., Crengle, S., & Perese, L. (2007). Prevalence of child sexual abuse reported by a cross-sectional sample of New Zealand women. *Child Abuse and Neglect, 31*, 935–945.

Farkas, M. S., & Grolnick, W. S. (2010). Examining the components and concomitants of parental structure in the academic domain. *Motivation and Emotion, 34*, 266–279.

Farr, R. H., & Patterson, C. J. (2013). Co-parenting among lesbian, gay, and heterosexual couples: Associations with adopted children's outcomes. *Child Development, 84*, 1226–1240.

Farver, J. A., Narang, S. K., & Bhadha, B. R. (2002). East meets West: Ethnic identity, acculturation, and conflict in Asian Indian families. *Journal of Family Psychology, 16*, 338–350.

Farwell, S. (2013, October 20–28). The girl in the closet: A survivor's story. *Dallas Morning News*. Retrieved June 18, 2014, from http://res.dallasnews.com/interactives/2013_October/lauren/#.U6JitPldXCY

Feemster, K. A., & Offit, P. (2013). Delaying vaccination is not a safer choice. *JAMA Pediatrics, 167*, 1097–1098.

Feeney, J. A. (2008). Adult romantic attachment: Developments in the study of couple relationships. In J. Cassidy & P. R. Shaver (Eds.), *Handbook of attachment* (2nd ed., pp. 456–481). New York, NY: Guilford.

Feinberg, M. (2002). Co-parenting and the transition to parenthood: A framework for prevention. *Clinical Child and Family Psychology Review, 5*, 173–195.

Feinberg, M. E., Brown, L. D., & Kan, M. L. (2012). A multi-domain self-report measure of co-parenting. *Parenting: Science and Practice, 12*, 1–21.

Feinberg, M. E., Solmeyer, A. R., Hostetler, M. L., Sakuma, K-L., Jones, D., & McHale, S. M. (2013). Siblings Are Special: Initial test of a new approach for preventing youth behavior problems. *Journal of Adolescent Health, 53*, 166–173.

Feldman, D. H., & Piirto, J. (2002). Parenting talented children. In M. H. Bornstein (Ed.), *Handbook of parenting. Vol. 5: Practical issues in parenting* (2nd ed., pp. 195–219). Mahwah, NJ: Lawrence Erlbaum Associates.

Felitti, V. J., Anda, R. F., Nordenberg, D., Williamson, D. F., Spitz, A. M., Edwards, V., . . . Marks, J. S. (1998). Relationship of childhood abuse and household dysfunction to many of the leading causes of death in adults: The Adverse Childhood Experiences (ACE) study. *American Journal of Preventive Medicine, 14*, 245–258.

Ferguson, C. J. (2013). Spanking, corporal punishment and negative long-term outcomes: A meta-analytic review of longitudinal studies. *Clinical Psychology Review, 33*, 196–208.

Fergusson, D. M., McLeod, G. F. H., & Horwood, J. L. (2013). Parental separation/divorce in childhood and partnership outcomes at age 30. *Journal of Child Psychology and Psychiatry, 55*, 352–360.

Fernald, A., & O'Neill, D. K. (1993). Peekaboo across cultures: How mothers and infants play with voices, faces, and expectations. In K. MacDonald (Ed.), *Parent-child play: Descriptions and implications* (pp. 259–286). Albany: State University of New York Press.

Field, T. (2010). Postpartum depression effects on early interactions, parenting, and safety practices: A review. *Infant Behavior and Development, 33*, 1–6.

Field, T., Hernandez-Reif, M., & Diego, M. (2006). Intrusive and withdrawn depressed mothers and their infants. *Developmental Review, 26*, 15–30.

Fiese, B. H. (2006). *Family routines and rituals*. New Haven, CT: Yale University Press.

Fiese, B. H., Foley, K. P., & Spagnola, M. (2006). Routine and ritual elements in family mealtimes: Contexts for child well-being and family identity. *New Directions for Child and Adolescent Development, 111*, 67–89.

Finer, L. B., & Sonfield, A. (2013). The evidence mounts on the benefits of preventing unintended pregnancy. *Contraception, 87*, 126–127.

Fingerman, K. L., Cheng, Y-P., Tighe, L., Birditt, K. S., & Zarit, S. (2012). Relationships between young adults and their parents. In A. Booth, S. L. Brown, N. S. Landale, W. D. Manning, & S. M. McHale (Eds.), *Early adulthood in a family context* (pp. 59–85). New York, NY: Springer.

Finkelhor, D., Ormrod, R. K., & Turner, H. A. (2007). Polyvictimization and trauma in a national longitudinal cohort. *Development and Psychopathology, 19*, 149–166.

Finkelhor, D., Ormrod, R. K., Turner, H. A., & Hamby, S. L. (2005). The victimization of children and youth: A comprehensive, national survey. *Child Maltreatment, 10*, 5–25.

Finkelhor, D., Turner, H., Ormrod, R. K., Hamby, S. L., & Kracke, K. (2009). Children's exposure to violence: A comprehensive national survey. *Juvenile Justice Bulletin: National Survey of Children's Exposure to Violence*. Washington, DC: OJJDP.

Finucane, R. C. (1997). *The rescue of the innocents: Endangered children in medieval miracles*. New York, NY: St. Martin's.

Firstman, R., & Talan, J. (1997). *Death of innocents*. New York, NY: Bantam Books.

Fisher, L., Ames, E. W., Chisholm, K., & Savoie, L. (1997). Problems reported by parents of Romanian orphans adopted to British Columbia. *International Journal of Behavioral Development, 20*, 67–82.

Flaks, D. K., Ficher, I., Masterpasqua, F., & Joseph, G. (1995). Lesbians choosing motherhood: A comparative study of lesbian and heterosexual parents and their children. *Developmental Psychology, 31*, 105–114.

Flanders, J. L., Simard, M., Paquette, D., Parent, S., Vitaro, F., Pihl, R. O., & Séguin, J. R. (2010). Rough-and-tumble play and the development of physical aggression and emotion regulation: A five-year follow-up study. *Journal of Family Violence, 25*, 357–367.

Flykt, M., Lindblom, J., Punamäki, R-L., Poikkeus, P., Repokari, L., Unkila-Kallio, L., . . . Tulppala, M. (2011). Prenatal expectations in transition to parenthood: Former infertility and family dynamic considerations. *Couple and Family Psychology: Research and Practice, 1*, 31–44.

Fogel, A., & Melson, G. F. (Eds.). (1986). *Origins of nurturance: Developmental, biological, and cultural perspectives on caregiving*. Hillsdale, NJ: Lawrence Erlbaum Associates.

Follan, M., & McNamara, M. (2013). A fragile bond: Adoptive parents' experiences of caring for children with a diagnosis of reactive attachment disorder. *Journal of Clinical Nursing, 23*, 1076–1085.

Fonagy, P., Steele, H., & Steele, M. (1991). Maternal representations of attachment during pregnancy predict the organization of infant-mother attachment at one year of age. *Child Development, 62*, 891–905.

Forgatch, M. S., Patterson, G. R., & Gewirtz, A. H. (2013). Looking forward: The promise of widespread implementation of parent training programs. *Perspectives on Psychological Science, 8*, 682–694.

Forste, R., & Haas, A. (2002). The transition of adolescent males to first sexual intercourse: Anticipated or delayed? *Family Planning Perspectives, 34*, 184–190.

Foster, H., & Brooks-Gunn, J. (2009). Toward a stress process model of children's exposure to physical family and community violence. *Clinical Child and Family Psychology Review, 12*, 71–94.

Foster, J. M., & Carson, D. K. (2013). Child sexual abuse in the United States: Perspectives on assessment and intervention. *American Journal of Humanities and Social Sciences, 1*, 97–108.

Fouts, H. N., Roopnarine, J. L., & Lamb, M. E. (2007). Social experiences and daily routines of African American infants in different socioeconomic contexts. *Journal of Family Psychology, 21*, 655–664.

Fox, N. A., Kimmerly, N. L., & Schafer, W. D. (1991). Attachment to mother/Attachment to father: A meta-analysis. *Child Development, 62*, 210–225.

Fox, N. A., Nelson, C. A., III, & Zeanah, C. H., Jr. (2013). The effects of early severe psychosocial deprivation on children's cognitive and social development: Lessons from the Bucharest Early Intervention Project. In N. S. Landale, S. M. McHale, & A. Booth (Eds.), *Families and child health* (pp. 33–41). New York, NY: Springer.

Fraiberg, S. (1987). Ghosts in the nursery: A psychoanalytic approach to the problems of impaired infant-mother relationships. In L. Fraiberg (Ed.), *Selected writings of Selma Fraiberg* (pp. 100–136). Columbus: Ohio State University Press.

Fraley, R. C., Griffin, B. N., Belsky, J., & Roisman, G. I. (2012). Developmental antecedents of political ideology: A longitudinal investigation from birth to age 18 years. *Psychological Science, 23*, 1425–1431.

Fraley, R. C., & Heffernan, M. E. (2013). Attachment and parental divorce a test of the diffusion and sensitive period hypotheses. *Personality and Social Psychology Bulletin, 39*, 1199–1213.

Frankel, D. G., & Roer-Bornstein, D. (1982). Traditional and modern contributions to changing infant-rearing ideologies of two ethnic communities. *Monographs of the Society for Research in Child Development, 47*(4, Serial No. 196).

Frazier, A., Camargo, C. A., Jr., Malspeis, S., Willett, W. C., & Young, M. C. (2013). Prospective study of peripregnancy consumption of peanuts or tree nuts by mothers and the risk of peanut or tree nut allergy in their offspring. *JAMA Pediatrics, 168*, 156–162.

Fredricks, J. A., & Eccles, J. S. (2004). Parental influences on youth involvement in sports. In M. R. Weiss (Ed.), *Developmental sport and exercise psychology: A lifespan perspective* (pp. 145–164). Morgantown, WV: Fitness Information Technology, Inc.

Freeman, D. (1983). *Margaret Mead and Samoa: The making and unmaking of an anthropological myth*. Cambridge, MA: Harvard University Press.

French, V. (2002). History of parenting: The ancient Mediterranean world. In M. H. Bornstein (Ed.), *Handbook of parenting, vol. 2: Biology and ecology of parenting* (2nd ed., pp. 345–376). Mahwah, NJ: Lawrence Erlbaum Associates.

Freud, S. (1936). *The ego and the mechanisms of defense*. New York, NY: International Universities Press.

Fridlund, A. J., Beck, H. P., Goldie, W. D., & Irons, G. (2012). Little Albert: A neurologically impaired child. *History of Psychology, 15*, 302–327.

Friedman, T. L. (2006). *The world is flat: A brief history of the twenty-first century*. New York, NY: Farrar, Straus, & Giroux.

Fries, A. B. W., Shirtcliff, E. A., & Pollak, S. D. (2008). Neuroendocrine dysregulation following early social deprivation in children. *Developmental Psychobiology, 50*, 588–599.

Fronek, P., & Crawshaw, M. (2014). The "new family" as an emerging norm: A commentary on the position of social work in assisted reproduction. *British Journal of Social Work, 44.*

Frosh, S. (2004). Religious influences on parenting. In M. Hoghughi & N. Long (Eds.), *Handbook of parenting: Theory research for practice* (pp. 98–109). Thousand Oaks, CA: SAGE.

Fruzzetti, A. E., Shenk, C., & Hoffman, P. D. (2005). Family interaction and the development of borderline personality disorder: A transactional model. *Development and Psychopathology, 17*, 1007–1030.

Fulkerson, J. A., Story, M., Mellin, A., Leffert, N., Neumark-Sztainer, D., & French, S. A. (2006). Family dinner meal frequency and adolescent development: Relationships with developmental assets and high-risk behaviors. *Journal of Adolescent Health, 39*, 337–345.

Fuller-Thomson, E., & Minkler, M. (2000). African American grandparents raising grandchildren: A national profile of demographic and health characteristics. *Health and Social Work, 25*, 109–118.

Funk, J. B., Baldacci, H. B., Pasold, T., & Baumgardner, J. (2004). Violence exposure in real-life, video games, television, movies, and the Internet: Is there desensitization? *Journal of Adolescence, 27*, 23–39.

Furman, W., & Lanthier, R. (2002). Parenting siblings. In M. H. Bornstein (Ed.), *Handbook of parenting, vol. 1: Children and parenting* (pp. 165–188). Mahwah, NJ: Lawrence Erlbaum Associates.

Furnham, A., & Weir, C. (1996). Lay theories of child development. *Journal of Genetic Psychology, 157*, 211–226.

Furstenberg, F. F. J. (1993). How families manage risk and opportunity in dangerous neighborhoods. In W. J. Wilson (Ed.), *Sociology and the public agenda* (pp. 231–258). Newbury Park, CA: SAGE.

Furstenberg, F. F. J. (2003). Teenage childbearing as a public issue and private concern. *Annual Review of Sociology, 29*, 23–39.

Furstenberg, F. F. J., Cook, T. D., Eccles, J., Elder, J., G. H., & Sameroff, A. (1999). *Managing to make it: Urban families and successful youth.* Chicago, IL: University of Chicago Press.

Gagne, M-H., & Bouchard, C. (2004). Family dynamics associated with the use of psychologically violent parental practices. *Journal of Family Violence, 19*, 117–130.

Galinsky, E. (1981). *Between generations: The six stages of parenthood.* New York, NY: Times Books.

Galton, F. (1883/1911). *Inquiries into human faculty and its development.* New York, NY: Macmillan.

Gangoli, G., McCarry, M., & Razak, A. (2009). Child marriage or forced marriage? South Asian communities in north east England. *Children & Society, 23*, 418–429.

Garbarino, J., Kostelny, K., & Barry, F. (1997). Value transmission in an ecological context: The high-risk neighborhood. In J. E. Grusec & L. Kuczynski (Eds.), *Parenting and children's internalization of value: A handbook of contemporary theory* (pp. 307–332). Hoboken, NJ: Wiley.

Garbarino, J., Kostelny, K., & Dubrow, N. (1991). *No place to be a child: Growing up in war zone.* Lexington, MA: Lexington Books.

Garcia Coll, C. K., Crnic, K., Lamberty, G., Wasik, B. H., Jenkins, R., Garcia, H. V., & McAdoo, H. P. (1996). An integrative model for the study of developmental competencies in minority children. *Child Development, 67*, 1891–1914.

Garcia Coll, C., & Garrido, M. (2000). Minorities in the United States. *Handbook of developmental psychopathology* (pp. 177–195). New York, NY: Springer.

Garcia Coll, C., & Pachter, L. M. (2002). Ethnic and minority parenting. In M. H. Bornstein (Ed.), *Handbook of parenting, vol. 4: Social conditions and applied parenting* (2nd ed., pp. 1–20). Mahwah, NJ: Lawrence Erlbaum Associates.

Gartrell, N., Deck, A., Rodas, C., Peyser, H., & Banks, A. (2005). The National Lesbian Family Study: 4. Interviews with the 10-year-old children. *American Journal of Orthopsychiatry, 75*, 518–524.

Gates, G. J. (2012). Family formation and raising children among same-sex couples. *National Council on Family Relations: Family Focus on . . . LGBT Families, FF51*, F1–F4.

Gates, G. J., & Newport, F. (2012). *Special report: 3.4% of U.S. adults identify as LGBT.* Princeton, NJ: Gallup Inc.

Gattario, K. H., Frisén, A., & Anderson-Fye, E. (2014). Body image and child well-being. In A. Ben-Arieh, F. Casas, I. Fones, & J. E. Korbin (Eds.), *Handbook of child well-being* (pp. 2409–2436). New York, NY: Springer.

Gauvain, M., & Perez, S. M. (2005). Parent-child participation in planning children's activities outside of school in European American and Latino families. *Child Development, 76,* 371–383.

Geary, D. C. (2006). Evolutionary developmental psychology: Current status and future directions. *Developmental Review, 26,* 113–119.

Gecas, V. (1979). *The influence of social class on socialization.* New York, NY: Free Press.

Gerard, J. M., Krishnakumar, A., & Buehler, C. (2006). Marital conflict, parent-child relations, and youth maladjustment: A longitudinal investigation of spillover effects. *Journal of Family Issues, 27,* 951–975.

Gerber, J. S., & Offit, P. A. (2009). Vaccines and autism: A tale of shifting hypotheses. *Clinical Infectious Diseases, 48,* 456–461.

Gershoff, E. T. (2002). Corporal punishment by parents and associated child behaviors and experiences: A meta-analytic and theoretical review. *Psychological Bulletin, 128,* 539–579.

Gershoff, E. T. (2013). Spanking and child development: We know enough now to stop hitting our children. *Child Development Perspectives, 7,* 133–137.

Gershoff, E. T., Grogan-Kaylor, A., Lansford, J. E., Chang, L., Zelli, A., Deater-Deckard, K., & Dodge, K. A. (2010). Parent discipline practices in an international sample: Associations with child behaviors and moderation by perceived normativeness. *Child Development, 81,* 487–502.

Gershoff, E. T., Miller, P. C., & Holden, G. W. (1999). Parenting influences from the pulpit: Religious affiliation as a determinant of parental corporal punishment. *Journal of Family Psychology, 13,* 307–320.

Ghuman, J. K., & Ghuman, H. S. (2013). Pharmacologic intervention for attention-deficit hyperactivity disorder in preschoolers. *Pediatric Drugs, 15,* 1–8.

Giedd, J. N. (2004). Structural magnetic resonance imaging of the adolescent brain. *Annals of the New York Academy of Sciences, 1021,* 77–85.

Giesbrecht, G. F., Miller, M. R., & Müller, U. (2010). The anger-distress model of temper tantrums: Associations with emotional reactivity and emotional competence. *Infant and Child Development, 19,* 478–497.

Gilligan, M., Suitor, J. J., Kim, S., & Pillemer, K. (2013). Differential effects of perceptions of mothers' and fathers' favoritism on sibling tension in adulthood. *The Journals of Gerontology Series B: Psychological Sciences and Social Sciences, 68,* 593–598.

Gillis, J. R. (1996). *A world of their own making: Myth, ritual, and the quest for family values.* Cambridge, MA: Harvard University Press.

Gipson, J. D., Koenig, M. A., & Hindin, M. J. (2008). The effects of unintended pregnancy on infant, child, and parental health: A review of the literature. *Studies in Family Planning, 39,* 18–38.

Giridharadas, A. (Feb. 20, 2008). The uncoupling of India: Divorce rises, as notions of love change. *The International Herald Tribune,* p. 1.

Glaser, D. (2000). Child abuse and the brain—A review. *Journal of Child Psychology and Psychiatry, 41,* 97–116.

Glasgow, K. L., Dornbusch, S. M., Troyer, L., Steinberg, L., & Ritter, P. L. (1997). Parenting styles, adolescents' attributions, and educational outcomes in nine heterogeneous high schools. *Child Development, 68,* 507–529.

Glass, J. C. J., & Huneycutt, T. L. (2002). Grandparents parenting grandchildren: Extent of situation, issues involved, and educational implications. *Educational Gerontology, 28,* 139–161.

Glenday, C. (Ed.). (2006). *Guinness world records 2007.* London, England: Guinness World Records.

Glover, V. (2011). Annual research review: Prenatal stress and the origins of psychopathology: An evolutionary perspective. *Journal of Child Psychology and Psychiatry, 52,* 356–367.

Godbout, N., Briere, J., Sabourin, S., & Lussier, Y. (2014). Child sexual abuse and subsequent relational and personal functioning: The role of parental support. *Child Abuse and Neglect, 38,* 317–325.

Goeke-Morey, M. C., Papp, L. M., & Cummings, E. M. (2013). Changes in marital conflict and youths' responses across childhood and adolescence: A test of sensitization. *Development and Psychopathology, 25*, 241–251.

Goldberg, W., & Keller, M. A. (2007). Co-sleeping during infancy and early childhood: Key findings and future directions. *Infant and Child Development, 16*, 457–469.

Goldenberg, R. L., Culhane, J. F., Iams, J. D., & Romero, R. (2008). Epidemiology and causes of preterm birth. *The Lancet, 371*, 75–84.

Goldstein, S., & Brooks, R. B. (2013). Why study resilience? *Handbook of resilience in children* (pp. 3–14). New York, NY: Springer.

Golombok, S., Blake, L., Casey, P., Roman, G., & Jadva, V. (2013). Children born through reproductive donation: A longitudinal study of psychological adjustment. *Journal of Child Psychology and Psychiatry, 54*, 653–660.

Gonzales, N., Coxe, S., Roosa, M., White, R. B., Knight, G., Zeiders, K., & Saenz, D. (2011). Economic hardship, neighborhood context, and parenting: Prospective effects on Mexican-American adolescent's mental health. *American Journal of Community Psychology, 47*, 98–113.

Goodman, R. (1997). The strengths and difficulties questionnaire: A research note. *Journal of Child Psychology and Psychiatry, 38*, 581–586.

Goodman, S. H., & Gotlib, I. H. (1999). Risk for psychopathology in the children of depressed mothers: A developmental model for understanding mechanisms of transmission. *Psychological Review, 106*, 458–490.

Goodnow, J. J. (1997). Parenting and the transmission and internalization of values: From sociocultural perspectives to within-family analyses. In J. E. Grusec & L. Kuczynski (Eds.), *Parenting and children's internalization of values: A handbook of contemporary theory* (pp. 333–361). New York, NY: John Wiley.

Goodnow, J. J., & Collins, W. A. (1990). *Development according to parents: The nature, sources, and consequences of parents' ideas.* Hillsdale, NJ: Lawrence Erlbaum Associates.

Goossens, L., Beyers, W., Emmen, M., & Van Aken, M. A. G. (2002). The imaginary audience and personal fable: Factor analyses and concurrent validity of the "New Look" measures. *Journal of Research on Adolescence, 12*, 193–215.

Gordon, I., & Feldman, R. (2008). Synchrony in the triad: A microlevel process model of co-parenting and parent-child interactions. *Family Process, 47*, 465–479.

Gottfried, A. E., Gottfried, A. W., & Bathurst, K. (2002). Maternal and dual-earner employment status and parenting. In M. H. Bornstein (Ed.), *Handbook of parenting, vol. 2: Biology and ecology of parenting* (2nd ed., pp. 207–230). Mahwah, NJ: Lawrence Erlbaum Associates.

Gottlieb, A. (2006). Non-Western approaches to spiritual development among infants and young children: A case study from West Africa. In E. C. Roehlkepartain, P. E. King, L. Wagener, & P. L. Benson (Eds.), *The handbook of spiritual development in childhood and adolescence* (pp. 150–162). Thousand Oaks, CA: SAGE.

Gottlieb, G. (2003). On making behavioral genetics truly developmental. *Human Development, 46*, 337–355.

Graham, A. M., Fisher, P. A., & Pfeifer, J. H. (2013). What sleeping babies hear: A functional MRI study of interparental conflict and infants' emotion processing. *Psychological Science, 24*, 782–789.

Granger, R. C. (2008). After-school programs and academics: Implications for policy, practice, and research. *Social Policy Report, 22*, 3–19.

Granic, I., & Patterson, G. R. (2006). Toward a comprehensive model of antisocial development: A dynamic systems approach. *Psychological Review, 113*, 101–131.

Grasso, D. J., Ford, J. D., & Briggs-Gowan, M. J. (2013). Early life trauma exposure and stress sensitivity in young children. *Journal of Pediatric Psychology, 38*, 94–103.

Graue, E., Kroeger, J., & Brown, C. (2002). Living the "gift of time." *Contemporary Issues in Early Childhood, 3*, 338–352.

Gray, P. (2011). The decline of play and the rise of psychopathology in children and adolescents. *American Journal of Play, 3*, 443–463.

Green, J. A., Gustafson, G. E., Irwin, J. R., Kalinowski, L. L., & Wood, R. M. (1995). Infant crying: Acoustics, perception and communication. *Early Development and Parenting, 4*, 161–175.

Greenberger, E., Goldberg, W. A., Hamill, S., O'Neil, R., & Payne, C. K. (1989). Contributions of a supportive work environment to parents' well-being and orientation to work. *American Journal of Community Psychology, 17,* 755–783.

Greene, S. M., Anderson, E., Hetherington, E. M., Forgatch, M. S., & DeGarmo, D. S. (2003). Risk and resilience after divorce. In F. Walsh (Ed.), *Normal family processes: Growing diversity and complexity* (3rd ed., pp. 96–120). New York, NY: Guilford Press.

Gregory, J., & Feldman, M. D. (2003). *Sickened: The memoir of a Munchausen by proxy childhood.* New York, NY: Random House.

Greven, P. J. (1973). *Child-Rearing concepts, 1628-1861.* Itasca, IL: Peacock.

Greven, P. J. (1977). *The Protestant temperament: Patterns of child-rearing, religious experience, and the self in early America.* New York, NY: Alfred A. Knopf.

Greven, P. J. (1991). *Spare the child: The religious roots of punishment and the psychological impact of physical abuse.* New York, NY: Alfred A. Knopf.

Groat, H. T., Giordano, P. C., Cernkovich, S. A., Pugh, M. D., & Swinford, S. P. (1997). Attitudes toward childbearing among young parents. *Journal of Marriage and Family, 59,* 568–581.

Grolnick, W. S. (2003). *The psychology of parental control: How well-meant parenting backfires.* Mahwah, NJ: Lawrence Erlbaum Associates.

Gross, J. J. (2014). Emotion regulation: Conceptual and empirical foundations. In J. J. Gross (Ed.), *Handbook of emotion regulation* (2nd ed., pp. 3–20). New York, NY: Guilford.

Grossman, K., Thane, K., & Grossman, K. E. (1981). Maternal tactual contact of the newborn after various postpartum conditions of mother-infant contact. *Developmental Psychology, 17,* 158–169.

Grotevant, H. D., McRoy, R. G., Wrobel, G. M., & Ayers-Lopez, S. (2013). Contact between adoptive and birth families: Perspectives from the Minnesota/Texas Adoption Research Project. *Child Development Perspectives, 7,* 193–198.

Grusec, J. E. (1992). Social learning theory and developmental psychology: The legacies of Robert Sears and Albert Bandura. *Developmental Psychology, 28,* 776–786.

Grusec, J. E. (2011). Socialization processes in the family: Social and emotional development. *Annual Review of Psychology, 62,* 243–269.

Grusec, J. E., Chaparro, M. P., Johnston, M., & Sherman, A. (2013). Social development and social relationships in middle childhood. In R. M. Lerner, M. A. Easterbrooks, & J. Mistry (Eds.), *Developmental psychology* (2nd ed., vol. 6, pp. 243–264). New York, NY: John Wiley & Sons.

Grusec, J. E., & Davidov, M. (2007). Socialization in the family: The roles of parents. In J. E. Grusec & P. D. Hastings (Eds.), *Handbook of socialization: Theory and research* (pp. 284–308). New York, NY: Guilford Press.

Grusec, J. E., & Goodnow, J. J. (1994). Impact of parental discipline methods on the child's internalization of values: A reconceptualization of current points of view. *Developmental Psychology, 30,* 4–19.

Grusec, J. E., Goodnow, J. J., & Kuczynski, L. (2000). New directions in analyses of parenting contributions to children's acquisition of values. *Child Development, 71,* 205–211.

Grusec, J. E., & Kuczynski, L. (1980). Direction of effect in socialization: A comparison of the parent's versus the child's behavior as determinants of disciplinary techniques. *Developmental Psychology*, 16, 1–9.

Grych, J. H. (2002). Marital relationships in parenting. In M. H. Bornstein (Ed.), *Handbook of parenting, vol. 4: Social conditions and applied parenting* (2nd ed., pp. 203–226). Mahwah, NJ: Lawrence Erlbaum Associates.

Grych, J. H., & Fincham, F. D. (1990). Marital conflict and children's adjustment: A cognitive-contextual framework. *Psychological Bulletin, 108,* 267–290.

Grych, J. H., Harold, G. T., & Miles, C. J. (2003). A prospective investigation of appraisals as mediators of the link between interparental conflict and child adjustment. *Child Development, 74,* 1176–1193.

Gunnoe, M. L., Hetherington, E. M., & Reiss, D. (1999). Parental religiosity, parenting style, and adolescent social responsibility. *Journal of Early Adolescence, 19,* 199–225.

Guttmacher Institute. (2013). *Unintended pregnancy in the United States.* New York, NY: Guttmacher Institute.

Guttmacher Institute. (2014). *American teens' sexual and reproductive health. Fact sheet.* Retrieved June 14, 2014, from http://www.guttmacher.org/pubs/FB-ATSRH.html

Halgunseth, L. C., Ispa, J. M., & Rudy, D. (2006). Parental control in Latino families: An integrated review of the literature. *Child Development, 77*, 1282–1297.

Halim, M. L., Ruble, D., Tamis-LeMonda, C., & Shrout, P. E. (2013). Rigidity in gender-typed behaviors in early childhood: A longitudinal study of ethnic minority children. *Child Development, 84*, 1269–1284.

Hall, D. E., Eubanks, L., Meyyazhagan, S., Kenney, R. D., & Johnson, S. C. (2000). Evaluation of covert video surveillance in the diagnosis of Munchausen syndrome by proxy: Lessons from 41 cases. *Pediatrics, 105*, 1305–1312.

Hall, G. S. (1904). *Adolescence: Its psychology and its relations to physiology, anthropology, sociology, sex crime, religion, and education* (vols. 1 & 2). New York, NY: D. Appleton.

Haller, M., & Chassin, L. (2011). The unique effects of parental alcohol and affective disorders, parenting, and parental negative affect on adolescent maladjustment. *Merrill-Palmer Quarterly, 57*, 263–292.

Halpern, R. (1990). Poverty and early childhood training: Toward a framework for intervention. *American Journal of Orthopsychiatry, 60*, 6–18.

Hamby, S., Finkelhor, D., Turner, H., & Ormrod, R. (2011). Children's exposure to intimate partner violence and other family violence. *Juvenile Justice Bulletin: National Survey of Children's Exposure to Violence.* Washington, DC: U.S. Department of Justice.

Hankin, B. L., Nederhof, E., Oppenheimer, C. W., Jenness, J., Young, J. F., Abela, J. R. Z., . . . Oldehinkel, A. J. (2011). Differential susceptibility in youth: Evidence that 5-HTTLPR x positive parenting is associated with positive affect "for better and worse." *Translational Psychiatry, 1*, e44.

Hannan, K., & Luster, T. (1991). Influence of parent, child, and contextual factors on the home environment. *Infant Mental Health Journal, 12*, 17–30.

Hansen, D. J., Pallotta, G. M., Christopher, J. S., Conaway, R. L., & Lundquist, L. M. (1995). The parental problem-solving measure: Further evaluation with maltreating and nonmaltreating parents. *Journal of Family Violence, 10*, 319–336.

Hansen, M., Kurinczuk, J. J., Milne, E., de Klerk, N., & Bower, C. (2013). Assisted reproductive technology and birth defects: A systematic review and meta-analysis. *Human Reproduction Update, 19*, 330–353.

Harkness, S., & Super, C. M. (Eds.). (1996). *Parents' cultural belief systems: Their origins, expressions, and consequences*. New York, NY: Guilford.

Harkness, S., & Super, C. M. (2006). Themes and variations: Parental ethnotheories in western cultures. In K. H. Rubin & O. B. Chung (Eds.), *Parenting beliefs, behaviors, and parent-child relations: A cross-cultural perspective* (pp. 61–79). New York, NY: Psychology Press.

Harlow, H., Dodsworth, R. O., & Harlow, M. K. (1965). Total isolation in monkeys. *Proceedings of the National Academy of Sciences, 54*, 90–96.

Harmon, D., & Brim, O. G. J. (1980). *Learning to be parents: Principles, programs, and methods.* Beverly Hills, CA: SAGE.

Harris, J. R. (1995). Where is the child's environment? A group socialization theory of development. *Psychological Review, 102*, 458–489.

Harris, J. R. (1998). *The nurture assumption: Why children turn out the way they do.* New York, NY: Free Press.

Harris, L. J. (2006). An empirical study of parental responsibility laws: Sending messages, but what kind and to whom? *Utah Law Review, 5*, 5–34.

Harrison, J. R., Vannest, K., Davis, J., & Reynolds, C. (2012). Common problem behaviors of children and adolescents in general education classrooms in the United States. *Journal of Emotional and Behavioral Disorders, 20*, 55–64.

Harrist, A. W., Topham, G. L., Hubbs-Tait, L., Page, M. C., Kennedy, T. S., & Shriver, L. H. (2012). What developmental science can contribute to a transdisciplinary understanding of childhood obesity: An interpersonal and intrapersonal risk model. *Child Development Perspectives, 6*, 445–455.

Harrist, A. W., & Waugh, R. M. (2002). Dyadic synchrony: Its structure and function in children's development. *Developmental Review, 22*, 555–592.

Hart, B., & Risley, T. R. (1995). *Meaningful differences in the everyday experience of young American children*. Baltimore, MD: Brookes Publishing Co.

Hart, S. N. (1991). From property to person status: Historical perspective on children's rights. *American Psychologist, 46*, 53–59.

Hart, S. N., Brassard, M. R., Binggeli, N. J., & Davidson, H. A. (2002). Psychological maltreatment. In J. E. B. Myers, L. Berliner, J. Briere, C. T. Hendrix, & C. Jenny (Eds.), *The APSAC handbook on child maltreatment* (2nd ed., pp. 79–103). Thousand Oaks, CA: SAGE.

Harter, S. (2006). The self. In N. Eisenberg (Ed.), *Handbook of child psychology, vol. 3: Social, emotional, and personality development* (6th ed., pp. 505–570). New York, NY: Wiley.

Hartos, J. L., Eitel, P., Haynie, D. L., & Simons-Morton, B. G. (2000). Can I take the car? Relations among parenting practices and adolescent problem-driving practices. *Journal of Adolescent Research, 15*, 352–367.

Harwood, R., Leyendecker, B., Carlson, V., Asencio, M., & Miller, A. (2002). Parenting among Latino families in the U.S. In M. H. Bornstein (Ed.), *Handbook of parenting, vol. 4: Social conditions and applied parenting* (2nd ed., pp. 21–46). Mahwah, NJ: Lawrence Erlbaum Associates.

Hastings, P. D., & Grusec, J. E. (1998). Parenting goals as organizers of responses to parent-child disagreement. *Developmental Psychology, 34*, 465–479.

Hastings, P. D., & Rubin, K. H. (1999). Predicting mothers' beliefs about preschool-aged children's social behavior: Evidence for maternal attitudes moderating child effects. *Child Development, 70*, 722–741.

Hastings, P. D., Zahn-Waxler, C., Robinson, J., Usher, B., & Bridges, D. (2000). The development of concern for others in children with behavior problems. *Developmental Psychology, 36*, 531–546.

Hatcher, D. L. (2007). Child support harming children: Subordinating the best interests of children to the fiscal interests of the state. *Wake Forest Law Review, 42*, 1029–1086.

Hauck, F. R., Signore, C., Fein, S. B., & Raju, T. N. K. (2008). Infant sleeping arrangements and practices during the first year of life. *Pediatrics, 122*(Supplement 2), S113–S120.

Haugaard, J., & Hazan, C. (2002). Foster parenting. In M. H. Bornstein (Ed.), *Handbook of parenting, vol. 1: Children and parenting* (2nd ed., pp. 313–328). Mahwah, NJ: Lawrence Erlbaum Associates.

Hawes, J. M. (1991). *The children's rights movement: A history of advocacy and protection*. Boston, MA: Twayne.

Hawk, C. K., & Holden, G. W. (2006). Meta-parenting: An initial investigation into a new parental social cognition construct. *Parenting: Science & Practice, 6*, 321–342.

Hayes, S. A., & Watson, S. L. (2013). The impact of parenting stress: A meta-analysis of studies comparing the experience of parenting stress in parents of children with and without autism spectrum disorder. *Journal of Autism and Developmental Disorders, 43*, 629–642.

Hayford, S. R., & Guzzo, K. B. (2013). Racial and ethnic variation in unmarried young adults' motivation to avoid pregnancy. *Perspectives on Sexual and Reproductive Health, 45*, 41–51.

Haynie, D. L., Farhat, T., Brooks-Russell, A., Wang, J., Barbieri, B., & Iannotti, R. J. (2013). Dating violence perpetration and victimization among U.S. adolescents: Prevalence, patterns, and associations with health complaints and substance use. *Journal of Adolescent Health, 53*, 194–201.

Haynie, D. L., Nansel, T., Eitel, P., Crump, A. D., Saylor, K., Yu, K., & Simons-Morton, B. (2001). Bullies, victims, and bully/victims: Distinct groups of at-risk youth. *Journal of Early Adolescence, 21*, 29–49.

Hays, J., Power, T. G., & Olvera, N. (2001). Effects of maternal socialization strategies on children's nutrition knowledge and behavior. *Applied Developmental Psychology, 22*, 421–437.

He, M., Irwin, J. D., Sangster Bouck, L. M., Tucker, P., & Pollett, G. L. (2005). Screen-viewing behaviors among preschoolers: Parents' perceptions. *American Journal of Preventive Medicine, 29*, 120–125.

Heimlich, J. (2011). *Breaking their will: Shedding light on religious child maltreatment*. Amherst, NY: Prometheus Books.

Hendrick, H. (2002). Constructions and reconstructions of British childhood: An interpretive survey, 1800 to the present. In A. James & A. Prout (Eds.), *Constructing and reconstructing childhood: Contemporary issues in the sociological study of childhood* (2nd ed., pp. 34–62). New York, NY: Routledge.

Henry, M., Cortes, A., & Morris, S. (2013). *The 2013 Annual Homeless Assessment Report (AHAR) to Congress: Part 1 Point-in-time estimates of homelessness*. Washington, DC: U.S. Department of Housing and Urban Development.

Henry K. Kaiser Family Foundation. (2013). *Total fertility rate*. Retrieved May 17, 2014, from http://kff.org/global-indicator/total-fertility-rate/

Herbers, J. E., Cutuli, J., Lafavor, T. L., Vrieze, D., Leibel, C., Obradović, J., & Masten, A. S. (2011). Direct and indirect effects of parenting on the academic functioning of young homeless children. *Early Education and Development, 22*, 77–104.

Hernandez, D. J., Denton, N. A., & Macartney, S. E. (2008). Children in immigrant families: Looking to America's future. *Social Policy Report, 22*, 3–22.

Hetherington, E. M., & Stanley-Hagan, M. (2002). Parenting in divorced and remarried families. In M. H. Bornstein (Ed.), *Handbook of parenting, vol. 3: Being and becoming a parent* (pp. 287–316). Mahwah, NJ: Lawrence Erlbaum Associates.

Hewlett, S. A. (1991). *When the bough breaks: The cost of neglecting our children*. New York, NY: Basic Books.

Heyman, J., Earle, A., & Hayes, J. (2007). *The work, family, and equity index: Where does the United States stand globally?* Boston, MA: Project on Global Working Families.

Heywood, C. (2001). *A history of childhood: Children and childhood in the West from medieval to modern times*. Malden, MA: Polity.

Hibel, L. C., Mercado, E., & Trumbell, J. M. (2012). Parenting stressors and morning cortisol in a sample of working mothers. *Journal of Family Psychology, 26*, 738–746.

Hill, N. E. (2001). Parenting and academic socialization as they relate to school readiness: The roles of ethnicity and family income. *Journal of Educational Psychology, 93*, 686–697.

Hill, N. E., Murry, V. M., & Anderson, V. D. (2005). Sociocultural contexts of African American families. In V. C. McLoyd, N. E. Hill, & K. A. Dodge (Eds.), *African American family life: Ecological and cultural diversity* (vol. 2, pp. 21–44). New York, NY: Guilford.

Hill, N. E., & Taylor, L. C. (2004). Parental school involvement and children's academic achievement: Pragmatics and issues. *Current Directions in Psychological Science, 13*, 161–164.

Hill, N. E., & Tyson, D. F. (2009). Parental involvement in middle school: A meta-analytic assessment of the strategies that promote achievement. *Developmental Psychology, 45*, 740–763.

Hill, N. E., & Witherspoon, D. (2011). Race, ethnicity, and social class. In M. K. Underwood & L. H. Rosen (Eds.), *Social development: Relationships in infancy, childhood, and adolescence* (pp. 316–346). New York, NY: Guilford Press.

Hilton, J. M., & Desrochers, S. (2000). The influence of economic strain, coping with roles, and parental control on the parenting of custodial single mothers and custodial single fathers. *Journal of Divorce & Remarriage, 33*, 55–76.

Hingson, R., Heeren, T., Winter, M., & Wechsler, H. (2005). Magnitude of alcohol-related mortality and morbidity among U. S. college students ages 18–24: Changes from 1998 to 2001. *Annual Review of Public Health, 26*, 259–279.

Hinshaw, S. P., & Scheffler, R. M. (2014). *The ADHD explosion: Myths, medication, money, and today's push for performance*. New York, NY: Oxford University Press.

Hinton, S., & Cassel, D. (2013). Exploring the lived experiences of homeless families with young children. *Early Childhood Education Journal, 41*, 457–463.

Hock, E., DeMeis, D., & McBride, S. (1988). Maternal separation anxiety: Its role in the balance of employment and motherhood in mothers and infants. In A. E. Gottfried & A. W. Gottfried (Eds.), *Maternal employment and children's development: Longitudinal research* (pp. 191–229). New York, NY: Plenum.

Hock, E., & Lutz, W. J. (1998). Psychological meaning of separation anxiety in mothers and fathers. *Journal of Family Psychology, 12*, 41–55.

Hodges, E. A., Smith, C., Tidwell, S., & Berry, D. (2013). Promoting physical activity in preschoolers to prevent obesity: A review of the literature. *Journal of Pediatric Nursing, 28*, 3–19.

Hoekstra-Weebers, J. E. H. M., Jaspers, J. P. C., Kamps, W. A., & Klip, E. C. (2001). Psychological adaptation and social support of parents of pediatric cancer patients: A prospective longitudinal study. *Journal of Pediatric Psychology, 26*, 225–235.

Hoeve, M., Dubas, J. S., Eichelsheim, V., Laan, P. H., Smeenk, W., & Gerris, J. R. M. (2009). The relationship between parenting and delinquency: A meta-analysis. *Journal of Abnormal Child Psychology, 37*, 749–775.

Hoff-Ginsburg, E. (1998). The relation of birth order and socioeconomic status to children's language experience and language development. *Applied Psycholinguistics, 19*, 603–629.

Hofferth, S. L., & Curtin, S. C. (2006). Parental leave statutes and maternal return to work after childbirth in the United States. *Work and Occupations, 33*, 73–105.

Hofferth, S. L., Kinney, D. A., & Dunn, J. S. (2006). *The "hurried" child: Middle-class phenomenon or value shift?* College Park: University of Maryland.

Holden, G. W. (1983). Avoiding conflict: Mothers as tacticians in the supermarket. *Child Development, 54*, 233–240.

Holden, G. W. (1985). How parents create a social environment via proactive behavior. In R. Garling & J. Valsiner (Eds.), *Children within environments: Towards a psychology of accident prevention* (pp. 193–215). New York, NY: Plenum Press.

Holden, G. W. (1988). Adults' thinking about a childrearing problem: Effects of experience, parental status, and gender. *Child Development, 59*, 1623–1632.

Holden, G. W. (2002). Perspectives on the effects of corporal punishment: Comment on Gershoff (2002). *Psychological Bulletin, 128*, 590–595.

Holden, G. W. (2003). Children exposed to domestic violence and child abuse: Terminology and taxonomy. *Clinical Child and Family Psychology Review, 6*, 151–160.

Holden, G. W. (2010). Childrearing and developmental trajectories: Positive pathways, off-ramps, and dynamic processes. *Child Development Perspectives, 4*, 197–204.

Holden, G. W., Barker, E. D., Appel, A. E., & Hazlewood, L. (2010). Partner-abusers as fathers: Testing hypotheses about their child rearing and the risk of physical child abuse. *Partner Abuse, 1*, 186–199.

Holden, G. W., Bayan, D., Baruah, J., & Holland, G. W. O. (2013). Parents' roles in guiding children's educational, religious, and other trajectories. *Journal of Educational and Developmental Psychology, 3*, 244–252.

Holden, G. W., & Buck, M. J. (2002). Parental attitudes toward childrearing. In M. H. Bornstein (Ed.), *Handbook of parenting, vol. 3: Being and becoming a parent* (2nd ed., pp. 537–562). Mahwah, NJ: Lawrence Erlbaum Associates.

Holden, G. W., Coleman, S., & Schmidt, K. L. (1995). Why 3-year-old children get spanked: Parent and child determinants in a sample of college-educated mothers. *Merrill-Palmer Quarterly, 41*, 431–452.

Holden, G. W., & Hawk, C. (2003). Meta-parenting in the journey of child rearing: A cognitive mechanism for change. In L. Kuczynski (Ed.), *Handbook of the dynamics in parent-child relations* (pp. 189–210). Thousand Oaks, CA: SAGE.

Holden, G. W., & Miller, P. C. (1999). Enduring and different: A meta-analysis of the similarity in parents' child rearing. *Psychological Bulletin, 125*, 223–254.

Holden, G. W., & Ritchie, K. L. (1991). Linking extreme marital discord, child rearing, and child behavior problems: Evidence from battered women. *Child Development, 62*, 311–327.

Holden, G. W., & West, M. J. (1989). Proximate regulation by mothers: A demonstration of how differing styles affect young children's behavior. *Child Development, 60*, 64–69.

Holden, G. W., & Williamson, P. A. (2014). Religion and child well-being. In A. Ben-Arieh, F. Casas, I. Fones, & J. E. Korbin (Eds.), *Handbook of child well-being* (pp. 1137–1208). New York, NY: Springer.

Holden, G. W., Williamson, P. A., & Holland, G. W. O. (2014). Eavesdropping on the family: A pilot investigation of corporal punishment in the home. *Journal of Family Psychology, 28*, 401–406.

Holden, G. W., & Zambarano, R. J. (1992). Passing the rod: Similarities between parents and their young children in orientations toward physical punishment. In I. E. Sigel, A. V. McGillicuddy-DeLisi, & J. J. Goodnow (Eds.), *Parental belief systems: The psychological consequences for children* (2nd ed.; pp. 143–172). Hillsdale, NJ: Lawrence Erlbaum Associates.

Holland, A. S., & McElwain, N. L. (2013). Maternal and paternal perceptions of co-parenting as a link between marital quality and the parent-toddler relationship. *Journal of Family Psychology, 27*, 117–126.

Holmbeck, G. N., Johnson, S. Z., Wills, K. E., McKernon, W., Rose, B., Erklin, S., & Kemper, T. (2002). Observed and perceived parental overprotection in relation to psychosocial adjustment in preadolescents with a physical disability: The mediational role of behavioral autonomy. *Journal of Clinical and Consulting Psychology, 70*, 96–110.

Holmes, E. K., Sasaki, T., & Hazen, N. L. (2013). Smooth versus rocky transitions to parenthood: Family systems in developmental context. *Family Relations, 62*, 824–837.

Holmes, M. R. (2013). Aggressive behavior of children exposed to intimate partner violence: An examination of maternal mental health, maternal warmth and child maltreatment. *Child Abuse and Neglect, 37*, 520–530.

Holt, L. (1929). *The care and feeding of children* (14th ed.). New York, NY: Appleton.

Holtrop, K., McNeil, S., & McWey, L. M. (2014). "It's a struggle but I can do it. I'm doing it for me and my kids": The psychosocial characteristics and life experiences of at-risk homeless parents in transitional housing. *Journal of Marital and Family Therapy, 40*.

Hook, J. L., & Chalasani, S. (2008). Gendered expectations? Reconsidering single fathers' child-care time. *Journal of Marriage and Family, 70*, 978–990.

Hoover-Dempsey, K. V., Battiato, A. C., Walker, J. M. T., Reed, R. P., DeJong, J. M., & Jones, K. P. (2001). Parental involvement in homework. *Educational Psychologist, 36*, 195–209.

Horowitz, F. D. (1992). John B. Watson's legacy: Learning and environment. *Developmental Psychology, 28*, 360–367.

Horwitz, B. N., & Neiderhiser, J. M. (2011). Gene-environment interplay, family relationships, and child adjustment. *Journal of Marriage and Family, 73*, 804–816.

Howard, J. A., Smith, S. L., & Ryan, S. D. (2004). A comparative study of child welfare adoptions with other types of adopted children and birth children. *Adoption Quarterly, 7*, 1–30.

Hsu, H-C. (2004). Antecedents and consequences of separation anxiety in first-time mothers: Infant, mother, and social-contextual characteristics. *Infant Behavior and Development, 27*, 113–133.

Hsueh, J., Principe Alderson, D., Lundquist, E., Michalopoulos, C., Gubits, D., Fein, D., & Knox, V. (2012). *OPRE Report: The Supporting Healthy Marriage evaluation: Early impacts on low-income families*. Washington, DC. Department of Health and Human Services, Administration for Children and Families, Office of Planning, Research and Evaluation.

Hudson, J. I., Hiripi, E., Pope, H. G., Jr., & Kessler, R. C. (2007). The prevalence and correlates of eating disorders in the National Comorbidity Survey Replication. *Biological Psychiatry, 61*, 348–358.

Huesmann, L. R., & Taylor, L. D. (2006). The role of media violence in violent behavior. *Annual Review of Public Health, 27*, 393–415.

Hughes, A. R., Sherriff, A., Lawlor, D. A., Ness, A. R., & Reilly, J. J. (2011). Incidence of obesity during childhood and adolescence in a large contemporary cohort. *Preventive Medicine, 52*, 300–304.

Hughes, D. (2003). Correlates of African American and Latino parents' messages to children about ethnicity and race: A comparative study of racial socialization. *American Journal of Community Psychology, 31*, 15–33.

Human Rights Watch. (2009). *Impairing education: Corporal punishment of students with disabilities in U.S. public schools*. Retrieved June 20, 2014, from https://www.aclu.org/human-rights/impairing-education-corporal-punishment-students-disabilities-us-public-schools

Husain, A. (1979). *Muslim parents: Their rights and duties*. Karachi, Pakistan: International Islamic Publishers.

Husain, A. (2006). *Islamic psychology: Emergence of a new field*. New Delhi, India: Global Vision Publishing House.

Huston, A. C., & Bentley, A. C. (2010). Human development in societal context. *Annual Review of Psychology, 61*, 411–437.

Huston, A. C., & Rosenkrantz Aronson, S. (2005). Mothers' time with infant and time in employment as predictors of mother-child relationships and children's early development. *Child Development, 76*, 467–482.

Huysman, A. (2003). *The postpartum effect: Deadly depression in mothers*. New York, NY: Seven Stories Press.

Hwang, W-C., Wood, J. J., & Fujimoto, K. (2010). Acculturative family distancing (AFD) and depression in Chinese American families. *Journal of Consulting and Clinical Psychology, 78*, 655–667.

Ice, C. L., & Hoover-Dempsey, K. V. (2011). Linking parental motivations for involvement and student proximal achievement outcomes in homeschooling and public schooling settings. *Education and Urban Society, 43*, 339–369.

ICF International. (2009). *Protecting children in families affected by substance use disorders*. Washington, DC: U.S. Department of Health and Human Services: Office on Child Abuse and Neglect.

Inglehart, R., & Baker, W. E. (2000). Modernization, cultural change, and persistence of traditional values. *American Sociological Review, 65*, 19–51.

Institute of Medicine. (2006). *Preterm births: Causes, consequences, and prevention*. Retrieved June 4, 2014, from http://www.iom.edu/Reports/2006/Preterm-Birth-Causes-Consequences-and-Prevention.aspx

Isenberg, E. J. (2007). What have we learned about homeschooling? *Peabody Journal of Education, 82*, 387–409.

Ispa, J. M., Sable, M. R., Porter, N., & Csizmadia, A. (2007). Pregnancy acceptance, parenting stress, and toddler attachment in low-income Black families. *Journal of Marriage and Family, 69*, 1–13..

Itard, J. M. G. (1962). *The wild boy of Aveyron* (G. Humphrey & M. Humphrey, Trans.). New York, NY: Appleton-Century-Crofts.

Jabès, A., & Nelson, C. A. (2014). Neuroscience and child well-being. In A. Ben-Arieh, F. Casas, I. Frones, & J. E. Korbin (Eds.), *Handbook of child well-being* (pp. 219–247). New York, NY: Springer.

Jaccard, J., Dittus, P. J., & Gordon, V. V. (2000). Parent-teen communication about premarital sex: Factors associated with the extent of communication. *Journal of Adolescent Research, 15*, 187–208.

Jackson, B. (1997). *Splendid slippers: A thousand years of an erotic tradition*. Berkeley, CA: Ten Speed Press.

Jacob, J., Gray, B., & Johnson, A. (2013). The Asian American family and mental health: Implications for child health professionals. *Journal of Pediatric Health Care, 27*, 180–188.

Jaffe, A. E., Eaton, W. W., Straub, R. E., Marenco, S., & Weinberger, D. R. (2013). Paternal age, de novo mutations and schizophrenia. *Molecular Psychiatry, 19*, 274–275.

Jain, A., Chamberlin, L. A., Carter, Y., Powers, S. W., & Whitaker, R. C. (2001). Why don't low-income mothers worry about their preschoolers being overweight? *Pediatrics, 107*, 1138–1146.

Jalongo, M. R. (2006). The story of Mary Ellen Wilson: Tracing the origins of child protection in America. *Early Childhood Education Journal, 34*, 1–4.

Jankowski, P. J., Hooper, L. M., Sandage, S. J., & Hannah, N. J. (2013). Parentification and mental health symptoms: mediator effects of perceived unfairness and differentiation of self. *Journal of Family Therapy, 35*, 43–65.

Jansen, J., de Weerth, C., & Riksen-Walraven, J. M. (2008). Breastfeeding and the mother–infant relationship—A review. *Developmental Review, 28*, 503–521.

Jansen, P. W., Mensah, F. K., Clifford, S. A., Tiemeier, H., Nicholson, J. M., & Wake, M. (2013). Development of mental health problems and overweight between ages 4 and 11 years: A population-based longitudinal study of Australian children. *Academic Pediatrics, 13*, 159–167.

Japel, C., Tremblay, R. E., & Côté, S. (2005). Quality counts! Assessing the quality of daycare services based on the Quebec Longitudinal Study of Child Development. *IRPP Choices* (vol. 11, pp. 1–42).

Jayanthi, N., Pinkham, C., Dugas, L., Patrick, B., & LaBella, C. (2013). Sports specialization in young athletes: Evidence-based recommendations. *Sports Health: A Multidisciplinary Approach, 5*, 251–257.

Jenni, O. C., & O'Connor, B. B. (2005). Children's sleep: An interplay between culture and biology. *Pediatrics, 115*, 204–216.

Jiang, Y., Ekono, M., & Skinner, C. (2014). Basic facts about low-income children. *National Center for Children in Poverty*. New York, NY: Mailman School of Public Health, Columbia University.

Johns, C. H. (1903). *The oldest code of laws in the world: The code of laws promulgated by Hammurabi, King of Babylonia*. Edinburgh, Scotland: T. & T. Clark.

Johnson, D. J. (2005). The ecology of children's racial coping: Family, school, and community influences. In T. S. Weisner (Ed.), *Discovering successful pathways in children's development: Mixed methods in the study of childhood and family life* (pp. 87–109). Chicago, IL: University of Chicago Press.

Johnson, S. L., & Benson, K. E. (2014). "It's always the mother's fault": Secondary stigma of mothering a transgender child. *Journal of GLBT Family Studies, 10*, 124–144.

Johnson, S. L., Li, J., Kendall, G., Strazdins, L., & Jacoby, P. (2013). Mothers' and fathers' work hours, child gender, and behavior in middle childhood. *Journal of Marriage and Family, 75*, 56–74.

Johnston, L. D., O'Malley, P. M., Bachman, J. G., & Schulenberg, J. E. (2011). *Monitoring the future national results on adolescent drug use: Overview of key findings, 2010*. Ann Arbor: Institute for Social Research, University of Michigan.

Jones, D. J., Forehand, R., Brody, G., & Armistead, L. (2002). Psychosocial adjustment of African American children in single-mother families: A test of three risk models. *Journal of Marriage and Family, 64*, 105–115.

Jones, J., & Mosher, W. D. (2013). Fathers' involvement with their children: United States, 2006–2010. *National Health Statistics Reports, 71*. Atlanta, GA: Center for Disease Control and Prevention.

Jones, T. L., & Prinz, R. J. (2005). Potential roles of parental self-efficacy in parent and child adjustment: A review. *Clinical Psychology Review, 25*, 341–363.

Juffer, F., Bakermans-Kranenburg, M. J., & van IJzendoorn, M. H. (Eds.). (2008). *Promoting positive parenting: An attachment-based intervention*. New York, NY: Lawrence Erlbaum Associates.

Julian, T. A., & Kominski, R. A. (2011). Education and synthetic work-life earnings estimates. *American Community Survey Reports, ACS-14*. Washington, DC: U.S. Census Bureau.

Kabat-Zinn, M., & Kabat-Zinn, J. (1997). *Everyday blessings: The inner work of mindful parenting*. New York, NY: Hyperion.

Kalmijn, M. (2013). Long-term effects of divorce on parent-child relationships: Within-family comparisons of fathers and mothers. *European Sociological Review, 29*, 888–898.

Kalmus, V., Siibak, A., & Blinka, L. (2014). Internet and child well-being. In A. Ben-Arieh, F. Casas, I. Frones, & J. E. Korbin (Eds.), *Handbook of child well-being* (pp. 2093–2133). New York, NY: Springer.

Kamerman, S., & Kahn, A. (1989). Family policy: Has the United States learned from Europe? *Policy Studies Review, 8*, 581–598.

Kang, J. (2013). Instrumental social support, material hardship, personal control and neglectful parenting. *Children and Youth Services Review, 35*, 1366–1373.

Karakurt, G., & Silver, K. E. (2014). Therapy for childhood sexual abuse survivors using attachment and family systems theory orientations. *American Journal of Family Therapy, 42*, 79–91.

Kasser, T. (2002). *The high price of materialism*. Cambridge, MA: MIT Press.

Kasser, T., Ryan, R. M., Zax, M., & Sameroff, A. J. (1995). The relations of maternal and social environments to late adolescents' materialistic and prosocial values. *Developmental Psychology, 31*, 907–914.

Katz, L. F., Maliken, A. C., & Stettler, N. M. (2012). Parental meta-emotion philosophy: A review of research and theoretical framework. *Child Development Perspectives, 6*, 417–422.

Kawabata, Y., Alink, L. R., Tseng, W-L., van IJzendoorn, M. H., & Crick, N. R. (2011). Maternal and paternal parenting styles associated with relational aggression in children and adolescents: A conceptual analysis and meta-analytic review. *Developmental Review, 31*, 240–278.

Kay, C., & Green, J. (2013). Reactive attachment disorder following early maltreatment: Systematic evidence beyond the institution. *Journal of Abnormal Child Psychology, 41*, 571–581.

Keller, H., & Greenfield, P. M. (2000). History and future of development in cross-cultural psychology. *Journal of Cross-Cultural Psychology, 31*, 52–62.

Keller, H., Miranda, D., & Gauda, G. (1984). The naive theory of the infant and some maternal attitudes. *Journal of Cross-Cultural Psychology, 15*, 165–179.

Keller, H., Voelker, S., & Yovsi, R. D. (2005). Conceptions of parenting in different cultural communities: The case of West African Nso and northern German women. *Social Development, 14*, 158–180.

Keller, H., & Zach, U. (2002). Gender and birth order as determinants of parental behavior. *International Journal of Behavioral Development, 26*, 177–184.

Keller, P. S., Cummings, E. M., Davies, P. T., & Mitchell, P. M. (2008). Longitudinal relations between parental drinking problems, family functioning, and child adjustment. *Development and Psychopathology, 20*, 195–212.

Kelley, B., & Carchia, C. (2013). Hey data data—Swing!: The hidden demographics of youth sports. Retrieved June 10, 2014, from http://espn.go.com/espn/story/_/id/9469252/hidden-demographics-youth-sports-espn-magazine

Kelley, B. T., Loeber, R., Keenan, K., & DeLamatre, M. (1997, December). Developmental pathways in boys' disruptive delinquent behavior. *Juvenile Justice Bulletin*. Retrieved May 27, 2014, from https://www.ncjrs.gov/pdffiles/165692.pdf

Kelley, R. (2007, September 3). Dollars for scholars: A bold experiment pays parents to do the right thing. *Newsweek*, p. 39.

Kellogg, N. D., & Hoffman, T. J. (1997). Child sexual revictimization by multiple perpetrators. *Child Abuse and Neglect, 21*, 953–964.

Kempe, C. H., Silverman, F. N., Steele, B. B., Droegemueller, W., & Silver, H. K. (1962). The battered child syndrome. *Journal of the American Medical Association, 181*, 17–24.

Kendall-Tackett, K. (2013). *Treating the lifetime health effects of childhood victimization* (2nd ed.). Kingston, NJ: Civic Research Institute.

Kendler, K. S., Neale, M. C., Kessler, R. C., Heath, A. C., & Eaves, L. J. (1993). A test of the equal-environment assumption in twin studies of psychiatric illness. *Behavior Genetics, 23*, 21–27.

Kerig, P. K. (1998). Moderators and mediators of the effects of interparental conflict on children's adjustment. *Journal of Abnormal Child Psychology, 26*, 199–212.

Kersting, A., Dölemeyer, R., Steinig, J., Walter, F., Kroker, K., Baust, K., & Wagner, B. (2013). Brief Internet-based intervention reduces posttraumatic stress and prolonged grief in parents after the loss of a child during pregnancy: A randomized controlled trial. *Psychotherapy and Psychosomatics, 82*, 372–381.

Khaleque, A. (2013). Perceived parental warmth, and children's psychological adjustment, and personality dispositions: A meta-analysis. *Journal of Child and Family Studies, 22*, 297–306.

Khaleque, A., & Rohner, R. P. (2002). Perceived parental acceptance-rejection and psychological adjustment: A meta-analysis of cross-cultural and intracultural studies. *Journal of Marriage and Family, 64*, 54–64.

Kiff, C., Lengua, L., & Zalewski, M. (2011). Nature and nurturing: Parenting in the context of child temperament. *Clinical Child and Family Psychology Review, 14*, 251–301.

Kim, P., Leckman, J. F., Mayes, L. C., Feldman, R., Wang, X., & Swain, J. E. (2010). The plasticity of human maternal brain: Longitudinal changes in brain anatomy during the early postpartum period. *Behavioral Neuroscience, 124*, 695–700.

Kim, S. Y., Chen, Q., Wang, Y., Shen, Y., & Orozco-Lapray, D. (2013). Longitudinal linkages among parent-child acculturation discrepancy, parenting, parent-child sense of alienation, and adolescent adjustment in Chinese immigrant families. *Developmental Psychology, 49*, 900–912.

Kim, S. Y., Nordling, J. K., Yoon, J. E., Boldt, L. J., & Kochanska, G. (2013). Effortful control in "hot" and "cool" tasks differentially predicts children's behavior problems and academic performance. *Journal of Abnormal Child Psychology, 41*, 43–56.

Kim, S. Y., Wang, Y., Orozco-Lapray, D., Shen, Y., & Murtuza, M. (2013). Does "tiger parenting" exist? Parenting profiles of Chinese Americans and adolescent developmental outcomes. *Asian American Journal of Psychology, 4*, 7–18.

Kimbro, R. T. (2006). On-the-job moms: Work and breastfeeding initiation and duration for a sample of low-income women. *Maternal and Child Health Journal, 10*, 19–26.

King, P. E., & Furrow, J. L. (2004). Religion as a resource for positive youth development: Religion, social capital, and moral outcomes. *Developmental Psychology, 40*, 703–713.

Kirby, J. N., & Sanders, M. R. (2013). The acceptability of parenting strategies for grandparents providing care to their grandchildren. *Prevention Science, 13*, e1–14.

Kiselica, M. S., & Morrill-Richards, M. (2007). Sibling maltreatment: The forgotten abuse. *Journal of Counseling & Development, 85*, 148–160.

Klaus, M. H., Jerauld, R., Kreger, N. C., McAlpine, W., Steffa, M., & Kennel, J. H. (1972). Maternal attachment: Importance of the first post-partum days. *New England Journal of Medicine, 286*, 460–463.

Klemetti, R., Sevón, T., Gissler, M., & Hemminki, E. (2006). Health of children born as a result of in vitro fertilization. *Pediatrics, 118*, 1819–1827.

Knight, G., Virdin, L., & Roosa, M. (1994). Socialization and family correlates of mental health outcomes among Hispanic and Anglo American children: Consideration of cross-ethnic scalar equivalence. *Child Development, 65*, 212–224.

Kochanska, G. (1997). Multiple pathways to conscience for children with different temperaments: From toddlerhood to age 5. *Developmental Psychology, 33*, 228–240.

Kochanska, G. (2002). Mutually responsive orientation between mothers and their young children: A context for the early development of conscience. *Current Directions in Psychological Science, 11*, 191–195.

Kochanska, G., Aksan, N., Penney, S. J., & Boldt, L. J. (2007). Parental personality as an inner resource that moderates the impact of ecological adversity on parenting. *Journal of Personality and Social Psychology, 92*, 136–150.

Kochanska, G., Aksan, N., Prisco, T. R., & Adams, E. E. (2008). Mother-child and father-child mutually responsive orientation in the first 2 years and children's outcomes at preschool age: Mechanisms of influence. *Child Development, 79*, 30–44.

Kochanska, G., & Kim, S. (2013). Early attachment organization with both parents and future behavior problems: From infancy to middle childhood. *Child Development, 84*, 283–296.

Kodituwakku, P., & Kodituwakku, E. L. (2013). Fetal alcohol syndrome. In D. W. Pfaff (Ed.), *Neuroscience in the 21 century* (pp. 2411–2430). New York, NY: Springer Science+Business Media.

Koenen, M. A., & Thompson, J., J. W. (2008). Filicide: Historical review and prevention of child death by parent. *Infant Mental Health Journal, 29*, 61–75.

Kohn, M. L. (1979). The effects of social class on parental values and practices. In D. Reiss & H. Hoffman (Eds.), *The American family: Dying or developing* (pp. 45–68). New York, NY: Plenum.

Kohn, M. L., Naoi, A., Shoenbach, C., Schooler, C., & Slomczynski, K. M. (1990). Position in class structure and psychological functioning: A comparative analysis for the United States, Japan, and Poland. *American Journal of Sociology, 90*, 964–1008.

Kolko, D. J. (1996). Child physical abuse. In J. Briere, L. Berliner, J. A. Bulkley, C. Jenny, & T. Reid (Eds.), *The APSAC handbook on child maltreatment* (pp. 21–50). Thousand Oaks, CA: SAGE.

Koplan, J. P., Liverman, C. T., & Kraak, V. A. (Eds.). (2005). *Preventing childhood obesity: Health in the balance*. Washington, DC: National Academies Press.

Kost, K., & Henshaw, S. (2013). US teenage pregnancies, births and abortions, 2008: State trends by age, race and ethnicity. *Guttmacher Institute*. Retrieved June 1, 2014, from http://www.guttmacher.org/pubs/USTPtrendsState08.pdf

Kotchick, B. A., Dorsey, S., & Heller, L. (2005). Predictors of parenting among African American single mothers: Personal and contextual factors. *Journal of Marriage and Family, 67*, 448–460.

Kotila, L. E., Schoppe-Sullivan, S. J., & Kamp Dush, C. M. (2013). Time in parenting activities in dual-earner families at the transition to parenthood. *Family Relations, 62*, 795–807.

Kovac, J. R., Addai, J., Smith, R. P., Coward, R. M., Lamb, D. J., & Lipshultz, L. I. (2013). The effects of advanced paternal age on fertility. *Asian Journal of Andrology, 15*, 723–728.

Kowal, A. K., Kramer, L., Krull, J. L., & Crick, N. (2002). Children's perceptions of the fairness of parental preferential treatment and their socioemotional well-being. *Journal of Family Psychology, 16*, 297–306.

Kowal, A. K., Krull, J. L., & Kramer, L. (2006). Shared understanding of parental differential treatment in families. *Social Development, 15*, 276–295.

Kowalski, R. M., & Limber, S. P. (2013). Psychological, physical, and academic correlates of cyberbullying and traditional bullying. *Journal of Adolescent Health, 53*, S13–S20.

Kozuki, N., Lee, A. C., Silveira, M. F., Victora, C. G., Adair, L., Humphrey, J., . . . Katz, J. (2013). The associations of birth intervals with small-for-gestational-age, preterm, and neonatal and infant mortality: A meta-analysis. *BMC Public Health, 13*(Supplement 3), S3.

Kramer, L., & Baron, L. A. (1995). Parental perceptions of children's sibling relationships. *Family Relations, 44*, 95–103.

Krishnakumar, A., & Buehler, C. (2000). Interparental conflict and parenting behaviors: A meta-analytic review. *Family Relations, 49*, 25–44.

Krishnamoorthy, J. S., Hart, C., & Jelalian, E. (2006). The epidemic of childhood obesity: Review of research and implications for public policy. *Social Policy Report, 20*, 3–17.

Kuczynski, L., & De Mol, J. (2014). Social relational theory: Dialectical models of transaction in parent-child relationships and socialization. In W. F. Overton & P. C. M. Molenaar (Eds.), *Theory and method* (7th ed., vol. 1). Hoboken, NJ: Wiley.

Kuhn, J. C., & Carter, A. S. (2006). Maternal self-efficacy and associated parenting cognitions among mothers of children with autism. *American Journal of Orthopsychiatry, 76*, 564–575.

Kunz, J. H., & Grych, J. H. (2013). Parental psychological control and autonomy granting: Distinctions and associations with child and family functioning. *Parenting: Science and Practice, 13*, 77–94.

Kuo, Z-Y. (1967). *The dynamics of behavioral development: An epigenetic view*. New York, NY: Plenum Press.

Kuppens, S., Grietens, H., Onghena, P., & Michiels, D. (2009). Measuring parenting dimensions in middle childhood: Multitrait-multimethod analysis of child, mother, and father ratings. *European Journal of Psychological Assessment, 25*, 133–140.

Kurdek, L. A. (2003). Correlates of parents' perceptions of behavioral problems in their young children. *Applied Developmental Psychology, 24*, 457–473.

Kurdek, L. A. (2004). Are gay and lesbian cohabiting couples really different from heterosexual married couples? *Journal of Marriage and Family, 66*, 880–900.

Kurdek, L. A., Fine, M. A., & Sinclair, R. J. (1995). School adjustments in sixth graders: Parenting transitions, family climate, and peer norm effects. *Child Development, 66*, 430–445.

Kwok, S. Y., Cheng, L., Chow, B. W., & Ling, C. C. (2013). The spillover effect of parenting on marital satisfaction among Chinese mothers. *Journal of Child and Family Studies, 22*, 1–12.

Ladd, G. W., & Pettit, G. S. (2002). Parenting and the development of children's peer relationships. In M. H. Bornstein (Ed.), *Handbook of parenting, vol. 5: Practical issues in parenting* (2nd ed., pp. 269–309). Mahwah, NJ: Lawrence Erlbaum Associates.

Ladd, G. W., Profilet, S. M., & Hart, C. H. (1992). Parents' management of children's peer relations: Facilitating and supervising children's activities in the peer culture. In R. D. Parke & G. W. Ladd (Eds.), *Family-peer relationships: Modes of linkage* (pp. 215–253). Hillsdale, NJ: Lawrence Erlbaum Associates.

LaFollette, H. (1980). Licensing parents. *Philosophy and Public Affairs, 9*, 182–197.

LaFreniere, P. J., & Sroufe, L. A. (1985). Profiles of peer competence in the preschool: Interrelations between measures, influence of social ecology, and relation to attachment history. *Developmental Psychology, 21*, 56–69.

Laible, D. J., & Thompson, R. A. (2000). Mother-child discourse, attachment security, shared positive affect, and early conscience development. *Child Development, 71*, 1424–1440.

Laible, D. J., & Thompson, R. A. (2007). Early socialization: A relationships perspective. In J. E. Grusec & P. D. Hastings (Eds.), *Handbook of socialization* (pp. 181–207). New York, NY: Guilford.

Lamb, M. E. (1982). Early contact and maternal-infant bonding: One decade later. *Pediatrics, 70*, 763–768.

Lamb, M. E. (Ed.). (2010). *The role of the father in child development* (5th ed.). New York, NY: Wiley.

Lamb, M. E., & Tamis-LeMonda, C. S. (2004). The role of the father: An introduction. In M. E. Lamb (Ed.), *The role of the father in child development* (4th ed., pp. 1–31). New York, NY: John Wiley & Sons.

Lamborn, S., Mounts, N. S., Steinberg, L., & Dornbusch, S. (1991). Patterns of competence and adjustment among adolescents from authoritative, authoritarian, indulgent, and neglectful families. *Child Development, 62*, 1049–1065.

Lang, A., & Carr, T. (2013). Bereavement in the face of perinatal loss: A hardiness perspective. In D. S. Becvar (Ed.), *Handbook of family resilience* (pp. 299–319). New York, NY: Springer.

Lang, S. N., Schoppe-Sullivan, S. J., Kotila, L. E., Feng, X., Dush, C. M. K., & Johnson, S. C. (2014). Relations between fathers' and mothers' infant engagement patterns in dual-earner families and toddler competence. *Journal of Family Issues, 35*, 1107–1127.

Lansford, J. E. (2009). Parental divorce and children's adjustment. *Perspectives on Psychological Science, 4*, 140–152.

Lansford, J. E., Bornstein, M. H., Dodge, K. A., Skinner, A. T., Putnick, D. L., & Deater-Deckard, K. (2011). Attributions and attitudes of mothers and fathers in the United States. *Parenting: Science and Practice, 11*, 199–213.

Lansford, J. E., & Deater-Deckard, K. (2012). Childrearing discipline and violence in developing countries. *Child Development, 83*, 62–75.

Lansford, J. E., & Dodge, K. A. (2008). Cultural norms for adult corporal punishment of children and societal rates of endorsement and use of violence. *Parenting: Science and Practice, 8*, 257–270.

Lansford, J. E., Lei, C., Dodge, K. A., Malone, P. S., Oburu, P., Palmérus, K., . . . Quinn, N. (2005). Physical discipline and children's adjustment: Cultural normativeness as a moderator. *Child Development, 76*, 1234–1246.

Lansford, J. E., Wager, L. B., Bates, J. E., Dodge, K. A., & Pettit, G. S. (2012). Parental reasoning, denying privileges, yelling, and spanking: Ethnic differences and associations with child externalizing behavior. *Parenting: Science and Practice, 12*, 42–56.

Larzelere, R. E., & Baumrind, D. (2010). Are spanking injunctions scientifically supported? *Law & Contemporary Problems, 73*, 57–87.

Larzelere, R. E., Morris, A. S., & Harrist, A. W. (2013). *Authoritative parenting: Synthesizing nurturance and discipline for optimal child development.* Washington, DC: American Psychological Association.

Lasko, J. K. (1954). Parent behavior toward first and second children. *Genetic Psychology Monographs, 49*, 97–187.

Laughlin, L. (2011). *Maternity leave and employment patterns of first-time mothers: 1961–2008 Current Population Reports.* Washington, DC: United States Census Bureau, U.S. Department of Commerce.

Laughlin, L. (2013). *Who's minding the kids? Child care arrangements: Spring 2011 Current population reports (vol. P70–135).* Washington, DC: U.S. Census Bureau.

Laukkanen, J., Ojansuu, U., Tolvanen, A., Alatupa, S., & Aunola, K. (2014). Child's difficult temperament and mothers' parenting styles. *Journal of Child and Family Studies, 23*, 312–323.

Laursen, B., Coy, K. C., & Collins, W. A. (1998). Reconsidering changes in parent-child conflict across adolescence: A meta-analysis. *Child Development, 69*, 817–832.

Lawrence, E., Rothman, A. D., Cobb, R. J., Rothman, M. T., & Bradbury, T. N. (2008). Marital satisfaction across the transition to parenthood. *Journal of Family Psychology, 22*, 41–50.

Leaper, C. (2002). Parenting boys and girls. In M. H. Bornstein (Ed.), *Handbook of parenting, vol. 1: Children and parenting* (pp. 189–225). Mahwah, NJ: Lawrence Erlbaum Associates.

Leaper, C. (2013). Gender development during childhood. In P. D. Zelazo (Ed.), *The Oxford handbook of developmental psychology, vol. 2: Self and other* (pp. 326–377). New York, NY: Oxford University Press.

Leaper, C., Anderson, K. J., & Sanders, P. (1998). Moderators of gender effects on parents' talk to their children: A meta-analysis. *Developmental Psychology, 34*, 3–27.

Leaper, C., & Bigler, R. S. (2011). Gender as a context for social development. In M. K. Underwood & L. H. Rosen (Eds.), *Social development: Relationships in infancy, childhood, and adolescence* (pp. 289–315). New York, NY: Guilford Press.

Leaper, C., & Friedman, C. K. (2007). The socialization of gender. In J. E. Grusec & P. D. Hastings (Eds.), *Handbook of socialization* (pp. 561–587). New York, NY: Guilford.

Lee, C-T., McClernon, F. J., Kollins, S. H., Prybol, K., & Fuemmeler, B. F. (2013). Childhood economic strains in predicting substance use in emerging adulthood: Mediation effects of youth self-control and parenting practices. *Journal of Pediatric Psychology, 38,* 1130–1143.

Lee, S. J., Altschul, I., & Gershoff, E. T. (2013). Does warmth moderate longitudinal associations between maternal spanking and child aggression in early childhood? *Developmental Psychology, 49,* 2017–2028.

Lee, S. J., Altschul, I., Shair, S. R., & Taylor, C. A. (2011). Hispanic fathers and risk for maltreatment in father-involved families of young children. *Journal of the Society for Social Work and Research, 2,* 125–142.

Lee, Y. (2009). Early motherhood and harsh parenting: The role of human, social, and cultural capital. *Child Abuse and Neglect, 33,* 625–637.

Leen-Feldner, E. W., Feldner, M. T., Knapp, A., Bunaciu, L., Blumenthal, H., & Amstadter, A. B. (2013). Offspring psychological and biological correlates of parental post-traumatic stress: Review of the literature and research agenda. *Clinical Psychology Review, 33,* 1106–1133.

Leerkes, E. M., Parade, S. H., & Burney, R. V. (2010). Origins of mothers' and fathers' beliefs about infant crying. *Journal of Applied Developmental Psychology, 31,* 467–474.

Leibenluft, E., Gobbini, M. I., Harrison, T., & Haxby, J. V. (2004). Mothers' neural activation in response to pictures of their children and other children. *Biological Psychiatry, 56,* 225–232.

Leibham, M. E., Alexander, J. M., Johnson, K. E., Neitzel, C. L., & Reis-Henrie, F. P. (2005). Parenting behaviors associated with the maintenance of preschoolers' interests: A prospective longitudinal study. *Applied Developmental Psychology, 26,* 397–414.

LeMasters, E. E. (1957). Parenthood as crisis. *Marriage and Family Living, 19,* 352–355.

LeMoyne, T., & Buchanan, T. (2011). Does "hovering" matter? Helicopter parenting and its effects on well-being *Sociological Spectrum, 31,* 399–418.

Lengua, L. J. (2006). Growth in temperament and parenting as predictors of adjustment during children's transition to adolescence. *Developmental Psychology, 42,* 819–832.

Lenhart, A. (2012). *Teens, smartphones & texting, Pew Research Internet Project.* Washington, DC: Pew Research Center.

Lenhart, A., Purcell, K., Smith, A. B., & Zickuhr, K. (2010). *Social media and young adults, Pew Research Internet Project.* Washington, DC: Pew Research Center.

Lenhart, A., Rainie, L., & Lewis, O. (2001). *Teenage life online: The rise of the instant-message generation and the Internet's impact on friendships and family relationships.* Washington, DC: Pew Internet & American Life Project Washington, DC.

Lepore, S. J., & Kliewer, W. (2013). Violence exposure, sleep disturbance, and poor academic performance in middle school. *Journal of Abnormal Child Psychology, 41,* 1179–1189.

Lereya, S. T., Samara, M., & Wolke, D. (2013). Parenting behavior and the risk of becoming a victim and a bully/victim: A meta-analysis study. *Child Abuse and Neglect, 37,* 1091–1108.

Lerner, R. M., Easterbrooks, M. A., & Mistry, J. (Eds.). (2013). *Handbook of psychology: Developmental psychology* (2nd ed., vol. 6). New York, NY: John Wiley & Sons.

LeRoy, M., Mahoney, A., Boxer, P., Gullan, R. L., & Fang, Q. (2014). Parents who hit and scream: Interactive effects of verbal and severe physical aggression on clinic-referred adolescents' adjustment. *Child Abuse and Neglect, 38,* 893–901.

Le Sage, L., & De Ruyter, D. (2008). Criminal parental responsibility: Blaming parents on the basis of their duty to control versus their duty to morally educate their children. *Educational Philosophy and Theory, 40,* 789–802.

Lesane-Brown, C. L. (2006). A review of race socialization within Black families. *Developmental Review, 26,* 400–426.

Leslie, L. A., Smith, J. R., Hrapczynski, K. M., & Riley, D. (2013). Racial socialization in transracial adoptive families: Does it help adolescents deal with discrimination stress? *Family Relations, 62,* 72–81.

Letiecq, B. L., & Koblinsky, S. A. (2004). Parenting in violent neighborhoods: African American fathers share strategies for keeping children safe. *Journal of Family Issues, 25,* 715–734.

Levendosky, A. A., & Graham-Bermann, S. A. (2001). Parenting in battered women: The effects of domestic violence on women and their children. *Journal of Family Violence, 16*, 171–192.

Levin, H. M., & Rouse, C. E. (2012, January 25). The true cost of high school dropouts. *New York Times*, p. A31. Retrieved May 27, 2014, from http://www.nytimes.com/2012/01/26/opinion/the-true-cost-of-high-school-dropouts.html?_r=0

Levine, J. A., Emery, C. R., & Pollack, H. (2007). The well-being of children born to teen mothers. *Journal of Marriage and Family, 69*, 105–122.

Levy-Shiff, R., Goldshmidt, I., & Har-Even, D. (1991). Transition to parenthood in adoptive families. *Developmental Psychology, 27*, 131–140.

Lewin, A., Mitchell, S. J., & Ronzio, C. R. (2013). Developmental differences in parenting behavior: Comparing adolescent, emerging adult, and adult mothers. *Merrill-Palmer Quarterly, 59*, 23–49.

Lewin, K. (1935). *A dynamic theory of personality*. New York, NY: McGraw-Hill.

Lewis, C. C. (1981). The effects of parental firm control: A reinterpretation of the findings. *Psychological Bulletin, 90*, 547–563.

Lewis, M., & Kreitzberg, V. S. (1979). Effects of birth order and spacing on mother-infant interactions. *Developmental Psychology, 15*, 617–625.

Leyendecker, B., Lamb, M. E., Harwood, R. L., & Schölmerich, A. (2002). Mothers' socialization goals and evaluations of desirable and undesirable everyday situations in two diverse cultural groups. *International Journal of Behavioral Development, 26*, 248–258.

Li, X., & Lamb, M. E. (2013). Fathers in Chinese culture: From stern disciplinarians to involved parents. In D. W. Schwalb, B. J. Schwalb, & M. E. Lamb (Eds.), *Fathers in cultural context* (pp. 15–41). New York, NY: Routledge.

Lillard, A. S., & Peterson, J. (2011). The immediate impact of different types of television on young children's executive function. *Pediatrics, 128*, 644–649.

Limber, S. P., Olweus, D., & Luxenberg, H. (2013). *Bullying in US schools*. Center City, MN: Hazelden Foundation.

Lin, C-Y. C., & Fu, V. R. (1990). A comparison of child-rearing practices among Chinese, immigrant Chinese, and Caucasian-American parents. *Child Development, 61*, 429–433.

Linares, L. O., Jimenez, J., Nesci, C., Pearson, E., Beller, S., Edwards, N., & Levin-Rector, A. (2014). Reducing sibling conflict in maltreated children placed in foster homes. *Prevention Science, 15*, 1–11.

Linebarger, D. L., & Walker, D. (2005). Infants' and toddlers' television viewing and language outcomes. *American Behavioral Scientist, 48*, 624–645.

Lino, M. (2013). *Expenditures on children by families, 2012*. U.S. Department of Agriculture, Center for Nutrition Policy and Promotion. Miscellaneous Publication No. 1528–2012.

Lippman, L. H., Moore, K. A., & McIntosh, H. (2011). Positive indicators of child well-being: A conceptual framework, measures, and methodological issues. *Applied Research in Quality of Life, 6*, 425–449.

Livingston, G. (2010, June 25). *Childlessness up among all women; down among women with advanced degrees. Pew research: Social & demographic trends.* Retrieved May 18, 2014, from http://www.pewsocialtrends.org/2010/06/25/childlessness-up-among-all-women-down-among-women-with-advanced-degrees/

Livingston, G. (2013). *At grandmother's house we stay: One-in-ten children are living with a grandparent*. Washington, DC: Pew Research Center.

Livingston, G., & Cohn, D. V. (2010, May 6). *The new demography of American motherhood. Pew Research: Social & demographic trends.* Retrieved May 18, 2014, from http://www.pewsocialtrends.org/2010/05/06/the-new-demography-of-american-motherhood/

Locke, J. (1693/1996). *Some thoughts concerning education* (4th ed.). London: A. & J. Churchill.

Loeber, R., & Stouthamer-Loeber, M. (1998). Development of juvenile aggression and violence: Some common misconceptions and controversies. *American Psychologist, 53*, 242–259.

Loehlin, J. C. (1997). A test of J. R. Harris' theory of peer influences on personality. *Journal of Personality and Social Psychology, 72*, 1197–1201.

López-Alarcón, M., Villalpando, S., & Fajardo, A. (1997). Breast-feeding lowers the frequency and duration of acute respiratory infection and diarrhea in infants under six months of age. *The Journal of Nutrition, 127*, 436–443.

Lorenz, K., & Kickert, R. W. (1981). *The foundations of ethology*. New York, NY: Springer.

Lovejoy, M. C., Graczyk, P. A., O'Hare, E., & Neuman, G. (2000). Maternal depression and parenting behavior: A meta-analytic review. *Clinical Psychology Review, 20*, 561–592.

Luby, J. L., Barch, D. M., Belden, A., Gaffrey, M. S., Tillman, R., Babb, C., . . . Botteron, K. N. (2012). Maternal support in early childhood predicts larger hippocampal volumes at school age. *Proceedings of the National Academy of Sciences, 109*, 2854–2859.

Lucassen, P. L. B. J., Assendelft, W. J. J., Gubbels, J. W., van Eijk, J. T. W., van Geldrop, W. J., & Knuistingh Neven, A. (1998). Effectiveness of treatments for infantile colic: Systematic review. *British Medical Journal, 316*, 1563–1569.

Lund, T. J., & Dearing, E. (2013). Is growing up affluent risky for adolescents or is the problem growing up in an affluent neighborhood? *Journal of Research on Adolescence, 23*, 274–282.

Lundahl, B. W., Nimer, J., & Parsons, B. (2006). Preventing child abuse: A meta-analysis of parent training programs. *Research on Social Work Practice, 16*, 251–262.

Lundberg, S., McLanahan, S., & Rose, E. (2007). Child gender and father involvement in fragile families. *Demography, 44*, 79–92.

Lupien, S. J., McEwen, B. S., Gunnar, M. R., & Heim, C. (2009). Effects of stress throughout the lifespan on the brain, behavior and cognition. *Nature Reviews Neuroscience, 10*, 434–445.

Luthar, S. S. (2003). The culture of affluence: Psychological costs of material wealth. *Child Development, 74*, 1581–1593.

Luthar, S. S., & Latendresse, S. J. (2005). Children of the affluent: Challenges to well-being. *Current Directions in Psychological Science, 14*, 49–53.

Lykken, D. T. (2001). Parental licensure. *American Psychologist, 56*, 885–894.

Lysell, H., Runeson, B., Lichtenstein, P., & Langstrom, N. (2014). Risk factors for filicide and homicide: 36-year national matched cohort study. *Journal of Clinical Psychiatry, 75*, 127–132.

Lytton, H. (1979). Disciplinary encounters between young boys and their mothers and fathers: Is there a contingency system? *Developmental Psychology, 15*, 256–268.

Lytton, H., & Gallagher, L. (2002). Parenting twins and the genetics of parenting. In M. H. Bornstein (Ed.), *Handbook of parenting, vol. 1: Children and parenting* (2nd ed., pp. 227–254). Mahwah, NJ: Lawrence Erlbaum Associates.

Lytton, H., & Romney, D. M. (1991). Parents' differential socialization of boys and girls: A meta-analysis. *Psychological Bulletin, 109*, 267–296.

Maccoby, E. E. (2000). Parenting and its effects on children: On reading and misreading behavior genetics. *Annual Review of Psychology, 51*, 1–27.

Maccoby, E. E. (2007). Historical overview of socialization research and theory. In J. E. Grusec & P. D. Hastings (Eds.), *Handbook of socialization* (pp. 13–41). New York, NY: Guilford Press.

Maccoby, E. E., & Martin, J. A. (1983). Socialization in the context of the family: Parent-child interaction. In P. Mussen & E. M. Hetherington (Eds.), *Handbook of child psychology: Vol. 4, socialization, personality, and social development* (4th ed., pp. 1–101). New York, NY: Wiley.

MacDonald, K. (1992). Warmth as a developmental construct: An evolutionary analysis. *Child Development, 63*, 753–773.

MacDorman, M. F., Declercq, E., Menacker, F., & Malloy, M. (2006). Infant and neonatal mortality for primary Cesarean and vaginal births to women with "no indicated risk," United States, 1998–2001 birth cohorts. *Birth, 33*, 175–182.

MacDougall, K., Beyene, Y., & Nachtigall, R. (2013). Age shock: Misperceptions of the impact of age on fertility before and after IVF in women who conceived after age 40. *Human Reproduction, 28*, 350–356.

MacKenzie, M. J., Nicklas, E., Brooks-Gunn, J., & Waldfogel, J. (2011). Who spanks infants and toddlers? Evidence from the Fragile Families and Child Well-being study. *Children and Youth Services Review, 33*, 1364–1373.

MacPhee, D., Fritz, J., & Miller-Heyl, J. (1996). Ethnic variations in personal social networks and parenting. *Child Development, 67*, 3278–3295.

Mahoney, A., Pargament, K. I., Tarakeshwar, N., & Swank, A. B. (2001). Religion in the home in the 1980s and 1990s: A meta-analytic review and conceptual analysis of links between religion, marriage, and parenting. *Journal of Family Psychology, 15*, 559–596.

Mahoney, J. L., & Zigler, E. F. (2006). Translating science to policy under the No Child Left Behind Act of 2001: Lessons from the national evaluation of the 21st-century community learning centers. *Journal of Applied Developmental Psychology, 27*, 282–294.

Malkin, C. M., & Lamb, M. E. (1994). Child maltreatment: A test of sociological theory. *Journal of Comparative Family Studies, 25*, 121–133.

Manning, W. D., & Brown, S. (2006). Children's economic well-being in married and cohabiting parent families. *Journal of Marriage and Family, 68*, 345–362.

Marceau, K., Horwitz, B. N., Narusyte, J., Ganiban, J. M., Spotts, E. L., Reiss, D., & Neiderhiser, J. M. (2013). Gene-environment correlation underlying the association between parental negativity and adolescent externalizing problems. *Child Development, 84*, 2031–2046.

March, C. (2005). Academic redshirting: Does withholding a child from school entrance for one year increase academic success. *Issues in Educational Research, 15*, 69–85.

March of Dimes. (2012). *Teen pregnancy*. Retrieved June 11, 2014, from http://www.marchofdimes.com/glue/files/teenage-pregnancy.pdf

March of Dimes. (2014). *Smoking, alcohol, and drugs*. Retrieved January 21, 2014, from http://www.marchofdimes.com/pregnancy/smoking-during-pregnancy.aspx

Marini, V. A., & Kurtz, J. E. (2011). Birth order differences in normal personality traits: Perspectives from within and outside the family. *Personality and Individual Differences, 51*, 910–914.

Marini, Z. A., Spear, S., & Bombay, K. (1999). Peer victimization in middle childhood: Characteristics, causes and consequences of school bulling. *Brock Education, 9*, 32–47.

Marsiglio, W., & Roy, K. (2012). *Nurturing dads: Social initiatives for contemporary fatherhood*. New York, NY: Russell Sage.

Martin, J., Kochanek, K. D., Strobino, D. M., Guyer, B., & MacDornan, M. F. (2005). Annual summary of vital statistics–2003. *Pediatrics, 115*, 619–634.

Martin, J. A., Hamilton, B. E., Osterman, M. J. K., Curtin, S. C., & Mathews, M. S. (2013). Births: Final data for 2012. *National Vital Statistics Reports, 62*(9).

Martin, J. A., Hamilton, B. E., Ventura, S. J., Osterman, M. J. K., & Matthews, T. J. (2013). Births: Final data for 2011. *National Vital Statistics Reports, 62*(1). Retrieved May 18, 2014, from http://www.cdc.gov/nchs/data/nvsr/nvsr62/nvsr62_01.pdf

Martins, C., & Gaffan, E. A. (2000). Effects of early maternal depression on patterns of infant-mother attachment: A meta-analytic investigation. *Journal of Child Psychology and Psychiatry, 41*, 737–746.

Martorell, G. A., & Bugental, D. B. (2006). Maternal variations in stress reactivity: Implications for harsh parenting practices with very young children. *Journal of Family Violence, 20*, 641–647.

Marvin, R. S., & Britner, P. A. (2008). Normative development: The ontogeny of attachment. In J. Cassidy & P. R. Shaver (Eds.), *Handbook of attachment* (pp. 269–294). New York, NY: Guilford.

Mason, C., Cauce, A., Gonzales, N., & Hiraga, N. (1996). Neither too sweet nor too sour: Problem peers, maternal control, and problem behavior in African American adolescents. *Child Development, 67*, 2115–2130.

Masse, L. N., & Barnett, W. S. (2002). A benefit cost analysis of the Abecedarian Early Childhood Intervention. In H. M. Levin & P. J. McEwan (Eds.), *Cost effectiveness and educational policy* (pp. 157–176). Larchmont, NY: Eye on Education.

Masten, A. S. (2011). Resilience in children threatened by extreme adversity: Frameworks for research, practice, and translational synergy. *Development and Psychopathology, 23*, 493–506.

Masten, A. S., & Narayan, A. J. (2012). Child development in the context of disaster, war, and terrorism: Pathways of risk and resilience. *Annual Review of Psychology, 63*, 227–257.

Matheny, A. P., Jr., Wachs, T. D., Ludwig, J. L., & Phillips, K. (1995). Bringing order out of chaos: Psychometric characteristics of the confusion, hubbub, and order scale. *Journal of Applied Developmental Psychology, 16*, 429–444.

Mathews, T., & MacDorman, M. (2011). Infant mortality statistics from the 2007 period linked birth/infant death data set. *National Vital Statistics Reports, 59*.

Matjasko, J. L., & Feldman, A. F. (2006). Bringing work home: The emotional experiences of mothers and fathers. *Journal of Family Psychology, 20*, 47–55.

Mattanah, J. F., Pratt, M. W., Cowan, P. A., & Cowan, C. P. (2005). Authoritative parenting, parental scaffolding of long-division mathematics, and children's academic competence in fourth grade. *Applied Developmental Psychology, 26*, 85–106.

Mattis, J. S., Ahluwalia, M. K., Cowie, S. E., & Kirkland-Harris, A. M. (2006). Ethnicity, culture, and spiritual development. In E. C. Roehlkepartain, P. E. King, L. Wagener, & P. L. Benson (Eds.), *The handbook of spiritual development in childhood and adolescence* (pp. 283–296). Thousand Oaks, CA: SAGE.

Mauras, C. P., Grolnick, W. S., & Friendly, R. W. (2013). Time for "the talk." Now what? Autonomy support and structure in mother-daughter conversations about sex. *The Journal of Early Adolescence, 33*, 458–481.

McAdoo, H. P. (2002). African American parenting. In M. H. Bornstein (Ed.), *Handbook of parenting, vol. 4: Social conditions and applied parenting* (pp. 47–58). Mahwah, NJ: Lawrence Erlbaum Associates.

McDonald, R., Jouriles, E. N., Ramisetty-Mikler, S., Caetano, R., & Green, C. E. (2006). Estimating the number of American children living in partner-violent families. *Journal of Family Psychology, 20*, 137–142.

McElhaney, K. B., & Allen, J. P. (2001). Autonomy and adolescent social functioning: The moderating effect of risk. *Child Development, 72*, 220–235.

McEvoy, M., Lee, C., O'Neill, A., Groisman, A., Roberts-Butelman, K., Dinghra, K., & Porder, K. (2005). Are there universal parenting concepts among culturally diverse families in an inner-city pediatric clinic? *Journal of Pediatric Health Care, 19*, 142–150.

McGrath, M., Cann, S., & Konopasky, R. (1998). New measures of defensiveness, empathy, and cognitive distortions for sexual offenders against children. *Sexual Abuse, 10*, 25–36.

McGuire, S. (2003). The heritability of parenting. *Parenting: Science and Practice, 3*, 73–94.

McGuire, S., Segal, N. L., & Hershberger, S. (2012). Parenting as phenotype: A behavioral genetic approach to understanding parenting. *Parenting: Science and Practice, 12*, 192–201.

McHale, J., Khazan, I., Erera, P., Rotman, T., DeCourcey, W., & McConnell, M. (2002). Co-parenting in diverse family systems. In M. H. Bornstein (Ed.), *Handbook of parenting, vol. 3: Being and becoming a parent* (2nd ed., pp. 75–108). Mahwah, NJ: Lawrence Erlbaum Associates.

McHale, J., & Lindahl, K. (2011). *Co-parenting: Theory, research, and clinical applications*. Washington, DC: American Psychological Association.

McHale, S. M., Crouter, A. C., & Whiteman, S. D. (2003). The family contexts of gender development in childhood and adolescence. *Social Development, 12*, 125–148.

McHale, S. M., Updegraff, K. A., Jackson-Newsom, J., Tucker, C. J., & Crouter, A. C. (2000). When does parents' differential treatment have negative implications for siblings? *Social Development, 9*, 149–172.

McLanahan, S., & Sandefur, G. (1994). *Growing up with a single parent: What hurts, what helps*. Cambridge, MA: Harvard University Press.

McLanahan, S., Tach, L., & Schneider, D. (2013). The causal effects of father absence. *Annual Review of Sociology, 39*, 399–427.

McLaren, C., Null, J., & Quinn, J. (2005). Heat stress from enclosed vehicles: Moderate ambient temperatures cause significant temperature rise in enclosed vehicles. *Pediatrics, 116*, 109–112.

McLoyd, V. C. (1990). The impact of economic hardship on Black families and children: Psychological distress, parenting, and socioemotional development. *Child Development, 61*, 311–346.

McLoyd, V. C., Jayaratne, T. E., Ceballo, R., & Borquez, J. (1994). Unemployment and work interruption among African American single mothers: Effects on parenting and adolescent socioemotional functioning. *Child Development, 65*, 562–589.

McMahon, C., Boivin, J., Gibson, F., Hammarberg, K., Wynter, K., Saunders, D., & Fisher, J. (2013). Pregnancy-specific anxiety, ART conception and infant temperament at 4 months post-partum. *Human Reproduction, 28*, 997–1005.

McNeely, C., Shew, M. L., Beuhring, T., Sieving, R., Miller, B. C., & Blum, R. W. (2002). Mothers' influence on the timing of first sex among 14- and 15-year-olds. *Journal of Adolescent Health, 31*, 256–265.

Mead, M. (1928). *Coming of age in Samoa*. New York, NY: Morrow.

Medina, A. M., Lederhos, C. L., & Lillis, T. A. (2009). Sleep disruption and decline in marital satisfaction across the transition to parenthood. *Families, Systems, & Health, 27*, 153–160.

Medina, J. (2010). *Brain rules for baby: How to raise a smart and happy child from zero to five.* Seattle, WA: Pear Press.

Meijer, A. M., & van den Wittenboer, G. L. H. (2007). Contribution of infants' sleep and crying to marital relationship of first-time parent couples in the 1st year after childbirth. *Journal of Family Psychology, 21*, 49–57.

Melton, G. B. (2008). Beyond balancing: Toward an integrated approach to children's rights. *Journal of Social Issues, 64*, 903–920.

Mennen, F. E., Kim, K., Sang, J., & Trickett, P. K. (2010). Child neglect: Definition and identification of youth's experiences in official reports of maltreatment. *Child Abuse and Neglect, 34*, 647–658.

Mensah, F. K., Bayer, J. K., Wake, M., Carlin, J. B., Allen, N. B., & Patton, G. C. (2013). Early puberty and childhood social and behavioral adjustment. *Journal of Adolescent Health, 53*, 118–124.

Mewse, A. J., Eiser, J. R., Slater, A. M., & Lea, S. E. G. (2004). The smoking behaviors of adolescents and their friends: Do parents matter? *Parenting: Science and Practice, 4*, 51–72.

Meyers, S. A., & Battistoni, J. (2003). Proximal and distal correlates of adolescent mothers' parenting attitudes. *Applied Developmental Psychology, 24*, 33–49.

Miall, C. (2013). 10,000 hours to perfection. *Nature Neuroscience, 16*, 1168–1169.

Mikelson, K. S. (2008). He said, she said: Comparing mother and father reports of father involvement. *Journal of Marriage and Family, 70*, 613–624.

Mikulincer, M., & Shaver, P. R. (2008). Adult attachment and affect regulation. In J. Cassidy & P. R. Shaver (Eds.), *The handbook of attachment* (2nd ed., pp. 503–531). New York, NY: Guilford.

Milan, S., Snow, S., & Belay, S. (2007). The context of preschool children's sleep: Racial/ethnic differences in sleep locations, routines, and concerns. *Journal of Family Psychology, 21*, 20–28.

Milburn, N. G., & Lightfoot, M. (2013). Adolescents in wartime US military families: A developmental perspective on challenges and resources. *Clinical Child and Family Psychology Review, 16*, 266–277.

Milkie, M. A., Mattingly, M. J., Nomaguchi, K. M., Bianchi, S. M., & Robinson, J. P. (2004). The time squeeze: Parental statuses and feelings about time with children. *Journal of Marriage and Family, 66*, 739–761.

Milkie, M. A., Simon, R. W., & Powell, B. (1997). Through the eyes of children: Youths' perceptions and evaluations of maternal and paternal roles. *Social Psychology Quarterly, 60*, 218–237.

Mill, J. S. (1859/1956). *On liberty*. New York, NY: Liberal Arts.

Miller, A. (1984). *For your own good: Hidden cruelty in child-rearing and the roots of violence* (H. Hannum & H. Hannum, Trans.). New York, NY: Farrar Straus Giroux.

Miller, A. L., McDonough, S. C., Rosenblum, K. L., & Sameroff, A. J. (2002). Emotion regulation in context: Situational effects on infant and caregiver behavior. *Infancy, 3*, 403–433.

Miller, B. C., Benson, B., & Galbraith, K. A. (2001). Family relationships and adolescent pregnancy risk: A research synthesis. *Developmental Review, 21*, 1–38.

Miller, C., Riccio, J., & Smith, J. (2009). *A preliminary look at early educational results of the Opportunity NYC-Family Rewards Program*. MDRC. Retrieved June 12, 2014, from http://www.mdrc.org/publication/preliminary-look-early-educational-results-opportunity-nyc-%E2%80%93-family-rewards-program

Miller, P. (2011). *Theories of developmental psychology* (5th ed.). New York, NY: Worth Publishers.

Miller, P. C., Shim, J. E., & Holden, G. W. (1998). Immediate contextual influences on maternal behavior: Environmental affordances and demands. *Journal of Environmental Psychology, 18*, 387–398.

Miller, S. A. (1995). Parents' attributions for their children's behavior. *Child Development, 63*, 1557–1584.

Miller-Day, M. A. (2002). Parent-adolescent communication about alcohol, tobacco, and other drug use. *Journal of Adolescent Research, 17*, 604–616.

Miller-Day, M. A. (2008). Talking to youth about drugs: What do late adolescents say about parental strategies? *Family Relations, 57*, 1–12.

Mills, R. S. L. (2005). Taking stock of the developmental literature on shame. *Developmental Review, 25*, 26–63.

Mills, R. S. L., Arbeau, K. A., Lall, D. I. K., & De Jaeger, A. E. (2010). Parenting and child characteristics in the prediction of shame in early and middle childhood. *Merrill-Palmer Quarterly, 56*, 500–528.

Milner, J. S., & Dopke, C. (1997). Child physical abuse: Review of offender characteristics. In D. A. Wolfe, R. J. McMahon, & R. D. Peters (Eds.), *Child abuse: New directions in prevention and treatment across the life span* (pp. 25–52). Thousand Oaks, CA: SAGE.

Minnett, A. M., Vandell, D. L., & Santrock, J. W. (1983). The effects of sibling status on sibling interaction—Influence of birth-order, age spacing, sex of child, and sex of sibling. *Child Development, 54*, 1064–1072.

Mintz, S. (2004). *Huck's raft: A history of American childhood*. Cambridge, MA: Harvard University Press.

Mintz, S., & Kellogg, S. (1988). *Domestic revolutions: A social history of American family life*. New York, NY: Free Press.

Minuchin, P. (1985). Families and development: Provocations from the field of family therapy. *Child Development, 56*, 289–302.

Mistry, J., Contreras, M., & Dutta, R. (2013). Culture and child development. In R. M. Lerner, M. A. Easterbrooks, & J. Mistry (Eds.), *Developmental psychology* (2nd ed., vol. 6, pp. 265–285). New York, NY: John Wiley & Sons.

Mitchell, K. J., Finkelhor, D., & Wolak, J. (2003). The exposure of youth to unwanted sexual material on the Internet: A national survey of risk, impact, and prevention. *Youth & Society, 34*, 330–358.

Moffitt, T. E. (1993). Adolescence-limited and life-course-persistent antisocial behavior: A developmental taxonomy. *Psychological Review, 100*, 674–701.

Moffitt, T. E. (2013). Childhood exposure to violence and lifelong health: Clinical intervention science and stress-biology research join forces. *Development and Psychopathology, 25*(25th Anniversary Special Issue 4, Pt. 2), 1619–1634.

Moffitt, T. E., Arseneault, L., Belsky, D., Dickson, N., Hancox, R. J., Harrington, H., . . . Caspi, A. (2011). A gradient of childhood self-control predicts health, wealth, and public safety. *Proceedings of the National Academy of Sciences, 108*, 2693–2698.

Moffitt, T. E., Caspi, A., Rutter, M., & Silva, P. A. (2001). *Sex differences in antisocial behavior*. New York, NY: Cambridge University Press.

Momper, S. L., & Jackson, A. P. (2007). Maternal gambling, parenting, and child behavioral functioning in Native American families. *Social Work Research, 31*, 199–209.

Mond, J., van den Berg, P., Boutelle, K., Hannan, P., & Neumark-Sztainer, D. (2011). Obesity, body dissatisfaction, and emotional well-being in early and late adolescence: findings from the project EAT study. *Journal of Adolescent Health, 48*, 373–378.

Monn, A., Casey, E., Wenzel, A., Sapienza, J., Kimball, A., Mack, B., III, . . . Michaels, C. (2013). *Risk and resilience in homeless children: Children's mental health ereview*. Minneapolis: University of Minnesota Extension.

Monthly Labor Review. (2013). *Marriage and divorce: Patterns by gender, race, and educational attainment*. Washington, DC: United States Department of Labor; Bureau of Labor Statistics.

Moore, M. R., & Brooks-Gunn, J. (2002). Adolescent parenthood. In M. H. Bornstein (Ed.), *Handbook of parenting, vol. 3: Being and becoming a parent* (2nd ed., pp. 173–214). Mahwah, NJ: Lawrence Erlbaum Associates.

Morawski, J. G., & St. Martin, J. (2011). The evolving vocabulary of the social sciences: The case of "socialization." *History of Psychology, 14*, 1–25.

Morgan, M., & Spock, B. M. (1989). *Spock on Spock: A memoir of growing up with the century*. New York, NY: Alfred A. Knopf.

Morin, R. (2013). *Study: More men on the "daddy track." Facttank: News in the numbers*. Washington, DC: Pew Research Center.

Morris, A. S., Cui, L., & Steinberg, L. (2013). Parenting research and themes: What we have learned and where to go next. In R. E. Larzelere, A. S. Morris, & A. W. Harrist (Eds.), *Authoritative parenting:*

Synthesizing nurturance and discipline for optimal child development (pp. 35–58). Washington, DC: American Psychological Association.

Morris, A. S., Silk, J. S., Steinberg, L., Myers, S. S., & Robinson, L. R. (2007). The role of the family context in the development of emotion regulation. *Social Development, 16*, 361–388.

Morris, T. (2013). *Cut it out: The C-section epidemic in America*. New York, NY: New York University Press.

Morrongiello, B. A., Klemencic, N., & Corbett, M. (2008). Interactions between child behavior patterns and parent supervision: Implications for children's risk of unintentional injury. *Child Development, 79*, 627–638.

Moster, D., Lie, R. T., & Markestad, T. (2008). Long-term medical and social consequences of preterm birth. *New England Journal of Medicine, 359*, 262–273.

Mrug, S., Elliott, M. N., Davies, S., Tortolero, S. R., Cuccaro, P., & Schuster, M. A. (2014). Early puberty, negative peer influence, and problem behaviors in adolescent girls. *Pediatrics, 133*, 7–14.

Mueller, C. M., & Dweck, C. S. (1998). Praise for intelligence can undermine children's motivation and performance. *Journal of Personality and Social Psychology, 75*, 33–52.

Murray, A. D. (1979). Infant crying as an elicitor of parental behavior: An examination of two models. *Psychological Bulletin, 86*, 191–215.

Murray, D. W. (2010). Treatment of preschoolers with attention-deficit/hyperactivity disorder. *Current Psychiatry Reports, 12*, 374–381.

Nathanson, A. (2001). Mediation of children's television viewing: Working toward concept clarity and common understanding. In W. Gudykunst (Ed.), *Communication yearbook* (pp. 115–151). Mahwah, NJ: Lawrence Erlbaum Associates.

National Center for Education Statistics. (2014). *Fast facts*. Retrieved May 21, 2014, from http://nces.ed.gov/fastfacts/display.asp?id=91

Neal, A. G., Groat, H. T., & Wicks, J. W. (1989). Attitudes about having children: A study of 600 couples in the early years of marriage. *Journal of Marriage and Family, 51*, 313–327.

Nelsen, J. (2006). *Positive discipline*. New York, NY: Ballantine Books.

Nelson, C. A. (2007). A neurobiological perspective on early human deprivation. *Child Development Perspectives, 1*, 13–18.

Nelson, L. J., Padilla-Walker, L. M., Carroll, J. S., Madsen, S. D., Barry, C. M., & Badger, S. (2007). "If you want me to treat you like an adult, start acting like one!" Comparing the criteria that emerging adults and their parents have for adulthood. *Journal of Family Psychology, 21*, 665–674.

Nelson, L., Padilla-Walker, L., Christensen, K., Evans, C., & Carroll, J. (2011). Parenting in emerging adulthood: An examination of parenting clusters and correlates. *Journal of Youth and Adolescence, 40*, 730–743.

Nelson, S. K., Kushlev, K., English, T., Dunn, E. W., & Lyubomirsky, S. (2013). In defense of parenthood: Children are associated with more joy than misery. *Psychological Science, 24*, 3–10.

Nepomnyaschy, L. (2007). Child support and father-child contact: Testing reciprocal pathways. *Demography, 44*, 93–112.

Newton, M. (2002). *Savage girls and wild boys: A history of feral children*. London, England: Faber and Faber.

Ng, F. F-Y., Pomerantz, E. M., & Deng, C. (2014). Why are Chinese mothers more controlling than American mothers? "My child is my report card." *Child Development, 85*, 355–369.

Nichols, M. P., & Schwartz, R. C. (2007). *Family therapy: Concepts and methods* (8th ed.). New York, NY: Allyn and Bacon

Nielsen, J. (2008, August 12). Dad wins custody of abused girl; state to care for her half-sisters. *Dallas Morning News*. Retrieved November 5, 2008, from http://www.dallasnews.com/index.html

Niemark, E. (1975). Intellectual development during adolescence. In F. D. Horowitz (Ed.), *Review of child development research* (vol. 4, pp. 541–594). Chicago, IL: University of Chicago Press.

Nievar, M. A., & Luster, T. (2006). Developmental processes in African American families: An application of McLoyd's theoretical model. *Journal of Marriage and Family, 68*, 320–331.

Nizza, M. (2007). Germany plays with procreation's price point. *The Lede: The New York Times News Blog*. New York, NY: New York Times.

Nsamenang, A. B., & Lamb, M. E. (1995). The force of beliefs: How the parental values of the Nso of northwest Cameroon shape children's progress toward adult models. *Journal of Applied Developmental Psychology, 16*, 613–627.

O'Connor, T., & Zeanah, C. (2003). Current perspectives on attachment disorders: Rejoinder and synthesis. *Attachment & Human Development, 5,* 321–326.

Offer, S. (2013). Assessing the relationship between family mealtime communication and adolescent emotional well-being using the experience sampling method. *Journal of Adolescence, 36,* 577–585.

Office of Applied Studies. (2009). *Adolescent behavioral health in brief*. U.S. Department of Health and Human Services: Substance Abuse and Mental Health Services Administration. Retrieved May 27, 2014, from http://www.samhsa.gov/data/StatesInBrief/2k9/OASTeenReportUS.pdf

Offit, P. (2008). *Autism's false prophets: Bad science, risky medicine, and the search for a cure*. New York, NY: Columbia University Press.

Ogbu, J. U. (1988). Cultural diversity and human development. In D. T. Slaughter (Ed.), *Black children and poverty: A developmental perspective. New Directions for Child Development* (vol. 42, pp. 11–28).

Ogden, C. L., Carroll, M. D., Kit, B. K., & Flegal, K. M. (2014). Prevalence of childhood and adult obesity in the United States, 2011–2012. *JAMA, 311,* 806–814.

Ojha, H., & Pramanick, M. (1992). Religio-cultural variation in childbearing practices. *Psychological Studies, 37,* 65–72.

Olds, D. L. (2006). The nurse-family partnership: An evidence-based preventive intervention. *Infant Mental Health Journal, 27,* 5–25.

O'Leary, S. G. (1995). Parental discipline mistakes. *Current Directions in Psychological Science, 4,* 11–13.

O'Leary, S. G., & Vidair, H. B. (2005). Marital adjustment, child-rearing disagreements, and overreactive parenting: Predicting child behavior problems. *Journal of Family Psychology, 19,* 208–216.

Olney, J. W. (2000). New insights and new issues in developmental neurotoxicology. *NeuroToxicology, 23,* 659–668.

Olvera-Ezzell, N., Power, T. G., & Cousins, J. H. (1990). Maternal socialization of children's eating habits: Strategies used by obese Mexican-American mothers. *Child Development, 61,* 395–400.

Olweus, D., & Breivik, K. (2014). Plight of victims of school bullying: The opposite of well-being. In A. Ben-Arieh, F. Casas, I. Frones, & J. E. Korbin (Eds.), *Handbook of child well-being* (pp. 2593–2616). New York, NY: Springer.

O'Malley, P. M., & Johnston, L. D. (2013). Driving after drug or alcohol use by us high school seniors, 2001–2011. *American Journal of Public Health, 103,* 2027–2034.

Ommundsen, Y., Løndal, K., & Loland, S. (2014). Sports, children, and well-being. In A. Ben-Arieh, F. Casas, I. Frones, & J. E. Korbin (Eds.), *Handbook of child well-being* (pp. 911–940). New York, NY: Springer.

Ordoñez, J. (2007, May 14). Baby needs a new pair of shoes. *Newsweek*, 50–54.

Oshima-Takane, Y., Goodz, E., & Derevensky, J. L. (1996). Birth order effects on early language development: Do secondborn children learn from overheard speech? *Child Development, 67,* 621–634.

Österman, K., Björkqvist, K., & Wahlbeck, K. (2014). Twenty-eight years after the complete ban on the physical punishment of children in Finland: Trends and psychosocial concomitants. *Aggressive Behavior, 40,* 1–14.

Ottoni-Wilhelm, M., Estell, D. B., & Perdue, N. H. (2014). Role-modeling and conversations about giving in the socialization of adolescent charitable giving and volunteering. *Journal of Adolescence, 37,* 53–66.

Oyserman, D., Bybee, D., & Mowbray, C. (2002). Influences of maternal mental illness on psychological outcomes for adolescent children. *Journal of Adolescence, 25,* 587–602.

Padilla-Walker, L. M., & Nelson, L. J. (2012). Black hawk down? Establishing helicopter parenting as a distinct construct from other forms of parental control during emerging adulthood. *Journal of Adolescence, 35,* 1177–1190.

Pagani, L. S., Fitzpatrick, C., & Barnett, T. A. (2013). Early childhood television viewing and kindergarten entry readiness. *Pediatric Research, 74,* 350–355.

Pagliocca, P. M., Melton, G. B., Lyons, J., P. M., & Weisz, V. (2002). Parenting and the law. In M. H. Bornstein (Ed.), *Handbook of parenting, vol. 5: Practical issues in parenting* (pp. 463–486). Mahwah, NJ: Lawrence Erlbaum Associates.

Paikoff, R. L., & Brooks-Gunn, J. (1991). Do parent-child relationships change during puberty? *Psychological Bulletin, 110,* 47–66.

Paley, B., Lester, P., & Mogil, C. (2013). Family systems and ecological perspectives on the impact of deployment on military families. *Clinical Child and Family Psychology Review, 16*, 245–265.

Palkovitz, R., & Palm, G. (1998). Fatherhood and faith in formation: The developmental effects of fathering on religiosity, morals, and values. *Journal of Men's Studies, 7*, 33–51.

Pandya, N. H., Mevada, A., Patel, V., & Suthar, M. (2013). Study of effect of advanced maternal age related risks for Down syndrome & other trisomies. *International Journal of Biomedical and Advance Research, 4*, 123–127.

Paquette, D. (2004). Theorizing the father-child relationship: Mechanisms and developmental outcomes. *Human Development, 47*, 193–219.

Parham, A. K. (2005). Perchance to soar: Raising a child with Down syndrome. *Parent: Wise Austin, 2*, 8–13.

Park, N. (2011). Military children and families: Strengths and challenges during peace and war. *American Psychologist, 66*, 65–72.

Parke, R. D. (2013). *Future families: Diverse forms, rich possibilities*. Malden, MA: John Wiley.

Parker, G. (1983). *Parental overprotection: A risk factor in psychosocial development*. New York, NY: Grune & Stratton.

Parker, K., & Wang, W. (2013). *Modern parenthood: Roles of moms and dads converge as they balance work and family*. Washington, DC: Pew Research Center.

Pastor, P. N., Reuben, C. A., & Duran, C. R. (2012). *Identifying emotional and behavioral problems in children aged 4–17 years: United States, 2001–2007 National Health Statistics Reports*. Washington, DC: National Center for Health Statistics.

Patrick, H., & Nicklas, T. A. (2005). A review of family and social determinants of children's eating patterns and diet quality. *Journal of American College of Nutrition, 24*, 83–92.

Patterson, C. J. (2002). Lesbian and gay parenthood. In M. H. Bornstein (Ed.), *Handbook of parenting, vol. 3: Being and becoming a parent* (2nd ed., pp. 317–338). Mahwah, NJ: Lawrence Erlbaum Associates.

Patterson, C. J. (2004). Gay fathers. In M. E. Lamb (Ed.), *The role of the father in child development* (pp. 397–416). New York, NY: John Wiley & Sons.

Patterson, G. R. (1982). *Coercive family process*. Eugene, OR: Castalia.

Patton, G. C., & Viner, R. (2007). Pubertal transitions in health. *The Lancet, 369*, 1130–1139.

Payne, K. K. (2013). Children's family structure, 2013. *NCFMR Family Profiles* (vol. FP-13-19). Bowling Green, OH: Bowling Green State University. Retrieved May 30, 2014, from http://www.bgsu.edu/content/dam/BGSU/college-of-arts-and-sciences/NCFMR/documents/FP/FP-13-19.pdf

Pearce, L. D., & Haynie, D. L. (2004). Intergenerational religious dynamics and adolescent delinquency. *Social Forces, 82*, 1553–1572.

Pellegrini, A. D., & Smith, P. K. (1998). Physical activity play: The nature and function of a neglected aspect of play. *Child Development, 69*, 577–598.

Peper, J. S., & Dahl, R. E. (2013). The teenage brain: Surging hormones—Brain-behavior interactions during puberty. *Current Directions in Psychological Science, 22*, 134–139.

Perozynski, L., & Kramer, L. (1999). Parental beliefs about managing sibling conflict. *Developmental Psychology, 35*, 489–499.

Perrin, E. C., & Committee on Psychosocial Aspects of Child and Family Health. (2002). Technical report: Coparent or second-parent adoption by same-sex parent. *Pediatrics, 109*, 341–344.

Perry, B. D. (1997). Incubated in terror: Neurodevelopmental factors in the "cycle of violence." In J. Osofsky (Ed.), *Children, youth, and violence: The search for solutions* (pp. 124–148). New York, NY: Guilford Press.

Perry, B. D., & Szalavitz, M. (2007). *The boy who was raised as a dog*. New York, NY: Basic Books.

Peschel, E. R., & Peschel, R. E. (1987). Medical insights into the castrati in opera. *American Scientist, 75*, 578–583.

Pettit, G. S., & Arsiwalla, D. D. (2008). Commentary on special section on "Bidirectional parent-child relationships": The continuing evolution of dynamic, transactional models of parenting and youth behavior problems. *Journal of Abnormal Child Psychology, 36*, 711–718.

Pettit, G. S., & Bates, J. E. (1989). Family interaction patterns and children's behavior problems from infancy to four years. *Developmental Psychology, 25*, 413–420.

Pettit, G. S., Bates, J. E., & Dodge, K. A. (1997). Supportive parenting, ecological context, and children's adjustment: A seven-year longitudinal study. *Child Development, 68*, 908–923.

Pew Hispanic Center. (2013). *A nation of immigrants: A portrait of the 40 million, including 11 million unauthorized*. Washington, DC: Pew Research Center.

Pew Research Center. (2012). *The global religious landscape: A report on the size and distribution of the world's major religious groups as of 2010*. Washington, DC: Pew Research Center.

Pew Research Center. (2014). *The rising cost of not going to college*. Retrieved February 12, 2014, from http://www.pewsocialtrends.org/2014/02/11/the-rising-cost-of-not-going-to-college/

Pianta, R. C., Sroufe, L. A., & Egeland, B. (1989). Continuity and discontinuity in maternal sensitivity at 6, 24, and 42 months in a high-risk sample. *Child Development, 60*, 481–487.

Pidd, H. (2011). Generous payments to parents aim to make Germany more family friendly. *The Guardian*. Retrieved June 12, 2014, from http://www.theguardian.com/world/2011/mar/16/germany-payments-to-parents

Pike, A. (2004). Behavioral genetics, shared and nonshared environment. In P. K. Smith & C. H. Hart (Eds.), *Blackwell handbook of childhood social development* (pp. 27–43). Malden, MA: Blackwell.

Pinderhughes, E. E., Dodge, K., Bates, J. E., Pettit, G. S., & Zelli, A. (2000). Discipline responses: Influences of parents' socioeconomic status, ethnicity, beliefs about parenting, stress, and cognitive-emotional processes. *Journal of Family Psychology, 14*, 380–400.

Pinker, S. (1998). Foreword. In J. R. Harris, *The nurture assumption: Why children turn out the way they do* (pp. xxiii–xxvi). New York, NY: Free Press.

Pinneau, S. R. (1955). The infantile disorders of hospitalism and anaclitic depression. *Psychological Bulletin, 52*, 429–452.

Pinquart, M., Stotzka, C., & Silbereisen, R. K. (2008). Personality and ambivalence in decisions about becoming parents. *Social Behavior and Personality, 36*, 87–96.

Pleck, J. H., & Masciadrelli, B. P. (2004). Paternal involvement by U.S. residential fathers. In M. E. Lamb (Ed.), *The role of the father in child development* (4th ed., pp. 222–271). Hoboken, NJ: John Wiley & Sons.

Plomin, R. (1990). *Nature and nurture: An introduction to human behavioral genetics*. Pacific Grove, CA: Brooks/Cole.

Plomin, R., & Daniels, D. (1987). Why are children in the same family so different from each other? *Behavioral and Brain Sciences, 10*, 1–60.

Plomin, R., DeFries, J. C., McClearn, G. E., & McGuffin, P. (2001). *Behavioral genetics* (5th ed.). San Francisco, CA: W. H. Freeman.

Pluess, M., & Belsky, J. (2013). Vantage sensitivity: Individual differences in response to positive experiences. *Psychological Bulletin, 139*, 901–916.

Poehlmann, J., & Eddy, J. M. (2013). Relationship processes and resilience in children with incarcerated parents. *Monographs of the Society for Research in Child Development, 78*(3), vii–viii.

Pollard, L. A. (1983). *Forgotten children: Parent-child relations from 1500 to 1900*. New York, NY: Cambridge University Press.

Pollard-Sacks, D. (2009). State actors beating children: A call for judicial relief. *UC Davis Law Review*. Retrieved June 12, 2014, from http://lawreview.law.ucdavis.edu/issues/42/4/articles/42-4_Sacks.pdf

Pomeroy, S. B. (1998). *Families in classical and Hellenistic Greece: Representations and realities*. New York, NY: Oxford University Press.

Popenoe, D. (2005). *War over the family*. New Brunswick, NJ: Transaction Publishers.

Popenoe, R. (2004). *Feeding desire: Fatness, beauty, and sexuality among Saharan people*. New York, NY: Routledge.

Population Reference Bureau. (2014). *PRB and Casey Foundation create index of child well-being*. Retrieved June 2, 2014, from http://www.prb.org/Publications/Articles/2014/casey-index-child-wellbeing.aspx

Potegal, M., & Davidson, R. J. (2003). Temper tantrums in young children: 1. Behavioral composition. *Journal of Developmental & Behavioral Pediatrics, 24*, 140–147.

Powell, D. R. (2005). Searches for what works in parenting interventions. In T. Luster & L. Okagaki (Eds.), *Parenting: An ecological perspective* (pp. 343–376). Mahwah, NJ: Lawrence Erlbaum Associates.

Power, T. G. (2004). Stress and coping in childhood: The parents' role. *Parenting: Science and Practice, 4*, 271–317.

Power, T. G., & Shanks, J. A. (1989). Parents as socializers: Maternal and paternal views. *Journal of Youth and Adolescence, 18*, 203–220.

Protzko, J., Aronson, J., & Blair, C. (2013). How to make a young child smarter: Evidence from the database of raising intelligence. *Perspectives on Psychological Science, 8*, 25–40.

Psychogiou, L., Daley, D., Thompson, M. J., & Sonuga-Barke, E. J. (2008). Parenting empathy: Associations with dimensions of parent and child psychopathology. *British Journal of Developmental Psychology, 26*, 221–232.

Puff, J., & Renk, K. (2014). Relationships among parents' economic stress, parenting, and young children's behavior problems. *Child Psychiatry & Human Development, 45*.

Pumroy, D. K., & Pumroy, S. S. (1978). *Modern child-rearing: A behavioral approach*. St. Louis, MO: Burnham Inc Pub.

Putnam, F. W. (2003). Ten-year research update review: Child sexual abuse. *Journal of the American Academy of Child and Adolescent Psychiatry, 42*, 269–278.

Putnam, S. P., Sanson, A. V., & Rothbart, M. K. (2002). Child temperament and parenting. In M. H. Bornstein (Ed.), *Handbook of parenting, vol. 1: Children and parenting* (2nd ed., pp. 255–278). Mahwah, NJ: Lawrence Erlbaum Associates.

Quintana, S. M., Aboud, F. E., Chao, R. K., Contreras-Grau, J., Cross, W. E., Hudley, C., . . . Vietze, D. L. (2006). Race, ethnicity, and culture in child development: Contemporary research and future directions. *Child Development, 77*, 1129–1141.

Radford, L., & Hester, M. (2001). Overcoming mother blaming? Future directions for research on mothering and domestic violence. In S. A. Graham-Bermann & J. L. Edleson (Eds.), *Domestic violence in the lives of children: The future of research* (pp. 135–155). Washington, DC: American Psychological Association.

Raley, S., & Bianchi, S. (2006). Sons, daughters, and family processes: Does gender of children matter? *Annual Review of Sociology, 32*, 401–421.

Rankin, J. L. (2005). *Parenting experts: Their advice, the research, and getting it right*. Westport, CT: Praeger.

Rao, P. A., & Beidel, D. C. (2009). The impact of children with high-functioning autism on parental stress, sibling adjustment, and family functioning. *Behavior Modification, 33*, 437–451.

Rauscher, F. H., Shaw, G. L., & Ky, K. N. (1993). Music and spatial task performance. *Nature, 365*, 611.

Regalado, M., Sareen, H., Inkelas, M., Wissow, L. S., & Halfon, N. (2004). Parents' discipline of young children: Results from the National Survey of Early Childhood Health. *Pediatrics, 113*, 1952–1958.

Regnerus, M. (2012a). How different are the adult children of parents who have same-sex relationships? Findings from the New Family Structures Study. *Social Science Research, 41*, 752–770.

Regnerus, M. (2012b). Parental same-sex relationships, family instability, and subsequent life outcomes for adult children: Answering critics of the new family structures study with additional analyses. *Social Science Research, 41*, 1367–1377.

Reid, M. J., Webster-Stratton, C., & Baydar, N. (2004). Halting the development of conduct problems in Head Start children: The effects of parent training. *Journal of Clinical Child and Adolescent Psychology, 33*, 279–291.

Reijntjes, A., Kamphuis, J. H., Prinzie, P., & Telch, M. J. (2010). Peer victimization and internalizing problems in children: A meta-analysis of longitudinal studies. *Child Abuse and Neglect, 34*, 244–252.

Reinelt, E., Stopsack, M., Aldinger, M., John, U., Grabe, H. J., & Barnow, S. (2013). Testing the diathesis-stress model: 5-HTTLPR, childhood emotional maltreatment, and vulnerability to social anxiety disorder. *American Journal of Medical Genetics Part B: Neuropsychiatric Genetics, 162*, 253–261.

Renk, K., Roberts, R., Roddenberry, A., Luick, M., Hillhouse, S., Meehan, C., . . . Phares, V. (2003). Mothers, fathers, gender role, and time parents spent with their children. *Sex Roles, 48*, 305–315.

Rentz, E. D., Martin, S. L., Gibbs, D. A., Clinton-Sherrod, M., Hardison, J., & Marshall, S. W. (2006). Family violence in the military a review of the literature. *Trauma, Violence, & Abuse, 7*, 93–108.

Resnick, M. D., Bearman, P. S., Blum, R. W., Bauman, K. E., Harris, K. M., Jones, J., . . . Udry, J. R. (1997). Protecting adolescents from harm: Findings from the national longitudinal study on adolescent health. *Journal of the American Medical Association, 278*, 823–865.

Resolve. (2014). *The costs of infertility treatment*. Retrieved January 21, 2014, from http://www.resolve.org/family-building-options/insurance_coverage/the-costs-of-infertility-treatment.html

Respers, L. (1996, February 24). Boy's stint in dress has dad fuming. *Austin American Statesman*, p. 1.

Reves, R. R., Morrow, A. L., Bartlett, A. V., Caruso, C. J., Plumb, R. L., Lu, B. T., & Pickering, L. K. (1993). Child day care increases the risk of clinic visits for acute diarrhea and diarrhea due to rotavirus. *American Journal of Epidemiology, 137*, 97–107.

Reynolds, A. J., Temple, J. A., Robertson, D. L., & Mann, E. A. (2002). Age 21 cost-benefit analysis of the Title 1 Chicago Child-Parent centers. *Educational Evaluation and Policy Analysis, 24*, 267–303.

Rheingold, H. L. (1973). To rear a child. *American Psychologist, 28*, 42–46.

Rhoades, K. A. (2008). Children's responses to interparental conflict: A meta-analysis of their associations with child adjustment. *Child Development, 79*, 1942–1956.

Rhodes, J. E., & DuBois, D. L. (2006). Understanding and facilitating the youth mentoring movement. *Social Policy Report, 20*, 3–19.

Rhodes, K. W., Orme, J. G., & Buehler, B. (2001). A comparison of family foster parents who quit, consider quitting, and plan to continue fostering. *Social Service Review, 75*, 84–114.

Richman, S. B., & Mandara, J. (2013). Do socialization goals explain differences in parental control between Black and White parents? *Family Relations, 62*, 625–636.

Rideout, V. J., Foehr, U. G., & Roberts, D. F. (2010). *Generation M2: Media in the lives of 8- to 18-year-olds: Kaiser Family Foundation*. Retrieved May 27, 2014, from http://kff.org/other/event/generation-m2-media-in-the-lives-of/

Rideout, V. J., Roberts, D. F., & Foehr, U. G. (2005). *Generation M: Media in the lives of 8–18 year-olds*. Washington, DC: Kaiser Family Foundation.

Riggs, S. A., & Riggs, D. S. (2011). Risk and resilience in military families experiencing deployment: The role of the family attachment network. *Journal of Family Psychology, 25*, 675–687.

Rilling, J. K. (2013). The neural and hormonal bases of human parental care. *Neuropsychologia, 51*, 731–747.

Rind, B., Tromovitch, P., & Bauserman, R. (1998). A meta-analytic examination of assumed properties of child sexual abuse using college samples. *Psychological Bulletin, 124*, 22–53.

Ritchie, K. L. (1999). Maternal behaviors and cognitions during discipline episodes: A comparison of power bouts and single acts of noncompliance. *Developmental Psychology, 35*, 580–589.

Robbins, J. M., Khan, K. S., Lisi, L. M., Robbins, S. W., Michel, S. H., & Torcato, B. R. (2007). Overweight among young children in the Philadelphia health care centers. *Archives of Pediatric and Adolescent Medicine, 161*, 17–20.

Robbins, R., Robbins, S., & Stennerson, B. (2013). Native American family resilience. In D. S. Becvar (Ed.), *Handbook of family resilience* (pp. 197–213). New York, NY: Springer.

Robinson, B. E., & Carroll, J. J. (1999). Assessing the offspring of workaholic parents: The children of workaholics screening test. *Perceptual and Motor Skills, 88*, 1127–1134.

Robinson, B. E., Flowers, C., & Carroll, J. (2001). Work stress and marriage: A theoretical model examining the relationship between workaholism and marital cohesion. *International Journal of Stress Management, 8*, 165–175.

Rochlen, A. B., McKelley, R., Suizzo, M., & Scaringi, V. (2008). Predictors of relationship satisfaction, psychological well-being, and life satisfaction among stay-at-home fathers. *Psychology of Men and Masculinity, 9*, 17–28.

Rochlen, A. B., Suizzo, M-A., McKelley, R. A., & Scaringi, V. (2008). "I'm just providing for my family": A qualitative study of stay-at-home fathers. *Psychology of Men & Masculinity, 9*, 193–206.

Rodger, S., Cummings, A., & Leschied, A. W. (2006). Who is caring for our most vulnerable children? The motivation to foster in child welfare. *Child Abuse and Neglect, 30*, 1129–1142.

Rodgers, J. L. (2001). What causes birth order–intelligence patterns? The admixture hypothesis, revived. *American Psychologist, 56*, 505–510.

Rodgers, J. L. (2014). Are birth order effects on intelligence really Flynn Effects? Reinterpreting Belmont and Marolla 40 years later. *Intelligence, 42*, 128–133.

Rodriguez, A., & Adamsons, K. (2012). Parenting expectations: Younger and older first-time parents. *Marriage & Family Review, 48*, 248–271.

Rodriguez, B. L., & Olswang, L. B. (2003). Mexican-American and Anglo-American mothers' beliefs and values about child rearing, education, and language impairment. *American Journal of Speech-Language Pathology, 12*, 452–462.

Rohner, R. P. (1986). *The warmth dimension: Foundations of parental acceptance-rejection theory.* Thousand Oaks, CA: SAGE.

Rollins, B. Y., Loken, E., Savage, J. S., & Birch, L. L. (2014). Measurement of food reinforcement in preschool children: Associations with food intake, BMI, and reward sensitivity. *Appetite, 72*, 21–27.

Roopnarine, J. L. (2004). African American and African Caribbean fathers: Level, quality, and meaning of involvement. In M. E. Lamb (Ed.), *The role of the father in child development* (4th ed., pp. 1–31). New York, NY: Wiley.

Rosemond, J. (2007). *Parenting by the took: Biblical wisdom for raising your child.* New York, NY: Howard Books.

Roth, J., & Brooks-Gunn, J. (2000). What do adolescents need for healthy development? Implications for youth policy. *Social Policy Report, 14*, 3–19.

Rothbart, M. K. (1971). Birth order and mother-child interaction in an achievement setting. *Journal of Personality and Social Psychology, 17*, 113–120.

Rothbart, M. K., & Bates, J. E. (2006). Temperament. In N. Eisenberg (Ed.), *Handbook of child psychology. Vol. 3: Social, emotional, and personality development* (6th ed., pp. 99–166). New York, NY: Wiley.

Rothbaum, F., Pott, M., Azuma, H., Miyake, K., & Weisz, J. (2000). The development of close relationships in Japan and the United States: Paths of symbiotic harmony and generative tension. *Child Development, 71*, 1121–1142.

Rothbaum, F., & Trommsdorff, G. (2007). Do roots and wings complement or oppose one another? The socialization of relatedness and autonomy in cultural context. In J. E. Grusec & P. D. Hastings (Eds.), *Handbook of socialization* (pp. 461–489). New York, NY: Guilford.

Rothbaum, R., & Weisz, J. R. (1994). Parental caregiving and child externalizing behavior in nonclinical samples: A meta-analysis. *Psychological Bulletin, 116*, 55–74.

Rousseau, J. J. (1762/1956). *Emile* (W. Boyd, Trans.). New York, NY: Columbia University.

Routh, C. H. F. (1879). *Infant feeding and its influence on life.* New York, NY: William Wood.

Rowe, D. C. (1994). *The limits of family influence: Genes, experience, and behavior.* New York, NY: Guilford Press.

Rubin, J. Z., Provenzano, F. J., & Luria, Z. (1974). The eye of the beholder: Parents' views on the sex of newborns. *American Journal of Orthopsychiatry, 44*, 512–519.

Rubin, K. H., Bukowski, W. M., & Parker, J. G. (1998). Peer interactions, relationships, and groups. In N. Eisenberg (Ed.), *Handbook of child psychology, vol. 3: Social, emotional, and personality development* (5th ed., pp. 619–700). New York, NY: Wiley.

Rubin, K. H., Nelson, L. J., Hastings, P., & Asendorpf, J. (1999). The transaction between parents' perceptions of their children's shyness and their parenting styles. *International Journal of Behavioral Development, 23*, 937–957.

Rudolph, K. D., Lansford, J. E., Agoston, A. M., Sugimura, N., Schwartz, D., Dodge, K. A., . . . Bates, J. E. (2014). Peer victimization and social alienation: Predicting deviant peer affiliation in middle school. *Child Development, 85*, 124–139.

Rudy, D., & Grusec, J. E. (2006). Authoritarian parenting in individualist and collectivist groups: Associations with maternal emotion and cognition and children's self-esteem. *Journal of Family Psychology, 20*, 68–78.

Ruhrah, J. (1925). *Pediatrics of the past.* New York, NY: Paul Hoeber.

Runyan, D. K., Shankar, V., Hassan, F., Hunter, W. M., Jain, D., Paula, C. S., . . . Bordin, I. A. (2010). International variations in harsh child discipline. *Pediatrics, 126*, e701–e711.

Russell, A., & Russell, G. (1989). Warmth in the mother-child and father-child relationships in middle childhood. *British Journal of Developmental Psychology, 7*, 219–235.

Russell, A., & Saebel, J. (1997). Mother-son, mother-daughter, father-son, and father-daughter: Are they distinct relationships? *Developmental Review, 17*, 111–147.

Russell, G. (1999). Primary caregiving fathers. In M. E. Lamb (Ed.), *Parenting and child development in "nontraditional" families* (pp. 57–82). Mahwah, NJ: Lawrence Erlbaum Associates.

Russell, G., & Radojevic, M. (1992). The changing role of fathers? Current understandings and future directions for research and practice. *Infant Mental Health Journal, 13*, 296–311.

Rutgers, A. H., Bakermans-Kranenburg, M. J., van IJzendoorn, M. H., & van Berckelaer-Onnes, I. A. (2004). Autism and attachment: A meta-analytic review. *Journal of Child Psychology and Psychiatry, 45*, 1123–1134.

Rutter, M., Colvert, E., Kreppner, J., Beckett, C., Castle, J., Groothues, C., . . . Sonuga-Barke, E. J. S. (2007). Early adolescent outcomes for institutionally-deprived and non-deprived adoptees. I: Disinhibited attachment. *Journal of Child Psychology and Psychiatry, 48*, 17–30.

Rutter, M., Moffitt, T. E., & Caspi, A. (2005). Gene-environment interplay and psychopathology: Multiple varieties but real effects. *Journal of Child Psychology and Psychiatry, 47*, 226–261.

Rutter, M., & Silberg, J. (2002). Gene-environment in relation to emotional and behavioral disturbance. *Annual Review of Psychology, 53*, 463–490.

Ryan, A. S., Wenjun, Z., & Acosta, A. (2002). Breastfeeding continues to increase into the new millennium. *Pediatrics, 110*, 1103–1109.

Ryan, R. M., & Deci, E. L. (2000). Self-determination theory and the facilitation of intrinsic motivation, social development, and well-being. *American Psychologist, 55*, 68–78.

Rymer, R. (1993). *Genie: A scientific tragedy* New York, NY: Harper Collins.

Sabiruddin. (1990). *A Muslim husband and wife*. New Delhi, India: Kitab Bhavan.

Sameroff, A. (Ed.). (2009). *The transactional model of development: How children and contexts shape each other.* Washington, DC: American Psychological Association.

Sameroff, A. J., & Chandler, M. J. (1975). Reproductive risk and the continuum of caretaking casualty. In F. D. Horowitz, M. Hetherington, S. Scarr-Salapatek, & G. Siegal (Eds.), *Review of child development research* (vol. 4, pp. 187–244). Chicago, IL: University of Chicago Press.

Sameroff, A. J., & Feil, L. A. (1985). Parental concepts of development. In I. E. Sigel (Ed.), *Parental belief systems: The psychological consequences for children* (pp. 83–105). Hillsdale, NJ: Lawrence Erlbaum Associates.

Sampson, R. J., & Laub, J. H. (1993). *Crime in the making: Pathways and turning points through life*. Cambridge, MA: Harvard University.

Sanders, M. R. (2013). The promotion of self-regulation through parenting interventions. *Clinical Child and Family Psychology Review, 16*, 1–17.

Sandin, B. (2014). History of children's well-being. In A. Ben-Arieh, F. Casas, I. Frones, & J. E. Korbin (Eds.), *Handbook of child well-being* (vol. 1, pp. 31–86). New York, NY: Springer.

Sandler, I. N., Schoenfelder, E. N., Wolchik, S. A., & MacKinnon, D. P. (2011). Long-term impact of prevention programs to promote effective parenting: Lasting effects but uncertain processes. *Annual Review of Psychology, 62*, 299–329.

Sandman, C. A., Davis, E. P., & Glynn, L. M. (2012). Prescient human fetuses thrive. *Psychological Science, 23*, 93–100.

Sanghavi, D. M. (2006). Wanting babies like themselves, some parents choose genetic defects. *New York Times*. Retrieved May 18, 2014, from http.//www.nytimes.com/2006/12/05/health/05essa.html?_r=0

Sarche, M. C., & Whitesell, N. R. (2012). Child development research in North American native communities—Looking back and moving forward: Introduction. *Child Development Perspectives, 6*, 42–48.

Saroglu, V., Delpierre, V., & Dernelle, R. (2004). Values and religiosity: A meta-analysis of studies using Schwartz's model. *Personality and Individual Differences, 37*, 721–734.

Savage, S. L., & Gauvain, M. (1998). Parental beliefs and children's everyday planning in European-American and Latino families. *Journal of Applied Psychology, 19*, 319–340.

Scal, P., Ireland, M., & Borowsky, I. W. (2003). Smoking among American adolescents: A risk and protective factor analysis. *Journal of Community Health, 28*, 79–97.

Scarr, S. (1992). Developmental theories for the 1990s: Development and individual differences. *Child Development, 63*, 1–19.

Scarr, S., & McCartney, K. (1983). How people make their own environments: A theory of genotype -> environment effects. *Child Development, 54*, 424–435.

Scarr, S., Phillips, D., & McCartney, K. (1989). Working mothers and their families. *American Psychologist, 44*, 1402–1409.

Scheidt, P. C., Harel, Y., Trumble, A. C., Jones, D. H., Overpeck, M. D., & Bijur, P. E. (1995). The epidemiology of nonfatal injuries among U.S. children and youth. *American Journal of Public Health, 85*, 932–938.

Scherrer, J. L. (2012). The United Nations Convention on the Rights of the Child as policy and strategy for social work action in child welfare in the United States. *Social Work, 57*, 11–22.

Schleider, J. L., Chorpita, B. F., & Weisz, J. R. (2014). Relation between parent psychiatric symptoms and youth problems: Moderation through family structure and youth gender. *Journal of Abnormal Child Psychology, 42*, 195–204.

Schoenmaker, C., Juffer, F., van IJzendoorn, M. H., & Bakermans-Kranenburg, M. J. (2014). Does family matter? The well-being of children growing up in institutions, foster care and adoption. In A. Ben-Arieh, F. Casas, I. Frones, & J. E. Korbin (Eds.), *Handbook of child well-being* (pp. 2097–2228). New York, NY: Springer.

Schoppe-Sullivan, S. J., Kotila, L. E., Jia, R., Lang, S. N., & Bower, D. J. (2013). Comparisons of levels and predictors of mothers' and fathers' engagement with their preschool-aged children. *Early Child Development and Care, 183*, 498–514.

Schoppe-Sullivan, S. J., & Mangelsdorf, S. C. (2013). Parent characteristics and early co-parenting behavior at the transition to parenthood. *Social Development, 22*, 363–383.

Schor, J. (2004). *Born to buy: The commercialized child and the new consumer culture*. New York, NY: Simon and Schuster.

Schreier, H. (2002). Munchausen by proxy defined. *Pediatrics, 110*, 985–988.

Schwartz, K., D'Arcy, H. J. S., Gillespie, B., Bobo, J., Longeway, M., & Foxman, B. (2002). Factors associated with weaning in the first 3 months postpartum. *Journal of Family Practice, 51*, 439–445.

Schwartz, L. L. (2003). A nightmare for King Solomon: The new reproductive technologies. *Journal of Family Psychology, 17*, 229–237.

Schwartz, S. J., Donnellan, M. B., Ravert, R. D., Luyckx, K., & Zamboanga, B. L. (2013). Identify development, personality, and well-being in adolescence and emerging adulthood: Theory, research, and recent advances. In R. M. Lerner, M. A. Easterbrooks, & J. Mistry (Eds.), *Developmental psychology* (2nd ed., vol. 6, pp. 339–364). New York, NY: John Wiley & Sons.

Schwarz, A., & Cohen, S. (2013, March 31). ADHD seen in 11% of U.S. children as diagnoses rise. *New York Times*, p. A1.

Sears, C. H. (1899). Home and school punishments. *Pedagogic Seminary, 6*, 159–187.

Sears, R. R. (1975). Your ancients revisited: A history of child development. In E. M. Hetherington (Ed.), *Review of child development research* (vol. 5, pp. 1–73). Chicago, IL: University of Chicago.

Sears, R. R., Maccoby, E. E., & Levin, H. (1957). *Patterns of child rearing*. Evanston, IL: Row, Peterson.

Sedlak, A. J., Mettenburg, J., Basena, M., Petta, I., McPherson, K., Greene, A., & Li, S. (2010). *Fourth National Incidence Study of Child Abuse and Neglect (NIS-4): Report to Congress, executive summary*. Washington, DC: U.S. Department of Health and Human Services, Administration for Children and Families.

Segal, N. L. (2000). *Entwined lives: Twins and what they tell us about human behavior*. New York, NY: Penguin Putnam.

Sege, I. (2007, July 24). Marry, marry? Quite contrary. The number of cohabiting couples with kids is on the rise. *Boston Globe*. Retrieved June 14, 2014, from http://www.boston.com/yourlife/family/articles/2007/07/24/marry_marry_quite_contrary_/?page=full

Segrin, C., Woszidlo, A., Givertz, M., & Montgomery, N. (2013). Parent and child traits associated with overparenting. *Journal of Social and Clinical Psychology, 32*, 569–595.

Selvaratnam, T. (2014). *The big lie: Motherhood, feminism, and the reality of the biological clock*. Amherst, NY: Prometheus Books.

Seng, A., & Prinz, R. (2008). Parents who abuse: What are they thinking? *Clinical Child and Family Psychology Review, 11*, 163–175.

Serbin, L. A., & Karp, J. (2004). The intergenerational transfer of psychosocial risk: Mediators of vulnerability and resilience. *Annual Review of Psychology, 55*, 333–363.

Serbinski, S., & Shlonsky, A. (2014). Is it that we are afraid to ask? A scoping review about sons and daughters of foster parents. *Children and Youth Services Review, 36*, 101–114.

Settles, B. H., Sheng, X., Zang, Y., & Zhao, J. (2013). The one-child policy and its impact on Chinese families. *International Handbook of Chinese Families* (pp. 627–646). New York, NY: Springer.

Seward, R. R., & Stanley-Stevens, L. (2014). Fathers, fathering, and fatherhood across cultures. In H. Selin (Ed.), *Parenting across cultures* (vol. 7, pp. 459–474). New York, NY: Springer.

Sewell, W. H., & Mussen, P. H. (1952). The effects of feeding, weaning, and scheduling procedures on childhood adjustment and the formation of oral symptoms. *Child Development, 23*, 185–191.

Shahar, S. (1990). *Children in the Middle Ages*. New York, NY: Routledge.

Shanahan, S. (2007). Lost and found: The sociological ambivalence toward childhood. *Annual Review of Sociology, 33*, 407–428.

Shapiro, A., & Lambert, J. D. (1999). Longitudinal effects of divorce on the quality of the father-child relationship and on fathers' psychological well-being. *Journal of Marriage and Family, 61*, 397–408.

Shealy, C. N. (1995). From Boys Town to Oliver Twist: Separating fact from fiction in welfare reform and out-of-home placement of children and youth. *American Psychologist, 50*, 565–580.

Shiffman, S., Stone, A. A., & Hufford, M. R. (2008). Ecological momentary assessment. *Annual Review of Clinical Psychology, 4*, 1–32.

Shin, H., Park, Y. J., Ryu, H., & Seomun, G. (2008). Maternal sensitivity: A concept analysis. *Journal of Advanced Nursing, 64*, 304–314.

Shonkoff, J. P., Garner, A. S., The Committee on Psychosocial Aspects of Child Family Health, . . . Wood, D. L. (2012). The lifelong effects of early childhood adversity and toxic stress. *Pediatrics, 129*, e232–e246.

Shonkoff, J. P., & Meisels, S. J. (2000). *Handbook of early childhood intervention*. New York, NY: Cambridge University.

Shonkoff, J. P., Richter, L., van der Gaag, J., & Bhutta, Z. A. (2012). An integrated scientific framework for child survival and early childhood development. *Pediatrics, 129*, e460–472.

Shope, J. T. (2007). Graduated driver licensing: Review of evaluation results since 2002. *Journal of Safety Research, 38*, 165–175.

Shumow, L., & Lomax, R. (2002). Parental efficacy: Predictor of parenting behavior and adolescent outcomes. *Parenting: Science and Practice, 2*, 127–150.

Shwalb, D. W., Nakazawa, J., Yamamoto, T., & Hyun, J-H. (2004). Fathering in Japanese, Chinese, and Korean cultures: A review of the research literature. In M. E. Lamb (Ed.), *The role of the father in child development* (pp. 146–181). New York, NY: Wiley.

Sierau, S., Jungmann, T., & Herzberg, P. Y. (2013). First-time parenthood under socially disadvantaged conditions: Linking caregivers' experiences of avoidance and relationship satisfaction with feelings of closeness to the infant. *Journal of Family Studies, 19*, 196–206.

Sikora, D., Moran, E., Orlich, F., Hall, T. A., Kovacs, E. A., Delahaye, J., . . . Kuhlthau, K. (2013). The relationship between family functioning and behavior problems in children with autism spectrum disorders. *Research in Autism Spectrum Disorders, 7*, 307–315.

Silk, J. S., Morris, A. S., Kanaya, T., & Steinberg, L. (2003). Psychological control and autonomy granting: Opposite ends of a continuum or distinct constructs? *Journal of Research on Adolescence, 13*, 113–128.

Simons, R. L., Lei, M. K., Beach, S. R. H., Brody, G. H., Philibert, R. A., & Gibbons, F. X. (2011). Social environment, genes, and aggression: Evidence supporting the differential susceptibility perspective. *American Sociological Review, 76*, 883–912.

Simons, R. L., Lorenz, F. O., Conger, R. D., & Wu, C-I. (1992). Support from spouse as mediator and moderator of the disruptive influence of economic strain on parenting. *Child Development, 63*, 1282–1301.

Singer, A., & Wilson, J. H. (2006). *From "there" to "here": Refugee resettlement in metropolitan America*. Washington, DC: The Brookings Institution. Retrieved June 6, 2014, from http://www.brookings.edu/~/media/research/files/reports/2006/9/demographics%20singer/20060925_singer.pdf

Singh, I. (2004). Doing their jobs: Mothering with Ritalin in a culture of mother-blame. *Social Science & Medicine, 59*, 1193–1205.

Singh, S., Sedgh, G., & Hussain, R. (2010). Unintended pregnancy: Worldwide levels, trends, and outcomes. *Studies in Family Planning, 41*, 241–250.

Skinner, B. F. (1938). *The behavior of organisms: An experimental analysis*. New York, NY: Appleton-Century.

Skinner, B. F. (1948). *Walden two*. New York, NY: MacMillan.

Skinner, D. G., Correa, V., Skinner, M., & Bailey, D. D. (2001). Role of religion in the lives of Latino families of young children with developmental delays. *American Journal on Mental Retardation, 106*, 297–313.

Slater, M. A., & Power, T. G. (1987). Multidimensional assessment of parenting in single-parent families. *Advances in Family Intervention, Assessment, and Theory, 4*, 197–228.

Slep, A. M. S., & O'Leary, S. G. (1998). The effects of maternal attributions on parenting: An experimental analysis. *Journal of Family Psychology, 12*, 234–243.

Smetana, J. G., Campione-Barr, N., & Daddis, C. (2004). Longitudinal development of family decision making: Defining healthy behavioral autonomy for middle-class African American adolescents. *Child Development, 75*, 1418–1434.

Smetana, J. G., Campione-Barr, N., & Metzger, A. (2006). Adolescent development in interpersonal and societal contexts. *Annual Review of Psychology, 57*, 255–284.

Smetana, J. G., Daddis, C., & Chuang, S. S. (2003). "Clean your room!" A longitudinal investigation of adolescent-parent conflict and conflict resolution in middle-class African American families. *Journal of Adolescent Research, 18*, 631–650.

Smetana, J. G., Metzger, A., Gettman, D. C., & Campione-Barr, N. (2006). Disclosure and secrecy in adolescent–parent relationships. *Child Development, 77*, 201–217.

Smock, P. J. (2000). Cohabitation in the United States: An appraisal of research themes, findings, and implications. *Annual Review of Sociology, 26*, 1–20.

Smyke, A. T., Koga, S. F., Johnson, D. E., Fox, N. A., Marshall, P. J., Nelson, C. A., & Zeanah, C. H. (2007). The caregiving context in institution-reared and family-reared infants and toddlers in Romania. *Journal of Child Psychology and Psychiatry, 48*, 210–218.

Solmeyer, A. R., & Feinberg, M. E. (2011). Mother and father adjustment during early parenthood: The roles of infant temperament and co-parenting relationship quality. *Infant Behavior and Development, 34*, 504–514.

Solomon, J., & George, C. (2008). The measurement of attachment security and related constructs in infancy and early childhood. In J. Cassidy & P. R. Shaver (Eds.), *Handbook of attachment* (2nd ed., pp. 383–416). New York, NY: Guilford.

Somerville, L. H. (2013). The teenage brain: Sensitivity to social evaluation. *Current Directions in Psychological Science, 22*, 121–127.

Somerville, L. H., Jones, R. M., Ruberry, E. J., Dyke, J. P., Glover, G., & Casey, B. J. (2013). The medial prefrontal cortex and the emergence of self-conscious emotion in adolescence. *Psychological Science, 24*, 1554–1562.

Sommerville, C. J. (1982). *The rise and fall of childhood*. Beverly Hills, CA: SAGE.

Sorbring, E. (2014). Parents' concerns about their teenage children's Internet use. *Journal of Family Issues, 35*, 75–96.

Sotomayor, S. (2013). *My beloved world*. New York, NY: Alfred A. Knopf.

Spitz, R. A. (1945). Hospitalism: An inquiry into the genesis of psychiatric conditions in early childhood. *Psychoanalytic Study of the Child, 1*, 53–74.

Spock, B. (1945). *The common sense book of baby and child care*. New York, NY: Duell, Sloan, & Pearce.

Spock, B. (1946). *The pocket book of baby and child care*. New York, NY: Pocket Books.

Spock, B., & Needlman, R. (2012). *Dr. Spock's baby and child care* (9th ed.). New York, NY: Pocket Books.

Squires, J. E., & Squires, R. H. (2013). A review of Munchausen syndrome by proxy. *Pediatric Annals, 42*, 67–71.

Stacer, M. J., & Perrucci, R. (2013). Parental involvement with children at school, home, and community. *Journal of Family and Economic Issues, 34*, 340–354.

Stacey, J., & Biblarz, T. J. (2001). (How) does the sexual orientation of parents matter? *American Sociological Review, 66*, 159–183.

Stallard, P., & Salter, E. (2003). Psychological debriefing with children and young people following traumatic events. *Clinical Child Psychology and Psychiatry, 8*, 445–457.

Stang, J., & Loth, K. A. (2011). Parenting style and child feeding practices: Potential mitigating factors in the etiology of childhood obesity. *Journal of the American Dietetic Association, 111*, 1301–1305.

Stanton, J., & Simpson, A. (2002). Filicide: A review. *International Journal of Law and Psychiatry, 25*, 1–14.

Stattin, H., & Kerr, M. (2000). Parental monitoring: A reinterpretation. *Child Development, 71*, 1072–1085.

Stattin, H., & Klackenberg-Larsson, I. (1991). The short- and long-term implications for parent-child relations of parents' prenatal preferences for their child's gender. *Developmental Psychology, 27*, 141–147.

Steelman, L. C., Powell, B., Werum, R., & Carter, S. (2002). Reconsidering the effects of sibling configuration: Recent advances and challenges. *Annual Review of Sociology, 28*, 243–269.

Steinberg, L. (2001). We know some things: Parent-adolescent relationships in retrospect and prospect. *Journal of Research on Adolescence, 11*, 1–19.

Steinberg, L., Blatt-Eisengart, I., & Cauffman, E. (2006). Patterns of competence and adjustment among adolescents from authoritative, authoritarian, indulgent, and neglectful homes: A replication in a sample of serious juvenile offenders. *Journal of Research on Adolescence, 16*, 47–58.

Steinberg, L., Elmer, J. D., & Mounts, N. S. (1989). Authoritative parenting, psychosocial maturity, and academic success among adolescents. *Child Development, 60*, 1424–1436.

Steinberg, L., & Morris, A. S. (2001). Adolescent development. *Annual Review of Psychology, 52*, 83–110.

Steinberg, L., Mounts, N., Lamborn, S., & Dornbusch, S. (1994). Over-time changes in adjustment and competence among adolescents from authoritative, authoritarian, indulgent, and neglectful families. *Child Development, 65*, 754–770.

Stern, D. (1977). *The first relationship: Infant and mother*. Cambridge, MA: Harvard University Press.

Stern, M., & Karraker, K. H. (1989). Sex stereotyping of infants: A review of gender labeling studies. *Sex Roles, 20*, 501–522.

Stevens, M. (2014). The cost-effectiveness of UK parenting programmes for preventing children's behaviour problems—A review of the evidence. *Child & Family Social Work, 19*, 109–118.

Stewart, S. M., Bond, M. H., Zaman, R. M., McBride-Chang, C., Rao, N., Ho, L. M., & Fielding, R. (1999). Functional parenting in Pakistan. *International Journal of Behavioral Development, 23*, 747–770.

Stice, E., Marti, C. N., & Rohde, P. (2013). Prevalence, incidence, impairment, and course of the proposed *DSM-5* eating disorder diagnoses in an 8-year prospective community study of young women. *Journal of Abnormal Psychology, 122*, 445–457.

Stipek, D. (2002). At what age should children enter kindergarten? A question for policy makers and parents. *Social Policy Report, 16*, 3–16.

Stolz, L. M. (1967). *Influences on parent behavior*. London, England: Tavistock Publications.

Stover, C. S., Easton, C. J., & McMahon, T. J. (2013). Parenting of men with co-occurring intimate partner violence and substance abuse. *Journal of Interpersonal Violence, 28*, 2290–2314.

Stowman, S. A., & Donohue, B. (2005). Assessing child neglect: A review of standardized measures. *Aggression and Violent Behavior, 10*, 491–512.

St. Peters, M., Fitch, M., Huston, A. C., Wright, J. C., & Eakins, D. J. (1991). Television and families: What do young children watch with their parents? *Child Development, 62*, 1409–1423.

Straus, M. A., Douglas, E. M., & Medeiros, R. A. (2014). *Primordial violence: Spanking and its relation to psychological development, violence, and crime*. New York, NY: Routledge.

Straus, M. A., & Field, C. J. (2003). Psychological aggression by American parents: National data on prevalence, chronicity, and severity. *Journal of Marriage and Family, 65*, 795–808.

Straus, M. A., & Stewart, J. H. (1999). Corporal punishment by American parents: National data on prevalence, chronicity, severity, and duration in relation to child and family characteristics. *Clinical Child and Family Psychology Review, 2*, 55–70.

Substance Abuse and Mental Health Services Administration. (2004). *Overview of findings from the 2003 National Survey on drug use and health*. Rockville, MD: Office of Applied Studies, NSDUH Series H-24, DHHS Publication No. SMA 04-3963.

Substance Abuse and Mental Health Services Administration. (2008). *Results from the 2007 National Survey on Drug Use and Health: National findings.* Rockville, MD: Office of Applied Studies.

Substance Abuse and Mental Health Services Administration. (2012). *Results from the 2010 National Survey on Drug Use and Health: Mental health findings NSDUH Series H-42, HHS Publication No. (SMA) 11-4667.* Rockville, MD: Author.

Suchman, N. E., Pajulo, M., & Mayes, L. C. (Eds.). (2013). *Parenting and substance abuse: Developmental approaches to intervention.* New York, NY: Oxford University Press.

Suizzo, M-A. (2007). Parents' goals and values for children: Dimensions of independence and interdependence across four U.S. ethnic groups. *Journal of Cross-Cultural Psychology, 38,* 506–530.

Sullivan, P. M., & Knutson, J. F. (2000). Maltreatment and disabilities: A population-based epidemiological study. *Child Abuse and Neglect, 24,* 1257–1273.

Sulloway, F. J. (1996). *Born to rebel: Birth order, family dynamics, and creative lives.* New York, NY: Pantheon Books.

Sundby, J., Essén, B., & Johansen, R. E. B. (2013). Female genital mutilation, cutting, or circumcision. *Obstetrics and Gynecology International, 2013,* 1–2.

Sung, V., Collett, S., de Gooyer, T., Hiscock, H., Tang, M., & Wake, M. (2013). Probiotics to prevent or treat excessive infant crying: Systematic review and meta-analysis. *JAMA Pediatrics, 167,* 1150–1157.

Susman, E. J., & Dorn, L. D. (2012). Puberty: Its role in development. In R. M. Lerner, M. A. Easterbrooks, & J. Mistry (Eds.), *Handbook of psychology, vol. 6: Developmental psychology* (2nd ed., pp. 289–320). Hoboken, NJ: John Wiley & Sons.

Sweet, M. A., & Applebaum, M. I. (2004). Is home visiting an effective strategy: A meta-analytic review of home visiting programs for families with young children. *Child Development, 75,* 1435–1456.

Swing, E. L., Gentile, D. A., Anderson, C. A., & Walsh, D. A. (2010). Television and video game exposure and the development of attention problems. *Pediatrics, 126,* 214–221.

Symonds, P. (1949). *The dynamics of parent-child relationships.* New York, NY: Columbia University.

Tamis-LeMonda, C. S., Wang, S., Koutsouvanou, E., & Albright, M. (2002). Childrearing values in Greece, Taiwan, and the United States. *Parenting: Science and Practice, 2,* 185–208.

Tamis-LeMonda, C. S., Way, N., Hughes, D., Yoshikawa, H., Kalman, R. K., & Niwa, E. Y. (2008). Parents' goals for children: The dynamic coexistence of individualism and collectivism in cultures and individuals. *Social Development, 17,* 183–209.

Tamm, L., Holden, G. W., Nakonezny, P. A., Swart, S., & Hughes, C. W. (2012). Metaparenting: Associations with parenting stress, child-rearing practices, and retention in parents of children at risk for ADHD. *ADHD: Attention Deficit Hyperactive Disorder, 4,* 1–10.

Tandon, P. S., Zhou, C., Lozano, P., & Christakis, D. A. (2011). Preschoolers' total daily screen time at home and by type of child care. *Journal of Pediatrics, 158,* 297–300.

Tasker, F. (2005). Lesbian mothers, gay fathers, and their children: A review. *Journal of Developmental & Behavioral Pediatrics, 26,* 224–240.

Taylor, J. S., Risica, P. M., & Cabral, H. J. (2003). Why primiparous mothers do not breastfeed in the United States: A national survey. *Acta Paediatrica, 92,* 1308–1313.

Taylor, R. D., & Wang, M. C. (Eds.). (2008). *Social and emotional adjustment and family relations in ethnic minority families.* New York, NY: Routledge.

Taylor, Z. E., Eisenberg, N., Spinrad, T. L., Eggum, N. D., & Sulik, M. J. (2013). The relations of ego-resiliency and emotion socialization to the development of empathy and prosocial behavior across early childhood. *Emotion, 13,* 822–831.

Teicher, M. H. (2000). Wounds that time won't heal: The neurobiology of child abuse. *Cerebrum, 2,* 50–67.

Teicher, M. H. (2002). Scars that won't heal: The neurobiology of child abuse. *Scientific American, 286,* 68–75.

Teicher, M. H., Polcari, A., Anderson, S. L., Anderson, C. M., & Navalta, C. (2003). Neurobiological effects of childhood stress and trauma. In S. W. Coates, J. L. Rosenthal, & D. S. Schechter

(Eds.), *September 11: Trauma and human bonds* (pp. 211–238). New York, NY: Routledge.

Tejada-Vera, B., & Sutton, P. D. (2010). *Births, marriages, divorces, and deaths: Provisional data for 2009 National vital statistics reports* (vol. 58). Hyattsville, MD: National Center for Health Statistics.

Thakkar, R. R., Garrison, M. M., & Christakis, D. A. (2006). A systematic review for the effects of television viewing by infants and preschoolers. *Pediatrics, 118*, 2025–2031.

Thelen, E., & Adolph, K. E. (1992). Arnold L. Gesell: The paradox of nature and nurture. *Developmental Psychology, 28*, 368–380.

Theule, J., Wiener, J., Tannock, R., & Jenkins, J. M. (2013). Parenting stress in families of children with ADHD: A meta-analysis. *Journal of Emotional and Behavioral Disorders, 21*, 3–17.

Thomas, A., & Chess, S. (1977). *Temperament and development*. New York, NY: Brunner/Mazel.

Thomas, A., Chess, S., Birch, H. G., & Hertzig, M. E. (1963). *Behavioral individuality in early childhood*. New York, NY: Wiley.

Thomas, J. L., Sperry, L., & Yarbrough, M. S. (2000). Grandparents as parents: Research findings and policy recommendations. *Child Psychiatry and Human Development, 31*, 3–22.

Thomassin, K., & Suveg, C. (2014). Reciprocal positive affect and well-regulated, adjusted children: A unique contribution of fathers. *Parenting: Science and Practice, 14*, 28–46.

Thompson, A. L., Adair, L. S., & Bentley, M. E. (2013). Maternal characteristics and perception of temperament associated with infant TV exposure. *Pediatrics, 131*, e390–e397.

Thompson, R. A. (1998). Early sociopersonality development. In N. Eisenberg (Ed.), *Handbook of child psychology. Vol. 4: Social, emotional, and personality development* (5th ed., pp. 25–104). Hoboken, NJ: John Wiley & Sons Inc.

Thompson, R. A. (2006). The development of the person: Social understanding, relationships, conscience, self. In N. Eisenberg (Ed.), *Handbook of child psychology, vol. 3: Social, emotional, and personality development* (6th ed., pp. 24–98). New York, NY: Wiley.

Tichenor, V., McQuillan, J., Greil, A. L., Contreras, R., & Shreffler, K. M. (2011). The importance of fatherhood to U.S. married and cohabiting men. *Fathering: A Journal of Theory, Research, and Practice About Men as Fathers, 9*, 232–251.

Tinsley, B. J., Markey, C. N., Ericksen, A. J., Ortiz, R. V., & Kwasman, A. (2002). Health promotion for parents. In M. H. Bornstein (Ed.), *Handbook of parenting, vol. 5: Practical issues in parenting* (2nd ed., pp. 311–328). Mahwah, NJ: Lawrence Erlbaum Associates.

Tittle, P. (Ed.). (2004). *Should parents be licensed? Debating the issues*. Amherst, NY: Prometheus Books.

Tolan, P., Gorman-Smith, D., & Henry, D. (2006). Family violence. *Annual Review of Psychology, 57*, 557–583.

Tomarken, A. J., & Waller, N. G. (2005). Structural equation modeling: Strengths, limitations, and misconceptions. *Annual Review of Clinical Psychology, 1*, 31–65.

Touchette, E., Dionne, G., Forget-Dubois, N., Petit, D., Pérusse, D., Falissard, B., . . . Montplaisir, J. Y. (2013). Genetic and environmental influences on daytime and nighttime sleep duration in early childhood. *Pediatrics, 131*, e1874–e1880.

Tremblay, R. E. (2006). Prevention of youth violence: Why not start at the beginning? *Journal of Abnormal Child Psychology, 34*, 480–486.

Tremblay, R. E., Japel, C., Perusse, D., McDuff, P., Boivin, M., Zoccolillo, M., & Montplaisir, J. (1999). The search for the age of "onset" of physical aggression: Rousseau and Bandura revisited. *Criminal Behavior and Mental Health, 9*, 8–23.

Tremblay, R. E., Nagin, D. S., Sequin, J. R., Zoccolillo, M., Zelazo, P. D., Boivin, M., . . . Japel, C. (2004). Physical aggression during early childhood: Trajectories and predictors. *Pediatrics, 114*, 43–50.

Trickett, P. K., & Negriff, S. (2011). Child maltreatment and social relationships. In M. K. Underwood & L. H. Rosen (Eds.), *Social development: Relationships in infancy, childhood, and adolescence*. New York, NY: Guilford Press.

Trivers, R. L. (1974). Parent-offspring conflict. *American Zoologist, 14*, 249–264.

Tronick, E. Z., Morelli, G., & Ivey, P. K. (1992). The Efe forager infant and toddler's pattern of social relationships: Multiple and simultaneous. *Developmental Psychology, 28*, 568–577.

Troxel, W. M., & Matthews, K. A. (2004). What are the costs of marital conflict and dissolution to children's physical health? *Clinical Child and Family Psychology Review, 7*, 29–57.

Trull, T. J., & Ebner-Priemer, U. W. (2009). Using experience sampling methods/ecological momentary assessment (ESM/EMA) in clinical assessment and clinical research: Introduction to the special section. *Psychological Assessment, 21*, 457–462.

Trumpeter, N. N., Watson, P. J., O'Leary, B. J., & Weathington, B. L. (2008). Self-functioning and perceived parenting: Relations of parental empathy and love inconsistency with narcissism, depression, and self-esteem. *Journal of Genetic Psychology, 169*, 51–71.

Trussell, J. (2011). Contraceptive failure in the United States. *Contraception, 83*, 397–404.

Tucker, C. J., Finkelhor, D., Shattuck, A. M., & Turner, H. (2013). Prevalence and correlates of sibling victimization types. *Child Abuse and Neglect, 37*, 213–223.

Tucker, C. J., & Kazura, K. (2013). Parental responses to school-aged children's sibling conflict. *Journal of Child and Family Studies, 22*, 737–745.

Turner, H. A., & Muller, P. A. (2004). Long-term effects of child corporal punishment on depressive symptoms in young adults. *Journal of Family Issues, 25*, 761–782.

Underwood, M. K. (2011). Aggression. In M. K. Underwood & L. H. Rosen (Eds.), *Social development: Relationships in infancy, childhood, and adolescence* (pp. 207–234). New York, NY: Guilford Press.

Underwood, M. K., Beron, K. J., & Rosen, L. H. (2009). Continuity and change in social and physical aggression from middle childhood through early adolescence. *Aggressive Behavior, 35*, 357–375.

Underwood, M. K., Ehrenreich, S. E., More, D., Solis, J. S., & Brinkley, D. Y. (2014). The BlackBerry Project: The hidden world of adolescents' text messaging and relations with internalizing symptoms. *Journal of Research on Adolescence, 23*.

Underwood, M. K., & Rosen, L. H. (2011). *Social development: Relationships in infancy, childhood, and adolescence*. New York, NY: Guilford Press.

United Nations Office of the High Commissioner for Human Rights. (1990). *The convention on the rights of the child*. Retrieved June 19, 2014, from http://www.ohchr.org/en/professionalinterest/pages/crc.aspx

Ursache, A., Blair, C., & Raver, C. C. (2012). The promotion of self-regulation as a means of enhancing school readiness and early achievement in children at risk for school failure. *Child Development Perspectives, 6*, 122–128.

U.S. Census Bureau. (2008). *Facts for features: Unmarried and single Americans week: Sept. 21–27, 2008*. Retrieved June, 4, 2014, from https://www.census.gov/newsroom/releases/archives/facts_for_features_special_editions/cb08-ff16a.html

U.S. Census Bureau. (2011). Statistical abstract of the United States: 2011. Washington, DC: U.S. Census Bureau.

U.S. Census Bureau. (2012). *Mother's day: May 13, 2012 Profile America: Facts for features* (Vol. CB12-FF.08). Retrieved June 4, 2014, from http://www.census.gov/newsroom/releases/archives/facts_for_features_special_editions/cb12-ff08.html

U.S. Census Bureau. (2013). *Annual social and economic supplement, current population survey*. Washington, DC: Author.

U.S. Census Bureau. (2014). *State & county quickfacts*. Retrieved June 17, 2014, from http://quickfacts.census.gov/qfd/states/00000.html

U.S. Department of Defense. (2012). *2011 demographics: Profile of the military community*. Washington, DC: Office of the Deputy Under Secretary of Defense (Military Community and Family Policy).

U.S. Department of Education. (2013). *The condition of education, 2013*. (NCES 2013-037): Status Dropout Rates. Retrieved June 11, 2014, from http://nces.ed.gov/pubs2013/2013037.pdf

U.S. Department of Health and Human Services. (1999). *Mental health: A report of the Surgeon General*. Rockville, MD: National Institute of Mental Health.

U.S. Department of Health and Human Services. (2001). *Adoption and foster care analysis and report system (AFCARS) report, No. 6*. Washington, CD: Children's Bureau.

U.S. Department of Health and Human Services. (2008). *Child health USA 2007*. Rockville, MD: U.S. Department of Health and Human Services.

U.S. Department of Health and Human Services. (2012). *Child maltreatment 2012*. Washington, DC: Administration on Children, Youth and Families.

U.S. Department of Health and Human Services. (2014). *Trends in teen pregnancy and childbearing*. Retrieved June 11, 2014, from http://www.hhs.gov/ash/oah/adolescent-health-topics/reproductive-health/teen-pregnancy/trends.html

van de Glind, H., & Kooijmans, J. (2008). Modern-day child slavery. *Children & Society, 22*, 150–166.

Vandell, D. L. (2000). Parents, peer groups, and other socializing influences. *Developmental Psychology, 36*, 699–710.

van der Veer, R., & Valsiner, J. (1994). *The Vygotsky reader*. Cambridge, MA: Blackwell.

Vandewater, E. A., Park, S-E., Huang, X., & Wartella, E. A. (2005). "No—You can't watch that." Parental rules and young children's media use. *American Behavioral Scientist, 48*, 608–623.

Van Gils, J. (2014). Play and well-being in children's life. In A. Ben-Arieh, F. Casas, I. Frones, & J. E. Korbin (Eds.), *Handbook of child well-being* (vol. 2, pp. 895–910). New York, NY: Springer.

van IJzendoorn, M. H. (1992). Intergenerational transmission of parenting: A review of studies in nonclinical populations. *Developmental Review, 12*, 76–99.

van IJzendoorn, M. H., & Juffer, F. (2005). Adoption is a successful natural intervention enhancing adopted children's IQ and school performance. *Current Directions in Psychological Science, 14*, 326–330.

van IJzendoorn, M. H., Schuengel, C., & Bakermans-Kranenburg, M. J. (1999). Disorganized attachment in early childhood: Meta-analysis of precursors, concomitants, and sequelae. *Development and Psychopathology, 11*, 225–250.

van Toledo, A., & Seymour, F. (2013). Interventions for caregivers of children who disclose sexual abuse: A review. *Clinical Psychology Review, 33*, 772–781.

van Zeijl, J., Mesman, J., Koot, H. M., Stolk, M. N., Alink, L. R. A., van IJzendoorn, M. H., . . . Juffer, F. (2007). Differential susceptibility to discipline: The moderating effect of child temperament on the association between maternal discipline and early childhood externalizing problems. *Journal of Family Psychology, 21*, 626–636.

Verhoeven, M., Junger, M., Van Aken, C., Deković, M., & Van Aken, M. A. G. (2007). Parenting during toddlerhood. *Journal of Family Issues, 28*, 1663–1691.

Vermeer, H. J., & van IJzendoorn, M. H. (2006). Children's elevated cortisol levels at daycare: A review and meta-analysis. *Early Childhood Research Quarterly, 21*, 390–401.

Vespa, J., Lewis, J. M., & Kreider, R. M. (2013). *America's families and living arrangements: 2012 Population characteristics*. Washington, DC: U.S. Department of Commerce, U.S. Census Bureau.

Visher, C. A., & Travis, J. (2011). Life on the outside: Returning home after incarceration. *The Prison Journal, 91*, 102S–119S.

Vittrup, B., & Holden, G. W. (2011). Exploring the impact of educational television and parent-child discussions on children's racial attitudes. *Analyses of Social Issues and Public Policy, 11*, 82–104.

Vittrup, B., Holden, G. W., & Buck, J. (2006). Attitudes predict the use of physical punishment: A prospective study of the emergence of disciplinary practices. *Pediatrics, 117*, 2055–2064.

von der Lippe, E., Rattay, P., & Domanska, O. (2013). Depression of single parents in Germany. Results from the 2009/10 GEDA-study. *The European Journal of Public Health, 23*(Supplement 1), 114.

Vondra, J., Sysko, H. B., & Belsky, J. (2005). Developmental origins of parenting: Personality and relationship factors. In T. Luster & L. Okagaki (Eds.), *Parenting: An ecological perspective* (pp. 35–71). Mahwah, NJ: Lawrence Erlbaum Associates.

Wachs, T. D., Bishry, Z., Sobhy, A., McCabe, B., Galal, O., & Shaheen, F. (1993). Relation of rearing environment to adaptive behavior of Egyptian toddlers. *Child Development, 64*, 586–604.

Waddell, C., & Shepherd, C. (2002). *Prevalence of mental disorders in children and youth*. Vancouver, BC: University of British Columbia.

Wagner, M. E., Schubert, H. J. P., & Schubert, D. S. P. (1985). Family size effects: A review. *Journal of Genetic Psychology, 146*, 65–78.

Wainright, J. L., Russell, S. T., & Patterson, C. J. (2004). Psychosocial adjustment, school outcomes, and romantic relationships of adolescents with same-sex parents. *Child Development, 75*, 1886–1898.

Waldfogel, J. (2001). International policies toward parental leave and child care. *The Future of Children, 11*, 99–111.

Walker, M., Moreau, D., & Weissman, M. M. (1990). Parents' awareness of children's suicide attempts. *American Journal of Psychiatry, 147*, 1364–1366.

Walsh, C., MacMillan, H., & Jamieson, E. (2002). The relationship between parental psychiatric disorder and child physical and sexual abuse: Findings from the Ontario health supplement. *Child Abuse and Neglect, 26*, 11–22.

Wang, M-T., & Sheikh-Khalil, S. (2013). Does parental involvement matter for student achievement and mental health in high school? *Child Development, 85*, 610–625.

Watkins, S. A. (1990). The Mary Ellen myth: Correcting child welfare history. *Social Work, 35*, 500–503.

Watson, J. B. (1928). *Psychological care of infant and child*. New York, NY: Norton.

Watson, J. B. (1930). *Behaviorism*. New York, NY: Norton.

Watson, J. B., & Rayner, R. (1920). Conditioned emotional reactions. *Journal of Experimental Psychology, 3*, 1–14.

Watson, L. F., Rayner, J-A., & Forster, D. (2013). Identifying risk factors for very preterm birth: A reference for clinicians. *Midwifery, 29*, 434–439.

Weber, D. A., & Reynolds, C. R. (2004). Clinical perspectives on neurobiological effects of psychological trauma. *Neuropsychology Review, 14*, 115–129.

Weed, K., Keogh, D., & Borkowski, J. (2006). Stability of resilience in children of adolescent mothers. *Applied Developmental Psychology, 27*, 60–77.

Weininger, E. B., & Lareau, A. (2009). Paradoxical pathways: An ethnographic extension of Kohn's findings on class and childrearing. *Journal of Marriage and Family, 71*, 680–695.

Weinraub, M., Horvath, D. L., & Gringlas, M. B. (2002). Single parenthood. In M. H. Bornstein (Ed.), *Handbook of parenting, vol. 3: Being and becoming a parent* (pp. 109–140). Mahwah, NJ: Lawrence Erlbaum Associates.

Weisleder, A., & Fernald, A. (2013). Talking to children matters: Early language experience strengthens processing and builds vocabulary. *Psychological Science, 24*, 2143–2152.

Weisman, A. (2007). *The world without us*. New York, NY: Macmillan.

Weisner, T. S. (2011). Culture. In M. K. Underwood & L. H. Rosen (Eds.), *Social development: Relationships in infancy, childhood, and adolescence* (pp. 372–399). New York, NY: Guilford.

Weisz, J. R., Sigman, M., Weiss, B., & Mosk, J. (1993). Parent reports of behavioral and emotional problems among children in Kenya, Thailand, and the United States. *Child Development, 64*, 98–109.

Wentzel, K. R., & Caldwell, K. (1997). Friendships, peer acceptance, and group membership: Relations to academic achievement in middle school. *Child Development*, 68, 1198–1209.

Wentzel, K. R., & Looney, L. (2007). Socialization in school settings. In J. E. Grusec & P. D. Hastings (Eds.), *Handbook of socialization: Theory and research* (pp. 382–403). New York, NY: Guilford.

Westerman, J. C. (1994). *Licensing parents: Can we prevent child abuse and neglect?* New York, NY: Plenum.

Weston, R., & Qu, L. (2001). Men's and women's reasons for not having children. *Family Matters, 58*, 10–15.

Wheaton, L., & Sorensen, E. (1998). Reducing welfare costs and dependency: How much bang for the child support buck? *Georgetown Public Policy Review, 4*, 23–37.

Wheeler, S. M., Williams, L., Beauchesne, P., & Dupras, T. L. (2013). Shattered lives and broken childhoods: Evidence of physical child abuse in ancient Egypt. *International Journal of Paleopathology, 3*, 71–82.

Whitehurst, G. J., & Lonigan, C. J. (1998). Child development and emergent literacy. *Child Development, 69*, 848–872.

Whiteman, S. D., McHale, S. M., & Crouter, A. C. (2003). What parents learn from experience: The first child as first draft? *Journal of Marriage and Family, 65*, 608–621.

Whitesell, N. R., Asdigian, N. L., Kaufman, C. E., Crow, C. B., Shangreau, C., Keane, E. M., . . .

Mitchell, C. M. (2014). Trajectories of substance use among young American Indian adolescents: Patterns and predictors. *Journal of Youth and Adolescence, 43*, 437–453.

Whiting, J. W. M., & Child, I. L. (1953). *Child training and personality: A cross-cultural study*. New Haven, CT: Yale University Press.

Whitton, S. W., Stanley, S. M., Markman, H. J., & Johnson, C. A. (2013). Attitudes toward divorce, commitment, and divorce proneness in first marriages and remarriages. *Journal of Marriage and Family, 75*, 276–287.

Wickes, I. G. (1953). A history of infant feeding: Part 1. Primitive peoples: Ancient works: Renaissance writers. *Archives of Disease in Childhood, 28*, 151–158.

Wigfield, A., Eccles, J. S., Schiefele, U., Roeser, R. W., & Davis-Kean, P. (2006). Development of achievement motivation. In N. Eisenberg (Ed.), *Handbook of child psychology, vol. 3: Social, emotional, and personality development* (6th ed., pp. 933–1002). New York, NY: Wiley.

Wilcox, W. B. (2002). Religion, convention, and paternal involvement. *Journal of Marriage and Family, 64*, 780–792.

Wildsmith, E., Steward-Streng, N. R., & Manlove, J. (2011). *Childbearing outside of marriage: Estimates and trends in the United States Child Trends research briefs*. Washington, DC: Child Trends.

Wilson, B. J., & Gottman, J. M. (2002). Marital conflict, repair, and parenting. In M. H. Bornstein (Ed.), *Handbook of parenting, vol. 4: Social conditions and applied parenting* (pp. 227–258).

Wilson, K., Fyson, R., & Newstone, S. (2006). Foster fathers: Their experiences and contributions to fostering. *Child & Family Social Work, 12*, 22–31.

Wilson, S., & Durbin, C. E. (2010). Effects of paternal depression on fathers' parenting behaviors: A meta-analytic review. *Clinical Psychology Review, 30*, 167–180.

Wilson, S. L., Kuebli, J. E., & Hughes, H. M. (2005). Patterns of maternal behavior among neglectful families: Implications for research and intervention. *Child Abuse and Neglect, 29*, 985–1001.

Wisner, K., Parry, B., & Piontek, C. (2002). Postpartum depression. *New England Journal of Medicine, 347*, 194–198.

Wolfenstein, M. (1951). Fun morality: An analysis of recent American child-training literature. *Journal of Social Issues, 7*, 15–25.

Wolke, D. (1998). Psychological development of prematurely born children. *Archives of Disease in Childhood, 78*, 567–570.

Wolke, D., Copeland, W. E., Angold, A., & Costello, E. J. (2013). Impact of bullying in childhood on adult health, wealth, crime, and social outcomes. *Psychological Science, 24*, 1958–1970.

Woods, J. J., & Wetherby, A. M. (2003). Early identification of and intervention for infants and toddlers who are at risk for autism spectrum disorder. *Language, Speech, and Hearing Services in Schools, 34*, 180–193.

Woolley, J. D. (1995). The fictional mind: Young children's understanding of imagination, pretense, and dreams. *Developmental Review, 15*, 172–211.

World Health Organization. (2012). *Born too soon: The global action report on preterm birth*. Geneva, Switzerland: World Health Organization.

World Health Organization. (2014a). *Child maltreatment*. Retrieved June 17, 2014, from http://www.who.int/mediacentre/factsheets/fs150/en/

World Health Organization. (2014b). *Commission on ending childhood obesity*. Retrieved June 6, 2014, from http://www.who.int/dietphysicalactivity/end-childhood-obesity/en/

Wu, P., Robinson, C. C., Yang, C., Hart, C. H., Olsen, S. F., Porter, C. L., . . . Wu, X. (2002). Similarities and differences in mothers' parenting of preschoolers in China and the United States. *International Journal of Behavioral Development, 26*, 481–491.

Yang, C. K., & Hahn, H. M. (2002). Cosleeping in young Korean children. *Journal of Developmental and Behavioral Pediatrics, 23*, 151–157.

Yang, F., Helgason, A. R., Sigfusdottir, I. D., & Kristjansson, A. L. (2013). Electronic screen use and mental well-being of 10–12-year-old children. *The European Journal of Public Health, 23*, 492–498.

Yang, J., Campo, S., Ramirez, M., Krapfl, J. R., Cheng, G., & Peek-Asa, C. (2013). Family communication patterns and teen drivers' attitudes toward driving safety. *Journal of Pediatric Health Care, 27*, 334–341.

Yarrow, A. L. (2009). *History of U.S. children's policy, 1900–present*. Retrieved June 19, 2014, from http://www.firstfocus.net/sites/default/files/r.2009-5.1.yarrow.pdf

Yirmiya, N., & Shaked, M. (2005). Psychiatric disorders in parents of children with autism: A meta-analysis. *Journal of Child Psychology and Psychiatry, 46*, 69–83.

Yopp, J. M., & Rosenstein, D. L. (2012). Single fatherhood due to cancer. *Psycho-Oncology, 21*, 1362–1366.

Yoshikawa, H. (2011). *Immigrants raising citizens: Undocumented parents and their young children*. New York, NY: Russell Sage.

Yu, S. M., & Singh, G. K. (2012). High parenting aggravation among US immigrant families. *American Journal of Public Health, 102*, 2102–2108.

Zahn-Waxler, C., Duggal, S., & Gruber, R. (2002). Parental psychopathology. In M. H. Bornstein (Ed.), *Handbook of parenting, vol. 4: Social conditions and applied parenting* (2nd ed., pp. 295–328). Mahwah, NJ: Lawrence Erlbaum Associates.

Zahn-Waxler, C., Radke-Yarrow, M., Wagner, E., & Chapman, M. (1992). Development of concern for others. *Developmental Psychology, 28*, 126–136.

Zahn-Waxler, C., Shirtcliff, E. A., & Marceau, K. (2008). Disorders of childhood and adolescence: Gender and psychopathology. *Annual Review of Clinical Psychology, 4*, 275–303.

Zeanah, C. H., Egger, H., & Smyke, A. (2009). Institutional rearing and psychiatric disorders in Romanian preschool children. *American Journal of Psychiatry, 166*, 777–785.

Zeanah, C. H., Scheeringa, M., Boris, N. W., Heller, S. S., Smyke, A. T., & Trapani, J. (2004). Reactive attachment disorder in maltreated toddlers. *Child Abuse & Neglect, 28*, 877–888.

Zeman, J., Cassano, M., Perry-Parrish, C., & Stegall, S. (2006). Emotion regulation in children and adolescents. *Journal of Developmental & Behavioral Pediatrics, 27*, 155–168.

Zentner, M., & Bates, J. E. (2008). Child temperament: An integrative review of concepts, research programs, and measures. *European Journal of Developmental Science, 2*, 7–37.

Zhai, F., Waldfogel, J., & Brooks-Gunn, J. (2013). Estimating the effects of Head Start on parenting and child maltreatment. *Children and Youth Services Review, 35*, 1119–1129.

Zhan, Q-T., Pan, P-P., Xu, X-R., Lou, H-Y., Lou, Y-Y., & Jin, F. (2013). An overview of studies on psychological well-being in children born following assisted reproductive technologies. *Journal of Zhejang University, 14*, 947–960.

Zhou, F., Santoli, J., Messonnier, M. L., Yusuf, H. R., Shefer, A., Chu, S. Y., . . . Harpaz, R. (2005). Economic evaluation of the 7-vaccine routine childhood immunization schedule in the United States, 2001. *Archives of Pediatrics and Adolescent Medicine, 159*, 1136–1144.

Zhou, Q., Tao, A., Chen, S. H., Main, A., Lee, E., Ly, J., . . . Li, X. (2012). Asset and protective factors for Asian American children's mental health adjustment. *Child Development Perspectives, 6*, 312–319.

Zigler, E., & Hall, N. W. (1989). Physical abuse in America: Past, present, and future. In D. Cicchetti & V. Carlson (Eds.), *Child maltreatment* (pp. 38–75). New York, NY: Cambridge University Press.

Zigler, E., & Muenchow, S. (1984). How to influence social policy affecting children and families. *American Psychologist, 39*, 415–420.

Zigler, E., & Styfco, S. J. (1994). Head Start: Criticisms in a constructive context. *American Psychologist, 49*, 127–132.

Zimet, D. M., & Jacob, T. (2002). Influences of marital conflict on child adjustment: Review of theory and research. *Clinical Child and Family Psychology Review, 4*, 319–335.

Zimmer, B. (2013, March 24). Providence's $5 million plan to shrink the "word gap." *Boston Globe*. Retrieved June 19, 2014, from http://www.bostonglobe.com/ideas/2013/03/23/providence-million-plan-shrink-word-gap/zwVX3JKvmsZChHVPimovbN/story.html

Zimmerman, F. J., Christakis, D. A., & Meltzoff, A. N. (2007). Television and DVD/video viewing in children younger than 2 years. *Archives of Pediatric and Adolescent Medicine, 161*, 473–479.

Ziol-Guest, K. M., & McKenna, C. C. (2014). Early childhood housing instability and school readiness. *Child Development, 85*, 103–113.

Žukauskienė, R. (2014). Adolescence and well-being. In A. Ben-Arieh, F. Casas, I. Fones, & J. E. Korbin (Eds.), *Handbook of child well-being* (pp. 1713–1738). New York, NY: Springer.

Author Index

Note: Page references followed by (box), (photograph), and (table) indicate names in display material.

Subject Index

Note: Pages references followed by (box), (photograph), (figure), and (table) indicate display material.